PRAISE FOR *DUPES*

"The press, the universities, and the elites on both coasts got the Cold War, fundamentally, wrong. Ordinary Americans—the kinds of people who devoted their energy to making ends meet, not to shaping received opinion—got the conflict, fundamentally, right. Paul Kengor presents an utterly invaluable study of this struggle here at home. Self-delusion and malaise versus good sense and courage; détente and weakness versus peace through strength; Jimmy Carter versus Ronald Reagan. Read *Dupes* and you'll understand how we finally won—and how very close we came to losing."

— **PETER ROBINSON**, author of *How Ronald Reagan Changed My Life*

"During my time as Ronald Reagan's national security adviser, we saw the crucial need to stand up to the Soviets and the international Communist movement. Too many people on our side, while well-intentioned, did not see that need and were often misled. At long last, here is a book that explores this intriguing and troubling aspect of the Cold War. Paul Kengor has written a lively, thoroughly documented book bringing a much greater breadth to an accurate understanding of America's battle against a truly evil empire."

— **WILLIAM P. CLARK**, former national security adviser

"As he did in his masterpiece on Ronald Reagan, *The Crusader*, Paul Kengor applies meticulous research to peeling back the layers of lies and obfuscation the American Left has used for years in claiming that its associations with the Soviets and other tyrants were just coincidental. But this is far from an across-the-board condemnation of every liberal. Kengor offers a favorable revision of Woodrow Wilson as a staunch anti-Bolshevik; exposes the thorough corruption of John Dewey; examines the CPUSA's targeting of the New Deal as 'fascist'; and exposes with reproduced photocopies the duplicity of American Communists in aiding and abetting Adolf Hitler with their antiwar efforts in the 1930s. A great contribution."

— **LARRY SCHWEIKART**, bestselling author of *A Patriot's History of the United States* and *Seven Events That Made America America*

"*Dupes* is an enormously important book that will forever change the way you think about liberals and how they deal with America's enemies. Kengor has unearthed eye-popping new information that left me amazed and a bit frightened. By the way, *Dupes* is especially relevant in the era of Obama."

— **FRED BARNES**, executive editor of the *Weekly Standard*

"The Crusades? The Inquisition? Forget about it. The greatest killer in human history has been Communism. In this engaging and important book, Kengor shows us who was duped by Communism, why, and the sad results. This is a significant addition to our historical understanding of the past hundred years—not to be missed by either the Right or the Left."

—**DINESH D'SOUZA**, bestselling author of *What's So Great About America*

"In the twentieth century it was Whittaker Chambers's *Witness* that alerted the West to the actions of those who were secretly serving the enemy. Now Paul Kengor gives us the twenty-first-century equivalent to *Witness*: a detailed, riveting history of those who were duped into doing the same. *Dupes* is not to be missed!"

—**PETER SCHWEIZER**, bestselling author of *Do as I Say (Not as I Do)*

"A book so fascinating and so revealing that I couldn't put it down. Kengor gives us a fabulous tour of Communist dupes in America from FDR through SDS, Carter, Kerry, and Ted Kennedy. The gullibility of FDR and others would be comical if it weren't so tragic for U.S. foreign policy. Key American leaders, as Kengor shows clearly, ultimately strengthened and extended the life of a totalitarian regime that thrived on deceit, oppression, and mass murder."

—**BURTON FOLSOM JR.**, author of *New Deal or Raw Deal?*

"*Dupes* is an extraordinary book that alters our understanding of the twentieth century."

—**HERB MEYER**, Special Assistant to CIA Director William Casey, 1981–87

"Face it. You are going to have to read this book. This book will be questioned and attacked, and it should be. It raises some crucial and extremely uncomfortable questions. It makes some very strong accusations that need to be answered—for instance, those about Senator Kennedy offering to help the Soviets against President Reagan. Some of the documentation is here. Start arguing."

—**MICHAEL NOVAK**, American Enterprise Institute

Dupes

Also by the author

The Crusader: Ronald Reagan and the Fall of Communism
God and Ronald Reagan: A Spiritual Life
God and George W. Bush: A Spiritual Life
God and Hillary Clinton: A Spiritual Life
The Judge: William P. Clark, Ronald Reagan's Top Hand
      (with Patricia Clark Doerner)
The Reagan Legacy: Assessing the Man and His Presidency
      (with Peter Schweizer)
Wreath Layer or Policy Player? The Vice President's Role in Foreign Policy

DUPES

*How America's Adversaries Have
Manipulated Progressives for a Century*

PAUL KENGOR, PH.D.

ISI BOOKS

WILMINGTON, DELAWARE

Kengor, Paul, 1966-
　　　　Dupes : how America's adversaries have manipulated progressives for a century / Paul Kengor.
　　　　p. cm.
　　　　Includes bibliographical references.
　　　　ISBN 978-1-935191-75-9

　　　　1. United States—Politics and government—20th century. 2. United States—Foreign relations—20th century. 3. Cold War. 4. Enemies—Political aspects—United States—History. 5. Deception—Political aspects—United States—History. 6. Progressivism (United States politics)—History. 7. Communism—United States—History. 8. Communism—Soviet Union—History. 9. United States—Politics and government—2001–2009. 10. United States—Foreign relations—2001–2009. I. Title.

E743.K425 2010
973.91—dc22　　　　　　　　　　2010020117

ISI Books
Intercollegiate Studies Institute
3901 Centerville Road
Wilmington, DE 19807-1938
www.isibooks.org

Manufactured in the United States of America

While Communists make full use of liberals and their solicitudes, and sometimes flatter them to their faces, in private they treat them with that sneering contempt that the strong and predatory almost invariably feel for victims who volunteer to help in their own victimization.

—Whittaker Chambers, *Witness*

For the time will come when people . . . will stop listening to the truth and will be diverted to myths.

—2 Timothy 4: 3–4

Dedicated to two *human* Cold War archives:

Herb Romerstein,
who chose the right side,

and

Arnold Beichman (1913–2010),
the cheerful Cold Warrior

CONTENTS

Introduction

THE OVERLOOKED ROLE OF THE DUPE

T his is a book about dupes, about those Americans who have unwittingly aided some of the worst opponents of the United States.[1] Misled about the true aims of foreign adversaries, many Americans (and other Westerners) have allowed themselves to be manipulated to serve opponents' interests. Most notably, after the Bolshevik Revolution and throughout the Cold War, Communists took full advantage of Western dupes. Indeed, Communist propagandists in the Soviet Union, around the world, and within America itself conducted this duping on a remarkable, deliberate scale and with remarkable, deliberate craftsmanship—with America's liberals and progressives as the prime target. Yet the story does not stop with the end of the Cold War. Unfortunately, dupes have surfaced in the War on Terror—including some of the very same Americans who unknowingly played the role of sucker to the Soviets—occasionally providing fodder for Middle East enemies, although the periods, and the processes, are quite different.

Pointing out this ongoing phenomenon is not a matter of beating up on the gullible. Using the word "dupes" may come across as name calling or sensationalism, but the reality is that it is the best term to describe those who are deceived by, and therefore unknowingly assist, foreign adversaries. The word has, in fact, been widely used throughout American history and up to the present to characterize the tools of foreign influence. President George Washington used the term "dupes" in his historic 1796 Farewell Address, for example.[2] And like the associated phrase "useful idiots"—widely attributed to Vladimir Lenin[3]—"dupes" became especially prominent in the Cold War: many of those misled by the Communists said they regretted having been duped; others spoke openly of fears of being duped.

The plain, undeniable—but historically unappreciated[4]—fact is that the dupe has played a significant role in the recent history of America and in the nation's ability to deal with destructive opponents. This book aims to shine light on this troubling aspect of our history. Of course, the phenomenon of the dupe is not merely of historical interest. Because it persists today, we must understand how the duping occurs—both how our opponents exploit the American home front and how some Americans allow themselves to be manipulated.

When I began this project, I did not recognize the extent to which duping still occurs, or how duping in the distant Cold War past has emerged as very relevant in today's politics. I initially conceived of the book as strictly a Cold War project. But it was nothing short of stunning to research this book during the presidential bid of Barack Obama and hear so many of the names in my research surface repeatedly in the background of the man who became president of the United States of America. The names included the likes of Frank Marshall Davis, a mentor to the young Obama in Hawaii; the controversial, well-publicized Bill Ayers; and the marquee figures in the 2008 group "Progressives for Obama," which read like a Who's Who of the '60s radicals called to testify before the House Committee on Internal Security. It was impossible for me to have foreseen this, given that I decided to pursue this project in 2006, when no one on the planet would have predicted the 2008 presidential election of a young politician named Barack Obama.[5] The way in which so many names and themes from the Cold War past aligned and made their way into Obama's orbit was chilling. This was the most fascinating, frustrating, and unanticipated aspect of the research for this project.[6] Though I had not expected to extend the narrative beyond the Cold War, I concluded that this information could not be ignored. It would be a worse sign of bias to ignore it than include it.

Nor is Obama is the only such contemporary case. Other political leaders today are products of the Vietnam era or the political godchildren of notable Marxist radicals, and they seek to lead America in a new war against a new kind of foreign totalitarianism.[7] Here, too, the Cold War past is not entirely disconnected from current threats. In key ways, past is prologue.

Lenin's "Deaf-Mutes"

It would be easy to dismiss dupes as gullible but ultimately harmless. But in fact, they have proven indispensable to America's adversaries. Most significantly, dupes were front and center—even when unaware of their position—in the longest-running ideological battle of the twentieth century, which began in October 1917 and did not end until the period of 1989–91, and which saw the deaths of an unprecedented volume of human beings at the bloody hands of Communism.

The pervasiveness of the dupe, and of Communist efforts to manipulate Americans, has become fully apparent only with the massive declassification of once-closed Cold War archives, from Moscow to Eastern Europe to the United States—the central factor that made this book possible and demanded it be done in the first place.[8] These voluminous archives, especially those of the Soviet Communist International (Comintern) on the Communist Party USA, are the primary source for this book, and were its heart and motivation.

From these records we now know that American Communists and their masters in Moscow (and "masters" is not too strong a word, as this book will show) were acutely aware that they could never gain the popular support they needed to advance their goals. Instead they concealed their intentions and found clever ways to enlist the support of a much wider coalition that could help them push their private agenda. The Communists carefully ensured that the coalition was kept unaware of that agenda. The larger coalition was duped—or at least targeted to be duped.

The Communists could not succeed without the dupes. If they flew solo, operating without dupes at their rallies, at their protests, in their petitions and ads in newspapers, then the Communists would reveal themselves to be a tiny minority. They also would be open to immediate exposure.

The dupes lent a presence, an apparent legitimacy, credibility, and generally a helping hand to the pro-Moscow agenda. Without the dupes, the Communists were dead in the water. Thus, they sought out the dupes desperately.

From the outset of the Bolshevik Revolution, the Soviet Union specialized in this unique form of outreach. Vladimir Lenin himself preached the mode of recruitment: "The so-called cultural element of Western Europe and America," averred Lenin, speaking of the elite, "are incapable of comprehending the present state of affairs and the actual balance of forces; these elements must be regarded as deaf-mutes [idiots] and treated accordingly." These so-called useful idiots—the title of a bestselling book on the Cold War by Mona Charen[9]—were to be major components of the Communists' campaigns.

The Communists targeted naïve individuals—usually on the left, and nearly always liberals/progressives[10]—for manipulation. Whittaker Chambers, a long-time Soviet spy who later renounced Communism, wrote in his memoir, *Witness,* that "Communists make full use of liberals and their solicitudes." These liberals were prey, typically made vulnerable by their misplaced trust in the far left. They mistakenly saw American Communists as their friends and as simply another group of citizens practicing civil liberties in a democratic society based on First Amendment freedoms. Most liberals, obviously, were not themselves Communists, but in sharing the left portion of the ideological spectrum, they shared with the Communists many key sympathies: workers' rights, the redistribution of wealth, an expansive federal government, a favoring of the public sector over the private sector, class-based rhetoric (often demagoguery) toward the wealthy, progressively high tax rates, and a cynicism toward business and capitalism, to name a few. The differences were typically matters of degree rather than principle.

Communists also zeroed in on American liberals with a strong distaste for *anti*-Communists. As James Burnham, the great convert to anti-Communism, famously remarked, for the Left, "the preferred enemy is always to the right."[11] To this day, much of the Left views anti-Communists as worse than Communists. Professors Richard Pipes of Harvard and Robert Conquest of Stanford's Hoover Institution—deans of contemporary Sovietology, Communism, and the Cold War, and both conservatives—have spoken at length of how liberals, particularly within academia, have tended to be not pro-Communist as much as *anti*-anti-Communist. This anti-anti-Communism led many liberals to forsake their better judgment and to be taken in by the Communists. The Communists prized the dupes, then, because these Americans helped not only advance a pro-Moscow agenda but also *discredit* the anti-Communists who opposed that agenda.

The Communists' "Sneering Contempt" Toward Dupes

Here is how the process of duping typically worked: The Communists would engage in some sort of unpopular, unsavory work that they would be prepared to publicly deny. (I will give plenty of examples in the pages ahead.) Deceit was a deliberate element of a larger, carefully organized campaign. As Lenin said, in a favorite quote of Ronald Reagan, the only morality that Communists recognized was that which furthered their interests.[12]

At some point as the Communists pursued their intentions, someone or some group—usually moderate to conservative Republicans or conservative Democrats—would catch on and blow the whistle. When the alarm was sounded, the Communists typically lied about whatever they were doing. They claimed not to be guilty of the charges and said they were victims of right-wing, "Red-baiting" paranoia. They relied on non-Communist liberals to join them in attacking their accusers on the right.

Contrary to public perception, this process actually preexisted the McCarthy era, although it was particularly after Senator Joe McCarthy that liberals often came to dismiss, dislike, and even detest the anti-Communists on the right. Despite the fact that the warnings of anti-Communists were borne out in the twentieth-century slaughter otherwise known as Marxism-Leninism, anti-anti-Communism was always a powerful tool for the true Communists who relied on liberals as their dupes.

For instance, liberals were unaware that their harsh criticisms of President Ronald Reagan, who was rightly seeking to counter and undermine the USSR, often were thrust onto the front page of *Pravda* and cut and pasted into releases from TASS, the official Soviet news agency. This happened all the time. These liberals inadvertently added fodder to the Kremlin's propaganda machine. To be fair, many of them were offering sincere criticisms of the president—legitimate dissent. Only now, however, are we aware of the level to which the enemy exploited such dissent.

The same happened in the 1960s with the Vietnam War. As readers will see, some of the antiwar movement's marches and statements were organized behind the scenes by American Communists. Some of their published work was actually appropriated by the Vietcong prison guards and laid into the hands of American POWs. Some of the worst, most irresponsible antiwar material was used for the attempted indoctrination of American soldiers held in odious places like the Hanoi Hilton.

Sadly, these liberals did not recognize that the Communists, at home and abroad, were privately contemptuous of them, viewing them as comically credulous. As Whittaker Chambers noted, Communists privately treated dupes "with that sneering contempt that the strong and predatory almost invariably feel for victims who volunteer to help in their own victimization." In this sense, the greatest victim in this equation—aside from truth itself—has always been the duped liberals. They failed to recognize that the Communists were not their friends—that, indeed, the Communists often hated what they loved.

More than that, the Communists hated those *whom* the liberals loved. As this book will make clear, the Communists maligned the Democratic presidents whom liberals adored. Throughout the twentieth century, each and every Democratic leader was a target for Communist vilification, beginning with Woodrow Wilson, whom Lenin called a "shark" and a "simpleton." The Communists, whether American or Soviet, demonized icons of the Democratic Party. They claimed, for instance, that Franklin Roosevelt was responsible for a "Raw Deal" and that Harry Truman was pursuing "World War III" in the name of an emerging American fascist-racist state. Obama mentor Frank Marshall Davis is an unimaginably outrageous case in point—one that must be read to be appreciated. Davis's brutal demonization of, and vile accusations against, Democratic Party heroes like Truman, a man of true courage and character, ought to disgust modern Democrats. His accusations against Truman and his secretary of state, George Marshall—Davis dubbed the Marshall Plan "white imperialism" and "colonial slavery"—make Joe McCarthy's accusations look mild by comparison.

The Communists frequently sought to undermine not only individual Democratic presidents but the Democratic Party en masse. At one point—in an episode either misrepresented or ignored by modern historians and journalists—American Communists targeted the 1968 Democratic National Convention, in part for the purpose of trying to advance their own far-left third party. Bear in mind that they did not target the Republican National Convention that year. It was the Democrats they looked to unravel. In the revolution, it would be their brothers on the left who were put against the wall first.

Then there were the Communist betrayals of the causes dearest to liberals' hearts. For instance, because of their lockstep subservience to the Soviet Comintern—also illustrated in these pages—American Communists flip-flopped on issues as grave as Nazism and World War II based entirely on whether Hitler was signing a nonaggression pact with Stalin or invading Stalin's Soviet Union. The disgusting about-face by Communist Party USA (CPUSA) on this matter was unforgivable.

Moreover, Communists repeatedly lied to and exploited the Roosevelt and Truman administrations as they sought victory for Communist leader Mao Tsetung in China. Mao prevailed in 1949, which led to the single greatest concentration of corpses in human history: at least sixty million dead Chinese, and probably many more.[13] When Republican congressmen in the 1950s were furious at the Truman State Department for allegedly having "lost" China, those Republicans were—whether they fully understood it or not—really angry over how some good liberal people in the Truman State Department were manipulated by underhanded forces within their midst.

To this day, liberals need to be reminded again and again: *the Communists were not your friends.* Quite the contrary, American Communists were for the most part a strikingly intolerant, angry bunch—a point well known to anyone who joined, survived, and fled the Communist movement or has studied it closely.[14]

Nonetheless, the Communists found that they could deflect charge after charge—*"Red herring!" "Red-baiter!" "Witch-hunter!" "McCarthyism!"*—and immediately count on an echo chamber from liberals who were more suspicious of right-wing anti-Communists than of far-left Communists.

Standing Against Dupery

Fortunately, and importantly, there have always been non-Communist liberals and (more generally) Democrats who refused to be duped. These were shrewd individuals who deserve to be commended for playing a pivotal, positive role during the Cold War. They figured out, some sooner than others, that the Communists often undermined genuine liberal/Democratic Party causes—including workers' rights and civil rights.

Consequently, this book certainly does not indict the entirety of the Democratic Party. Democrats like Henry "Scoop" Jackson, Sam Nunn, Thomas Dodd, Zbigniew Brzezinski, John F. Kennedy, James Eastland, Francis Walter, Edwin Willis, Richard Russell, and Harry Truman—plus certain union leaders like the AFL-CIO's Lane Kirkland, some key players in the NAACP, and savvy intellectuals like Sidney Hook and Lionel Trilling[15]—were hardly dupes. Rather, they were committed Cold Warriors or chastened anti-Communist liberals who stood apart in their willingness to confront the Kremlin and not be hoodwinked. Some of them led America in intense Cold War showdowns.

Interestingly, some of their inheritors—for example, Senator Ted Kennedy, brother of Senator John F. Kennedy (both Massachusetts Democrats), or Senator Chris Dodd, son of Senator Thomas Dodd (both Connecticut Democrats)—bear little political resemblance.[16] It is impossible to picture Ted Kennedy in the 1980s borrowing the words of his late brother, who had alerted America to the perils of its "atheistic foe," of the "fanaticism and fury" of the "godless" "communist conspiracy," possessed by an "implacable, insatiable, unceasing . . . drive for world domination" and "final enslavement."[17] Ted Kennedy instead torched presidents like Ronald Reagan, who sounded more like Ted's brother than Ted did. Likewise, Ted Kennedy's pal and Senate colleague Chris Dodd would have never in the 1980s chastised his fellow liberals as "deluded" "innocents," as "unwitting" and "muddle-headed" "naïve sentimentalists," saddled with "confusion" over Communism and "communist political warfare"—as had Dodd's father.[18] For these modern liberals, the apple fell far from the tree.

The point, though, is that Democrats should not be painted with a broad brush; the views of the son (or the brother) were not necessarily identical to the father's. The 2008 Democratic senator from the Northeast was not the 1960 Democratic senator from the Northeast. The Democratic Party fifty years ago was more conservative than today. Similarly, the Republican Party then was more liberal than today. Just as Democrats like JFK and Scoop Jackson took hawkish or at least measured stances on Communism, there were liberal to moderate Republicans (like Senator Mark Hatfield) who pushed for accommodation and "freezes" with the Soviets. In fact, détente, which was the essence of Soviet accommodation, was begun by two Republican presidential administrations—those of Richard Nixon and Gerald Ford—before Democrat Jimmy Carter picked it up. Thus, this book is not a one-sided partisan rant against or in favor of a particular political party. Democrat Harry Truman is defended in these pages as much as, if not more than, Republican Ronald Reagan.

Often, too, prominent Democrats tried to stop other members of their party from being duped by the Soviets. For example, in the 1940s diplomat George Earle, the former governor of Pennsylvania, informed FDR that he was being badly misled by the Soviets on the infamous Katyn Wood massacre. Earle was far from the only Democrat to warn FDR.

In fact, large sections of this book could not have been completed without the digging of the Democrats who headed the House and Senate committees that collected information on certain indigenous threats. The House Committee on Un-American Activities was launched by Democrats in the 1930s, and for almost all of its nearly forty-year history it was chaired by Democrats—from Congressman Martin Dies of Texas in the 1930s, to Congressman Francis Walter of Pennsylvania in the 1950s, to Congressman Richard Ichord of Missouri in the late 1960s and early 1970s. Likewise, Democratic Party champions Senator James Eastland of Mississippi and Senator Thomas Dodd of Connecticut served as anti-Communist pillars on the Judiciary Committee, and chair and vice chair, respectively, of the Subcommittee on Internal Security, which produced numerous investigative analyses. It is crucial to understand that Democratic stalwarts played an important role in standing against the Soviet threat throughout the Cold War—or at least, until Democrats in Congress took a significant turn to the left after Watergate and Vietnam.

Of course, many liberals today have nothing good to say about the likes of the House Committee on Un-American Activities. In fact, many accounts lump together—quite inaccurately—the work of this *House* committee with the investigations of *Senator* Joe McCarthy, as M. Stanton Evans ably demonstrates in his 2007 book on McCarthy.[19] Frequently, too, the House committee is dismissed as conducting nothing more than "witch hunts." But in truth, the House Committee on Un-American Activities did much commendable work, from exposing traitors like Alger Hiss to blowing the whistle on insidious Communist-front groups such as the American Peace Mobilization, which unapologetically appeased Nazi Germany simply because Hitler had signed a pact with Stalin—and did so as the Nazis mercilessly pounded Britain. (The American Peace Mobilization will be documented at length in this book.) The House Committee on Un-American Activities—run by Democrats—played an indispensable role in casting light on this and other loathsome Communist fronts.

Further along those lines, some of the best work exposing the crimes and treasonous duplicity of American Communists—and thereby illuminating the dupes—has come from journalists and scholars who are on the left, or who at least are not right-wingers. To give just a few examples cited in the pages ahead: Arthur M. Schlesinger Jr., Allen Weinstein, Sam Tanenhaus, George F. Kennan, Ron Radosh, Anne Applebaum, John Lewis Gaddis, Mark Kramer, Jerry and Leona Schecter, not to mention leftist sources like *The New Republic,*[20] and leading academic publishing houses like Yale University Press and Harvard University Press.[21] Remarkably, the longtime editorial director of Yale University Press who launched the invaluable Annals of Communism series, Jonathan Brent, has been the Alger Hiss Professor at Bard College (no kidding).[22] This book builds on the foundation laid by these historians, journalists, and publishers.

The book further draws—and heavily so—on Communist literature and even the post–Cold War books and memoirs of Soviet officials as high ranking as Mikhail Gorbachev and his close aide Alexander Yakovlev. This is likewise (and especially) true for memoirs of American Communists, from CPUSA officials in the 1930s to the student radicals of the 1960s—the latter including Bill Ayers and Mark Rudd as well as ex-Communists such as David Horowitz, Peter Collier, and Ron Radosh. I have also drawn on the testimony of a long line of former Communists, from Arthur Koestler to J. B. Matthews to Whittaker Chambers.

The sterling investigative work of certain Democrats and liberals, and the eye-opening testimony of former Communists, should speak to all Americans—conservatives and liberals, Republicans and Democrats. In fact, it is my most sincere wish that liberals and Democrats will read this book carefully. It offers a cautionary tale for my friends on the left—the non-Communist left. For the best of my country, I want the dupery to stop. I plead with liberals to consider this book with an open mind, and be ready to be surprised and even occasionally encouraged.

The Duped, the Innocent, and the Redeemed

This book covers a wide cast of Cold War types and characters: Communists and non-Communists, left-wingers and right-wingers, fellow travelers, legitimate dissenters, anti-Communist liberals, duped and unduped liberals, and even full-fledged traitors. Some hopped across various of these categories at different points in their lives: For example, when Roger Baldwin founded the ACLU he was the prototype dupe and seemingly a small "c" communist—though prudent enough not to join CPUSA—but later he cooperated with the FBI in identifying Americans working for the KGB. More famously, Whittaker Chambers sojourned from KGB spy to conservative Republican. Even a wild progressive like educational reformer John Dewey ultimately learned (but only later) not to say the utterly stupid things about Joseph Stalin gushed by the likes of George Bernard Shaw and H. G. Wells, or by Dewey's student Corliss Lamont—men who forever embarrassed themselves with the most luscious praise for Soviet dictators.

Some folks who were duped on occasion were, on other occasions, sensible in recognizing the latest Soviet sham and bravely denounced Moscow's newest set of lies. Eleanor Roosevelt joined Stalin in blasting Winston Churchill's prophetic, courageous "Iron Curtain" speech, but two years later rightly called Stalin and Molotov liars because of their outrageous claims about America's treatment of Europe's "Displaced Persons." Others, like diplomat William C. Bullitt and Senator Paul Douglas, were once duped but made a 180-degree turn, emerging as brilliant observers who spoke to the brutal reality of the USSR. A major thrust of this narrative is the possibility of political redemption by former dupes. Indeed, three of the four dupes profiled in this book's early chapters later redeemed themselves, and did so while remaining Democrats and liberals in good standing.

The goal in this book is to be truthful. This means that I have not shied away from exploring how President Franklin Roosevelt was duped by certain aides, possibly including the enigmatic Harry Hopkins. But it also means that I defend FDR against the villainous charges leveled by Communists, not to mention certain inaccurate assertions made by anti-Communists. For instance, this book clarifies the record on FDR's relationship with Comrade Earl Browder, general secretary of CPUSA, a complicated issue subject to longtime, lingering misinterpretation.

In this book I also acknowledge that some people whom I admire were once dupes. In particular I have in mind the president on whom I began my career as an author: Ronald Reagan. Reagan obviously changed, and later acknowledged that he had been duped early in his Hollywood days. Even ex-Communists like Morris Childs and Ben Gitlow changed. Some of the once duped, who remained liberals to their dying day, have had a profound impact on me spiritually, and still do, such as Thomas Merton.

In short, I have tried to write this history as objectively as possible. I am open to the possibility that herein I myself have been duped on occasion: it may later emerge from FBI files and Soviet archives that one or more of the "innocent" characters in this book was not a gullible liberal but in fact a hard-line KGB spy. Time will tell.

Dupes: Defending the "Most Colossal Case of Political Carnage in History"

The compelling reason why this story needs to be told is that the dupes, the fellow travelers, the traitors, and whoever else wittingly or unwittingly aided and abetted the Communist movement in the last century also knowingly or unknowingly contributed to the most destructive ideology in the history of humanity. That is no small malfeasance. Whether they knew it or not, these folks defended or helped defend the indefensible. Some of them expressed regret, while many others did not. Many of the unrepentant instead attacked those who asked questions or shed light on their wrongdoings—and still do to this day.

No form of government or ideology in history killed so many innocents in such a short period as Communism. Stéphane Courtois, editor of the French journal *Communisme* and also of the seminal volume *The Black Book of Communism,* published by Harvard University Press, notes that government-orchestrated crime against its own citizens was a defining characteristic of the Communist system throughout its existence. Communism was responsible for an unfathomable amount of murder—a "multitude of crimes not only against individual human beings but also against world civilization and national cultures," writes Courtois. "Communist regimes turned mass crime into a full-blown system of government."[23]

Martin Malia, who wrote the preface to *The Black Book of Communism,* agrees. "Communist regimes did not just commit criminal acts," writes Malia, noting that non-Communist states have done likewise, "but they were criminal enterprises in their very essence: on principle, so to speak, they all ruled lawlessly, by violence, and without regard for human life." Here is a critical point and lesson: Under Communism, totally different national cultures, from all over the globe, sharing only Communism as their common characteristic, all committed mass violence against their populations. This violence was an institutional policy of the new revolutionary order. Its scope and inhumanity far exceeded anything in the national past of these cultures.[24]

Malia aptly writes that the Communist record offers the "most colossal case of political carnage in history."[25] *The Black Book of Communism* tabulates a total Communist death toll in the twentieth century of roughly 100 million.[26] And these frightening numbers actually underestimate the total, especially within the USSR.[27] The late Alexander Yakovlev, the lifelong Soviet apparatchik who in the 1980s became the chief reformer and close aide to Mikhail Gorbachev, and who, in the post-Soviet 1990s, was tasked with the grisly assignment of trying to total the victims of Soviet repression, estimated that Stalin alone was responsible for the deaths of 60 to 70 million, a stunning number two to three times higher than estimates in *The Black Book of Communism*.[28] Mao Tse-tung, as noted, was responsible for the deaths 60 to 70 million in China.[29] And then there were the killing fields of North Korea, Cambodia, Cuba, Eastern Europe, and more. In fact, the *Black Book* went to press too early to catch the 2 to 3 million who starved to death in North Korea in the late 1990s.[30]

A mountain of skulls of at least 100 million blows away Hitler's genocide in sheer bloodshed, and is actually twice the death toll of World War I and II combined.[31] It is difficult to identify any ideology or belief system in history that has killed more people, let alone in such a concentrated period of time—a roughly seventy-year period that equates to almost four thousand dead victims per *day*.[32] It boggles the mind to imagine how one ideology could cause so much pain and suffering. The very worst moments of the entirety of the Spanish Inquisition come nowhere near the level of death in Stalin's purges or even Lenin's first year in power.[33]

To be duped on, say, a poorly written piece of pork-barrel legislation submitted to Congress is one thing, but to be duped on the most horrific slaughter in human history is quite another.

Compounding the tragedy is that this murderous ideology was expansionary and dedicated to global revolution. While the commitment to that mission varied from Communist country to country, it had been a central tenet in the writings of Marx and Lenin and was the basis for the formation of the Soviet Comintern— the Communist International—which directed Communist parties worldwide from a central headquarters in Moscow. CPUSA was not merely another political party; its founding members considered themselves loyal Soviet patriots committed to this goal.

This fact—laid out in Chapter 1—is of enormous significance in understanding why fears over domestic Communism in the United States were not unduly obsessive but completely legitimate. And the dupes obliviously helped to advance the savage interests of Soviet Communism.

A debate still rages to this day: would American Communists have fought for the Soviets in a war between the United States and the USSR? The answer is not black-and-white, and ranged from individual to individual; many American Communists were torn on the matter. An easier question would be whether they would refuse to fight *against* the USSR. Their loyalties were with Moscow—certainly that was true for formal Communist Party members. They were blindly loyal patriots and parrots for the Soviet cause. As George F. Kennan put it, Communists faithfully obeyed only "the master's voice."[34] As will be seen in the pages ahead, this sentiment is especially pervasive in Comintern archives on CPUSA, declassified by the Russian government in the early 1990s.

In short, American Communists were defending a barbarous machine of genocidal class warfare, committed to the overarching goal of spreading itself all over the world, with the ultimate intention of a single Communist state directed from Moscow. Their naïve accomplices—the dupes—were sadly, dangerously unaware of how they were helping to advance that horrid system and its interests. That is why all of this still matters. And that is why the role of the dupe should never be laughably dismissed from our history or from discussions of where America, as a nation, goes from here.

The Dupe Today

Finally, that brings us from history—the past—to the present and future. America today finds itself fighting another form of totalitarianism in another global battle: radical Islamic fundamentalism, which brews the hate that the United States confronts in the War on Terror. In the twentieth century, the malignant force America confronted was militant, atheistic, murderous, expansionary communism; in the twenty-first century, it seems to be the scourge of suicidal/homicidal Islamism.

President George W. Bush, the 9/11 president, described the ten-year period after the fall of the Soviet Union in 1991 as the "hiatus" before the "day of fire" that exploded on September 11, 2001. In the mid-1990s, the emergent players on the world's stage were not clear to the United States. These were "years of repose, years of sabbatical," said Bush in his second inaugural address. What would come next? The answer came abruptly and violently, compliments of Osama bin Laden's suicide bombers, with three thousand Americans blown to pieces in the process.

The dupes of the War on Terror are not precisely the same as the dupes of the Cold War. That is especially so because the dupers are not nearly as adept at duping, or even at trying to dupe; the modern-day Islamist does not focus on honing the crass art of propaganda at which the twentieth-century Communist excelled. Moreover, it would never be right to assert that, say, a liberal critic of Bush policy in Iraq in 2006 was a dupe simply because that criticism pleased the enemy. That would be extremely unfair. Legitimate, proper dissent, especially at time of war, is a hallmark of American democracy. I had my own criticisms of Bush policy in Iraq, which I do not think made me a liberal dupe; no doubt, President Bush too often hurt himself—his own worst enemy in making himself the most unpopular president in modern times.[35]

Furthermore, in contrast to the Cold War, there is no centrally headquartered Comintern—such as, say, a "Khomeintern" in Iran—or al-Qaeda equivalent to CPUSA, cooking up propaganda to feed to the field workers, in careful coordination with ringmasters in Tehran.

In the War on Terror, then, the examples of dupery can be much more difficult to define. Nonetheless, clear cases of dupery have emerged since September 11, 2001, and especially since the U.S. invasion of Iraq in 2003. What's more, in plenty of situations certain Americans—including leading politicians—have said and done some really dumb things that were not legitimate, had no basis in fact, and no doubt elated the enemy.

Remarkably, some of those voices said things in the 2000s nearly identical to what they had said as much younger war protesters in the 1960s and 1970s. Some of the same figures who accused U.S. soldiers of war crimes and burning down villages in the Middle East in 2005 made the same irresponsible, incorrect, and deleterious allegations against U.S. soldiers in Southeast Asia thirty years earlier. Their transition from "Cold War dupe" to "War on Terror dupe" appears to have been almost seamless. Moreover, many of the radicals and war protesters of the '60s have suddenly reemerged as politicians, tenured professors, and even associates of the current president of the United States.

Those details will be provided in the pages ahead. What it means is that the dupe has not gone the way of the Cold War. The role of the dupe continues to be profoundly important, dangerous, and unappreciated. This book endeavors to show how and why.

1

WORLD REVOLUTION, THE COMINTERN, AND CPUSA

A merican Communists explicitly committed themselves to a systematic effort to promote and expand Communism throughout the world, with the violent, nondemocratic, totalitarian leadership in Moscow the guiding light of that effort. Of this, there is no question whatsoever. It was especially true of those who were actual members of the Communist Party USA (CPUSA), but applied even to some who never joined the party but were dedicated small "c" communists.

Of course, it was in the interest of American Communists to publicly deny this bold ambition, which patently ran contrary to U.S. interests. They scoffed at claims of any global ambition, so as to try to diminish the American public's fears, and to frame their accusers as paranoid. And they realized early on that they could count on many liberals/progressives to defend them against charges raised by anti-Communists.

Even to this day, much of the American academy downplays, if not outright denies, the Communists' international objective. Rather, it is the claims of the *anti*-Communists that are immediately held suspect, and tend to be rejected almost out of hand. That is to say, a Lillian Hellman or Earl Browder is reflexively given the benefit of the doubt, whereas a Whittaker Chambers or Ronald Reagan is not.

Yet the international objectives of the Communists are undeniable. The historical record on this matter is abundantly clear. It is unfortunate that space needs to be devoted to illustrating the most basic facts regarding the Communists' global ambitions. It would be like beginning a book on Hitler and World War II with a lengthy chapter trying to establish that the führer had expansionary designs on Europe. Tragically, the gross failure to teach these most elementary realities about Communism requires such a treatment.

The World According to Marx and Lenin

From the outset, Marxism-Leninism was expansionary, openly calling for Communism throughout the world. Even the typical college freshman can probably recognize the bumper-sticker slogan of Karl Marx: "Workers of the world, unite!" These triumphant final words of *The Communist Manifesto* (1848) are immediately preceded by Marx's proclamation that the proletarians of the revolution "have a world to win."[1]

In his 1850 Address of the General Council to the Communist League, Marx candidly explained, "It is our interest and our task to make the revolution permanent, until the proletariat has conquered state power and until the association of the proletarians has progressed sufficiently far—not only in one country but in all the leading countries of the world."[2]

There was no mistaking the universality of Marx's project, or that of Vladimir Lenin and the Bolsheviks. The Bolsheviks seized power in Russia in their October 1917 revolution. Richard Pipes, emeritus professor of Russian history at Harvard and the author of seminal books on the Russian Revolution and Communism, emphasizes that the Bolsheviks took the reins in Russia only because that country happened to be a ripe target of opportunity. They never had any intention, writes Pipes, of staying strictly within those borders. Quite the contrary: the Bolsheviks were convinced that the capitalist powers would quickly snuff out their revolution unless it rapidly spread to the industrial countries of the West.[3]

Lenin himself frankly explained that Communism must extend beyond Russia's borders: "We have always emphasized that one cannot achieve such a task as a socialist revolution in one country."[4] Indeed, he said that "the final victory of socialism in a single country is impossible."[5]

In a decree published in December 1917, only a few weeks after launching the Bolshevik Revolution, Lenin and cohort Leon Trotsky announced that they would appropriate the huge sum of two million rubles "for the needs of the revolutionary internationalist movement."[6] At the time their own revolution was far from secure, with the treacherous Russian Civil War (1918–21) imminent. Still, the urgent need to protect themselves did not deter them from their paramount priority: global revolution.

In a major speech in 1920, Lenin could not have been clearer about the international scope of his and his party's ambitions: "[In October 1917] we knew that our victory will be a lasting victory only when our undertaking will conquer the whole world, because we had launched it exclusively counting on the world revolution."[7] When he gave this speech, the Bolsheviks were embroiled in the Russian Civil War, but tellingly, Lenin defined victory as occurring when Communism had triumphed not only in Russia but around the globe.

Comrades immediately endorsed Lenin's words. Trotsky, who himself professed the "proletarian world revolution" and the goal of "overturning the world," declared that in regard to the Bolsheviks' ultimate objectives, "more unassailable testimony could not be asked."[8]

America in the Communists' Crosshairs

For decade upon decade of the Cold War, the American Left angrily denied a point made by many sources on the right, from *National Review* to President Ronald Reagan: Vladimir Lenin and his Bolsheviks had their eyes not only on Europe but even on America.[9]

Of course, that point should hardly be controversial. After all, Lenin spoke of *world* revolution, as had Marx. But given the many times this elemental point has been challenged over the years, it is worth revisiting exactly what Lenin and others said on the subject.

As early as August 1918, less than a year after seizing control in Russia, Lenin took the time to write an open letter to American workers. The remarkably frank letter, laden with his notorious bile, was a classic Lenin diatribe.[10] He railed against America's so-called imperialists and multimillionaires, who, he said, were "disgusting" hypocrites, slanderous "vultures," "scoundrels," "sharks," and "modern slave-owners" who arrogantly wallowed in "filth and luxury," holding Americans on the verge of "pauperism." "Every dollar" they earned was "stained with blood."

Yes, said Lenin, these Americans might think that they are "geographically the most secure" of the world's "bloodsuckers," but, alas, assured the Bolshevik, invoking revolutions from Jacobin France to Bolshevik Russia, they were not secure from his "invincible" proletariat: "The American workers will not follow the bourgeoisie. They will be with us, for civil war against the bourgeoisie." He urged: "We are banking on the inevitability of world revolution. . . . We are in a besieged fortress until other armies of the world socialist revolution come to our aid."

This was a direct appeal to the worker-troops of the United States of America. And violence would be necessary: "The truth," explained Lenin, a moral relativist, "is that no revolution can be successful unless the resistance of the exploiters is crushed." A few months later, in November 1918, Lenin warned that "Anglo-French and American imperialism will inevitably strangle the independence and freedom of Russia unless world-wide socialist revolution, unless world-wide Bolshevism, conquers."[11] He insisted that "the Soviet government triumph in every advanced country in the world," particularly over "Anglo-American imperialism." "One or the other" must triumph. "There is no middle course."[12]

There it was, in the plainest language, addressed to Americans: global revolution and conquest, worldwide Communism and Bolshevism, capitalist encirclement and confrontation. There was never any doubt about Lenin's intentions, or his belligerence.

Violence Is Necessary

The language that Lenin and his followers used—seeing the opposition "crushed," calling for Bolshevism to "conquer," "overturning the world"—is instructive. Lenin, Trotsky, and others insisted that to achieve the Bolsheviks' goals, force was necessary, from sparking revolts to fomenting full-scale civil wars. As early as January 1919, Moscow instigated a revolt in post–World War I Germany, though it was quickly quelled. By July 1920, the Communists had sparked uprisings in Hungary, Finland, and Poland. Lenin, Trotsky, Nikolai Bukharin, and Grigori Zinoviev all excitedly signed a manifesto announcing that "world Civil War" was the "watchword" and "the order of the day."[13]

Lenin went so far as to favor another world war to advance his cause, precisely the strategy Stalin adopted in 1939.[14] It is uncanny to read secret Lenin missives from the 1920s on spreading Communism to Poland, Italy, Hungary, Germany, and other countries, and then to read Stalin's secret speech to his Central Committee advocating the same two decades later.[15] Stalin was truly Lenin's disciple.

Lenin, like Stalin after him, foresaw inevitable military conflict with the West. He forthrightly explained this view in a March 1919 report to the Eighth Party Congress: "We live not only in a state but in a system of states, and the existence of the Soviet Republic side by side with the imperialist states for an extended period is unthinkable. In the end either one or the other will conquer. And before this result, a series of horrible conflicts between the Soviet Republic and the bourgeois states is inevitable."[16] One cannot casually skip over the phrase "horrible conflicts," which was no small statement. Lenin had deduced that "as long as capitalism and socialism exist, we cannot live in peace: in the end, one or the other will triumph—a funeral dirge will be sung either over the Soviet Republic or over world capitalism."[17]

Later, in a major 1946 article for *Life* magazine, the prominent liberal historian Arthur M. Schlesinger Jr. underscored this crucial Lenin quotation. Schlesinger noted that Lenin and his followers, including Stalin and his associates, were bound to regard the United States as the enemy not because of a particular American deed but because of the "primordial fact" that America was the leading capitalist power and thus, by "Leninist syllogism," unappeasably hostile. Lenin assumed that America would seek to oppose, encircle, and destroy Soviet Russia.[18] Perhaps Schlesinger hoped to spare his fellow liberals the embarrassment of denying such obvious facts, particularly since Republican anti-Communists they disliked were loudly citing the Communists' frank statements. Like Schlesinger, other esteemed men of the left wrote candidly of the Communists' ambitions at the time. A notable example was George F. Kennan in his historic "X" article, in which he outlined the policy of containment.[19]

Not surprisingly, Lenin frequently expressed a favorable view of war. "To reject war in principle is un-Marxist," he wrote in July 1914, knowing full well that Marx himself said the same. Lenin also stated: "Who objectively stands to gain from the slogan 'Peace'? In any case, not the revolutionary proletariat." He reaffirmed this one year later, in July 1915: "We cannot support the slogan 'Peace' since it is a totally muddled one and a hindrance to the revolutionary struggle."[20]

Lenin and Trotsky fondly harked back to the most barbarous group of killers prior to the Bolsheviks: the French fanatic Maximilien Robespierre and his guillotine-dropping Jacobins, who beheaded forty thousand French citizens from 1793 to 1794, with special attention to persecuting the religious.[21] "It will be necessary to repeat the year 1793," wrote Lenin. "After achieving power, we'll be considered monsters, but we couldn't care less."[22] Lenin and his self-described group of "glorious Jacobins" would monstrously do just that, and, indeed, could not care less.

Here one sees a commitment to world revolution at truly any cost, including any carnage necessary. Lenin biographer Dmitri Volkogonov, a former Red Army general, stated that "world revolution" was "a matter to which he [Lenin] devoted unprecedented effort."[23] The unprecedented effort required unprecedented means.

Establishing the Comintern

To achieve his "full-fledged political project: world socialist revolution," Lenin established the Communist International (Comintern) in March 1919.[24] Writing in *Pravda* at the time, Lenin declared, "The founding of the . . . Communist International heralds the international republic of Soviets, the international victory of communism."[25] In his concluding speech to the congress at which the Comintern was established, Lenin proclaimed that "the victory of the Proletarian revolution on a world scale is assured."[26]

The Comintern was centralized under Moscow leadership, which was to have "uncontested authority" over the Communist parties that would soon be established all over the world, including in the United States.[27] The entire physical apparatus for the Comintern, which included several buildings and the radio school that served as its all-important source for mass communication, was located exclusively in Moscow. Every country with a Communist Party would have a representative stationed in Moscow.[28]

The USSR's leadership was to be the conductor of the global Communist symphony, orchestrating an international association of Communist parties, all dedicated to the goal of a global revolution. Those parties were to march in lockstep with Moscow. The master's foreign-policy goals were to be theirs.

By 1919, already impressed with the "dizzying speed" of the Communists' progress, Grigori Zinoviev, the first head of the Comintern, confidently predicted that "in a year all Europe shall be Communist. And the struggle for Communism shall be transferred to America, and perhaps Asia and other parts of the world."[29]

The military-minded Trotsky described the Comintern as the "General Staff of the World Revolution."[30] Lenin himself left no doubt that he envisioned the Comintern as (in Richard Pipes's words) "a branch of the Russian Communist Party, organized on its model and subject to its orders." The 1920 Comintern Congress made this clear, demanding that its foreign delegates enforce "iron military discipline" on party members in their home countries. Directing delegates to take over mass organizations and especially trade unions in their home countries, Lenin said that Communists should, by "necessity," not hesitate to "resort to every kind of trick, cunning, illegal expedient, concealment, suppression of truth."[31]

The Comintern made clear that any members of Communist parties around the world who did not give total subservience to Moscow, "who reject in principle the conditions and theses put forward by the Communist International, are to be expelled from the party." The 1920 Congress spelled out the necessity of total fealty to Moscow with the following stated condition for admission to the Comintern: "Every party which wishes to join the Communist International is obligated to give unconditional support to any Soviet republic in its struggle against counter-revolutionary forces."[32]

Here we see the pattern established: members of Communist parties around the world, including in the United States, would see themselves as loyal Soviet patriots. The slogan, in effect, was "Moscow first." Soviet interests reigned supreme, holding sway over those of any other regime. "Party discipline" would become an infamous trademark of Communist parties everywhere, including in the United States. Discipline was harsh, more fiercely dogmatic than any religious excommunication.

In keeping with Lenin's goals, the 1920 Comintern Congress explicitly stated that violence was central to the Communist mission. It instructed its delegates to support "armed insurrection" against non-Communist governments in order to supplant them with Communist regimes. As Pipes notes, these Communist regimes "would ultimately fuse into a worldwide Soviet Socialist Republic."[33] And among the twenty-one requirements for membership that the Comintern Congress issued, point seventeen declared bluntly, "The Communist International has declared war on the entire bourgeois world."[34]

The Comintern continued that pledge after Lenin departed this world. In 1924, a year that began with the Bolshevik godfather's death in January, the Fifth Congress reiterated the Comintern's global objectives: "The ultimate aim of the Communist International is to replace the world capitalist economy by a world system of Communism." The "successful struggle" for the "dictatorship of the proletariat presupposes the existence in every country of a compact Communist Party, hardened in the struggle, disciplined, centralized and closely lined up with the masses."[35]

The Comintern was to be the permanent platform of the Soviet Communist state. Thus, when asked to pick a date for the start of the Cold War, some historians have chosen not customary dates like 1945 or 1947 or 1948, but 1920—the year the Comintern took flight.[36]

The Comintern Comes to America: CPUSA

In America, many within the non-Communist Left shrugged off the Comintern. For years, some questioned whether the organization had ever existed, let alone whether it harbored such global ambitions. These deniers were precariously susceptible to Communist manipulation.

And yet it did not take long before the tentacles of Vladimir Lenin and the Comintern reached all the way into America.

The Communist Party established in the United States was, like other Communist parties around the world, expected to thrive on lawlessness and deceit. This was made official at that first major Comintern Congress in July 1920. Point three of the twenty-one requirements for membership in the Comintern called on Communists in every country, including in America, to create a "parallel illegal apparatus," which, "at the decisive moment," would take charge of the revolution. When the moment was right, those comrades would assist the masters in Moscow in "performing [their] duty to the revolution." Lest there be any doubt that the Soviets intended American Communists to understand this duty, Moscow widely disseminated these orders within the United States, in English, in a document titled "The Twenty-one Conditions of Admission into the Communist International."[37]

The American effort started in September 1919, only months after the establishment of the Comintern in Moscow. At a convention in Chicago, two U.S. Communist parties were formed: the Communist Labor Party and the Communist Party of America. After a few additional mergers and name changes, the American Communists in 1929 formed a single Communist Party USA (CPUSA). CPUSA became the political party for American Communists throughout the entirety of the Cold War.[38]

It cannot be emphasized enough that American members of the Communist Party saw themselves as subservient to the Comintern and to Moscow. This is the single most important point in understanding the party, its positions, and why it was indeed a threat—and why anti-Communists were rightly concerned.

From the outset, the Comintern micromanaged the party in America. It created an "Anglo-American Secretariat," and stationed a representative of the American party in Moscow. This liaison delivered orders from Moscow to American Communists.[39]

Moscow's control of the American party was constant and total, in ways far too numerous to summarize here. Historian and former Communist Theodore Draper provided a simple but telling indicator in his eye-opening account of CPUSA. Draper recalled that when a new member (like himself) joined the party in, say, New York in the 1920s, he signed a party registration card inscribed with these words: "The undersigned, after having read the constitution and program of the Communist Party, declares his adherence to the principles and tactics of the party and the Communist International, agrees to submit to the discipline of the party as stated in its constitution, and pledges to engage actively in its work."[40]

New members swore a loyalty oath, which stated: "I pledge myself to rally the masses to defend the Soviet Union, the land of victorious socialism. I pledge myself to remain at all times a vigilant and firm defender of the Leninist line of the party, the only line that insures the triumph of Soviet Power in the United States." This particular oath was issued in 1935, during the height of Stalin's terror, which annihilated tens of millions.[41]

Unflagging allegiance to the Bolsheviks was the mission of Americans who joined the Communist Party. They swore to it. They literally carried it with them. It is self-evident that this allegiance was not "American"; it most certainly stood in contrast to the principles of the American republic as conceived by its founders.

The Comintern Archives on CPUSA

CPUSA subservience to the Comintern/Moscow was so total that when CPUSA picked leaders for its own Central Committee, it first sent a list to the Comintern for permission. These lists exist for viewing today, declassified in the Comintern Archives on CPUSA.[42] Portions of those archives are available for examination at the Library of Congress, which in the early 1990s purchased from the post-Soviet Russian government (of Boris Yeltsin) a sizable reservoir of material. Each reel of microfiche from those archives contains a day's worth of viewing material, compliments of CPUSA's fastidious reporting to bosses at the Comintern. And each details the American party's shocking subservience to Moscow. The files include reports to the Comintern from the American party's Central Executive Committee, instructions from the Comintern to CPUSA, financial reports, correspondence among the heads of the groups, and much more.[43]

From the countless examples that can be drawn from those archives, here are three from the immediate September 1919 to November 1919 period when the American party was first created. These examples are significant in demonstrating the level of Comintern control over the American party and, in turn, the loyalty of those party members to Moscow.

The first example, which is among the earliest documents in the massive Comintern Archives on CPUSA, is from the summer of 1919, just prior to the party's formation in Chicago in September. The heading on the double-spaced document states, "Soviet Power and the Creation of a Communist Party of America." The three-page report, described as a "Thesis of the Executive Committee of the Third International," carries two authoritative signatures: "For the Bureau of the Communist International, N. Bucharin, J. Bersin (Winter)."[44]

PARLIAMENTARISM, SOVIET POWER AND THE CREATION OF A
COMMUNIST PARTY OF AMERICA.
(Thesis of the Executive Committee of the Third International) 1

1) For the purpose of attaining an immediate success of the revolutionary class struggle, of systematically organizing it, of uniting and co-ordinating its all really revolutionary forces, and for the purpose of unifying principles and organization, it is necessary to form a Communist Party which should be affiliated with the Communist International. This party may be the result of the union of the left elements of the A. S. P., S. L. P., I. W. W., Socialist Propaganda League, etc..

2) The cardinal unifying and directing idea should be the recognition of the necessity for proletarian dictatorship, that is, Soviet power, through revolutionary mass action (strikes and insurrections) which destroys the old machinery of the capitalist state, transforming xxxxxxxxxxxxxxxxxxxxxxx and creates a new proletarian state, transforming the organs of mass action (Soviets of Workers Deputies) into organs of power over the resisting bourgeoisie.

This cardinal idea can unite the left elements of the disentegrating Socialist Party and the I. W. W.

The negative attitude of the I. W. W. toward political action was always based upon their opposition to parliamentarism. From the view-point of revolutionary Marxism, every class struggle aiming at the destruction of the bourgeois state machinery is a political struggle, whether the groups and classes conducting this struggle recognize it or not. The crux of the struggle centers just now

Moscow orders "the creation of a Communist Party of America": Excerpts from the 1919 Comintern report calling for an American Communist Party loyal to "Soviet power."

3.

any such vivid examples of revolutionary parliamentarism as the Liebknecht and bolshevik examples, precipitated the negative attitude toward parliamentarism. However, this issue does not warrant a split in the movement.

We call the attention of the comrades to the necessity of creating illegal underground machinery side by side with the legally functioning apparatus.

For the Bureau of the Communist International,

N. Bucharin

J. Bersin (Winter)

(See pages 24–25.) This refers to Nikolai Bukharin, one of the core Bolshevik founders, and Jan Berzin, who later became head of the GRU (Soviet military intelligence).

The document begins by affirming that the American party will not be independent from the Soviet Comintern. It orders: "1) For the purpose of attaining an immediate success of the revolutionary class struggle, of systematically organizing it, of uniting and co-ordinating all really revolutionary forces, and for the purpose of unifying principles and organizations, it is necessary to form a Communist Party which should be affiliated with the Communist International." The next line makes the allegiance clear: "2) The cardinal unifying and directing idea should be the recognition of the necessity for proletarian dictatorship, that is, Soviet power."[45] The document commits both the Soviet and American representatives to the Soviet superstructure.

The Comintern concludes with a telling reminder to the "comrades" in America: "We call the attention of the comrades to the necessity of creating illegal underground machinery side by side with the legally functioning apparatus." Here we see the essence of the third requirement of membership that the Comintern Congress delineated—but in a document issued months *before* the Congress produced its twenty-one-point manifesto. Moscow's order to the American comrades is unambiguous: you must carry forth your work of "revolutionary Marxism"— aimed at "the destruction of the bourgeois state machinery"—by all means available, legal *and* illegal.

This was quintessential Leninist morality. "To speak the truth is a petit-bourgeois habit," said Lenin. "To lie, on the contrary, is often justified by the lie's aim."[46] The good comrades in America would agree.

A second document in the Comintern Archives from the period appears to have been issued from the Chicago convention of September 1–7, 1919.[47] (See page 27.) It is printed on the letterhead of the newly established Communist Party of America, at 1219 Blue Island Avenue, Chicago, Illinois. In this letter, the Communist Party of America's executive secretary, Charles Ruthenberg, an international hero of the Communist movement, addresses "International Delegates" and the Comintern in Moscow.[48] The brief, celebratory letter bears four simple sentences:

> In the name of the Communist Workers of the United States organized in the Communist Party of America I extend greetings to the Communist Party of Russia.
>
> Hail to the Dictatorship of the Proletariat!

COMMUNIST PARTY OF AMERICA
1219 Blue Island Avenue
CHICAGO. ILL.

;.B.Ruthenberg
   Executive Secretary

                                        Official Organ
                                        THE COMMUNIST
                                        Issued Weekly
                                        Louis C. Fraina
                                                  Editor
                                        I.E.Ferguson
                                                  Associate Editor

          In the name of the Communist Workers of the United States organized in the Communist Party of America I extend greetings to the Communist Party of Russia.

          Hail to the Dictatorship of the Proletariat!

          Long Live the Russian Socialist Soviet Republic!

          Long Live the Communist International!

                              Fraternally Yours,
                                   C.Ruthenberg
                              Executive Secretary.

Isaac Edw. Ferguson.

Alexander Steklitsky.   International Delegates

C.Ruthenberg

NOTE:Comrade Louis C.Fraina,International Secretary and comrade Nicholas I Hourwich,International Delegate,not in Chicago at this time).

Celebrating the birth of the American Communist Party: The brand-new Communist Party of America proudly proclaims its loyalty to Soviet Russia.

Long live the Russian Socialist Soviet Republic!
Long live the Communist International!

The level of loyalty to Moscow speaks for itself. The respect was mutual: upon Ruthenberg's death a decade later, his body was placed in memoriam at the wall of the Kremlin near Lenin's tomb, alongside other "heroes" of Bolshevism.[49] This American chose to spend eternity in the cold bosom of his beloved USSR, as close as possible to the rotting breast of Vladimir Lenin.

A third document, a remarkable seven-page letter dated November 24, 1919, is addressed "To the Bureau of the Communist International." Sent from Chicago, the letter is signed by "International Secretary, Louis C. Fraina," and attested to by "C. [Charles] Ruthenberg, Executive Secretary," both with the Communist Party of America. (See page 29.) The letter begins, "Comrades: As International Secretary, I make application for admission of the Communist Party of America to the Bureau of the Communist International." Noting that the Communist Party of America was officially organized on September 1, 1919, with "approximately 55,000 members," Fraina and his comrades are now filing their official application.[50]

And as they do, Fraina and friends make their loyalties frighteningly clear. Here is their close on page seven:

The Communist Party realizes the immensity of its task; it realizes that the final struggle of the Communist Proletariat will be wage[d] in the United States, our conquest of power alone assuring the world Soviet Republic. Realizing all this, the Communist Party prepares for the struggle.

Long live the Communist International! Long live the World Revolution!!

Fraternally yours,
International Secretary,
Louis C. Fraina (signature)

In absorbing this letter, consider that a long line of dupes would later defend the American Communist Party against charges that it was battling for the USSR, the Comintern, and global revolution. Those individuals simply did not know what they were talking about.

As for Louis C. Fraina, he was one of the core founders of the American party, credited as the first Communist editor in the United States. Fraina edited *Revolu-*

final struggle of the Communist Proletariat will be wages in the United States, our conquest of power alone assuring the world Soviet Republic. Realizing all this, the Communist Party prepares for the struggle.
Long live the Communist International ! Long live the World Revolution

Fraternally Yours,

International Secretary.

Attest
C. Ruthenberg.
Executive Secretary.

Preparing for the "final struggle": An excerpt from the Communist Party of America's application for Comintern membership. Here, on the last page, the American party commits itself to the "conquest of power" in the United States.

tionary Age, a Boston-based magazine that in its first edition, July 5, 1919—the day after America's birthday—devoted itself to the overthrow of the American government and "the annihilation of the fraudulent democracy of the parliamentary system."[51] Fraina's next issue, in August, called for a "dissolution and collapse of the whole capitalist world system" and "world culture," to be "replaced by communism." It advocated "an international alliance of the Communist Party of the United States only with the communist groups of other countries, such as the Bolsheviki of Russia." These, said Fraina's *Revolutionary Age,* would be the principles to be adopted by the comrades at their convention in Chicago in September.[52]

With Soviet Communism, Fraina had found his system and his calling—and so had his friends. Their servility lasted throughout the existence of the American party, which was and would remain a Bolshevik puppet.[53] Herb Romerstein, a leading authority on Communism in America, sums it up: "From 1919, when it [the American Communist Party] was formed, to 1989, when the Soviet Union collapsed, it was under total Soviet control."[54]

Further Subservience to Moscow: Year Two

Again, these examples of subservience to Moscow are only a tiny sampling of the evidence. Bear in mind, too, that this mountain of evidence comes from just a few months in 1919 immediately surrounding the formation of the American Communist Party. A similarly voluminous dossier can be assembled from practically any other time period covered in the Comintern Archives on CPUSA. To suggest the extensiveness of this evidence, I will cite a handful of additional remarkable cases, these from the second year of existence of the American Communist Party and the Comintern—the year 1920. These, too, are extremely telling. They are critical to understanding that American Communists were not members of a conventional political party.

The first example is a three-page document titled "TO THE CENTRAL COMMITTEES OF THE AMERICAN COMMUNIST PARTY AND THE AMERICAN COMMUNIST LABOUR PARTY." Dated January 12, 1920, the letter is issued from Moscow by "President of the Executive Committee of the Communist International, Zinoviev"—that is, Comintern chief Grigori Zinoviev.[55] In the letter, Zinoviev indicates that the relationship between American Communists and the Soviet Union is to be underground, illicit, and insidious. The head of the Comintern suggests that Communists engage in all sorts of clandestine activity in America, ranging from "revolutionary propaganda among the masses" to "an underground printing-plant and distribution machinery." Zinoviev closes the letter with this final order from the Comintern: "The Executive Committee urges the American Comrades immediately to establish an underground organisation, even if it is possible for the party to function legally."[56] So the clear order from the Comintern was that Communists in America needed to develop covert capabilities *even when they were legally permitted to assemble as a political party.* Here was another explicit instruction from the Comintern to establish an illegal "underground" in America, issued months in advance of the Comintern Congress's formal requirement that Communist parties overseas create a "parallel illegal apparatus."

The Comintern edicts that followed throughout 1920 displayed a similarly dictatorial tone. Among them is a caustic memo addressed "To All Members of the Socialist Party of the United States," dealing with the May 1920 report issued at the National Convention of the American Socialist Party.[57] In this seven-page memo, the Comintern expresses its frustration at the lack of centralization among America's comrades. It barks:

> The Communist International is not a hotel, where travellers may come with their baggage and carry on their private affairs. The Communist International is an army in wartime; volunteers who join the Army of the Revolution must adopt its principles and obey its orders, submit to its discipline. None but revolutionary, Communist parties are accepted in the Communist International.

The Comintern demands a "strongly centralized form of organization, a military discipline." This is "war," after all—or, as the memo puts it, the party is "an army in wartime." Getting testy, Moscow wants to know: are the American comrades on the side of Bolshevism, or not?

Right on cue, the United Communist Party of America (a merger of the two previous parties) called a convention on May 31, 1920, where it responded with a brief one-and-a-half page resolution for the Comintern.[58] (See page 32.) The delegates concluded by adopting this specific resolution:

> The United Communist Party, in its program, form of organization and methods of party activity conforms to every requirement of the Communist International; and it is a first desire of our party to make itself an [sic] native unit of the International in every possible respect.
> Greetings to the Communists of all countries!
> Long live the Communist International!

- 2 -

Party will omit no effort to join to itself all of the members of these
Federation groups, no longer, however, as loosely federated units of a de-
centralized party, but as members of a centralized party.

The United Communist Party, in its program, form of organization and
methods of party activity conforms to every requirement of the Communist
International; and it is a first desire of our party to make itself an
active unit of the International in every possible respect.

Greetings to the Communists of all countries!

Long live the Communist International!

                                        The delegates of the first
                                        convention of the United
                                        Communist Party of America.

Adopted by the convention, May 31st, 1920.

Received in Holland July 3rd will a letter signed J. E. Ferguson requesting transmission to M. Mailed from H. to Berlin on July 5th. Another copy has been forwarded throught special occasion on the same date. Holland July 5th

A "native unit of the International": The conclusion of the resolution adopted at the American Communist Party's May 1920 convention, at which the party declared its absolute dedication to Moscow.

This resolution ought to be a chilling wake-up call to those who have claimed that the American Communist Party was just another political party. Here the American Communists unequivocally declared their absolute dedication to the supreme party in Moscow and to the worldwide revolution.

Moscow Money to CPUSA

The most salient illustration of Soviet control over American Communists was the fact that the American party all along received funding from the Soviet government, beginning in 1919 and continuing until the collapse of the Soviet empire in 1989.

This fact publicly emerged only after the Cold War ended. We now know, however, that the Soviets did not provide some piddling sum; rather, they kept CPUSA afloat with massive stipends. By 1980 the funding had reached nearly $2.8 million annually. In the 1920s, when cash from the USSR was especially scarce, the Comintern supplied the American Communist movement with an enormous sum in valuables: several million dollars' worth of gold, silver, jewels, much or perhaps all of which the Soviet regime had stolen, and in some cases had probably removed from sacred relics from ransacked churches.[59]

The significance of this support cannot be overstated: a foreign government, with which America was effectively at war by the late 1940s, was funding an American political party, and that party concealed the funding. This was illegal at both ends, on the Soviet side and CPUSA side.

And yet the dupes shrugged off suspicions of funding as "inordinate fear" of Communism, as the latest Red-under-every-bed theory of extremists such as those from the John Birch Society. They refused to concede the possibility that such a nightmare existed under Uncle Sam's nose. In fact, as made clear by documentation that has emerged since the end of the Cold War, the funding was real, it was deep, it was illicit, and it most assuredly proved that CPUSA was an arm of the Soviet regime.

That financial connection likewise applied to the *Daily Worker,* the house organ of CPUSA, which received heavy cash infusions from the Comintern from the earliest days of its existence.[60] That, too, is no surprise, given that, as the U.S. Congress affirmed, the *Daily Worker* was "founded in response to direct instructions from the Communist International in Moscow."[61] It was a creature of the Comintern, which exercised control over the publication, either directly or through CPUSA, or both. The editor of the *Daily Worker* was approved by the Comintern.

So intertwined was the *Daily Worker* with Moscow that editors of the American paper ended up as top Comintern officials (Morris Childs, to name just one) and as employees of the official Soviet news agency, TASS (Harry Freeman, among others).[62] Quite a few members of CPUSA worked for TASS and were recruited (some successfully) by Soviet intelligence—Samuel Krafsur, Paul Burns, and Beatrice Heiman, to name a few.[63]

These Communists served not America but the Soviet Union. Their loyalties were elsewhere. As Lincoln Steffens, the popular journalist for *The New Republic,* unforgettably put it, "I am a patriot for Russia; the Future is there; Russia will win out and it will save the world."[64]

Herb Romerstein repeatedly stresses this loyalty point: "Communist Party members were loyal Soviet patriots. . . . Most were not qualified to be spies, but those who were qualified were recruited through Party channels and made available to Soviet intelligence for classic espionage, agent-of-influence operations, or as couriers." He says that "almost every spy" tapped by the Soviets was a member of the American party.[65] CPUSA was a major recruiting ground for Soviet espionage, and some of those American Communists saluted the Red flag and consciously collaborated with Moscow.

Romerstein clarifies that these individuals in CPUSA "were not the useful idiots," not the "suckers"—that is, they were not the dupes. Quite the contrary, he affirms: "They were fully aware of exactly what they were doing. They manipulated the useful idiots on behalf of Soviet interests. Trusted Party members in the front organizations controlled them and recruited suckers to promote Soviet interests."[66]

Lenin's Dupes

Sadly, many Americans, especially liberals, neglected these vital points of distinction. Too often, they defended CPUSA as just another political group with the traditional right to practice civil liberties and form a political party, and dismissed allegations that the party was collaborating with the Comintern. In doing so, the dupes became a huge asset to the American Communists, who covered up the truth about their operations not just out of caution but in keeping with explicit orders from Moscow. While the Communists dissembled, the dupes aided their denials.

Vladimir Lenin had brilliantly foreseen this assistance by dupes, whom he referred to as "deaf-mutes"—an expression that, in less sensitive times, has been translated as "idiots." He cynically but shrewdly saw dupes—drawn from the

Western cultural elite—as useful specifically on matters involving the Comintern. He stated:

> We must (a) In order to placate the deaf-mutes, proclaim the fictional separation of our government . . . from the Comintern, declaring this agency to be an independent political group. The deaf-mutes will believe it. (b) Express a desire for the immediate resumption of diplomatic relations with capitalist countries on the basis of complete non-interference in their internal affairs. Again, the deaf-mutes will believe it.[67]

They will believe it. Lenin confidently predicted that these *idiots*—this is the basis for the "useful idiots" phrase attributed to Lenin—would believe the denials and therefore help advance the Communist conspiracy. Added Lenin: "They will even be delighted and fling wide-open their doors through which the emissaries of the Comintern and Party Intelligence agencies will quickly infiltrate into these countries disguised as our diplomatic, cultural, and trade representatives."[68]

In his typical crude fashion, Lenin laughed at these people. He really did see these elites as useful idiots. He held them in greater contempt than did anyone on the right.

Lenin saw huge potential in America, telling a meeting of activists in December 1920, "Thus we have before us the greatest state in the world."[69] And the "deaf-mutes" were a big part of his plan for that greatest state in the world.

Murdering the Masses in Moscow

In the meantime, Lenin and his minions had some killing to do. As American Communists pledged their heart and soul to Moscow, their new gods were gunning down the masses. Those who dared possess property were especially reviled—for Marx had written, "The theory of the Communists may be summed up in the single sentence: Abolition of private property."[70] Landowners like the kulaks were carted off or simply expunged on the spot, and they were merely one category of Lenin's identified "harmful insects."

The Soviet slaughter largely credited to Joseph Stalin was begun by Lenin, the man who instituted the gulag labor-camp system and established the secret police, first called the Cheka. By 1918–19, within just months of the October 1917 revolution, the Cheka was averaging a thousand executions per month, without trial, for political offenses alone.[71] The Cheka proudly self-reported this number in its documents. In fact, it apologized that its data was incomplete, and boasted that the number was likely much higher.

In the 1920s, the Cheka introduced a quota method: each region and district had to arrest, deport, or shoot a certain percentage of people who were deemed denizens of several "enemy" social classes.[72] Members of certain groups from within the bourgeoisie were targeted in the USSR as Jews were in Nazi Germany—that is, for isolation and liquidation.

Here are excerpts from three contemporaneous reports on Cheka brutality, filed not by Bolshevik enemies but by Communist officials themselves:

(1) I have checked up on the events surrounding the kulak uprising in the Nova-Matryonskaya *volost*. The interrogations were carried out in a totally chaotic manner. Seventy-five people were tortured, but it is impossible to make head or tail of any of the written reports. . . . The local Cheka leader [said]: We didn't have time to write the reports at the time. What does it matter anyway when we are trying to wipe out the bourgeoisie and the kulaks as a class?

(2) The Cheka are looting and arresting everyone indiscriminately. Safe in the knowledge that they cannot be punished, they have transformed the Cheka headquarters into a huge brothel where they take all the bourgeois women. Drunkenness is rife. Cocaine is being used quite widely among supervisors.

(3) It is impossible to get any clear idea of who was shot or why. . . . Orgies and drunkenness are daily occurrences. Almost all the personnel of the Cheka are heavy cocaine users. They say this helps them deal with the sight of so much blood on a daily basis. Drunk with blood and violence, the Cheka is doing its duty.[73]

W. H. Chamberlain, the journalist who became probably the first historian of the revolution, said that by 1920 the Cheka had carried out 50,000 executions.[74] Historian Robert Conquest, drawing exclusively on Soviet sources, tallies 200,000 executions at the hands of the Bolsheviks under Lenin from 1917 to 1923, and 500,000 when combining deaths from execution, imprisonment, and insurrection.[75]

Across the board, the leading Bolsheviks preached the necessity of "mass terror," from Lenin—in a direct, written order to the Comintern's Zinoviev[76]—to

Felix Dzerzhinsky, founder of the Soviet secret police, to G. I. Petrovskii, commissioner of home affairs, to the pages of *Izvestia*. All of this was prior to the bloodthirsty Stalin. As one historian wrote, "Terror was implicit in Bolshevism from the start."[77] And Vladimir Lenin was its godfather. Page after page of this book could be filled with bloodcurdling directives that Lenin wrote in longhand, order after order whereby this political gangster requested that various groups and peoples, from kulaks to priests, be hanged or shot.[78]

The chief of Lenin's killing machine, the ferocious Latvian Martin (M. Y.) Latsis, explained this early Red Terror with deadly candor in his orders to underlings in the field:

> We are exterminating the bourgeoisie as a class. In your investigations don't look for documents and pieces of evidence about what the defendant has done, whether in deed or in speaking or acting against Soviet authority. The first question you should ask him is what class he comes from, what are his roots, his education, his training, and his occupation. These questions define the fate of the accused [79]

We are exterminating the bourgeoisie as a class. Like Nazism, Bolshevism was fueled by hatred.

Defending the Indefensible

Those who manage to say, even today, that Communism is a *good idea* in theory, since it allegedly purports to help one's fellow man, are badly deceived, clearly having read no Marx or Lenin.[30] Communism was never about love and brotherhood; Communism was built on a specific type of hatred: *class* hatred. Certain classes were targeted not only for envy and rage but also for genocidal destruction. It was a system constructed on the most wretched vices; it was vicious.

Over time, most Americans figured this out. Too many, however, were hoodwinked from the start.

Typical of the bad thinking on the American left was the author, poet, and playwright Langston Hughes, who once joined the Communist side but later abandoned it. Writing in 1934, Hughes captured American Communists' love for the Soviet Union, their Soviet patriotism, their atheism, their desire to spread the ideology worldwide through the Comintern, and their ultimate dream of remaking America into a Soviet sister state. "Put one more 'S' in the USA to make it

Soviet," declared Hughes. "The USA when we take control will be the USSA."[81] Hughes urged his comrades to rise and fight for the "great red flag . . . of the Internationale." Or, as he put it in one of his most famous poems:

> Goodbye Christ, Lord Jehovah,
> Beat it on away from here, make way for a new guy with no religion at all,
> A real guy named Marx, Communism, Lenin, Peasant, Stalin, worker, me.[82]

As segments of the American Left persisted with this homicidal sophistry, the ideology of global Communism had begun a rampage of hate, violence, and mass murder that would claim at least a hundred million lives worldwide.

How long would it take for American Communists to wake up and smell the corpses? How long would it take for their fellow travelers on the left to realize the true nature and horrific brutality of the experiment in Moscow? Sadly, in many cases the answer to that question was *too long*.

Instead, a parade of Communists and their dupes marched proudly, blindly along after the founding of the Comintern and American Communist Party. And the first target in their sights was a liberal president—no less than a progressive icon.

2

WOODROW WILSON:
"UTTER SIMPLETON"

President Woodrow Wilson stands astride history as the progressive's progressive. He advanced a vigorous, activist federal government in both domestic and foreign policy, creating a host of new regulatory agencies, implementing the income tax, establishing the Federal Reserve, and pioneering an interventionist foreign policy—so much so that liberal internationalism is often summed up simply as "Wilsonianism."

President Wilson's impact is undeniable. Winston Churchill described Wilson's influence at the end of World War I: "Writing with every sense of respect, it seems no exaggeration to pronounce that the action of the United States with its repercussions on the history of the world depended, during the awful period of Armageddon, upon the workings of this man's mind and spirit to the exclusion of almost every other factor; and that he played a part in the fate of nations incomparably more direct and personal than any other man."[1]

While Wilson is a liberal icon, many conservatives decry his influence. They argue that he excessively wielded—even abused—state power, particularly during wartime.[2] They cite his appalling, retrograde views on race and segregation, long concealed by his liberal hagiographers. And, particularly relevant at this current juncture in American history, they see in Wilson the beginning of a long march leftward, of an ever-expanding and ever-more-powerful federal government. In the progressive Wilson, in other words, they see the seeds of groups like today's "Progressives for Obama," discussed at length later in this book.

Yet neither Wilson's progressive admirers nor his conservative critics typically take account of a crucial aspect of Wilson's presidency: his response to Communism. It was during his administration that the Bolsheviks took power in Russia, the Comintern was established, and the Communist Party was founded in America. Wilson watched all of this intently, with deep concern. Unlike the liberals/progressives who today uphold his name, Wilson was not an anti-anti-Communist. He detested Marxism-Leninism, and never made excuses for its disciples. He would not denounce the anti-Communists as worse than the Communists. That is because he *was* an anti-Communist.

Wilson paid a price for his opposition to the Communists. While many on the Right do not like Wilson, their distaste is nothing compared to the oozing hatred expressed by the far Left—a hatred that few Americans are aware of.

Yes, Woodrow Wilson was a man of the Left, but he knew that Bolshevism was a very bad thing—and he did not hesitate to say so or to act accordingly.

Barbarians, Terrorists, Tyrants

Throughout the 1980s, liberals denounced conservative Ronald Reagan as a paranoid, hysterical, Red-baiting Commie hater. Those critics would be quite surprised that the liberal Woodrow Wilson used language every bit as harsh as Reagan's in describing Communism.

Wilson loathed Communism for its aggression, expansionary tendencies, and denial of basic civil liberties. As the world's foremost voice for democracy, he had opposed the czarist autocracy that the Bolsheviks replaced in Russia. Yet he understood that the Bolsheviks were not a force for democracy, but in fact were the worst of anti-democrats. Perhaps most importantly, the inherent godlessness of the Marxist-Leninist ideology repelled Wilson, who was an extremely religious man—a devout Calvinist who had what biographer Arthur Link described as a "superb command of Reformed theology."[3]

Where Reagan rebuked the USSR as an "evil empire," the genteel Wilson dubbed the Bolsheviks "barbarians," "terrorists," and "tyrants." He said they were engaged in a campaign of "mass terrorism," of "blood and terror," of "brutal force," of "indiscriminate slaughter" through "cunning" and "savage oppression." The "violent and tyrannical" Bolsheviks were "the most consummate sneaks in the world," and Bolshevism was an "ugly, poisonous thing" that "feeds on the doubt of man." President Wilson used such language openly and frequently, including in remarks to a joint session of Congress. He warned of how the Bolsheviks were "poisoning" (probably his most common metaphor) the Russian people (and people elsewhere) with an "expansionist" ideology that they wanted to export throughout the world and against the United States. They aimed for "the promotion of Bolshevist revolutions throughout the world."[4]

"Bolshevism is a mistake and it must be resisted," insisted Wilson. "It is wrong."[5] It was wrong, he averred, for Russia, for America, and for the world. "No man in his senses would think that a lot of local soviets could really run a government."[6]

So repugnant were Lenin and his agitating, conspiratorial ilk that Wilson and his State Department refused to engage in diplomatic relations or even try to find common ground with the Bolsheviks. "In the view of this Government," the Wilson State Department announced in an official statement, "there cannot be any common ground upon which it can stand with a Power whose conceptions of international relations are so entirely alien to its own, so utterly repugnant to its moral sense. . . . We cannot recognize, hold official relations with, or give friendly reception to the agents of a government which is determined to conspire against our institutions; whose diplomats will be the agitators of dangerous revolt; whose spokesmen say that they sign agreements with no intention of keeping them."[7]

One of the more striking displays of Wilson's anti-Bolshevism was a September 6, 1919, speech in Kansas City. Here he expressed his "abhorrence" of Bolshevism and reiterated his "hope" that "there won't be any such a thing growing up in our country as international Bolshevism, the Bolshevism that destroys the constructive work of men."[8] Ironically, Wilson said this precisely at the moment that American Communists were meeting in Chicago and "growing up" a form of international Bolshevism in their country.

Wilson was speaking in Kansas City to rally support for the Treaty of Versailles, which was being opposed by isolationist Republicans in the Senate. In the speech, Wilson slyly compared the Republican opposition to the Bolshevik "spirit." He told his critics to "put up or shut up," and then stated: "Opposition constructs nothing. Opposition is the specialty of those who are Bolshevistically inclined. And again, I assure you I am not comparing any of my respected colleagues to Bolsheviki; but I am merely pointing out that the Bolshevistic spirit lacks every element of constructive opposition."[9]

This was a stunning statement. No doubt, had a *Republican* president so characterized his *liberal* opponents, it would have prompted liberal journalists and historians to forever tag the president a Red-baiting reprobate. In Wilson's case, however, the comments have been conveniently sunk into a historical black hole.

That is likewise true for another arresting assertion by Wilson. Dr. Cary Grayson, Wilson's esteemed friend, physician, and adviser, recorded an expression of Wilson's concerns about Bolshevism that also reflected the great progressive's highly regressive views of ethnic minorities. In a diary entry of March 10, 1919, Grayson noted that Wilson feared "the American negro returning from abroad . . . would be our greatest medium in conveying bolshevism to America." As evidence, Wilson pointed to a single anecdotal example of a "negro laundress," a "negress," who was demanding a higher wage than she had been offered. From this one case, reported to him personally the liberal icon projected a pandemic of "negro"-imported Bolshevism.[10]

Despite his inherent bigotries and misplaced analogies, Wilson's characterization of Bolshevism in and of itself was not some ill-informed rant. Quite the contrary, Wilson was arguably America's best-educated president, with a law degree from the University of Virginia and a Ph.D. in political science from Johns Hopkins. In addition to practicing law, he taught for years at such prestigious institutions as Bryn Mawr, Wesleyan, and Princeton—he also served as college president of the last—and he published landmark journal articles and books that remain seminal works in their fields even today.[11] The well-read, scholarly Wilson studied Bolshevism with a discerning eye. He was not given to childish delusions about Marxism-Leninism. He knew the bad guys were bad guys, and that a genuine liberal should not support or defend them.

President Wilson backed up his anti-Bolshevik rhetoric with action. He wanted Bolshevism out of power, and was willing to dedicate American force to help make it happen. In the Russian Civil War he aided the "White" Menshavik forces fighting the "Red" Bolsheviks. He supported a naval blockade of a Red-controlled area inside the USSR, and even joined a multinational Western coalition in sending troops—including a huge contingent of more than ten thousand American boys[12]—to fight the Bolsheviks. So intense (and forgotten) was Wilson's sustained military action against the Bolsheviks that historian Robert Maddox has called it America's "Unknown War with Russia."[13]

Wilson was a man of the liberal Left who understood the vicious hazard posed by these men of the Communist Left. He knew that Communism was a terrible threat to all of humanity.

And that is why Communists, from Chicago to New York to Moscow, despised Wilson.

Lenin on Wilson

Vladimir Lenin's words were always remarkably militant, and President Wood-row Wilson was hardly exempted from the dictator's caustic tongue and pen.[14]

In an August 1918 letter to American workers, Lenin employed bloodcur-dling language to describe the American system, economy, culture, form of gov-ernment, way of life, and president. Lenin counted Wilson among the slanderous "vultures," "bloodsuckers," "scoundrels," "sharks," "modern slave-owners," and wallowers in "filth and luxury" who held Americans on the verge of "pauperism." Wilson was among those "bandits" who ensured that "every dollar" Americans earned was "stained with blood."

Just in case it was not completely clear that Lenin was calling out Wilson in particular, the Russian leader took explicit aim at the American president. Of the liberal's liberal, the great internationalist, the Bolshevik gangster wrote: "I am not surprised that Wilson, the head of the American multimillionaires and servant of the capitalist sharks, has thrown [socialist leader Eugene] Debs into prison. Let the bourgeoisie be brutal to the true internationalists, to the true representatives of the revolutionary proletariat! The more fierce and brutal they are, the nearer the day of the victorious proletarian revolution." It was in this same letter—this direct appeal to the worker-troops of the United States of America—that Lenin pledged that violence would be necessary: "The truth is that no revolution can be successful unless the resistance of the exploiters is crushed."

It was nothing at all for the Communists to call for President Wilson's head on a platter. Such an unapologetically violent missive provides still more evidence that it was absurd to defend the Communist Party in America—wholly dedicated to Lenin—as just another political party.

Lenin also mocked Wilson's "empty phrases about the 'great importance' of 'democracy.'" In his October 1919 "Greeting to the German, Italian, and American Communists," which was reprinted in American Communist publications that fall, Lenin declared that such "designations" of "democracy" were mere empty designs of "the exploiters" and the "Philistines" and the "petty bourgeois." This, and Wilsonian-ism generally, had to be resisted, said Lenin, so that "victory will be ours." The leader of the worldwide revolution concluded: "The victory of Communism is inevitable."[15]

Lenin had expressed all of these sentiments together the previous year, in November 1918, when he warned that "Anglo-French and American imperialism will inevitably strangle the independence and freedom of Russia unless world-wide socialist revolution, unless world-wide Bolshevism, conquers."[16]

Was Wilson up to the task of stopping this inevitable Communist take-over of America and the world? No, not in Lenin's mind. The highly educated American president was too stupid, the Bolshevik said. Lenin told a meeting of activists in December 1920 that this "greatest state in the world," standing before them as a grand prize in waiting, was led by a president who was "an utter simpleton."[17]

America's Comrades

Of course, the Communists at home, being subservient to their masters in Moscow, saluted the red flag. That meant that they also shook their fist at Woodrow Wilson and the American flag.

Consider the case of Communist editor Louis C. Fraina, who dedicated the first edition of *Revolutionary Age,* printed in Boston on July 5, 1919, to the overthrow of the U.S. government and "the annihilation of the fraudulent democracy of the parliamentary system."[18] Who was Fraina's target at the moment? The administration of the great liberal Democrat Woodrow Wilson.

Similarly, a 1920 flier produced by the United Communist Party (see page 45) called for not only a boycott of the 1920 election in America but an actual "overthrow" of the American "capitalist government" and the establishment of a "Soviet government." The party widely disseminated this flier and other materials that unflinchingly urged this mission; there was nothing secret about the Communists' objectives.

Such fliers were not only found on buildings, in mailboxes, and on doorsteps throughout America in 1920 but also on the desks of the Comintern in Moscow. In fact, this exact flier today resides in the Comintern Archives on CPUSA.[19] America's comrades were reporting their noble efforts to their bosses in Moscow. They wanted Lenin's men to know they were working hard for the USSR—working hard on the American front, against America itself, just as Lenin wanted.

As revealed in official United Communist Party proclamations (also sent to the Comintern),[20] the comrades' ultimate goal was to "STAND BY SOVIET RUSSIA"—not by the United States, but by Russia. (See page 46.) Bolshevik Russia was their country, their love, their home—not Woodrow Wilson's America.

Worse, bemoaned the party, was that Wilson's America opposed Russia in solidarity with the allegedly murderous minions of England, France, and Poland. Yes, innocent Bolshevik Russia was under relentless assault from vicious, imperialist-driven Poland. The party was irate that Wilson's America, Lloyd George's England,

Don't Vote! Strike!

BOYCOTT THIS ELECTION!

The whole election business is a FAKE to fool you.

The government is a part of the capitalist machine to keep you down, so the capitalists can oppress and rob you.

When you strike — THE COURTS ENJOIN YOU — THE POLICE BEAT YOU — THE SOLDIERS SHOOT YOU. — That is what the capitalist government is for.

Overthrow the Capitalist Government!
Establish the Soviet Government!

The capitalist government will fight your every effort to free yourself from wage slavery whether Republicans, Democrats, Socialists or Farmer-Laborites are elected.

Workers should vote ONLY for candidates who will propagate the destruction of capitalist government.

The UNITED COMMUNIST PARTY is the ONLY party which puts up candidates for this purpose.

The UNITED COMMUNIST PARTY has no candidates this election because of government persecution.

THEREFORE: BOYCOTT THIS ELECTION!
DON'T VOTE! STRIKE!

THE UNITED COMMUNIST PARTY.

"Overthrow the Capitalist Government!": In this 1920 flier the American Communist Party makes no secret of its objectives.

STAND BY SOVIET RUSSIA

Proclamation by the United Communist Party of America.

WORKINGMEN OF THE UNITED STATES!

THE World War of the capitalists fighting to destroy their rivals in the struggle for profit, cost millions of lives and billions in treasures. All Europe still suffers the fearful misery produced by that war.

The bloody struggle really never came to an end.

Ever since the workers of Russia overthrew the capitalists and landowners who robbed and exploited them, the capitalist governments of the world have been scheming to destroy the Soviet Government the workers established.

The capitalists are constantly lying to you about the conditions in Russia. They dare not let you know what the workers and peasants have achieved in spite of the blockade and the never-ending war against them. They know that, with such example before them, the workers of every other country will destroy their capitalist governments and put an end to the capitalist system.

In order to preserve their system of exploitation, the capitalists, therefore, attack the Soviet Government with every means at their command. They financed all the czarist generals who would act as their tools. Kolchak, Denikin, Yudenich were only tools of Lloyd George, Clemenceau and Woodrow Wilson. It was English, French and American gold that paid for their work of murdering Russian workers and peasants. But in place of destroying the government of the workers and peasants, these czarist generals and their armies have been destroyed.

Then the Allied imperialists drove Poland to attack Russia.

Soviet Russia desired peace with Poland. But the Polish brigands had their orders from London, Paris and Washington. Without warning, they invaded the Ukraine, destroying cities, murdering women and children.

But the Russian workers and peasants have hurled back the bloodthirsty invaders and almost wiped out their armies paid and supplied by the Allies.

NOW THAT THE IMPERIALIST ALLIANCE IS BEATEN, IT IS TRYING TO AROUSE YOU ONCE MORE AGAINST THE SOVIET GOVERNMENT OF RUSSIA.

England and France are going to send their armies to help the Polish bandits. The United States will furnish money and munitions to Poland.

Workingmen of the United States, this is only the beginning of a new great war—a war to crush the first Workers' Republic. As before the world war, first this country will furnish money and munitions. Then it will call upon the youth of the nation to go forth and

"Stand by Soviet Russia": An excerpt from an official proclamation of the American Communist Party, which calls on "workingmen of the United States" to resist the "imperialist alliance."

and Clemenceau's France were sending "their armies," money, and munitions to "Polish bandits."

Wilson's "Stupid" Dream

Another reason American Communists so stridently objected to President Wilson was his faith. The Marxists sneered that Wilson thought he was doing the *"Lord's"* work in seeking to establish the League of Nations.

Lord? The Communists knew where to look for supreme authority and inspiration—to Vladimir Lenin. They would do *Lenin's* work. And a rich area in that mission field was to demonize Woodrow Wilson's loftiest ambition.

Wilson's dream was the League of Nations. Today it is common for conservatives to beat up Wilson for establishing this international "peace" organization, the precursor to the United Nations. But it was the far *Left* that first attacked him for this effort.

The League of Nations was the crowning touch on Wilson's historic "Fourteen Points," the principles for which, he said, the Great War was fought. Establishing the league was deeply personal for him; doing so would fulfill his lifelong ambition to leave his mark on history. His relentless campaign for Senate approval of American membership in the league, against staunch Republican opposition, was so physically and mentally debilitating that it arguably killed him.

And yet Wilson steamed ahead, filled with the spirit, as the devout five-point Calvinist saw his effort as sanctified and predestined by Providence. He believed the League of Nations was God's will. Wilson intoned:

> The stage is set, the destiny is closed. It has come about by no plan of our conceiving, but by the hand of God who led us this way. We cannot turn back. We can only go forward, with lifted eyes and freshened spirit, to follow the vision. It was of this that we dreamed at our birth. America shall in truth show the way. The light streams upon the path ahead, and nowhere else.[21]

The Communists saw this clatter as "stupid," as they did any "superstitious" belief in a deity. They perceived it as spiritual pabulum, as "Wilson the simpleton" at his most simplistic, at his pious worst. The godless already had a vampiric reaction to the God-fearing. And now Wilson was endeavoring to create a world based on democratic freedom—the antithesis of the world for which the comrades were crusading.

Wilson famously wanted to "make the world safe for democracy." American Communists framed Wilson's talk of democracy as bunk, since it was not Bolshevik "democracy." For real democracy, opined Anton Pannekork in the May 15, 1920, edition of *Communist Labor,* the official organ of the Communist Labor Party of America, the world should look to Soviet Russia. "The question of Democracy appears to be a great and debatable one," wrote Pannekork in a piece titled "Bolshevism and Democracy." Yet, said Pannekork, toeing the Party line, it was not debatable as to which country and leader shone forth the guiding light; it was Lenin and his Russia, not Wilson and his America. Wrote Pannekork: "There is no people in the world today (except the Russian people) which has the right to decide its fate."[22]

The United Communist Party of America drove home this message in fliers it circulated before the 1920 elections. One of them noted that the "main issue" between Republicans and Democrats was whether the United States should join the League of Nations. The "big international banking interests" and the "industrial capitalists," America's comrades said, were behind Wilson's crusade. The Communist Party said that the political debate over the league amounted to "a fight between two groups of capitalist interests," neither of which would ever "improve the conditions under which [Americans] live and work."[23]

Wilson's entire prospect was so ridiculous, concluded America's Marxist-Leninists, that Americans should boycott the 1920 elections.

Thus, Woodrow Wilson's indefatigable effort to launch the League of Nations, with America as a member, was another liberal cause vilified by the Communists.

Wilson and "The Fighting Quaker"

Even as Lenin and his fellow Communists around the world baldly stated their violent, expansionist ambitions, the Communist Party accused the Wilson administration of overreacting to the Communist threat. That Communist line in the 1920s became the party line among liberals/progressives in America, and remains a common view even today.

The principal target for the Left has been Wilson's controversial attorney general, Alexander Mitchell Palmer.

The vigorous Palmer was in his late forties when he served Wilson as the nation's fifty-first attorney general from March 1919 to March 1921. Palmer was a progressive from the old school: a moralist, a social reformer, a pacifist, a Christian (he was a Quaker). Elected to Congress in 1908, he had pushed a number of major progressive causes, from the abolition of child labor to the advancement of women's suffrage. He became a star in the Democratic Party constellation, a delegate to the Democratic National Convention in 1912 and 1916 and a member of the Democratic National Committee from 1912 to 1920.

Palmer was close to Wilson personally and, even more so, ideologically. Both men had been very much against American entry into World War I. Wilson, in 1916, had stumped on a platform to keep America out of the war, but ultimately changed course after Germany provoked the United States through a series of complicated international incidents. Eventually, Wilson sought and secured war authorization from Congress in April 1917.

For his part, Palmer remained opposed to the war, committed to his Quaker convictions. He refused Wilson's offer to be secretary of war. Instead, after the war, Palmer took the position of attorney general. One of his first postwar acts was to release some ten thousand aliens of German ancestry whom the Wilson administration had seized during the war out of suspicion that they harbored loyalties to the kaiser.

By then, in 1919, it was no longer Germany but the Communists who threatened the American way of life. As would be the case after World War II, it was a Democratic president and his administration that fingered the threat and developed strategies to counter it, with American Communists crying foul and seeking out liberals to join the chorus.

Likewise posing a danger was the rising anarchist movement. The Wilson administration struggled to make distinctions between anarchists and Communists and to respond appropriately. The attorney general's office was at the tip of the spear.

In April 1919, only weeks into Palmer's tenure as attorney general, anarchists sent a booby-trapped bomb to his home. The bomb was intercepted and defused, but a few months later they successfully exploded another bomb on his porch. It killed one of the plotters but failed to injure Palmer, his wife, or his child, who were home in bed at the time.

"The Fighting Quaker," as Palmer became known, was ready to fight back. He and Wilson saw the anarchists as part of a witches' brew of radical-Left elements endangering America. He was particularly concerned about Red activity during May Day 1920. With the encouragement—in fact, mandate—of his president, Palmer began wiretapping suspected indigenous threats and rounding them up. More than ten thousand people were arrested, and some were deported.

The reaction to the "Palmer Raids" was multifaceted. Traditional Democrats applauded his actions, whereas many liberals decried what they saw as a flagrant abuse of civil liberties. No doubt, some "suspects" were wrongly suspected, and treated quite harshly and unfairly, but others were genuinely dangerous and anti-American. One can debate each and every case of alleged sedition, from smaller names to bigger fish like Emma Goldman, but there is no debate that some anarchists were assembling and exploding bombs, or that the leadership of the Communist Party in America was hell-bent on overthrowing the U.S. government. Both Palmer and Wilson understood that the Communists in particular were "revolutionists," as the Reds' own bombastic literature stated unequivocally, and that they were absolutely dedicated to the USSR.

Palmer did show some mercy. He had asked Wilson to pardon the great socialist Eugene Debs. The Quaker viewed his request as, among other things, an act of compassion toward a man of declining health. The liberal president angrily refused, reportedly shouting, "Never!"[24]

But the Communists showed no such mercy toward Palmer. The Reds detested him. From the start they had used their publications to blast the attorney general, and the attacks became even more intense once he began seeking to hold them accountable for their obvious advocacy of violence and antigovernment activity. They published caricatures of Palmer as a stomping, bloodthirsty American Indian, carrying a long, sharp knife in his left hand and hoisting a dripping, bloody scalp in his right hand. (See page 51.) That picture, splashed across the February 25, 1920, issue of *Communist Labor,* was sent to the Comintern.[25] The American comrades surely hoped to impress their mentors in Moscow with their dedicated demonization of Palmer.

In truth, Palmer had never killed anyone. Lenin was doing the killing. Palmer himself had been targeted for murder, as had his wife and child. To the Communists, however, it was the attorney general who was unhinged.

And how is Palmer remembered today? Not as victim but as victimizer.

For example, the popular reference website Encyclopedia.com features several entries on Palmer, including one from *The Encyclopedia of World Biography* that begins: "As U.S. attorney general, Alexander Mitchell Palmer (1872–1936) was instrumental in creating the 'red scare' of internal Communist subversion after World War I."[26]

Note that Palmer is described not as one who early on recognized the subversive intent of Communists in America and around the world, but instead as progenitor in a long line of "scare" mongers. Note, too, that this is the very first line of the entry, clearly signaling that Palmer unfairly maligned Communists.

It is no accident that "Red scare" gets attached to Palmer's name. From the outset of the American Communist threat, the Left accused major government

Demonizing the attorney general: The front page of the February 25, 1920, issue of *Communist Labor* featured this vicious caricature of Woodrow Wilson's attorney general, Alexander Mitchell Palmer.

officials who looked into the legitimate problem of subversion and infiltration, of overreaching, of paranoia, and of drumming up "inordinate" fears of Communism. Most famously, Senator Joe McCarthy was accused of fomenting a "Red scare" in the 1950s, but before McCarthy, there was FBI director J. Edgar Hoover, Congressman Martin Dies (Texas Democrat), and, yes, Attorney General Palmer and President Woodrow Wilson. The Left has characterized just about every major pursuit of the Marxist menace as an unsavory, regrettable "Red scare" by paranoid U.S. government officials—Democrats and Republicans.

To cite merely one case in point, consider Dr. Harry F. Ward, a liberal Methodist preacher, seminary professor, ACLU founder, and dupe of dumbfounding proportions. Writing in *Protestant Digest* in January 1940, long before Senator McCarthy descended on the scene, Reverend Ward admonished the liberal faithful of the perils of "anti-communism," which was being employed "under the leadership of [Congressman] Dies in a new red hunt" that promised to be even "more ruthless than that of Mitchell Palmer." Practically any anti-Communism was deemed ruthless, and every new attempt was worse than its vulgar predecessor.[27]

As demonstrated by the case of Palmer and his president, Woodrow Wilson, this was the Left's line from day one of the American Communist movement. The Communists could count on liberals to push that line, even against Democratic presidents and administrations.

The Eternal Villain

Woodrow Wilson was the first in a long line of liberal Democratic presidents whom the Communists attacked ferociously. They wasted no time finding their eternal villain: the anti-Communist blowing the whistle.

Thus began the peculiar situation of American liberals defending Communist subversives against investigations by anti-Communists even as the Communists blistered the liberals/progressives. The bizarre dynamic of anti-anti-Communism, which has infected liberals from the very beginning, has mangled their ability to best react to the extremists on their far left.

President Wilson was an exception to this rule—a progressive who understood that the Communists were not the friends of liberals. Some of his inheritors understood that, too, but far too many did not—and never have.

3

POTEMKIN PROGRESSIVES

From the very start of their movement, Communists looked to liberals for assistance—that is, to liberals they could dupe. The strategy began in late 1919, with the founding of their party in Chicago, and picked up full force in 1920–21, the final stretch of Woodrow Wilson's presidency.

Liberal dupery by Communists lasted throughout the history of the Soviet Union, but it was never as widespread or successful as in the 1920s and 1930s. This should not be a surprise. The 1920s was the first full decade for the Soviet Communist Party, the Communist Party in America, the Comintern, and Communist parties around the world. In the early 1920s Stalin had not yet taken the helm, and many leftists had been hoodwinked into thinking that Lenin was a friendly fellow—despite what should have been obvious from his writings and public statements.[1] Of course, even in the late 1920s, once the brutal Stalin had fully assumed power, many liberals were still being taken, seeing him, too—unbelievably—as a jovial chum.

To some liberals of the day, the brave new world being charted by the men in Moscow seemed like it might dovetail with the growing progressive movement in the United States, which had taken off in the first decades of the twentieth century. There was a sense among many liberals/progressives—ubiquitous in their writings at the time—that they and the Soviets were traveling along a similar path, "fellow travelers" on a shared road toward a better world based on the collective, on redistribution of wealth, on public ownership of "the means of production," on a devotion to the state and central planning. No matter what their goal, progressives almost always looked to the federal government for resolution. Such thinking made progressives particularly easy prey for Communists, especially through front groups, which the Communists created for the specific purpose of deceiving the broader public. It is instructive that when the U.S. Congress later published its major investigation of front groups, titled "Guide to Subversive Organizations and Publications," many of the organizations featured the word "Progressive" in their names. Those groups originated in this period.[2]

No dummies, the statists running the USSR saw a giant opportunity. They invited progressives to the Soviet Union and, among other forms of propaganda, subjected them to carefully managed tours of "Potemkin villages." In the late eighteenth century, Russian official Grigori Aleksandrovich Potemkin had purportedly constructed fake settlements in the Crimea to impress Catherine II during her visit there. The Communists embraced this tactic as a way to convince visitors that Communism was producing a glorious new world. The Soviets built not only villages but, more often, showplace buildings, factories, and farms. Just as important was what they *prevented* visitors from seeing.[3] Through this artful stagecraft the Soviets manipulated legions of gullible Westerners. I call these dupes "Potemkin Progressives."

Potemkin Progressives were usually people of impact—educators, academics, journalists, union organizers. The Soviet strategy was not to convince the duped to sign up as Soviet citizens and stay, but rather to send them back home to the non-Communist world raving about Lenin, Stalin, and the alleged grand achievements of Bolshevik Russia. Many of these Western elites did precisely that.

"I've never met a man more candid, fair, and honest," marveled author H. G. Wells after meeting with Stalin in 1934, at the start of the Great Purge. "Everyone trusts him." Wells had likewise been impressed by Lenin, whom he called a "frank," "refreshing," and "amazing little man" who had "almost persuaded me to share his vision."[4]

Wells's fellow socialist, playwright George Bernard Shaw, was fully persuaded, piping up with an even more outrageous assessment after meeting with Stalin: "We cannot afford to give ourselves moral airs when our most enterprising neighbor [the Soviet Union] . . . humanely and judiciously liquidates a handful of exploiters and speculators to make the world safe for honest men."[5]

That shameful, deadly serious statement was an almost verbatim regurgitation of the line Stalin had fed him as justification for Soviet mass murder.[6] Shaw praised not only the dictator's "utilitarian killing" but also the henchmen who pulled the triggers, such as Cheka founder Felix Dzerzhinsky.[7] Shaw's repeated rationalizations of Bolshevik manslaughter, which he deemed necessary to fulfill the USSR's "gifted" "economic conscience," were unconscionable.[8] He defended purges. He dismissed reports of famine as a "lie" and as "inflammatory irresponsibility"—as no less than a "slander" of Stalin's Five-Year Plan.[9] Most remarkably, he backed the willful extermination of the intelligentsia—a "persecution," said Shaw, that "was, I think, justified at the time."[10]

Shaw was not alone. Some of the very brightest of the West's feted intellectuals were taken in by Stalin's gaze and faux villages. There to observe the curious spectacle of these Potemkin Progressives was Malcolm Muggeridge, the British journalist and commentator. Muggeridge would become an intellectual giant of the twentieth century and, most unlike Shaw, one of the century's illustrious converts to Christianity. At this time, Muggeridge was a man of the Left, but, true to his curmudgeon nature, he was not taken by anyone, least of all Soviet handlers. He was bewildered by the credulity of his friends, of whom he recorded:

> They are unquestionably one of the wonders of the age, and I shall treasure till I die as a blessed memory the spectacle of them travelling with radiant optimism through a famished countryside, wandering in happy bands about squalid, over-crowded towns, listening with unshakable faith to the fatuous patter of carefully trained and indoctrinated guides, repeating like schoolchildren a multiplication table, the bogus statistics and mindless slogans endlessly intoned to them.[11]

Elsewhere Muggeridge wrote:

> There were earnest advocates of the humane killing of cattle who looked up at the massive headquarters of the OGPU [the successor to the Cheka as the Soviet secret police] with tears of gratitude in their eyes, earnest advocates of proportional representation who eagerly assented when the necessity of the Dictatorship of the Proletariat was explained to them, earnest clergymen who walked reverently through anti-God museums and reverently turned the pages of atheistic literature, earnest pacifists who watched delightedly tanks rattle across Red Square and bombing planes darken the sky, earnest town-planning specialists who stood outside overcrowded ramshackle tenements and muttered: "If only we had something like this in England!"[12]

"The almost unbelievable credulity of these mostly university-educated tourists," Muggeridge added, "astonished even Soviet officials used to handling foreign visitors."[13]

Muggeridge noted that the common bond among these Western visitors was not nationality but that they were all "progressives." He recorded: "These fellow-passengers provided my first experience of the progressive elite from all over the world who attached themselves to the Soviet regime, resolved to believe anything they were told by its spokesmen." He noted that they were mostly academics and writers, and "all upholders of progressive causes and members of progressive organizations," ecstatic about playing a part in this "drama of the 20th century. Ready at any moment to rush on to stage, cheering and gesticulating . . . a Western version of the devotees of Krishna who throw themselves under the wheels of the great Juggernaut."[14]

For all their acclaimed cynicism, these Western intellectuals, these high-minded progressives, were putty in the hands of Bolshevik molders and shapers—precisely as Lenin had predicted.

The Soviets practiced this Potemkin manipulation so frequently that it is not unusual to peruse documents from the Comintern Archives on CPUSA and encounter memos from Communist officials spelling out strategies for influencing specific officials via these tours. Consider a July 8, 1936, missive from Sam Darcy, CPUSA's representative to the Comintern (using his code name, "Randolph") to "Comrade Shvernik" at Comintern headquarters in Moscow. The purpose, as expressed in the title of the memo, was to influence two American union officials visiting the USSR. The letter began, "The above two American trade union officials [Joseph Schlossberg and David Dubinsky] are coming to the USSR and should be given special attention." The confidential letter noted that both Americans "are on the whole friendly to the USSR." The memo ended, "I propose they be received by Comrade Shvernik and the trade unions and every effort made to influence them."[15] (See page 57.)

The "influence" here was not the coercion that Stalin employed against millions of suffering souls captive to the prison nation he was erecting; rather, it was the sweet, seductive lie of the Potemkin village, with its cakes and pies, teeming caviar, booming factories, fine ballets and museums. This was standard operating procedure.

Oftentimes, the dupes came by the literal boatload, as the naïve shoved themselves onto ships like the SS *President Roosevelt* and SS *Europa,* launched from New York City en route to the workers' paradise. When we look back at these fellow travelers, it is often hard to tell whether the duped were liberals, communists, liberals becoming communists, or some other variant of progressives/leftists. Moreover, while some of the passengers were plainly duped, sometimes for life, others did not take the bait; still others redeemed themselves later, learning valu-

```
 8"
1416/3
эn 13.7.36                                    Confidential
```

Jomrade Shvernik;   July 8, 1936

<u>Regarding</u> – Tour of Joseph Schlossberg
and David Dubinsky

The above two American trade union officials are coming to
the USSR and should be given special attention:

<u>David Dubinsky</u>: President of the International Ladies Garment
Workers Union – 3rd largest union in the AFL
with 200,000 members. He was born in Poland, is
of Jewish descent, and was arrested several times
in Poland for political activities. He was exiled
to Siberia in 1908 and escaped to the U.S. in 1911.
He has been a Right wing Socialist until several
months ago, when he resigned from the Socialist
Party in order to support Roosevelt for President.

<u>Joseph Schlossberg</u>: Secretary of the Amalgamated Clothing Workers
Union, which has 150,000 members. Born in Russia
in 1875. Came to the U.S.A. in the 1890s. He is
a support of the movement for the Farmer Labor
Party.

Both the above people are on the whole friendly to the USSR.
Their coming is in line with the coming of many of the same type of
conservative Socialists such as Held (President of the Forwarts
Association), Cahan (one of the reactionary leaders of the Socialist
Party) Vladek (also a Right winger in the SP). There is a great

Practiced manipulation: In this July 1936 confidential memo, the American representative to the Comintern urges Moscow to make "every effort . . . to influence" two union officials traveling to the USSR.

able life lessons put to good use in the service of opposing Moscow as stalwart anti-Communist Democrats.

What is clear is that the manipulation was done on an incredible scale, with sweeping success, and with many victims, each a fascinating and sad story in itself. The scale was so vast, in fact, that it would be impossible to limit the cases to a single chapter. Among the schools of suckers swirling in the waters, this chapter focuses on three individuals, covered chronologically according to their voyages to the Motherland: William C. Bullitt, Paul H. Douglas, and Corliss Lamont. All three men will resurface later in this book, with two of them experiencing remarkable turnabouts, moving so far as to warn Democratic presidents about the Communist menace.

These case studies serve as cautionary tales as well as (in two instances) hopeful examples of personal and political redemption.

William C. Bullitt: Man of "Deep Wisdom and Liberality"

Among the first to set sail for the red horizons of Russia was William Christian Bullitt. Born on January 25, 1891, to a wealthy, high-society family in Philadelphia, Bullitt studied at Yale, where he earned Phi Beta Kappa honors and was voted "most brilliant" in his 1912 class.[16] That latter achievement, no small feat for any year at Yale, was particularly notable given the steep competition in 1912, a class that included Averill Harriman and Cole Porter.[17] Initially, Bullitt followed the family tradition by pursuing law, enrolling at Harvard Law School, but he withdrew upon the untimely death of his father.

After leaving Harvard, he traveled to Europe, where he had summered as a child. He became fluent in French and German—and in the left-wing politics that dominated European culture. He drank up the Marxism that prevailed among the continent's chattering classes.

In Europe, Bullitt put his Yale mind and connections to work, becoming a foreign correspondent for the *Philadelphia Public Ledger* in 1915. In *The New Republic,* editor Walter Lippmann christened him "the sharpest of the American correspondents" covering the Great War.[18]

Through that war coverage Bullitt became close to some of President Woodrow Wilson's most influential advisers, including Colonel Edward House. This led to a prestigious appointment: as an assistant secretary of state in December 1917, only weeks after the outbreak of the Bolshevik Revolution. The young man was rising quickly. By the time of the Versailles Conference in 1919 he was advising President Wilson. It was at Versailles that Bullitt's growing adoration for Bolshevism became clear to Wilson.

As a member of Wilson's staff, Bullitt pushed hard for recognition of Russia—very, very hard. Like many other liberals/progressives of the era, Bullitt saw the Soviet state as nothing less than the future itself, and wanted the U.S. government to recognize the regime. President Wilson, however, did not share the infatuation of many of his progressive friends. He rebuffed Bullitt's requests to recognize the Soviet state. Devastated, the young State Department official resigned.

"Enthusiastic Supporter of the Bolshevik Experiment"

When it came to matters Bolshevik, William Bullitt felt that President Wilson's staff needed "men of deep wisdom and liberality," such as himself, to understand the fine efforts that Moscow was undertaking on behalf of all humanity.[19] He was quite disappointed that Wilson did not appreciate the utopia laid out before them. How could this erudite president of Ivy League pedigree be so shallow? After all, stressed Bullitt, Vladimir Lenin was a "genial" man of "large humor and serenity." The Bolshevik godfather and his Communist Party were "strong politically and morally."[20]

How did Bullitt come to this naïve thinking about the Soviets?

First and foremost, there was the stilted experience of Bullitt's many trips abroad, including to Lenin's Russia. In March 1919 he was dispatched to Russia on a special diplomatic mission that included a week and a half of meetings with high-level Soviet officials, meaning he was wined and dined in the best, select places, and got nowhere near an accurate representation of life in the real Soviet Russia. He met with the likes of diplomat Maxim Litvinov, Foreign Minister Georgi Chicherin, and, on March 14, Lenin himself. The meeting with Lenin apparently made Bullitt swoon. After this trip Bullitt became, in the apt description of diplomatic historian Francis Sempa, "among the first Americans and Westerners to be hoodwinked by Soviet leaders."[21]

It did not help that Bullitt had been accompanied by *The New Republic*'s Lincoln Steffens and the well-known Swedish Marxist Karl Kilbom. He could not have picked two worse travel companions. Kilbom was already a true believer, and Steffens was even more gullible than Bullitt. Steffens's magazine, *The New Republic,* which became the political bible of the Left, was filled with gibberish on Soviet Russia. The magazine dubbed the Russian Revolution "one of the great enterprises in the history of human liberation."[22] Recall, too, that it was Steffens who, upon his return from Russia, scribbled that he had seen "the Future," and that Russia would "save the world." Steffens was moved to verse: "I would like to spend the evening of my life watching the morning of a new world."

Thus, William Bullitt made his Soviet foray with friends who were not exactly dubious of Bolshevism. Not surprisingly, he was duped. He became so enamored with the Soviet Union and such a bleeding-heart Red that he divorced his first wife in 1923 and in 1924 married Louise Bryant, the widow of Marxist playboy John Reed. Reed, the namesake of the infamous Communist John Reed Clubs, was (like Charles Ruthenberg) buried under the wall of the Kremlin as a foreign Communist hero.

By the 1920s Bullitt had unmistakably become "an enthusiastic supporter of the Bolshevik experiment," in the words of historians Douglas Brinkley and Townsend Hoopes.[23] Now outside the Wilson administration and far removed from the Republican administrations that followed, he continued—like so many other progressives in the 1920s—to fight for U.S. diplomatic recognition of the Soviet Union. Even after Lenin died, Bullitt's enthusiasm for the Soviet system and its "genial," "moral" leaders—including the newly elevated Joseph Stalin—remained undiminished.

When a new Democratic administration came to power under Franklin Roosevelt in 1933, Bullitt was rewarded for his patience and dedication to Soviet Russia. Incredibly, in November 1933, FDR appointed this giddy member of Stalin's fan club as America's first U.S. ambassador to the Soviet Union.

What an extraordinary accomplishment for the forty-two-year-old Bullitt. And what an extraordinarily naïve decision by an American president. It remains unclear what, or who, compelled FDR to pick a man of such insatiable Soviet sympathies as America's ambassador to the USSR.

And it was only a short time before Bullitt's new boss did what Bullitt and his fellow "men of liberality" had been urging for more than a decade: he recognized Russia. The president thrilled progressives everywhere. William Bullitt was their boy.

And he was not only *their* boy. Bullitt celebrated with a dinner date with Joseph Stalin. This date was more intimate than any he had shared with Lenin. It was December 30, 1933, and the author of the Great Purge wined and dined Bullitt. At the end of a lovely evening together, FDR's new ambassador bade Stalin goodnight with a tender kiss on the cheek; the doting despot dutifully reciprocated.[24]

When some anti-Communists charged that Bill Bullitt and Joe Stalin were "in bed" together, they were closer to the truth than even they realized. It was a budding Russian romance.

Or so it seemed. Bullitt's fling was more puppy love than a lasting marriage. His path ahead would take some surprising turns. Neither Bullitt nor his friends and foes could possibly see it then, but he was about to learn some hard lessons regarding the country and dictator he loved. They were lessons gleaned from a longer, deeper look at the real Russia, not the quick head fake of a Potemkin-village tour.

William Christian Bullitt had a Saul-like conversion ahead of him.

Paul H. Douglas: An Early Target

A likewise compelling story is that of Paul H. Douglas.[25]

Paul Howard Douglas was born a Quaker in Salem, Massachusetts, on March 26, 1892. The young man of New England stock made his way to graduate school at Columbia University, where he earned a master's degree in 1915 and a doctorate in economics in 1921, en route to becoming a longtime college professor. Also in 1915, he married Dorothy Wolff, a non-Quaker (Jewish), who likewise earned a Ph.D. from Columbia. The politics of both Paul and Dorothy were staunchly on the left; Dorothy would drift even further in that direction as time went on. The two would divorce in 1930 after having four children together.

As will be abundantly evident in the pages ahead, Columbia was home to an inordinate number of not mere progressives but committed Marxists. That toxic Columbia milieu of extreme-Left politics infected the mind of the young Douglas. It would take decades, including two wars, one hot, one cold—plus hot wars within the Cold War—to goad the lifelong Democrat away from the Columbia perspective.

But that was later. For now, Paul Douglas was on the Reds' radar.

A List of "Liberal" Professors

Among the first indications that Communists targeted Douglas is a fascinating December 2, 1920, letter that today resides in the Comintern Archives.[26] The letter was sent by "Paul Stolt," executive secretary of the "National Office" of the United Communist Party, to a recipient identified only as "Latimer,"which was typical of the cryptic surnames used by the Communist movement.[27] (Even the fuller "Paul Stolt" was a pseudonym.)[28] The cover page of the four-page letter includes only two sentences: "Some time ago we received word from the Comint

[Comintern] that they wanted the names and addresses of 'liberal' college professors in this country, so as to be able to send them literature for college libraries.
Such a list is enclosed." (See page 63.)

Within the archives, the letter rests amid other party documents that stress
the importance of disseminating Communist literature inside the United States—
the better to educate the masses.[29] The letter is written in that spirit. Clearly, the
Communists thought these professors could help place their materials in American college libraries—places of study for the nation's youth, who were long a hot
target for Marxists. Given the brevity of the cover letter, it is unclear whether
the party saw these academics as potentially helpful because they were civil liber-
tarians, progressives, liberals who were soft on Communism, liberals who were
easily duped, or some combination thereof. At least some were pro-Communist,
though none jump off the page as leading Communist Party members.

Seventy-eight academics are listed in the pages that follow Stolt's cover letter. They cover a wide range of institutions, from Smith College to Swarthmore
to Vassar to Wellesley to Amherst, from Bates to Brown to Bryn Mawr. Cornell
University won the most mentions. The most common cities of residence for the
professors were New York City, Chicago, Berkeley, and Boston/Cambridge. And
"social justice" professors from such institutions of the Religious Left as General
Theological Seminary, Mount Holyoke, Trinity College, and Union Theological
Seminary received a disproportionate share.

Some of the names on the list are recognizable to this day, ninety years later:

Arthur M. Schlesinger Sr. In the document, Dr. Schlesinger is listed as "A.
M. Schlesinger—University of Iowa City. Iowa [sic]."[30] This refers to the late,
esteemed Schlesinger (1888–1965), father of the equally renowned Arthur M.
Schlesinger Jr. (1917–2007) and husband of the noted feminist Elizabeth Bancroft
Schlesinger. Schlesinger received his Ph.D. in history from Columbia. He first
taught at Ohio State University and, as the letter suggests, briefly at the University of Iowa (1919–1922), before landing at the faculty of Harvard, where he
became an institution.

Harry F. Ward. Ward, listed with Union Theological Seminary in New York
City, was not only a staunch liberal but also one of the best-known fellow travelers of the Communist Party among clergymen. A Methodist minister, Ward, at
the time of this letter, was working with Roger Baldwin to establish the American Civil Liberties Union (ACLU), which was launched that same year. The
ACLU's Baldwin was an atheist initially enamored with Soviet Communism, as
was evident in his 1928 book *Liberty under the Soviets,* which was based on his two-
month Potemkin-village tour of the USSR in 1927. Ward and Baldwin were such

Архив
КОМ...
№ 114
МОСКВА.

December 1 1920

Latimer:—

    Some time ago we received word from the Comint that they wanted the names and addresses of "liberal" college professors in this country, so as to be able to send them literature for college libraries.

    Such a list is enclosed.

                                    Fraternally,

                                    Paul Holt
                                    Executive Secretary.

Moscow targets "liberal" professors: The American Communist Party provides "the names and addresses of 'liberal' college professors" that the Comintern previously requested.

extraordinary cases of dupery throughout the 1920s—though Baldwin, to his credit, turned around considerably later[31]—that they merit a book in and of themselves, and cannot be given due justice here. Put simply, the Reverend Ward may well have been the single greatest sucker in the entire history of the American Religious Left.[32]

Irving Fisher. Fisher (1867–1947) is listed with Yale University, where he became a recognized economist. After getting his Ph.D. in economics from Yale in 1891 (reportedly the first doctorate Yale awarded in economics), Fisher went on to serve in a number of fields, including mathematics—and eugenics. He once served as secretary of the American Eugenics Society.

Harold Laski. Designated on the list as "Harold J. Laski—Cambridge, Mass," Laski was on his way to becoming one of the most influential socialists of the twentieth century. He ended up as a major player in British politics and a long-time professor at the London School of Economics (1926–1950). One of Laski's famous students was a young American named John F. Kennedy, who enrolled in Laski's course in the summer of 1935. JFK, a hawkish anti-Communist Democrat, referred to Laski as a "radical of the left," a "discontented spirit," and a man "filled with bitterness" and "great venom."[33]

Also on the list is Paul Douglas.

He is identified as "Paul H. Douglas—University of Washington, Seattle, Wash." (See page 65.) It is telling that the Communists knew Douglas's proper location. Between 1915 and 1920 he had moved six times, shifting throughout the country to various academic posts; he was at the University of Washington for only a very short time (1919–1920).[34] In short, Stolt and Latimer knew Douglas before he had become an academic star (he would make his name at the University of Chicago later in the 1920s). They almost certainly knew him from his time at Columbia in the 1910s.

Aboard the SS Useful Idiot

In July 1927, six and a half years after being placed on this Communist Party list, Douglas set off for the USSR on the ultimate progressive voyage. A mix of progressives, varying sorts of liberals, and (mostly closet) communists traveled aboard the aptly titled SS *President Roosevelt,* named for the first progressive president, Teddy Roosevelt. The human cargo was replete with professors, union officials, left-wing journalists (including contributors to *The New Republic* and *The Nation*), ACLU staff, and members of the "social justice" Christian Left from such

Chas. P. Steinmetz — Union College, Bendell Ave. Schenectady, N.Y.

Harry F. Ward — Union Theological Seminary, 600 W.122 St.N.Y.C.

Winifred Smith — Vassar College, Poughkeepsie, N.Y.

George G. Groat — University of Vermont, Burlington, Vt.

J.D. Eggleston — Virginia Politechnic Institute, Blacksburg, Va.

Prof. Tyson — 5504 Wilkens St. Pittsburg, Pa.

Morris C. Croll — Princeton University, Princeton, N.J.

Prof. Campbell — University of Rochester, Rochester, N.Y.

Prof. Hunt — University of Southern Cal. Los Angeles, Cal.

Sara H. Stites — Simmons College, Boston, Mass.

Samuel Weir — Simpson College, Indianola, Iowa.

Prof. Sessions — Smith College, Northampton, N.E.

Josah Morse — University of So. Carolina, Columbia, S.

H.M. Burr — Springfield Y.M.C.A., Springfield, Mass.

Prof. Leonard — Wabash College, Crawfordsville, Ind.

Prof. Osborne — Washington Jefferson, Washington, Pa.

Harold J. Laski — Cambridge, Mass.

G.D. Hancock — Washington, Lee Univ. Lexington, Va.

S.H. Stevens — Washington University, St. Louis, Mo.

Paul H. Douglas — University of Washington, Seattle, Wash.
Vida Scudder — Wellesley College, Wellesley, Mass.
Charles Elmer Gehlke — Western Reserve Col. Cleveland, Ohio.

E.A. Ross — Wisconsin Univ. Madison, Wisconsin.

Home Address 1941 Arlington Place.

Irving Fisher — Yale University, New Haven, Conn.

Walton H. Hamilton — Amherst College, Amherst, Mass.

President Ware — Atlanta University, Atlanta, Ga.
J. Murray Carroll — Bates College, Lewiston, Maine.
Jas. E. Wright — Baylor University, Waco, Texas.
Marion H. Hedges — Beloit College, Beloit, Wis.
W.F. Ladd — Berkeley Divinity School, Middletown, Conn.
Warren H. Catlin — Bowdoin College, Brunswick, Maine.
Alvin H. Hansen — Brown University, Providence, R.I.
Gladys Boone — Bryn Mawr College, Bryn Mawr, Pa.
Ira C. Cross — University of California, Berkeley, Cal.

Douglas makes the list: Paul H. Douglas appears on the Comintern's list of "liberal" professors, alongside such noted academics as Harold Laski and Irving Fisher.

institutions as Yale Divinity School and Mount Holyoke College. Among the professoriate on the expedition, economists and teachers of education dominated. Predictably, Columbia University served up more passengers than any other college, including not only Douglas but also economist Rexford Guy Tugwell, Carlos Israels of Columbia's School of Law, and George Counts of Columbia Teachers College, an earnest disciple of Professor John Dewey.[35]

Too often today, professors teach their students that it was the Great Depression that compelled American interest in Communism.[36] In reality, American Communism was launched, and attracted hordes of elite admirers, well before the Great Depression—in fact, during one of the most prosperous decades in American history, the 1920s. The trip that Paul Douglas and his fellow political pilgrims took aboard the SS *President Roosevelt* is a case in point. They could hardly have pointed to fears of depression as the reason for their soul-searching in Lenin land; at the time of their voyage, the unemployment rate was a stellar 3.3 percent, and the stock market was solid.[37] They had no good excuse for their impressionability.

The Soviets worked hard to take advantage of their gullibility. As author Sylvia Margulies reported some forty years later, the Comintern was secretly involved in planning the SS *President Roosevelt* trip from the beginning, instructing the Communist Party in America on which individuals to send along. Soviet officials arranged not only stops at Potemkin villages but also interviews with innumerable Soviet conspirators.

Unfortunately, neither Douglas nor Rex Tugwell nor most of the others seemed to have any idea of the level of Communist involvement, at home or in the USSR.[38] They were primed to be duped, so much so that the SS *President Roosevelt* ought to be posthumously rechristened the SS *Useful Idiot*.

"Useful Things" for Useful Idiots

One of the most dramatic examples of liberal dupery in Communist history occurred during this 1927 voyage. As Amity Shlaes chronicled in her bestselling book *The Forgotten Man: A New History of the Great Depression,* the dupery was done by no less than Joseph Stalin.

Stalin met with the Potemkin Progressives from the SS *President Roosevelt* on September 9, 1927, at 1 P.M.[39] This was no quick meet-and-greet. The dictator and his guests chatted for more than six hours. Clearly, Stalin saw this as an investment worth his precious time, well worth a break from bludgeoning kulaks.

During the meeting, Paul Douglas and company tepidly asked the dictator about the matter of religion. Did a Communist have to be an atheist? Yes, Stalin said—but at the very moment he answered, church bells began ringing across the street. The dupes all laughed, while Stalin smiled, as if, Shlaes wrote, "to signal the tolerance he could not articulate officially."[40]

Though the bells elicited a chuckle from Stalin's guests, the truth of Soviet intolerance of religion would have shocked them. That intolerance was so vast, petty, and intrusive that it actually extended as far as, yes, the ringing of church bells. Stalin and his officials worked feverishly to silence those bells, as documents from the Soviet archives reveal.[41] For example, from January to February 1930, Soviet official Alexander Likhachev exchanged a series of letters with Ivan Tovstukha, personal secretary to Stalin, in which they examined the ongoing "problem" of the ringing of church bells in villages. Such noise had already been strictly prohibited. As usual, however, the Bolsheviks had to grapple with the stubborn faith of Orthodox Christians. Likhachev and Tovstukha discussed removing the church bells and recasting them into more "useful things." But in the end, the Communist regime chose to do what it did best: destroy. The bells were rolled down steeples and smashed into shards or blown up.

Of course, church bells were hardly the only target of the Soviet regime. In one of the letters between Likhachev and Tovstukha, the good comrades considered the transformation of the glorious Cathedral of Christ the Savior, an eyesore to the atheists that stood just a few blocks away from the Kremlin. Czar Alexander I had dedicated the church in gratitude to Divine Providence for saving Russia from Napoleon in 1812. It was the pride of Russia, with Michelangelo-like artwork adorning the towering ceilings. Yet Stalin, like Lenin before him, found all this reverence "stupid." He envisioned morphing the historic cathedral into a museum, maybe a museum to atheism, as had been done with many Russian churches since the 1920s, one of the pet initiatives of Lenin's League of the Militant Godless.

Stalin grew tired of the debate over what to do with the cathedral. In December 1931 he had the ornate structure dynamited and reduced to rubble. In its place, he planned to erect a sacred Palace of Soviets. Fittingly, however, the central planners could never get the project off the ground. They ultimately converted the mess into a large municipal swimming pool.

Despite what was really happening outside the walls of the Kremlin, Stalin charmed his American callers during their marathon meeting in September 1927. As the afternoon progressed, Paul Douglas and his group chatted and laughed, and ate—sausage, cheese, caviar. The caviar was so thick that the progressives gobbled it up on sandwiches, as crackers offered an insufficiently small platform. They did so as the proletariat outside scoured the earth for potatoes and turnips.[42]

When the visitors tried to leave, a gracious Stalin urged them to stay, and then posed some questions of his own, which were transcribed by official Soviet note takers. Just a few days later *Pravda* published the amiable exchange.[43] For Moscow, this meant a double propaganda effect from the visit: not only did the Soviets publish the dialogue in their government-controlled press, but also the progressives filed pleasant dispatches in the American media when they returned home.

At the end of the long session, Paul Douglas stared off at a bust of Karl Marx in the corner of the room, apparently somewhat unsettled by the experience. Stalin, the master of manipulation, seemed to sense this whiff of ambivalence among one of his Potemkin Progressives.

Douglas suddenly felt a hand on his shoulder. He spun around and saw Generalissimo Stalin, who cracked a joke about whether Marx had worn a necktie.[44] The progressive friends all shared a parting laugh. It had been a delightful afternoon.

Paul Douglas's Skepticism

Many of the American visitors left Moscow satisfied. These hopeful progressives could not wait to get home to spread the gospel about the exciting new world they had encountered in Mother Russia. They would give Stalin what he wanted.

But as Amity Shlaes noted, "Several of the travelers sensed that they had been used to an extent they had not foreseen."

Paul Douglas was one who emerged skeptical. He argued with one of his duped colleagues about the recollection they were jointly composing for publication back home. Douglas felt his partner was painting a far-too-rosy scenario.[45] He was not so comfortable putting his name atop a whitewash.

Douglas was not quite as taken with the Soviet Union as many of his comrades. His unease was a bellwether of things to come.

Corliss Lamont: The Soviets' Gushing Admirer

Emblematic of the hopelessly naïve was Corliss Lamont. Unlike Paul Douglas and William Bullitt, Lamont never veered from the pro-Soviet path.

Lamont was the son of wealthy New York banker Thomas W. Lamont, chairman and partner at J. P. Morgan, and a giant of Wall Street.[46] Born in Englewood,

New Jersey, in March 1902, this blueblood attended the elite prep school Phillips Exeter Academy before heading off to Harvard, where he earned a bachelor's degree in 1924. He then spent a year studying at Oxford. Ultimately, like many progressives of his day (including Paul Douglas), he settled in New York City and landed at Columbia University, a fateful turn. At Columbia he imbibed Marxism and atheism, as well as progressive philosophy from John Dewey and colleagues, who were busy reshaping America not through its political institutions but through education.

Lamont earned his Ph.D. in philosophy from Columbia in 1932. He turned his dissertation into a book titled *The Illusion of Immortality* (1935); it became an immediate atheist classic and is still in print.[47] That book launched him as a leading "humanist" of the twentieth century. He also emerged as a vocal advocate for American civil liberties, becoming a director of the ACLU.

During this same period Lamont became enamored with the Great Experiment in Moscow.

It is difficult (and controversial) to assess whether Lamont was himself a communist, and if so, to what degree—nothing has ever shown that he joined CPUSA, for instance. What is undeniable is that he was pro-Communist, supporting both Communist causes and the USSR itself.

Indeed, he was a prototype Potemkin Progressive.

Corliss and Friends

One of the clearest examples of Corliss Lamont's pro-Soviet work was his leadership role in one of the worst Communist front groups, Friends of the Soviet Union, which—unbeknownst to the American public at the time—had been created by the Communist Party in America.[48] Originally called Friends of Soviet Russia, the group went through a slight name change in 1929 under orders from the Comintern. That same mandate from the Comintern also directed the group to push the U.S. government to recognize, and support, the USSR.[49] That push for diplomatic recognition attracted many progressives to the group, just as the Communists who controlled the group knew it would.

Friends of the Soviet Union was headquartered in New York City, at 80 East 11th Street. The organization's masthead carried this slogan: "HAIL the glorious achievements of the workers and peasants of the U.S.S.R.—where STARVATION AND UNEMPLOYMENT HAVE BEEN ABOLISHED." (See page 70.) The group also published a propaganda work called *Soviet Russia Today*. A simple

NATIONAL OFFICE

FRIENDS OF THE SOVIET UNION

(UNITED STATES SECTION)

80 EAST 11TH STREET

ROOM 221

NEW YORK CITY

490

HAIL the glorious achievements of the workers and peasants of the U. S. S. R., — where STARVATION AND UNEMPLOYMENT HAVE BEEN ABOLISHED.

November 21, 1931.

CRETARIES OF THE FSU
MBERS OF EXECUTIVE COMMITTEES AND ACTIVE
RIES OF THE FSU

ades:

sed bulletin from the national secretary is intend-
tion by our locals. We ask that everyone of these.
are taken up in the meetings of the executive and
ship meetings, and that the active functionaries
her as soon as possible to discuss and make proposals.

less for us in the National Office to hold meetings,
e directives from our International Office and to make
stions without securing the active participation and
f our members.

mication is not intended for the secretaries alone
eral information. It is very specific and we look
wards a reply from every branch and also individual
from our active members. From such replies we can
whether or not we are alive and able to build up the
ization that we want.

orm us as soon as possible of any decision you make,
e that on the magazine regular reports are sent in

Fraternally yours,

FRIENDS OF THE SOVIET UNION

Corliss Lamont's Communist front: The Friends of the Soviet Union celebrates the "glorious achievements" of the USSR, where "STARVATION AND UNEMPLOYMENT HAVE BEEN ABOLISHED."

glance at the inside cover of the magazine shows that the organization was thoroughly penetrated by Marxists. The short list of contributing editors featured names and photos of such usual suspects as Maxim Gorky, Theodore Dreiser, Anna Louise Strong, Karl Radek, and longtime CPUSA head and hard-line Soviet loyalist William Z. Foster—who in 1932 openly professed, "The American Soviet government will join with the other Soviet governments in a world Soviet Union."[50]

Other notable contributing editors to the magazine included non-Communist liberals/progressives such as the writer Upton Sinclair. (See page 72.) Sinclair, who was an extraordinary dupe, somehow managed to avoid ever seeing the correspondence that the national offices of Friends of the Soviet Union sent to locals in Chicago, Cleveland, Detroit, Los Angeles, Minneapolis, Philadelphia, San Francisco, Seattle, and elsewhere.[51] In these letters, correspondents openly greeted each other as "comrade."[52]

As a nonofficer, Sinclair might be excused for such ignorance. But it is difficult to claim ignorance for Corliss Lamont, who was not only a leader of the group but often its keynote speaker at events like its first national "Soviet Union Day," held in New York City on December 17, 1933.[53] (See page 73.)

Where did Corliss Lamont *really* stand?

Russia Day by Day

One thing is certain: like atheistic humanism, the USSR became one of Corliss Lamont's loves. In 1932 he and his wife, Margaret—comrades-in-arms-and-marriage—shoved off for the earthly utopia that was the Soviet Union. The pair put their experiences to paper and in 1933 published a book called *Russia Day by Day*.[54] It was Corliss Lamont's first published work, even before *The Illusion of Immortality*.

The goal of *Russia Day by Day*, as the Lamonts stated in the opening paragraph, was to provide a work of "value for persons who are interested in the Soviet, especially those planning to go there for the first time." They hoped the book would both inspire and guide wayfarers to the USSR. It was tailor-made for Potemkin Progressives.

Russia Day by Day is a work that needs to be seen to be believed. Page after page features examples of how horribly the Lamonts were duped.

The Lamonts set sail for the workers' paradise from New York on July 1, 1932, aboard the SS *Europa*, along with 250 other passengers. Their book was not exactly transparent as to who was managing the trip, other than to point to "group

CONTRIBUTING EDITORS:

ALBERT INKPIN
International Sec'y, F.S.U.

"Our task is to aid in securing the victory of Socialism by means of making known to the workers of all capitalist countries the achievements of Socialist construction."

MARCEL SCHERER
National Sec'y, F.S.U.

"The growing war-danger today necessitates a fearless voice to broadcast the truth about the Soviet Union."

MAXIM GORKY

Hailed as the greatest internationally known revolutionary writer. Author of the famous novel "Mother."

KARL RADEK

Famous Soviet journalist, authority on Russia's foreign policy. Author of "Story of Shock Brigades."

UPTON SINCLAIR

Novelist, journalist, lecturer and critic.
—"Will do my part to expose the lies and slanders against Soviet Russia. Your publication will bring the true facts to light."

ANNA LOUISE STRONG

Well known American lecturer on the New Russia. Now Associate Editor of the "Moscow News." Author of "Russia Conquers Wheat."

WM. Z. FOSTER

National Secretary, Trade Union Unity League, says:
—"It is necessary to bring before the workers of this country the achievements of the Soviet Union and the genuine peace policy of the Proletarian State."

Sinclair does his part: Well-known writer Upton Sinclair, a contributing editor to the propaganda work *Soviet Russia Today*, vows to "expose the lies and slanders against Soviet Russia."

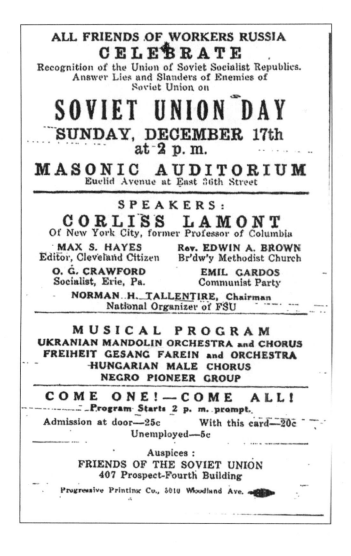

Lamont, main attraction: Corliss Lamont was the keynote speaker at the 1933 event held to celebrate "Soviet Union Day."

tours" engineered by "travel agencies" or by "experienced American travelers in Russia." Nor did the book say anything about the "interpreters" supplied to the Lamonts.[55]

Upon their arrival in Leningrad on July 11, the Lamonts wrote, they were whisked from spot to spot in "brand-new" and "big shiny" Lincoln Eight limousines. Presumably, this was not the typical method of transportation for the Russian proletariat. The Lamonts—true limousine liberals—acknowledged that "some of the Americans object strongly and assert that this is the naïve Soviet way of trying to impress visitors," but then they quickly dismissed the possibility. Such was the tone of their book from the outset.

The Lamonts downplayed practically every criticism of the USSR. At each stop in Bolshevik Russia, they found more "evidence" of American "misperception." This started with the moment the Soviet secret police rifled through their bags. Lamont, the noted champion of American civil liberties, simply shrugged at the search. The "dreaded G.P.U.," he and his wife wrote, did not look "either formidable or ferocious"; rather, the secret police were "courteous and efficient," and "good-natured."

Of course, some negatives were undeniable, even to the Lamonts. In 1932 poverty and starvation were everywhere in the Soviet Union—even a blind man would recognize it. The Lamonts' handlers, no matter how much they strove to stage every encounter and control every move, could not avoid scenes of desperation. And, indeed, the Lamonts noted that one of their "first impressions of Leningrad is that a considerable amount of begging is going on." They glimpsed a ragged woman on a house-step holding a tiny baby in one arm and pleading for food with the other. So much for the USSR's having "abolished" starvation, as Corliss Lamont's organization the Friends of the Soviet Union claimed.

Yet the Lamonts blissfully accepted the explanation of their interpreter/handler, who said "that most of these beggars are people who are too lazy to work, since every Russian can get a job if he wants to." They further justified the situation to readers by explaining that the deprivation had been "bequeathed by the Tsarist regime." All that starvation left over from the czars "cannot be completely eliminated all at once," the Lamonts said. But the Bolsheviks had made progress: the Lamonts claimed that Czar Nicholas had left a trail of one million "professional beggars" but that this figure was now down to just forty thousand.

This was the first of innumerable Soviet statistics that the Lamonts cited unquestioningly. On this, at least two noteworthy corrections are in order: First, this report of forty thousand beggars contradicted the Lamonts' own claim, made later in the book, that there was "no unemployment" in the USSR—unless begging was considered a form of employment. Second, had any nation in human history achieved such a dramatic reduction in begging, it would have been an astounding achievement. But the inconvenient truth—unmentioned by the Lamonts—was that as a result of Stalin's policies, forty thousand people were starving to death practically every two weeks in the Ukraine alone.

Corliss and Margaret Lamont were just like the Potemkin Progressives Malcolm Muggeridge spoke of, "repeating like schoolchildren" the Soviets' "bogus statistics."

Smelly Saints

Many Potemkin Progressives of this period shrugged off the Soviet repression of religion, claiming that it wasn't as bad as simple-minded American anti-Communists made it out to be. The Lamonts went further in *Russia Day by Day:* they not only failed to condemn the Soviet hatred of God and persecution of worshipers but actually seemed to affirm it.

The Lamonts' militant atheism shines through in their book, particularly in its later stages. They laughed scornfully at the "trivial religious mumbo-jumbo" they encountered. Chronicling their visit to one chapel, the couple dispassionately recorded how the house of worship was being torn down: "The workmen hack away unconcernedly, burying their picks with nonchalance in the head of Jesus or in the face of an apostle." The Lamonts also noted approvingly that the Bolsheviks' anti-religion museum inside St. Isaac's Cathedral in Leningrad mocked every imaginable aspect of religious life: "the fragments of the true cross, the bottles of the holy tears, and so on." More than once the couple ridiculed the Russian Orthodox Church's teaching that the bodies of some saints resisted decomposition, divinely protected on earth even in death. They took pains to show that the remains of saints "crumble away after all." Of the corpse of one "old priest-saint" they saw on display, they wrote, "The profound smell of it and the numerous worm-holes in the face and hands do not indicate that the Lord has been watching over his body with any particular care."

On July 14, the Lamonts ventured to the Leningrad headquarters of the Union of Militant Atheists, where they were impressed by a "very alert" young atheist. They noted approvingly that the Soviet propaganda work "against God" was "always tied up with other superstitions such as the idea of immortality." Their agreeable atheist host sent them off by proudly presenting husband and wife with the "Militant Atheist insignia," an official button of the "Atheists Union." The Lamonts consented.

Many God-fearing liberals like Paul Douglas and William Bullitt were ultimately appalled by what they saw in the Soviet assault on religion. Malcolm Muggeridge was so horrified by what he witnessed (in 1932, the same year as the Lamonts' trip) that his experience put him on the road to becoming a leading Christian convert and apologist.[56] But Corliss Lamont and his wife embraced the Soviets' anti-religion campaigns.

At the Foot of Lenin

As soon as the Lamonts arrived in Moscow via their limousine, they headed for their source of spiritual sustenance: Lenin's Tomb. The plate at the foot of the tomb declared the former Soviet leader to be "the immortal one"—a statement that Corliss Lamont, soon to publish *The Illusion of Immortality,* did not lampoon or even acknowledge. Though Lenin had been dead and encased in a glass box for more than eight years, the Lamonts saw no signs of corruptibility, as they had with the decaying saints. They recorded: "Lenin's face is strong, calm, and refined in the fundamental sense. His hand rests on a red pillow and his hands, clasped on his chest in a tranquil way, appear delicate and intellectual."

The secular pilgrims expressed their devotion to Lenin—indeed, their love for the deceased leader. They "want[ed] to stop" and gaze longingly at Lenin's body, but they had to "keep moving." They ached for more. One trip was simply "not enough," so they got in line again. They paid "homage," "taking strength from [Lenin's] impersonally beautiful and resolute face," which seemed "perfectly natural and wholly desirable."

"Collective Nurseries" and "Factory Kindergartens"

The Lamonts also admired the Soviets' treatment of children. They especially appreciated how Soviet boys and girls were separated from their mothers, since that separation "liberated" moms to perform "activities of real significance." The Lamonts praised the mass youth group Young Pioneers; Komsomol, the Communist Party youth organization; "collective nurseries"; "factory kindergartens"; and communes. Most stunning, they found "charming" the sight of uniformed, androgynous children—boys and girls alike had their heads shaved—marching in formation, singing in unison under banners.

At one commune, the Lamonts were enamored with the children freed from their mothers and their "bourgeois toys." They were overwhelmed when the kids humored them with a question. "The comrades of the commune are very loath to let us go," reported the teary-eyed couple, "and only do so after we have sung with them the [Communist] *Internationale,* all three verses."

The Lamonts apparently had no trouble with the lyrics.

The couple also wrote of a strange "Children's Village" where four-year-old boys and girls—"left by their mothers for the day in the care of qualified nurses"—participated in a "mimic war" against dastardly capitalists, replete with firecrackers, fake guns, gas masks, a pretend gas attack that scared even the "shivering" police dogs on hand, and "damnable smoke" everywhere.

The Lamonts asked the obvious question: "Is this a pernicious militarization of young boys and girls?" The civil-liberties heroes, though, were quick to set the record straight. The Soviet government, they explained, needed to "teach its citizens, young and old, how to defend themselves against foreign attack." Besides, "most other governments, it may be said, do not spend much time or money on peace propaganda," as did (allegedly) the Soviet government. In other words, the Bolsheviks, in the minds of the Lamonts, struck a perfect balance in teaching children about war and peace. The authors then began a long discourse on how and why "the sincerity of the Soviet's desire for peace can hardly be questioned."

"A Tremendous Positive Factor for Peace"

Practically nothing escaped the attention—or praise—of the Lamonts. They covered birth control and legalized abortion (here the Soviets were way ahead of American liberals); John Dewey and Karl Marx; the supposedly incomparable reporting of Anna Louise Strong and the *New York Times's* Walter Duranty; "no unemployment"; science "fast triumphing over superstition"; racial prejudice that had "all but disappeared"; divorce and mental health; rapidly diminishing problems of prostitution and "homosexualism"; "jolly" women's prisons where "some of the prisoners act as guards"; priest-less Red funerals; a solemn visit to John Reed's grave; a governing "true international spirit"; the flourishing of "minority languages and cultures"; and marvelous Five-Year Plans.

The Lamonts challenged the view that Russians were unhappy under the Soviets. In fact, they reported—repeating what their tour guide had told them—there were folks everywhere, from Romania to Finland, dying to cross the border to enter Russia. And the Lamonts informed readers that the Comintern was "a tremendous positive factor for peace in the world as a whole."

The Lamonts' tour took them from city to city throughout the USSR. They wrapped up their stage-managed journey in late August, as they boarded the SS *Lenin* en route to Yalta on the Crimea. It was a fitting site, though the couple could not have known it: Yalta would be the site where, in the final months of World War II, the major powers set up the postwar division of Europe that laid the groundwork for the Cold War. In another chilling portent the Lamonts could not have comprehended, they disembarked at Yalta seven years to the day before the signing of the Hitler-Stalin Pact, which precipitated World War II.

After wrapping up their tour of the USSR, the Lamonts headed to Poland. They left the Soviet Union on September 1, 1932—exactly seven years before the Germans, newly allied with the USSR through the Hitler-Stalin Pact, invaded Poland, thus launching World War II. Once the Lamonts got to Poland their tone shifted from ebullient to sour. They no longer gave everything the benefit of the doubt. No, they perceived the Polish soldiers as haughty and brutish—so unlike the gentle, affable souls in the Soviet secret police. For the first time in the entire book, the Lamonts at long last utter the word "dictatorship"—in regard to Poland.

"The New World"

As the Lamonts steamed back to America aboard the SS *Europa,* they relaxed for a friendly card game. They felt their hearts "fill with envy" at a pack of "Soviet anti-religious playing cards" presented by one of their travel mates, purchased back in the city of Rostov. The deck included "satires of the four main religions of Russia: Greek Orthodox, Catholic, Mohammedan, and Buddhist." The cards featured priests and nuns "shown up as hypocrites who eat, drink, and live in luxury; and who cast glances of suppressed desire at each other and everyone else." It was a rollicking fun card game.

Once in New York, Corliss and Margaret Lamont reflected that things in the USSR had been "much more comfortable than expected." This was not, they concluded, because they had been driven to Potemkin villages in limousines, fed caviar and wine, and manipulated by Soviet handlers. No, they assured their readers that "no person" ready for an "expedition to Russia" should fear simply being "'shown' special apartments, people, and villages dressed up to impress the tourist mind." "So as far we know," they told their readers, "we were permitted to see everything we wanted to see and had time to see. . . . As someone else has said, you see in Russia what the Russians want you to see, but they want you to see *everything.*"

What the Lamonts saw, in sum, was "a great deal of happiness"—a "new human nature." They ended their book with, in effect, a plea for more duped

American progressives to visit more Potemkin villages: "The new world of the twentieth century is the Soviet Union. And no one who is seriously interested in the progress of the human spirit can afford to miss it."

Big Fish

The Kremlin must have been positively elated with the Lamonts' chronicle of the Soviet Union. The Comintern itself could not have produced a better book. The Soviet Department of Agitprop could not have commissioned anything as important as this piece of wild Soviet propaganda composed by a respected professor at an Ivy League school for mass American consumption.

Was Corliss Lamont a communist? Reading *Russia Day by Day* makes it extremely difficult to believe that he was not. Yet let us accept the claims of liberals, made for more than three-quarters of a century, that he was a man of the Left, nothing more.

If that is the case, then we must conclude that Corliss Lamont was a dupe of *staggering* proportions. And if some hidden file or document one day emerges to reveal that he was secretly a Communist Party member, then it is his liberal stalwart defenders who were duped. Whatever the truth, there is a lot of duping in this picture.

Russia Day by Day was hardly Lamont's last encomium to the experiment in Moscow. He was not done being duped.

Nor was his alma mater, Columbia University, which offered up another esteemed progressive from the Teachers College and the pragmatist school of the Philosophy Department, another professor to assert the unbelievable—another sucker for the Soviet experiment. This sucker would be the biggest fish of them all.

4

JOHN DEWEY:
THE KREMLIN'S FAVORITE EDUCATOR

To Moscow, one of the most important dupes among those boatloads of Americans who came to witness the Soviets' grand experiment was the renowned John Dewey, a progressive pillar and icon.

Dewey—educator, philosopher, professor, reformer—was a liberal's man for all seasons. His impact on education and philosophy, most notably during his long tenure at Columbia University, is difficult to overstate. His influence has been felt for more than a century, as he inspired sweeping changes in education, from K–12 to higher education, especially involving the training of college students to become public-school teachers. He is the father of modern public education.

As early as the 1920s, he was already being referred to as the "venerable" John Dewey, as "America's philosopher." To this day there exists a long line of Dewey devotees, mainly liberals/progressives, whose respect borders on adoration. But there are nearly as many Dewey detractors, mainly from the political Right, whose disrespect borders on demonization.

It is in the realm of education that Dewey receives his most loving praise and damning criticism. Consider Dewey's best-known work, *Democracy and Education* (1916). This book would find itself on practically any list of top "progressive" books. Moreover, it is required reading in graduate programs in education, and in many courses in philosophy, history, and political science. But the reception is quite different at the other end of the political spectrum. For instance, the conservative publication *Human Events* placed *Democracy and Education* at number five on its list of the "Ten Most Harmful Books of the 19th and 20th Centuries"—trailing only *The Communist Manifesto, Mein Kampf, Quotations from Chairman Mao,* and *The Kinsey Report. Human Events* judged Dewey's book worse than Marx's *Das Kapital,* Betty Friedan's *The Feminine Mystique,* and Nietzsche's *Beyond Good and Evil* (itself a Dewey favorite).[1]

More broadly, critics have held Dewey accountable for the decline of education in the United States. Professor Henry Edmondson III, an expert on education, writes that the degree to which American education is "unsound" is "largely attributable to the influence of John Dewey."[2] Similarly, Georgetown University political theorist George W. Carey says that "we cannot come close to understanding why our public education is in such a wretched state without examining John Dewey's philosophy." Carey laments that "the degenerative effects of Deweyism" still "thrive in the schools of education on our college campuses across the country."[3]

Clearly, more than a half century after his death, John Dewey remains a lightning rod.

Yet, as in the case of Woodrow Wilson, there are equally important aspects of Dewey's career and legacy that neither his admirers nor his detractors have properly explored. The purpose here is to uncover the crucial, underemphasized elements of his politics and worldview, and to reveal the profound effect of his educational ideas in a most surprising part of the world: Soviet Russia. Dewey was very proud of that influence, but his hagiographers have missed—or worse, covered up—this part of the story.

Further, of course, the purpose here is to show how badly John Dewey was duped by the men in Moscow.

Dewey on Education

Before we consider where John Dewey came from, where he went, and how and where he was duped, it is important to understand his perspective on public education, since those ideas were what appealed to the Soviets and brought him into contact with the architects of the Bolshevik state.

John Dewey is often claimed as the "father" of a number of concepts, many of which overlap, and some of which are run together or confused. He has been called a founding father of "pragmatism," and of "experimentalism" or "instrumentalism" in the classroom.[4] Today we can see the spirit of Dewey in the constant experimentation that prevails in modern public education, the always-changing methods, programs, terms and trends, fads and fashion, and "research" into "bettering" education.[5]

Dewey also favored, and in some respects helped shape, the secular relativism that has come to dominate public education. When it came to repudiating religion and moral absolutes in the public schoolroom, he was way ahead of his time. He rejected the notion of a single fixed, transcendent reality.[6] He also dismissed time-honored concepts like "virtue," asserting that honesty, chastity, courage, and industry were not the private possessions of the individual but, instead, what he called "working adaptations of personal capacities with environing forces." Dewey underscored the allegedly indispensable formative role of the "collective," the "public," and "socialization." He preached that "all morality is social," as are all ethics. He opposed traditional notions of *individual* character.[7]

To Dewey, the student was seen not as an individual human being, with private thoughts or feelings, but as part of the "collective"—the collective experience of human beings.[8] He or she was a product of the "public," of the larger society. Thus, "socialization" was a driving principle of Dewey's ideas about education. Not coincidentally, socialization remains at the crux of public education.

As Henry Edmondson observes, Dewey's views on an individual's education cannot be separated from his broader worldview. Dewey was a political progressive, which at its core means that he viewed humanity and history as constantly being refined and moving forward, as inexorably *progressing*. His sweeping plans for the child were just an element of his sweeping plans for the nation and the world. Dewey believed that for the United States to survive, "American democracy" must be transformed first by a revolution in education, which would be followed by a social and economic revolution.[9]

Significantly, Dewey judged that pursuing political and social change through politics was frustratingly slow, whereas doing so through education could be much quicker and more efficient.[10] This was a central theme in his *Democracy and Education*. His primary focus, then, was the schoolhouse, not the houses of legislature.

That is no small point. As we shall see, so many radical children of the 1960s embraced this thinking, heading to places like Columbia to earn graduate degrees in education and ultimately becoming the tenured professors of today. They eschewed politics for education, ascertaining that they could be more directly effective in the classroom. Here, too, John Dewey was their forerunner.

The Life and Career of Dewey

John Dewey was born in Burlington, Vermont, on October 20, 1859, and died in New York City on June 1, 1952. He was the third of four sons to Lucina Artemisia

Rich and a shopkeeper named Archibald Sprague Dewey. Dewey's father was not an academic but pursued books and the life of the mind; he was known to be partial to British literature, and introduced the boy to faculty friends at the University of Vermont. His mother was said to be strict and devoutly religious.[11] Some scholars maintain that the mother's (supposed) overbearing piety—a common caricature by Dewey's secular-progressive admirers—ultimately turned away the son.[12]

The question of religious impact was no small thing, not only to Dewey and his fellow progressives but also, later, to the Soviets.

Dewey, at age eleven, joined the First Congregational Church in Burlington, with a membership application written by his mother.[13] One could argue that Dewey's slow departure from the faith, barely perceptible at first, began when he was an undergraduate at the University of Vermont, where—along with his reading of "progressive" journals outside the classroom—he was exposed to an intoxicating brew of agnosticism, positivism, and Darwinian evolution.

Though undecided about his profession when he graduated, he accepted a teaching position in Oil City, Pennsylvania, and then, two years later, took another back in Vermont. At Lake View Seminary in Charlotte, Vermont, he met a philosopher named H. A. P. Torrey, who introduced him to Immanuel Kant. Still a Christian, even an orthodox one, Dewey read Kant as a corrective to the scientific skepticism of faith that was prevailing in much of the academic world.[14]

Dewey's professional life as a scholar also began to take flight at this time. In 1882 he published an essay in the *Journal of Speculative Philosophy,* which encouraged him to pursue graduate studies. That same year he entered the doctoral program in philosophy at Johns Hopkins University, where he encountered another mentor, George Sylvester Morris, a leading neo-Hegelian philosopher. Dewey ate up Hegel, referring to Hegel's thought as a kind of personal liberation. "At the same time," writes Dewey scholar Jared Stallones, "Hegel allowed Dewey to stay within the intellectual camp of theism, albeit a type of philosophical pantheism. He was not yet ready to cut loose the moorings of his religious upbringing."[15] Indeed, even after Dewey earned his doctorate and joined the faculty at the University of Michigan, he became an active member of the First Congregational Church and, on campus, involved himself with several student Christian groups and Bible classes.[16]

Over the long term, however, Dewey's infatuation with Hegel would have other effects—especially involving his sympathies for Marxism.

A turning point came in his marriage in 1886 to Harriet Alice Chapman, who was raised with a deep skepticism of organized religion and any form of what she swiftly dubbed "dogma." Harriet, who felt that theology and "ecclesiastic institutions" had "benumbed rather than promoted" religious attitudes, had an abiding effect on her husband's faith and politics, lasting long after her death.[17] It appears that Dewey had abandoned organized religion by the mid-1890s.[18]

His wife was not the only important influence on his thinking. As his academic career took off, he entered a series of environments that fostered radical-Left thinking. In 1894 he earned a major promotion by being named head of the department of philosophy at the University of Chicago. By this point deeply interested in education and pedagogical reform, Dewey thrived under the social progressivism and left-wing thinking that dominated the city of Chicago's intellectual life. He participated in the lectures at Jane Addams's "progressive" Hull House, which attracted popular speakers such as Clarence Darrow and young professors like Paul H. Douglas. Chicago was a hotbed of radical politics; it is no coincidence that the Communists would, a quarter-century later, choose this "progressive" city for the formal launch of the Communist Party in America.

In 1905 Dewey moved to another radical hotspot, New York City. He became professor of philosophy at Columbia University, with a joint appointment at Columbia Teachers College, the university's school of education. It was there— at Columbia and in New York City—that Dewey began to shape progressivism. Joining up with like-minded politicos, he became a founding member of groups like the Teachers League of New York (1913), the American Association of University Professors (1915), and the American Civil Liberties Union (1920). He also became president of the American Philosophical Society and the American Psychological Association.

Over the next few decades, Dewey wrote the works that made him an academic celebrity and philosopher-educator extraordinaire—one of the most recognized names in American education, culture, and politics. His books included such classics as *Essays in Experimental Logic* (1916), *Democracy and Education* (1916), *Human Nature and Conduct* (1922), *Experience and Nature* (1925), *The Public and Its Problems* (1927), *The Quest for Certainty* (1929), *Individualism, Old and New* (1930), *A Common Faith* (1934), *Liberalism and Social Action* (1935), *Logic: The Theory of Inquiry* (1938), *Theory of Valuation* (1939), and *Freedom and Culture* (1939). His articles could be found throughout major publications of the day, including the liberal flagship, *The New Republic*. Disciples like William H. Kilpatrick made sure that Dewey's ideas became the blueprint for instructing thousands of education majors; *Democracy and Education,* in fact, became a veritable "bible of Columbia Teachers [College]."[19]

God and Man at Columbia

Like so many other secular progressives, John Dewey expressed a hearty distaste—bordering on contempt—for religion. This trait would appeal to the God-
haters in Moscow.

The onetime Bible-study-teaching son of a devout mother took such a hard-
left turn that he came to agree with Karl Marx on religion. In April 1935, in a
glowing review of a book by a prized student, Columbia colleague, and unflagging
atheist and Stalin apologist—none other than Corliss Lamont—Dewey asserted
that "religion is the opium of peoples."[20] Elsewhere he judged that religion "has
lost itself in cults, dogmas, and myths."[21] The remark on "dogma" seemed to
reflect his wife's influence, while the language on "cults" and "myths" was no
doubt what he had heard from Marxist colleagues in Chicago and New York and,
as we shall see, during his visit to the Soviet Union. The Bolshevik government
created an actual Department of Cults, charged with monitoring the dangerous
"myths" and "superstitions" of Christians.

Religion, Dewey maintained, had a crippling, degenerating effect, instill-
ing "a slavery of thought and sentiment." He devoured Nietzsche, who called the
morality of Christian religion a "slave morality." Dewey wrote that religion is "an
intolerant superiority on the part of the few and an intolerable burden on the part
of the many."[22] Christianity, in particular, was a "dying myth," he said. He commended those wise enough to have "escaped this delusion" of "supernatural com-
mands, rewards, and penalties" connected with "Christendom as a whole." And
those who subscribed to more orthodox forms of Christianity were especially
foolish, desperately needing to be "progressively liberated from [their] bondage to
prejudice and ignorance."[23]

Was Dewey an atheist? Numerous atheist websites proudly claim him as one
of their own, while several conservative Christian websites call him an atheist for
very different reasons. Some of these sites (pro and con) employ an atheistic quote
attributed to Dewey, but the quotation is not reliably sourced.[24] We do know that
in addition to being a harsh critic of religion, Dewey was also the most prominent
philosopher to sign the 1933 *Humanist Manifesto,* which declared, among other
things, that humanists "regard the universe as self-existing and not created," that
"the time has passed for theism [and] deism," and that "the distinction between the
sacred and the secular can no longer be maintained."[25]

Corliss Lamont, who had studied under Dewey while getting his Ph.D. at
Columbia, seemed to affirm that Dewey had rejected God. In his atheist classic

The Illusion of Immortality, which, as noted, began as Lamont's doctoral dissertation, Lamont fondly called Dewey "one of my earliest teachers in philosophy" and then declared that Dewey was "convinced that this life is all."[26]

The elder philosopher not only did not object to this characterization but even wrote an endorsement for the book; it was the only endorsement that appeared on the dust jacket. Further, Dewey wrote a glowing review of Lamont's book (the review in which he called religion "the opium of peoples").[27] Lamont liked the review so much that he asked Dewey's permission to use it as the introduction to subsequent editions of the book. Dewey happily agreed, and the introduction was carried into the book's fifth edition (1990), many years after his death.[28]

Dewey's hostility to religion seemed to spike the more he ran with fellow travelers and admirers of the Great Experiment in Moscow, of which there were many in New York. Columbia University, in particular, was an extremely secular and politically radical place, no doubt the worst of the Ivy League schools in that regard, far ahead of the secular-left drift of universities later in the century. For a Dewey already moving away from conventional religion, and whose politics were already on the left, Columbia was an explosive environment.

One of the better sources on this political zoo—many others could be cited— was the late, great Catholic writer Thomas Merton, who was a student at Columbia in the 1930s. Merton was a man of the Left throughout his life. He was a vocal peace activist, a prolific author and poet, the world's best-known Trappist monk, and eventually a prominent Vietnam War critic. The very liberal International Thomas Merton Society today bears his name. Merton attested to the extreme secular-left bent of the campus in this period, and to the abnormally high number of Communists at Columbia, especially among students. Merton himself joined the Communist Party while there, and wrote that "there were, at that time, quite a few communists or communist sympathizers among the undergraduates."[29] The Communists at Columbia actually had full control of the student newspaper and other groups on campus.[30]

The faculty, said Merton, were mostly liberals, not Communists, and that included the professors at Teachers College, who, wrote Merton, with an edge, "always stood for colorlessness and mediocrity and plain, hapless behaviorism."[31] But secularism was dominant at Columbia, he said. In his brilliant spiritual autobiography, *The Seven Storey Mountain* (1948), Merton wrote:

> Poor Columbia! It was founded by sincere Protestants as a college predominantly religious. The only thing that remains of that is the university motto: *In lumine tuo videbimus lumen*—one of the deepest and most beautiful lines of the psalms. "In Thy light, we shall see light." It is, precisely, about grace. It is

a line that might serve as the foundation stone of all Christian and Scholastic learning, and which simply has nothing whatever to do with the standards of education at modern Columbia.[32]

This spiritual vacuum, combined with the radical leftism on campus, offered ample opportunities for CPUSA and front-group recruiters who worked the street corners hunting for intelligent but immature recruits. Merton's narrative helps explain why someone like Whittaker Chambers, who attended Columbia in the 1920s, could enter the college as a Taft Republican and leave a Marxist who not only joined the Communist Party and edited its publications but also became a KGB spy.

John Dewey spent decades in this secular-progressive environment. Of course, he came to influence it as well. By the time Merton arrived on campus, Dewey had been a fixture there for three decades. Dewey towered over Columbia, inspiring near worship. The school's secularism, Merton said, was part of the prevailing Deweyan zeitgeist.

In fact, Merton suggested that Columbia's motto—*In lumine tuo videbimus lumen*—"might profitably be changed to: *In lumine Randall videbimus Dewey*" (here referring to John Dewey and to another influential Columbia philosophy professor, John Herman Randall).[33]

Dewey's Politics

Clearly, John Dewey's politics were on the left—but exactly how *far* to the left has long been a matter of dispute.

One source of the confusion is that much of his written work was ambiguous. Oliver Wendell Holmes called Dewey's writing "inarticulate." Jacques Maritain said the innumerable "ambiguities" in Dewey's work fostered "a disastrous confusion of ideas." Lionel Trilling listened to a Dewey lecture at Columbia and "found him incomprehensible."[34] Political scientist Leo R. Ward noted that "it is difficult to say for sure in what Dewey believed."[35] All of this is true.

Here Dewey had much in common with Karl Marx. As with Marx, a cottage industry arose in trying to ascertain what Dewey meant; when he was being practical or abstract; what kind of a blueprint, if any, he left for his form of utopia; and the degree to which the implementers of his vague concepts had successfully executed his ideas.

Dewey and Marx also shared a connection to Hegel, notes William Brooks, a scholar at Canada's St. Lawrence Institute for the Advancement of Learning.

Marx drew from the German philosopher his view of the dialectic. Dewey, too, was influenced by Hegel, and he created his own dialectic—educational where Marx's was economic. Dewey's educational dialectic owed a debt not just to Hegel but also to Marx himself, Brooks points out: "Dewey found Marxism useful, if not indispensable, in the formulation of his educational theories."

Like Marx, Dewey was convinced that economics was central to determining the course of society and history. He also indicated that he thought Marx had correctly applied Hegel's dialectic to the realm of economics. "We are in for some kind of socialism, call it whatever name we please," averred Dewey. "And no matter what it will be called when it is realized"—some called it socialism, some called it communism—"economic determinism is now a fact, not a theory."[36]

Of course, Dewey and Marx were united in their hostility to religion, too. According to Brooks, Dewey believed that schools needed to be liberated from religious influences in order to demonstrate that it was not Providence but man's labor that was responsible for progress. His apostles would take up the charge of banning religion from public schools.

Dewey, like so many other leftists of the era, closely considered Marxism and was influenced by it to a substantial degree. He had many Marxist sympathies and might have been a Marxist for a period. As for the Communist movement, he was an intimate of many of the chief figures involved and fell in with a number of front groups.

True, for various reasons (as we shall see) this man of the Left ended up repudiating *official* Communism. But his sympathies placed him in a number of socialist groups—including, reportedly, the Socialist Party.[37] And as a result he was in position to be suckered by the Communists into supporting their causes.[38]

Whatever John Dewey's politics actually were, he was, indisputably, a dupe.

Embracing Comrade Dewey

For a time, at least, John Dewey and the Bolsheviks formed a mutual-admiration society. His ideas influenced the Bolsheviks from the very start of their revolution. In fact, the Soviets embraced Dewey's ideas for their schools before American liberals did. As William Brickman, a colleague at Columbia's Teachers College, wrote in a gushing but authoritative introduction to Dewey's book *Impressions of Soviet Russia,* "The number of translations of Dewey's works was quite impressive during the initial decade [of the Russian Revolution]."[39]

No question about that. The Bolsheviks wasted no time getting John Dewey's works into Russian. In 1918, only three years after it was published in the United States, Dewey's *Schools of Tomorrow* was published in Moscow.[40] Given what was happening in Russia at the time, this is staggering. The Bolshevik Revolution had begun only months earlier and the devastating Russian Civil War was in full swing. Millions of people were on the verge of poverty, starvation, and death by war and execution. What's more, the Bolsheviks were broke; they did not have the money to be translating American books into Russian. The fact that they managed to make Dewey's work such a high priority at that perilous moment is compelling testimony to how much they emphasized education as the way to build the Communist state, and to how utterly indispensable Lenin, Trotsky, and Stalin considered Dewey's teachings.

Only a year after *Schools of Tomorrow* was published came a Russian translation of Dewey's *How We Think* (1919) and then, in 1920, *The School and Society*.[41] These, too, came during the misery of the Russian Civil War (1918–21), which, according to historian W. Bruce Lincoln, snuffed out the lives of *seven million* men, women, and children.[42] Dewey's ideas were apparently judged as crucial to the revolution as any weapon in the arsenal of the Red Army.

And so several more translations immediately followed, including a big one: in 1921, even before the civil war had ended, the Soviet government published a sixty-two-page pamphlet excerpted from Dewey's *Democracy and Education*.[43]

Remember, *Democracy and Education* stands as John Dewey's most significant work. It remains the most common choice of schools of education as an introduction to Dewey's thought. It became the bible of Columbia Teachers College, and a guidepost for educational programs across the country. It was the book in which the philosopher himself said he attempted to summarize his "entire philosophical position."[44] Liberals and progressives adore the book; it is one of the classics in their movement.

And it was a Bolshevik favorite.

Dewey's impact on the Soviet Union was immediate and pervasive. A witness to this was Anna Louise Strong, who worked and lived in the USSR in the early 1920s and closely observed Soviet education.[45] Strong was one of the eight contributing editors to the flagship publication of the front group Friends of the Soviet Union. She was close to Corliss Lamont. She was (in the words of the U.S. Congress) "for years one of the most active agents for the Communist International."[46] She was a splendid duper of Protestant clergymen in particular.[47] Even Corliss and Margaret Lamont could not avoid calling Strong an "American supporter of the Communist cause." She was author of the pamphlet "The Soviets

Conquer Wheat" and coeditor of the English-language *Moscow Daily News,* along with "Michael Borodin," whom the Lamonts identified in their book only as "of Chinese fame."[48] In fact, *Mikhail* Borodin was widely known in Communist circles as "Stalin's Man in China," having helped forge the Chinese Marxist movement in the 1920s.[49] (This was another of those crucial facts the Lamonts neglected to mention to their readers.)

Note Strong's testimony on Dewey's impact on the Soviets: contemporary school reform in Stalin's state, she said, was "modeled more on the Dewey ideas of education than on anything else we have in America. Every new book by Dewey is seized and early translated into Russian for consultation. Then they make their own additions."[50]

The Soviets themselves said this quite candidly. In a 1929 book, Albert P. Pinkevich, rector of the Second State University of Moscow, stated that Dewey had a "tremendous influence" on Soviet education. Pinkevich compared Dewey's impact to that of leading educators in Germany, where Marxism was particularly prevalent; German was often the first Western language of translation for Soviet documents. Compared to even the Germans, "Dewey comes infinitely closer to Marx and the Russian communists," asserted Pinkevich.[51]

The Soviets were lavish in their praise of Dewey. Professor Stanislav T. Shatskii, a leading Soviet educational "reformer," told Dewey's close Columbia colleague Thomas Woody that he "drew greatest assistance" from Dewey and was "deeply impressed by his 'philosophy of pragmatism.'"[52] It was Shatskii who translated Dewey's magnum opus, *Democracy and Education,* into Russian for the Soviet pamphlet.

Was Dewey embarrassed to be heartily embraced by totalitarians? Not at all. As his admiring colleague William Brickman discerned, "This was fulsome praise indeed for Dewey."[53]

The Soviets reached out to Dewey directly to convey their praise. In 1928 Professor A. G. Kalashnikov of the pedagogical department of Moscow Technical University sent Dewey a two-volume set of the most recent *Soviet Pedagogical Encyclopedia,* which owed a great debt to Dewey's progressive work.[54] Kalashnikov included a warm personal note to Dewey that read, "Your works, especially 'School and Society' and 'The School and the Child,' have very much influenced the development of the Russian pedagogy and in the first years of [the] revolution you were one of the most renowned writers." The "concrete shapes of pedagogical practice" that Dewey had developed, wrote an appreciative Kalashnikov, "will be for a long time the aim of our tendencies."[55]

VIP

In sum, the apparatchiks commandeering the Soviet educational bureaucracy were dazzled by John Dewey. Surely, too, they appreciated his evolving view of the menace of religion to young people.

Soviet officials practically begged Dewey to come pay them a visit—a *special* visit. This was a man, after all, who merited VIP treatment. He had already helped the Bolsheviks tremendously with their education system. Now they sensed that the Columbia professor could be an even bigger help: here was a progressive who could communicate the Soviets' worldview to America and who, more than that, could help them with some major political objectives in Washington, D.C.—well beyond the province of education.

The Kremlin needed John Dewey to come to the USSR to be shown around. Precisely that would happen in the summer of 1928.

5

John Dewey's Long, Strange Trip

By 1928 John Dewey could no longer resist the blandishments of the Soviet Union. That summer he embarked on a pilgrimage to the USSR.

He set sail as part of an unofficial delegation of twenty-five American educators from various universities, including, naturally, Columbia Teachers College, where colleagues like Dr. J. McKeen Cattell joined the voyage. According to State Department records, Dewey and crew launched on June 23; they would return home on or around July 20.[1]

Dewey should have known the obvious: the purpose of these invitations from the Soviet government was to try to dupe high-level American leftist intellectuals into favorable impressions of the Great Experiment, and then to enlist them in a campaign to get the U.S. government to officially recognize Stalin's dystopia. The progressives would be paraded from Potemkin village to Potemkin village in the hopes that they would share their exciting experiences with the masses back home.

But Dewey downplayed the potential for political exploitation, even scoffing at the paranoia of those who suggested it. In his account of the trip, he paused to acknowledge that some "kindly friends" had tried to warn him "against being fooled by being taken to see show places." This warning "appears humorous in retrospect," he said.[2] Although the Soviets were masters of propaganda and manipulation—as Dewey himself recorded in his notes—he explained that they "had enough to do on their own account without bothering to set up show establishments to impress a few hundred—or even thousand—tourists."[3]

This was disingenuous at best. Dewey knew he was no mere tourist, and neither were the nearly two dozen university presidents and experts of American higher education traveling with him on this guided tour. The Bolsheviks saw him as the world's preeminent educator, a fact conveyed to Dewey quite clearly.

Perhaps to spare himself the charge of extreme gullibility, Dewey conceded in his next breath that indeed certain "places and institutions . . . were 'shown' us," and that they may well have been "the best of their kind." But he saw no manipulation there; these places and institutions were merely "representative of what the new regime is trying to do."[4]

When Dewey got back to America, he did not disappoint the Soviets. Between November and December the professor filed a six-part series of glowing reports in *The New Republic*. The next year these epistles to the faithful and seekers alike were eventually compiled into a book, *Impressions of Soviet Russia and the Revolutionary World*.[5]

That book, more than any *allegation* that the philosopher-educator was a Marxist, was the most damning indictment of Dewey's views on the USSR. What it reported was nothing short of breathtaking.

Love That Leningrad

Dewey's dispatches on Russia were evocative and full of colorful detail, at times almost lyrical. He was occasionally ambivalent about his subject, uncertain whether to commend or criticize the Bolshevik experiment. But his hesitation typically gave way to the former—usually quite easily.

Consider, for example, the very first lines of his first epistle. As with the Lamonts, Dewey's first staged stop was at Leningrad. The city had been renamed in 1924, after having been previously called Petrograd (1914) and, historically, St. Petersburg. "The alteration of Petrograd into Leningrad is without question a symbol," began Dewey, "but the mind wavers in deciding of what." On one hand, he mused, "it seems to mark a consummation, a kind of completed transmigration of souls. Upon other occasions, one can imagine it a species of mordant irony."[6]

The mordant irony, of course, was that the decaying city was a fitting tribute to the decaying corpse of Vladimir Lenin. But Dewey dismissed that idea as something in which an "enemy" of the Bolsheviks would find "malicious satisfaction." He was much more charitable. Though the city was admittedly "unkempt," he sensed an "impression of movement, vitality, energy. The people go about as if some mighty and oppressive load had been removed, as if they were newly awakened to the consciousness of released energies."[7]

In Dewey's mind, the Bolsheviks had thoroughly liberated the Russian people. He could see it himself. Then again, he was on a staged tour. He should have expected nothing else from a totalitarian country that would have shielded from him—or jailed—any poor soul (or dissident) who might have begged him for a minute of concealed conversation or a nugget of bread.

Here again he expressed momentary hesitation. "I am willing to believe what I have read," he said, "that there is a multitude of men and women in Russia who live in immured and depressed misery, just as there is a multitude in exile." But he quickly countered that there was another "multitude," those "of a new life," a new multitude that "walks the streets, gathers in parks, clubs, theaters, frequents museums." Those people, this "reality," as he called it, invigorated Dewey. They constituted not only "the present and the future" but also "the essence of the Revolution in its release of courage, energy and confidence in life."[8]

Dewey almost swooned: "My mind was in a whirl of new impressions in those early days in Leningrad. Readjustment was difficult, and I lived somewhat dazed."[9]

Critics of the Soviets had it all wrong, he suggested. "I have heard altogether too much about Communism, about the Third International [the Comintern], and altogether too little about the Revolution," he wrote. Never mind the millions of lives claimed in that Revolution; to Dewey, the Bolsheviks had ushered in not any sort of dangerous dictatorship, but rather a "revolution of heart and mind" and a "liberation of a people to consciousness of themselves as a determining power in the shaping of their ultimate fate."[10]

"Such a conclusion may seem absurd," he added. True enough—the Bolsheviks' brutal, unelected dictatorship was constructing history's vastest system of what Lenin and Trotsky termed "concentration camps." Yet Dewey simply compounded the absurdity by invoking a Marxist refrain. The most important reality, he claimed, was that the "dialectic of history" was happening right under everyone's nose. Here, John Dewey, student of the Hegelian dialectic, seemed to endorse the basic Bolshevik worldview:

> My conviction is unshaken that this phase of affairs [in Russia] is secondary in importance to something else that can only be termed a revolution. That the existing state of affairs is not Communism but a transition to it; that in the dialectic of history the function of Bolshevism is to annul itself; that the dictatorship of the proletariat is but an aspect of class-war, the antithesis to the thesis of the dictatorship of bourgeois capitalism existing in other countries; that it is destined to disappear in a new synthesis.[11]

These, wrote Dewey, "are things the Communists themselves tell us. The present state . . . is necessarily a state of transition to the exact goal prescribed by the Marxian philosophy of history."[12]

The Columbia professor was absolutely right in his understanding of Marxist theory and philosophy of history. Yes, the current phase of a revolution did not matter as much as the direction and end goal; as Marx himself argued, it was merely a way-station, a transition to the eventual world revolution that would usher in a classless society. But Dewey was not simply *describing* Marxist theory; he seemed to be endorsing it—though, as usual, his language made him hard to pin down.

Sometimes Dewey's reports contradicted themselves. For example, he said that the Russian people "are well nourished" and that "there are no marked signs of distress," though he was forced to acknowledge that "fairly long lines are seen waiting at some shops, especially where food is sold," and that items in store windows were "usually of the quality associated with cheap bazaars."[13]

Dewey concluded this first report in *The New Republic* with a parting rush of enthusiasm: "The outstanding fact in Russia is a revolution, involving a release of human powers on such an unprecedented scale that it is of incalculable significance not only for that country, but for the world."[14]

Dewey was right about the scale and significance, but the tragic consequences stood in direct contrast to the Brave New World he envisioned.

The Safety of the Masses

Dewey's second article in his *TNR* series featured more of the same. In it he praised "the orderly and safe character of life in Russia," an odd contention that, as he correctly noted, "would be met with incredulity by much more than half of the European as well as the American public."[15] Indeed.

Dewey had clearly digested the Communist Party dogma regarding the Bolsheviks' annihilation of certain despised groups. He wrote: "In spite of secret police, inquisitions, arrests and deportations of *Nepmen* and *Kulcks*"—businessmen, industrialists, and farmers—"exiling of party opponents, including divergent elements in the party, life for the masses goes on with regularity, safety and decorum." There was *no* country in *all* of Europe, said the unflinching professor, in which "the external routine of life is more settled and secure."[16]

Summing up his stroll through Leningrad, he again momentarily considered the possibility that he was being managed by Soviet handlers. He and his delegation had been free to "sight-see," but only in a controlled or "favorable" environment. But, following his already-familiar pattern, he dismissed the likelihood of manipulation. The Soviet-directed tour of Leningrad may have been "carried on under most favorable auspices," but, he insisted, he and his group had been free to "form our own ideas from what we saw and had contact with."[17]

Dewey Discovers the "New World"

Each article in Dewey's series for *The New Republic* progressed to a new level of absurdity, as if the professor himself was following a kind of personal Hegelian dialectic. His third piece, aptly titled "A New World in the Making," described his pilgrimage to Moscow. He was nearly reverential in his account of the capital city, much as the Lamonts had venerated Lenin's cold flesh. As he got physically closer to Joseph Stalin and Felix Dzerzhinsky and M. Y. Latsis, to the headquarters of the Cheka and the Comintern, to the rumblings of Red Square and the Kremlin, to the dead body of Lenin, he detected "the heart of the energies that go pulsing throughout all of Russia." He had the "feeling" that he "was coming into intimate contact, almost a vicarious share, in a creative labor, in a world in the making." He and his fellow travelers "were now suddenly let into the operative process itself"—and it was invigorating. The philosopher took in the "deepening" "sense of energy and vigor released by the Revolution."[18]

What he saw came "as a shock," Dewey professed. What he recorded next no doubt would surprise his readers back home, especially those in the pews: the pragmatist hailed the Bolsheviks' commitment to historical and cultural "conservation," especially in regard to the "temples of the Orthodox Church and their art treasures." This commitment was real, assured Dewey, and stood "contrary, again, to the popular myth." Oh, sure, he conceded, "the anti-clerical and atheistic tendencies of the Bolshevist" were "true enough," but "the churches and their contents that were of artistic worth are not only intact, but taken care of with scrupulous and even scientific zeal."[19]

This statement displayed a bracing ignorance. It was so misguided that William Brickman, the uncritical editor of Dewey's *Impressions of Soviet Russia,* where this passage was included, was compelled to insert a gentle footnote: "Dr. Dewey, evidently, had no knowledge of the desecration of churches and synagogues."[20]

Dewey also, evidently, had no knowledge of how many houses of worships had been shut down, forcibly stripped of relics and gems, and blown up, and how many priests and nuns had been carted off and locked up. Most offensive, Dewey hailed these "conservations" during his trips to Moscow and Leningrad, where the infamous Church Trials had taken place just a few years earlier (1921–22). In those show trials, priests and patriarchs had been forced to surrender to the state the Church's most sacred materials, much of which was melted down or turned into cash for Bolshevik coffers. The church officials were then imprisoned and often executed.[21]

Dewey's terrible mistakes and misinformation did not stop there. In the next line, he conceded that it was "true that many [of these churches] have been converted into museums." On this, however, he added no clarifying information. What *kind* of museums? one might ask. Even the Lamonts had conceded that the Soviets turned churches into atheist museums. Here, too, Dewey's editor was forced to add some crucial missing detail: "One example was the conversion of the Cathedral of Our Lady of Kazan . . . into the Museum of the History of Religion and Atheism."[22]

Further justifying the Soviets' anti-religious actions, Dewey then maintained that "to all appearances there are still enough [open churches] to meet the needs of would-be worshippers."[23] The Lamonts had said the same. Surely their Soviet handlers had fed them this line.

In truth, the Soviet authorities were in the process of shutting down the vast majority of the 657 churches that had been operating in Moscow on the eve of the Bolshevik Revolution. According to the Moscow Russian Orthodox Patriarchy, only 46 churches remained open by the 1970s, and those churches operated with little to no freedom, subject to the constant monitoring of KGB "church watchers" and other government authorities seated throughout church sanctuaries.[24]

Of course, according to the Soviets, the Russian "new man" had been unshackled from religion, freed from so-called superstitions and dogma. Naturally, then, the number of "would-be worshippers," as Dewey put it, had decreased, meaning that many fewer churches were needed. To Dewey, who would later write that religion was the "opium of the peoples," this logic must have made sense.

Dewey went so far as to celebrate the confiscation of Russia's priceless religious icons and paintings as wonderful "restoration" projects done with meticulous care by the nation's academic establishment—"experts, antiquarians, scholars of history, chemists."[25] In reality, the Bolsheviks took these things and locked them up, removing them from sight. These images of Christ, the Blessed Virgin, the angels and saints, were a threat to the transformation of human nature that the Bolsheviks sought via totalitarian Communism, and of which Christianity was a formidable foe. It would take nearly seventy years before the icons would again see the light of day.[26]

In no other matter was the intellectual John Dewey so remarkably ignorant as in the area of religion in Soviet Russia. Here, in particular, the esteemed professor played the role of supreme dupe. As Mikhail Gorbachev would acknowledge decades later, the Bolsheviks waged an all-out "war on religion."[27] Even after the Civil War had ended, noted Gorbachev, in a time of "peace," they had "continued to tear down churches, arrest clergymen, and destroy them. This was no longer understandable or justifiable. Atheism took rather savage forms in our country at that time."[28]

Gorbachev was describing precisely the time that John Dewey was in the Soviet Union.

Dewey finished his third *New Republic* article by proclaiming the Bolshevik Revolution "a great success."[29]

The "Great Experiment"

In the fourth and fifth articles in the *New Republic* series, Dewey provided lengthy treatises on Soviet education. He perceived in Russia nothing short of an "educational transformation," which he wholeheartedly endorsed—in fact, envied.

The leading progressive concluded, "The Russian educational situation is enough to convert one to the idea that only in a society based upon the cooperative principle can the ideals of educational reformers be adequately carried into operation."[30] In other words, he seems to have viewed Bolshevik Russia—a "society based upon the cooperative principle"—as the *only* sort of society where his kind of educational reform could be adequately implemented. This assessment ought to give pause to Dewey's foes and admirers alike. It means following not only his progressive models for education but also his progressive notions for society; both education and society must be reshaped.

In his reports on Soviet education, Dewey frequently used the terms "democracy" and "democratic"—an odd choice of words to describe Stalin's state, but one in keeping with the Bolsheviks' cynical use of language and Dewey's own often enigmatic, exasperating usage of the terms.[31] He consistently hailed the Soviet collective over the individual, and glowingly reported that "the activities of the schools dovetail in the most extraordinary way, both in administrative organization and in aim and spirit, into all other [Soviet] social agencies and interests."[32] He summed up: "I think the schools are a 'dialectic' factor in the evolution of Russian communism."

Russian schools were the "ideological arm of the Revolution," as he rightly put it. Dewey did not seem to sense the dangers with this. Quite the contrary—

he appeared highly impressed with what he witnessed in Russian education. This should not come as a surprise, given his own views about how public schools must serve a socialization function, with the collective standing superior to the individual, and about how these schools must be devoid of a religious foundation. The real question is how much he *learned* from Russia's educators and how much he *taught* Russia's educators; the degree to which he was pupil or professor remains unclear.

Dewey was especially impressed with how the Bolshevik regime seemed so willing to pursue reform and "progress." The father of experimentalism in American public education was thrilled with the "experimentation" thriving in Russian public education, which he saw as "flexible, vital, creative." In fact, his final *New Republic* article was titled "The Great Experiment and the Future"—cleverly tying the phrase "Great Experiment," which progressives usually applied to Soviet Communism generally, to Soviet education.

Moscow, Dewey reported, had "cleared the way" of impediments to pedagogical reform that the czars had allegedly put in place. As an example of such hurdles, he informed readers that the czars had blocked top Soviet educator Stanislav Shatskii from something as benign as introducing football to young people. The czarist authorities, Dewey reported, had concluded that instruction in football was actually thinly veiled training for the art of bomb-throwing. Dewey lampooned the thought, which was intended to illustrate the anti-Communist, Red-baiting paranoia of the "reactionary" Czar Nicholas II.[33]

Whether the football story is accurate is hard to say. No doubt, Dewey could have heard it only from his Bolshevik handlers.

One thing, however, is certain, and gets closer to the truth of the matter: as editor Brickman pointed out in a footnote, Shatskii was a committed Communist and rabble-rouser whom the czarist authorities had arrested not for teaching football but for "trying to plant socialism in the minds of little children."[34] That was another minor detail that Dewey did not share with readers of *The New Republic*.

To Dewey, all of that czarist closed-mindedness was in the past—dead with the *ancien régime*. Now, he hailed, it was a new day for Russia. The "reformers" were free, severed from the "conservative" past and joined with Stalin in running a better Russia. Shatskii himself now "found his advice and even his criticisms welcomed" by the open-minded, tolerant men who guided the new Russia.[35]

This bright new day would not last long. Several years after Dewey's dispatch for *The New Republic,* these open-minded, tolerant men would purge Stanislav Shatskii in the rampage of the Great Purge. In 1934 he became one of the first placed before the firing squad.

But that was later. In all, opined John Dewey, in what he treated as yet another pleasant surprise—sure to shock the sensibilities of unsophisticated American critics of Bolshevism—this new way of life, this dawn of a new day for Russian education, was extremely healthy for "the masses" (Dewey used this term often). The "masses" awoke to discover many "doors" opened to them "that were formerly shut and bolted."

Why such benevolence from the Bolsheviks? Because the present government, he maintained, "is as interested in giving [Russians] access to sources of happiness"—*sans,* one must surmise, freedom of speech, press, assembly, religion, and property—as the czarist government "was [interested] to keep them in misery." "This fact," explained the professor, "and not the espionage and police restrictions, however excessive the latter may be, explains the stability of the present government."[36]

As this statement indicates, it cannot be argued that Dewey was *unaware* of the brutality of the Soviet state. He frequently acknowledged Moscow's strong-arm tactics, only to dismiss or rationalized them. Here it was the Soviets' "excessive" "espionage and police restrictions," which, he asserted without providing any evidence, had nothing to do with the "stability" of the Bolshevik regime. Earlier it had been his odd statement that "in spite of secret police, inquisitions, arrests and deportations of *Nepmen* and *Kulaks,* exiling of party opponents, including divergent elements in the party, life for the masses goes on with regularity, safety and decorum." That is quite an "in spite of."

Did Dewey's students read any of this? Probably so, given the ideological closeness between Columbia and *TNR.* Upon reading such ruminations, a freshman in Dewey's philosophy course at Columbia might figure that the Bolsheviks were held together though some sort of elected parliamentary coalition, rather than a brutal dictatorship. The freshman would be warmed, *pleasantly surprised,* by the Bolsheviks' educational experimentation.

For Dewey, education was a bulwark of Bolshevik benevolence. He felt so positive because of "the marvelous development of progressive educational ideas and practices under the fostering care of the Bolshevist government—and I am speaking of what I have seen and not just been told about."[37]

"A Crime Against Humanity"

The views that Dewey expressed about his Soviet tour were so flattering—and so gruesomely misguided—that even his daughter, Jane, conceded they were "very sympathetic in tone with the USSR."[38] He made his sympathies abundantly clear in his final article for *The New Republic* series, in which he offered a recommendation to the U.S. government: full diplomatic recognition of Bolshevik Russia.

Diplomatic recognition had, of course, been Stalin's primary international political objective for years. It was the Soviets' prime motivation for hosting such visits by Western intellectuals. In other words, Dewey did exactly what Stalin wanted. That he concluded the series by pushing this objective illustrates the extent to which the Bolsheviks had duped the father of modern American public education.

"Political recognition of Russia on the part of the United States," Dewey wrote, was "at least a necessary antecedent step" in "bringing about the kind of relations that are in the interest of both countries and of the world." Dewey candidly admitted that his trip had brought him to that conclusion: "I went to Russia with no conviction on that subject. . . . I came away with the feeling that the maintenance of barriers that prevent intercourse, knowledge and understanding is close to a crime against humanity."

That admission bears repeating: Dewey conceded that he had gone to Russia without an opinion on the matter of recognition, but he returned with the conviction that the United States should extend recognition—indeed, that to fail to do so would be "close to a crime against humanity." His Soviet handlers had convinced him. He took the bait—hook, line, and sinker.

Dewey went so far as to charge that Britain's *withdrawal* of recognition of Russia "had done more than any other one thing to stimulate the extremists and fanatics of the Bolshevist faith, and to encourage militarism and hatred of bourgeois nations."[39]

This was an amazing charge. If only Britain and other Western nations granted Russia the recognition for which the Soviets and their progressive friends pleaded, Dewey was saying, then nonextremists and nonfanatics—like General Secretary Stalin—could be aided in their struggles against the militants. In short, we in the West were encouraging extremism among the Communists—within an otherwise idyllic USSR. Communist militancy was at least in part our fault.

The pragmatist's argument was hauntingly similar to that made decades later by members of the political Left after September 11, 2001, when endeavoring to explain why militant, extremist Muslims hated the West. Mistrust was not the fault of the violent extremists—whether jihadist Muslims or despotic Bolsheviks—but somehow of the West, because of its very mistrust of the extremists in the first place.

In all, Joseph Stalin and his henchmen could not have been more satisfied with John Dewey's pleas in *The New Republic*. From the first Dewey dispatch to the last, the professor did what the Soviets hoped, and then some. For Dewey to close with a push for diplomatic recognition was ideal, from the Soviet perspective.

John Dewey had been a dupe, and so had the editors at *The New Republic,* which provided him a mighty platform—six separate issues—from which to issue this pro-Soviet propaganda. The Soviets should have considered awarding some kind of commendation to Dewey and the editors of *The New Republic.* The only remaining question on hopeful Soviet minds was just how many additional dupes Dewey and *TNR* could drum up in the United States through this high-profile series of articles.

Legwork for Stalin

Fortunately, America, unlike Russia, was a real *democracy*—to borrow a favorite word that dominated Dr. Dewey's musings. That is to say, Americans enjoyed a genuinely free and diverse press, with real freedom of thought. As such, little time was wasted in throwing cold water on Dewey's burning enthusiasm for Stalin's state. Soon the conservative press in the United States, especially the Hearst newspapers—which the American Left derided as "reactionary" and hysterically anti-Communist—was labeling Dewey a "Bolshevik" and a "Red."[40]

And yet Dewey's service to the Soviet cause was not over. He went further on the recognition issue: in late January 1933 the professor signed a letter urging the American president-elect, Franklin Delano Roosevelt, to recognize Russia. Some eight hundred professors and university presidents joined Dewey in signing the letter, including the usual suspects from Columbia—Carlos Israels, R. G. Tugwell, and George Counts, all of whom had traveled to the Soviet Union with Paul Douglas aboard the SS *President Roosevelt* in 1927.[41] Naturally, too, Corliss Lamont heartily supported all these efforts (and then some), and Margaret Lamont organized a separate committee to recognize Russia, generating yet more petitions. Women were her chief target, and she managed to get such well-known figures as Jane Addams and Amelia Earhart to sign on.[42] The Potemkin Progressives had launched an all-out effort for Stalin's top priority. They were truly doing Stalin's legwork.

Ironically, this influential letter from the American academy came right as news emerged that the Soviet central-planner-in-chief was collectivizing agriculture in the North Caucasus, an utterly disastrous project that would usher in one of the worst episodes of mass starvation in human history. The progressives, however, viewed Stalin's intentions with considerable optimism. Dewey—and those of similar mind—saw the coming collectivization as quite promising, possibly the future for economic development.[43]

In short, then, John Dewey's insights on Bolshevik Russia from roughly 1928 to 1933 were not merely naïve but appalling. What explains his credulity?

To the best of our knowledge, he was not a member of the Communist Party, nor was he even a small "c" communist.[44] This seems true despite his repeated expressions of admiration and sympathy for Marxist ideas. Dewey was far Left but not a communist, not a member of CPUSA, and not under the control of the party.

He was, however, most definitely a dupe, and in that capacity he provided invaluable aid to the Soviets.

Yet there is more to John Dewey's story. Like many duped leftists, he moved in and out of the "dupe" category—sometimes suckered, other times not. He was fooled for a while, but, like certain other leftists, he found redemption in the truth—namely, the truth about Stalin. As with so many leftists, it would take some time. For all their brilliance, the enlightened professors were not exactly quick studies. For all their celebrated cynicism and erudition, they were extremely gullible—at least when it came to their "friends" on the left.

Dewey, nonetheless, would come around. He would eventually reject what a later, savvier intellectual, Vaclav Havel, would call "the communist culture of the lie."

6

THE REDEMPTION OF PROFESSOR DEWEY

Although the swift rebuke of John Dewey's "impressions" of the Soviet Union did not immediately change the educator's views, the backlash may have prompted him to revisit his conclusions about the Great Experiment. In 1934, the first year of Stalin's Great Purge, Dr. Dewey delivered another written surprise, but this one far more grounded in reality.

In April of that year he published a short but sweet essay called "Why I Am Not a Communist" in *Modern Monthly;* soon thereafter it was reprinted in hardcover in a printed symposium edited by the leftist intellectual Sidney Hook.[1] Dewey actually wrote the piece in 1933, and said it was the culmination of "reservations" that had begun to swirl in his mind back in 1931.[2]

It was clear from the essay that Dewey's problems were not so much with "communism" as a philosophy as with "Communism, official Communism, spelt with a capital letter," as the professor put it. In other words, he objected to how Soviet Russia was putting the ideology put into practice.

The despiser of "dogma" also took umbrage at the dogmatism of a regime that had become "the dictatorship *of* the proletariat and *over* the proletariat." This dictatorship and "the suppression of the civil liberties of all non-proletarian minorities" had become "integral parts of the standard Communist faith and dogma," Dewey wrote. There was, in fact, an "excess of dogma and indoctrination" under Communism.

He was realizing what many anti-Communists (like Ronald Reagan) would later point out: atheistic Communism was, ironically, like a religion to the Marxist faithful.

Dewey finally recognized what Vladimir Lenin had preached from the out-set: the inevitability of class war, the need for violent revolution, party infallibil-ity, and the use of lying and deception to achieve the party's purposes. "One of the reasons I am not a Communist," he explained, "is that the emotional tore and methods of discussion and dispute which seem to accompany Communism at present are extremely repugnant to me." He said that Communists, and especially "Communist spokesmen," harbored a "systematic, persistent and seemingly inter-tional disregard" for "fair play" and "elementary honesty in the representation of facts." The Communists believed that "the end justifies the use of *any* means," he concluded. Some fifty years later Ronald Reagan would say much the same thing in his first presidential press conference—to the guffaws of liberals who derided him for his supposedly crass anti-Communism. The Soviets, Reagan said, "reserve unto themselves the right to commit any crime, to lie, to cheat, in order to attain" their goal of "world revolution and a one-world Socialist or Communist state."[3]

The ends-justify-the-means approach, Dewey said, also applied to how the Communists treated their opponents and to how they used liberals—that is, their dupes. The Soviets engaged in "hysteria" in "their denunciations," attempted "character assassination of their opponents," and employed a "policy of 'rule or ruin.'" Then, surely thinking of how he and his duped liberal friends had been treated, he condemned the Communists' "misrepresentation of the views of the 'liberals' to whom they also appeal for aid in their defense campaigns."

John Dewey, erstwhile sucker, had wised up.

The Dewey Commission

From there, the education of John Dewey continued its upward trajectory. Like many leftists of his generation, he came to see the sheer brutality of the Soviet system. In the mid-1930s millions were killed in Stalin's Great Purge, in the gulags, and in the Ukraine's forced famine. For Dewey, the most galling example of Soviet injustice came in the Moscow show trials.

While Stalin simply stacked kulaks in boxcars and shipped them off to the gulag, he used elaborate "show trials" to eliminate political and military rivals. The idea was to accord these higher-profile figures some semblance of apparent justice—though the trials were rigged, with the verdict predetermined. It was more farce—the Potemkin village taken into the courtroom.

One of the earliest victims of these show trials was Pavel P. Blonskii, with whom Dewey was quite familiar. Blonskii had been one of Dewey's advocates on

Soviet education in the 1920s. Blonskii was purged in 1931, well before Stalin really ramped up the killing machine.[4]

But it was Stalin's actions toward Leon Trotsky that really set off Dewey. In December 1927 Stalin had exiled Trotsky—his chief competitor as Lenin's former second in command—to Alma Ata, Kazakhstan, in Soviet Central Asia. This move had the crucial effect of splitting the international Communist movement into two polarized factions, pro-Trotsky versus pro-Stalin. Trotsky eventually made his way to Mexico, where he made a lot of noise—to Stalin's chagrin. The Soviet supreme leader persecuted his rival in exile, putting Trotsky on "trial" in Moscow in absentia.

In 1937 Dewey organized a tribunal of American leftists to examine the Moscow trials, with special focus on Trotsky's case. The philosopher-educator became the chairman of the Commission of Inquiry into the Charges Made Against Leon Trotsky in the Moscow Trials, which ran from 1937 to 1938.[5] The Dewey Commission was a coalition of liberals/progressives, socialists, and even Trotskyites. The last category included many unwavering comrades motivated to expose Stalin's crimes by their love of Trotsky and what they perceived as Trotsky's "better" version of global Communism. This was hardly commendable, as Trotsky himself had advocated violence and world revolution, was a thug, and was as militantly atheistic as Stalin (if not more so), having launched with Lenin the League of the Militant Godless. He was not a good man.

But while the Dewey Commission was encouraged by Trotskyites, it was not a Trotskyite body. In fact, many members of the commission disliked Trotsky because he had persecuted non-Communist leftists when he was Lenin's partner in crime. Dewey himself was neither a Trotskyite nor a Trotskyite sympathizer. The same could be said for his right-hand man on the commission, Sidney Hook, a liberal who was no dupe.[6]

The Dewey Commission became a battleground, reflecting the bitterly opposed factions and microfactions of the political Left. Nonetheless, with the good professor trying to keep the commission together, this gaggle of leftists started accumulating evidence against Stalin.

The Right Side of History

Transcripts of the rigged hearings in Moscow made their way to the West. As they did, many leftists were shocked at the transparent phoniness of the proceedings. Notably, they included Whittaker Chambers, who was in the process of leaving his life as a Communist and KGB spy. Shaken by the transcripts, Chambers sought out Dewey, through Sidney Hook—a sign that Chambers approved of where Dewey stood on Stalin. These two men—a former Columbia undergrad and a current Columbia professor—had changed dramatically over the previous decade. To borrow from Chambers's language, both were now on "the right side of history."

Chambers's request for a meeting was rebuffed because Hook and Dewey knew of his recent checkered history—as did much of the New York Left—and were not certain he had rejected that past. They feared that leaked word of a meeting could compromise the impact of the Dewey Commission. Dewey (and Hook especially) understood that the judgment of the commission could really rankle the USSR. Stalin feared the verdict of their report, which could have lasting implications for the global Communist movement.[7]

As the commission took up the issue of the alleged guilt of Leon Trotsky, Dewey and other members traveled to Coyoacan, Mexico, where the exiled Communist had been living as a guest of Diego Rivera. The professor personally interviewed Trotsky there. Dewey also sent a telegram to Clarence Hathaway, editor of the *Daily Worker,* inviting the Communists to send an attorney to participate in a preliminary hearing in Mexico City on whether Trotsky was guilty of the charges that Stalin's cronies had made against him. Hathaway reported the telegram and invitation at a Communist Party Politburo meeting on April 2, 1937. Typical of CPUSA behavior, the Communists opted not to participate but instead to vilify Dewey in the *Daily Worker*—and to send at least one secret agent.[8]

The commission's hearing degenerated into political infighting, but Dewey's crew still managed to produce some solid findings in the form of two published reports: "The Case of Leon Trotsky" (1937) and "Not Guilty" (1938).[9] The commission rightly determined that the trials were frame-ups, in which the outcomes had been predetermined. The "trials" had been a feeble attempt to paint a veneer of justice to convince gullible outsiders.

The findings were international news—exactly as Stalin had feared. They were covered in the *New York Times* for three straight days—December 12–14, 1937—and the coverage was favorable to the commission's conclusions. Stalinists worldwide reacted with palpable rage, vilifying Dewey as a "warmonger" and an "enemy of the working people." The overheated reaction was testimony to the quality of the Dewey Commission's work.[10]

Stalin's American "Friends"

This is not to say that Joseph Stalin no longer had friends among American liber-als. Predictably, dupes were there to defend Stalin when the Dewey Commission published its findings. One was former Dewey student Corliss Lamont, head of the odious front group Friends of the Soviet Union, which was full of closet Com-munists and duped liberals.

Lamont went on the radio immediately after Dewey had finished reading his broadcast statement on the commission's findings. He was also quoted as a coun-terpoint to the Dewey Commission in the widely read *New York Times* articles on the subject. Lamont eagerly attacked the findings of his mentor while simultaneously excusing the Georgian bandit spearheading (to that point) history's bloodiest regime.

As usual, Moscow appreciated Lamont's work, as is today evident in Comin-tern documents. Sidney Bloomfield, an American Communist stationed at the Comintern in Moscow, had been tasked with monitoring the American press reaction to the workings of the Dewey Commission and the Trotsky issue gener-ally. In one memo for the Comintern, dated February 3, 1937, and headed "NOT TO BE PUBLISHED," Bloomfield expressed his disappointment with the *New York Times,* especially the reporting of Joseph Shaplen, whom Bloomfield called a "Right-wing Socialist." Bloomfield was let down even by the reporting of Walter Duranty, the notorious Soviet apologist at the *Times,* who seemed overly sympa-thetic to Trotsky.[11] Of course, Bloomfield most reviled the coverage of the Hearst press, which, he said, was the "most vicious of all . . . the bourgeois papers." "The Hearst press," he reported, "out-did all the others in collecting the filth from all the fascist and reactionary press of the world."[12]

But there was a ray of hope, Bloomfield reported in a second memo for the Comintern. Fortunately for the Communists, Corliss Lamont was on Stalin's side. Lamont, Bloomfield noted approvingly, had taken "issue with Dewey on the important questions," cited the "poisonous campaign of Trotyskism" around the world, and called for "American sympathy to be continued 'towards the heroic efforts of the Soviet Republic to construct a new world whose basic ethical prin-ciple is loyalty to the welfare and progress of all mankind.'"[13]

Those last glowing words for Stalin's Russia were Lamont's. The Commu-nists in Moscow were not the only ones who took note of the remarks. Lamont's pals at the *Daily Worker* published his radio address in the December 14 issue.

John Dewey may have seen the light, but Corliss Lamont continued to wallow in darkness.

The Mother of All Epitaphs

Dewey would later say of the Trotsky commission episode, "It was the most interesting single experience of my life."[14] For his work with the commission, the professor earned the enmity of Joseph Stalin and the evil empire. So much so that by 1952, the year of Dewey's death—and one year before Stalin's—the "scholars" in the Soviet Ministry of Education published a "study" titled "The Pedagogy of J. Dewey in the Service of Contemporary American Reaction."[15] A far cry from the encomiums that had poured forth from Moscow in the 1920s, this Soviet "study" portrayed Dewey as a promoter of "obscurantism," a spreader of "vile ideology," a "thorough enemy of science," a "henchman of the contemporary world of imperialist reaction," and a defender of "imperialist barbarism." In their typical flair for understatement, the Soviets judged Dewey the "wicked enemy" not merely "of the American people, but also of all the freedom-loving peoples of the entire earth." Dewey stood in contrast to the "freedom-loving" men in the Kremlin, who by this point had annihilated anywhere from twenty million to sixty million people. He especially stood in contrast to "the great leader of the Soviet people and of all progressive mankind, J. V. Stalin."[16]

In truth, this was the finest of tributes to Dewey—the mother of all epitaphs.

In the end, then, John Dewey is a prototype for the experience of so many of the duped "progressives" of his era: he had been a complete dupe, but had awakened to the real horrors of Soviet Communism, and then made reparation. To be sure, he could still be counted on to offer the occasional naïve reflection on communist ideology, but he had awoken to the vicious nature of the Stalin regime. Life affords plenty of second chances, and Dewey made the best of his.

And as we shall see in a later chapter, John Dewey's long, strange trip was not even finished. Another opportunity for political redemption was waiting around the bend.

7

SMEARING ANOTHER LIBERAL ICON:
CPUSA's ASSAULT ON "FASCIST" FDR
AND THE NEW DEAL

In the 1930s, with the rise of Hitler in Germany, the Communist Party USA (CPUSA) and its members adamantly opposed the Nazis—for a while, anyway. At the same time, they shamelessly tried to frame President Franklin Delano Roosevelt and his New Deal as an American form of the same fascism. In addition to smearing that liberal icon—the next in line after Woodrow Wilson—they were also considerably unkind to a third liberal icon, Eleanor Roosevelt.

Those positions, unbelievable as they may seem to modern readers, will be demonstrated in this and subsequent chapters. Throughout, American Communists marched in lockstep with the Soviet line—and occasionally succeeded in enlisting gullible liberals. These machinations formed another insidious side of the American Communist movement. Liberal Americans should have been—and should remain—outraged by this.

But here is yet another ugly aspect of the history of American Communism that has been given short shrift by historians. The vast majority of Americans have no knowledge of the horrible treatment CPUSA doled out to liberal icons. Too often, historians have focused instead on the alleged evils and excesses of the anti-Communists; as usual, the enemy for the Left is always to the right.

Notably, the trashing of FDR was not permanent: once the president joined sides with Joseph Stalin to fight the Nazis, he was the toast of American Communists. CPUSA twisted and turned based on instructions from the Comintern.

In addition, the shabby treatment of FDR included slashing from inside as well as outside: covert Communist operatives sought to penetrate the Roosevelt administration at the same time that their comrades were attacking the new president and his policies in their protests and publications.

And then there was the peculiar relationship between the president and hardened Communist Party operatives like Earl Browder.

In short, the matter of Communists and the Roosevelt administration is a multifaceted one.

The 1932 Presidential Campaign

One might think that in the 1932 election, American Communists would see the decidedly left-leaning Franklin Roosevelt as the lesser of two evils, surely preferable to Republican Herbert Hoover.[1] That was not the case. CPUSA and many of its members began attacking FDR months before a single American cast a ballot.

The extent of the Communist assault on Roosevelt in 1932 is evident in multiple files from the Soviet Comintern archives on CPUSA.[2] CPUSA seemed proud of its efforts aimed at then–New York governor Roosevelt, eagerly reporting its successes to the comrades at the Comintern. Of course, the reporting to the Comintern was the secretive component of the effort. The shots at FDR, in contrast, were done quite openly.

This was particularly clear in an August 6, 1932, press release distributed by CPUSA, which alerted journalists to a coming damning series of articles on the major party presidential candidates: FDR, Hoover, and even Socialist Party candidate Norman Thomas, who was too far to the right for CPUSA's tastes. The first of the articles, the press release announced, would focus on FDR. It would be no less than a five-thousand-word treatise that, CPUSA helpfully offered, newspapers could choose to run as a single article or in several installments.[3]

Circulated by CPUSA's Information Bureau, the press release was sent to America's newspapers, large and small. It stated:

WATCH FOR THIS SERIES OF ARTICLES!!!

To the Editor: We shall shortly release for publication in your paper a series of articles disclosing the inner machinery of the three political parties of the ruling classes, Republican, Democrat, and Socialist.

The first of the series will be on Roosevelt and the Democratic Party. The article will be about 5,000 words in length and can be published in 5 separate installments or in one printing, if you are a weekly.

The articles will contain material previously unpublished, factual in nature, and will be of great interest to your readers. The chapters in the Roosevelt series will be titled:

1. Who is Roosevelt?
2. Roosevelt as Imperialist
3. Roosevelt and Tammany
4. Roosevelt and the Power Companies
5. Roosevelt and Labor

—Information Bureau

In answer to the first question—who is Roosevelt?—CPUSA had the answer in short order: He was a corrupt imperialist from Tammany Hall, in bed with the "Power Companies." He didn't give a damn about the little guy. He was a Wall Street kingpin in the pocket of Big Business.

The guys and gals at CPUSA crafted a little "Campaign Song" for the 1932 presidential race, one that continued the attack.[4] It went like this:

Tweedle dee, tweedle dum, tweedle doodle
Elephant, donkey, and poodle
Hoover, Roosevelt, Thomas
Whatever you want they'll promise
Prosperity, bunk, and booze,
Heads they win, tails we lose
Tweedle dee, tweedle dum, tweedle doodle
Elephant, donkey, and poodle
The fakers are playing the same old game,
The difference is only in the name
But workers' and farmers' Communist votes
Will prove that they are tired of being the goats

Whether Franklin Roosevelt was the bunker or boozer is not completely clear, but he was no doubt deemed a faker.

Assailing FDR and the New Deal

Roosevelt was elected president in a landslide in November 1932. To liberals and traditional Democrats everywhere, he was more than just a new face at 1600 Pennsylvania Avenue. He was a kind of political savior at the most desperate time in their lives. It was the Great Depression, the worst economic crisis in American history, marked by saw soup lines, dust bowls, closed shops, bank panics, skyrocketing unemployment (the rate reached an unprecedented 25 percent), and plummeting national morale. So for countless Americans—not only Democrats—Roosevelt's emergence was a lifeline.

But that was not how American Communists saw it. They wasted no time assailing the new president and his New Deal.

FDR was inaugurated on March 4, 1933. Less than two months later, the Communists seized the opportunity to denounce the new president as a fascist. Yes, a *fascist*—and at a time when the world was hardly ignorant of fascism. This was no small charge.

Communists routinely—and loudly—employed this obviously unjustified, over-the-top language throughout their literature at the time. Once again, CPUSA proudly shipped copies of such vulgar nonsense to the Comintern, as if to brag to the masters in Moscow that the good comrades on the American front were doing their best to undermine the new U.S. "regime." The examples that follow are drawn exclusively from the Comintern archive, and are a mere sliver of what is available in those files. CPUSA was so prolific in its demonization of FDR that an entire book would be needed to lay out all the exhibits.

May Day, which was also International Workers Day, was a major event for the Communists. CPUSA used this day to carry out its anti-FDR campaign on many fronts, not only on the streets of New York or San Francisco—the usual suspects—but also in smaller towns in the Heartland. For example, the Communists scheduled a May Day event at the courthouse in Terre Haute, Indiana. The flier promoting the occasion (see page 114) proclaimed to workers and farmers that this May Day would be "an inspiration for a UNITED FRONT of all impoverished masses against the Hunger, Forced Labor, Terror and War Government of the Roosevelt McNutt Dictatorship." (Paul McNutt was the Democratic governor of Indiana.)

FDR had been in power for less than two months, but somehow it was clear to Communist Americans that he was pursuing a terrorist dictatorship seeking war and forced labor. What was more, the flier announced, Roosevelt was deploying "the humiliating tactics of relief agencies." FDR, it seemed, was not seeking

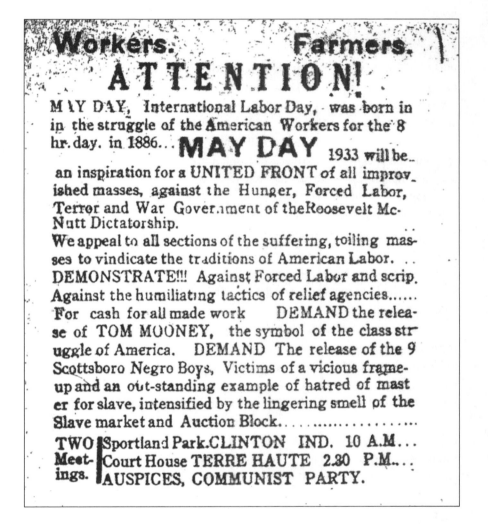

Resisting FDR's "dictatorship": On May Day 1933 the Communist Party organized nationwide demonstrations to protest the "Terror and War Government" of President Roosevelt—who had been in office two months.

relief for the downtrodden suffering under the Great Depression; he was out to humiliate them.

The Roosevelt administration would have been amazed that it was being so harshly criticized for such good intentions, and so rapidly into the presidency. Strangely, too, its method—an unprecedented expansion of central government—was the kind of thing that Communists usually would hail. No presidential administration had ever moved so far to the left, and so quickly, but it was not enough for the comrades.

In the next line in the Terre Haute flier, the Communists squeezed in a short reminder of the tragic case of the Scottsboro Boys. In 1931 a group of African-American teenagers were wrongly accused of gang raping two white girls, and nearly lynched. After the boys were convicted by all-white juries and sentenced to death, the American Communists vigorously exploited this miscarriage of justice. To the Communists, the alarming case not only indicated that America was racist (in contrast to the USSR) but was even related to the new Democratic administration in Washington. The Terre Haute flier included this line: "DEMAND The release of the 9 Scottsboro Negro Boys, Victims of vicious frame-up and an out-standing example of hatred of master for slave, intensified by the lingering smell of the Slave market and Auction Block." Somehow the Scottsboro boys were linked to the new policy of "Forced Labor" (mentioned twice in the flier) and the "Auction Block" of FDR's new America.[5]

The Communists led May Day celebrations all across America, from Terre Haute to Wilkes-Barre, Pennsylvania, to Rockford, Illinois, from St. Louis to Philadelphia to Chicago. Newspaper ads promoting the events took the opportunity to bludgeon the new Democratic administration.

One ad, plugging a May 1 workers' "celebration" at the Scottish Rite Auditorium in San Francisco, insisted that "Roosevelt's 'New Deal' far from bringing relief to Labor, has turned out to be a program which includes forced labor for the unemployed at a wage scale of $1.00 a day." Listing a host of FDR's alleged economic crimes, the ad claimed that Roosevelt's policies had only "reduc[ed] our real wages yet farther."[6] (See page 116.)

But this Democratic Party reptile was not only seeking "forced labor," the comrades assured. He and his "capitalist class" were "preparing to plunge us into a new WORLD WAR." It was Woodrow Wilson all over again—only worse.

According to the Communist ad, these capitalists were conspiring "hand in hand with this brutal program of hunger and war"—that is, FDR's New Deal. The real "danger" was that America would launch a merciless attack on, of all places, the Soviet Union.

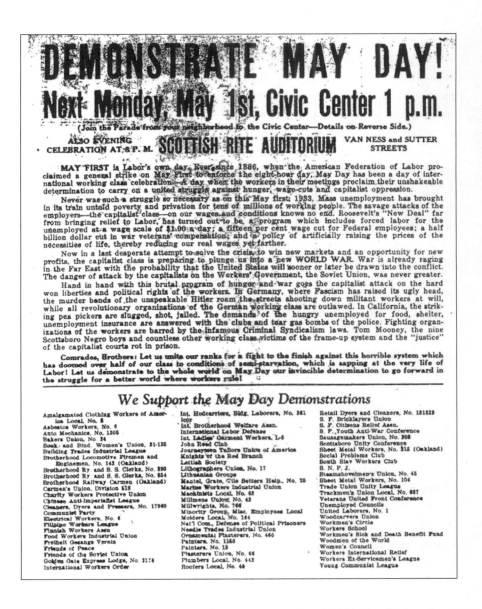

At war with the New Deal: From the start the Communists rejected FDR's New Deal, as shown in this ad for May Day 1933 protests, which condemns Roosevelt's program as "forced labor for the unemployed."

This is stunning to read today. CPUSA was portraying FDR—who had been president for only a matter of weeks—as a warmonger bent on wreaking havoc on the poor USSR. The claims were nothing short of ridiculous. Keep in mind, this was 1933, more than eight years before the United States was compelled to enter the Second World War after being attacked by Imperial Japan. And when the United States did finally enter the fight, it did not attack the Soviet Union; the two countries were part of an alliance against the Axis powers.

The Communists' May Day ad then likened FDR's vicious America to Hitler's fascist Germany by invoking the supposedly harsh American tactics against striking "pea pickers" in California. For good measure the Communists threw in a reference to the Scottsboro case.

The message was clear: America was speeding toward fascism, with a nefarious capitalist ruling class that was targeting the Soviet Union. By the reckoning of the Reds, the United States of 1933 was a diabolical place—very unlike Stalin's Russia (where the Great Purge was getting under way). The ad closed: "Comrades, Brothers: Let us unite our ranks for a fight to the finish against this horrible system which has doomed over half of our class to conditions of semi-starvation, which is sapping the very life of Labor!"

And who found themselves among the "comrades" and "brothers" united in the "ranks"? The dupes.

Among the more than seventy endorsing groups, unions, and civics clubs listed at the bottom half of the ad, a few were predictable: the Communist Party, the John Reed Club, the Young Communist League, not to mention Corliss Lamont's Friends of the Soviet Union. But many more "comrades" and "brothers" were rather benign organizations, certainly non-Communist. The Asbestos Workers, No. 6; Painters, No. 19; Plumbers Local, No. 442; Roofers Local, No. 40; Millwrights, No. 766; the Lettish Society—these and other groups had been duped. They innocently thought they were joining some friends likewise concerned about wages and the Great Depression. But their "friends," they discovered when this ad ran, had other motives, based on loyalties far away.

The roofers and painters and Lettish Society would be more careful next time around. Their antennae would be raised for the next May Day. By then, however, the Communists would have a whole new gathering of suckers to sign on as fellow endorsers.

"Headlong Towards Fascism"

In that advertisement for the San Francisco rally can be seen the template for fliers and ads the Communists distributed around America for May Day 1933. In promotional material for a demonstration in Chicago's Union Park, Communists decried "the Roosevelt forced labor camps" (this at a time when *real* forced labor camps existed in the Soviet Union). The Union Park rally spelled out FDR's alleged warmongering: "Billions of dollars are being spent for war. Yet our relief is out."

It didn't matter that there was not a kernel of truth to these claims; these were the kind of irresponsible falsehoods spun by CPUSA offices. An ad announcing a May Day event in St. Louis was similarly irresponsible, calling FDR a "fascist dictator."

Yet another ad, this one promoting a May Day parade and mass meeting in Minneapolis, was as transparent as it was brutal. (See page 119.) Under the giant heading "DEMONSTRATE Against HUNGER, FASCISM, WAR," the ad accused the New Deal of seeking "a total abolition of the workers' right to strike," of having "viciously attacked" unions, and of developing "the biggest war construction program ever known in the United States." "ALL THIS WAS DONE," screamed the flier, "AS THE CAPITALIST WAY OUT OF THE CRISIS. ALL THIS SHOWS HOW THE AMERICAN GOVERNMENT IS MOVING HEADLONG TOWARDS FASCISM AND WAR."

The ad ended with this final demand by "the workers of Minneapolis": "For the Defense of the Soviet Union and Soviet China."[7]

To the Communists, Roosevelt was so unlike their iconic leader, Lenin. It was a comparison they made continually, well beyond May Day 1933. Throughout America in January 1934, the comrades held "Lenin Memorial Meetings" to commemorate the tenth anniversary of the death of their beloved leader. As one flier declared, it had been Lenin alone, "the greatest leader," who showed "the only road to freedom," not only for workers but also for the racially oppressed, especially blacks in the segregated South. (See page 120.) FDR was a grim departure from Lenin, given the "whole Roosevelt program of preparation for fascism and war." That program did not "set aside one cent for unemployment insurance"; rather, it spent "billions" for "battleships, war planes and munitions for a war in which we will be asked to shoot down workers so Wall Street can make more profits."[8]

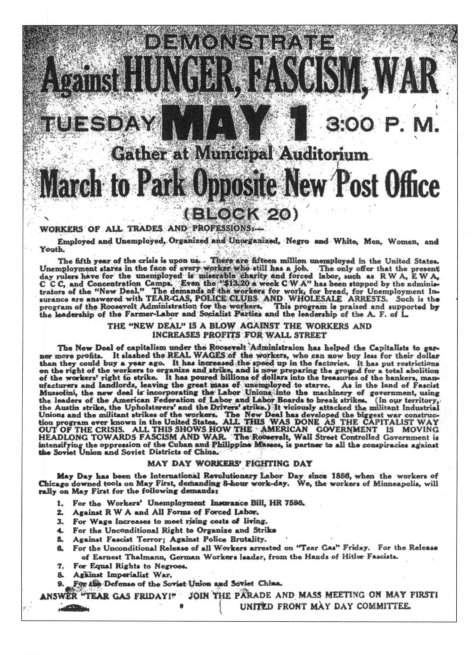

DEMONSTRATE
Against HUNGER, FASCISM, WAR
TUESDAY MAY 1 3:00 P. M.
Gather at Municipal Auditorium
March to Park Opposite New Post Office
(BLOCK 20)

WORKERS OF ALL TRADES AND PROFESSIONS:—

Employed and Unemployed, Organized and Unorganized, Negro and White, Men, Women, and Youth.

The fifth year of the crisis is upon us. There are fifteen million unemployed in the United States. Unemployment stares in the face of every worker who still has a job. The only offer that the present day rulers have for the unemployed is miserable charity and forced labor, such as R W A, E W A, C C C, and Concentration Camps. Even the "$13.20 a week C W A" has been stopped by the administrators of the "New Deal." The demands of the workers for work, for bread, for Unemployment Insurance are answered with TEAR-GAS, POLICE CLUBS AND WHOLESALE ARRESTS. Such is the program of the Roosevelt Administration for the workers. This program is praised and supported by the leadership of the Farmer-Labor and Socialist Parties and the leadership of the A. F. of L.

THE "NEW DEAL" IS A BLOW AGAINST THE WORKERS AND INCREASES PROFITS FOR WALL STREET

The New Deal of capitalism under the Roosevelt Administraion has helped the Capitalists to garner more profits. It slashed the REAL WAGES of the workers, who can now buy less for their dollar than they could buy a year ago. It has increased the speed up in the factories. It has put restrictions on the right of the workers to organize and strike, and is now preparing the ground for a total abolition of the workers' right to strike. It has poured billions of dollars into the treasuries of the bankers, manufacturers and landlords, leaving the great mass of unemployed to starve. As in the land of Fascist Mussolini, the new deal is incorporating the Labor Unions into the machinery of government, using the leaders of the American Federation of Labor and Labor Boards to break strikes. (In our territory, the Austin strike, the Upholsterers' and the Drivers' strike.) It viciously attacked the militant Industrial Unions and the militant strikes of the workers. The New Deal has developed the biggest war construction program ever known in the United States. ALL THIS WAS DONE AS THE CAPITALIST WAY OUT OF THE CRISIS. ALL THIS SHOWS HOW THE AMERICAN GOVERNMENT IS MOVING HEADLONG TOWARDS FASCISM AND WAR. The Roosevelt, Wall Street Controlled Government is intensifying the oppression of the Cuban and Philippine Masses, is partner to all the conspiracies against the Soviet Union and Soviet Districts of China.

MAY DAY WORKERS' FIGHTING DAY

May Day has been the International Revolutionary Labor Day since 1886, when the workers of Chicago downed tools on May First, demanding 8-hour work-day. We, the workers of Minneapolis, will rally on May First for the following demands:

1. For the Workers' Unemployment Insurance Bill, HR 7598.
2. Against R W A and All Forms of Forced Labor.
3. For Wage Increases to meet rising costs of living.
4. For the Unconditional Right to Organize and Strike
5. Against Fascist Terror; Against Police Brutality.
6. For the Unconditional Release of all Workers arrested on "Tear Gas" Friday. For the Release of Earnest Thalmann, German Workers leader, from the Hands of Hitler Fascists.
7. For Equal Rights to Negroes.
8. Against Imperialist War.
9. For the Defense of the Soviet Union and Soviet China.

ANSWER "TEAR GAS FRIDAY!" JOIN THE PARADE AND MASS MEETING ON MAY FIRST!
UNITED FRONT MAY DAY COMMITTEE.

FDR the warmonger: In this ad for a May Day rally, the Communists declare that the Roosevelt administration "IS MOVING HEADLONG TOWARDS FASCISM AND WAR."

LENIN
Shows The South The Only Way To
JOBS LAND and FREEDOM

Today the conditions of the Southern working-people are miserable. That is why every worker is looking for a way out. Lenin, the greatest leader of the workers of the world, shows us the only road to freedom.

It was Lenin who called on the Russian workers and farmers to fight for land, peace and bread, under the leadership of the Russian Communist Party. That is how the workers there overthrew the Czar and the capitalists and established a workers' and farmers' (Soviet) government in 1917.

On January 21, 1924, this great leader died. But his memory and his teachings live on in the hearts of tens of millions of toilers led by Lenin's Party, the Communist International. Surely Lenin's teachings are for us Southern toilers, who are the most oppressed workers in our country. The whole Roosevelt program of preparation for fascism and war crushes the Southern masses. Our wages are worse than elsewhere, and the NRA differentials are starving us on the job as prices go sky-rocketing.

The CWA is throwing thousands out and threatening to cut off all cash relief soon. The cutting of the cotton acreage is a death-blow to hundreds of thousands of toiling farmers. The Roosevelt program does not set aside one cent for unemployment insurance, billions are spent for battleships, war planes and munitions for a war in which we will be asked to shoot down workers so Wall Street can make more profits.

The Negro people are inhumanly oppressed, segregated and jim-crowed. And the lynch-rope of the bosses, the bullets of the police, are always ready if they protest. The bosses' policy of dividing the workers keeps both white and colored toilers in bondage with conditions getting worse and worse.

Lenin's way to freedom is UNITY AND STRUGGLE. Only we, the white and Negro workers of the South, ourselves, will do it. Lenin said: Organize a strong Communist Party as the leader of the working-people. Organize a real trade union movement and kick out the big labor fakers of the A F of L who mislead the A F of L rank and file in their fight for better conditions.

Lenin said: Organize a powerful movement to break down race prejudice, to struggle for equal rights for the Negro people, and for the right of the Negroes to govern the Black Belt as they see fit. He said: the revolutionary way out, following the example of the Soviet Union, is the only way out, for the white and Negro workers and farmers of the South and for our fellow workers all over the United States and throughout the entire world. This is the way to jobs and land, to peace and freedom.

Attend
LENIN MEMORIAL MEETINGS
On Jan. 21st---In All Parts Of The South This
Year.
Join The Party of Lenin— The Communist Party
For More Information Write To Box 1813, B'ham, Ala.

Roosevelt versus Lenin: Communists vilified FDR in part because he was no Lenin. This 1934 flier slams Roosevelt while hailing Lenin as "the greatest leader of the workers of the world."

Working Women of the World, Unite!

Aside from fliers and meetings and memorials, the Communists kept up the propaganda campaign against FDR in their publications. One such publication prominent in the Comintern's holdings was *The Working Woman,* which billed itself as the "magazine for working women, farm women, and working class housewives." CPUSA pushed to make *The Working Woman* its leading American publication for women. Its writers took special aim at women in the Roosevelt administration, and particularly Mrs. Roosevelt, who was not left-leaning enough for CPUSA.

A case in point was the January 30, 1934, issue, copies of which CPUSA dutifully sent to the Comintern. The lead story, titled "Mrs. Roosevelt's 'Sweet' Promises," mocked Eleanor Roosevelt's "boasted relief" as phony "sweet charity," a series of broken promises.[9] It slammed two New Deal projects, one at Bear Mountain, New York, and another in Morgantown, West Virginia, as mere "publicity stunt[s] for the Roosevelts." The article, by reporter Sadie Van Veen, even zinged highly friendly voices from the administration, like Secretary of Labor Frances Perkins[10] and top FDR adviser Harry Hopkins, who, said Van Veen, joined Eleanor and the rest of the Roosevelt crew in a display of "contemptible hypocrisy."

The Working Woman followed that story with such touching female-friendly pieces as an update on the health of the aged mother of Comintern general secretary Georgi Dimitroff and a glowing review of Clara Zetkin's *Reminiscences of Lenin,* including praise for the late despot's "warm smile," "keen joy" for workers, "clear thinking," and "masterly eloquence."

The magazine also included a preview of International Women's Day on March 8, 1934, a day that Comrade Lenin and the Comintern had established in 1919. This preview, written by *The Working Woman*'s Anna Damon, blasted the New Deal as the "Raw Deal"—the "new chains of slavery being forged by the 'liberal' Roosevelt administration." The future, said Damon, was not in the "Roosevelt program of hunger and war"; no, she averred, the "Soviet Union shows the way."

With Franklin and Eleanor desiring "hunger and war," was there any American who understood the right model for the United States? Who understood that the New Deal was really the *Raw* Deal, and that FDR's National Recovery Administration (NRA) was not about recovery but about rip-off?

The Working Woman did find one source in America who deserved to be commended: Clarence Darrow.

Darrow, the great atheist lawyer who took on William Jennings Bryan in the Scopes Monkey Trial, had also defended Ben Gitlow and other Communist Party members in a historic case protecting their right to be Communists in America—back during the "fascist" days of Woodrow Wilson. The Communist movement adored Darrow, for his advocacy on behalf of atheism as much as for his defense of Communism. Now he earned praise from *The Working Woman* for taking on the Roosevelt administration. Darrow chaired a commission that studied the NRA's operation. His resulting report, *The Working Woman* raved, "tells more truth about the N.R.A. than Miss [Frances] Perkins does. It says what the Communists have been saying from the beginning."[11]

Praise the Lord for Clarence Darrow.

Infiltrating the Roosevelt Administration

Bear in mind that liberals who idolized FDR later defended Communist agitators who trashed their beloved president—defended them, that is, against the *anti*-Communists. Despite the Communist attacks on a liberal icon, it was the anti-Communists who earned progressives' wrath for insisting that these Communist agitators were un-American, pro-Soviet, and dedicated to interests outside of the United States.

The attacks on the greatest liberal president, his administration, his policies, and his wife—a historic first lady with a policy role—were clear even at the time. A more sinister Communist tactic would not be discovered until after World War II, and in fact we are still learning details to this day. The Communists, it turns out, were toiling behind the scenes to infiltrate the Roosevelt administration on behalf of Moscow. Sometimes closet CPUSA members were penetrating the administration, but frequently actual spies for the Soviet KGB infiltrated the upper reaches of government. Alger Hiss is the most infamous example of the latter.

Perhaps the most thoroughly penetrated area of FDR's administration was agriculture, and specifically the Agricultural Adjustment Administration (AAA). FDR had formed this new wing of the Department of Agriculture to solve the nation's farm crisis, at a time when agriculture was still America's most pervasive industry. Soon AAA was bursting with a huge staff of five thousand, and included top talent from Ivy League faculties and Wall Street, as well as such liberal dynamos as Adlai Stevenson, Abe Fortas, and Thurman Arnold.[12]

This elite intellectual powerhouse was ready to rescue America's farmers. As a group, writes Sam Tanenhaus in his seminal biography of Whittaker Chambers, this crew "knew little, if anything, about farming or farmers." They didn't need to; they were America's progressives. They had been self-anointed and self-appointed; it was their job to change America via the New Deal.[13]

Unfortunately, within that powerhouse of traditional Democrats were secret Communists like John Abt and Alger Hiss.[14] There was also Hal Ware, who would create an entire Communist cell within AAA. These clandestine Communists duped many of the liberals in the organization—big time.

The Communists keyed in on AAA because they knew that agriculture was the backbone of the American economy, as well as the Soviet economy, the Chinese economy, and the world economy. As usual, *The New Republic* was there to champion the Communist cause, editorializing: "The only groups in the country that have given serious attention to the plight of the tenant farmer are the Socialists and the Communists."[15] But some of the comrades, eager to revamp American agriculture, privately became restless when it appeared the New Deal would not go as far as they had envisioned: no mass collectivization. Some of them had begun referring to FDR as "the 'Kerensky' of the U.S.A.," referring to the liberal official who briefly ruled Russia after the fall of the czar but who was ousted when Lenin and the Bolsheviks seized power.[16]

Hal Ware jumped in. Ware was no Potemkin Progressive; he was a committed Communist. As a paid consultant to the U.S. Department of Agriculture, he had traveled to Russia in the 1920s and ended up supplying statistics on the agricultural utopia organized from Moscow. In 1931 he returned to the United States from the Soviet Union to organize farmers into what he called "an agrarian wing to the proletarian movement." He was initially frustrated, but that changed with the advent of the Roosevelt administration. In 1933, sensing an opportunity, he began canvassing government agencies for new recruits for the Communist Party.[17]

Though no longer with the Department of Agriculture, Ware "became a familiar figure at the AAA," according to Tanenhaus, as he virtually "camped out in the lunchroom." He began exerting real influence. As Tanenhaus rightly notes, Ware "assembled a secret Communist network in Washington," a cluster of seven cells or more, each with a leader who also belonged to an "elite nucleus" that wielded substantial influence. These separate but coordinated cells were created as part of a deliberate, viable Communist apparatus operating within the Roosevelt administration. Each cell leader was tasked with organizing a "study group" within his government agency. From those cells, Commissar Ware and his comrades thrust their swords deep.[18]

How successful was the penetration?

Alger Hiss, Harry Dexter White, Lauchlin Currie, and Harold Glasser are a few of the more notorious KGB agents who we now know were doing the work of the USSR, and who preyed upon unsuspecting liberals throughout the Roosevelt administration. Other suspects ranged from John Abt to Charles Kramer, and even to Harry Hopkins.

Harry Hopkins: Agent 19?

Because of his remarkable influence with FDR, Harry Hopkins stands as the most sensational case among the potential Soviet agents.

Born in 1890 in Sioux City, Iowa, to a small businessman father and devout Methodist mother, Hopkins was a leading progressive of his day. He left the Midwest for New York City in the 1910s, where he was caught up in the left-wing politics of the city. By the 1920s he was active in a number of liberal causes, with special interest in social work. He ended up executive director of the Temporary Emergency Relief Administration under New York's governor, Franklin Delano Roosevelt. His management of welfare policy impressed not only the governor but also the governor's wife, Eleanor.

In March 1933, soon after taking over the White House, FDR summoned Hopkins to Washington to spearhead relief at the federal level. The adviser quickly gained influence with FDR, so much so that he became one of the principal architects of the New Deal, particularly the relief programs within the Works Progress Administration (WPA). Under Hopkins, the WPA became one of the largest employers in all of the United States.

Only after his death in 1946 did we begin learning more concrete information on Hopkins's dealings with Communists. He seems to have first had contact with the Communist underground in the 1930s, and to have fallen in with Hal Ware's cells within the Department of Agriculture. The researchers of the Venona transcripts—communiqués between the Soviet Union and American Communists intercepted by the U.S. government—have concluded that Hopkins was a member of a Department of Agriculture "study group" run by Lee Pressman.[19]

Of course, participation in Pressman's group would not by itself guarantee that Hopkins was a Communist, let alone a KGB mole. Hopkins's activities are more instructive. Many of his actions were so helpful to the Soviets that he was at a minimum a terribly naïve dupe, and possibly something much worse.[20]

The evidence from the Soviet side, suggesting that he was something much worse, began emerging in the 1960s. The sources include Oleg Gordievsky, a former KGB officer and one of the most knowledgeable defectors ever to leave the Soviet Union, and Iskhak Akhmerov, a high-level Soviet official who worked inside the United States during World War II. Gordievsky began working undercover for British intelligence in 1974, a decade before his defection, until he was exposed by CIA traitor Aldrich Ames. Gordievsky called Hopkins an agent of "major significance."[21] Akhmerov, who was in contact with the likes of Alger Hiss, described Hopkins as "the most important of all Soviet wartime agents in the United States."[22] He knew Hopkins dating back to the 1930s.

Much more information on Hopkins emerged decades later, specifically with the revelations from the Venona transcripts. Many Venona messages contain messages to or from Hopkins. He was in contact with such high-level Soviet officials as General A. I. Belyaev, Ambassador Maxim Litvinov, Andrei Gromyko—and Stalin himself. Some of his discussions with Stalin were conducted in FDR's presence, but others were not. Many of those interactions were obviously appropriate for a representative to the American president, but others seem suspicious. In one Venona report, dated May 29, 1943, Akhmerov reported to Moscow on secret discussions between FDR and Churchill. According to the report Soviet agent "19" channeled this secret information to the USSR. Researchers who have studied Venona make a convincing case that agent 19 was Harry Hopkins.[23]

The leading authority on Venona, Herb Romerstein, is convinced that Hopkins actively worked for the other side. "He was a dedicated Soviet agent," states Romerstein, categorically. "He was both a spy—that is, he supplied information—and an agent of influence." Hopkins was not a "useful idiot," says Romerstein, but rather one who sought out useful idiots: "Some of those he conned in the White House and outside were useful idiots."[24]

Having secured the ear and deep trust of Roosevelt, Hopkins arguably became the president's right-hand man during World War II. He was essentially FDR's chief political adviser, confidant, troubleshooter, and sometimes diplomat. He literally lived in the White House, with FDR seeing him more than any other aide. "You'll learn what a lonely job this is," said a vulnerable Roosevelt to presidential aspirant Wendell Wilkie, "and you'll discover the need for somebody like Harry Hopkins, who asks for nothing except to serve you."[25]

The common claim is that Hopkins alone wielded more power than the entire State Department. That certainly seemed the case as he accompanied Roosevelt to all the major conferences of World War II: Casablanca, Tehran, Yalta. Nowhere was he more instrumental than on policy toward Stalin's state and via the Lend-Lease program, which directed tens of billions of dollars to U.S. allies in the war effort. He was the unofficial chief emissary to Britain, where he worked directly with Churchill, and was also sent to Moscow to negotiate with Stalin.

Hopkins became close to the Soviets; precisely *how* close remains the big question, and a source of controversy. He still has loyal defenders who say any suggestion that he was a Soviet agent is an ugly smear. The latest declassified material, however, plus the research of Romerstein and others, raises legitimate concerns that Harry Hopkins was serving Soviet interests.

And if he was not a Soviet spy, then he was a dupe of disturbing proportions. As we shall see, he aided the Soviets in two areas in particular: the atomic bomb and the future of postwar Eastern Europe.

FDR and Comrade Browder

Before we consider more on Harry Hopkins, it is important to take notice of another curious, and controversial, FDR relationship: the president's connection to Earl Browder, the face of American Communism.

Browder (1891–1973), general secretary of CPUSA from 1934 to 1945, was no minor figure with minor notions. "Above all," he had stated in his 1934 CPUSA convention report, "we arm ourselves with the political weapons forged by the victorious Communist Party of the Soviet Union, with the mighty sword of Marx-ism-Leninism, and are strengthened and inspired by the victories of socialist con-struction won under its Bolshevik leadership headed by Stalin." The pro-Stalin, pro-Soviet patriot continued: "Our World Communist Party, the Communist International, provides us the guarantee not only of our victory in America, but of the victory of the proletariat throughout the world."[26]

To that end, the Comintern of the 1930s had not backed down from its ear-lier triumphant and militaristic pronouncements. In its recently published "condi-tions for admission," the Comintern stated that its members—which, of course, included CPUSA—"must render every possible assistance to the Soviet Republics in their struggles against counter-revolutionary forces. They should conduct an organized and definite propaganda to induce the workers to refuse to make or handle any kind of military equipment intended for use against the Soviet Repub-lics, and should also carry on, by legal or illegal means, a propaganda among any troops sent against the Workers' Republics."[27]

For members of CPUSA, things remained crystal clear: Their first priority was the Soviet Union. Period.

For its part, CPUSA stated candidly: "We want our Party to become like an army, a Bolshevik army, who while understanding the policy behind each deci-sion is prepared to carry it out with military promptness, without any hesitation or question, and further, to carry out the decisions with Bolshevik judgment and maximum effectiveness."[28]

Given such bold statements, *any* relationship between Browder and the sitting president of the United States was nothing to be shrugged off. Understandably, then, the nature of the Browder-FDR relationship has long been one of intense speculation, from both the Right and the Left. The wildest speculation, in fact, was rooted in exaggerations begun on the far Left—ironically, begun by Browder and his party.

The Speculation

My first angle into the worst of the speculation was a knowledgeable source involved in Cold War intelligence. By then in his eighties, the source was tight-lipped, insisted on anonymity, would not go on the record, and clearly seemed bound by security restrictions—both ancient and unnecessary—in terms of what he could say or even suggest. It seemed apparent, however, that my source's source was Browder himself.

Asked if Browder had "advised FDR or pushed him toward wrongly trusting Stalin," my source said, "I can't say. I don't know the nature. There were rumors that he [Browder] met with FDR. . . . These claims came after the war. FDR was dead by then, so he couldn't confirm anything."

My source continued, "The claim was that he [Browder] was a conduit of information between top-level Communist Party people around the world and FDR—and our government. That, I think I can say, is true." He added: "There's no doubt that they had contact. The key is how, where, and when."

As my source noted, the questions about Browder's connection to President Roosevelt were crucial because Browder was not only head of CPUSA but also a "Comintern agent," one who actively recruited Red Americans as official Soviet agents.[29] Moreover, the source said, Browder in the 1930s "was trying to organize the world for Moscow," as he had been "a Communist loyal to the Soviet Union." So it is crucial to know to what extent he was in touch with the president of the United States, who was being lobbied to make policy changes favorable to Stalin's Russia.

I include this anonymous source only because it is representative of the speculation, and because his information checks out. Consider:

Early published information on an FDR-Browder relationship surfaced in the 1940s. We know that the president's contact with Browder went back to the 1930s, on issues ranging from domestic politics—even presidential elections—to international relations, including, yes, relations with the USSR. The most famous and open exchanges between the two came when FDR granted Browder a full and unconditional pardon and (later) a commutation of a prison sentence. As for the latter, the Communist leader had been sentenced to four years in prison for passport fraud; in 1940 he had falsified his passport so he could travel to the USSR.[30]

But the exchanges between the two men went well beyond legal matters, as shown by letters between FDR and Browder, and communications between Browder and the Comintern. For instance, Roosevelt and Browder exchanged four letters between June 14 and July 12, 1943; these have been declassified and are available from the FDR Library. We can now observe what FDR could not at the time: that on June 12, just before the exchange of letters began, Comintern head and Stalin stooge Georgi Dimitroff,[31] communicating with Browder via clandestine radio, told his loyal American servant to use his influence with the Roosevelt administration to try to secure the release of a Communist Party apparatchik held in Argentina and about to be deported to Spain.[32] The apparatchik was Victorio Codovilla (1894–1970), early founder of the International Socialist Party, a forerunner to the Communist Party,[33] and an international troublemaker. Codovilla had been the Comintern representative in Spain—a spot of major interest to the Soviets in the 1930s, to say the least. Sure enough, Comrade Browder cabled FDR just two days later, on June 14, 1943, requesting that the president step in to prevent the sure execution of Codovilla in Spain.

The mere fact that Browder would directly cable the president bespeaks both bravado and influence. That Roosevelt would respond is a confirmation of Browder's confidence. In FDR's first response, on June 23, he said that this was a matter of "exclusive jurisdiction of the Argentine Government," but that he would nonetheless talk to the U.S. ambassador to Argentina. Just three days later, on June 26, the president wrote Browder with good news from the ambassador: Codovilla would not be deported. Two weeks later, on July 12, a pleased Browder wrote a letter thanking the president.[34]

Anyone who claims that there was no substance to the relationship between Browder and FDR, or that the CPUSA leader exerted no influence on the White House, needs to read correspondence such as this. The exchanges are undeniable, and significant.

In the Codovilla case and others, Browder dutifully reported the information he obtained to his friends at the Comintern. Often he communicated by cable or radio, but sometimes he traveled to Moscow to connect with Dimitroff and associates. In those sessions with Dimitroff, Browder discussed such matters as the Codovilla situation, as well as foreign policy, international events, the prospects for FDR's reelection, the coalition of American groups and political parties supporting Roosevelt, and even whether CPUSA should back the president's reelection bids. Browder and Dimitroff considered whether the Communists should be a part of the big-tent, left-wing coalition supporting FDR.[35]

From the Comintern files and declassified Venona transcripts, it is clear what the Comintern knew; what the KGB, GRU (military intelligence), and NKVD (secret police) knew; and what Browder knew. It is not always clear what FDR knew. But we know—from Venona and Comintern files, as well as presidential papers and letters, and the private papers of Eleanor Roosevelt, Earl Browder, former Communist (and noted historian) Theodore Draper, and others—that Browder was the link among them all.

At first blush, it seems quite disturbing that the CPUSA chief had such access to the president of the United States, especially if FDR had no idea that Browder was running the information to Moscow. This would be yet more evidence that too many liberal Democrats—including their president—failed to recognize that CPUSA was not merely another political party.

That said, all of this is not as odd as it may seem. The timing is important: The USSR, like America, did not want a war with the Nazis. The Soviets also wanted better relations with Washington. The USSR and the United States had positions that sometimes ran along a parallel track. As the 1930s progressed, it became clearer that the priority was to stop Hitler. Thus it was not surprising that some Communists, from America to the Soviet Union, would endorse FDR's presidential bid, even after the Comintern and its operatives had viciously attacked the American president.[36]

Franklin, Earl, and Comrade Josephine

The speculation about the FDR-Browder relationship only intensified because of the claims of one Josephine Adams. Adams was the source of more explosive rumors—and of much misinformation.

Venona authorities John Earl Haynes and Harvey Klehr write, "Although Browder performed many valuable services for Soviet intelligence, he also inadvertently provided it with misinformation about President Roosevelt." Specifically, in July 1943, Browder told KGB and GRU representatives in the United States, who in turn informed their superiors in Moscow, that he had a friend, a secret CPUSA member, who was surreptitiously meeting with FDR. This friend, Browder told his comrades, was a back channel between him and the White House. The friend was Josephine Truslow Adams.[37]

Various forms of documentation reveal how Soviet intelligence in the United States reported this revelation to Moscow. For example, the GRU's Georgi Bolshakov excitedly relayed the information in an August 21, 1943, memo to Dimitroff at the Comintern (which, incidentally, Stalin, in the middle of the war, claimed to have a dissolved—another phony Communist claim accepted by many liberals, including FDR).[38] "According to information we have received," transmitted Bolshakov, "an American citizen, Josephine Truslow, on instructions from Browder is meeting systematically with the president of the U.S. Roosevelt. Please advise whether this is in fact the case, and whether you have any information on this issue."[39]

Was it in fact the case? And who was Josephine Adams?

Public awareness of Adams's claims surfaced as early as Robert Sherwood's highly sympathetic 1948 book on Harry Hopkins, in which Browder was quoted taking pride in the fact that he presented his "views on world events" to the president, and adding that the president "appreciated the service I gave him."[40] The mode of this presentation, plus additional details, were reported in an influential 1959 book by conservative author George Crocker, titled *Roosevelt's Road to Russia*. Crocker, after underscoring that Roosevelt "was no . . . Communist," reported that FDR had "clandestinely obtained the recommendations of Earl Browder."[41]

"We know now that President Roosevelt maintained a secret liaison with Browder," noted Crocker. "One Josephine Adams, an artist, acted as a courier between the two men. She relayed information, and even documents, between them, conveying to each the views of the other. She saw Roosevelt between thirty-eight and forty times during the three year period preceding his death." "These meetings," he added, "were held either at the White House or at Roosevelt's Hyde Park home. (Years later, Miss Adams so testified under oath before a subcommittee of the United States Senate.)"[42] Crocker noted that Browder had confirmed this, and cited Sherwood's book on Harry Hopkins.[43]

What Crocker did not know, and Browder and others did not know, was that Josephine Truslow Adams was a woman of questionable sanity who seems to have misled everyone, including Browder, into believing that she was Browder's conduit to the White House.

This is not to say she existed in an entirely alternate universe. She met and knew Mrs. Roosevelt and even exchanged letters with her, as Browder himself had exchanged letters with FDR—most or all of which (Browder-FDR) are now on file at the FDR Library.[44] The best sources on this, who have looked into the matter extensively, through interviews and primary sources, including declassified archives, are Haynes and Klehr and Browder biographer James G. Ryan.[45]

Ryan notes that by 1941 Josephine Truslow Adams had already become a minor cause célèbre in the Communist Party. Born in Brooklyn in 1897, Adams was a leftist and art teacher at Swarthmore College. She had testified before the House Judiciary Committee against a bill to legalize wiretapping; she had done so in defense of civil liberties for Communists. She later claimed that her position had led "someone" to bug her office and home telephones.

Swarthmore, for various reasons, refused to renew Adams's teaching contract. The Reds portrayed this as discrimination against her for speaking out, but more likely it was motivated by reasons relating to her mental fitness. She looked for work, and was helped by a woman named Esther Lape, who also happened to be a friend of Eleanor Roosevelt. The first lady was impressed by Adams's artistic work and met with her, at Swarthmore, in April 1941.[46]

Thus began somewhat of a friendship between Eleanor Roosevelt and Adams. Yet it was Adams who was the main driver behind the relationship, sending the first lady not only artwork but also a deluge of letters. As Ryan put it, this was "a largely one-sided correspondence" that lasted "throughout the war years."[47]

Meanwhile, Adams continued her "civil liberties" activism on behalf of Communists and their causes. Later that year, in December 1941, she sent a plea to the White House urging a presidential pardon of Earl Browder. She was a visible member of the Free Browder Committee. According to Ryan, Adams received a "short, noncommittal reply" from "the White House" (Ryan does not identify the writer or signer of the White House letter). A few months later, in April 1942, she sent another dispatch pressing Mrs. Roosevelt to meet with the prominent Communist and ACLU board member Elizabeth Gurley Flynn, again on the Browder issue. This time, the first lady was more firm, explaining that Flynn's Communist reputation gave her no credibility on the issue. Adams backed off when FDR commuted Browder's sentence.[48]

Some authors have suggested that the relationship ended there. In fact, documentation shows that Josephine Adams wrote a letter to Mrs. Roosevelt on July 4, 1944, asking her to assist Raisa Browder (Earl's wife) on a matter of travel and immigration. The letter was sent on to Earl Harrison, the commissioner of the Immigration and Naturalization Service, and Mrs. Browder's problem was resolved. Even then, Adams sent Mrs. Roosevelt still more letters regarding the Browders.[49]

As these details clearly show, there was a relationship between Adams and the Roosevelt White House—or, at least, between Adams and the first lady. The main issue of contention is the extent of the relationship—and how close it got to FDR.

Adams began claiming in 1942, and through 1943, that she was meeting with the president. Yet, according to Ryan, her only White House visit took place in 1939, and it was with a "lobbying organization."[50] Indeed, that one occasion seems the only documentable White House visit by Adams.

Importantly, however, people in the Communist movement believed Adams's claims of repeated visits and counsel with the president. Among her most notable believers was Earl Browder, with whom she met frequently. It certainly helped Adams's credibility with Browder when she showed off her letters from Mrs. Roosevelt. When she and Browder met at a July 4, 1942, CPUSA "Independence Day" gathering, she told Browder that she had helped negotiate and secure his release from prison. They became friends, with Adams, in Browder's words, becoming a "frequent family visitor." She convinced the CPUSA chief that she had, as Ryan put it, "an intimate White House relationship." According to Ryan, "Browder displayed unprecedented gullibility."[51]

Haynes and Klehr, having reviewed the primary documents, write that through Adams, "Browder believed he had a private pipeline to the White House. Browder gave Adams material on various political matters to discuss with President Roosevelt during their (as he thought) frequent chats." Some of Browder's information on politics, they maintain, went directly into letters that Adams sent to Eleanor Roosevelt. Mrs. Roosevelt, in turn, "recognized the political interest of some of Adams's letters and forwarded them to her husband—noting in one, however, 'I know nothing of her reliability.'" The first lady, report the authors, sent "polite responses" to Adams, the most encouraging—and eyebrow-raising—being a note that claimed, "Your letters go directly to the president. What then happens I do not know."[52]

Mrs. Roosevelt's ambiguity was not what Josephine Adams imparted to Earl Browder. To Browder, she insisted that she actually met with FDR, in person and often. She then gave the CPUSA leader important, substantive messages that she vowed were the president's responses to Browder.

Was this the case? No, apparently not.

In fact, write Haynes and Klehr, Adams "simply made up FDR's responses, basing them on the analysis offered by political commentators and on what Browder wanted to hear." They say that Adams did such a convincing job that even in the 1950s, when Adams's mental instability was apparent, "Browder had difficulty believing that he had been hoodwinked." He judged the messages too politically sophisticated for Adams to have fabricated them.[53]

Thus, Earl Browder himself—Communist kingpin, duper of liberals—had been duped.

Browder, at first, could not have known that Adams had major psychiatric issues. Even J. Edgar Hoover's FBI talked to Adams well into the 1950s, and she was called to testify in closed session to Congress. Eventually the FBI would dismiss her, with one agent stating that she suffered from an "emotional and intellectual state of unbalance."[54]

Still, given her involvement with the FBI and even Congress, certain journalists picked up on her claims about the Roosevelts. With such shocking revelations going public, it was only a matter of time before Adams had herself a book deal. The book was never published, however, as her ghostwriter and editor discovered the unreliability of much of what she said and killed the project.

Adams started going in and out of mental institutions around 1956, and spent the final years of her life permanently confined.

Haynes and Klehr are excellent sources not only on all the details of these complicated relationships but also, central to the thesis of this chapter, on the *effect* of all this misinformation. As they note, this bad information, as it became public, "contributed to the souring of postwar American politics." The bad information began with Browder, who both hinted and boasted of his relationship with Roosevelt, which led to rumors of his "back channel" to the White House— rumors that first circulated in the upper echelons of CPUSA. From there, chronicle Haynes and Klehr, the story "seeped out" to "Popular Front liberal allies" of the party.

In short order, the rumor mill reached anti-Communists, including prominent defectors like John Lautner, Louis Budenz, and Frank Meyer. And while many anti-Communists (including J. Edgar Hoover himself) discounted the rumors, others, particularly those who despised both Browder and FDR, believed what they hoped to be true—the better to tear down Roosevelt. In certain circles on the political Right, theories began to circulate of the late, great FDR-Browder-CPUSA-Comintern conspiracy.[55]

FDR and the Communists

Overall, FDR's dealings with Earl Browder were not the things of grand conspiracy—or at least were nothing to match Josephine Adams's fevered imaginings.

Nonetheless, they were troubling enough, as was the whole of American Communist penetration of the president's administration. Here again, the trouble stemmed largely from the common liberal failure to distinguish between the Left and the far Left, and to appreciate that the Communist Party was not simply another political party. This time around, the failure was Franklin Roosevelt's as well, even as there is no evidence that FDR was advancing Moscow's agenda through Earl Browder.

If FDR was duped, it was not by Browder. The president left himself vulnerable to duping by close advisers like Harry Hopkins—and even by "Uncle Joe" Stalin himself.

But before any of those charades could transpire, CPUSA had some grand manipulation planned for liberals who could help the Communist cause for "peace" . . . or for "war" . . . or for both.

8

WAR COMMUNISM:
HATING FDR, LOVING FDR

Perhaps the single most egregious example of American Communist duplicity was the appalling manner in which CPUSA and its acolytes flip-flopped on Adolf Hitler and World War II, based entirely on marching orders from Moscow—that is, on loyalty to the USSR, not to the United States. This meant that they alternately hated FDR, loved FDR, and sought to dupe FDR, as well as the beloved president's supporters.

In the early to mid-1930s, CPUSA adamantly opposed Hitler's Germany. But the party stance shifted dramatically in 1939 with the shocking revelation of the Hitler-Stalin Pact, the joint "nonaggression" agreement between Nazi Germany and Bolshevik Russia. The pledge of nonaggression pertained only to the two countries; it hardly applied to the nations the dictators sought to devour. Only a week after signing the agreement, Germany invaded Poland from the west (September 1), and just two weeks later the USSR invaded from the east (September 17). This pact sent shockwaves throughout the world, nowhere more so than in the American Communist movement.

How did CPUSA respond? As always, it followed Moscow's lead. It did whatever Stalin and the Comintern ordered.

Thus, CPUSA was suddenly allied with Hitler. These Communists no longer marched against Hitler. Instead, they vilified American allies under Hitler's siege, such as Britain, and attacked President Roosevelt for providing aid to those allies. On the American home front, the Communists positioned themselves as being on the side of "peace," even though they sided with the aggressors who started the Second World War.

But those were only the first twists and turns: CPUSA did another about-face once Hitler betrayed Stalin, violating his agreement of nonaggression by invading the Soviet Union in June 1941. With that, CPUSA could again (and did) become anti-Hitler, and magically morphed into being pro-Britain and even pro-Roosevelt.

Still later, after World War II, there would be another flip-flop. When the United States and USSR emerged as antagonists in the Cold War, CPUSA demonized Roosevelt's successor, President Harry Truman. This time, CPUSA framed America as the renegade aggressor.

To be sure, some American Communists were so horrified by the 1939 Hitler-Stalin Pact that they bolted CPUSA. Many Jewish-American Communists, for example, parted with Moscow. Of course, many of the disaffected turned to Trotsky (before he was murdered by Stalin's henchmen) and remained Communists under his roof, rather than Stalin's. Others remained small "c" communists, but withdrew their membership from CPUSA.

But CPUSA itself, and its devoted faithful, marched in lockstep with the USSR. If Stalin's Soviet Union was against it, so were they. If Stalin was for it, so were they. The record is perfectly clear. This pattern provides plain evidence that CPUSA was a creature of the Comintern—that members of the party considered themselves first and foremost loyal Soviet patriots.

And all along, the Communists looked for—and found—dupes. Many liberals, they discovered, could be swayed into thinking that the bad guys were not the Communists, who hopped in and out of bed with Hitler and trashed liberal presidents, but, amazingly enough, the *anti*-Communists who saw the Communists as agents of a foreign power. As had been the case throughout the Depression, the Communists frequently could count on the dupes to come to their defense against the anti-Communists.

Sadly, CPUSA's sordid behavior before and during World War II is rarely taught today. That omission makes it much easier for contemporary liberal academics to defend the Communists as they denounce the anti-Communists in a one-sided attack.

"For the Defense of the Soviet Union"

A good starting point in revealing the Communists' wartime shell game is a March 23, 1936, document in the Comintern archives on CPUSA. The memo,

titled "DIRECTIVES ON ANTI-WAR CAMPAIGN," was sent "TO ALL DIS-
TRICT BUROS" by the Central Committee of CPUSA.[1] (See page 138.) The goal
of the directive was to "mobilize the masses" and organize "big mass meetings and
demonstrations" on April 7, 1936. CPUSA's Central Committee issued talking
points: "The chief slogan around which our agitation shall be carried on for the
April 7th occasion shall be 'Keep America out of war by keeping the world out of
war. Against the Roosevelt war budget. For the support of the peace policy of the
Soviet Union. For the defense of the Soviet Union.'"

It is useful to recall that this campaign for "peace" fell smack in the middle of
Stalin's Great Purge. The USSR's "peace policy" was in truth an unprecedented
policy of orchestrated, systemic domestic terror. But in CPUSA's account it was
President Roosevelt who was a warmonger.

The memo provided an excellent example of how CPUSA sought out front
groups and dupes to further its agenda. "Every effort should be made," ordered
CPUSA's Central Committee, "to organize these actions on April 7th on a
united front basis. Party organizations should, first of all, strive to get the local
organizations of the American League Against War and Fascism to take the
initiative in organizing these demonstrations and meetings." The local Communist parties "should make a special effort . . . to approach the various peace
organizations."

In truth, the American League Against War and Fascism was one of the most
notorious and subversive Communist-front organizations. It was organized in
New York City from September 29 to October 1, 1933, emerging the same year
that Hitler and FDR entered office.[2] The group was anti-Hitler, anti-FDR, and
pro-Stalin. It cleverly adopted a public platform that stood against Hitler, fascism,
and war, perfect for appealing to non-Communist liberals. The Religious Left,
in particular, would be prime ground for duping, eagerly supplying speakers and
marchers for the league's rallies.

The March 1936 memo carefully emphasized the need to ensure that the
message of the Communist Party was expressed at these meetings, even as they
were carried out under the name of peace organizations. It was imperative to get
out the pro-Soviet message while extending the umbrella of "peace."

The Central Committee told the comrades to watch their *Daily Worker* over
the next few days, as it would carry a statement from the Central Committee
"calling for demonstrations and mass meetings on April 7th." CPUSA's district
organizers did as they were told.

March 23rd, 1936

TO ALL DISTRICT BUROS

DIRECTIVES ON ANTI-WAR CAMPAIGN

On April 7th, 1917, America entered the World War. The Central Committee has decided to make this April 7th, the occasion for big mass meetings and demonstrations to mobilize the masses in the struggle for peace and against war. The chief slogan around which our agitation shall be carried on for the April 7th occasion shall be "Keep America out of war by keeping the world out of war. Against the Roosevelt war budget. For the support of the peace policy of the Soviet Union. For the defense of the Soviet Union."

Every effort should be made to organize these actions on April 7th on a united front basis. Party organizations should, first of all, strive to get the local organizations of the American League Against War and Fascism to take the initiative in organizing these demonstrations and meetings with our full support. We should make a special effort on this occasion to approach the various peace organizations that are also contemplating the holding of meetings and discussions in connection with the anniversary of the entrance of American imperialism into the last World War. Should our efforts, however, fail in the organization of joint united front meetings on April 7th, the Party must under all circumstances independently hold and organize anti-war meetings on April 7th.

It is very important that, at these anti-war meetings we make clear before the masses the role of the Roosevelt administration in the present developing war situation throughout the world, and to make clear also the policy of the Party on the question of the struggle for peace. It is, therefore, advisable that at all united front meetings, we should strive for a Party speaker; and at the meetings held under the auspices of the Party, there should be not more than two speakers with one principal speaker who will have an opportunity to clearly present to the assembled workers the facts of the present war situation and the position of the Party for the struggle for peace.

We advise that special functionaries conferences shall be held at which the D.O.'s and other leading members of the Buro shall make a report on the present war situation and the policy of the Party. Such meetings will help to clarify the Party membership itself and to mobilize it in the struggle against war and for the preparations for May 1st. These functionaries conferences shall be followed up with unit discussions.

Within the next few days the Daily Worker will carry a statement of the Central Committee, calling for demonstrations and mass meetings on April 7th.

Comradely yours,

CENTRAL COMMITTEE CPUSA

In search of dupes: This 1936 directive from the Communist Party's Central Committee emphasizes the need to involve "the various peace organizations"—non-Communist liberals—in "demonstrations and mass meetings."

Which Side to Fight For?

There were compelling exceptions to this stance of "peace," as seen in another remarkable CPUSA document in the Comintern archives, titled "WHAT ARE WE TO DO IN CASE OF WAR?"[3] This internal party memo, dated September 9, 1938, conceded that there were "several possibilities in the alignment of states in any coming war"—a war which at that point was exactly one year away. Notably, the document never mentioned the United States, perhaps out of fear that the document might get into the hands of U.S. officials, though it no doubt included America among the "capitalist states" it mentioned.

And therein came a bracing (albeit not surprising) declaration: "If only capitalist (and, therefore, necessarily Imperialist) states are at war," said the document, "it is obvious that the communist slogan of the proletariat turning their guns against their own bourgeoisie is the only correct one." And what if the USSR was at war with the capitalist states? The document explained, "If Russia, the Workers' State, has to defend itself against capitalist aggression, this slogan is even more urgently necessary for the workers in the capitalist states."

In other words, if America, a "capitalist-imperialist" state, went to war with Russia, then American Communists should take up arms against their own "bourgeoisie." The goal, according to the CPUSA document, was always to establish "a workers' state in any one of the capitalist countries," a "Dictatorship of the Proletariat in their respective countries." The USSR would be the supreme overseer of that state, of that dictatorship.

It was the Revolution first. It was Communism first. It was Russia first. It was never America first, as America's principles and its Constitution were antithetical to those of Soviet Communism and the Bolshevik Revolution.

For decades, anti-Communists openly expressed their fear that American Communists would side with the Soviet Union if it came to blows with the United States. As CPUSA documents such as this one reveal, those fears were hardly misplaced.

The American "Peace" Mobilization

Publicly, CPUSA's message was quite different. The party and its front groups made "peace" the focus of their campaign. That way, the Communist Party could attract a lot of peace-loving, non-Communist liberals to their rallies, at which it promoted Soviet foreign-policy objectives, of course. This push got more intense, and scared up more recruits, as Hitler began his sweep through Europe in the late 1930s.

The most insidious manifestation of this effort was the organization known as the American Peace Mobilization. This group was exposed as a Communist front only later, after World War II, thanks to investigative work by President Truman's attorney general, Tom Clark, and by the House Committee on Un-American Activities. The House committee would dub the American Peace Mobilization "one of the most seditious organizations which ever operated in the United States," "one of the most notorious and blatantly Communist fronts ever organized in this country," and an "instrument of the Communist Party line."[4] That is precisely correct. The American Peace Mobilization was created in the summer of 1940, after the Hitler-Stalin Pact, to sway American opinion against going to war against Nazi Germany. Because Stalin was (at that point) in a pact with Hitler, the American Peace Mobilization sought to stop America from resisting Nazi Germany or even from aiding Western allies who were desperately defending themselves against Hitler's hellacious assault. Consequently, the American Peace Mobilization protested Lend-Lease, a Roosevelt administration policy to provide U.S. aid to Britain and other embattled allies in their resistance to the Nazi onslaught. The Communist-front organization did this even as British citizens faced Germany's widespread, intentional bombing of noncombatants. The Communists hid behind the high-road claim that they simply favored "peace," the better to attract genuine peace activists and isolationists.

Of course, the American Peace Mobilization concealed its true intentions at the time. Today, however, we can discover the scope of its ambitions from documents in the Comintern archives—documents not available even to the fine investigators in Attorney General Clark's office or on the House Committee on Un-American Activities.

One such document is an April 2, 1941, memo prepared by Comrade "T. Ryan."[5] Tim Ryan, born Francis Waldron (1905–1961), was a major Comintern operative active in the Communist Party all over the world, from New York to Washington to Manila to Peking. He moved to Moscow in the 1920s, but in 1938 the Comintern sent him back to America to serve as a key player in CPUSA's national leadership, and as a central liaison to the Soviet leadership. Later, in 1946, he would replace Earl Browder—another major Comintern agent/operative—as general secretary of CPUSA.[6] Typical of Communist operatives of that era, he went by at least a couple of names: Tim Ryan was his Comintern/Soviet name; in America he went by yet another name, Eugene Dennis.[7]

Ryan/Dennis prepared his April 2, 1941, memo for Comintern general secretary Georgi Dimitroff. Typed, six pages in length, the document offered a candid, revealing explanation of the purposes and roots of the American Peace Mobilization. (See page 142.) It opened by stating flatly that the American Peace Mobilization "was organised on the initiative of our Party in Chicago in September, 1940 at a national anti-war conference representing approximately 12 million working people," ranging from "the progressive labor, youth, farm and Negro movements" to "Progressive Protestant church organisations."[8] The American Peace Mobilization was organized, wrote Ryan/Dennis, to oppose "the imperialist character of the war and the policies of the Roosevelt administration," and to "popularise on a wide scale the need of establishing friendly relations between the USA and the USSR." To his Soviet superiors, Ryan/Dennis marveled at the party's success in organizing this coalition, especially the ability to attract a "committee of 800 progressive Protestant ministers."

Ryan/Dennis and his comrades particularly sought out the turn-the-other-cheek Christian Left—innocent, trusting liberals who took up Jesus's mandate that "Blessed are the peacemakers"—at least when working for a cause embraced by the Left. These sheep were delivered into the mouths of wolves.

Christian Dupes

The American Peace Mobilization was agitating and getting headlines almost from the moment it was founded. This is evident in one of the earliest news clips on the group, a very brief October 11, 1940, article in the *Washington Post*, aptly titled "Peace Group Assails Roosevelt," where the American Peace Mobilization denounced the "semi-Fascist" character of FDR's appointments to the "entire selective service machinery."[9] This was a strident position—perhaps too aggressive for the front group. Someone within the mobilization stepped up to muzzle the big mouths, reminding them to stay on message: the group's focus was the war/peace issue. (The comrades would generate plenty of other opportunities to call FDR a fascist.)

The group organized another major meeting just two months after the September 1940 Chicago conference that Ryan/Dennis noted in his memo. Held in Chicago the weekend of November 9–10, this assembly employed another popular Communist front issue, racial discrimination; it was dubbed the 1st Illinois Conference of the National Negro Congress. The YMCA played the role of sucker, offering its building, on the corner of 38th and Wabash streets, as the host site.[10]

"8"
3546/3
vt-copy
2.iv.41   Confidential - USA

THE AMERICAN PEACE MOBILISATION.

The American Peace Mobilisation (APM) -- which was organised
on the initiative of our Party in Chicago in September, 1940 at a
national anti-war conference representing approximately 12 million
working people from the progressive labor, youth, farm and Negro movements, the Townsend Old Age pension movement, and progressive Protestant church organisations -- has become the main coordinating and leading center of the people's anti-imperialist and anti-war movement. The
national leadership of the organisation is of a broad, anti-war, people's
front character, under militant labor influence, and includes progressive ministers, authors, etc. and left-wing and Communist leaders from
the progressive unions, farm groups, youth and Negro movements.

In its formative period, the program of APM was built around
the following main slogans of action: a) Keep America out of the war;
Get out and stay out of the war; No aid to Either Belligerent group;
Against Yankee Imperialism in Latin America; Aid the Chinese People;
b) Defeat Militarisation and Regimentation; c) Restore the Bill of
Rights; d) Stop war profiteering; e) Guarantee a decent standard of
living to all.

But in the first days of its existence, the APM did not take
a clear-cut anti-imperialist position on such questions as the character
of the war, national defence and the issue of peace. And it evaded
taking an official stand on, or raising the, burning question of friendship with the great Land of Socialism.

In the six months since its existence, APM has initiated and
set in motion important mass activities and campaigns against the en-
actment of military conscription, and subsequently for the improvement
of the wages, conditions and democratic rights of those conscripted for
military service; for the defeat of the War Powers Bill; for the defence of the right to strike and the enforcement of labor legislation

Rooted "in the principles of Marxism-Leninism": Excerpts from the confidential 1941 memo from
Tim Ryan (a.k.a. Eugene Dennis) to the Comintern explaining the Communist origins and
objectives of the American Peace Mobilization.

- 6 -

energetically, skillfully and widely undertaken. And in this connection our Party must strengthen its independent role and activities,
must further fortify itself organisationally and politically in the
principles of Marxism-Leninism; must utilise the rich experiences of
the masses in the anti-war movement and the developing economic and
political struggles to educate the working class in the spirit of the
class struggle, of proletarian internationalism, of socialism.

                              T. Ryan

Listed on the letterhead for the event were national officers for American Peace Mobilization like Max Yergan—a well-known YMCA figure and a Communist[11]—and John P. Davis, as well as endorsers like Frank Marshall Davis (discussed at length later in this book). The Religious Left was again a major target, with local religious leaders going along for the ride. Especially important were black pastors from the community, such as the Reverend Mary G. Evans, an active pastor who left the African Methodist Episcopal church in the early 1930s to join the Community Church Movement and became pastor of Cosmopolitan Community Church in 1932. Evans was among what has been called the "African Diaspora."[12] Likewise adding their names as endorsers were union representatives such as Henry Roberts, president of the Federation of Hotel Waiters, No. 356; John J. Ryan, an organizer for the Transport Workers Union; and Peter Davis of the PWOC (Packinghouse Workers Organizing Committee) division of the CIO.

The fliers for the November 9–10, 1940, event at the Wabash YMCA protested, "Negroes and the whole American population are being called upon to 'sacrifice for national defense.'" Black Americans, the conference organizers urged, should not send their money, their bodies, or their bonds to support this "wave of war hysteria" by FDR and his cronies. They should not be "bludgeoned into situations against their best interest." The powers-that-be in Washington were pining for "another war," contrary to the interests and well-being of the poor masses.

The Communists' argument that young black men were being prepared to die in an unjust war perpetrated by white politicians would be rehearsed again and again in the decades to come. For example, liberal African-American leaders such as Jesse Jackson and Congressman Charles Rangel (NY-Democrat) would protest the 1991 Gulf War and 2003 Iraq War making almost precisely the same case. CPUSA and its front group honed this tactic as early as 1940.

The number of Religious Left figures involved in the Communist-initiated American Peace Mobilization was remarkable. Some were open Communists, some closet communists, some non-Communist liberals, some dupes. Amid the grand schemers who were doing the duping was a much larger group of victims from across multiple denominations. Particularly vulnerable were folks from the United Methodist Church, the Presbyterian Church USA, the Quakers, and especially the Episcopal Church.

The American Peace Mobilization seemed to draw more individuals from the Episcopalian denomination than any other. In March 1958 a team of researchers led by J. B. Matthews, the ex-Communist who became one of America's foremost experts on the movement, and Archibald Roosevelt, the son of President Theodore Roosevelt, released a report on Episcopalian "rectors" who were active participants

in the mobilization. The report identified many participants, including Frank Bancroft, Richard T. S. Brown, Eliot White, Charles Coker Wilson, and the vigorously
active Walter Mitchell. Mitchell, the bishop of Arizona, was prominent in Communist organs like the *Daily Worker*, the *Chicago Star*, and *Daily People's World*. His name
appeared in such publications upwards of thirty times in this period, including
twice early in 1941 for his work for the American Peace Mobilization.[13]

The American Peace Mobilization got much press at the time. And while
those clips are today conveniently forgotten, especially among the people in the
pews at the mainline Protestant denominations, they are alive and well in the
Soviet Comintern files on CPUSA. CPUSA had incredible success recruiting
these dupes, and proudly sent details of this successful campaign to its masters at
the Comintern.

Duping the Press: The *New York Times*'s "Group of Clergymen"

The comrades in the "peace" mobilization also generated their share of dupes
among reporters. The *New York Times* was particularly susceptible.

On January 10, 1941, the *Times* ran an article deceptively titled "Clergymen Group Charges War Aim."[14] The piece discussed a letter sent to FDR by
a "group of clergymen" representing "religious denominations" throughout the
country. This purported peace epistle claimed that the president's foreign policy
"will inevitably lead to war and the destruction of democracy." The "clergymen,"
reported the *Times*, had asked the president "to put an end to what we deem is
an aggressive, militant foreign policy." Prompted by their closet comrades, they
argued that Roosevelt's policies were "aggressive" and "militant," and in fact constituted an "unjust war."

Of course, this argument was preposterous. Pearl Harbor was nearly a year
away when the clergymen sent their letter to FDR. The "militant" policies they
decried were nothing more than aid to Britain. The Communists must have been
amazed that this unbelievable position could attract the support of "progressive"
clergy—as well as serious attention by the nation's top newspaper. The *Times*
went so far as to publish the entire text of the "peace" mobilization's "appeal."
Meanwhile, the word "communism" or "communist" was not found in the *Times*'s
article. The Gray Lady was completely duped.

Two weeks later, a much smarter *Washington Post* did a piece on the American
Peace Mobilization, with special focus on whether it was a Communist front.
The *Post* reporter, Edward T. Folliard, noted that among the sixteen sponsors of a

recent "working conference for peace" run by the mobilization, there were "several well-known Communists or Communist sympathizers."[15]

Had this article run in, say, 1955, liberals in Washington might have denounced the *Post* reporter as a McCarthyite Red-baiter—a loathsome anti-Communist. But that phenomenon was down the road. For now, it was 1941, well before the Left dismissed every claim of Communist infiltration. A world war was on the horizon.

Though the *Post*'s Folliard did good work, he missed the elephant in the room. The main source he quoted was American Peace Mobilization executive secretary Fred V. Field, described in the article as "a bespectacled young man with a Harvard accent," who cheerfully laughed off charges of Communist infiltration. Folliard did not mention that Field's middle initial, "V.," stood for "Vanderbilt," as Field's grandmother was a member of the fabulously wealthy Vanderbilt dynasty.[16] More importantly, the *Post* story did not point out that this millionaire Ivy Leaguer was himself a devout Communist, and quite the rabble-rouser.

Field was a contributor to the *New Masses* and *Daily Worker,* and founder of the subversive publication *Amerasia.* Worst of all, he had been executive secretary of the odious American Council of the Institute of Pacific Relations (IPR).

IPR was an international group, a sort of think tank, with affiliates in ten countries. It had many members and contacts within the U.S. government, in addition to American colleges, newspapers, and foundations. IPR was arguably one of the most destructive entities of the entire 1940s, causing enormous damage in Asia and China in particular, actively working for the overthrow of Chiang Kai-shek's government and its replacement with Mao Tse-tung and the Red Chinese. IPR's officers, contributors, and members included some of the worst spies, subversives, dupes, and questionable characters of the entire Cold War, including the infamous Harry Dexter White, Lauchlin Currie, Laurence Duggan, Owen Lattimore, and Alger Hiss—plus, naturally, Corliss Lamont.[17] As the Senate Judiciary Committee and House Committee on Un-American Activities would later affirm, "Members of the small core of officials and staff members who controlled IPR were either Communist or pro-Communist," and both CPUSA and Soviet officials considered IPR "an instrument of Communist policy, propaganda and military intelligence."[18]

In 1940 Fred Field had resigned as executive secretary at IPR in order to assume leadership of the American Peace Mobilization. But he helped keep IPR afloat with his own money—that is, Vanderbilt money—and would return to the organization after the American Peace Mobilization had done its work. More accurately, he would return to IPR after the mobilization finished flip-flopping on "peace," based on whether Stalin was allied with or against Hitler.[19]

So when the *Post* did its January 1941 article on the American Peace Mobilization, Fred Field was a closet Communist, although his sympathies were hardly a secret. Eventually he would openly admit that he was a Communist. He made that admission only well after Lauchlin Currie and Owen Lattimore nearly succeeded in placing the zealous Moscow apparatchik in a major job with U.S. military intelligence, which would have made Field a top Soviet agent.[20]

The *Washington Post* reported none of this on Fred Field. Nonetheless, Folliard had begun the digging on the American Peace Mobilization. This reporter, in particular, was now on guard, and a few months later he would do another article exploring whether the group was a Communist front.[21]

The same cannot be said for the *New York Times*.[22]

"Let Our Foreign Policy Wage Peace!"

With only mild scrutiny coming from the press, the American Peace Mobilization pulled off some impressive public displays from early April to late June 1941. In New York City it engineered several demonstrations and one large rally, and in Washington it staged demonstrations at the Capitol and picketed the White House.

In advance of a major demonstration in New York City held April 5–6, 1941, the mobilization sent out a formal statement addressed "To all Friends of Peace and Liberty." (See page 148.) The statement warned "fellow Americans" that they were in great danger. Americans, it seemed, were being duped—not by Communists but by the villainous FDR.

"This is not a war to wipe out the evils of Hitlerism and tyranny," explained the American Peace Mobilization. "It is not a war to defend democracy. It is a war to line the pockets of corporate interests at the expense of the peoples of the World."[23] Pearl Harbor was still seven months away, but the closet comrades said that President Roosevelt was itching to "drag America more deeply into this war . . . to get us into total war against the will of the people."

Scaling the highest limits of hyperbole, the American Peace Mobilization concluded that mere U.S. aid to the barely surviving "British Empire" constituted a form of "total war" by "the American people"; it was Britain that was a "warring empire." America needed to "get out and stay out of World War II"—Britain's war.

By this point, Britain had been under siege from the Nazi Blitz for eight long months; it was not conducting total war but suffering under total war. How could American Communists possibly take this position? The answer, again, is because it was Stalin's position.

Call AMERICAN PEOPLE'S MEETING

New York City • April 5-6, 1941

To all Friends of Peace and Liberty

Fellow Americans:

We Are in Danger.

The tragic days of 1917 and an AEF are almost here again.

Our trade unions are under attack. The right to strike is being taken away.

Our farmers are being driven from their land; their products are selling below cost. We are paying more for food.

Our rents are being increased. Our wages are being held down. Unemployment continues and our relief is being cut.

Discrimination against our Negro people is increasing. Attacks against the Jewish people are being intensified. Our non-citizens have been fingerprinted.

There are virtually no jobs for youth. Four million people are being place under military law.

Congress continues to deney the vote to ten million American citizens. Minority parties are being rapidly suppressed.

We are being intimidated and spied upon. Our persons and our papers are being seized without warrant.

Our Constitutional rights are being taken from us.

This is how democracy was blacked out in Germany and in France, how it is being blacked out in England, and how it will be blacked out here unless labor and the people unite and act.

These things have happened to us because our statesmen and economic royalists are violating the will of the people. Men in high places are dragging us into a war three thousand miles away.

This is not a war to wipe out the evils of Hitlerism and tyranny. It is not a war to liberate the peoples of Germany or France, India or Ireland, Africa or Asia. It is not a war to defend democracy. It is a war to line the pockets of corporate interests at the expense of the peoples of the World.

The Tory bill 1776 would enable these corpo-

Turn Page

☆   ☆   ☆

"A war to line the pockets of corporate interests": This 1941 statement from the American Peace Mobilization bears the obvious marks of Communist agitprop but nonetheless was endorsed by more than eighty influential Americans.

More incredible is how anyone on the American Left could have taken the bait. The American Peace Mobilization's resolution was so in defiance of reality that it bore the obvious marks of Communist agitprop. Nonetheless, more than eighty influential Americans lined up to sign their names to the statement.

The signers included the two vice chairmen of the American Peace Mobilization, both well-known Communist sympathizers: novelist Theodore Dreiser and Congressman Vito Marcantonio. Not surprisingly, the Communists on the list—that is, the formal CPUSA members—were identified on the endorsement sheet by their non-Communist affiliations. The Reds included Fred Field, Abe Flaxer, and Donald Henderson. (Henderson met often with Harold Ware, architect of the Ware cell that had penetrated FDR's AAA.)[24] The list also included a host of unsuspecting dupes: union heads, journalists, pastors, professors (Columbia University, Howard University), and representatives of reputable organizations like the YMCA, most unaware of how they were being used by the Communists.[25]

The single largest represented group among the signers was Christians from the mainline Protestant denominations, including the overall chairman of the American Peace Mobilization, the Reverend John B. Thompson, and, predictably, Episcopal bishop Walter Mitchell. Eighteen of the eighty signers—nearly 25 percent—carried the titled "Reverend" in front of their name.[26]

There was even a rabbi on the list, Rabbi Moses Miller, chairman of the Jewish People's Committee. This is remarkable, especially given that after the Hitler-Stalin Pact the Communists had lost a lot of fellow travelers who were Jewish. Indeed, the Communist Party's Jewish-language newspaper, the *Daily Morning Freiheit,* whose building stood right aside the *Daily Worker*'s, lost half its readers after Stalin made his pact with Hitler.[27] But its stalwart editor, M. J. Olgin, a Jewish immigrant and Columbia Ph.D., remained unwavering in his fanatical devotion to the Marxist vision.[28]

Still, Rabbi Miller was there, plus a litany of liberal Christian friends, urging no "war" assistance against Hitler's bid to turn Europe into (as the führer put it) "a vast botanical garden in which Germans of pure Aryan extraction can breed." In pursuing his "Final Solution," Hitler would "liquidate" some six million Jews. For the Communists, however, all of that was secondary to Hitler's alliance with Stalin. It was Stalin first—*always* Stalin first.

As for the dupes to the Communists, they desired "peace." "Let our foreign policy wage peace!" was the battle cry of the group's formal declaration, issued April 5, 1941.

But the meeting was not all formality. The (closet) party members threw a party in hopes of widening their net to catch more suckers. After Fred Field

offered introductory remarks, the brethren joined the musical troupe the Almanacs in belting out a song called "Get Out and Stay Out of War," which was followed by a keynote speech from the Reverend John B. Thompson. Then, after an
intermission, more frivolity followed, before Dr. Max Yergan, the well-known
Communist, spoke. After Yergan came more music to lighten the atmosphere,
this time from the great African-American musical performer (and Communist)
Paul Robeson. Representative Marcantonio finished the day, adding the legitimacy of a congressional endorsement. (See the event program, page 152.)

The American Peace Mobilization cleverly promoted the musical acts as a way
to attract outsiders—non-Communists who could join the cause. The nationally
known Robeson was a big draw. So were the Almanacs, a group that featured (at
differing times) famous singers/actors like Burl Ives, Woody Guthrie, Will Geer,
and Pete Seeger, some of whom were Communists and others who left the party
(or the movement) and became liberals.[29] Almost every "folk ballad" by the Almanacs was a swipe at FDR and his "unjust war"—not just "Get Out and Stay Out of
War" but also "Franklin, Oh Franklin."

In adjoining rooms, various breakout sessions were held, on topics ranging
from "The Church and the War" to "Civil Rights in Wartime" to "The Negro
People and the War."

Marching Orders from Moscow

Most shocking regarding the April 5–6 rally in New York City, and sobering to
observe today, are the related documents in the Comintern archives on CPUSA,
which show how the organizers of the rally took marching orders directly from
Moscow. At least two documents are worth noting.

One was the previously mentioned memo by Tim Ryan/Eugene Dennis
(April 2, 1941). That memo not only traced the Communist roots of the American Peace Mobilization, as noted, but also excitedly anticipated the coming April
5–6 celebration in New York City. In the final line of the memo, Ryan/Dennis
concluded that the international Communist Party "must utilise the rich experiences of the masses in the anti-war movement and the developing economic and
political struggles to educate the working class in the spirit of the class struggle,
of proletarian internationalism, of socialism."

The other document is even more intimately tied to the rally. It is a one-page,
handwritten document in the Comintern archives; specifically, it is the text of a
secret radio message that Comintern head Georgi Dimitroff sent to CPUSA gen-

eral secretary Earl Browder with instructions for the New York conference. Comrades "Marty and Ryan," meaning Andre Marty and Tim Ryan/Eugene Dennis, who were the American representatives to the Comintern, had written an initial draft of a "directive" to CPUSA on the position the American Peace Mobilization should take at its April 5–6 rally. Dimitroff rewrote that draft.

On March 29, 1941, Dimitroff gave his final, handwritten directive (see page 154) to the Comintern's radio operator to be sent in secret code to CPUSA.[30] At CPUSA headquarters in New York City, party member Rudy Baker received the message, decoded it, and gave it to Earl Browder. Browder, in turn, passed it on to the proper party figures within the American Peace Mobilization.[31]

The document began, "Regarding April sixth anti-war conference, we recommend. . . ." It then listed at least four principles that became part of the formal resolution the conference organizers adopted several days later; one of the principles ultimately adopted was the final point (point "VII"), which called for a "people's peace." (See page 156.) Interestingly, Dimitroff seemed concerned about offending the Roosevelt administration, and showed greater tact than the bomb-throwing radicals in CPUSA. (Yes, the Soviet Communist was more responsible than American Communists.) In one line calling for a "struggle against the war-policy of administration," Dimitroff crossed out the word "administration" and replaced it with "government." It was a minor change, but it softened the tone, not so directly implicating FDR and his administration. The Comintern chief concluded by calling for the "establishment of friendly relations with great Soviet country of socialism."[32]

The White House Picket

Aside from the April 5–6 rally in New York, many other American Peace Mobilization demonstrations took place in this period. On May 10 some 150 women from the mobilization's "women's division" paraded along the sidewalks near Broadway in New York City.

The ladies easily suckered the *New York Times*. These "mothers," as the *Times* called them—again not once using the word "Communist" in the article—carried placards with phrases like "Keep our fleet home" and "Rockefeller's war is not our war. Our sons shall not die for Standard oil."[33] (Fifty years later, this statement would be echoed in the "No blood for oil" mantra popularized by the American Left during the first Persian Gulf War.)

Around the same time the American Peace Mobilization began its "permanent peace vigil" outside the White House. This was a protest against Lend-Lease

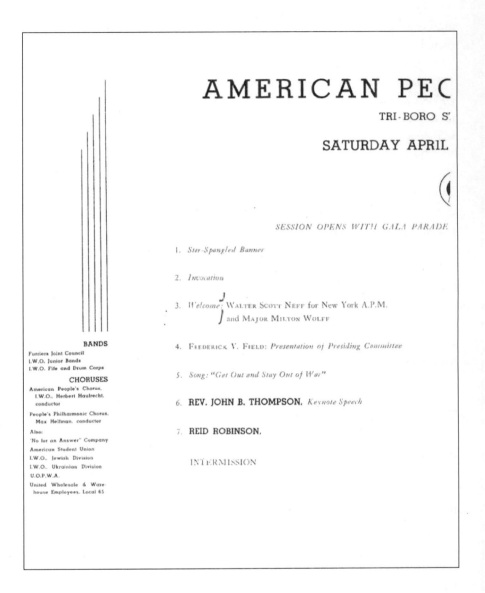

AMERICAN PEC

TRI-BORO S'

SATURDAY APRIL

SESSION OPENS WITH GALA PARADE

1. *Star-Spangled Banner*

2. *Invocation*

3. *Welcome:* WALTER SCOTT NEFF for New York A.P.M.
   and MAJOR MILTON WOLFF

BANDS
Furriers Joint Council
I.W.O. Junior Bands
I.W.O. Fife and Drum Corps

4. FREDERICK V. FIELD: *Presentation of Presiding Committee*

CHORUSES
American People's Chorus,
  I.W.O., Herbert Haufrecht,
  conductor
People's Philharmonic Chorus,
  Max Helfman, conductor

5. *Song:* "Get Out and Stay Out of War"

Also:
'No for an Answer" Company
American Student Union
I.W.O., Jewish Division
I.W.O., Ukrainian Division
U.O.P.W.A.
United Wholesale & Ware-
  house Employees, Local 65

6. **REV. JOHN B. THOMPSON,** *Keynote Speech*

7. **REID ROBINSON,**

INTERMISSION

Casting the net: The April 1941 American Peace Mobilization rally attracted major non-Communist support with popular performers like Paul Robeson and the Almanacs.

LE'S MEETING

JM RALLY

941 — 1:30 P. M.

IE DELEGATES INTO THE STADIUM

8. Songs:"*Plough Under*"
   "*Franklin, Oh Franklin*"
   "*Ballad of October 16*"

9. Dances: Italian Tarantella, Schottische, American Folk Dance

10. **DR. MAX YERGAN**
    Introduced by GEORGE F. BROWN, Organizer, Dining Car Employes Local 370, A.F.L.

11. **PAUL ROBESON** Songs

12. American People's Chorus: "*Billy Boy*"

13. People's Philharmonic Chorus: "*Spring 1941*"
    No for an Answer Chorus: "*No for an Answer*"

14. **CONGRESSMAN VITO MARCANTONIO**

15. *Battle Hymn of the Republic*

SONGS
The Almanacs
Earl Robinson
Marc Blitzstein
Saul Aarons
Max Helfman

DANCES
Jewish School Division, I.W.O.
Parents Assoc., P. S. 157

Signs and Decorations:
Charles Keller

PRODUCTION STAFF
Lem Ward, Director
Lou Leif, Manager
Jess Kruger, Stage Manager
John Randolph, Announcer
Jack Zilbert, Band Director
Ralph Avery, Assistant
Edith Segal, Dance Director

Regarding April sixth anti-war conference,
we recommend that major attention be
focused on immediate economic and political
demands and these should be closely connected
with the struggle against the involvement of the
american people in the war. American labour
and people should, in opposition to war-policy
of ~~Administration~~ Government, strive to make impossible
extention and prolongation of war and support
with all means efforts of peoples in Europe
and in other continents for a peoples' peace
without violence and without imperialist
annexations. X The struggle for peoples' peace,
starting from the interests of the american
people, means first of all struggle against
war-policy of ~~Administration~~ Government and against
reactionary imperialist policy of american
bourgeoisie and common struggle of
toiling masses in America and with peoples'
masses of other countries especially England,
Germany and France, as well as establishment
of friendly relations with great sowjet-
country of socialism.

29.3.41.

on N 39-40

Marching orders: This handwritten message from Comintern head Georgi Dimitroff, sent via secret radio transmission to CPUSA, reveals the extent to which Moscow directed the American Peace Mobilization's April 1941 rally.

in particular but, really, the entirety of the Roosevelt defense program. Mobilization organizers Dr. Walter Scott Neff, a Cornell Ph.D. and professor, and Dr. Annette Rubenstein, principal of Robert Louis Stevenson School, had led the expedition from New York City to Washington. Once at the White House, the protesters made quite a scene, especially when a group of Army soldiers and Marines showed up to tear apart their placards and disrupt the line.[34]

No matter, the comrades were committed. They continued their vigil nonstop, day after day, week after week. It was resoundingly successful in that it generated a lot of press attention—just what the comrades had wanted. How long would it last? The momentum kept rising. Press attention kept coming. The "peace vigil" was working wonderfully.

But then something happened.

The round-the-clock American Peace Mobilization picket of the White House had continued for well over a month, lasting an impressive 1,029 hours. But suddenly the "peace" marchers departed. Just like that, the protest was over. Why? What had happened?

"The line was disbanded," reported the New York Times. Endeavoring to explain why, the Gray Lady sought out a reliable source for its faithful readers: Fred Field. The unbreakable picket was suddenly disbanded, explained the Times, because, "according to Frederick Field," the American Peace Mobilization had "fulfilled" its "overwhelming" mission of bringing a message of "peace" to the president.[35] And now it was time to go home.

Curiously, though, the marchers departed while singing "You Gotta Get Tough, You Gotta Get Tough."[36]

"Gotta Get Tough"? That did not sound like the conventional peace tune. It sounded like a summons to swords rather than ploughshares. What was going on?

When the American Peace Mobilization suddenly ended its protest outside the White House, it was June 22, 1941, Moscow time.[37]

American People's Mobilization

The venerable New York Times failed to make yet another connection for its readers: the peace contingent finally broke up the moment that news hit of the German invasion of the Soviet Union, which occurred in the very early morning hours of June 22, 1941.[38]

Thus this "peace movement" took another sharp turn. Suddenly it was no longer in favor of peace. These American doves were instantly transformed into

Declaration

of the

American

People's Meeting

══════ APRIL 5-6, NEW YORK CITY ══════

People of America!

These are the people's planks to defend America. These are the step back to peace.

I. **Get out and stay out of World War II.**
Oppose every step toward further involvement; no convoys of and by ships; no A.E.F. to any foreign shore. End military alliance with the British Empire.

II. **Defend and improve the American standard of living.**
Adequate social security, protection against unemployment, sickness and old age, training and education for America's youth.
Guarantees of adequate wages and incomes to the working people and farmers of America.

III. **Regain and strengthen our constitutional liberties.**
Defend the right to strike; resist attacks on free education; defend every victim of Hitler-like persecution; equal rights for the Negro people and an end to anti-Semitism.

IV. **Take the burden of the war off the backs of the poor.**
Make the rich pay. Conscript wealth; confiscate war profits; stop profiteering; end unjust taxation of the poor.

V. **Protect the rights of the conscripts.**
Higher wages; job protection; adequate health safeguards and full democratic rights for all draftees.

"For a People's Peace": The final resolution adopted at the American Peace Mobilization's April 1941 rally reflects at least four points Dimitroff had specifically suggested.

VI. Let our foreign policy wage peace.

For the friendliest relations with the peoples of Latin America, based on their right to fully resist exploitation of American monopoly; no help to the foes of China within or without; but real aid to United China's struggle for freedom; genuine independence of Puerto Rico and the Philippines; friendly relations with the Soviet Union to prevent further extension of war.

VII. For a People's Peace.

For a peace without indemnities, without annexations, based upon the right of all peoples in subjugated or colonial countries to determine their own destinies.

In seeking this peace we need and solicit the cooperation of all the American People. These are our tasks. In these tasks we shall have no fear. We shall not grow weary. We are the Power. We are the People.

⦿ ⦾ ⬤

Shall it be war or shall it be peace?

In the solemn presence of the American people, Roosevelt and Willkie took the pledge for peace. Both of them by cynical words and deeds have betrayed that pledge.

Behind our backs the peace and future prosperity of our land have been bartered for world empire and the imperial ambitions of the lords of Wall Street.

A hundred times our voices have given clear expression to our will for peace. But with cunning and fraud men who hold political power, by virtue of our decision, have brought our country to the brink of disaster; have inched our people toward the folly of war.

Lifting the embargo on munitions to countries at war was called an act 'or peace. Trading 50 of our destroyers for naval bases was hailed as shrewd Yankee statesmanship. Conscription was coated with the sugary label of peace-time army training for home defense. And the 5,200 rain-soaked youth delegates to the Youth Citizenship Institute were accused by the President of uttering "twaddle" for expressing a fear that they might be forced to die on foreign battlefields. Each step toward war has been muffled and disguised. But now the juggernaut of war moves more quickly.

With the passage of the Lend-Lease bill, "All Aid Short of War" became "All Out Aid to the British Empire." Now "All Out Aid to the British Empire" has become "Total War for America." Armed convoys are an imminent danger. And no one is longer accused of "twaddle" who speaks of an A.E.F. Every move of foreign policy has been designed to increase the hostility of other nations against us; has been calculated to drag Latin America into the conflict and to spread the blood-soaked theatre of war to

hawks. That was because their true country—Stalin's Russia—was now under siege.

A telling testimony came from Henry Winston of the Young Communist League. "When the news of the attack came over the air," said a breathless Winston in a July 1941 report to the league, "many of our young comrades were coming home tired and ready for a good sleep. Yet, these comrades . . . sat up all night eagerly waiting until the headquarters would be open, ready for activity in the fight to crush Hitlerism."[39]

Now that "Hitler's barbaric hordes attacked the land of socialism" (in Winston's words), the peace-professing comrades were eager "to help win the people in support of the Soviet Union and Britain in the fight to smash and wipe Hitlerism from the face of the earth." After loudly denouncing American "war hysteria" and condemning Britain as a "warring empire," the American Communist movement quite abruptly started calling for immediate American entrance into a war against Nazi Germany and full-blown American aid to the Brits.

Groups like the Young Communist League pledged to work day and night "to win the mass of youth to a broad front against Hitler." Comrade Winston addressed an emergency two-day "enlarged meeting" of the National Committee of the Young Communist League, USA. He and his friends outlined an all-out drive to organize a broad coalition "among the masses"—nationally, "state and city-wide," inside buildings, "open-air," wherever necessary to defend the Soviet Motherland. "The new situation," explained Winston, "tremendously increases our responsibility and calls for the greatest amount of heroism and courage on the part of each and every one of our members. It calls for a readiness to sacrifice even to the point of death."[40]

The young American comrades pledged their lives and sacred honor to their country—that is, to the USSR.

The American Peace Mobilization faced one problem: making this 180-degree turn overnight would be so blatant that even the most gullible of its dupes might notice that the organization was nothing more than a Stalinist front. The Communists surely figured that no one, not even the normally reliable Religious Left, would fail to connect these giant red dots.

Nonetheless, they gave it a shot.

The group changed its name to the American *People's* Mobilization, adopted a pro-war policy, and called for complete U.S. assistance not only to Britain but even to Chiang Kai-shek's China—and of course to the USSR. In short, the new "APM" reversed all of its former positions the moment that Hitler betrayed Stalin.

Mercifully, some of the more battle-hardened liberals—that is, chastened observers of Communist schemes who had been suckered before—were not falling for this one.

Civil-rights leaders like NAACP acting secretary Roy Wilkins, who was still seething over how the Communists had hijacked the Scottsboro case, lambasted them for this flip-flop. Most appalling to Wilkins was the fact that in dropping their antiwar pose, the Communists had abandoned their pursuit of civil rights for blacks, too. "They abandoned the fight for Negro rights on the ground that such a campaign would 'interfere with the war effort,'" Wilkins later wrote. "As soon as Russia was attacked by Germany they dropped the Negro question and concentrated all effort in support of the war in order to help the Soviet Union. During the war years the disciples of the extreme Left [Communists] sounded very much like the worst of the Negro-hating southerners."[41]

The Communists' earlier support for civil rights was exposed as a gambit simply to bring in new recruits and advance the larger cause. That cause—the Soviet Motherland—was always the first priority. Now civil rights was no longer as useful to them; the war effort would be a much better cause for recruitment and advancement of their global purposes.

About-Face

Roy Wilkins was exactly right. Few about-faces were so revealing and so despicable. Of course, it has largely been forgotten. For the American Left, it was not the acronym "APM" that would acquire infamy, but "HUAC"—its favored label for the House Committee on Un-American Activities. The reprobates were not the pro-Communists but the anti-Communists, even as the latter exposed the former.

Even at the time, the American *People's* Mobilization did not suffer as might be expected from such a transparent flip-flop. The Communist manipulators would find a whole new round of dupes.

They would have to wait a bit, however. The problem in the summer of 1941 was that many regular Americans were not ready for war, since their country—the United States—had not been attacked. For American Communists, however, *their* country—the USSR—had been attacked. They were gung ho.

The Communists would gain traction in their new pro-war campaign six months later—after December 7, 1941.

9

Duping FDR:
"Uncle Joe" and "Buddies"

ate's day of infamy arrived December 7, 1941. Once Pearl Harbor was
bombed by the Japanese, who, along with the Nazis, were part of a *real*
fascist-imperialist Axis—not the Rooseveltian concoction stirred up by
American Communists—Uncle Sam was instantly thrust into the war. This
meant that America found itself formally, albeit uncomfortably, on the same side
as the totalitarian USSR.

CPUSA was thrilled. It was free to be pro-American. It could be pro-FDR.
This was a political liberation in many ways. Perhaps most importantly, any
Soviet sympathizers, or even Soviet spies, working for the Roosevelt adminis-
tration could openly endorse a pro-Moscow line from within their department
or agency, or within the White House. That may have been the case for Harry
Hopkins.

The "Buddies"

Well before Pearl Harbor, Harry Hopkins was singing the praises of Joseph Stalin
and the need for an alliance and even friendship with the dictator. Not long after
the June 22, 1941, Nazi invasion of the Soviet Union, done in violent defiance
of the Hitler-Stalin Pact that had launched the dual German-Soviet invasion of
Poland and started World War II, Hopkins eagerly headed to Moscow. Unlike
Senator Harry Truman, who responded to the Nazi assault on Russia by stating,

"If we see that Germany is winning we ought to help Russia, and if Russia is winning we ought to help Germany, and that way let them kill as many as possible,"[1] Hopkins had no trouble picking sides.

On July 31, 1941, Hopkins met with General Secretary Stalin. He was quite taken by the dictator. Conversing with the tyrant was like "talking to a perfectly coordinated machine," he said.[2] He immediately cabled FDR with his impression of the "intelligent" Stalin.[3]

Overall, Hopkins was elated to report to the president that he and Stalin had become chums, and FDR was delighted to hear that. The president relayed the exciting news to others: "Harry and Uncle Joe got on like a house afire. They have become buddies."[4]

After this meeting—the first of several Hopkins visits to Moscow—the presidential adviser began advising Roosevelt that Generalissimo Stalin should *not* be viewed as a Communist bent on the Marxist-Leninist doctrine of world revolution. "It is ridiculous to think of Stalin as a Communist," Hopkins scoffed. "He is a Russian nationalist."[5] This "nationalism, not Communism" argument had also been made by Roosevelt's former ambassador to the Soviet Union, Joseph Davies—who, as we will see later in the chapter, was a remarkable dupe of Stalin and the Soviets. Receiving such advice from his inner circle surely colored the president's views on Stalin's USSR.[6]

Harry Hopkins's primary mission was to determine what Stalin needed in wartime to repel Hitler, and thus what the despot wanted from America. On its face, that certainly was understandable, given the wartime alliance and given Hopkins's position as head of the Lend-Lease program. Yet Hopkins seems to have relished the chance to go well beyond the call of duty.

"Lending" a Hand

General John Deane, who was in Moscow to observe the budding political romance between Hopkins and Stalin, commented on how Hopkins carried out his mission with a zeal bordering on fanaticism.[7] Sure enough, FDR's key aide commandeered Lend-Lease to provide Stalin with extraordinary benefits, to the tune of some $1.5 billion.

To be sure, the primary U.S. goal was to stop Nazi Germany, and thus it was imperative for the United States to aid Stalin's USSR militarily in order to slow Hitler. American military aid—that is, *conventional* military aid—was especially necessary given that Stalin, under his recent bloody Great Purge, had annihilated tens of thousands of Soviet military officers—the human capital needed to defend against the Nazis.[8]

On the other hand, no one on the American side would begin to consider *non*conventional aid in the form of atomic-weapon assistance. Anyone who did that would surely be at least a dupe, and perhaps even a traitor. Early in the war the United States began the super-secret Manhattan Project, a crash program to develop the atomic bomb. It was so secretive that even Roosevelt's (later) vice president, Harry Truman, was not told of the project. We now know that by 1943 the Soviets had initiated their own program, and looked to America for "assistance."

The Soviets sought that assistance in several ways, including through intense espionage. In fact, some scholars have determined that the Soviets could not have gotten the bomb without the work of a network of spies pilfering the Manhattan Project design.[9] Less well known is that the Soviets at times *openly* sought materials that could aid their nuclear development. In some cases they did this quite directly, almost as if to see what they could get away with.

One notable example, based on newly available Venona transcripts, was laid out in the seminal work *The Venona Secrets*.[10] This episode could not have been justified as merely another component of aiding Stalin with conventional means to repel Hitler.

On February 1, 1943, an American chemical company called Chemator received its first Soviet request for various forms of uranium. Harry Hopkins's Lend-Lease program had approved Soviet requests for other chemicals via Chemator. Of course, a request for uranium, the element necessary for producing a nuclear bomb, was something altogether different.

The loyal Americans working at Chemator did not know of the secret American atomic-bomb project, but nonetheless went to the U.S. government as standard operating procedure for such an unusual request. They were fully willing to deny the request if Uncle Sam said so. Instead, Hopkins's Lend-Lease granted permission to give the Soviets what they asked for—specifically, 220 pounds of uranium nitrate, 220 pounds of uranium oxide, and 25 pounds of uranium metal.[11]

With that green light, the Soviets went wild, one month later ordering tons of uranium. This caught the attention of General Leslie Groves, the colorful, fiery military director of the Manhattan Project. Groves voiced angry concern to Lend-Lease officials about what was being so easily approved for Soviet purchase. It seemed to Groves, an engineer as well as a military general, that Lend-Lease was going far beyond conventional assistance to a wartime ally. Later he went public with his concerns in testimony before Congress. The general complained that Lend-Lease officials were exerting a "great deal of pressure . . . to give the

Russians everything they could think of," including "this uranium material." Groves said he had personally wanted to veto the requests, but Hopkins and crew were doing their best to push the orders through. "We didn't want this material shipped," Groves said during his congressional in testimony, "yet they [Lend-Lease] kept coming back and coming back."[12]

Groves did not say, and the congressmen did not ask, to what extent "they" at "Lend-Lease" were being directed by the director of the program, Harry Hopkins, the president's close friend and adviser.

The Soviets, of course, got their atomic bomb—in 1949, far quicker than anyone had anticipated. In a flash, America lost its nuclear monopoly, and Stalin suddenly had enormous bargaining power.

"He Likes Me Better"

As a liberal Democrat pursuing the greatest expansion of federal power in the history of the republic, Franklin Roosevelt was like a magnet to people on the left side of the political spectrum. They surrounded him, enthusiastically signing up for the progressive cause. Many of these individuals, of course, were red-white-and-blue, God-and-country Democrats—obviously, in no way Communists. But there were others, some within the president's close orbit, who had Soviet interests at heart, or who at the very least were sympathetic to the Soviets. This made the task of dealing with the world's multiple threats even more difficult for the non-Communist/anti-Communist Democrats.

That task was exacerbated as Stalin himself underwent a makeover at the hands of friends in the White House and certain left-leaning factions of the American press. Soon the Marxist autocrat became known as "Uncle Joe," an egregious term of endearment intended to hoodwink Americans into thinking that Stalin was a gentle ally.

President Roosevelt frequently used the moniker. Though it is hard to say whether he coined the term, it is clear that FDR was describing this ruthless killer in ingratiating terms long before the war—that is, before such warm words could be justified as necessary to strengthen a formal military alliance. As early as January 1934, less than a year into his presidency, and shortly after he extended diplomatic recognition to Russia—a step refused by his predecessors, Democrat and Republican—FDR referred to Stalin as "His Excellency."[13]

The form of address was hardly necessary. The phrase might be acceptable if the authoritarian were a king, but he was not. He was a Communist despot.

This was a harbinger of the unnecessarily flattering tone Roosevelt would adopt toward the totalitarian.

Some FDR historians and biographers have portrayed a president deeply torn over "crossing the bridge" with the "devil" Stalin.[14] In truth, Roosevelt seemed more often enchanted than conflicted by Stalin, as can be seen in the historical record. A search of the *Presidential Documents* reveals that FDR was frequently more upbeat than ambivalent about the Soviet dictator.[15] The president very often used words of eye-opening personal affection.

Only three months after Pearl Harbor, for example, FDR wrote a note to Winston Churchill in anticipation of his first meeting with Stalin. "I think I can personally handle Stalin better than either your Foreign Office or my State Department," FDR boasted to Churchill on March 18, 1942. "Stalin hates the guts of all your people. He thinks he likes me better."[16]

Roosevelt and Stalin had never met. How would FDR have surmised that the Soviet leader liked him? This must have been the impression the president had been receiving around the White House, almost surely from Harry Hopkins directly. Likewise, Roosevelt had probably received this word from Joe Davies, his former ambassador to the USSR, whom he continued to consult.[17]

The British prime minister must have raised an eyebrow upon reading that missive.

Franklin, Harry, and a "Hunch"

Another telling incident along this troubled road occurred in August 1943. FDR was contemplating the counsel of one of his truly expert Soviet advisers, a man who had been his first Soviet ambassador, from 1933 to 1936, and who now presciently warned the president of the "domination of Europe by Stalin's communist dictatorship."[18]

Who was this far-sighted adviser? None other than William C. Bullitt.

Bullitt had come a long way since his Bolshevik romance three decades earlier—since the kiss he had planted on Stalin's pockmarked cheek. He had awakened to the reality of Soviet Communism: the purges, the forced famine in the Ukraine, the pervasive terror and desire for conquest. Bullitt also recognized the horror of the Soviet assault on religion, and the painful thrust of Marxist-Leninist morality and expansionary ideology. He was now one of the shrewdest observers of the Soviet Union.[19]

As early as 1941 Bullitt had begun warning FDR that Communists were a threat not only abroad but also within the president's midst. In a July 1, 1941, letter, he cautioned the president: "Communists in the United States are just as dangerous enemies as ever, and should not be allowed to crawl into our productive mechanism in order later to wreck it when they get new orders from somewhere abroad." Bullitt most assuredly knew of what he was speaking. He had been on their side. He warned FDR of a Stalinist "Fifth Column," and of "public or underground Communist Parties."[20]

Bullitt was inspiring proof of a liberal who saw the evidence and was duped no more. He had lived up to his Yale undergraduate billing as "most brilliant." He was not only informed but also prophetic.

Sadly, though, he was a prophet unrecognized in his own land. President Roosevelt had other, more influential advisers who took a decidedly different view of Joe Stalin. What Bullitt told the president was not what Roosevelt wanted to hear. FDR replied:

> Bill, I don't dispute your facts [or] the logic of your reasoning. I just have a hunch that Stalin is not that kind of man. Harry [Hopkins] says he's not and that he doesn't want anything but security for his country, and I think that if I give him everything I possibly can and ask nothing from him in return, *noblesse oblige,* he won't try to annex anything and will work with me for a world of democracy and peace.[21]

A stunned Bullitt argued with the president, informing the Hyde Park patrician that he was dealing not with a British duke but rather with "a Caucasian bandit, whose only thought when he got something for nothing was that the other fellow was an ass."

This was Bullitt's not-so-subtle way of instructing the leader of the free world—his president and commander in chief—that he was being duped, or, even less subtly, being made into Uncle Joe's jackass. He tried to tell FDR that there was no "factual evidence" that Stalin was a good or changed man, and to think otherwise was to be guilty of "the fatal vice in foreign affairs—the vice of wishful thinking."[22]

FDR, however, felt differently. As Bullitt's account suggests, Roosevelt liked Stalin. The Caucasian bandit had struck him as a good guy just looking out for his country—one he would work with to advance democracy and peace.

The president told Bullitt: "It's my responsibility, not yours, and I'm going to play my hunch."

"We Are Going to Get Along Very Well"

FDR's "hunch" was terribly misguided. It was not mere wishful thinking but a fatally flawed diagnosis from start to finish. Indeed, his appraisal of Stalin was one of the most naïve assessments of any major foreign leader in the history of the American presidency.

But few liberal historians bother to include that statement in their accounts of Roosevelt and his relationship with Joseph Stalin. And the rare historians who do quote FDR's "hunch" typically remove the sentence "Harry [Hopkins] says he's not," putting in an ellipsis instead.[23] Of course, the Hopkins line is the most damning part of an extremely damning quotation, since ample evidence suggests that Hopkins's loyalty may have been divided. It is as if historians have not wanted to validate any allegations of anti-Communists who have maintained that FDR was duped by some of his closest advisers.

The FDR-Bullitt exchange is, as we will see, just one of many instances in which Roosevelt conveyed a woefully misguided impression of Stalin. Obviously, the commander in chief's top priority was to defeat Hitler, and he needed Stalin's help to do that. To that end, he correctly ensured flows of U.S. materiel to help the USSR fight Germany. Allying with the Soviet Union was certainly justified in the circumstances of world war, given the lack of better options.

Still, FDR's misplaced trust in Stalin cannot be attributed entirely to a difficult foreign-policy decision made in the interest of America's national security. The situation is more complicated than that.

Some historians have argued that Roosevelt knew that Stalin was a thug but tried to assuage him to keep the Soviet dictator happy and away from further mischief. Unfortunately, to make this case is to rely on assumptions that the historical record does not seem to support.

It is not simply that FDR frequently stated that he thought he could work with Stalin and that Stalin was a reasonable and good man. The New Dealer went much further, working proactively to promote a positive image of Stalin in America—in his radio addresses, and also (as we will see in the next chapter) through books and even a major film.

Particularly disturbing was a fireside chat Roosevelt delivered on Christmas Eve 1943, shortly after he got cozy with the Caucasian bandit at the Tehran conference. At a time when countless Russian Christians prepared to celebrate Christmas in the gulag—by then, upwards of 90 percent of Soviet churches, monasteries, priests, monks, bishops, and nuns had been eliminated or imprisoned[24]—the American president offered this warm account of the Soviets to his fellow Americans:

> To use an American and somewhat ungrammatical colloquialism, I may say that "I got along fine" with Marshal Stalin. He is a man who combines a tremendous, relentless determination with a stalwart good humor. I believe he is truly representative of the heart and soul of Russia; and I believe that we are going to get along very well with him and the Russian people—very well indeed.[25]

FDR had, in effect, placed a Christmas candle in the window for Uncle Joe. Not only had Roosevelt been fooled by Stalin, but now he was fooling tens of millions of his own countrymen, who hung on his every word as they gathered around their radios for these chats.

Nor can it be argued that the president's glowing words were mere public diplomacy, intended to boost the American public's wartime morale. FDR spoke of Stalin precisely that way in private as well. Even in his private correspondence to Churchill, Roosevelt had taken to calling Stalin "Uncle Joe."[26]

Getting "Fresh" with "Uncle Joe"

The Tehran conference offers a window into FDR's efforts to win the heart of Stalin. When the Big Three leaders met at noon on November 30, 1943, Roosevelt deployed a plan to loosen up Stalin. He had bought a birthday gift for Churchill. "Winston," he said, as he huddled with Churchill, Stalin, and representatives, "I hope you won't be sore at me for what I am going to do." He began ribbing Churchill, who, as FDR later put it, "just shifted his cigar and grunted." The president turned to Stalin and whispered, with an impish smile, "Winston is cranky this morning, he got up on the wrong side of the bed."[27]

FDR seemed to strike a chord with the villainous tyrant—one that enlivened the president. As Roosevelt later recalled to his secretary of labor, Frances Perkins, "A vague smile passed over Stalin's eyes, and I decided I was on the right track." FDR pushed on, "teasing" Churchill about his Britishness, about John Bull, about his cigars. "It began to register with Stalin," the president told Perkins with delight. "Winston got red and scowled, and the more he did so, the more Stalin smiled. Finally Stalin broke into a deep hearty guffaw, and for the first time in three days I saw light."[28]

Rewarded for his efforts, and invigorated, FDR now ramped up the charisma: "I kept it up until Stalin was laughing with me, and it was then that I called him 'Uncle Joe.' He would have thought me fresh the day before, but that day he laughed and came over and shook my hand." This broke the ice, said the president, with brotherly love set to follow: "From that day on, our relations were personal, and Stalin himself indulged in occasional witticism. The ice was broken and we talked like men and brothers."[29]

FDR would leave Tehran "moved" by what he perceived as brother Stalin's sincerity, and by what he called "Stalin's magnificent leadership" of Russia. The patrician was impressed that such magnificence could radiate from a mere peasant who hailed from "one of the least progressive parts of Russia." "He is a very interesting man," summed up the president. More than that, said FDR, Stalin "had an elegance of manner that none of the rest of us [at Tehran] had."[30]

Again and again we see Roosevelt mischaracterizing Stalin. How could the American president hail this brutal totalitarian's "magnificent" leadership skills and his "elegance of manner"? The question has vexed FDR's admiring biographers.

Conrad Black, a highly sympathetic biographer of President Roosevelt, finds the Tehran episode "particularly alarming"—so much so that he does not want to believe it. Black somewhat dismissively notes that the episode is based on the account of Frances Perkins, though FDR told it to Perkins, and though, as Black acknowledges, Perkins was "generally a reliable source." Black judges that the details of the story were "undoubtedly embellished"—not by Perkins but by FDR. Thus, says Black, any smidgen of "damage to Roosevelt's reputation" ought to come from the possibility that the president would be so "self-serving to have given such a fraudulent account to a valued colleague."[31]

In fact, nothing from this account is hard to believe. There is no reason to think it was fraudulent. No one is on record claiming that it was fraudulent, including the subject and the witness. To the contrary, it is consistent with FDR's record toward Stalin.

Again, it is understandable that Roosevelt, locked in an unavoidable alliance with the Soviet Union, would do what he could to try to forge a relationship with Stalin for the sake of America and its vital foreign relations. Using his charm to soften the tyrant, the president would make the best of a bad situation in order to advance peace. As Frances Perkins put it, "He had gone prepared to like Stalin," but he also had gone "determined to make himself liked."[32] That door had to swing both ways. To focus on this aspect of Roosevelt's career is not to dismiss his entire presidency, which most presidential scholars—this historian included[33]—have judged successful, even great.

Even conceding this, however, one must acknowledge that FDR never seemed to see the brutality of Stalin. The evidence, going back to the first twelve months of his presidency, sometimes suggests admiration. And it is not as if indications of Soviet totalitarianism were not available at the time. Remember, FDR's Democratic predecessor Woodrow Wilson had recognized the viciousness of the Bolsheviks years earlier.

After discounting Frances Perkins's account of Tehran, Black does not deal with Roosevelt's own, written account of the meeting one year later in a letter to Churchill. In a note dated November 30, 1944, FDR celebrated: "I shall never forget the party with you and UJ [Uncle Joe] a year ago and we must have more of them that are even better."[34]

The president wanted more such unforgettable parties with Uncle Joe—now nicknamed with an even more affectionate "UJ," another FDR term of endearment.[35] Publicly and privately, Franklin Roosevelt conveyed little skepticism toward the mad tyrant.

In fact, in the days immediately following Tehran, Roosevelt estimated that after the war his biggest area of difficulty would involve not Stalin and the Soviets but Churchill and the British. "The President said he thought we would have more trouble in the Post War world with the English than with the Russians," recorded Attorney General Francis Biddle.[36]

"Everything" Stalin Wanted

The key question is whether President Roosevelt went overboard to get Uncle Joe to like him—and if so, when and where.

On this, Frances Perkins had more to say. Conrad Black does not report these interesting thoughts either, despite the fact that they can be found in the exact paragraphs from which he quotes other Perkins material. FDR lamented to his labor secretary that "for the first three days [at Tehran] I made absolutely no progress. I couldn't get any personal connection with Stalin, *although I had done everything he asked me to do* [emphasis mine]."[37]

If Roosevelt had done everything Stalin asked of him, that would be a real problem.

FDR did not stop there. He continued expressing his frustrations to Perkins: "I had come there [to Tehran] to *accommodate Stalin.* I felt pretty discouraged because I thought I was making no personal headway [emphasis mine]."[38]

The president had gone to Tehran to *accommodate* Stalin? Yes.

That was Perkins's prelude to FDR's account that followed—his teasing of Churchill and breaking the ice with Stalin, his getting "fresh" with "UJ."

No matter how noble FDR's wartime intentions—and his wartime goal was indisputably a good one—real dangers lay in his misjudgment of Joseph Stalin, particularly if the president did "everything [Stalin] asked me to do" and whatever he could to "accommodate Stalin."

Consider the recent conclusion of historian Wilson D. Miscamble:

> He [FDR] either downplayed or simply failed to appreciate the ideological chasm that divided the democracies from Stalin's totalitarian regime. He largely ignored the evidence of Soviet culpability for the appalling Katyn Massacre [in Poland] and, in general, he refrained from criticizing the Soviets. . . . Roosevelt's complaisance cannot be explained away simply by his recognition of the military necessities for defeating Germany. It rested upon the tragic misperception that he could build a bond of friendship with his Soviet opposite.[39]

It is difficult to dispute any of Miscamble's statement.

Roosevelt's poor judgment of Stalin would have tragic consequences. What was the source of his misperception? It seems clear that FDR was misled—that is, duped—into a terribly naïve view of Stalin at least in part by bad advisers, some of whom may have had loyalties elsewhere.

Katyn Cover-up

In the previous quotation, Wilson Miscamble makes reference to another regrettable FDR misjudgment, one frequently ignored by historians: the president's refusal to concede Soviet culpability in the Katyn Wood massacre, one of the worst war crimes of the twentieth century.

The roots of this atrocity date back to September 1939, when the Nazis and Bolsheviks jointly annihilated and partitioned Poland. The Soviets seized thousands of Polish military officers as prisoners of war. The Poles' fate was sealed on March 5, 1940, when Stalin signed their death warrant, condemning 21,857 of them to "the supreme penalty: shooting." The surviving NVKD document, sent by the diabolical Lavrenti Beria to "Comrade Stalin," features Stalin's handwritten signature on top, followed by signatures from Politburo members Marshal Voroshilov, Vyacheslav Molotov, and Anastas Mikoyan. Corresponding signatures also appear in the left margin from "M. [Mikhail] Kalinin" and "L. [Lazar] Kaganovich."[40]

In that spring of 1940 the prisoners were taken to three primary execution sites, the most infamous of which became the namesake of the crime: the Katyn Forest, located twelve miles west of Smolensk, Russia. There, these Polish men were slaughtered like farm animals. The Bolsheviks covered their crime with a thin layer of dirt.

In April 1943, after the Germans had betrayed the Hitler-Stalin Pact and advanced with lightning speed into Soviet territory, they discovered the mass graves and immediately tried to turn the atrocity into a wartime propaganda coup to split the Big Three Allies. The Soviets, being masters of lies, responded by blaming the massacre on Hitler and *his* goons. Stuck in between was the rest of the civilized world, which sought to determine which of the two sets of devils had done the dirty deed.

Not helping the situation on the American side was the Office of War Information (OWI). This group was penetrated by Communists and filled with liberal dupes, who through their information campaigns generated many more dupes among the wider public.

OWI was one of the Communists' greatest infiltration successes of the 1930s and 1940s.[41] Elmer Davis, a liberal, had been a popular radio commentator when FDR hired him to run OWI, where he was plainly duped on matters related to the Russians and Poland, and on Katyn especially. Davis and his agency's reporting on certain aspects of Poland's experience was so egregious that as early as June 1943 it caught the attention of Ambassador Jan Ciechanowski of the Polish government-in-exile and also of Congressman John Lesinski of Michigan. Congressman Lesinski, another Democrat alert to the chicanery of Communists, went to the House floor to denounce OWI's lousy coverage of the Soviet crimes in Poland. Lesinski's complaints riled Davis.

Lesinski and Ciechanowski decried the Communist penetration at OWI, especially the Polish-language section. These charges were accurate, though Davis attacked them as "lies."[42] The head of OWI was apparently unable to distinguish the kings of lies (in Moscow) from the truth-tellers (in America).[43]

OWI's dubious reporting on Katyn became a scandal. Davis had personally gone on-air giving the Soviet spin. Polish exile groups rightly accused OWI of a blackout on the real story of Kremlin complicity. Ambassador Ciechanowski said OWI's broadcasts on Katyn were so bad that they "could only be termed pro-Soviet propaganda." He maintained that "notorious pro-Soviet propagandists and obscure foreign communists and fellow travelers were entrusted with these broadcasts." This further infuriated Elmer Davis.[44]

Aside from OWI, other leftists followed the Soviet line on Katyn. One was Corliss Lamont, who in May 1943 produced a pamphlet dismissing the Katyn Wood massacre as a "Nazi-inspired charge."[45] Lamont's response was no surprise, given his dim view of Poland, which he had portrayed as a "fascist" aggressor toward the USSR in *Russia Day by Day*.[46]

So where did President Roosevelt stand on Katyn?

The president was inclined to give "UJ" the benefit of the doubt. Nonetheless, he realized the need to delegate an official who could take a close look. In 1944 he dispatched George Earle as a presidential special emissary on the Balkans to conduct an investigation into Katyn.

George Howard Earle III was an interesting character. Born in December 1890, he had been an excellent athlete, outdoorsman, adventurer, and all-around fun-loving guy. He first served FDR as a minister to Austria in 1933 and 1934 before being elected governor of Pennsylvania. He served one term as governor, from 1935 to 1939, and then during World War II he became a lieutenant commander in the U.S. Navy. President Roosevelt chose his fellow Democrat as emissary to the Balkans in part because Earle maintained informed contacts there, especially in Bulgaria and Romania.

Tasked with investigating Katyn, Earle soon learned the obvious truth: the Soviets had created the killing field. But when he brought his news home, FDR was not exactly agreeable. The president had already consulted with Elmer Davis's boys at OWI, and by this point he had made it a habit to turn a blind eye toward things anti-Soviet—especially anything that impugned Stalin's "elegance," "magnificence," and "stalwart good humor." Earle had been warned about this, as he later admitted in testimony during a congressional investigation of Katyn. An old friend, Joe Levy of the *New York Times,* had warned him: "George, you do not know what you are going to get over there [in the White House]. Harry Hopkins has complete domination over the president and the whole atmosphere over there is 'pink.'"[47]

Earle learned soon enough what he was going to get. He made his case to FDR: "About this Katyn massacre, Mr. President. I just cannot believe that the American president and so many people still think it is a mystery or have any doubt about it. Here are these pictures. Here are these affidavits and here is the invitation of the German government to let the neutral Red Cross go in there and make their examination. What greater proof could you have?"[48]

Earle was exactly right, as the Soviets decades later would concede under Mikhail Gorbachev. But Roosevelt disagreed, replying: "George, they [the Nazis] could have rigged things up. The Germans could have rigged things up."[49] FDR was accepting the Soviet line.

As Earle put it, Roosevelt was adamant that the Katyn claims were "entirely German propaganda and a German plot." The president said to his special emissary: "I'm absolutely convinced that the Russians didn't do this."

An amazed Earle responded: "Mr. President, I think this evidence is overwhelming."[50] It was.

And it was also no great surprise. The Soviets had been shipping captured Poles into Russian territory from the first months after the joint Soviet-German invasion of Poland in late 1939. This was hardly a secret. FDR (or his staff) could have opened the April 15, 1940, *New York Times* and read, "The Soviet authorities are transporting a large part of the population of Eastern Poland into inner Russia." Surely the Poles were not being escorted to a tea party with Uncle Joe at the Kremlin. They were given "only fifteen minutes to leave their homes," added the *Times,* and "even seriously ill persons are forced into the unheated emigration trains."[51]

But FDR refused to believe George Earle's report of Soviet war crimes against Polish military officers. Earle saw Roosevelt's denial of Katyn as a microcosm of an even greater and more dangerous denial. The emissary expressed his trepidation of the overall "Russian situation," describing how the USSR had done its best to "deceive" the American people. The Soviet leadership, he told FDR, had done this not only with Katyn but "also primarily, the most important of all, by this dreadful book of Joe Davies, *Mission to Moscow."* This "dreadful" book was written by FDR's former ambassador to the Soviet Union. Davies's book had "made Stalin out to be a benign Santa Claus," said Earle, and had sadly "made such an impression on the American people."[52] (Here, Earle could not have known that he was digging himself in an even deeper hole, since, as we shall see in the next chapter, the president was head of the Davies fan club, eager to promote the book on a grand scale.)

FDR was getting annoyed with Earle. "George," the president lectured his fellow Democrat, "you have been worried about Russia ever since 1942. Now let me tell you. I am an older man than you and I have had a lot of experience." Roosevelt then explained why his colleague's concerns were overblown.

The emissary again pressed the evidence on Katyn, urging the president to "please look over" the photos and affidavits. Roosevelt did, but to no avail. George Earle later expressed his great frustration with the president, saying he had felt "hopeless."[53]

The affair did not end gently. When Earle asked Roosevelt for permission to go public with his concerns about Katyn, Uncle Joe, and the workers' paradise, he got a testy rebuke from the grandfatherly New Dealer. On March 24, 1945, FDR wrote coldly to his fellow Democrat:

I have noted with concern your plan to publicize your unfavourable opinion of one of our allies, at the very time when such a publication from a former emissary of mine might do irreparable harm to our war effort. . . . To publish information obtained in those positions without proper authority would be all the greater betrayal. . . . I specifically forbid you to publish any information or opinion about any ally that you may have acquired while in office or in the service of the United States Navy.[54]

If the stern message was not clear enough, it was followed by a gesture far more disconcerting—an almost unbelievable response that FDR hagiographers have ignored for seven decades. According to Earle, shortly after he received this letter from the president, he was greeted by two FBI agents while fishing on a remote pond in Maryland. The agents delivered a letter announcing the former governor's immediate assignment to the island of Samoa, seven thousand miles away, where he had been appointed assistant head of the Samoan Defense Group. The president himself had made the assignment though the U.S. Navy.

FDR had exiled his old friend.[55]

Earle's surviving son candidly tells this story today. The son says that his father was bitterly disappointed, and "very upset that the president had done that to him." "I think it was very unusual and very autocratic," says his son. "Because, I mean, in a democracy you can't do that sort of thing, but the president thought in wartime he could do it and he did it. Of course, he got away with it."[56]

February 1945: Yalta

Franklin Roosevelt's misperception, his obviously misplaced trust in "Uncle Joe." was nowhere as destructive as at the Yalta Conference. The most damaging of FDR's dealings with Stalin came there, that first week of February 1945.

One agreement signed at Yalta provided for "free and unfettered elections . . . on the basis of universal suffrage and secret ballot" in the nations of Eastern Europe. But Stalin and his cronies snapped the agreement like a twig. For the next forty-plus years they made Eastern Europe the Soviet Communist bloc, with the totalitarian USSR dominating the historic, proud nations of the region, installing puppet leaders like Georgi Dimitroff in Bulgaria.

It should have been no surprise that Stalin would break his vow of elections. President Roosevelt—and certainly his advisers—should have known the Soviets' record of cynically exploiting words like "democracy" and "elections" without meaning them. The Soviets, in fact, had already staged phony elections in Poland, back in October 1939, one month after the USSR invaded eastern Poland. Then, as always, the discussion of elections was a sham.[57]

Thus, many have charged that FDR and crew "sold out" Eastern Europe at Yalta. Some scholars have made this case, and even Presidents Ronald Reagan and George W. Bush publicly expressed that perspective (in some form).[58] The view is especially common among the people of Eastern Europe. Nowhere is Yalta more hated, and FDR more cursed, than in Poland, even today.

Of course, not everyone agrees that Roosevelt was guilty of "selling out" Eastern Europeans. "The claim that Roosevelt betrayed Eastern Europe at Yalta," writes Jacob Heilbrunn, a fair, thoughtful writer from the political Left, "is an old right-wing canard." He dismisses the thought as "cheap historical revisionism," as a "slander against Roosevelt," that "belong[s] to the Ann Coulter school of history."[59] (Actually, long before Ann Coulter criticized FDR on Yalta, other popular conservative authors did so; for instance, John Flynn, in his 1948 book *The Roosevelt Myth,* called Yalta "The Final Betrayal.") Heilbrunn notes that the territory FDR supposedly ceded to the Soviets at Yalta "was already in their possession." He says that Roosevelt had no choice but to cut a deal with Stalin, since doing otherwise would have "seriously jeopardized" the first priority: the common battle to defeat Nazi Germany.

Heilbrunn is quite right about the primary goal of Yalta. That said, postwar boundaries and peace are not exactly minor concerns, as had been learned two-and-a-half decades earlier at Versailles. In fact, the post–World War I Treaty of Versailles was on many minds at the end of the Second World War, especially with the German surrender only months away. One can work on more than one priority. Leaders have staffs who work around the clock on such things.

There remain other issues of contention from Yalta.

A lingering, harsh criticism is that Alger Hiss, the infamous Soviet agent inside the State Department, was at Yalta and purportedly helped mislead the president, allowing Stalin to seize control of Eastern Europe. This is a common charge from the political Right, but some historians dispute it. Conrad Black, for example, claims that "Hiss had no influence whatever on Roosevelt or American policy at Yalta."[60] (On the same page, however, Black argues that Hiss made a positive contribution in constructing a "sensibly reasoned argument" against giving the USSR three votes at the United Nations.)[61]

But even if Hiss did not mislead Roosevelt, it is difficult to argue that certain advisers did not dupe, or at least poorly advise, the president.[62] The affirmation of Harry Hopkins alone would seem to bear witness to this.

Hopkins was pretty darned satisfied with Yalta, saying that both he and the president left the conference in a "mood of supreme exultation." "We really believed in our hearts," he later told his sympathetic biographer, Robert E. Sherwood, "that this was the dawn of the new day we all had been praying for and talking about for so many years. We were absolutely certain that we had won the first great victory of the peace—and by 'we' I mean all of us." That "we" most certainly included the president he served as right-hand man.[63]

Hopkins once again had been deeply impressed by Stalin and comrades. He was positively euphoric: "The Russians had proved that they could be reasonable and farseeing and there wasn't any doubt in the minds of the president or any of us that we could live with them and get along with them peacefully for as far into the future as any of us could imagine."[64] It was, Hopkins judged, perhaps a heavenly reward for which they had all been praying.[65]

One can surmise that Stalin, though not *praying*, also exulted in this great victory. Hopkins thought so. He said that Uncle Joe, too, was pleased with the results at Yalta, as was the whole of the Soviet delegation.

With some help from their American friends, Stalin's henchmen had pulled off quite a coup at Yalta. But the conference did not represent, as many FDR critics have maintained, a single moment of capitulation.[66] Rather, it was another stop—albeit the last and most important stop—on Roosevelt's potholed road of cooperation with Stalin. FDR had long misjudged the despot's slave state and the tyrant himself as a good-natured, constructive partner. That misperception would dramatically affect the postwar world.

There is an even more surreal postscript to all of this: President Roosevelt may have done the unthinkable by knowingly walking into Soviet surveillance traps—not once but twice, at Tehran and Yalta. At both conferences, FDR stayed in Soviet quarters and, according to historian Gary Kern, "was bugged like no other American president in history." Worse than that, Kern claims that Rooosevelt was aware of the trap.[67]

Kern, a translator, researcher, and author, painstakingly documents this in a scholarly paper so credible that it is posted at the official website of the CIA. He lays out FDR's acquaintance with bugs, the Soviet sources that confirm the surveillance, the eyewitnesses and "ear-witnesses," Soviet archives, interviews, and primary sources that include Russian memoirs never translated into English.

If accurate, this would be another mystifying, bracing component of a sad saga. The degree to which FDR seems to have deluded himself on Stalin and the Soviets is shocking.

Yalta Regrets—Sort Of

In a cabinet meeting shortly upon his return from Yalta, FDR waxed philosophical, even spiritual, as he groped for a richer understanding of the Bolshevik bandit's *magnificence*. There was, the president pondered aloud to his cabinet secretaries, "something else" he had detected in Stalin, something "besides this revolutionist Bolshevist thing." What might it have been?

The Episcopalian vestryman from Hyde Park looked upward for an answer: perhaps it had been the dictator's youthful training for the "priesthood."[68]

Never mind that Stalin, a militant atheist, had been expelled from seminary en route to his merciless destruction of religion in the Soviet Union. No, FDR mused to his cabinet secretaries, perhaps this seminary influence had communicated something to Stalin about the "way in which a Christian gentleman should behave."[69]

Christian gentleman, indeed. Even Conrad Black could not help but describe this FDR meditation as a rather odd reflection, though he immediately dismissed it by saying there was "not a shred of evidence that Roosevelt thought Christian decency predominated in Stalin's character."[70] Here again, FDR's owns words are not to be taken as evidence of his beliefs—at least when the words conflict with the process of constructing a saintly image of the man.

Soon, however, Roosevelt admitted having regrets about what he signed at Yalta. He realized the agreement had been far from perfect.

Among the modern FDR historians, Black shows this convincingly, marshaling two important quotations. First, the president told Adolf Berle, the State Department hand and learned adviser on things Soviet, "I didn't say the result [at Yalta] was good. I said it was the best I could do." Second, FDR agreed with criticisms that Admiral Bill Leahy leveled against the agreement on Poland. Admiral Leahy complained, "Mr. President, this is so elastic that the Russians can stretch it all the way from Yalta to Washington without technically breaking it." Roosevelt replied: "Bill, I know it. But it's the best I can do for Poland at this time."[71]

Then, on March 23, 1945, FDR confided to Anna Rosenberg, a well-known businesswoman and public official during the war: "Averell [Harriman] is right. We can't do business with Stalin. He has broken every one of the promises he made at Yalta."[72]

Yes, Stalin had broken them right away. That FDR assessment came only a month after Yalta. The Soviet leader had snapped the olive branch that quickly.

It took FDR only a few weeks to deduce that he may have failed postwar Eastern Europe at Yalta. He learned quickly, but only *after* the conference. He had been president for twelve years prior to Yalta—during which time the Soviet tyrant was murdering tens of millions of his own citizens for his classless "utopia"—but still he had not figured out Stalin's monstrous character. This was an odd learning curve, and a fatal one.

Those who defend FDR's actions at Yalta would do well to remember that FDR criticized *himself* on Yalta. Roosevelt's regrets were so heartfelt that he expressed them directly to the madman in Moscow. On April 1, 1945, the president wrote to Stalin, "I cannot conceal from you the concern with which I view the development of events of mutual interest since our fruitful meeting at Yalta."[73] FDR was particularly concerned about the fate of Poland. He must have had a sickening feeling.

Stalin surely laughed at the letter.

In any case, it was too late—too late for Poland, too late for Eastern Europe, and too late for FDR, who died only days after this note to "UJ." The whole rotten mess was now the problem of a former farmer and haberdasher from Missouri named Harry Truman.

Good Luck, Harry

This chapter on FDR cannot end with FDR. For Roosevelt's mistakes hounded his successor.

As has been well-documented, Roosevelt had told his vice president nothing about his private discussions with Churchill and Stalin, about Yalta, about the conduct of the war, about the atomic bomb, or about anything else of substance regarding the nation's security. Truman barely even saw FDR—at best a handful of times during his short stint as vice president.[74] Later, General Harry Vaughan, a Truman confidant who became White House chief of staff, remembered the daunting challenges this presented to Truman when he assumed the presidency under emergency conditions:

> [Truman] talked to everybody that had been to Yalta; everybody that had been to Tehran and everybody that had been to Casablanca, to any of those conferences; he talked to Mrs. Roosevelt and even talked to Anna Roosevelt, the president's daughter, because she had accompanied the president. I'm sure she wasn't in any of the conferences but he thought she might have overheard some casual conversation that might give him some pointers. It was a terrific job to try to prepare himself because the Potsdam Conference was scheduled.[75]

Vaughan recoiled at the sight of Stalin telling Truman, "Now the president [FDR] promised me that he would. . . ." Stalin was not shy about filling in his own blank. Said Vaughan, "Everybody within the sound of his [Stalin's] voice suspected it was a lie from start to finish but how could you prove it?"[76] (Vaughan's statement suggests that most others aside from FDR distrusted Stalin.)

With Roosevelt fully cognizant of his rapidly declining health, it is inexcusable that he did so little to prepare the president-in-waiting. Indeed, it was one of the most irresponsible things that FDR did. Truman, as president, would take legislative steps to ensure it never again happened to another vice president.

But that was later. For now, the Potsdam Conference, the final Big Three summit of World War II, was only weeks away. The end of the war and the fate of the postwar world hung in the balance. Where could Harry Truman turn? To *whom* could he turn?

Truman had to rely on anyone he could. As Vaughan indicated, he went to many people. Naturally, he figured the man to trust was Harry Hopkins, FDR's confidant, who had been a central player at Yalta. So Truman dispatched Hopkins to Moscow to meet with Stalin in May 1945, shortly after FDR's death. This means that FDR ill-served Harry Truman twice over, leaving the vice-president-turned-president ignorant and also in the nurturing hands of Hopkins.

Hopkins arrived in Moscow on May 25, 1945, and met with Stalin on May 26 and 27. Hopkins's representation of America in this instance is complex and hard to pin down. Some suspect him of nefarious motives, whereas others view him sympathetically, believing that Stalin, a man he had heretofore greatly admired, burned him.

On May 26 Hopkins insisted to Stalin that American "public opinion" toward Russia had been adversely affected by the "inability to carry into effect the Yalta agreement on Poland." Stalin, in turn, blamed that failure on the British, saying that they were building up a "cordon" along the Soviet border, presumably to keep the Red Army in check. According to Robert Sherwood and other historians, Hopkins responded by saying that the United States did not support a British perimeter, but instead was happy to see "friendly countries" placed along the Soviet border.[77]

For Stalin, of course, "friendly countries" were totalitarian Communist regimes, Soviet puppet governments, throughout Eastern and Central Europe. Stalin greeted this with a sudden cheerfulness, saying that if such were the case, they could "easily come to terms" on Poland.[78]

According to historians sympathetic to Hopkins—such as Sherwood, who is favorable to the point of being obsequious—this *misstep* by Hopkins allowed Stalin to roll over him the next day, even as Hopkins made an allegedly impassioned appeal to the Soviets to allow American-style democratic "freedoms" in the newly occupied territories. Even historian Laurence Rees, who is more skeptical of Hopkins and FDR, argues that a well-intentioned Hopkins was subject to the Soviet despot's "bruising performance" and was "genuinely hurt by Stalin's insults." Stalin "almost toy[ed] with the new president's emissary."[79]

If this was the case, then Harry Hopkins was not a clandestine agent—"Agent 19"—helping Moscow. Instead he was a fool, a dupe, one who, for whatever absurd reason, had nearly adored Stalin all along, only to finally learn—too late—that Uncle Joe was not exactly avuncular.

There is, however, another interpretation of the meetings. For that, one can look to actual witnesses, such as Assistant Secretary of State Charles "Chip" Bohlen.

Bohlen was there, and took minutes on the meeting. According to Bohlen's record, Hopkins did not forcefully represent the American position, which was to push for free and fair elections in Poland—what FDR had expected to come from Yalta. Rather, he informed Stalin "that the United States would desire a Poland friendly to the Soviet Union, and in fact desired to see friendly countries all along the Soviet borders." Hopkins spoke of a Soviet-"friendly" Poland in particular. Stalin, said Bohlen, responded (no doubt with a giant grin), "If that be so, we can easily come to terms in regard to Poland."[80]

Bohlen added a very important insight regarding the context of these times. He said that by May 1945, the dominant view of Harry Hopkins, as well as the State Department generally, was that Stalin was trustworthy and that any post-Yalta problems were the doings of some shadowy figures behind the scenes at the Kremlin—certain generic "Red Army Marshals," in the words of Averell Harriman, the ambassador to the Soviet Union. Hopkins was not alone when he asserted, "We felt sure we could count on him [Stalin] to be reasonable and sensible and understanding."[81]

Whether Hopkins had been unwittingly duped or had deliberately sought to assist Stalin, the fate of Eastern Europe was sealed regardless. An increasingly ailing Harry Hopkins could ready for his exit into the next world. He would die only eight months later, leaving another guy named Harry—Harry Truman—with a Cold War, and leaving the people of Eastern Europe in the calloused hands of Uncle Joe.

"What He Did Not Understand"

Perhaps the most learned observer of all this theater was Chip Bohlen. Bohlen was there as the Communist movement, both at home and abroad, maneuvered throughout the war period, from the Hitler-Stalin Pact in 1939, to the Nazi assault on Britain in 1940, to the German invasion of Russia in June 1941, to FDR's dealings with Stalin after December 1941, and on through Yalta in February 1945.

Bohlen was a renowned diplomat, admired by both Democrats and Republicans.[82] He was an insider at some of the great events of the twentieth century. One of FDR's top aides, he attended the wartime conferences from Tehran to Yalta. After Roosevelt's death he continued to meet with Stalin, along with Harry Hopkins, under the leadership of President Truman.

Bohlen had the warmest respect and affection for FDR. Thus his abiding regret over the president's handling of the Soviets carries real credibility. He later recorded: "As far as the Soviets were concerned, I do not think that Roosevelt had any real comprehension of the great gulf that separated the thinking of a Bolshevik from a non-Bolshevik, and particularly from an American." Somewhat sheepishly, Bohlen continued: "He [FDR] felt that Stalin viewed the world somewhat in the same light as he did, and that Stalin's hostility and distrust, which were evident in the wartime conferences, were due to the neglect that Soviet Russia had suffered at the hands of other countries for years after the [Bolshevik] Revolution."[83]

Those "other countries" included America. Under Woodrow Wilson, of course, the United States had sent thousands of troops to battle the Bolsheviks in the 1918–21 Russian Civil War. Also the Republican administrations of the 1920s had refused to recognize the Soviet Union. Stalin's Russia, FDR judged, had been misunderstood and unfairly maligned—a common view among American progressives at the time. But that view was badly misguided, as Bohlen explained: "What he [FDR] did not understand was that Stalin's enmity was based on profound ideological convictions."[84]

In other words, Stalin was an aggressive, mass-murdering, conquest-driven, ideological Marxist-Leninist. Uncle Joe and Uncle Sam had nothing in common. FDR didn't get that one quite right. And from the start to the finish of his administration, the great New Dealer was greatly trashed, hated, and duped by Communists at home and abroad, both far away and all too close.

10

THE HOLLYWOOD FRONT

It wasn't only politics, presidents, and Washington that the Communists aimed to disrupt. There was also culture, movies, and Hollywood. MGM was a target of opportunity every bit as much as FDR.

Vladimir Lenin said that "of all the arts, for us the most important is cinema."[1] Grigori Zinoviev, Lenin's head of the Comintern, declared that motion pictures "can and must become a mighty weapon of Communist propaganda and for the enlightening of the widest working masses."[2] The Soviet sense of the significance of film was made unmistakably clear in March 1928 at the first Party Conference on Cinema.[3]

The Soviets realized, of course, that nowhere was the movie industry as prolific, advanced, and influential as in the United States of America, especially in Hollywood's Golden Age: the 1930s and 1940s. Hollywood's stars and starlets were revered by adoring masses. Inevitably, then, Communists from Moscow to New York set their sights on Tinseltown; their penetration became much deeper and more pervasive than liberals dare acknowledge.

Taking a leadership role were Communist union heads and screenwriters, with the latter poised to provide indoctrination via their crafting of scripts. In 1946 Communist screenwriter Dalton Trumbo declared that "every screenwriter worth his salt wages the battle in his own way—a kind of literary guerrilla warfare."[4]

A fellow screenwriter who devoutly enforced that warfare was a nasty individual named John Howard Lawson, known as "Hollywood's commissar." In his revealingly titled book *Film in the Battle of Ideas,* which was published by the Communist house Masses & Mainstream, Lawson was candid in instructing his comrades: "As a writer do not try to write an entire Communist picture, [but] try to get five minutes of Communist doctrine, five minutes of the party line in every script that you write."[5]

This was precisely the advice that the Comintern and CPUSA gave to American Communists to best deliver propaganda. (Recall the use of this tactic at the American Peace Mobilization rallies.) The goal was to exploit a legitimate medium, a reputable non-Communist one, as a platform to disseminate a Communist message. For the screenwriter, the movie could serve as a kind of front in and of itself, as did certain "peace" rallies.

Lawson was combative in his cause. "It is your duty," he instructed his fellow Soviet patriots, "to further the class struggle by your performance." That struggle, he said, included the highest of Soviet priorities: the undermining of God. The commissar wanted to see in American movies a "campaign against religion, where the minister will be shown as the tool of his richest parishioner."[6]

For decades since, American liberals have tried to portray anti-Communists' concerns about Hollywood as brute hysteria. In fact, the anti-Communists were very well-informed of the Communists' intentions—far better informed than were the liberals duped by the Reds. As Kenneth Lloyd Billingsley, author of an excellent book on the subject, wrote of Hollywood's Communists: "They had enjoyed spectacular success using liberals to serve their causes." The movie industry, wrote Billingsley, "had played the role of what Lenin called 'useful idiots,' duped and bilked by militant Communists."[7]

Naïveté was the big issue among liberals, but not the only issue. Many simply could not bring themselves to criticize anyone on the left and thereby concede any ground to the anti-Communists. This was the case even after the hideous behavior of Communists during World War II—including harsh treatment of liberals, their causes, and their iconic president. Screenwriter Budd Schulberg, a former Communist Party member, admitted this to Arthur Koestler, the respected ex-Communist author who penned the seminal work Darkness at Noon. Although he detested Communists, Schulberg said, he did not want to attack anyone on the left. Koestler corrected Schulberg: "They're not left; they're East."[8]

Lies, Damned Lies, and Lillian Hellman . . . and Arthur Miller?

To fully chronicle the eclectic list of Hollywood Reds and dupes, and the troubling cases somewhere in between, is impossible in a chapter or two. There were, for starters, the unrepentant Stalin apologists, like writer Lillian Hellman; CPUSA member Dashiell Hammett, a famous mystery and script writer, and Hellman's longtime lover;[9] Lester Cole, a Communist writer who later excoriated those who wanted to forgive and forget, like Budd Schulberg, and who so enraged Louis B. Mayer that the MGM mogul screamed, "You're nuts! Goddamn crazy Commie! Get out! Goddamn it, *get out!*";[10] musician Artie Shaw, who, as we will see, could proudly recite the Soviet "constitution"; playwright Bertolt Brecht, later dubbed "Minstrel of the GPU";[11] performer Paul Robeson, Marx's musical mouthpiece;[12] the union thug Herb Sorrell; plus many, many more. Hollywood had not failed to produce a dramatic cast.

Hellman, whom producer Elia Kazan once described as a "coiled snake," was among the worst cases.

Until her dying days, Hellman insisted that she had not been a Communist.[13] But she did not exactly have a reputation for veracity. Writer Mary McCarthy publicly called Hellman a liar, saying, "Every word she writes is a lie—including 'and' and 'the'"—prompting a slander suit from Hellman.[14] British historian Paul Johnson, who said that for Hellman "falsehood came naturally," unforgettably quipped that "there are lies, damned lies, and Lillian Hellman."[15]

Not that Hellman, who referred to the USSR as "the Motherland," needed to prevaricate to infuriate. Her candor was maddening enough. She dismissed the very notion of Stalin's purges as "anti-Soviet propaganda," attacked the Dewey Commission for its findings on the Moscow show trials, and, in general, unerringly parroted the Stalinist line.[16] While unflinchingly defending Moscow's mass murderer, she viciously attacked Senator Joe McCarthy, the subject of her book *Scoundrel Time.*

If Lillian Hellman was not a Communist, then she was a dupe, and a crass, insufferable dupe at that.

The forerunner to Hellman's *Scoundrel Time* was Arthur Miller's classic play *The Crucible.*

Miller is an interesting case requiring careful study. The playwright was made famous and became a hero among the Left for many reasons, but especially for *The Crucible,* a political parable blasting McCarthyism and the "Red Scare." In many liberal circles it is tantamount to a crime merely to suggest that Miller was ever a Communist or Communist sympathizer. In truth, however, close investigation of Miller's complex story reveals that at one point he undeniably had Communist sympathies, if not loyalties.

Arthur Miller was born in New York City in October 1915 to Isidore and Augusta Miller, two Polish-Jewish immigrants. He attended the University of Michigan, where he began writing plays. Though much has been written on Miller, the best current research on his life, his politics, and his political-personal double life has been done by Dr. Alan M. Wald, English professor at the University of Michigan. In his insightful, probing 2007 book *Trinity of Passion,* Wald, himself a man of the Left, shows that Miller had been "a struggling Marxist playwright since the late 1930s."[17]

A genuine scholar, willing to do the hard digging, Wald took the time to look at old editions of the *Daily Worker, New Masses, Masses & Mainstream, Currents, Jewish Life,* the liberal *PM,* and other Communist, Communist-led, or Communist-friendly publications of the era. He found that Miller's byline frequently appeared in those publications, and that his plays were often glowingly reviewed by comrades.[18] But beyond that, Wald made a blockbuster discovery: Miller seems to have published in *New Masses* under the pseudonym of Matt Wayne from March 1945 to March 1946.[19]

Scouring those publications, as I have likewise done, reveals that Arthur Miller was an active participant. Two features stand out: Miller's open participation (under his real name) in a symposium splashed on the cover of *New Masses* on December 25, 1945 (along with well-known Communist screenwriter Albert Maltz),[20] and an interview/profile of Miller in the April 17, 1946, edition of the *Daily Worker,* along with an accompanying photograph of the proletarian playwright.[21] (See pages 186–87.)

By Wald's description, Miller's political writing in these publications was often "militantly angry."[22] It also reflected the party line and language. In the *Daily Worker* interview, Miller explained that "the main fight" in the postwar era was "the fight to raise the living standards of people all over the world and the enemy is imperialism."[23]

In addition to these two standout Miller contributions, other, lesser-noticed items buried inside these publications are likewise illuminating. For instance, Miller was highlighted as the first speaker in a public forum—cosponsored by *New Masses* and the new Communist journal *Mainstream* (before the two fused into one publication)—vigorously defending Hollywood screenwriter Howard Fast, who had caught the attention of the House Committee on Un-American Activities.[24] Fast was a writer for the *Daily Worker* and *New Masses,* became an editor for *Masses & Mainstream,* and wrote novels like *The Incredible Tito,* about Yugoslavia's Communist dictator. He would receive the Stalin Peace Prize in 1953.[25]

In its July 3, 1945, issue, *New Masses* offered its readers a special deal: The comrades-turned-capitalists advertised a reduced rate on a one-year subscription if purchased with a choice book by one of the listed authors. The options included

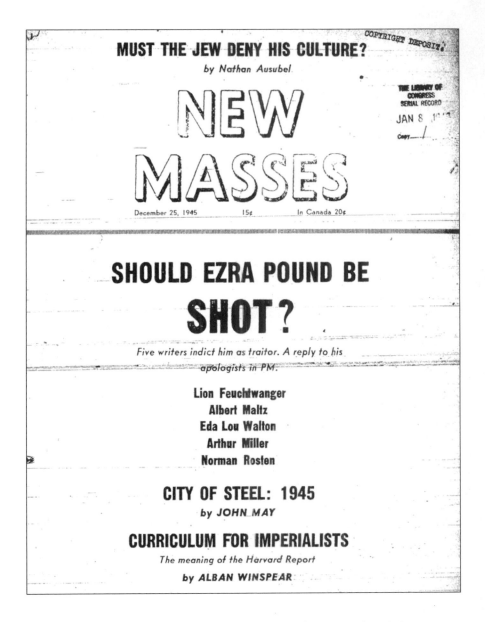

Miller in New Masses: Playwright Arthur Miller participated in a December 1945 symposium in the Marxist publication *New Masses*—and may well have written columns under a pseudonym.

Miller in the Daily Worker: Miller's writing was often glowingly reviewed by America's comrades, including in this April 1946 profile in the Soviet-funded *Daily Worker*.

Volume 23 of *The Collected Works of V. I. Lenin*; Owen Lattimore's *Solution in Asia*; Bertolt Brecht's *The Private Life of the Master Race*; Dr. Harry F. Ward's *The Soviet Spirit* (Ward was the Religious Left dupe of ACLU fame); and, among a handful of others, Arthur Miller's *Situation Normal*. (See page 189.)

Professor Wald notes that *New Masses* made such offers for no less than three books by Miller: *Situation Normal, Focus,* and *All My Sons.* "Usually," notes Wald, "the books offered with *New Masses* subscriptions were by well-known Communists; it was uncommon to see three by one author."[26] Miller was a special case. Apparently, his thinking fell that closely in line with the comrades at *New Masses.* Most interesting, this was still well before *The Crucible.*

Even this short list of Miller's work and interaction with the Communist Party, its front groups, and its publications contravenes claims by the likes of *The Nation,* which informed its readers at Miller's death: "He certainly wasn't a communist, and he wasn't a socialist."[27]

That statement is bizarre, given the totality of Arthur Miller's activities in the 1930s and 1940s. It could be defended only with the crucial caveat that Miller had left the party, the movement, the ideology, by the 1950s or later in life, as he likely did.[28] To claim he was never a Communist, or even a small "c" communist or a socialist, is to be very naïve.

The Crucible: "By Far Miller's Best Play"

And then, only after all of that, came *The Crucible.* The Communists loved *The Crucible* as much as liberals did. The review of *The Crucible* in the January 28, 1953, issue of the *Daily Worker* carried the unequivocal headline "'The Crucible,' Arthur Miller's Best Play."[29]

"It is by far Miller's best play," began reviewer Harry Raymond. It was "a case history" of "persecution" and "hysteria" against "innocent men and women sent to the gallows" in Salem, Massachusetts, in 1692. But make no mistake, explained Raymond, "It is impossible to view this play honestly without noting the awful parallel courses of two widely separated American persecutions: the Salem witchhunt and the current persecution of Communists and other progressives." The reviewer added: "Like the Salem persecution, the present one is directed by the ruling class of the land, its leaders of government, its judges, and what reactionary clergy they have been able to enlist." And what of these reactionaries? The atheist *Daily Worker* was inspired to invoke the image of Christ at this sober moment, perhaps for the benefit of its friends on the Religious Left:

publican Spain would leave Europe again to the destroyer of his cause. Can Koestler deny that the chief responsibility for the rearming of Germany, the rise of fascism and the delivery of Spain to Franco lies on Britain and specifically on its determination to be the arbiter in a balance-of-power Europe, weighted against the Soviet Union?

Koestler's ultimate solution lands him where most of the renegade flights from revolution and logic end—in mysticism. According to Koestler, history is the record of cyclic swings between the commissar, or scientific, thinking, and the Yogi, or contemplative, thinking. The former has been in the ascendant for three centuries, but is now on the down swing. Yogi thinking is returning into its "usurped" place. This rejection of the scientist for the mystic is managed by a *tour de force;* it is done entirely in scientific terminology. Scientists should not be surprised. Ex-revolutionists, on becoming counter-revolutionists, commonly manage the turn with citations from the revolutionary handbooks.

The heart of the book, however, is a morbid-minded attack on the Soviet Union that goes far beyond W. L. White in virulence and dishonesty. White grudgingly acknowledges some Soviet virtues; Koestler none. Koestler writes as if the Soviet Union exists in a vacuum and the choices imposed upon it by the capitalist encirclement were all voluntary choices. He has no mention of Soviet aid to Spain, or Soviet efforts for collective security, or the inter-racial fraternity in its federal structure. He does not scruple to use the discredited testimony of Leon Blatt, the Polish Socialist, not only denounced in the Polish and Czech democratic press in London but unintentionally refuted by the anti-Soviet Jan Karski in his book, *The Secret State.* Nor, since he spreads his anti-Soviet pitch over the entire Left, does he scruple about standing truth on its head. The renegades who staffed the European secret services and the European counterparts of the Dies Committee will chuckle at the Koestler version in which they are the victims and their victims the fingermen!

A REALLY comprehensive analysis of *The Yogi and the Commissar,* exposing all its offenses against logic and honesty, would require another book. I must limit myself, in conclusion, to a consideration of two other Koestler ideas.

One of them, the notion of the intelligentsia—supposedly the nervous system of the social organism—as neurotic in function, has already been effectively dealt with by Joel Bradford (NM, Dec. 19, 1944). This theory poses neurosis as a function of the nerves, which makes as much sense as asserting it to be a function of the digestive tract—to develop ulcers.

The other idea, wearisomely reiterated in all sorts of contexts, is that man's conscious life is poor, weak and indecisive as compared with his subconscious life. Despite reason and science and civilization the animal remains, by far the greater part of man. The failure of the Left, insists Koestler, lies in its reliance on reason, and neglect and misunderstanding of the forces of the unconscious—though, by a characteristic contradiction, Koestler elsewhere castigates the Left for acting too much under the spell of the unconscious.

Can Koestler, in the entire history of mankind, point to one instance of human advance achieved by anything but the directing force of reason? The power of the irrational is tremendous, of course, and to be reckoned with; but as regards human progress it has operated negatively. Its power is shown in the torments endured by the men of reason, the resistances they have had to overcome. Had it been otherwise more revolutions would have succeeded and fewer would have been bloody. Fortunately, for mankind, it was Czarism, not the Russian revolutionists, who resorted to mystics.

But an ex-radical, reduced to faith in Colonel Blimp and Yoga, will naturally wish to decorate the descent into the irrational. Radicals will continue on the difficult but ascending path of reason.

The Basic Guys

UP FRONT, by Bill Mauldin. Henry Holt, $3.

BILL MAULDIN, the cartoonist of the Army newspaper *Stars and Stripes,* explains that "I draw pictures for and about dogfaces because I know what their life is like and I understand their gripes." He confines himself to one group at the front because "riflemen . . . are the basic guys and the most important guys in a war." The fierce partisan attitudes of the cartoons speak for "The Benevolent and Protective Brotherhood of Them What Has Been Shot At."

July 3, 1945 NM

A favorite of the comrades: Here *New Masses* features Arthur Miller's book *Situation Normal* as part of a special subscription offer—one of at least three Miller works so promoted in the publication.

these reactionaries, the reviewer said, had "deserted the teachings of Jesus to follow the war god Mars."

Communists gushed over Miller's link between Salem witch-hunters and American anti-Communists, and could not hold back their applause, exhorting non-Communist liberals to the encore. To that end, the *Daily Worker,* on the same page of its review, posted an accompanying sidebar on "What Other Critics Said About 'Crucible.'" There, the *Daily Worker* led appreciatively with the endorsement of the *New York Times* reviewer, who dubbed Miller's play "powerful," and a "genuine contribution." "Neither Mr. Miller nor his audiences," wrote *Times* reviewer Brooks Atkinson, in a line underscored by the *Daily Worker,* "are unaware of certain similarities between the perversions of justice then and now."

Miller, always a favorite of the Communist press, saw his popularity with the general public skyrocket. Now a national figure, he came to the attention of the House Committee on Un-American Activities.

On June 21, 1956, Miller was called to appear before the committee. His testimony received tremendous attention. The *New York Times,* for example, ran the eye-catching headline "Arthur Miller Admits Helping Communist-Front Groups in '40s." The lead sentence of the *Times* story noted: "Arthur Miller, playwright, disclosed today a past filled with Communist-front associations."[30]

To Congress, Miller conceded that he had signed appeals and joined protests sponsored by Red-backed groups. He refused to name names of those who were there with him. Likewise, he would not name people who joined him during the four or five times that he said he had attended Communist Party writers' meetings. Miller also denied that he had ever been under "Communist discipline" and would not answer the question of whether he had ever joined the party.[31]

The most dramatic moment of the hearing came when the House committee's counsel asked Miller whether he had once signed an application to join the party. As Miller dissembled, the counsel presented the exact five-digit number on the party application form for "A. Miller," listed as a "writer," whose address was 18 Schermerhorn Street in Brooklyn—where Arthur Miller had in fact lived. Congress went so far as to publish a photocopy of the application card.[32] (See page 191.) Miller said he had "no memory of such a thing."[33]

That was then—when Arthur Miller kept a lot of things close to the vest. Among them was whether *The Crucible* was, in fact, an allegory about McCarthyism. For most of his life, Miller publicly explained the play as being simply about the Salem witchcraft trials. To be sure, the world had always surmised, and many teachers had long taught, that *The Crucible* was really about the anti-Communist "witch hunts" of the 1950s, but Miller did not openly concede such a link to the

An application for CPUSA membership: Congress published this copy of a Communist Party membership application form for "A. Miller," whose occupation is listed as "writer." and whose Brooklyn address matched Arthur Miller's own.

House Committee on Un-American Activities or Senator McCarthy's investiga-tions.[34] Even most reviewers (the Communist *Daily Worker* being a notable excep-tion) stopped short of explicitly linking Salem to anti-Communism.

But in June 2000, late in his life, Miller wrote an article for the British left-wing newspaper the *Guardian* in which he finally came clean about *The Crucible*.[35] In the opening line of the *Guardian* piece he admitted, "It would probably never have occurred to me to write a play about the Salem witch trials of 1692 had I not seen some astonishing correspondences with that calamity in the America of the late 40s and early 50s." If that was not clear enough, he added, "I refer to the anti-communist rage that threatened to reach hysterical proportions and sometimes did."[36]

Miller's long-overdue admission of the obvious opened the door for the *New York Times,* in its later obituary for Miller, to be able to report in 2005—which it did not in 1956—that *The Crucible* was "a 1953 play about the Salem witch trials inspired by his [Miller's] virulent hatred of McCarthyism."[37]

But even then Miller—whom the *Times* would call the "Moral Voice" of the American stage in its obituary—did not really come clean. In the *Guardian* he descended to Lillian Hellman levels when he stated that of "everyone I knew . . . one or two were Communist Party members."[38] If that was not a blatant lie, then Arthur Miller was unbelievably foolish. Recall that he had told Congress that he had attended Communist Party screenwriters' meetings; surely there were more than "one or two" party members at those. Recall, too, that he had been inter-viewed by the *Daily Worker* and written for *New Masses;* surely he encountered more than "one or two" party members there.

Miller was either fibbing or unbelievably gullible. One cannot lunge for the excuse that he was afraid of political persecution: This was the year 2000. Miller was free to be frank with no fear of reprisal by a long-defunct House Committee on Un-American Activities or a long-dead Joe McCarthy.

All of this ought to constitute a literary bombshell of sorts, contrary to liberal howls throughout the years that any suggestion that Arthur Miller was a Com-munist was baseless Red-baiting. And what if Miller had been a party member, or even a small "c" communist? It would mean that he was not a dupe but a duper, one who generated a cast of dupes, especially among those who defended him against accusations that he was sympathetic to the USSR. Liberals insisted that Miller was one of them, despite his innumerable unsightly instances of toeing the Commu-nist Party line, which often ran contrary to the official position of the Democratic administration—for example, on Red China, Korea, the Spanish Civil War, and atomic espionage; on President Truman's use of the atomic bomb; on capitalism, materialism, profits, wages, and religion; on American "civil rights" abuses and American "imperialism"; on Howard Fast; on the Smith Act; on the *illegitimacy* of the House Committee on Un-American Activities and the *legitimacy* of CPUSA; in signing his name as a sponsor to the USSR's first World Youth Festival in Prague in 1947, and in signing a statement defending controversial Communist Gerhart Eisler before the party apparatchik fled America to become a top official in East Germany; and, generally, in support of numerous Communist front groups.[39]

And if Miller had been a member of CPUSA, or even a communist who did not join the party, it would mean that he duped not only his liberal defenders but, in addition, all those millions, including generations of students, who read or watched *The Crucible,* relishing its delicious digs at anti-Communist "witch-hunters" who persecuted innocents—supposed innocents like Arthur Miller. If Miller was secretly a Communist (or communist) and knew which of the accused were guilty, were lying, were operating covertly, or were serving Moscow, then his classic play, and his classic denials, misled a lot of trusting readers and audience members, with whom he was never exactly forthcoming.

Perhaps time, and archives, will tell the whole truth about Arthur Miller. Maybe the answers reside in Miller's still-closed private papers at the University of Texas or in *The Crucible* collection held at Columbia University.

Whatever the case, countless readers and playgoers saw in Miller's fiction the facts about anti-Communist persecution. When concerns over Communists in Hollywood mounted, leftist actors such as Will Geer adopted the Miller line and moaned about "Salem witch-hunts."[40] But those who understood the Communists recognized that reality was far different from how Miller portrayed it. Criticizing Miller's allegory, Elia Kazan's wife, Molly, explained: "Those witches did not exist. Communists do. Here, and everywhere in the world. It's a false parallel." Molly Kazan shrewdly tried to inform the duped: "Witch hunt! . . . No one who was in the Party and left uses that phrase. They know better."[41] (For the record, Geer, later famous for playing "Grandpa" on the 1970s TV hit *The Waltons,* very likely was a Communist sympathizer and may well have been a party member at one point, probably when he was a master's student at Columbia University.)[42]

Molly and Elia Kazan tried to warn the duped because they did "know better"; Elia Kazan once had been a member of the Communist Party.[43] He and his wife were liberal anti-Communists who understood the horrors of Communism, recognized the Communist love of the lie, and said so with intelligence and nuance. They were ultimately crucified for their good sense and willingness to speak out.[44] Like Saturn, the Left eats its own children; it has devoured Elia Kazan, who even today is roundly booed by Hollywood's illiberal liberals.

The Angry and the Gullible

Molly Kazan's frank assessment reflects the reality of Hollywood Communists in the 1940s, though this reality has typically been obscured by historians.

Led by a hardcore group of writers and mansion Marxists whom Communist Party members knew as the "first team"—Dalton Trumbo, John Howard Lawson, Paul Jarrico, Howard Fast, Lester Cole, and Albert Maltz—Hollywood Communists could be an angry, discontented group. The great F. Scott Fitzgerald, who had worked on a 1939 script with Budd Schulberg, remarked on their viciousness: "The important thing is that you should not argue with them. Whatever you say, they have ways of twisting it into shapes which put you in some lower category of mankind, 'Fascist,' 'Liberal,' 'Trotskyist,' and disparage you both intellectually and personally in the process."[45]

Hollywood's Communists had the faith without the hope and the charity. They looked for dupes everywhere—among friends, relatives, associates, and especially actors, the perceived dummies who mouthed words that they, the ventriloquists, penned. They looked to the likes of Planned Parenthood progressives, such as celebrated actress Katharine Hepburn, who had been nurtured by the teachings of racial eugenicist Margaret Sanger,[46] and whom Communist screenwriters could count on to read a script or speech of their doing.[47] In one sorry incident, Hepburn was the opening speaker at a May 19, 1947, Progressive Party Rally at Hollywood Legion Stadium, where, draped in a long, flame-red dress, the liberal New Englander read a speech scripted by Trumbo—a speech so admired by *People's Daily World* that the Los Angeles–based Party organ reprinted the entire text.[48]

The comrades sought out whomever they could. We now know, courtesy of declassified FBI files, about the case of Lucille Ball, famed comedienne of *I Love Lucy*. Ball joined the Communist Party in the 1930s. She claimed that she did so simply because she wanted to "shut up" her overbearing grandfather, the radical "Red" Fred Hunt.[49] By the 1950s she had left the party and was voting for Eisenhower. In between, however, her proletarian pursuers in Hollywood were unrelenting, seeking not only to have her involved but even (reportedly) to use her home as a meeting place.[50]

Many of Hollywood's finest liberals were victimized by sustained manipulation. It is interesting that while many liberals have been concerned about the reputation of Communists, those same Communists had no qualms about tarnishing the reputations of the liberals they preyed upon—even when the liberals were friends and relatives.

"I was duped and used," said the celebrated actor Edward G. Robinson. "I was lied to." He had "acted from good motives," but was exploited nonetheless. "The Reds," lamented Robinson, "made a sucker out of me."[51]

The same could be said for a sad swath of liberals like Gene Kelly, Judy Garland, Myrna Loy, Melvyn Douglas, Danny Kaye, Gregory Peck, Lena Horne, John Garfield, Lauren Bacall, Humphrey Bogart, and many more. Each is a story in itself.

Gene Kelly, for instance, was misled in large part by his wife, Betsy Blair, a Red—or, as Louis B. Mayer called her, Kelly's "commie wife."[52] Kelly was a sizable dupe, a pleasant, likable, patriotic American counted on and rolled by the Reds, tasked to stand in front of a giant backdrop of the American flag and lead the Pledge of Allegiance or exhort a rally of "progressives" in reverential renditions of "America."[53] In one particularly sad display, the all-American boy was cast to provide the introduction at the initial meeting of the Communist front Progressive Citizens of America, held at the Embassy Auditorium in Los Angeles on February 11, 1947. The theme for the evening was established before Kelly spoke, as a large screen flashed photographs of Hiroshima before and after Harry Truman dropped the bomb, with rolling footage of the dead and maimed and overflowing hospitals. On the ballot for the election of the executive board members of Progressive Citizens that evening were closet hard-line Communists like John Howard Lawson and Dalton Trumbo, as well as (among others) non-Communist liberals like Edward G. Robinson, Humphrey Bogart, John Garfield, Gregory Peck, Lena Horne, Gene Kelly, and Melvyn Douglas.[54]

As in the case of Gene Kelly, Melvyn Douglas's politics were closely linked to those of his wife, Helen Gahagan Douglas, an actress who later became a Democratic senator from California, where she became known as the "Pink Lady" for her far-left views. Badly burned by front groups, Melvyn Douglas would later urge his fellow liberals to "not allow themselves to be confused or cajoled into joining hands with the Communists."[55]

Way too many Hollywood liberals were cajoled.

Confused Cagney, Crazily Confused Chaplin, and More

The categories of Hollywood duped and nonduped, of liberals and Communists, were never perfectly tight. They resist broad-brush characterizations, as life does.

Take the case of actor James Cagney, who in the 1930s was totally duped to the point of possibly having been a misled Communist, but certainly was not a

Communist in the end.[56] At one point in the process, Cagney expressed interest in meeting with Theodore Dreiser and Lincoln Steffens, the latter the resident Potemkin Progressive at *The New Republic.* Communist screenwriter John Bright, who had taken Mr. Yankee Doodle Dandy under his wing, brokered a dinner for the men in San Francisco.[57] But the Hearst press—which Hollywood's Reds always hated—caught wind of the meeting. When studio head Jack Warner read the Hearst story, he called Cagney and Bright into his office and reprimanded them for being "Communist dupes."[58]

Cagney learned a lesson. For whatever reasons, whether public relations or sincerity, he backed away. One who did not was Charlie Chaplin.

"Thank God for Communism!" Chaplin told the appreciative atheists at the *Daily Worker.* "They say Communism may spread all over the world. I say, *so what?*"[59] The comedian wasn't joking.

Chaplin, whom author Kenneth Lloyd Billingsley described as "not a conventional Party member," declined to do a movie about Napoleon because he said he "didn't like dictators." When a wag asked the silent-film star whether he considered Stalin a dictator, Chaplin demurred: "it hasn't been settled what that word means."[60]

At the same time, it must be noted that Hollywood had many strong anti-Communists: Robert Taylor, John Wayne, Gary Cooper, Olivia de Havilland, Jimmy Stewart, Clare Boothe Luce, Edward Arnold, George Murphy, Robert Montgomery, Adolphe Menjou, Ginger Rogers, Bob Hope, and William Holden, to name only a few. Menjou's denunciations of Communism were scathing. Taylor's were bold and unflinching. Luce, who wrote screenplays and for the stage, in addition to being a journalist, was eloquent in her informed criticisms of Communism.[61]

And, of course, some celebrities once fell into the category of dupe but wised up. De Havilland, a dedicated Democrat, is an example of someone who was duped once, but not again. As we will see, too, an actor friend of hers transformed from dupe into anti-Communist—arguably the greatest anti-Communist of them all.

Mission to Moscow

Communist infiltration of Hollywood, and the accompanying duping, reached a crisis point after World War II, but it actually began as early as the 1930s. By the time war erupted, the Communists, and more importantly their dupes, were able to pull off a startling work of pro-Soviet propaganda.

The film was *Mission to Moscow,* released in 1943 by Warner Brothers. The movie was based on the 1941 memoir of the same name by Joseph Davies, former

U.S. ambassador to the USSR. In 1936 Davies had replaced William C. Bullitt as FDR's ambassador, a coup for the closet comrades in the Roosevelt administration. It was as if the Bolshevik demon exorcised from Bullitt's body had leapt into Davies. The good ambassador was an extraordinary dupe and a notorious enabler of the "Uncle Joe," "noble ally" party line.

Not surprisingly, Davies's book, published by Simon & Schuster, was extremely pro-Soviet. The former ambassador portrayed a host of nefarious Bolshevik figures—including Stalin and Soviet foreign minister Molotov—in the best possible light. Davies failed to mention forced famine, the Great Purge, or anything else that would reflect poorly on Stalin and his thugs. He even defended the horrible miscarriage of justice that was the Moscow show trials, concluding that the accused had been guilty of "plotting" against Stalin.

The book was a smash hit, selling upwards of 700,000 copies. Between the copies sold and the buzz on radio and in newspapers, Davies's memoir duped a lot of Americans of its own accord. Actually, the duping did not stop at the water's edge: translated into at least a dozen languages, it misled countless others around the world. It was an insult to the real victims of Moscow's repression, from Finland to Poland, from the kulak farmer to the Ukrainian casualty to the show-trial victim.[62]

Bad as it was, Davies's book did not quite scale the Himalayan heights of hyperbole achieved by the screen version. The film was made in the authoritative style of a documentary, but in fact the purpose of the film was to rally American wartime support for the nation's new ally in the fight against Hitler: Stalin's Russia.

And Davies did not exactly repudiate the cinematic version. Quite the contrary—he oversaw and made it worse. Hollywood's mavens gave Davies veto power over any scenes that made him uncomfortable. He even recorded an introduction to the film.[63] In that introduction, in which he spoke while seated in an armchair, Davies set the tone for the 124 minutes of nonsense that followed. He began: "No leaders of a nation have been so misrepresented and misunderstood as those in the Soviet government during those critical years between the two world wars."

This was a stunning remark. In point of fact, at that time in history no leaders of a nation had maimed and murdered so many people in such a brief period. But Davies's words carried weight because he had served as America's ambassador to the USSR. From the outset, this major motion picture, which had the deliberate goal of molding public perception on Stalin's Soviet Union, was duping its viewers.

Incredibly, the movie got even worse. It advanced the myth that the USSR was leading the way to a new dawn of peace for all of humanity. This is no exaggeration; the film said such things almost verbatim. It portrayed Stalin as a grand-fatherly, pipe-smoking, unerringly calm wise man. The movie needs to be seen to be believed; to lay out the full litany of its outrages is beyond the space limitations of this book.[64]

The screenplay was written by Howard Koch, who was chosen on the basis of someone's (it is not clear whose) recommendation that he was "nonpolitical." In truth, Koch was at the least a fellow traveler, and had probably been a Communist Party member for a time in the 1930s. Some of his correspondents actually addressed him as "Comrade Koch."[65]

During the making of this masterpiece of manipulation, Koch seemed to relish every dig at the "fascists" who he knew would be uncomfortable with certain auda-cious scenes. As he watched the opening introduction by Davies, for instance, Koch shook his fist with righteous indignation and said, "Let the Soviet haters scream!"[66]

A Friend in the White House

Most troubling of all, responsibility for the film did not lie only with the former ambassador, the Hollywood screenwriter, and the studio. The chain of command ran directly into the Oval Office. The film was made at the request of the man who had appointed Davies in the first place—President Franklin Delano Roosevelt.

President Roosevelt was instrumental in ensuring that the book was con-verted into a major motion picture, as part of his ongoing effort to better the image of "Uncle Joe" in the United States.[67] The book had been a crash project for the same reason, rushed into print only weeks after Pearl Harbor. So keen was FDR on the film that he and Davies met several times during its production to discuss progress before it was released in May 1943.[68]

Though the president's decision to push the book and movie can be defended as an action taken to help win a terrible war, *Mission to Moscow*'s portrayal of Sta-lin's Soviet Union was so shockingly inaccurate, so delusional, that it duped the American viewing public.

Of course, to FDR's Office of Wartime Information (OWI)—which, as noted earlier, was heavily penetrated by Communists and loaded with dupes—*Mission to Moscow* was not inaccurate but rather was a "convincing means of helping Americans to understand their Russian allies."[69] According to OWI, the filmmak-ers had made "every effort" to "show that Russians and Americans are not so very different at all." This applied to living standards: "The Russians are shown to eat well and live comfortably," OWI noted approvingly. Here the Soviet Union was just five years removed from the Great Purge and facing starvation, rampant poverty, food lines, and five to ten million Ukrainian corpses—none of which was represented in the film.[70] OWI's claim was at best ludicrously false, and at worst a deliberate fabrication.

OWI also hailed *Mission to Moscow* for providing an *accurate* view of the Russian leadership. "One of the best services performed by this picture," the government agency stated, "is the presentation of Russian leaders not as wild-eyed madmen, but as far-seeing, earnest, and responsible statesmen." This was OWI's take on terrorists like Stalin, Molotov, and Lavrenti Beria, the last being the head of the Soviet secret police (and also a serial rapist). To the information agency, the film had wisely recognized that the Soviet leaders, just like U.S. leaders, "desire peace" and "possess a blunt honesty."

According to OWI, *Mission to Moscow* performed an invaluable service by fostering a necessary sense of "post-war cooperation."[71]

"An Expedient Lie"

Not everyone was so taken with the movie. One of the harshest critics was, amazingly, the film's producer, Robert Buckner.

Buckner was mortified by the movie, of which he had lost control. He felt little recourse but to attack his own film in a lengthy letter. He dubbed it "an expedient lie for political purposes."

He was especially livid about the scenes concerning the Moscow purge trials. Buckner said that he and Davies "had a rather violent argument" over these depictions. He was furious that the ambassador "insisted upon the guilt" of the wrongly accused. This outrage sent Buckner running to Jack and Harry Warner, the towering studio bosses who ran Warner Brothers. He warned them that "a great historic mistake" was being made.[72]

Buckner also took umbrage at, as he put it, Davies's "insinuation that Finland was not actually invaded by the USSR." He and Davies argued this point as well. When Buckner told the ambassador that the "opposite was true." Davies countered that he had "privileged knowledge" of the conflict.[73]

The producer instructed Davies that Jack Warner had already sunk a million dollars into the movie and would not tolerate such shabby work. At that point, according to Buckner, Davies pulled out his personal checkbook and said, "I will give you the million here and now, and will take over the negative of the film from you." Davies had the money; like Corliss Lamont, like Fred Field, he had inherited a fortune built on the hard work of American entrepreneurs. Specifically, his wife was a wealthy heiress (who, incidentally, demanded face time in the film).[74]

In the end, about the only sources who liked this piece of Stalinist agitprop, aside from Davies and FDR, were the Soviets and the *New York Times*. The long-time movie reviewer at the *Times,* Bosley Crowther, appreciated this "screen manifesto" and its "boldness unique in film ventures." The film, wrote Crowther, "comes out sharply and frankly for an understanding of Russia's point of view," and "says with a confident finality that Russia's leaders saw, when the leaders of other nations dawdled, that the Nazis were a menace to the world."

Stalin and crew, it turned out, were visionaries—prophets for peace.

The "most absorbing" part of the film, Crowther said, was Davies's "whirl-wind efforts to tell America the truth"—about the evil Nazis and the good Soviets—"before it is too late." Crowther had some criticisms of the film artistically, but not politically. The movie "says quite clearly," he noted without complaint, that "Russia, far from earlier suspicion, is a true and most reliable ally." While acknowledging that Davies's film would "obviously prove offensive to those elements which have challenged his views," Crowther seemed to feel that the depiction was dead-on—indeed, "a valuable influence to more clear-eyed and searching thought."[75]

Warner Brothers was the most unlikely of studios for this piece of pro-Soviet propaganda. Jack Warner was no dupe. He was a solid anti-Communist ever on the alert for cases of potential dupery among his studio's major stars. As the Jimmy Cagney episode demonstrates, he never hesitated to call a star into his office to warn about "hanging out with Reds."

Warner later told the House Committee on Un-American Activities that his motives for making the film were patriotic, to get behind the war effort to stop Hitler.[76] Moreover, he figured he could accept Ambassador Davies at his word. This was a completely reasonable assumption. After all, here was a highly accomplished political figure who had been the U.S. ambassador to the Soviet Union. He had spent years on the scene in Russia—certainly far more than had Jack Warner. Why should Warner doubt Davies?

For that matter, the president of the United States yearned for the film, and was briefed throughout its production cycle. Roosevelt surely had been briefed on Russia far more than had Warner. Why should Warner doubt Franklin Delano Roosevelt?

John Dewey's Ongoing Redemption

One unlikely hero in this Hollywood saga was erstwhile dupe John Dewey, proving again that dupery does not have to be a permanent condition, and that political life offers many opportunities for redemption.

Mission to Moscow set Dr. Dewey seething. The philosopher-educator, who had gotten the wake-up call with Stalin's purges and show trials, denounced the film in a letter to the *New York Times*. He wrote the letter with editor and scholar Suzanne La Follette, cousin of the famous progressive Senator Robert La Follette of Wisconsin. Their lengthy dispatch, published in its entirety, ran in the May 9, 1943, edition of the *Times,* two weeks before the movie hit the theaters, suggesting that Dewey and La Follette had seen a special preview.

The letter was smoking in its channeled indignation. It began: "The film 'Mission to Moscow' is the first instance in our country of totalitarian propaganda for mass consumption—a propaganda which falsifies history through distortion, omission or pure invention of facts, and whose effect can only be to confuse the public in its thought and its loyalties." Dewey and La Follette noted that even in a fictional film such misrepresentations "would be disturbing," but they were particularly "alarming" in a movie sold as nonfiction, using a documentary style.[77]

Drawing on his expertise from chairing the Trotsky Commission, Dewey dismantled the movie's incorrect claims about the purge trials. The professor and La Follette made a devastating case, juxtaposing quotations from letters and official reports that Davies wrote while ambassador with scenes from the film, many of which did not square up. The letter condemned "the make-believe Russia of the film," which was "gay, even festive." "Wherever Mr. Davies goes," Dewey and La Follette wrote, "he encounters a happy confidence in the regime."

The letter also attacked *Mission to Moscow* for suggesting that Stalin had been "driven into Hitler's arms" because the dictator had been unfairly slighted by the French and British. In fact, as Dewey and La Follette noted, the Allies had made a "desperate effort" to form a defensive alliance with Stalin early in the summer of 1939, prior to the August 1939 signing of the Hitler-Stalin Pact. There was even "an Allied military mission vainly waiting to confer with the Soviet General Staff at the very time when the Stalin-Hitler pact was announced." (If only Dewey and La Follette had known the full truth, which is even worse: Stalin and his hack Marshal Voroshilov cynically delayed and rebuffed the Anglo-French delegation because they were hoping for a better deal with the Nazis—a hideous deal that would have appalled the British and French, as the Nazis and the USSR divvied up much of Europe.)[78]

Dewey and La Follette pointed out an egregious omission in the film: "Hitler's armies are shown invading Poland, but not Stalin's." Yes, the faux documentary neglected to note that the Red Army invaded Poland just two and a half weeks after the Germans did, in compliance with the terms of the Hitler-Stalin Pact. How could that utterly crucial fact be omitted? Hitler and Stalin *together* launched World War II.

In a brilliant parting shot, Dewey and La Follette called *Mission to Moscow* a "major defeat for the democratic cause," adding that it "sabotaged" the Allied cause and "assailed the very foundations of freedom" by making "skillful use of the Hitler technique." The movie, they said, conveyed a false impression "that Soviet Russia is our ally in the same degree as Great Britain." It was a form of appeasement, a "gross misrepresentation," and an example of "moral callousness." More than that, the film was "anti-British, anti-Congress, anti-democratic and anti-truth." *Mission to Moscow*, Dewey and La Follette concluded, created a "moral callousness in our public mind" that was "profoundly un-American."

Think about that: these renowned liberals/progressives had declared this film, championed by the Democratic president and by his administration, to be *un-American* propaganda.

Of course, Dewey's motives were not totally without suspicion, as Jack Warner noted. When informed that Dewey had been disgusted by his studio's film, Warner shot back, "From what I read and heard, [Dewey] was a Trotskyite and they were the ones who objected mostly."[79]

Warner was right: The Trotsky movement objected strongly to the film, especially because *Mission to Moscow* defended Stalin's side in Leon Trotsky's show trial. It was also true that the American Trotskyist movement had grown powerful—the largest of the Trotskyist movements in existence. In sheer propaganda alone, the American movement was the most advanced of all world Trotskyist parties; in organizing and maintaining the world movement, it was second only to the French Trotskyist party.[80]

Had the Trotskyites trotted out Professor Dewey to do their bidding? Was the father of modern public education being duped yet again? Was he secretly a Trotsky follower? As always with John Dewey, there was a myriad of legitimate questions.

The fact remains, however, that Dewey was exactly right in his criticisms of *Mission to Moscow*, which had gone well beyond the show trials and anything to do with Trotsky. And Trotskyites were not alone in condemning the movie, which critics aptly slammed as *Submission to Moscow*. Ultimately, the film found itself blacklisted by the House Committee on Un-American Activities, a group Dewey (on other occasions) deemed "hysterical."

Here, then, were some strange bedfellows: John Dewey and the House Committee on Un-American Activities, momentarily, indirectly, uneasily, on the same team.

A Duped Liberal Named Ronald Reagan

Clearly, Hollywood in the 1940s produced some strange plots, including a political shift with profound implications for the Cold War.

Among the most interesting cases of this entire period was a fellow named Ronald Wilson Reagan. The actor would travel the road from liberal Democrat to moderate Democrat to moderate Republican to conservative Republican, from idolizing FDR to supporting Truman to voting for Eisenhower—his first vote for a Republican—and then on to Nixon and Goldwater. Eventually the actor became a politician and the very face of political conservatism and anti-Communism. Along that route, Reagan was never pro-Communist, but was once a dupe—as he openly confessed later.

Reagan was a victim of front groups during and immediately after World War II. Among them was the benignly named American Veterans Committee (AVC), which sought out Reagan for its speaking circuit. The speaking material provided to Reagan for AVC events was "hand-picked," he later realized, as were his audiences. He ultimately recognized that he was being "steered more than a little bit."[81] And Communists were doing the "steering." With fellow actors like Dick Powell warning him about being duped, Reagan began to suspect that AVC was a Communist front, one of the first suspect causes to which he was "awakened."[82]

That was likewise the case for the Hollywood Independent Citizens Committee of the Arts, Sciences, and Professions (HICCASP). This innocent-sounding group was another of those that Reagan later referred to when he admitted that he had "blindly and busily" joined "every organization I could find that would guarantee to save the world." He was "naïve," he confessed. He "was not sharp about communism." Reagan became "an active (though unconscious) partisan in what now and then turned out to be Communist causes." The Communists succeeded in Hollywood, he pointed out, "by reason of deception." The duped Reagan saw the folks at HICCASP, AVC, and similar organizations as nothing more than "liberals," and "being liberals ourselves," he and many of his fellow Hollywood liberals "bedded down with" the closet Marxists.[83] Reagan learned that the Reds were not under the bed, but in the bed.

Reagan came to his senses and took a bold stand at a HICCASP meeting on July 2, 1946. He had been asked to serve on the board of the group. He received a baptism by fire that hot summer day.

He teamed up with group member James Roosevelt, son of the recently deceased FDR. Like Reagan, James Roosevelt was a non-Communist liberal and a dedicated Democrat. Roosevelt had suggested a group statement repudiating Communism. At the very least, this would be a good PR move, given that HIC-CASP was being maligned as a suspected Communist front.

What Roosevelt and Reagan witnessed next was nothing short of a fusillade by the closet comrades. As Reagan described it, "a Kilkenny brawl" erupted. One writer (whom Reagan generously left unnamed in his account) barked that if a war broke out between the United States and the USSR he would voluntarily take up arms for Stalin. The popular musician Artie Shaw leapt up and saluted the Soviet flag, offering, on the spot, to recite the words of the Bolshevik "constitution" from memory, which, claimed Shaw, was "a lot more democratic" than the U.S. Constitution.[84]

Leading the assault were the interminably abusive John Howard Lawson and Dalton Trumbo, who led the peanut gallery in denouncing the young liberal actor as an "enemy of the proletariat," "capitalist scum," "witch-hunter," "Red-baiter," and that old standby of the Left—"Fascist." Reagan recalled that Lawson got in his face, "waving a long finger under my nose and telling me off." The atmosphere was so charged that one woman (a liberal) had a heart attack and had to be removed. The genial Reagan held firm, bravely endorsing Roosevelt's proposal amid the onslaught from his fellow "liberals."[85]

Not One of "Them": Olivia de Havilland

Joining Reagan in recognizing HICCASP's true colors was his friend Olivia de Havilland, an actress famed for many roles, including the saintly but naïve "Melanie" in the landmark Gone with the Wind. She discovered that the comrades wanted to use her as a pretty face and a mouthpiece.

A few days before the HICCASP blow-up, Dalton Trumbo handed de Havilland a speech to deliver at a rally in Seattle. The text seemed remarkably pro-Soviet, with no mention of any criticisms of Communism. On top of that, the speech vilified the Truman administration as an anti-Semitic, racist, union-busting, war-mongering, imperial regime ready for aggression against an angelic USSR.[86] It was the standard Soviet-CPUSA party line.

But de Havilland refused to be a stooge for Stalin. She ditched Trumbo's text, requesting and receiving another from writer Ernest Pascal; then she delivered a stern rejection of Communism. She told the rally, "We believe in democracy, and not in Communism." Even worse for Hollywood's apparatchiks, she warned liberals about being used by Communists, noting that secret Reds "frequently join liberal organizations" in order to prey on trusting liberals. And while such was "their right," noted de Havilland, it was also the right of liberals "to see that they do not control us, or guide us . . . or represent us."[87]

When Hollywood's Bolsheviks saw what de Havilland had done, they were enraged. True to form, Trumbo and Lawson launched into childish fits of hella-cious name-calling.[88] If the commissars had had their own mini-gulag somewhere between Seattle and Los Angeles, Olivia de Havilland would have been there with shaved head, shivering in a dark cell, by morning.

De Havilland was onto the Reds. And so after Reagan and James Roosevelt experienced the Lawson-Trumbo tirade at the HICCASP board meeting, Dore Schary, a non-Communist liberal and RKO executive, quietly invited them to a small gathering at de Havilland's apartment. When Reagan and Roosevelt arrived, a relieved Reagan told de Havilland that he had figured she was one of "them." She smiled and said she was not.

All three were ready to resign from HICCASP, but Reagan went back once more a few nights later. He offered a group statement that affirmed American free enterprise and repudiated Communism. John Howard Lawson went ballistic, leveling his finger and raising his voice at Reagan: "Never!"

Reagan stepped down that evening, with others soon following.

Reagan's Awakening

This was a serious awakening for Ronald Reagan. Something was not quite right in the "liberal" camp. The proud, self-proclaimed "FDR Democrat" was troubled.

That same year, 1946, Reagan got still more evidence that something was amiss. By then a popular after-dinner speaker in Hollywood, he mixed movies with politics in his talks. The politics focused mainly on the dangers of fascism, the totalitarian monster of the recent past.[89]

After one such speech to the men's club at his church, the Hollywood Beverly Christian Church, Reagan was gingerly approached by his pastor, the Reverend Cleveland Kleihauer. Dr. Kleihauer was not known to be a liberal or a conserva-tive. He had common sense, and as a man of the cloth, he knew that there were few more ferocious foes of religion, and Christianity in particular, than Soviet Communism. The pastor thanked his church member for his impassioned attack on the Nazis and fascism, and then counseled: "I think your speech would be even better if you also mentioned that if communism ever looked like a threat, you'd be just as opposed to it as you are to fascism."[90]

Good point, Reagan thought. He did seem to be falling a little behind the times. He began working some new material into his speech text—a little something on Stalin and the threat posed by Moscow. Who could possibly object?

The next speech Reagan gave, the audience whooped nearly every time he blasted the defeated Nazis. "In a forty-minute talk," Reagan later wrote, "I got riotous applause more than twenty times."

But then he condemned Soviet Communism.

The response? Dead silence. It was "ghastly," Reagan remembered. His fellow "liberals" glared at him.

Before Reagan spoke out against Communism, liberals had liked him and praised him as smart and articulate. Suddenly, with the choice he had made, they viewed him as a loathsome "reactionary," a "fascist," and stupid, to boot.[91] This was the beginning of an odd metamorphosis Reagan would undergo in the unforgiving eyes of the Left.[92]

After this incident and the HICCASP showdown, Reagan became more suspicious, more vigilant—and much less gullible. He also became more aggressive, as was evident in another confrontation a few months later, recalled at length by fellow actor Sterling Hayden.

Hayden is remembered for an unforgettable role as the Air Force general who launched nuclear war in *Dr. Strangelove.* His personal politics zigged and zagged, including his views on Communism.[93] As a young man, he had run away to sea, where he sailed the world several times—a man's man, much like the characters he played. As a Marine in World War II he parachuted behind enemy lines in Yugoslavia, and was decorated for his actions. While manifestly pro-American, he was also pro-Soviet, and after the war, in 1946, he joined the Communist Party.[94] (Reagan said of Hayden: "It bothered me a great deal to see him on that side. Here was a man with a magnificent war record.")[95]

This Communist sympathizer had his encounter with Ronald Reagan one evening in the fall of 1946. At that point, Reagan was head of the Screen Actors Guild (SAG). Along with prominent actor and fellow anti-Communist William Holden, Reagan decided to crash an important meeting convened by Hollywood Communists at the home of actress Ida Lupino. There the Communists and their fellow travelers planned to make a final push to organize the film industry, specifically through the thuggish Herb Sorrell's Red-dominated Conference of Studio Unions (CSU).

Reagan had had enough with the "large," "muscular," and "aggressive" Sorrell.[96] As head of SAG he had a responsibility to keep the union from being hijacked by Communists. Moreover, Sorrell's thugs had been harassing Reagan personally. They had threatened to throw acid in his face and to hurt his children, who now needed police protection. In one instance, the bus that Reagan was scheduled to ride through studio picket lines was bombed and burned just before he boarded.[97] He began carrying and sleeping with a Smith & Wesson.[98]

The word was out on the importance of the gathering at Lupino's place, which Sterling Hayden had been tasked to spearhead. Now more than seventy-five leftists assembled, including Communists like Howard Da Silva as well as good-hearted liberals like John Garfield, who was constantly being tugged and tormented by Reds at home (his wife) and at work. This crowd, Reagan later recalled, was "astonished and miffed" when he and Holden strolled into the room.[99]

Reagan had quickly become the enemy. Not only had he started criticizing Communism, but now he was openly fighting the Communists who were trying to hijack the unions. In a SAG report he had been preparing, he concluded that a looming major actors' strike was "jurisdictional" rather than over wages and hours—a position unwelcomed by Hollywood's Reds, and especially Herb Sorrell's CSU, who tried to frame the strike as the fault of fat-cat studio bosses.[100] Reagan was bucking the party line.

While the crowd at Ida Lupino's fixed them with icy stares, Reagan and Holden calmly took seats on the floor. Reagan politely waited for the right moment before rising to ask whether he could have the microphone. He proceeded to give a forty-minute presentation that was constantly booed and interrupted. Certain members of the audience, such as Garfield, defended Reagan's right to speak. At least some in the crowd actually believed in civility and free discourse.[101]

Reagan managed to keep his poise and was remarkably effective, to judge from those in attendance. As Hayden later put it, Reagan coolly "showed up and took over and ground me into a pulp. . . . He dominated the whole thing." Overall, said Hayden, Reagan was "very vocal and clear-thinking."[102]

Historians Ronald and Allis Radosh, who have written a book on the Communist movement in Hollywood, have shown this incident to be a seminal moment in helping to end the "golden era" of Hollywood Communists. Reagan had pulled off quite a coup. The Communists were foiled in their bid to try to hijack the unions.[103]

Reagan, Eleanor, and the DPs

Many liberals now began to wake up, from Hollywood to Washington. Even Eleanor Roosevelt smelled the coffee, which was no small switch.

Consider that as recently as March 1946, when a bold Winston Churchill came to America to warn of an "Iron Curtain" descending across the European landscape, Mrs. Roosevelt was among the most dubious.

The former British prime minister had spoken the truth about the creeping Soviet takeover of Eastern Europe. In response, Stalin blasted him: "To all intents and purposes, Mr. Churchill now takes his stand among the warmongers."[104] Churchill was not surprised by Stalin's reaction, nor would he have been taken aback at how CPUSA immediately pilloried his plans to launch "a new world war."[105] He was, however, struck to see that Mrs. Roosevelt agreed with Stalin and the Reds.[106] She accused the courageous Englishman of "desecrating the ideals for which my husband gave his life." She took direct aim at Churchill, with a personal swipe: "Perhaps it's just as well that he [FDR] is not alive today to see how you have turned against his principles."[107] As columnist Drew Pearson put it, "What she said was not friendly" and "was definitely critical" of Churchill.[108]

In short order, however, Mrs. Roosevelt received a series of wake-up calls. The first came when she took up the cause of the so-called Displaced Persons (DPs) of Eastern Europe. The DPs dominated world headlines in 1947. Initially survivors of Nazism, they included a very large number of displaced European Jews, including those longing for a homeland in "Palestine," which had not yet been partitioned into Israeli and Palestinian states. But the list of designated DPs mushroomed to 1.5 million as Stalin's Red Army moved into Central and Eastern Europe and people desperately fled from Soviet-occupied areas. The Eastern Europeans, the *New York Times* reported, would "dare not go back [to their native lands] . . . because they will not submit to the arbitrary governments which have been imposed on their homelands [by the USSR]."[109]

The United States attempted to come to the DPs' rescue, housing them in makeshift camps in Europe.[110] In response, the Soviets and the international Communist movement ramped up the agitprop, contending that these humanitarian centers were really a form of imperialistic "concentration camps." As unjust and ridiculous as these charges were—the United States spent at least $100 million annually to protect these displaced foreigners—the Communists had learned many times that they could count on a certain number of duped liberals to buy into their absurd allegations.

One liberal not biting was Eleanor Roosevelt. When Soviet officials insisted that the United States was holding the DPs as a source of semi-slave labor—a natural thought to Moscow, given the Soviet way of doing things—Mrs. Roosevelt fired back immediately, dismissing the accusation as "utterly untrue."[111]

The Kremlin upped the ante, demanding that the DPs be forcibly repatriated to Eastern Europe—the territories newly "liberated" by the USSR. The Truman administration did not back down: Secretary of State George C. Marshall, who would be criticized by many Republicans for major losses in the Communist world—including "losing China"—adamantly rejected the Soviet demand.[112] Leading Democrats, from Marshall to President Truman to former first lady Roosevelt, held firm, as did a politically active liberal actor named Ronald Reagan.

Reagan and Mrs. Roosevelt—both former dupes—publicly supported congressional legislation to permit entry of 400,000 DPs into the United States.[113] This legislation, introduced by Congressman William G. Stratton (Illinois Republican), faced opposition in Congress.[114] To the thirty-six-year-old Reagan, this opposition was immoral; these people needed to be saved from the clutches of Soviet Communism. As head of SAG, he took up the torch for the DPs. On May 7, 1947, through the New York–based Citizens Committee on Displaced Persons, he released a statement urging passage of the Stratton bill.[115]

The episode involving the DPs represented a bridge from Reagan's frequent wartime denunciations of Nazism to the opening of his longtime opposition to Communism, the new totalitarian threat facing Uncle Sam. This was Ronald Reagan's first open campaign against the Kremlin. It marked an important public turning point for Reagan, one missed by his biographers.[116] From here on he would be persona non grata in Red Square, and among certain impolite company in Hollywood. He would be duped no more. And he could count on Mrs. Roosevelt, duped often in the past, to join in standing up to the Communists—at least in this case.

Hollywood's Comrades

The threat from Berlin may have been vanquished, but, as more and more Americans were noticing by the mid-1940s, the threat from Moscow was growing. The commendable case of Ronald Reagan and Eleanor Roosevelt showed that the Hollywood Left and the Washington Left could join forces to resist the Soviet menace.

At the same time, that menace was alive and well in certain precincts in Hollywood, as the political class in Washington had become well aware. To confront that threat, Congress would summon the nation's movie stars, writers, and producers, friendly and unfriendly, for a dramatic series of hearings in the nation's capital.

11

OCTOBER 1947:
HOLLYWOOD V. "HUAC"

Exactly thirty years after Bolshevism consumed St. Petersburg and Moscow, it created a firestorm in Hollywood and Washington, D.C. In October 1947 the U.S. Congress held dramatic hearings on the subject of Communist infiltration in Hollywood.

The conflagration that ensued has long been a subject of heated debate, with conservatives perceiving the hearings as a long-overdue investigation of a genuine domestic threat, and with liberals portraying it as an intolerant infringement on American civil liberties, resulting in an infamous blacklist and ruined reputations among the accused. It was here that the House Committee on Un-American Activities became a liberal bogeyman—an anti-Communist menace long before Senator Joe McCarthy arrived on the scene.[1]

This congressional panel would be forever etched in liberal lore, and language, as "HUAC"—an incorrectly reordered acronym which not so subtly claimed that the *committee's* activities were "un-American." It is difficult to say who first coined "HUAC," but it is clear that CPUSA delighted in the pejorative, adopting (if not starting) it as the Communists' de facto name for the committee. CPUSA's organ, the *Daily Worker,* which put the word "communists" in quotes when referring to actual Communists fingered by the House committee, did not place the "HUAC" acronym in quotes, even though it was inaccurate and, in effect, slang. Sometimes the Left, both liberals and Communists, used the term "the Un-American Committee"—a pejorative found in Communist organs ranging from the *Daily Worker* to the *Chicago Star.*[2] The comrades had their talking points laid out neatly:

the anti-Communists were un-American; the American Communists in CPUSA—those pledged to the Soviet Comintern—were the *real* Americans.

Ironically, the Communists ultimately found the House committee's hearings useful for bringing liberals to their defense and for unifying the Left in ganging up on anti-Communism. They were shrewd as ever, knowing precisely which buttons to push to enlist liberals in their protection, all the while carefully avoiding Congress's central questions: Were they Communists? Which of them were Communists? Were they seeking to manipulate movies with Communist messages? Were they loyal to Moscow over America? Were they pro-Stalin? Did Stalin's stand dictate their stand?

For one week in late October 1947, both "friendly" and "unfriendly" Hollywood witnesses, from actors to producers to writers, filled hearing rooms in the Capitol building, where they engaged in riveting, at times blistering, exchanges. The whole scene was a spectacle, from the gaveling chairman of the committee, Congressman J. Parnell Thomas (New Jersey Republican), to the gaveled likes of John Howard Lawson and Dalton Trumbo; from stars like Gary Cooper, ogled by young girls outside the hearing room, to the oddest unforeseen development of them all: sitting in that room were two most unlikely future presidents—a freshman congressman named Richard Nixon and a young actor named Ronald Reagan.

These hearings were not just a major news story or fascinating political theater; they were major history.

Reagan and the Friendlies

Ronald Reagan was one of several actors called as friendly witnesses, along with leading men Robert Taylor, Gary Cooper, Adolphe Menjou, and Robert Montgomery.[3] Reagan testified on October 25, 1947. Referring to Hollywood Communists, the thirty-six-year-old head of the Screen Actors Guild (SAG) told Congress:

> We have exposed their lies when we came across them, we have opposed their propaganda, and I can certainly testify that in the case of the Screen Actors Guild we have been eminently successful in preventing them from, with their usual tactics, trying to run a majority of an organization with a well organized minority.
>
> So that fundamentally I would say in opposing those people that the best thing to do is to make democracy work. In the Screen Actors Guild

we make it work by insuring everyone a vote and by keeping everyone informed. I believe that, as Thomas Jefferson put it, if all the American people know all of the facts they will never make a mistake.

Whether the [Communist] Party should be outlawed, I agree with the gentlemen that preceded me that that is a matter for the government to decide. As a citizen I would hesitate, or not like, to see any political party outlawed on the basis of its political ideology. We have spent 170 years in this country on the basis that democracy is strong enough to stand up and fight against the inroads of any ideology. However, if it is proven that an organization is an agent of a power, a foreign power, or in any way not a legitimate political party, and I think the government is capable of proving that, if the proof is there, then that is another matter.

I do not know whether I have answered your question or not. I, like Mr. [Robert] Montgomery, would like at this moment to say I happen to be very proud of the industry in which I work; I happen to very proud of the way in which we conducted the fight [against Communism]. I do not believe the communists have ever at any time been able to use the motion-picture screen as a sounding board for their philosophy or ideology. I think that will continue as long as the people in Hollywood continue as they are, which is alert, conscious of it, and fighting. . . .

I abhor their [Communist] philosophy, but I detest more than that their tactics, which are those of the fifth column, and are dishonest, but at the same time I never as a citizen want to see our country become urged, by either fear or resentment of this group, that we ever compromise with any of our democratic principles through that fear or resentment. I still think that democracy can do it.[4]

It is difficult to argue with Reagan's assessment. He simultaneously championed civil liberties and condemned Communism. The committee chairman, J. Parnell Thomas, unhesitatingly told the young actor: "We agree with that. Thank you very much." Reagan was not gaveled or shouted down.

His testimony was widely reported as the best of the hearings. James Loeb, the executive secretary of the liberal lobby group Americans for Democratic Action (ADA), called Reagan's testimony "by all odds, the most honest and forthright from a decent liberal point of view." Loeb described Reagan as "the hero" of the hearings and summed up Reagan's closing statement as "really magnificent."[5]

Escaping notice at the time, and later by historians as well, was the *Daily Worker*'s response to Reagan's testimony. Remarkably, the Communist Party organ did not denounce the actor with its usual over-the-top rants. Actually, though it didn't praise Reagan, the paper was fairly content with his statement. The *Daily Worker* seemed impressed that he "proved a reluctant witness, refusing to parrot back to chairman J. Parnell Thomas his suggestion that outlawing the Communist Party was desirable."[6] That was no small thing, as Robert Taylor and Adolphe Menjou both favored banning the party.[7]

The one item of Reagan's statement that the *Daily Worker* highlighted was his quote from Thomas Jefferson and the remarks on making "democracy" work. From the beginning the Communists had cynically used terms like "democracy" to lure in the unsuspecting. In this case, Ronald Reagan's respect for America's *genuine* democratic traditions led him to resist a call for an outright ban on CPUSA—a stance the comrades applauded, obviously.

Yet Reagan had added a caveat that the *Daily Worker* did not quote: "If it is proven that an organization is an agent of a power, a foreign power . . . then that is another matter."

"Agent" is a loaded word. It can, and often does, imply outright spying. No doubt, most members of CPUSA were not spying as paid agents of the Kremlin, although some were, especially in the leadership. If that is what Reagan meant by "agent," then the *Daily Worker* was right to express satisfaction with his statement; in that case, Reagan was still struggling to connect the dots. But if by "agent" Reagan meant an instrument serving Soviet interests, then CPUSA unquestionably *was* an agent of the USSR, a foreign power. The party had been from the outset. It had saluted the dictates of the Comintern from the beginning.

Although the *Daily Worker* cited Reagan's testimony approvingly, the young actor may have already figured out the Communists' modus operandi. In his statement he included a crucial aside after saying, "If it is proven that an organization is an agent of a power, a foreign power, or in any way not a legitimate political party . . .": ". . . and I think the government is capable of proving that."

Ronald Reagan, the former dupe, may have been a quicker study than the Communists realized.

While Reagan earned a hat tip from the *Daily Worker,* he went on to receive lavish praise from his fellow actors for his work as SAG president, which included a systematic, extremely effective campaign to purge Hollywood of Communist influence—a "fight," said Reagan, "hand-to-hand combat."[8] Reagan's learning curve continued; he remained ever vigilant not to be duped again, and warned fellow liberals not to be duped.[9] And when he got it, he really got it.

"The Communist plan for Hollywood was remarkably simple," Reagan later explained. "It was merely to take over the motion picture business . . . [as] a

grand world-wide propaganda base." In those days before TV and mass production of foreign films, said Reagan, American movies dominated 95 percent of
the world's movie screens, with an audience of "500,000,000 souls" around the
globe. "Takeover of this enormous plant and its gradual transformation into a
Communist gristmill was a grandiose idea. It would have been a magnificent
coup for our enemies."[10]

In Reagan's view, that was what was at stake, with the "master scheme"
including a careful strategy "to line up big-name dupes to collect money and create prestige."[11] Liberals needed to wake up. They needed to follow the learning
curve that Reagan had, as did the rest of America.

Just Like Bogie and Bacall

While Ronald Reagan was making amends for past dupery, other Hollywood liberals were about to be publicly embarrassed that week in October 1947. That pool
of suckers was deep. And among the more prominent were two of the biggest stars
of the era, the hot Hollywood couple Humphrey Bogart and Lauren Bacall.

A brief comparison of Bogart to Reagan is telling.[12] Reagan reportedly had
been the first actor offered the part of "Rick" in the classic *Casablanca*. He turned
down the role to take another in *King's Row,* an acclaimed film that became one
of Reagan's best-known, though it lost to *Casablanca*—with Bogart in the lead
role—at the Academy Awards.[13] (One of the primary contributors to the *Casablanca* script was Howard Koch, the "Comrade Koch" of *Mission to Moscow* infamy.)[14]

Reagan and Bogart appeared to know each other pretty well. They were
close enough that Bogart was one of only fifteen "honorary members" of the official Ronald Reagan Fan Club,[15] one of the largest fan clubs in all of Hollywood
in the 1940s, as Reagan was among the top five box-office draws at Warner
Brothers. Bogart was the club's headliner male name; the lead female member
was Bette Davis.[16]

Bogart and Reagan also shared a passion for politics. Originally men of the
Left, both would move to the right, though Bogie only slightly—he always stayed
in the Democrat camp. That shift, however, came later. In the 1940s Bogart
shared something else with Reagan: he was duped, and badly so.

First Amendment Crusaders

After World War II, Bogart and Reagan were committed liberals, with brooding Communists desperate to find ways to use the two actors. By October 1947, however, Reagan had been burned once too often, and he went to the House Committee on Un-American Activities a chastened liberal. Hollywood's Reds knew he was long gone; he had chosen the *other side*. The liberal Democrat was now, according to the standard lexicon of the Reds, a "fascist" and "capitalist scum."

As Reagan and other friendly witnesses prepared to testify in Washington, Hollywood's Communists looked to other liberals in the movie industry for support. Bogart was still susceptible. The Communists appealed to him and other Hollywood liberals by wrapping themselves in the American flag.

A group of high-profile Tinseltown actors, writers, and producers planned a major public-relations trip to Washington to defend the First Amendment freedoms of their friends accused of being Communists, who were being summoned before the House committee as "unfriendly" witnesses. These liberals were more than game. After consulting with the unfriendlies, they changed the group's name from the confrontational Hollywood Fights Back, opting instead for the Committee for the First Amendment. This was a savvy PR move, signifying the high road to be taken: the Communists' case would be based on the U.S. Constitution, on the unimpeachable American Founders and their venerable First Amendment— in other words, on the antithesis of the USSR that the comrades secretly saluted. The Constitution-lovers at the *Daily Worker* were happy to join in, aiding the campaign by headlining it as a "Bill-of-Rights Tour."[17]

The liberal stars enlisted in the cause ran into the hundreds, including Katharine Hepburn, Henry Fonda, Gregory Peck, Myrna Loy, and Paulette Goddard. Roughly two dozen of them actually ventured to Washington for the hearings. The traveling troupe included big names: Danny Kaye, Ira Gershwin, Judy Garland, John Garfield, Sterling Hayden, Gene Kelly, Burt Lancaster, John Huston, Philip Dunne, Billy Wilder, and, of course, Bogie and Bacall.[18] Bogart topped the list, as he would any blockbuster movie.

The two dozen huddled with directors Dunne and Huston, their leaders, to coordinate and ensure that they spoke from the same script. The group took the position that questions from the congressional investigation did not merit responses because they violated the rights of the accused to believe what they wanted, to assemble as they wanted, and to say what they wanted as guaranteed under the First Amendment.[19] The liberals assumed that their accused friends were not Communists. They had convinced themselves—or allowed themselves to be convinced—that the deceivers were sitting in Washington, not Hollywood.

"Before we left Hollywood," Bogart said later, "we carefully screened every performer so that no red or pink could infiltrate and sabotage our purpose."[20] Bogie prided himself on his ability not to be tricked. He was street-wise, just like his movie image.[21] As one "First Amendment" crusader put it, Bogart "feels that he's the most politically sophisticated guy in our business."[22] The tough-talking Bogie seemed a most unlikely character to be duped.

The crew from the Committee for the First Amendment boarded a plane bearing the name *Red Star* (no kidding), which immediately raised suspicions among the liberals, though not enough to stop the voyage. "Coincidence or design?" Lauren Bacall puzzled to herself.[23]

As Bogie and Bacall led the expedition from California, a New York contingent readied to join them in Washington, including writer Arthur Miller, musicians Leonard Bernstein and Artie Shaw—proclaimer of the Soviet constitution—and producer Elia Kazan.[24] (See page 218.)

Along the route, the Hollywood stars had plenty of moments to talk to reporters. Bogart, a hard-drinking hothead, prone to speak for himself without coordinating with his friends, issued a personal statement to the press, insisting that the activities of the group had "nothing to do with Communism. It's none of my business who's a Communist and who isn't. . . . The reason I'm flying to Washington is because I am an outraged and angry citizen who feels that my civil liberties are being taken away."[25]

That line from Bogart, though honest and consistent with the American way of life, was a perfect parroting of the Communist Party line. Bogie and others had no idea how their words had, in essence, already been scripted by their closet-comrade friends. They would be unwitting mouthpieces for the Communist line, flawlessly echoing the Reds' talking points. This was clear once the unfriendlies—the so-called Hollywood Ten—began to testify.[26]

"Nazi" America

Once upon a time, when the Soviets signed a nonaggression pact with Hitler, American Communists actively appeased Nazi Germany, placing American interests and the American ideal and democratic way of life secondary to the goals of the Soviet totalitarian state allied with fascist Nazis. They even opposed aid to

Bogart, Bacall Lead 26 Notables

WASHINGTON, Oct. 26.—Twenty-seven movie stars, producers and press agents, led by Humphrey Bogart and Lauren Bacall, were flying here from Hollywood today to protest the Un-American tactics of the House Un-American Activities Committee investigating alleged film-land "Communists."

The expedition, scheduled to arrive at 8:20 p.m. EST, was planned two days ago over coffee which Bogart and his wife had with directors John Huston and William Wyler.

HUMPHREY BOGART

Other members include Jane Wyatt, Larry Adler, Marsha Hunt, Geraldine Brooks, Evelyn Keyes, Paul Henreid, Danny Kaye, Richard Conte, Sterling Hayden, Gene Kelly, lyricist Ira Gershwin, director John Huston, writers Joe Sistrom, Arthur Kober, Sheridan Gibney, Sheppard Strudwick, Philip Dunne, Robert Ardrey, Ernest Pascal, Jules Buck, Robert Presnell, Jr., Mel Frank and Ted Rader, press agents David Hopkins and Henry Rogers.

And from Broadway will come Leonard Bernstein, Louis Calhern, Agnes De Mille, John Garfield, Ted Harris, Garson Kanin, Richard Maney, Walter Huston, George S. Kaufman, Arthur Miller, Harold Rome, Canada Lee, Artie Shaw, Irwin Shaw, Richard Watts, Jr., Deems Taylor, Oscar Serlin, Paul Draper and Elia Kazan.

REPRESENT 500

The film group represents 500 members of the newly-founded Hollywood Committee for the First Amendment. It declared in its first public press release that "we are just Americans who believe in constitutional democratic government."

"We are protesting the nature of the hearings . . . because we defend the rights of individuals to be free from

Saluting the Hollywood "notables": The *Daily Worker* (October 27, 1947) praises Humphrey Bogart and the many other artists protesting "the Un-American tactics of the House Un-American Activities Committee."

democratic Britain as it was being mercilessly savaged by totalitarian-fascist Germany. And in the postwar period they did not object that the USSR was seizing Eastern Europe and rounding up Displaced Persons (DPs). Stalin's NKVD had, in fact, seized Nazi concentration camps and begun using them for Soviet purposes, with Buchenwald renamed Soviet Special Camp No. 2.[27]

But now, in October 1947, American Communist screenwriters—who refused to openly admit they were Communists and loyal Soviet patriots—invoked the spirit of Jefferson and Madison; their lodestar was no longer October 1917 but July 1776.

More than that, they denounced the congressmen who dared to question their loyalties as nothing less than goose-stepping stormtroopers seeking to establish a Nazi regime in the United States. *Yes, a Nazi regime.* This was a consistent Communist Party line, up and down the ranks. Again and again America's Communists and Communist sympathizers lashed out at these alleged homegrown "Nazis" and "fascists."

The *Daily Worker,* of course, was central to this coordinated campaign of outrageous name-calling. An excellent case in point is the October 29, 1947, issue, which led with an article by Washington editor Rob F. Hall. The piece trumpeted the combative words of unfriendlies John Howard Lawson, who testified on October 27, and Dalton Trumbo, Albert Maltz, and Alvah Bessie, who testified (in that order) on October 28.[28] Unbeknownst to their liberal friends, all four of these men were dedicated Communists; Hall and his colleagues at the *Daily Worker* knew the truth, surely, but made no mention of it in their paper.

Commissar Lawson was characteristically vicious. He informed Congress that it was behaving like "Hitler's Germany." "You are using the old technique, which was used in Hitler's Germany," explained Lawson, "in order to create a scare here." The House committee was, said the dedicated Stalinist, "trying to introduce fascism in this country."[29]

For his part, Dalton Trumbo did nothing to conceal his contempt for the congressmen, especially Chairman Thomas, who gaveled the writer repeatedly. "You have produced a capital city on the eve of its Reichstag fire," Trumbo lectured. "For those who remember German history in the autumn of 1932 there is the smell of smoke in this very room." As if that were not direct enough, Trumbo screamed as he left the hearing room: "This is the beginning of an American concentration camp!"[30]

The screenwriter said this at the very time that the Soviets were taking over Buchenwald from the Nazis.

Albert Maltz followed next. Though he was not as visibly angry, his words were incendiary. He accused Congressmen Thomas and John Rankin, the latter the racist New Deal Democrat from Mississippi, of a bipartisan effort to "carry out activities in America like those carried out in Germany by Goebbels and Himmler."[31] Meanwhile, in the USSR that Maltz advocated, Stalin boasted about his own vicious secret-police head (and serial rapist and mass murderer), Lavrenti Beria, whom Stalin dubbed "our Himmler."[32] This was not hyperbole on Uncle Joe's part. Sadly, Maltz (who was Jewish) and the others seemed incapable of making distinctions between true tyrants and murderers, on one hand, and elected representatives conducting a public inquiry, on the other.

Maltz also declared that the congressmen were full of "hatred of the very idea of democratic brotherhood"—though he said nothing about the antidemocratic USSR that he admired. The American politicians were carrying out "an evil and vicious procedure," a form of "official tyranny," according to this supporter of evil, vicious, and official *Soviet* tyranny.[33]

Maltz was followed by fellow screenwriter Alvah Bessie. Maltz and Bessie knew each other well; both were alumni of Columbia University and fellow contributors to *New Masses,* which had been edited by former KGB agent and Communist spy Whittaker Chambers. Bessie was so dedicated to international Communism that in the 1930s he volunteered for the International Brigades to fight alongside the Communists in the Spanish Civil War.[34] Bessie was literally willing to give his life for Communism.

These, too, were rather crucial details apparently not shared with Bogie and Bacall and friends.

Befitting his willingness to fight, Bessie was pugnacious before the House Committee on Un-American Activities. At one point he referred to chief investigator Robert E. Stripling as "Mr. Quisling." This implied that Stripling was guilty of privately serving an enemy government, and thus a traitor and a cretin—an ironic form of disparagement coming from Bessie. Over and over, Bessie warned that the committee was pushing America toward "fascism" and "foster[ing] the sort of intimidation and terror that is the inevitable precursor of a fascist regime."[35]

A decade later, Bessie would seek vengeance with a play he titled simply *The Un-Americans,* a morality play released the year Joe McCarthy died.[36]

The Nazi parallels were not only absurd but deeply offensive, given the very recent experience of the Holocaust. American Jews, in particular, should have been outraged by the comparison. Analogies between Congressman Thomas and Hitler, between Stripling and Goebbels, and between "HUAC" and the Third Reich were obscene; they trivialized the unprecedented, unspeakable evil inflicted by Hitler and his racist-fascist henchmen.

And yet the Communists' outrageous accusations worked. They allowed the closet comrades to deflect attention from the justifiable question of where their true loyalties lay—and for whom, and what, they were really working. Congress was conducting a legitimate inquiry, given the history, record, and professed beliefs of CPUSA, the Comintern, and their sworn members. Congressional investigators were well aware of that background. They also had documentation to back it up—everything from lengthy Comintern edicts to tiny CPUSA membership cards; detailed testimony from numerous former party members, such as Ben Gitlow and J. B. Mathews; and a cache of militant speeches from Soviet leaders beginning with Lenin. And, of course, there were the tens of millions of Soviets slaughtered at the hands of the current leader of the USSR.

The Communist tactic of deflection worked in large part because a host of duped liberals joined the chorus. As ridiculous as it was to call the Communists' accusers Nazis or fascists,[37] the CPUSA approach worked masterfully with liberals in Hollywood, especially when the unfriendlies were called to testify in Washington. The success of the campaign was stunning, given that many of these liberals had always recognized the evils of Hitlerism—unlike their comrade friends, whose position on the Nazis depended on what Stalin was saying at the moment. These liberals *knew what Nazis were really like,* and still they engaged in the smears.

Hollywood's liberals were a huge help to the Communists. The American public in the 1940s was not cynical toward Hollywood as it is today. In the 1940s, Hollywood's Golden Age, the actors and actresses were truly *stars.* The Communists knew that these were precisely the right cohorts to enlist.

Not every star could be fooled into repeating the Marxist agitprop about incipient "fascism" or a coming American "Nazi state." John Wayne, for example, would insist that America needed a "delousing" of Communists and their sympathizers.[38] But plenty of other celebrities did join the cause. To be fair, Hollywood's progressives generally stuck to the "First Amendment" script—but not all of them. Some celebrities took the bait, repeating the obscenities about fascism or Nazism, or some other infamous form of historical repression. And as they did, the secretly and illegally Soviet-funded *Daily Worker,* mouthpiece of the secretly and illegally Soviet-funded CPUSA, ran their words in banner headlines.

"I ask you when they put words in concentration camps, how long will it be before they put men there, too?" said Judy Garland in defense of the accused Communist screenwriters. The *Daily Worker* eagerly published her assessment—more than once.[39] "Dorothy" looked somewhere over the rainbow and saw nothing but barbed wire and gas chambers—an American Auschwitz, courtesy of Congress's anti-Communists.

"This is nothing new," lamented actor Frank Gervasi, quoted in a *Daily Worker* piece titled "Hollywood Fights Back." "We saw it before in Rome [under Mussolini] and Berlin [under Hitler]."[40]

Actor Larry Parks went for another analogy: he likened Congress's investigation to the "Spanish Inquisition." Sure enough, the *Daily Worker* ran with the quote, just as it ran with a similar quote from the first press release by the Committee for the First Amendment, which denounced this "political inquisition."[41] Similarly, the Communist newspaper quoted liberal actor John Garfield as being "sore, damn sore" at Congress's so-called heavy hand against the First Amendment. Garfield said he loved "this country and . . . want to see it set free"—as if America had returned to the days of slavery.[42] Judy Garland agreed with Garfield. She announced that Congress was "kicking the living daylights out of the Bill of Rights." Once again she got her name in the *Daily Worker*.[43]

Lillian Hellman provided great copy for the *Daily Worker* with her regular recitations of the party line. Speaking of the hearings, she snarled, "This past week has been sickening and degrading." The congressmen were "yes-men" and "Judas-goats," who would lead films, radio, press, publishers, trade unions, scientists, and churches "to the slaughter." And all of it was unnecessary, said the pro-Stalin writer, since "there's never been a communist idea in films."[44]

By this point, the House Committee on Un-American Activities had been likened to Hitler's Gestapo, to Spain's inquisitors, to Salem's "witch" drowners, to slaveowners, and to Judas, who handed over Jesus Christ for crucifixion. Hollywood's liberals and Reds alike were making Congress pay the price for daring to consider whether there were Communists in Hollywood seeking to secretly manipulate the film industry under orders from *true* henchmen like Stalin and Beria in Moscow.

No amount of truth injected into the debate seemed to make any difference. When Congressman Thomas suggested that Communist propaganda had been inserted into certain Hollywood films "during the past eight years," the *Daily Worker* dubbed Thomas's mere suggestion a "smear"—as if films like *Mission to Moscow* had never happened. Hollywood heroes stepped forward to back the *Daily Worker*'s disavowals. When Chairman Thomas asked Danny Kaye—who had done mocking imitations of Thomas during his trip to Washington aboard the *Red Star*—whether he had ever seen a Hollywood movie that seemed to include pro-Soviet propaganda, the dancing comedian replied flatly, "No, sir. I haven't."[45] Standing with Kaye was Paul V. McNutt, a special counsel for the movie industry, who sent a letter to Thomas protesting the congressman's insinuation.[46]

Seconding Kaye was Gene Kelly, who in an interview with the media said: "As

Mr. Kaye has remarked, it's pretty hard to find any propaganda in pictures. . . . You can't make a picture for entertainment that the American public will accept and inject any propaganda in it. So I think so far, we're pretty safe."[47]

While McNutt, Kaye, and Kelly challenged the notion that Communist propaganda could make it into a movie, John Howard Lawson was preparing to testify as an unfriendly before the House committee. It was Commissar Lawson, recall, who had ordered Communist writers that it was their "duty" to get "Communist doctrine" and "the party line in every script that you write." For now, however, Commissar Lawson was talking to Kaye and friends about one thing only: his awe of the First Amendment to the U.S. Constitution.

A Sprinkling of "Red" Pepper

This kind of rhetoric did not come strictly from actors. The *Daily Worker* also thrilled in the words of certain Democratic senators, such as Elbert Thomas of Utah, Glen H. Taylor of Idaho, Harley Kilgore of West Virginia, and Claude "Red" Pepper of Florida, who advised the unfriendlies not to answer questions from their congressional colleagues. Senator Thomas dubbed the committee's methods "unholy." Senator Taylor vowed "to battle this Un-American Committee."[48] Taylor said the committee members were "fascist-minded," in "parallel with those of pre-war leaders in Germany, Italy, and Japan." The *Daily Worker* gratefully ran these senatorial assessments on page one of its October 22, 1947, issue; it included them in other editions as well, under eye-catching headlines like "Liberals Question Committee's Legality."[49]

The *Daily Worker* was especially pleased with Senator Pepper's words, which it turned into a gigantic, front-page, above-the-fold headline that screamed, "SEN. PEPPER URGES FILM STARS DEFY HOUSE PROBE: Says Committee Helps Fascism." (See page 224.) The senator from Florida had long been accused of thinking like a Soviet official. Here, he did not disappoint the Bolshevik faithful: he told reporters that the "HUAC" investigation could be "the Stalingrad in the attack on civil liberties in this country." The imagery was clear: the senator was likening the so-called First Amendment fighters to the Soviet soldiers who turned back the Nazi assault at Stalingrad in late 1942 and shifted the momentum in the war. In this analogy, the members of the House Committee on Un-American Activities were the Nazis. The editors at the *Daily Worker* liked the analogy so much that they flagged it with a subhead, "STALINGRAD FOR FREEDOM."[50]

"Red" Pepper: The *Daily Worker* often celebrated American progressives' attacks on anti-Communists. Here (October 22, 1947) the Communist Party mouthpiece trumpets Senator Claude Pepper's condemnations of the House Committee on Un-American Activities.

Senator Pepper was doing yeoman's work in helping CPUSA rally the masses. He was extremely active, joining forces with the Progressive Citizens of America, which called for the abolition of the House Committee on Un-American Activities.[51]

Aside from Senator Pepper, another go-to source for the *Daily Worker* was FDR's former vice president Henry Wallace, a dupe of such incredible proportions that this book cannot do him justice. "Has America gone crazy?" the *Daily Worker* quoted Wallace summing up the Hollywood hearings. "Is the Un-American Activities Committee evidence that America is travelling the road to fascism?"[52]

The former vice president urged his fellow Americans that they "must destroy" the House committee—at the ballot box, of course. If they did not, the evil committee "will destroy many of the foundations of democracy and Christianity."[53] Wallace, a fond admirer of the Soviet experiment, was worried about threats to democracy and Christianity—in America, that is.

Don't Play It Again, Sam

Fortunately for the anti-Communist cause, all of this reckless insanity, spoken from the mouths of certain senators, actors, and screenwriters, created a backlash. One person weary of the cacophony was Humphrey Bogart, who seemed to grow less comfortable by the day, especially once the news turned against the crew of the *Red Star*.

Bogart was still expressing outrage at the congressional investigation after the Committee for the First Amendment arrived in Washington. He gave a radio broadcast in which he angrily declared: "We saw the gavel of a committee chairman cutting off the words of free Americans. The sound of that gavel, Mr. Thomas, rings across America! Because every time your gavel struck, it hit the First Amendment to the Constitution of the United States."[54]

Soon thereafter, however, the press reported that one of the group's members, actor Sterling Hayden, was a Communist. Among the whistleblowers was George Dixon in his "Washington Scene" column in the *Washington Times Herald*. Dixon got the scoop from "the blonde and beautiful Miss Mary Benton Gore," a "member of one of our most respected families." A cousin of Senator Albert Gore Sr. (Tennessee Democrat), Mary Benton Gore found herself the object of Hayden's attention and affection at a "little dinner party" arranged during the actor's stay in Washington. Hayden spoke too freely to Miss Gore, who, in turn, spoke freely to George Dixon, who then spoke freely to all of Washington and beyond, detailing Hayden's interest not only in Gore's beautiful blonde hair but also in Stalin's ugly Bolshevik Russia.[55]

Dixon's report was embarrassingly gossipy but, it turned out, embarrassingly correct, as Hayden later conceded when summoned back to Washington for testimony. Yes, Sterling Hayden was a Communist. So much for Bogie's having "carefully screened every performer" before they left Hollywood.

Worse, Bogie and friends learned that all those anti-Communist congressmen, investigators, and lawyers did not arraign people for fun; no, they actually had some evidence. It took mere minutes to show that the suspicious screenwriters were, in fact, Communists. Congress presented registration rolls, news clips, *Daily Worker* articles, *New Masses* bylines, front-group memberships, party applications, forms, cards, checks, cash, and even numbers. Consider the evidence the House committee unveiled:

Dalton Trumbo: Communist Party registration card, code no. "Dalt T." The committee presented a total of thirty-nine citations with Communist or Communist-front affiliations.

Albert Maltz: Communist Party registration card, no. 47196. The committee presented a total of fifty-eight citations with Communist or Communist-front affiliations.

Alvah Bessie: Communist Party registration card, no. 46836. The committee presented a total of thirty-two citations with Communist or Communist-front affiliations.

John Howard Lawson: Communist Party registration card, no. 47275. The committee found Lawson to be a one-man Communist front. Committee investigators presented the May 18, 1934, *Daily Worker,* which identified Lawson as one of its correspondents; a November 1946 issue of *Masses & Mainstream* listing Lawson as a member of its editorial board (along with Alvah Bessie and Dalton Tumbo);[56] the unsettling examples of Lawson (who was Jewish) flip-flopping on Hitler in lockstep with the CPUSA-Comintern-Moscow party line; and Lawson's position as a sponsor of the American Peace Mobilization,[57] the most insidious of Communist fronts, along with his Hollywood friends Albert Maltz, Budd Schulberg, Herbert Biberman,[58] Dashiell Hammett, Artie Shaw, and Will Geer.[59]

The evidence was shocking and undeniable—and only made Lawson, Trumbo, Maltz, and Bessie angrier.

"*Hitler Germany!*" yelped Lawson, when presented with irrefutable evidence. "*Hitler tactics!*" he screeched as six Capitol policemen led him from the witness stand.[60]

"*American concentration camp!*" moaned Trumbo, as he was escorted out of the room and away from the piles of embarrassing evidence.[61]

Only then did Bogart and Bacall recognize that they had been used. Unbelievable as it may seem, Bacall later said that as she and Bogie and the others flew to Washington, they did not know that most of the unfriendlies called to testify were in fact members of the Communist Party. "We didn't realize until much later," she admitted, "that we were being used to some degree by the Unfriendly Ten."[62] She conceded that they had been foolishly naïve, headstrong, emotional, and that they had hastily strolled into something "we knew nothing about."[63]

Bogie was not so gentle. He was furious that he had been made to look like an idiot—a useful idiot. "You f—ers sold me out!" he yelled at Danny Kaye.[64]

Many members of the group felt that way. Billy Wilder spoke up first: "We oughta fold."[65] They did. The Committee for the First Amendment fell silent, withered, and died.

So thorough had been the duping that the California state legislature, in an investigation and report a few months later, listed the Committee for the First Amendment as a Communist front, right alongside the American Peace Mobilization, HICCASP, and the Progressive Citizens of America.[66] This was not, of course, because most of those on the Committee for the First Amendment had been Communists—that is not how Communist fronts worked—but because the group's non-Communist liberals were snowed by the Reds. These liberals had been "suckers," as SAG head Ronald Reagan put it, victims of "one of the most successful operations in [the Communists'] domestic history."[67]

And with the committee and its members fully exploited, the Communists hung out to dry the liberals who had lent their names to defend individuals they thought had been honest with them. The stars' reputations had been tarnished by the closet Communists who used them. Now they endeavored to explain themselves. The celebrated lyricist Ira Gershwin, for instance, appeared before the California legislature to explain how he could be so oblivious as to host meetings for a Communist front at his home.[68]

Bogart, too, looked to repair the damage. He published a strong statement in which he declared, "I am not a Communist" or even "a Communist sympathizer." "I detest Communism just as any decent American does," wrote Bogie. "I'm about as much in favor of Communism as J. Edgar Hoover." He pledged that his name would never again "be found on any Communist front organization as a sponsor for anything Communistic."[69] He conceded that the trip to Washington had been "ill-advised," "foolish and impetuous." He told *Newsweek,* "We went green and they beat our brains out." Bogart also said that liberals like himself could no longer "permit ourselves to be used as dupes by Commie organizations."[70]

British commentator Alistair Cooke, an astute observer of Bogart, said the actor "was aghast to discover that several of them [unfriendlies] were down-the-line Communists coolly exploiting the protection of the First and Fifth Amendments to the Constitution."[71] The actor wanted to be viewed as a straight-shooter, speaking the truth candidly, even when it hurt. He had expected the same from his Hollywood associates. Instead, he had been duped, as had other actors, such as John Garfield ("I'm a sucker for a left hook").

All over the world, the press took potshots at Bogie: "Was Bogart's Face Red?" ran the headline in London's *News Chronicle*.[72] "Don't try to fox me again," columnist George Sokolsky warned Bogart in an open letter in the *New York Sun*.[73]

Communists and even some liberals lined up to blast Bogart for daring to say he had been duped.[74] Bogie was no longer a friend. Being on the side of anti-Communism, he was a mortal enemy. As Bogart's son, Stephen, later recalled, some of Bogie's liberal friends "felt that he was copping out, just trying to protect his career."[75] And his liberal friends were kind compared to his Communist "friends." Communist screenwriters like Lester Cole, Larry Adler, and Alvah Bessie all slammed Bogart, as did the *Daily Worker*. Adler said Bogie had "caved in in the most demeaning, debasing way." Adler, Cole, and Bessie accused him of (in Bessie's words) "provok[ing] a panic that rapidly destroyed the Committee for the First Amendment itself," since Gene Kelly, Danny Kaye, and others had quickly followed Bogart's lead.[76] "Bogart's about-face," lamented the *Daily Worker*, was a shame, given "all the good things" he had contributed "to the fight for a finer America," until, alas, he "decided to embrace Operation Mass Murder."[77]

Yes, Humphrey Bogart, former good man; now, *mass murderer* of civil liberties. Like Reagan, he had suddenly morphed into a "fascist," "capitalist scum." As F. Scott Fitzgerald had warned, Bogart had become a target for subhuman demonization.

Of course, that is how Communists had always treated their liberal "friends." But at least liberals learned a hard lesson this time.

Well, not all liberals. The *Washington Post* produced a surreal editorial rebuking not the unfriendlies for misleading their liberal friends but Bogart for his apology. "There is no reason for Mr. Bogart to apologize," lectured the *Post*. "Defense of the constitutional rights of fellow citizens is an excellent reason for making a trip to Washington." The editors conceived an exceedingly strange explanation for Bogart's apology: "One can scarcely help suspecting that what led Mr. Bogart to his interesting apologia and his gratuitous avowal that he had no use for Communism was fear of the consequences of being branded a Communist by the Thomas Committee." A patronizing *Post* sniffed: "We are rather sorry for Mr. Bogart. He had nothing at all to be ashamed of until he began to be ashamed."[78]

In the decades since, many liberals have adopted that same line—that Bogart caved in to fears of being labeled a Communist.[79] They are wrong: Bogart's reaction, as Lauren Bacall has repeatedly noted, stemmed from the undeniable fact that he had been sold a false bill of goods by the Reds. He thought the people he was defending were not Communists—but they were. The writers and performers he defended had lied to him, with no concern for his reputation. Bear in mind, too, that Bogart was not summoned to Washington or ordered to testify. He went there voluntarily. This was not the case of "right-wing" anti-Communists striking fear into the hearts of good liberals; rather, it was an example of naïve liberals waking up to the fact that Communists had duped them.

Needless to say, the *Daily Worker* was thrilled to see the *Washington Post*'s editorial. The CPUSA house organ gleefully reported how the *Post* "raked Humphrey Bogart over the coals editorially." The *Daily Worker* quoted the editorial at great length, dedicating seven full paragraphs to the *Post*'s criticisms.[80] The Communists saw that they could still count on liberals, even after everything that had happened.

They could count on liberals for many decades to follow. The torch would be passed to future generations of liberals—journalists at the *Washington Post* and the *New York Times,* professors in college classrooms—to call "HUAC" names, defend the likes of Lawson and Trumbo, and argue that anti-Communist "witch-hunters" had run roughshod over innocent liberals.

As for liberals like Bogart, like Garfield, like Wilder, like Reagan, they had learned their lesson.

Enemies at Home?

One of the Hollywood Ten called to testify before Congress in October 1947 was the director Edward Dmytryk. At the time he was an unfriendly witness, but he, too, would experience an awakening. The reflections he ended up sharing with Congress four years later shed light on the issue at the crux of the debate over domestic Communism, particularly when it became clear that the United States and the Soviet Union were adversaries. The question was whether American Communists, given their pledged loyalties to the USSR, would fight for the Soviet Union against America if the two countries ever went to war.

When Dmytryk testified in 1947, he had sincerely believed that Stalin's Russia and CPUSA wanted peace. But by the time he sat before the House Committee on Un-American Activities in April 1951, his view had changed. "I had never heard, before 1947, anybody say they would refuse to fight for this country in a war against Soviet Russia," Dmytryk told the committee.[81] In the intervening years, however, many developments—including a hot war on the Korean Peninsula and high-profile espionage cases like the Rosenbergs and Alger Hiss—had revealed to him that American Communists' "love of the party" and the USSR took precedence over any love he thought they had for America. He felt that the Communist Party encouraged this treachery as a natural result of its allegiance to the Soviet Union.

Dmytryk should not have been surprised. The party, of course, pledged itself to the Soviet Motherland, and had from the very beginning—since that founding meeting in Chicago in September 1919. As far back as 1944 CPUSA general secretary Earl Browder had frankly admitted his loyalty to the Soviet Union over the United States in testimony before Congress.[82] When Congress looked deeper into the matter, both Democrats and Republicans were mortified by the affirming testimonies they received from some American Communists.[83]

It was a hard lesson that many in Hollywood, including Edward Dmytryk, learned late. And it was an issue that the new Democratic president in Washington would have to confront in a new war—the Cold War.

12

TRASHING TRUMAN:
WORLD COMMUNISM AND THE COLD WAR

W hen Ronald Reagan testified before the House Committee on Un-American Activities in 1947, he and the entire world had been assured of the closing of the Comintern. Moscow had shut down the Comintern in 1943 in order to improve wartime relations with the United States—allegedly, anyway.[1]

In truth, the organization was not really abolished, as scholars such as Harvard's Mark Kramer have shown.[2] Herb Romerstein, who has spent decades examining the ongoing life of the Comintern after 1943, notes that the Comintern "continued to exist in various forms" after its supposed shuttering. As a young Communist, Romerstein learned this firsthand, and he confirmed it in his career as a government investigator and, today, as an archival researcher.

The Soviets continued the Comintern's critical functions. Certain entities like the Comintern radio school never ceased operations. Every country's Communist Party, Romerstein adds, continued to have a representative in Moscow who reported to what was a Comintern-like central structure, and did so both during and after World War II.[3] Romerstein cites the American representative, Maria Reiss,[4] who corresponded with the Comintern well after the war, writing memos to an organization that supposedly did not exist. (In the 1960s, Reiss would pledge her allegiance to Mao's China after the Sino-Soviet split.)[5] Many other such cases could be cited.

More importantly, the Comintern had merely morphed into a new entity: the International Department, which ran under the auspices of the all-powerful

Soviet Central Committee. The International Department would last until the dissolution of the Soviet Union, all along retaining the Comintern's primary function of maintaining relations with Communist parties all over the world and funding those parties wherever and whenever possible, including by providing military aid to Soviet clients in the Third World.[6]

In short, Moscow had not abandoned the objective for which the Comintern was created in the first place: to spread Communism around the globe. That goal was fundamental to Marxism-Leninism and would not change.

Thus, as Romerstein notes, CPUSA remained "under total Soviet control . . . from 1919, when it was formed, to 1989, when the Soviet Union collapsed."[7] The party's top officials were in constant contact with the head of the International Department once the Comintern was disbanded (in name).[8]

Stalin's War

It was Joseph Stalin who announced the closing of the Comintern, but he remained committed to the Soviet mission of spreading Communism worldwide. In fact, he had far greater success in the task than Lenin ever did.[9]

Greedily eyeing post–World War II Eastern Europe, Stalin said: "Whoever occupies the territory also imposes on it his own social system as far as his military can reach."[10] Years later his right-hand man, Molotov, said that his duty had been clear: "I saw my task as minister of foreign affairs as being how to expand the boundaries of our Fatherland. And it seems to me that we and Stalin did not cope badly with this task."[11]

Not badly at all: they got all of Eastern Europe.

Yet Stalin's gaze extended beyond Eastern Europe, a fact not appreciated even today. A recently declassified Soviet document reveals a secret speech that Stalin gave to the Plenum of the Politburo of the Central Committee of the All-Union Communist Party on August 19, 1939, only four days before signing the Hitler-Stalin Pact. The speech explains Stalin's motivation for trusting Hitler in such a pact, a seemingly inexplicable trust.

Stalin began his remarks by declaring, "The dictatorship of a Communist Party may be envisaged only as a result of a great war." He argued that a major war would be good for the USSR because it would help spread global Communism—or, in his words, "world Revolution." If and when a conflict started, he said, it would be "indispensable to prolong the war as long as possible." Stalin asserted:

We have before us a vast field of action to develop the world Revolution. Comrades! It is in the interests of the USSR—the Fatherland of the Workers—that war should break out between the Reich and the Franco-British capitalist bloc. We must do everything so that the war should last as long as possible with the aim of weakening both sides. It is for these reasons that we must give priority to the approval of the conclusion of the pact proposed by Germany, and to work so that this war, which will be declared within a few days, shall last as long as possible. It is therefore necessary to strengthen the work of propaganda in the countries that will have entered the war, so that they shall be ready for the after-war period.[12]

The "after-war period" would be the moment ripe for the "world Revolution."

Think about what this means: This diabolical man saw great advantage in a destructive major war, since the death and devastation would open the doors for "world Revolution." He thus hailed "the pact proposed by Germany," which would soon be known as the Hitler-Stalin Pact, because it would usher in such a prolonged and ruinous war. He was right that war was coming: World War II soon followed.

Four days after this statement, the Soviets and the Nazis signed the pact. One week after the signing, on September 1, 1939, Germany invaded Poland from the West; then, on September 17, the USSR invaded from the East. The nonaggression pact aggressively launched the Second World War, the most devastating war in history, which took the lives of at least fifty million people, and probably many more than that. Stalin got the agony he hoped for when he said he would do everything possible "so that the war should last as long as possible," but not exactly in the way he expected: this deadly war ended up claiming more lives from the USSR than from any other nation—a staggering total of at least twenty million Soviet deaths.

In the same speech Stalin excitedly addressed the possibilities of a "Sovietization of France"—the result of a "defeated France"—and a "Soviet Germany." In both cases, "the Communist revolution will happen inevitably," prophesied Stalin, and the USSR would sweep in to make each country its ally. Even "in the event of a German defeat," the Soviet dictator confidently predicted, "the Sovietization of Germany and the creation of a Communist government will follow inevitably." This would mean, however, that the USSR would need to "come to the aid of our Berlin comrades," because Britain and France would try to prevent the "emergence of a Soviet Germany." "Thus," insisted Stalin, "our task consists in making sure that Germany should be involved in war as long as possible, so that England

and France would be so exhausted that they would no longer be capable of presenting a threat to a Soviet Germany."[13]

The one factor that Stalin left out of his ideal scenario was the United States of America. Once Uncle Sam entered the fray in World War II, victory for the West was assured, and Stalin's dream of a Sovietized France, Germany, and more was foiled—or, at least, his *immediate* dream. The postwar chaos that plagued all of Europe gave Stalin another chance.

There was, however, one man who stood in the way: a rookie American president from a place called Independence, Missouri.

1946–49: Truman's Crash Course on Communism

President Harry Truman, who in April 1945 succeeded the deceased FDR, spent his first few years in the Oval Office getting a sobering education on America's wartime ally—that is, on Uncle Joe. First there had been Stalin's infamous Bolshoi Theater speech of February 9, 1946, which blamed capitalism and the West for starting World War II. This speech—widely covered by the press[14]—was an outrageous rewriting of history, given Stalin's culpability in launching the war. Truman advisers like the distinguished Paul Nitze interpreted the Bolshoi speech as tantamount to a Soviet declaration of World War III.[15]

Bolshoi was such a wake-up call that within days of the speech, a young staff officer named George Kennan submitted his historic Long Telegram, sent from the U.S. embassy in Moscow to the United States. Kennan's analysis would be credited for founding the doctrine of containment. And Winston Churchill, by then a *former* prime minister, headed to the United States, where on March 5, less than a month after the Bolshoi Theater speech, he warned Americans of that "Iron Curtain" closing across the European continent. The speech rattled not only Eleanor Roosevelt but even a green President Truman, not yet the Cold Warrior of history, who quickly distanced himself from the speech.[16]

The Bolshoi Theater speech came in the context of blatant Soviet violations of the Yalta agreement, as Moscow installed puppet governments and refused its promise of free elections throughout Eastern Europe. The USSR was also committing countless war crimes throughout defeated Europe, especially in the eastern portion of Germany, where Red Army soldiers were guilty of an estimated two million rapes. Thousands of the violated women committed suicide, and the abortion rate among impregnated German women shot up to *90 percent*.[17] Bolshoi came exactly one year after Yalta. It was fitting: one giant lie followed by another giant lie.

Meanwhile, all of postwar Europe was starving, mired in its most acute condition in centuries, compounded by droughts and blizzards. Some sixty million men were out of work, and projections held that a hundred million people would go hungry. By 1947 the United States was devising a plan to aid the recovery of all of Europe, Western and Eastern. Secretary of State George C. Marshall and President Truman saw the relief as humanitarian but also political, with the aim of trying to stop the whole continent from falling into the Communist camp.

The Marshall Plan, as it became known, was announced in June, and all European nations were invited to apply for aid. From East to West, there was tremendous appreciation for this act of American generosity. Upon the announcement of aid, Britain's Ernest Bevin cheered, "We grabbed the lifeline with both hands." Even Czechoslovakia's parliament, marked by a strong Communist presence, voted to apply for the much-needed aid.

But others were not quite so happy.

Secretary of State Marshall was stunned when he learned during a trip to Moscow that Stalin and the Soviets were totally opposed to any Marshall Plan aid for anyone, especially for Germany. The USSR delivered this message to the entire world when Foreign Minister Molotov, on orders from Stalin, stormed out of the Paris summit, where desperate nations met to discuss the full scope of assistance they needed. The Soviets denounced the Marshall Plan, which would provide desperately needed aid to a ravaged continent, as an example of American "belligerence," "aggression," and "imperialism."

The jaw-dropping Soviet response made it obvious to Marshall and Truman that the Soviets wanted all of Europe prostrate, to make possible the rise of Communist governments across the continent—just as Stalin had hoped and predicted in his August 1939 Central Committee speech. Stalin's dreams for Western Europe were on the verge of coming true, especially in vulnerable countries like Germany, Italy, and possibly France—on top of the gains already seized in Central and Eastern Europe. Only American aid stood in the way.

In March 1947, three months before the unveiling of the Marshall Plan, President Truman had announced a major military and economic aid package to Turkey and Greece. In doing so he had laid out what became known as the Truman Doctrine, as he declared, "It must be the policy of the United States to support free peoples who are resisting attempted subjugation by armed minorities or by outside pressures." Truman called the Truman Doctrine and Marshall Plan "two halves of the same walnut"; both were part humanitarian aid and part Soviet containment.[18] Together, they gave the Soviets much to complain about.

Opposing the Marshall Plan and any other form of American aid, the Soviet Union began a major propaganda push. The Kremlin and the Comintern—or, more specifically, the Comintern's successor organization—delivered orders to Communists around the world to repeat the line about American belligerence. It would be a hard sell, even to the most loyal comrades.

Stalin stepped up the resistance with aggressive action. In June 1948 the Red Army blocked all road and rail routes into Berlin (West and East). The Berlin Blockade was a brazen, bellicose act—a clear violation of Yalta.

Some U.S. military advisers suggested ramming through the Soviet blockade. President Truman rebuffed their advice and instead responded in the most nonaggressive way that he could: he ordered an unprecedented airlift of food, fuel, and medicine to the people trapped behind the blockade. The Berlin Airlift lasted into May 1949.

As for Czechoslovakia, which wanted Marshall Plan aid, a seething Stalin summoned its leaders to Moscow and ordered them to refuse the action of the parliament and reject Marshall Plan aid. Jan Masaryk, the son of the founder of the modern Czech state, lamented on the plane home that he had left Prague a free man and returned a slave to Stalin. Czechoslovakia's fate was sealed: a Communist coup followed, and by February 1948, the Red flag was flying over Prague. (Amid the tumult, Masaryk died in a "suicide" leap from his window, long suspected as murder.) With the the fall of Czechoslovakia, the isolationist Republican Congress finally began cutting checks for Marshall Plan aid.

In no time, the two sides were starkly divided. Two adversarial military alliances emerged: NATO (the North Atlantic Treaty Organization) in the West, and the Warsaw Pact in the East.

The Cold War was on.

Franklin Roosevelt had left Harry Truman in the dark on vital matters relating to Soviet Communism. The lack of crucial details left Truman confused about FDR's discussions with Stalin, and bewildered by Roosevelt's trust in Stalin. FDR's erstwhile chum, however, cleared up that confusion soon enough; "UJ" provided the new president a crash course in reality.

The Demonization of Harry Truman

There was no doubt in the mind of any fair, rational observer that the Soviets were starting the Cold War. Among the only skeptics were the irrepressibly naïve and those posing as doubters—that is, those with hidden agendas in support of

Moscow. This included American Communists, who parroted the Soviet line expressed in official statements and in publications like *Pravda* and *Izvestia*. And the chief audience for those American Communists was American liberals.

As the Communists set out to dupe liberals/progressives, the main target of Moscow's vicious propaganda campaign was not conservative Republicans. Rather, it was a Democrat—President Harry Truman. This is a crucial point that many modern Democrats and liberals have missed in their ardent anti-anti-Communism.

Lieutenant General Ion Mihai Pacepa, the highest-ranking intelligence official to defect from the Soviet bloc (he is still alive, and now a U.S. citizen), described in shocking candor the Soviets' campaign to demonize Truman around the world:

> The communist effort to generate hatred for the American president began soon after President Truman set up NATO and propelled the three Western occupation forces to unite their zones to form a West German nation. We were tasked to take advantage of the reawakened patriotic feelings stirring in the European countries that had been subjugated by the Nazis, in order to shift their hatred for Hitler over into hatred for Truman—the leader of the new "occupation power." Western Europe was still grateful to the U.S. for having restored its freedom, but it had strong leftist movements that we secretly financed. They were like putty in our hands.[19]

Unlike Western liberals—"putty in our hands"—Pacepa lived Communism and thus could not be fooled into some fantasy world. He grew up in Romania, stuck in the new Soviet Communist bloc. He and his family were among those "Captive Peoples" that later presidents such as Dwight Eisenhower and Ronald Reagan would describe, to the snickers of the American Left. Pacepa's father had a picture of Harry Truman, the face of freedom, hanging in their home in Bucharest. That was truth. But as an adult, needing to make a living in awful circumstances, Pacepa did not tell that truth; finding employment in Romanian intelligence, he helped spin the Soviets' web of lies.

In the West, the Left, said Pacepa, "needed a tangible enemy, and we gave them one. In no time they began beating their drums decrying President Truman as the 'butcher of Hiroshima.'" Pacepa and the Communist intelligence agencies would spend "many years and many billions disparaging subsequent presidents."

The Communists, in Moscow and in America, vilified President Truman in ways that made the most Red-baiting Republican look like a Truman campaign worker by comparison. The Communist criticism of Truman was brutal, blaming the man from Independence for everything from starting the Cold War to seeking World War III to looking to establish a racist-fascist state that sought an imperial-colonial empire.

One of the top functionaries in the American Communist Party, Philip Frankfeld, who headed the party in Maryland, disseminated a pamphlet urging his comrades to view Harry Truman as their primary enemy. "Truman is in the driver's seat," warned Frankfeld. "Truman determines both foreign and domestic policies." Frankfeld pressed the American party to "direct its main blows against Trumanism as the main enemy of the American people today."[20]

In their pamphlets and publications, American Communists attacked every Truman policy at odds with Stalin policy, from the "Truman-Marshall Plan" to the U.S. resistance of Communism on the Korean Peninsula. CPUSA head William Z. Foster dubbed Truman a "militant imperialist," and the *Daily Worker* urged comrades everywhere to see that "the center of the reactionary forces in the world today rests in the United States." Communists accused Truman of a form of "American fascism," of being a "warmonger," of being "another Hitler," of employing "Hitlerite tactics." Of course, they had once said such things about FDR—until he sided with Stalin during the war. Now they hailed Roosevelt, at least in contrast to Truman, whom they accused of betraying his predecessor. The comrades assailed Truman for his "abandonment of the policies of Franklin Roosevelt."[21]

And they searched diligently for dupes. As noted, in Hollywood, "liberals" like Dalton Trumbo wrote rally speeches for stars like Katharine Hepburn and Olivia de Havilland. De Havilland adamantly rejected Trumbo's June 1946 Seattle text because it had compared the United States to the Third Reich, blamed the Truman administration for all sorts of racial bigotries, and accused "certain interests" of pursuing a "drive toward war against the Soviet Union."[22] In the mind of the Communists—or, more pointedly, in their propaganda—those "interests" were Harry Truman's.

Communists also set up front groups wherever they could. In Los Angeles and Washington, the comrades created the benignly named Korean Culture Society, as well as the Korean Independent News Company, to protest American policy in Korea, where U.S. troops were engaged in a life-and-death struggle against the forces of global Communism. Both of these groups, cited as Communist fronts by the California Senate, not only opposed U.S. policy but also created pressure for a recall of U.S. troops from South Korea.[23] Pro–Red China organizations popped up as well, including American Friends of the Chinese People (and its official organ, *China Today*), later cited as a Communist front by the House Committee on Un-American Activities.[24]

Ultimately, a large group of disaffected liberals coalesced in the 1948 Progressive Party, which supported the presidential candidacy not of Democrat Harry Truman but of former vice president Henry Wallace, who was wildly pro-Soviet. As one scholar notes, the new party saw itself as "the inevitable outgrowth of liberals' profound disillusionment with the Truman administration and the only vehicle available for 'progressives' to combat the rightward drift of the nation's politics."[25]

The Soviets and their supporters around the world conducted slanderous campaigns against Truman and his administration, with the explicit intent of serving the expansionary aims of Soviet Communism. And it could succeed only by duping non-Communists from the Left into believing the lie.

A Peek Behind the Iron Curtain

The Communists faced one recurring challenge to their duping efforts: occasionally the truth about Soviet Communism trickled out. As successful as the Soviets were with Potemkin villages and agitprop, the ugly truth could not be repressed entirely. Revelations of the Stalin regime's brutal tactics had changed the minds of John Dewey and other dupes; the Communist movement's abrupt flip-flop on Hitler's Germany had awoken some party members and Communist sympathizers; the ample evidence that supposedly innocent Hollywood figures were, in fact, Communists had led Humphrey Bogart to see that he and his colleagues had been "used as dupes by Commie organizations."

Still more evidence came out—to the anger of the Communists—in the form of eyewitness testimony from a former top CPUSA figure, Ben Gitlow. Gitlow had twice run as the Communist Party's candidate for vice president of the United States (1924 and 1928) and had served on the Executive Committee of the Comintern. In 1948, as the Cold War intensified, he drew attention by publishing a major book reflecting what he had seen during his years in the party, *The Whole of Their Lives: Communism in America.*

This was actually the second book Gitlow had written, the first having been published in 1940—his autobiography, *I Confess: The Truth about American Communism.*[26] Even before that, in 1939, he had been called to testify before Congress, where he broke a long silence after leaving the Communist Party in 1929. In his testimony and writings Gitlow laid out a litany of disturbing facts on CPUSA's relationship with Moscow. For example, he bore witness to party members' "fanatical zeal" for the Soviet Union and their support for the USSR's "ultimate victory over the capitalist world."[27] He also revealed details about Soviet espionage and how the

Comintern funded the American party—sending, Gitlow said, between $100,000 and $150,000 *annually,* another $35,000 to launch the *Daily Worker* in 1924, and tens of thousands of dollars to American union bosses.

For blowing the whistle, Gitlow earned the enmity of the Comintern and its American hacks. In an October 1939 confidential memo to the Executive Committee of the Comintern, Pat Toohey, CPUSA's representative in Moscow, wrote a summary of Gitlow's congressional testimony and denounced Gitlow to his Soviet comrades as a "stool-pigeon and provocateur."[28] (See page 241.)

Toohey concluded his report by reassuring his bosses in Moscow that Gitlow's revelations would do little to harm the international Communist propaganda effort. He pointed out that "the anti-Soviet and reactionary forces" were trying to use testimony such as Gitlow's "as a shield behind which they are striving to draw the USA into the imperialist war." But, Toohey said confidently, "The ranks of the Party are apparently holding firm. . . . The membership is responding fine. With the exception of three desertions (two writers, one lower trade union functionary) the enemies of the Party can find no members to denounce the Party."

Of course, the Communists needed more than the party to hold firm; they also needed their dupes to continue naïvely supporting the Marxist-Leninist cause.

A Tutorial from Professor Schlesinger

Once again, however, it must be stressed that not all liberals were duped by the Communists. And among Cold War liberals, few did better early work warning their brethren about Soviet Communism than Arthur M. Schlesinger Jr., the later John F. Kennedy/"Camelot" court composer, longtime Harvard professor, partisan Democrat, liberal's liberal, and son of the esteemed—and earlier mentioned—Harvard historian Arthur M. Schlesinger Sr.

Early in the Truman years, the junior Schlesinger endeavored to educate those who disputed the fact that Lenin and Stalin saw the United States, as leader of the capitalist world, as unappeasably hostile—as a country with which conflict was inevitable. In his writing, the professor instructed Americans that this Leninist logic had always prevailed among the Soviets, and would continue to do so into the postwar world, regardless of what America's president did or failed to do. In fact, according to Schlesinger, nothing the United States could have done in 1944–45 in particular "would have abolished this mistrust, required and sanctified as it was by Marxist gospel—nothing short of the conversion of the United States into a Stalinist despotism."[29]

- 3 -

for the USA and the world. He fully explained the position of
the CP USA on immediate questions, on questions of Marxian
theory, Communist program and aims, on the struggle against war,
for Socialism, and thoroughly unmasked Trotskyism, whose agents
are aiding the Dies Committee.

In answer to the testimony of Comrade Browder, the Dies
Committee brougnt in Ben Gitlow, the expelled Lovestoneite, who
was held up as "former national secretary of the CP, former
vice-presidential candidate", etc. Gitlow performed the role
of stool-pigeon and provocateur. The gist of his "testimony",
upon which the Dies Committee declares it has the necessary
proof to destroy the CP USA, is as follows:

Gitlow declared that from 1922-1929 the CI sent to the CP
USA $100,000 to $150,000 yearly, that at times it came in forms
of "diamonds" and jewelry when valuta was unavailable; that
such money continues to come; that he has "documentary evidence".

2. That the CI sent $35,000 to start the Daily Worker in
1924 and an equal amount every year afterwards; that he, himself, received money in Berlin to bring to the USA.

3. That the CI sent $50,000 to finance the campaign of
Brophy (now director of the CIO) who was opposing Lewis for
Miners' Union Presidency in 1927; that the CI sent money to
finance two big farmer-labour conventions in 1924 and 1925.
(Brophy issued an indignant denial.)

Gitlow the "stool-pigeon and provocateur": In this excerpt from a confidential 1939 memo to the Comintern, CPUSA representative Pat Toohey denounces the congressional testimony of former party official Ben Gitlow.

Schlesinger's most trenchant, widely read admonition to this effect was his excellent July 1946 piece for *Life* magazine.[30] At that point, he was in his first year as an associate professor of history at Harvard.

"For better or for worse," the article began, "the Communist Party of the U.S. is here to stay." CPUSA, Schlesinger said, pointing to its headquarters on Twelfth Street in New York City, "controls an active and disciplined following through the country. . . . Communists are working overtime to expand party influence."

To describe this unique threat, the professor used religious metaphors, as he commonly did in his writings on the USSR.[31] The party's appeal, he said, "is essentially the appeal of a religious sect—small, persecuted, dedicated, stubbornly convinced that it alone knows the path to salvation." To understand the Communists, he explained, one must think of them in terms "not of a normal political party, but in terms of the Jesuits, the Mormons or Jehovah's Witnesses."

Once the Communist was fully committed, his "world becomes totally the world of the party." Baptized into the faith, Communists voluntarily cut off nonparty friendships and activities. One CPUSA acolyte quoted by Schlesinger, explaining why he made the party the beneficiary of his insurance policy, said, "The reason I did that was, in the first place, I am not married and have nobody to leave anything like that to, and in the second place the Communist Party is more in the world to me than anything else." This total assimilation of the individual to the party, said Schlesinger, brings "consecration." Like members of a "religious order," CPUSA members "become so involved socially and psychologically that the threat of expulsion strikes them as excommunication would a devout Catholic. It is enough to keep them in line long after they begin to develop intellectual doubts about the infallibility of Russia."

The professor also wrote that members of the Communist Party in America served as "the unquestioning servants of the Soviet Union." CPUSA, Schlesinger noted, was for a long time billed as the American section of the Communist International, and he pointed out that it "has always received directives and in the past some funds from the U.S.S.R. via courier."

Schlesinger's arguments were entirely correct, but it was stunning to see such claims coming from a liberal Harvard professor in perhaps America's leading mainstream news magazine, *Life*. The allegation that CPUSA received not only marching orders from the USSR but also money—100 percent accurate, as we now know—was the kind of charge that many liberals ascribed to reactionary right-wingers, to "dumb" anti-Communists. In fact, Schlesinger was showing himself to be very well-informed, down to the details.

The party's activities, the professor contended, "will be turned on and off as the interests of an external power dictate." Schlesinger wrote that American Communists' goals were Moscow's goals: "In its own eyes the party has two main commitments: to support and advance the U.S.S.R., and to promote the establishment of socialism in the U.S. The second is necessarily subordinate to the first because Communists regard the preservation of the workers' state in Russia as indispensable to the spread of socialism through the world."

From the start, wrote Schlesinger, the party's operations were "conspiratorial, its activities largely clandestine." The Harvard professor added that the Communist Party felt "justified in using any methods to advance the cause." Here Schlesinger noted that the testimony of Harold Laski was especially telling, "since Communists can hardly write him off as a red-baiter or reactionary." Quite right: recall that Laski was one of those "liberal" academics listed with the senior Schlesinger in the 1920 Communist Party document cited in Chapter 3. Laski said: "The Communist parties outside Russia act without moral scruples, intrigue without any sense of shame, are utterly careless of truth, sacrifice without any hesitation. . . . The result is a corruption, both of the mind and of the heart, which is alike contemptuous of reason and careless of truth." These Communists, said Schlesinger, would substitute "any external standard for the truth." Indeed, they were sneaky liars: "The Communists spread their infection of intrigue and deceit wherever they go."

Schlesinger noted that the party worked through both secret members and fellow travelers, and that underground cells operating under party direction had become active in Washington in the 1930s. The professor then dropped a bombshell: some of these surreptitious party members "name several congressmen as reliable from the party point of view." More so, he added, "well-known Communist sympathizers are on the staffs of some senators and congressional committees."

This was quite a charge, at multiple levels. The liberal Ivy League historian's (accurate) portrayal of Communist penetration in Washington was precisely what the much-vilified Senator Joe McCarthy later alleged.

"The great present field of Communist penetration is the trade unions," added Schlesinger. The party had made "particular headway" among Hollywood intellectuals, "who find in the new faith a means of resolving their own frustration and guilt." "Second only to the unions," he added, "is the drive to organize the Negroes," with CPUSA busy "sinking tentacles into the National Association for the Advancement of Colored People."

Professor Schlesinger identified another Communist objective: the party sought to infiltrate "groups of liberals organized for some benevolent purpose, and because of the innocence, laziness and stupidity of most of the membership, perfectly designed for control by an alert minority."

These liberals were, of course, the dupes. In Schlesinger's description, they were not only naïve but also "lazy" and "stupid."

As that characterization suggests, Schlesinger was deeply troubled by what Communists were doing to unsuspecting dupes among his fellow liberals. He warned that it was to the American Left that Communism presented "the most serious danger." The methods of American Communists "are irreconcilable with honest cooperation, as anyone who has tried to work with them has found out the hard way. Communists have succeeded in hiding their true face from American liberals." These covert Red troops were engaged in a "massive attack on the moral fabric of the American left."

Dr. Arthur M. Schlesinger Jr. got it right. Unfortunately, many of his colleagues in the academy, and in the broader American Left, failed to heed his warnings. In the coming years, in fact, they would dismiss or attack anyone who made such claims. The Communists, therefore, continued to make victims of American liberals. The duping went on.

Duped No More: Paul H. Douglas Gets Religion

Another professor and partisan liberal Democrat who refused to be duped in this period was Paul H. Douglas. He, too, had been listed in that 1920 letter targeting "liberal" professors, along with the senior Schlesinger and Harold Laski.

By the time the Cold War started, it had been twenty years since Douglas made his Potemkin Progressive tour of the Soviet Motherland in July 1927. Of all those progressives who had been enchanted during that Soviet tour and their six-hour wine-and-dine session with Stalin, Douglas was perhaps the most ambivalent. His initial impressions were not those of a Corliss Lamont. And in the intervening years, he had headed more in the direction of William Bullitt and John Dewey.

What happened?

At first Douglas actually headed farther to the left. His experience in academia, as a professor at the University of Chicago, radicalized him. By 1932, five years after his sojourn to the Soviet Union, Douglas had found even FDR too conservative for his tastes. He cast his presidential ballot that year for the Socialist Party candidate, Norman Thomas.

Slowly but surely, though, Douglas gravitated to Roosevelt and the New Deal. As he moved closer to the center (though he would always be on the left), he found reasons to question the esteem in which FDR and other liberals held

Stalin. (His wife, Dorothy Wolff, remained to the far left; the couple ended up divorcing.)[32] Douglas was becoming an anti-Communist liberal Democrat, much like Arthur Schlesinger Jr.

The experience of combat seems to have jolted Douglas. In 1942 the fifty-year-old academic came out from behind his desk and enlisted in the Marines as a private, eager to serve his country in World War II. The professor became a war hero, twice earning the Purple Heart in the Pacific theater, including at the Battle of Okinawa. The labor economist was shot and grazed by shrapnel as he carried a flamethrower to the frontlines and uncovered and ignited Japanese enemy caves.

Douglas survived to emerge a staunch defender of America in the global war that followed the fight against Nazism: the Cold War. By 1947, he was an advocate of President Truman's containment policy, to the point that in 1950 he supported American military intervention in the Korean Peninsula to halt the spread of Communism in Asia. He was deeply concerned with the fall of China to Mao in 1949 and now even second-guessed U.S. recognition of the USSR, which he and his progressive comrades had lobbied for two decades earlier.

By 1948, Dr. Douglas set aside his lecture notes and made a bid for the U.S. Senate, running as a Democrat in the state of Illinois. He won. He was sworn into office in January 1949, with his new wife, Emily Taft Douglas—a soul mate of more sensible politics—at his side.

America would soon hear much more from Paul H. Douglas. This was a very different man from the one who had traversed Potemkin villages in 1927. Here was a liberal who desired to be duped no more.

Misplaced Loyalties

The Cold War was in full force. While liberals' loyalties lay with their president, Communists' loyalties lay with their dictator. Thus America's Communists saw no choice but to undermine Harry Truman; after all, the Democratic president was trying to counter the Soviet Union—their true motherland.

Truman's case offers this book's repeated reminder: To this day, many liberals do not understand that Communists were not their friends. The Communists used them, and viewed them as gullible, even stupid, and often deserving of contempt for their naïveté—a level of naïveté that never ceased to amaze the KGB.

In short order, America's comrades, with the handy enlistment of their dupes, would be taking to the streets and their typewriters to take down Harry Truman. Among them was a fellow named Frank Marshall Davis.

13

DREAMS FROM FRANK MARSHALL DAVIS

By 1949 the Cold War was raging, as Joseph Stalin's broken promises at Yalta fell like dominoes throughout Eastern Europe. It was obvious to any reasonable American, Democrat or Republican, that the Soviets had started the Cold War. But the Communists did diligent propaganda work blaming America, and hoping to win dupes to their side. They flawlessly followed the pattern described by the KGB's General Pacepa.

An excellent illustration of this process was Frank Marshall Davis, who in 1949 began writing a regular column—"Frank-ly Speaking"—for the Communist organ of Hawaii, the *Honolulu Record*. Raised in Kansas and Chicago, Davis moved to Hawaii in the late 1940s. He is a fascinating case to consider, given that his success depended on dupes. Even today he can count on dupes to cover for him, to ridicule his anti-Communist detractors as the equivalent of UFO conspiracy nuts, because he had a profound effect on the American politician who represents the hopes and aspirations of Democrats, who came out of nowhere to become the political phenomenon of our time: President Barack Obama.

As we move through this book's chronology, I will show where and when Davis and Obama forged their relationship. I will also show how liberals have grown more defensive about charges that Davis was a Communist, since they want to ensure that Obama is not publicly linked with a pro-Soviet Marxist mentor. As this chapter will show, it was clear by 1949–50 that Davis, if he was not a member of CPUSA, was at least a small "c" communist and was wildly pro-Soviet.

And if somehow, despite all those indications, Davis was not a communist, he was flatly the single greatest dupe in this book.

Enter Hawaii

The stage for this drama, this rendezvous with history, was Hawaii.

Off the beaten path of established Cold War history was the Soviet interest in Hawaii before the territory became part of the United States (it didn't become a state until 1959). Moscow did its best to keep this ambition under wraps, as did CPUSA, which aided and abetted Stalin in the endeavor.

On February 17, 1935, the Anglo-American Secretariat of the Comintern held a meeting in Moscow on the "Hawaiian Question." (The briefing on this meeting is another document with us today thanks to the archival digging of Herb Romerstein.)[1] Among the seventeen attendees at the meeting, the two most important players were "I. Mingulin," the head of the Anglo-American Secretariat, and William Schneiderman, alias "Sherman," an American agent of the NKVD, the predecessor to the KGB. Schneiderman was the CPUSA's representative in Moscow; his job was to pass information between the two sides, delivering marching orders from the Soviet Communist Party to the American Communist Party.[2] At the meeting, Mingulin conveyed the Comintern's order that a Communist Party apparatus be set up in Hawaii. Schneiderman was to draft the message to CPUSA on the Hawaiian question, which he did that day.[3] Later he would be made head of the Communist Party of California, the closest American port of interest to the Hawaiian theater of operations.

Hawaii landed on the Soviets' radar because the islands were becoming increasingly significant to U.S. foreign policy. The Soviet aim in Hawaii was as anti-American as imaginable. This is immediately apparent in a follow-up document, dated July 7, 1935, titled simply "Letter to the CPUSA on Hawaii," and written by Comintern officials.[4] The document shows how Communists saw the world upside down: Though Hawaiians had already made attempts to become part of the United States of America, and would eventually get statehood, the Communist letter opened by arguing that the alleged "growing discontent of the masses of the population in the Hawaiian Islands" was the result of "the regime of colonial oppression and the exploitation of American imperialism with its policy of militarisation of the Hawaiian Islands."[5]

The Communists had already used this charge of "imperialism" and "exploitation" in China in the 1920s, and it would become a Communist battle cry throughout the Cold War, from Cuba to Vietnam to El Salvador and beyond. They continually used the refrain, and non-Communist liberals could always be counted on to join the chorus.

To take advantage of the alleged discontent among the Hawaiian masses, Comintern officials said it was "essential" that American Communists "give every possible assistance to the development of the mass revolutionary movement in Hawaii, so that the foundations will be laid for the formation of a Communist Party as the leader of the emancipation movement in Hawaii." True emancipation of Hawaii, in their eyes, would be a Communist Hawaii, one that was a satellite in the Soviet orbit, and that would serve as a strategic base for the further spread of Marxism-Leninism into Asia.

To get there, the Comintern said the American Communist Party should "raise the slogan of 'Right of Self-determination of the Peoples of Hawaii, up to the Point of Separation.'" Communists were direly needed in Hawaii to advance specific Soviet policy goals, including "the withdrawal of the U.S. armed forces" from the islands. Among the "political slogans" of the "Hawaiian revolutionary movement," ordered the Comintern, should be an exhortation to join the "struggle against the yoke of American imperialism."[6]

Any student of Soviet history understands the tactic of sloganeering within Communist propaganda. The Communists excelled at boiling down their goals into a sheet of carefully articulated talking points that became the consistent party line at home and around the world. It is remarkable to observe their discipline *worldwide* in sticking to the script. It was impressive, achieved only because of that religious-like loyalty by the Marxist faithful.

As to the situation in Hawaii, any student of World War II understands that the U.S. forces cited in these documents were vital to the security of the United States, as the Japanese would make painfully clear at Pearl Harbor on December 7, 1941. To the Comintern, however, the presence of U.S. forces in Hawaii represented an obstacle to the Soviets' expansion of Communism into Asia and throughout the world—an obstacle to, as this Comintern decision-brief put it, the Communists' "revolutionary tasks in Hawaii."

Mingulin and Schneiderman strategized on the need to get Communists onto the islands to agitate against the various positions of the U.S. government and to promote the Soviet line wherever and whenever they could. This goal remains so explosive—so utterly contrary to American interests—that portions of the Comintern archives on this subject have been reclosed. American researchers—specifically, Romerstein—were able to obtain copies of some of this correspondence in Moscow during the brief period when the window was open.

The briefing document on the February 17, 1935, meeting finishes with this plan of action: "Responsible for Commission: Com. Sherman." This meant that Comrade Sherman—that is, William Schneiderman—would be in the field gathering recruits.[7]

With that, the process was under way. Though the momentum was sidetracked because of World War II, it would pick up in the late 1940s, as the Cold War took flight.

Enter Frank Marshall Davis

Among those who suddenly appeared in Hawaii in (apparent) service to the Soviets' objective was a transplant named Frank Marshall Davis. Davis had served as executive editor, columnist, and member of the board of directors for the *Chicago Star,* the Communist outlet of Chicago, known to locals as the *"Red" Star.*[8] There he shared the spotlight with a number of notable Reds, including Hollywood's Howard Fast, the illustrious Stalin Peace Prize winner defended by Arthur Miller, and even a rare contributing U.S. senator, Claude "Red" Pepper.[9]

Since the founding of the American Communist Party there in 1919, Chicago had remained a hotbed of Marxism. Davis was affiliated with several front groups there: the Abraham Lincoln School, American Youth for Democracy, the Chicago Committee for Spanish Freedom, the Civil Rights Congress, the League of American Writers, and the National Negro Congress.[10] While he was quiet about those affiliations, he was unrestrained in his admiration of the USSR, constantly hailing its achievements. For example, Davis, who was black, praised Stalin's alleged racial miracle: of all the nations in the world, he explained in the *Star,* it was "only the Soviet Union which has abolished racism and color prejudice."[11]

Davis was very active in Chicago, helping local Communist Party cadres with all kinds of causes and campaigns, many of which at first glance seemed nonpolitical. He often participated in initiatives to help various workers' groups, such as the Citizens' Committee to Aid Packing-House Workers, where he served as a committee member with Vernon Jarrett. (See page 250).[12] Jarrett would become a longtime popular media voice in Chicago, and father-in-law to Valerie Jarrett, who today is a close senior adviser to President Barack Obama.[13]

But Davis also got involved in explicitly political issues. He agitated against U.S. involvement in World War II and rejected aiding Britain against Germany— the party line of the American Peace Mobilization. He urged that "Negroes" resist "the wave of war hysteria." And he helped organize the crucial early American

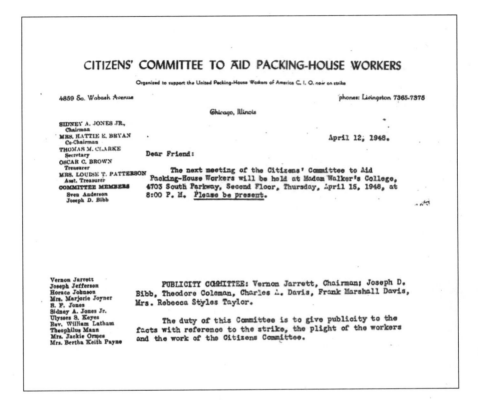

Davis and Jarrett: Frank Marshall Davis served on the Citizens' Committee to Aid Packing-House Workers alongside left-wing journalist Vernon Jarrett, who became the father-in-law of Valerie Jarrett, now a close adviser to President Obama.

Communist front: Davis formally endorsed the crucial November 1940 conference held in Chicago by the American Peace Mobilization, which was later exposed as a Communist front.

Peace Mobilization conference in Chicago in November 1940, where his name appeared on the letterhead as an endorser.[14] (See page 251). Of course, that was all prior to the Nazi invasion of the USSR in June 1941. Consistent with the American Communist movement, he flipped on the war once Hitler invaded the Soviet Union, suddenly morphing from dove to hawk.

Though Davis always sought to conceal his Communist affiliations, his writing for the *Star* was transparently sympathetic to the Bolshevik worldview, to Stalin, to the Soviet Union, and to American Communists. He gushed about his dear friend Paul Robeson, the most famous African-American Marxist, and proud recipient of the Stalin Peace Prize (1952).[15] Davis later conceded that it was at the "suggestion" of Robeson that he moved to Hawaii.[16]

And so in 1948 Davis just happened to arrive in Hawaii at the same time that leaders of the Communist Party in Hawaii—realizing the limits of national party organs like the *Daily Worker* and *People's Daily World*—established a weekly newspaper, the *Honolulu Record*. We now know (here again, thanks to Romerstein's archival research) that a resolution approving this idea was adopted at the "Territorial convention" of the Communist Party of Hawaii, held at Hauulu and Kuliouou Beach in April 1948. Playing a central role in that confab was the Communist-controlled International Longshoremen's and Warehousemen's Union (ILWU). Jack H. Kawano, a member of the executive board of the Communist Party of Hawaii, later testified: "The Party instructed its members to get the ILWU behind the *Honolulu Record,* and urge the union to buy subscriptions and ads. Every cell of the Communist Party was instructed to designate someone to handle the ads and subscriptions in the union for both the *People's World* and the *Honolulu Record.*"[17]

A key player in this, who needs to be mentioned here because of the frequency in which he would appear in Frank Marshall Davis's columns, was Harry Bridges, who ran the ILWU. The U.S. government repeatedly tried to deport Bridges back to his native Australia because of his alleged work for the global Communist movement. He denied being a member of the Communist Party, and got lots of help from friends and accomplices.

In fact, we now know that Bridges was so high up in CPUSA that he served on the Central Committee of the American Communist Party. Moscow itself approved the appointment: declassified documents in the Comintern archives show that CPUSA in 1938 sent Moscow a list of names of those it wanted on the Central Committee, one of which was identified as "Rossi (Bridges)—CPUSA Central Committee member and president of the Longshoremen's and Warehousemen's Union."[18]

The CIO, the great non-Communist trade union, knew about and reported publicly on Bridges's numerous Communist activities, including his secret meetings with party functionaries. The CIO was not bashful about its findings; one report was titled "Communist Domination of Certain Unions."[19] Perhaps not coincidentally, Frank Marshall Davis attacked the CIO in his columns.

Like CPUSA, Davis railed against the U.S. government's treatment of Harry Bridges, screeching that tyrants were illegally pursuing an innocent man. Bridges, portrayed as a yet another victim of anti-Communist hysteria, became a campaign issue for the Reds, a very useful one that enlisted the support of more than a few dupes.

Of course, Davis very likely knew the truth about Bridges, in which case he fibbed repeatedly in order to help serve Bridges's masters in Moscow. If he did not know the truth, then he was duped by his own comrades. There is surely no question that Davis's buddy Paul Robeson understood the real story about Bridges. Everyone in political circles in Hawaii knew the powerful ILWU and suspected that it was a Communist instrument.

Years later, in his autobiography, Davis wrote about Bridges and the circumstances under which he came to Hawaii in 1948. "I had also talked with Paul Robeson," wrote Davis, "who the previous year had appeared there [Hawaii] in a series of concerts sponsored by the International Longshoremen's and Warehousemen's Union (ILWU), the most powerful labor organization in the territory. Paul enthusiastically supported our pending trip and told me how much he wanted to return to that delightful place. I also wrote to Harry Bridges, head of the ILWU, whom I had met at Lincoln School. He suggested I get in touch with Koji Ariyoshi, editor of the *Honolulu Record,* a newspaper that was generally similar to the *Chicago Star.*"[20]

In that single paragraph Davis mentioned: (1) three prominent figures who were secret Communist Party members—Paul Robeson, Harry Bridges, and Koji Ariyoshi, all of whom operated under deceit and denial; (2) the Lincoln School, which was a Communist front that operated under deceit and denial; and (3) the "generally similar" *Honolulu Record* and *Chicago Star,* both party and/or party-line publications that operated under deceit and denial.[21]

Such deceit and denial was also standard policy of the Hawaii Communist Party. In 1947, a year before Davis's arrival, Ichiro Izuka, a Hawaii-born Japanese-American ex-Communist, warned his fellow islanders of this "conspiratorial Party, working against the welfare of the people of my native islands." Izuka emphasized how the party thrived on lies, deception, "hate [as] a weapon," "libel," and character assassination.[22]

"Yelping Stalinists and Their Dupes"

Soon after Frank Marshall Davis appeared in Hawaii, members of the local branch of the NAACP grew weary of him. Some NAACP members called him "Comrade Davis" and were irritated at how he "sneaked" into their meetings "with the avowed intent and purpose of converting it into a front for the Stalinist line."

Non-Communist liberals like Edward Berman, a local civil-rights activist who supported the Hawaii branch of the NAACP, and Roy Wilkins, of the national branch of the NAACP, understood that the likes of Davis were not their allies. Berman recalled how he was at a meeting when "one Frank Marshall Davis, formerly of Chicago (and formerly editor of the Chicago Communist paper, the *Star*), suddenly appeared on the scene to propagandize the membership about our 'racial problems' in Hawaii. He had just sneaked in here on a boat, and presto, was an 'expert' on racial problems in Hawaii."[23]

Berman, a Caucasian, wrote to Wilkins, emphasizing the racial unity and harmony on Hawaii: "There is no segregation here." He knew right away that Davis and others had come to agitate, to "create a mythical racial problem here." Such were "their tactics."[24] Indeed, the Communist goal was to create a facade of problems that could be blamed on American imperialism.

Berman warned Wilkins that the "influx of this element"—meaning "Communists" like Davis who had voyaged from the mainland—had "frightened away . . . scores of Negro members." Fearing that the Communists were out to "destroy the local branch of the NAACP," he said, "Only by a reorganization with a policy that will check this infiltration, can we hope to get former members back into a local NAACP branch."[25] Berman had already seen precisely this sort of Communist infiltration happen to an organization close to his heart, the Hawaiian Association for Civil Unity, and saw it unfolding again with the local branch of the NAACP.

Berman was deeply troubled by how Stalinists—he included Davis in this group—duped liberals into the Soviet line: "We are going to have to have the authority over here—otherwise you'll have a branch exclusively composed of yelping Stalinists and their dupes—characters who are more concerned about the speedy assassination of Tito [in Yugoslavia] than they are about the advancement of the colored people of these United States."[26]

"Frank-ly Speaking"

To advance the revolution, Frank Marshall Davis had more than a temporary podium at the local NAACP; he had a regular platform in the newspaper, and used it to its full extent.

The first issue of the *Honolulu Record* appeared on August 5, 1948.[27] In what Barack Obama supporters sixty years later would deem a striking coincidence (the few, that is, who knew of Davis), Davis arrived in Hawaii shortly thereafter, in December. He began his weekly "Frank-ly Speaking" column in May 1949. (See page 256). Just before he left Chicago, he had signed a petition urging Congress to abolish the House Committee on Un-American Activities and defending the Communist Gerhart Eisler, who (under constantly changing aliases) had carried out numerous Comintern missions around the world, including in the United States. (As noted, Eisler would ultimately flee America to become a top Communist official in East Germany.) Now, in Hawaii, Davis would continue to walk the Soviet line—over and over and over.[28]

A systematic look at Davis's "Frank-ly Speaking" columns in 1949 and 1950 reveals the extent to which he followed the Communist Party's talking points.

Consider his May 12, 1949, op-ed, "How Our Democracy Looks to Oppressed Peoples." Handed a regular column, he wasted no time in denouncing the Marshall Plan, in keeping with the Soviet line on the subject. (See page 257). "For a nation that calls itself the champion of democracy, our stupendous stupidity is equalled only by our mountainous ego," Davis complained. "Our actions at home and abroad are making American democracy synonymous with oppression instead of freedom."

This was two years after the announcement of the Marshall Plan, by which point it was universally understood as a gracious gesture by America, vital to the recovery of postwar Europe—which is precisely why the USSR opposed it. Nonetheless, Stalin and Molotov continued to attack the rescue plan, and the foot soldiers in the field were left to argue that it reflected America's imperial, neocolonial ambitions.

Davis went further, dubbing the American plan a form of slavery and racism. He wrote that since the end of World War II, "I have watched with growing shame for my America as our leaders have used our golden riches to re-enslave the yellow and brown and black peoples of the world." He pointedly added, "As the colonials see it, the Marshall plan is a device to maintain what they call 'white imperialism,' and no manner of slick phrases can convince them otherwise." He said that this

HONOLULU RECORD

Davis, New Columnist, Takes Over From WKB

n,
er

ht
te
t-
ip

rn
ie
bf
p-
r-
l-

ce
y,
t-

s.
n
n
ie
-
a

t-

n
s,

er
g
g

t-
l-

d.

W. K. Bassett, who has written a regular weekly column from the first issue of the RECORD, will not be able to continue his column because of pressure of work.

Frank Marshall Davis, who is known to RECORD readers for his frequent articles, will write a weekly column for us, headed FRANK-LY SPEAKING. His column will appear on the editorial page, in the space formerly devoted to A POINT OF VIEW by Mr. Bassett, whose provocative and interesting comments had wide following.

We hope he will again be able to write for us.

—The Editor

CHAMBER SEES NO DEPRESSION

WASHINGTON (FP)—Millions of U. S. workers watching diminishing pay envelopes and increasing unemployment might be thinking about the possibility of a depression.

But the 2,000 members of the U. S. Chamber of Commerce who gathered here for the 5-day 37th annual meeting ending May 5 in the patioed general headquarters and the Statler hotel don't see it that way at all.

As President Earl O. Shreve of the Chamber puts it: "A return to price controls and other market restraints would delay and perhaps halt the transition from abnormal boom conditions to a more solid and orderly pattern of prosperity."

ie
p
.o
-
a
.s
.s
y
ai
y,
n

Dangerous Thoughts

Overheard in a teachers' restroom after the annual visitation of Mrs. Ruth E. Black:

FRANK MARSHALL DAVIS, whose column "Frank-ly Speaking" will appear weekly on the RECORD's editorial page, has published several books of poetry. Formerly an editor of the Chicago Star, he is the executive editor of the Associated Negro Press. Also well known as a fighter for civil liberties, he is a member of the National Executive Board of the Civil Rights Congress.

PEARSON OFF T.H. AIR

Drew Pearson is off the air in Hawaii, temporarily at least, according to E. D. Beatie, production manager of station KULA.

"Due to change in program policy of KULA, Drew Pearson's program has been temporarily discontinued. At the first opportunity Station KULA hopes to bring the internationally known commentator back to island listeners," Mr. Beatie told the RECORD.

Asked if probable pressure on

"Public May In Anti-La

By ST.

Whether or Walter D. Ac ticed it, Sec HB 1142) of / law after the legislature pos lem. He wer intending to laws" of the thinks them U. S. Supreme seem to put h tion regarding supposed to p by "six or me

During her union represe bill was aime pecially agair

The new la "any use of fc turbing the p

But it does ing the publ omission mak ence in the o authority th: Roberts, who opinion in t vs. Connectic vah's Witnes "disturbing t stopping a m and playing a

Roberts wr mon law" co peace" was no viction in An

The new 11571, howev reference eve which would usage under

Roberts wa had a reputa servation.

"Frank-ly Speaking": In 1949 Davis began his regular column in the Communist organ the *Honolulu Record*. There he railed against President Truman, American "imperialism," and much more.

frank-ly speaking

By FRANK MARSHALL DAVIS

How Our Democracy Looks
To Oppressed Peoples

For a nation that calls itself the champion of democracy, our stupendous stupidity is equalled only by our mountainous ego. Our actions at home and abroad are making American democracy synonymous with oppression instead of freedom.

Four years ago, we had the opportunity for world leadership. This was near the end of World War II, a global conflict for freedom and liberation. We shouted our antagonism toward the "superior race" theories of the Nazis.

MR. DAVIS

But before the guns grew cold, we interpreted freedom and liberation to be the exclusive possession of the imperialist governments of Europe. I have watched with growing shame for my America as our leaders have used our golden riches to re-enslave the yellow and brown and black peoples of the world.

As the colonials see it, the Marshall plan is a device to maintain what they call "white imperialism," and no manner of slick phrases can convince them otherwise. They also see our congressional failure to pass the civil rights program as merely the domestic side of the same coin of the oppression of non-white peoples everywhere.

Billions To Bolster Empires

Under the Marshall plan, billions of U. S. dollars have been used to bolster the tottering empires of England, France, Belgium, Holland and the other western exploiters of teeming millions of humans. The Dutch have used their share to make war upon the Indonesians who are guilty of wanting self-government; France and England have gotten the financial means of crushing rebellions against white imperialism in Asia and Africa. With callous disregard for the natural rights of the subject peoples, we have told Western Europe to rebuild itself through taking out tremendous profits by robbing the 150,000,000 black Africans who get only ignorance and poverty and the print of the aggressors' heels stamped hard into the face.

With our usual genius for suppressing the common people, we backed the oppressors in China. We poured in a Niagara of cash to the corrupt Kuomintang, thus insuring the enmity of millions of Chinese who thereby faced a harder fight for freedom and the end of feudalism.

These crimes we have committed in the name

American "oppression": In this May 12, 1949, column, Davis condemns the United States for "stupendous stupidity" and for "making American democracy synonymous with oppression." The object of his outrage was the Marshall Plan.

nefarious "oppression of non-white peoples everywhere" was being purchased via Secretary of State George Marshall's "billions of U.S. dollars . . . to bolster the tottering empires of England, France, Belgium, Holland and the other western exploiters of teeming millions of humans."

Davis also echoed the Communists in their assault on Chiang Kai-shek's anti-Communist Kuomintang regime in China; the Communist goal was to bolster Mao Tse-tung and to try to incite a Marxist takeover of the world's most populous nation. He wrote: "With our usual genius for suppressing the common people, we backed the oppressors in China. We poured in a Niagara of cash to the corrupt Kuomintang, thus insuring the enmity of millions of Chinese who thereby faced a harder fight for freedom and the end of feudalism." These were "crimes" undertaken by the "same bi-partisan coalition" that had "wrecked the civil rights program" in America. The racist bunch included both Democrats, such as Harry Truman and George Marshall, and Republicans, such as Senators Robert Taft and Arthur Vandenberg.

To Davis, all of this was so utterly unlike that true bastion of freedom: the Soviet Union. In the USSR there was no racism: "Russia continues to point to the fact that discrimination and segregation based on race does not exist there."

Next, under a subhead titled "To Whom the Oppressed Look," Davis pointed to Paul Robeson, the obvious Communist who many liberals mysteriously insisted was not a Communist. Davis upheld Robeson as the symbol of aspiration for the oppressed peoples of the world. He quoted a "YMCA official" named Lawrence C. Burr, who said of a Robeson visit to India: "Well known for his part in the struggle for human freedom and equality through the years, Robeson will perhaps receive the greatest ovation ever accorded an American. In the minds of many Indian leaders, the noted singer symbolizes the aspirations of oppressed peoples in all sections of the world."[29]

Davis finished his piece: "We may as well face it. The oppressed peoples of the world are not looking to our Wall Streeters, our brass hats, our Trumans or our Vandenbergs for liberation. These leaders had their chance—and muffed it."

The Marshall Plan was a dead end for freedom. The hope of the world, Davis proclaimed, lay in the vision of Paul Robeson and the USSR.

Providing Cover for Dupes

A week later, Davis was back supporting the propaganda positions of the Communist movement. On May 26, 1949, he wrote a piece expressing his disappointment with the CIO, the great anti-Communist labor union. At the same time, he expressed approval of: (1) Vice President Henry Wallace, the notorious defender of the USSR; (2) the Communist front groups the National Lawyers Guild and the Civil Rights Congress; and (3) Eugene Dennis, national secretary of the Communist Party. Davis also hinted at his struggles with the liberals at the national and local branches of the NAACP.

This piece was followed by a sarcastic June 2 dispatch titled "How to Become a Communist," which had dupes as its target audience. He cried that anyone "who wants enough money to eat regularly, have sufficient clothes and a decent roof above his head is a 'dupe' who 'has been tricked by the Communist leadership of the union [Harry Bridges's ILWU].'" Any attacks on Bridges as a Communist, warned Davis, were essentially hate speech—"vicious hate propaganda directed against the ILWU and the working people." The "loud cry" of "subversive" and "Communist" is "a device used by the haves to block the onward march of the have-nots and maintain the status quo."

Personal attacks on Harry Bridges and other so-called innocents were merely a "divisive Big Business weapon of Red-baiting" aimed at "working people." Davis stoically assured his readers, "So long as I believe that my cause is just, I shall not be halted by name-calling"—presumably referring to accusations that Davis, too, was a Communist. People like Davis and those ILWU members "will be labeled Marxists," he lamented, simply because "they want higher pay and better working conditions."

This was a recurring theme in Davis's columns: supposedly unmerited allegations of being a Communist. On July 7, 1949, he wrote: "I don't know about you, but I personally am tired of the wolf cry of Communism raised by those in power to justify their refusal to grant equality, whether to a territory, a minority group, or an individual. And I am not alone in this stand. Increasing numbers of Americans are becoming angered when they are thrown the same old smelly Red herring each time they ask for a helping of democracy."

But with this plea for fairness, Davis was covering for truly suspicious individuals.

For instance, he went directly to the case of the Reverend Thomas S. Harten, whom he called "for many years one of the most noted Negro pastors." He quoted the pastor: "I say to America that before she preaches to Russia or to any other nation, she must remove the mote from her own eye, and clean up the dirt in her own backyard."

Davis did not mention the fact that Reverend Harten was a member of the board and general assembly of the radical, Communist-infiltrated National Council of Churches. Nor did he note that the reverend was an active supporter of the candidacy of Benjamin Davis Jr., the longtime Communist who campaigned for New

York congressman-at-large in 1942, and who was a regular in the *Daily Worker*.[30] Harten peered at the eye of the USSR from his pulpit and saw no mote there at all.

Davis said that Reverend Harten and his ilk "feel their cause is just and are ready to face crucifixion, if need be, for what they believe in. They have no fear of the Pontius Pilates of 1949." Yes, in Frank Marshall Davis's world, the Pontius Pilates were the anti-Communists, not the Communists conducting show trials of priests and bishops and sentencing them to execution or prison camps. Here he was making a bid for the support of the biggest suckers of them all: the Religious Left.

Sometimes Davis lashed out at "Red-baiters" for their "paranoia" over people he surely knew were Communists, whereas other times he did so when citing a liberal (often a duped liberal) who was defending the rights of Communists or, better, blasting anti-Communists.

Consider his reference to Dr. Robert Hutchins, chancellor of the University of Chicago, in his August 4, 1949, column. He hailed the renowned educator for "fearlessly" maintaining his "independence of thought" in an era "of rising reaction, of liberals being scared into silence by un-American committees and the weapon of Red-baiting." (There was the "un-American committee" again, a label Davis had also used at the *Chicago Star*.)[31] In a recent commencement address, Hutchins had excoriated the "dragnet philosophy of the witch-hunters," which he said ran contrary to the American way of life: "We do not throw people into jail because they are alleged to differ with the official dogma."[32]

Davis reveled in Hutchins's message to the graduating seniors. He seemed especially pleased that Hutchins had quoted Karl Marx. Davis recorded:

> [Hutchins stated:] "For example, the *Communist Manifesto* demands free education for all. Are we therefore, to recant and renounce the American doctrine of free education for all?" Speaking of the cold war, Dr. Hutchins said: "It has never been shown that there are so many spies and traitors in this country, or that the external danger is so great and imminent that we have to divert the entire attention of our people into one great repressive preoccupation, into one great counter-revolution in which the freedoms of our citizens must be thrown overboard as too burdensome for the floundering ship of state to carry."

What Dr. Hutchins apparently did not know, but Davis likely did, as did every member of CPUSA, is that nearly every American spy successfully recruited by the KGB came directly out of the American Communist Party.

Davis was thrilled that Hutchins had said what he said, with credibility that the columnist and his comrades did not possess.[33] This "significant speech," said Davis, was a sharp warning against "growing fascism here in America." And "if fascism and World War III are to be averted," he added, publications like the *Honolulu Record,* which had the courage to print the dire warnings of men such as Dr. Hutchins, "will play a leading role in their defeat."

Harry Truman's "Program for World War III"

Throughout August 1949, Davis insisted that President Truman was itching to launch World War III, targeting the innocent lambs running the Soviet Union and its affiliated "new democracies" in Eastern Europe.[34]

In his August 4 piece, he said that Truman was part of an American propaganda machine "aimed to deceive the American people into supporting a new world war, if need be, to bail Big Business out of a depression." This charge bore an uncanny resemblance to the Stalinist line. In the February 1946 Bolshoi Theatre speech, Stalin had claimed that capitalist countries had started World War II to advance big business. Now, with the advent of the Cold War, Communists worldwide had begun arguing that the capitalist countries were pining to repeat the crime—precisely the charge that Davis leveled here.

Two weeks later, on August 18, Davis stepped up the attack on "the double-talking Truman administration with its program for World War III." He said that the "the Truman doctrine in Greece and Turkey and then the Marshall Plan" were "based upon the continuation of colonial slavery by the ruling classes of Western Europe." He also blasted non-Communist labor unions, which he contrasted with the free-dom-loving folks at ILWU in Hawaii, for backing this neocolonialism: "Instead of leading the fight for peace and security"—that is, by siding with Stalin—"and opposing profit-grabbing and world domination by the billion-dollar corporations, the top leadership of organized labor still swoons to the siren songs of the Truman gang."

As Moscow stepped up its attack on the Marshall Plan, so did Davis. In his next column, on August 25, he zinged the Truman administration's alleged pro-war propaganda effort: "We Americans have no yearning for war despite the propaganda barrage intended to whip up hysteria. Leading scientists and military experts have warned that nobody can win the next global conflict, despite the pipe dreams of our Big Business and Big Brass."

Echoing a call that the American Peace Mobilization's closet Communists had used in opposing U.S. involvement in World War II—and that would resonate with the political Left for generations to come—Davis protested that he would not die for oil: "I have no desire to give my life to maintain high profits for Standard Oil. . . . I shall not help England and France keep millions of my colored brothers in Africa and Asia in colonial slavery. Yet that is what our dividend diplomats ask of you and me when they demand our support of the bi-partisan Marshall plan, Atlantic pact and a shooting war, if necessary, to bail us out of depression."

Once again Davis brought China into the picture, urging imperialist America to dump Chiang's Chinese nationalists. Of course, such would result in a Communist takeover of China, which, at the time of this article, was perilously close to becoming a reality. Davis urged that the Truman administration and Congress divert money from Chiang to more worthwhile endeavors, like inner-city poverty: "Billions poured down the rat-hole in China to aid the corrupt Nationalist regime of Chiang Kai-shek could have completely eliminated the slums in a number of major American cities, not only providing decent housing but employment in the construction of this housing."

Davis went a step further, suggesting that America not only abandon Chiang but also trade with a "Liberated China"—meaning Mao's China—with Russia, and with the "democracies" of the Soviet empire. To ensure trade with Eastern Europe, he advised, "We must reject all war alliances such as the Atlantic pact" and "fake 'recovery programs' such as the Marshall plan." So Davis wanted U.S. aid (in the form of trade) to Stalin's Russia, to Mao's China, and to the Soviet Communist bloc, but opposed U.S. aid to the non-Communist democracies of Western Europe.

Truman's "Aggression" Against Stalin

On September 1, 1949, Davis ratcheted up the vitriol. Going beyond even earlier claims of Truman warmongering, he suggested that the United States wanted to take over Russia: "It has also been asked how the U.S. expects to rule Russia when the federal government can't rule Mississippi."

The same column illustrated another tactic common among Communists, one that often duped liberals beautifully: Davis took the case of certain black Communists, who had been rightly suspected of Communist activities and foreign loyalties, and characterized their investigation as racially motivated. He pointed to a federal case against twelve known CPUSA leaders. Two of the twelve were black—just enough for Davis to convert the case into a racist junta. He borrowed language from an ad defending the two in an influential left-wing African-American weekly in Los Angeles, the *California Eagle*. The ad, here quoted by Davis, declared:

"While allowing those guilty of violent acts to go free, our government is now trying 12 national leaders of the Communist party. Among them are two of our brothers.

"They are Honorable Benjamin J. Davis, Communist member of the city council of New York, and Henry Winston [of the Young Communist League], youthful veteran of World War II, who holds one of the three leading posts in the Communist party nationally. . . . The Communist party has a long record of vigorous advocacy and struggle for the democratic rights of Negro citizens. We feel that this fact is not unrelated to the current persecution of its leaders. . . .

"Anyone who dares to think for himself and to say what he thinks is in danger of being fired from his job, branded as a Communist subversive, and thrown in jail.

"Freedoms guaranteed by the Bill of Rights are now, once more, in serious danger. There is no hope for Negro freedom if the liberties of our country are now snuffed out behind anti-Communist hysteria.

"If the freedom of Davis and Winston can be taken away today, the gains we have made in our battle for full equality will be taken away tomorrow. We therefore call upon you to stop this unconstitutional prosecution of Benjamin Davis, Henry Winston and their associates because of their political beliefs."

Note that neither Davis nor the *California Eagle* disputed that these black Americans were Communist Party leaders. They simply created a red herring, alleging that the Communist Party functionaries were enduring "persecution" only because they were black.

The cries of racism worked nicely with many non-Communist liberals.

Truman's "Fascism, American Style"

Davis picked up the race argument with vigor in his September 15 column, where he announced that anti-Communism was really veiled racism—and fascism: "Several weeks ago I pointed out that it was considered subversive in some quarters to fight against white supremacy, and that campaigning for peace was labeled 'un-American.' The advocates of peace and equality are termed 'Communists' and every attempt is made to silence them."

"This," declared Davis, "is fascism, American style."

Davis cited an incident from the summer in Peekskill, New York, which the Left immediately turned into a symbol of postwar repression by a "hysterically" anti-Communist culture.[35] Paul Robeson was scheduled to sing for the benefit of the Harlem chapter of the Communist front group the Civil Rights Congress. During a recent trip to Paris, Robeson had claimed that black Americans would be unwilling to fight in a war against the USSR. The party line ever since, which many liberals have dutifully echoed, was that Robeson (as Davis himself put it) was "taken out of context."[36] He was not. As Robeson carefully reiterated in a speech at a "Welcome Home Rally" in New York on June 19, 1949, "I said it was unthinkable that the Negro people of America or elsewhere in the world could be drawn into war with the Soviet Union. I repeat it with hundredfold emphasis: *they will not.*"[37] In the wake of such inflammatory comments, Robeson's Peekskill appearance was protested by angry local townspeople, or what Davis characterized as "a group of young white storm troopers . . . operating under Ku Klux Klan direction." Davis portrayed the townspeople as irate not because of a Robeson statement that many regarded as unpatriotic or even traitorous, but because they were driven by racist rage against a black man. Davis reported that "a lynching spirit was aroused" against Robeson, "but not a single policeman or state trooper was on hand to maintain law and order."

And who was to blame for this? The Democrats.

Davis fired at Harry Truman, and especially his former attorney general, Tom Clark, for having dared to label the Civil Rights Congress a subversive organization. "This was interpreted as government sanction for violence," argued Davis. He quoted Robeson, who likewise blamed Truman: "It's clear now who uses force and violence," said the singer. "Let it be equally clear who advocates its use. The money crowd pulls the strings, right up to the White House. President Truman talks a good game of civil rights, but that's just talk. He gives the lynchers the green light. More than 100 Negroes have been lynched since he fell into FDR's shoes. For doing nothing about that, his attorney general was promoted to the supreme court."

Davis agreed with Robeson, charging that this "fascism" had "the silent backing of President Truman, Democrat, whose loyalty order, witch-hunts and promotion of Tom Clark to the supreme court indicate his real attitude on civil rights."

To top off the point, Davis, as he and the Communist movement so often did, held up the USSR as an enlightened, multicultural polar opposite of the intolerant United States. In the Soviet Union, he averred, "racism is a serious crime," and "discrimination against colored peoples . . . has ended." He again borrowed from his friend Robeson: "In Paul's own words, what he admires most about the Soviet

Union is the abolition, by strict law, of racism and jim crow, the doctrine of equality regardless of color or race, and human dignity for all."[38]

One would think that Davis would show some level of appreciation to President Truman for his major efforts on behalf of civil rights and desegregation, including his call for federal antilynching legislation and his 1948 executive order integrating the armed forces.[39] Davis could not do that, however. Instead, writing in other columns, he dismissed Truman's "token support" on civil rights, saying the president (at best) "talked a good civil rights program."[40]

He couldn't give the president credit for one overriding reason: Harry Truman sat opposed to Joe Stalin, meaning that Truman had to be the enemy.

Once more we see Frank Marshall Davis parroting a favorite Soviet line. The USSR and the international Communist movement employed race on a grand scale to denigrate America. The Kremlin had a propaganda weapon to hold over the head of Uncle Sam—race, slavery, America's historical bigotry toward blacks—and it was not about to let that one go. For the Soviet Union, with an extremely small black population and without America's shameful history of enslaving Africans, the race issue was a convenient tool with which to bludgeon Uncle Sam.

Never mind that Soviet Russia had brutally discriminated against its minorities, and even targeted entire groups for forcible annihilation. The race argument enabled the Communists to claim the moral high ground.

The Devil and Harry Truman

In his next two columns, Davis made heavy use of the Christian Left. Some of these Christians were duped liberals, whereas others were closet Communists, predators encircling unsuspecting dupes.

To judge from the language in his columns, Davis was no fan of pastors, usually expressing a Leninist view of them as hucksters looking to take money from the poor, superstitious masses, who clung to their God like a drug, an "opiate."[41] Still, he was more than happy to accept the backing of gullible pastors for any cause close to the heart of CPUSA and Moscow.

To that end, the names in Davis's column of September 22, 1949, "Cold War in Church," read like a Who's Who of radical preachers. He cited the Reverend Dr. John Howard Melish, Walter Russell Bowie, Joseph F. Fletcher, and Bishop William Scarlett. These four were among the most prominent, longest entries in the investigative compilations put together by J. B. Matthews, the famed former-Communist-turned-government-investigator who served as director of research for the House Committee on Un-American Activities.[42] Among the more than 1,400 radical Protestant rectors on Matthews's list, none was as far to the left, and few took up as many pages, as Melish.[43]

Davis neglected to share such pertinent background information with his readers. His goal, after all, was to portray the pastors as mainstream. He tapped Melish for the opening to his September 22 column: "Remember the name of the Rev. Dr. John Howard Melish, rector of the Church of the Holy Trinity, Episcopalian, in Brooklyn. If civilization survives the threat of World War III, future generations will remember Dr. Melish as one of the great martyrs of 1949 in the fight against the flood-tide of American fascism." The good Dr. Melish, wrote Davis, was "a victim, on the religious front, of a Truman administration that talks like an angel and acts like the devil."

Davis condemned the "thought control police," referring not to the Soviet system of NKVD oppressors but to a supposed *American* operation. By this he meant "the bi-partisans"—the Truman administration and the Republican Congress—whose policies were "aimed against such Negroes as Paul Robeson, who think American democracy could learn about race relations from Russia, against such labor leaders as Harry Bridges who oppose Taft-Hartley and the imperialistic Marshall plan, and against such pastors as Dr. Melish, who believe the Soviet Union and the U.S. can live peacefully in the same world. This is pro-fascist ideology, pure and simple."

The seventy-four-year-old Melish was being vilified, Davis claimed. The bishop had relieved Melish of his duties as rector of New York's Episcopal Holy Trinity Church after forty-five years of service. Why? "Because he believed in applied Christianity, and because he and his son, the Rev. William Howard Melish, assistant rector, refused to join in the anti-Communist hysteria."

Davis also praised the son of the blessed father: "Long before V-J Day, the Rev. Melish, with the blessings and advice of his ageing father, began working toward friendly postwar relations between the Soviet Union and the U.S. He saw that the future of the world would largely be shaped by how these two powerful wartime allies got along in peace. He believed it was up to the Christian church to lead in this field."

In fact, William Howard Melish was so extreme that his father looked like a conservative Republican by comparison. To sugarcoat the politics of the radical son would be even more difficult. But Davis would try.

Davis noted that in 1946 William Howard Melish had become chairman of the National Council of American-Soviet Friendship (NCASF). He did not mention that this was a Communist front group, an active organization within CPUSA—

indeed, the American Communist Party had created the organization in 1943. NCASF picked up objectives previously undertaken by party-controlled groups like the American Council of Soviet Relations and Corliss Lamont's Friends of the Soviet Union. (This constant changing of names was a standard Comintern concealment tactic.)

The U.S. Congress later investigated NCASF and reported that the majority of its national officers and board of directors—that is, people who held positions like that of William Howard Melish—tended to be "functionaries and members of the Communist Party." Congress added that the organization's views were "invariably and markedly pro-Soviet and, except during the war years, anti–United States Government." The "primary purpose" of NCASF, the report stated, was to "advance and promote the objectives of the Soviet Union for the Communist Party behind a facade of being independent of the Party and interested only in developing friendship between the Soviet Union and the United States."[44]

Davis also failed to inform his readers that William Howard Melish's name frequently appeared in such publications as *Soviet Russia Today* and the *Daily Worker,* and on numerous Communist petitions,[45] and that Melish had recently started a column for *New Masses.* Ironically, that column began just about the same time that Matt Wayne—the suspected pseudonym of Arthur Miller—launched his column in *New Masses.* Melish and Arthur Miller, incidentally, were friends and neighbors in Brooklyn.[46]

Omitting all those facts, Davis reported instead that the NCSAF was "nonpolitical," and that the persecuted Dr. Melish became chairman of the organization "shortly before the nation announced, in effect, that it was out to conquer the globe for Big Business by thrusting the Truman Doctrine into the international arena."

Significantly, Davis noted that Melish was one of the committee of six clergy and two laymen who visited Yugoslavia and returned to make a "factual report giving the lie to the persecution propaganda surrounding the arrest and conviction of Archbishop Stepinac."

This remark will enrage any reader familiar with the Stepinac case, which was a very real and very vicious case of Communist persecution of a saintly man (decades later the Catholic Church declared him a martyr and beatified him). Stepinac was the victim of a classic Communist show trial—no question.[47] For Melish and his group not to know better was an example of either dupery or mendacity; for Davis, it was most likely the latter.

In the world of Davis and his comrades, the show trial and subsequent imprisonment of Archbishop Stepinac did not qualify as genuine persecution of a church official, but the supposedly harsh treatment of Dr. Melish somehow did.

Sensing he had a worthy campaign issue at hand, Davis in his next column again turned reality upside down, portraying Communism as friendly to Christianity, and anti-Communism as un-Christian. In "Challenge to the Church," published on September 29, 1949, he quoted extensively from a letter by "Benjamin D. Shaw, noted New York churchman."[48] He was so impressed with Shaw's letter that he wrote, "I wish every minister, every churchman, every Christian could read the entire statement." In one section that Davis cited, Shaw imagined Judgment Day, where anti-Communist Christians would be called to account for their attacks on Christ-loving Communists: "On your Judgment Day, when the Lord will ask you for an account of your stewardship, will you have to say, 'Lord, they were a pack of wolves'? If God will then ask you, 'My son, did you do all you could to humanize these wolves, to Christianize them, to teach them My Way?' will your answer be, 'Lord I was too busy Redbaiting'?"

Davis likewise trumpeted Shaw's claim that "the Christian churches, and the Catholic church in particular, are making a grievous error in their shortsighted belief that the major enemy of Christianity is Communism." Not only was Soviet Russia not antireligious, Shaw said, but it had saved the world from Hitler's "anti-Christian paganism." Christians everywhere should be thanking Stalin.

The late Lenin would have been astonished to learn Communism was *not* a "major enemy of Christianity"—or he would have thanked Davis and Shaw profusely for their propaganda work.

Davis Emboldened

As the fall of 1949 came around, Frank Marshall Davis must have been buoyed by global Communism's huge gains. While the Truman administration and Republican Congress were aghast at the "twin shocks" of 1949—the advent of the Soviet atomic bomb and the loss of China to Mao—CPUSA was delirious with success. Ex-Communist Whittaker Chambers had lamented that by leaving Communism, "I know that I am leaving the winning side for the losing side."

Davis grew more confident with the pen, making even more outlandish assertions. Before, he had floated the idea that anti-Communism was a form of racism. Now, in his November 24, 1949, column, he tried to link anti-Communism with the KKK. "For many years the Ku Klux Klan has been virtually inactive," he wrote. "But recently the groups have come alive. . . . They are trying at present to unite all under a single leadership with the slogan of 'Fight Communism to Maintain White Supremacy.' . . . To reaction, any attempt to change the status quo of discrimination is Communistic." A couple of columns later, on December 8, 1949, he said that "if you fight too hard for civil rights . . . you are likely to be branded a Communist."

Davis was constructing a clever defense for himself—an early, Cold War, Communist version of the race card. He was sending a signal that anyone who accused him of being a Communist should be prepared to be denounced as a white-hooded racist looking to stop him from advancing civil rights. "I, personally, have no intention of letting the cry of 'communism' sidetrack me from my goal of complete civil rights as guaranteed by the Constitution," he vowed. "The fight for absolute equality will continue. . . . I want civil rights for all people, and I shall not rest until that goal is achieved."

That was not his only goal, however. In the crucial year to come—which brought the race for the enormously powerful hydrogen bomb and a costly hot war on the Korean Peninsula—Frank Marshall Davis had much else in store.

Big Business, Bad Truman, and the H-Bomb

Davis had big issues on his mind as 1950 began. In his January 26 column—titled "Free Enterprise or Socialism?"—he painted a stark picture of an America on the verge of another Great Depression, the fault of a "virtual dictatorship of Big Business." He took special aim at General Motors, which he said would soon monopolize the entire auto industry. If he had the power to do so, he would have nationalized GM. And not just GM. He concluded the column by saying that in the face of "still rising unemployment and a mounting depression, the time draws nearer when we will have to decide to oust the monopolies and restore a competing system of free enterprise, or let the government own and operate our major industries." Given that he declared that "the backbone of free enterprise" had already been broken, it was pretty clear what option Davis was endorsing.

Soon Davis was taking up another weighty issue: America's potential manufacture of the hydrogen bomb. The prospects for the "super" bomb, the far more destructive successor to the atomic bombs that had been dropped on Hiroshima and Nagasaki, was a bracing thought for everyone. No one wanted to see the world erupt in a horrific nuclear war.

The American decision to pursue the H-bomb was especially troublesome to Communists, since it would mean a quick one-up on the Soviets, who by 1949 had reached effective parity with the United States after stealing enough Manhattan Project secrets to build their own atomic bomb. That pilfering was made possible by precisely the kind of clandestine Communist infiltration that concerned anti-Communists—and that Davis and CPUSA were hoping to convince duped liberals did not exist.

In America, Truman administration officials debated whether to pursue the hydrogen bomb; in Moscow, Stalin had no hesitation. President Truman ultimately decided to take the advice of science advisers like physicist Edward Teller and seek the H-bomb because he had been told that Stalin was seeking the weapon; in other words, his chief motivation was to get it before the Soviets did. This decision sent Communists scrambling to another propaganda campaign. It didn't matter that Stalin was hastily pursuing the H-bomb himself; the Soviets and their comrades framed Truman's strategic choice as yet another form of American belligerence. Their goal was to manipulate mass opinion, and especially to mobilize duped liberal "peace activists" into joining them in their protests against the "hell-bomb." It was an ideal propaganda point.

Davis took up the task right on cue with a brazen February 9, 1950, piece, "Onward with the Hydrogen Bomb." Referring to his native America, he wrote, "Never before in history has there been a nation that proclaimed more loudly its love of peace and yet used its might to lash peace from the door. When we dropped the atom bomb on Hiroshima, we believed the world was ours. Having defeated the Axis powers on the battlefront, we were ready to show the Russians who was boss of this world."

Here was a flagrant example of another Communist flip-flop on World War II, based entirely on where Moscow stood at any given time. In truth, the United States had dropped the bomb on Japan not to be "boss of this world" but to force Japan to surrender and to end World War II. At Potsdam in July 1945, Truman had actually informed Stalin that the United States had "a new weapon of unusual destructive force." Winston Churchill later wrote that Stalin "seemed to be delighted" by the news, and Truman recalled that the Soviet leader said he hoped the United States would make "good use of it against the Japanese."[49] The dropping of the bomb spared not only U.S. Marines but also the Red Army; they were saved from a massive land invasion that would have left millions dead, including huge numbers of Russian boys.

Davis ignored this history. Instead, he contended that America at the end of World War II, ungrateful for the Soviets' help in "curb[ing] the greatest threat to civilization the world had ever known," turned on the good Soviet leadership, unable to satiate its lust for violence. But Americans were aware "that Russia had lost an estimated 20,000,000 people fighting the Nazis," meaning, Davis claimed, that Truman and his "dividend diplomats" had to gin up crises involving the USSR: "If Molotov coughed, it threatened our 'security' in Iran. If Vishinsky laughed, we were 'endangered' in Korea." It was an American "propaganda barrage" of manu-factured crises.

In contrast to the hypocritical Americans—who claimed "we love peace" while "rattling our atom bombs," Davis said—stood the genuinely peace-loving Soviets. The columnist wrote: "But we, too, love peace, said the men in the Krem-lin." Davis appealed to readers' sympathies by highlighting the Soviets' postwar plight while showcasing their supposed magnanimity. Again speaking for Moscow (something he apparently had no difficulty doing), he wrote: "Your [America's] productive capacity was unscathed and came out of the war greater than ever before in the whole history of mankind. It will take us years to restore the losses sustained by Russian industry from the German blitz; let's get together, talk this thing out and settle our differences amicably so that we can all go about the busi-ness of making the world safe forever from another war. Peace we want above all else, said Uncle Joe in messages to America."

While the Soviet tyrant was cuddly "Uncle Joe" in Davis's rendering, Amer-ica was full of fat-cat capitalists, warmongering generals, and desperate politicians who "recoiled in horror" at Moscow's appeals for peace. Without a "brink-of-war economy," the column declared, America's "giant corporations" couldn't get "fat contracts to make materials of war and products for the anti-Communists of Europe." "No, real peace is an expensive luxury that the big stockholders and professional soldiers can't afford."

And Davis was not finished. He wrote that President Truman and Ameri-ca's "dividend diplomats wrung their hands" when they found out "the Russians had the atomic bomb." The American people—and presumably the peace-loving Soviets—"breathed more easily," recognizing that "maybe there would be peace at last" now that neither the United States nor the USSR "would start anything for fear of retaliation by the other."

Ah, but "ours is a resourceful land," Davis said. "Unless we have a threat better than the other fellow's, the crisis making business might go bankrupt, thus forcing us to cut our war budget, and you know what that would do to the incomes of the poor millionaires. Therefore, we will create a hydrogen bomb to shake at Russia, and then we can keep on making shiny new crises on a mass production basis."

And what would happen if the Soviets developed their own hydrogen bomb? "We shall have reached another stalemate, and the boys will have to think up a weapon guaranteed to destroy everything—that is, everything, not marked with the Stars and Stripes—in one global explosion."

What Davis wrote in this and other columns was so thoroughly in keeping with the official Soviet line that it defies imagination that liberals, then and today, could claim he was unfairly maligned as even a small "c" communist. In fact, given how closely he followed the Communist Party line, it seems inconceivable that he was not receiving orders from the party in some form, either from CPUSA officials or from erstwhile Comintern apparatchiks. Otherwise, somehow, by pure coincidence, he was mimicking the Soviet line without error, and without shame.

Frank's Enemies

In the columns that followed through 1950, Davis directed his strongest outbursts at anti-Communist members of Congress—such as Republican senators Karl Mundt of South Dakota and Homer Ferguson of Michigan, and Republican congressman Richard Nixon of California, whom he labeled "the three dictators" in a March 23, 1950, piece—and groups like the American Legion (March 16 column) and the CIO labor union (numerous columns). Meanwhile he praised the ACLU and Americans for Democratic Action, and defended Harry Bridges and his ILWU against the "witch-hunters" (columns of March 30, April 6, April 20, and May 11). And, of course, he bent over backwards to characterize the House Committee on Un-American Activities as a racist organization and anti-Communists generally as raving racists (April 13, April 20, April 27, May 18, and June 8).

One other Davis piece is worthy of special attention: a May 18, 1950, article on West Germany. This Davis missive illustrates where Moscow stood on postwar Germany and the shameless way in which American Communists followed the line. The American Communists' position on Germany has been too easily forgotten.

After World War II, the Soviets wanted a prostrate, permanently divided Germany. This objective was driven by two chief motivations: (1) that Germany would not again rise to attack Russia—an understandable motivation that prevailed even in the mind of Mikhail Gorbachev into the late 1980s[50]—and, (2) equally important, that a devastated Germany might turn to Communism. On the latter, recall that Stalin, in his August 1939 speech to the Central Committee, had hoped that one result of a "great war" in Europe would be a "Sovietized" Germany. This explains the Berlin Blockade of 1948–49. Stalin now had East Germany in the Soviet camp, but he wanted West Germany there as well. As a result, Communists around the world launched a systematic campaign to demonize West Germany.

Hopping into the fray was Frank Marshall Davis. Davis had been pushing the unbelievable Moscow line that the Soviet Union and its Eastern European satel-

lites were "democracies," an absurd but common tactic by Communists throughout the Cold War (and in Castro's Cuba even today). Now he employed a corollary
tactic, and even taller tale, by contending that nations allied with the United
States in its resistance to Communism were *not* democracies. In this case, his
target was West Germany; the May 18 column was mockingly titled "Our New
'Democratic' Partner."

Davis began: "We have the amazing spectacle of the foreign ministers of the
United States, Great Britain and France formally announcing that Western Germany is being brought in as a full fledged partner in the alliance of the 'western
democracies' against Russia. If there had been a sincere effort to democratize
Western Germany, I would feel much better about it." He offered no evidence
whatsoever for the claim that American officials were insincere about democratiz-
ing West Germany.

Even more irresponsibly, he invoked the outrageous Soviet line that Ameri-
can policy was bringing back the Third Reich. "It is a known fact that many honest
American officials have quit their posts in disgust over the way in which Western
Germany is being handed back to the Nazis." In fact, averred Davis, America's
policy of de-Nazification was a sham—"one of the big jokes of the 20th century."
He called the program a "sop" to an American public still outraged by the horrors
of Dachau and Buchenwald. "But the public has gradually forgotten in five years.
And as the memory of these atrocities faded, so did our denazification."

Worse, wrote Davis, American officials were instead making an enemy out
of Stalin: "Stalin has been built up as a greater menace than Hitler and tears have
been shed over the 'poor Nazis' who murdered tens of millions of human beings.
Jail doors have been opened and Nazi leaders have been almost invited to take up
business at the old stand." Here again, Davis alleged a racist-fascist-imperialist-
capitalist conspiracy: "The big industrialists who financed Hitler have been
handed back their factories and the old school ties with Wall Street are almost as
strong as they ever were."

The West Germany that America was trying to help to its feet was, Davis said,
"the Germany of the master race theory. . . . The fascists we sought to extermi-
nate in World War II as 'the greatest threat to mankind the globe has ever known,'
are now our partners." This "alliance with a revived Nazi Germany" would certainly please America's bigoted anti-Communists—"such persons as John Rankin
of Mississippi and John Wood of Georgia, two past and present chairmen of the
un-American committee whose ideas on race parallel those of Adolf Hitler."

Today, American politicians like Barack Obama travel to Germany to make
eloquent speeches on how the United States rightly stood beside Berliners in

resisting the Soviet Union in those scary, early days of the Cold War. "The only reason we stand here tonight," presidential candidate Obama told citizens of a unified Berlin in July 2008, "is because men and women from both of our nations came together" at a time when "the Soviet shadow swept across Eastern Europe" and "the Communists chose to blockade the western part of the city . . . in an effort to extinguish the last flame of freedom in Berlin." Germans and Americans had "learned to work together and trust each other less than three years after facing each other on the field of battle," thanks to such things as "the generosity of the Marshall Plan" that helped create "a German miracle." That "victory over tyranny gave rise to NATO, the greatest alliance ever formed to defend our common security," an alliance necessary "to face down the Soviet Union."[51]

Obama was spot-on, reflecting the consensus feeling of Americans, Republican and Democrat alike—including Presidents Ronald Reagan and John F. Kennedy, who also delivered historic speeches in Berlin conveying America's proud solidarity with West Germany against the Communists. And yet Obama's mentor in Hawaii in the 1970s, Frank Marshall Davis, had strenuously contested every one of these points in his propaganda work. None of what Obama rightly hailed was in any way thanks to the work of Davis.

Indeed, joining ranks with Stalin and his Communist acolytes, Davis trashed the vital yet precarious U.S.–West German friendship.

Bitter Mentor

To this day, many liberals pillory conservatives who have accused Harry Truman of turning a "blind eye" to Communist infiltration inside his administration, or of "losing China." And yet, as this chapter has shown, those accusations from the Right are timid compared to the nastiness that Frank Marshall Davis and the Communists displayed toward Truman and Marshall.

In column after column, Davis went after Truman and his administration, leveling accusations of warmongering, belligerence, hypocrisy, racism, fascism, capitalist exploitation, aid to Nazi leaders, and more. Meanwhile, he held up Stalin's Soviet Union as a paragon of peace, equality, and human dignity. Those liberals who have defended Davis were (and are) covering for a man who lied mercilessly about a great Democrat, Truman—and who did so on behalf of Stalin and Mao, the two greatest mass murderers in human history.

Davis's columns, stunning in their degree of pro-Soviet and anti-American sentiment, were designed to hoodwink non-Communist liberals into supporting

ᴌᴏ98   SCOPE OF SOVIET ACTIVITY IN THE UNITED STATES

possible self incrimination, to answer questions concerning his Communist affiliations before the House Un-American Activities Committee. He is indicted for conspiracy to violate the Smith Act.

Edward G. Rohrbough, reporter and principal stockholder of the Record, arrived in Honolulu from New York City during the summer Since that time he has been continuously in the employ of the Honolulu Publishing Co., Ltd. Rohrbough is the husband of Jeanette Nakama, also an employee of the Record, who has been identified as a member of the munist Party of Hawaii by many former Communists. Rohrbough contributor to such Communist publications as the Daily People's World New Masses. (The Daily People's World was cited as "the official organ Communist Party on the west coast" by the Special Committee on Un-American Activities in March 1944, and as the "west coast mouthpiece of the Communist Party" by the California Committee on Un-American Activities in 1948. Special Committee on Un-American Activities also cited New Masses "nationally circulated weekly journal of the Communist Party." New Masses has been cited as a "Communist periodical" by the United States Attorney General.)

During World War II, Rohrbough was stationed in China as a civilian employee of the Office of War Information. It was while serving in China that he became acquainted with Honolulu Record Editor Koji Ariyoshi, who at that time was also in the employ of the Office of War Information. Rohrbough's writings in the Daily People's World, and New Masses, during the postwar period have shown him to be in complete sympathy with the Chinese Communists, whom he has extolled as the "liberators" of China and the torchbearers of "democracy." Rohrbough also served as a consultant of the Committee for a Democratic Far Eastern Policy during 1948 and 1949. The United States Attorney General has cited the Committee for a Democratic Far Eastern Policy as a Communist organization.

Frank Marshall Davis, an identified member of the Communist Party and a resident of Hawaii since December 1948, has been a weekly contributor to the pages of the Honolulu Record since May 1949. His column, entitled "Frankly Speaking," has been devoted to unrelenting and unmitigated complaints of racial discrimination in the United States. Davis has revealed himself to be a bitter opponent of capitalism and a staunch defender of such prominent Communists and Communist sympathizers as Paul Robeson, W. E. B. DuBois, Langston Hughes, Howard Fast, Mary McLeod Bethune, Earl B. Dickerson, Carey McWilliams, Robert Morse Lovett, Herbert Aptheker, and A. Clayton Powell. Nor has Davis confined his inflammatory racial propaganda to the columns of the Honolulu Record alone. His story, Hawaii's Plain People Fight White Supremacy, appeared in the November 1951 issue of Freedom, a tabloid publication emanating from New York City, whose treatment of interracial problems strikingly conforms to Communist Party policy. The chairman of the editorial board of Freedom is Paul Robeson, an identified member of the Communist Party.

On March 3, 1947, while Davis was employed as executive editor of the Associated Negro Press with offices in Chicago, Ill., he was listed by the magazine PM as a signatory to a petition urging Congress to abolish the House Un-American Activities Committee and calling upon President Truman to effect the immediate release of Communist Gerhart Eisler. The petition referred to the work of the House Un-American Activities Committee as "undemocratic" activity and protested that the consequence of its program "would be the ultimate suppression of all traditional American liberties."

Prior to his arrival in the Territory, Frank Marshall Davis was affiliated with the Communist-line Chicago Star and the following Communist-front organizations: Civil Rights Congress, Chicago Committee for Spanish Freedom, American Youth for Democracy, Abraham Lincoln School, National Association for Constitutional Liberties, League of American Writers, and National Negro Congress. During the period of his residence in Hawaii he has played a prominent role in the activities of the Communist-front Hawaii Civil Liberties Committee and its successor the Hawaii Civil Rights Congress.

Davis is not known to receive any compensation from the Honolulu Record Publishing Co., Ltd. His income appears to be derived totally from his stationery and paper business which he has advertised in the Honolulu Record under the name Oahu Papeds, 867 Ahua Street.

Wilfred M. Oka, sports editor of the Honolulu Record, has been identified as a member of the Communist Party by 2 former Communists, while 3 other former

Frank Marshall Davis, Communist?: This 1957 Senate report calls Davis "an identified member of the Communist Party."

the Communist agenda. In particular, his twisted appeal to the racism allegedly inherent in anti-Communism was aimed at dupes.

Was Frank Marshall Davis a Communist? Within only months of these 1949–50 columns, Davis's name began appearing in various investigations of the Communist movement, beginning with a 1949 report by the California Senate, titled "Fifth Report of the Senate Fact-Finding Committee on Un-American Activities."[52] He was closely investigated by the International Security Subcommittee of the U.S. Senate Judiciary Committee, falling under several probes in a series of reports titled "Scope of Soviet Activity in the United States." In one such report, ultimately published by the U.S. Senate in 1957, Davis was listed as "an identified member of the Communist Party."[53] (See page 275). Most important is the transcript of Davis's December 1956 testimony to the U.S. Senate, where, when asked about his relationship with the Communist Party, he pleaded the Fifth Amendment.[54] (See pages 278–79). This was a pattern Davis followed throughout his life, and he could always count on dupes to back him. In typical searing fashion, Davis excoriated ex-comrades like the celebrated African-American writer Richard Wright, a courageous man who left and exposed the party in the classic work *The God That Failed*—a heresy that Davis denounced as an "act of treason."[55]

In subsequent decades, a smattering of books, reports, articles, and even Web postings added to the limited volume of material on Frank Marshall Davis. Books like James Edward Smethurst's *The New Red Negro* (1999) quoted Davis's poetry and noted his involvement as a teacher at CPUSA-sponsored schools; Smethurst, a professor at the University of Massachusetts who earned his Ph.D. at Harvard, concluded that Davis "was almost certainly a CPUSA member."[56] Most of the biographical works have been sympathetic and nonaccusatory, even those acknowledging Communist Party affiliations. Other citations have been not at all approving, especially those underscoring Davis's poetic works like "Smash on, victory-eating Red Army" and "Christ is a Dixie N—er." (In the latter poem, Davis shrugged off Jesus Christ as "another New White Hope," which was consistent with his other anti-Christian screeds, such as his mocking "Onward Christian Soldiers.")[57]

And as we will see, a few years after Smethurst's book was published, another biographer produced something of a smoking gun in regard to Davis's membership in the Communist Party.

The case of Frank Marshall Davis is more relevant today than ever before, given his relationship with America's forty-fourth president. The young man who would be president described Davis affectionately in his best-selling memoirs, calling him a mentor and thanking "Frank" for helping him find his identity as an African-American.

The relationship between Frank Marshall Davis and the future president, Barack Obama, will be visited later in this book.

2518   SCOPE OF SOVIET ACTIVITY IN THE UNITED STATES

TESTIMONY OF FRANK MARSHALL DAVIS

Mr. MORRIS. Give your name and address to the reporter, Mr. Davis.

Mr. DAVIS. Frank Marshall Davis, 47-388 Kam Highway.

Mr. MORRIS. Mr. Davis, when did you come to Honolulu?

Mr. DAVIS. In 1948.

Mr. MORRIS. 1948. Where were you born?

Mr. DAVIS. Arkansas City, Kans.

Mr. MORRIS. What has been your education?

Mr. DAVIS. Let's see. Through high school and a year at Friends University.

Mr. MORRIS. Where is Friends University?

Mr. DAVIS. And at Kansas State College. That is at Manhattan, Kans.

Mr. MORRIS. You are a columnist, are you not, for the Honolulu Record?

(The witness consults with his attorney.)

Senator WATKINS. Just a minute, Counsel. Did he ask you anything before you started to talk?

Mrs. BOUSLOG. Yes; he did, Senator.

Senator WATKINS. I couldn't see his lips move.

Mrs. BOUSLOG. He had his back to me.

Senator WATKINS. I could see that side of his face.

Mrs. BOUSLOG. I tell you, Senator, he did ask me.

Senator WATKINS. I have noticed the tendency, however, for counsel, not only in this hearing here but in the hearings on other days, before the witness could even open his mouth, to start to advise him. That amounts to what we call coaching the witness, and it is not permitted in this committee.

You see, the witnesses are not parties. They come in as any ordinary citizen would come in to testify in a matter in which the Senate is interested, as an ordinary witness would come in to testify in court. Such witnesses are not entitled to have counsel or register objections, and all of that sort of thing. They may come before the court to testify, as you know, with nobody there except the judge to advise them as to their rights as witnesses. Now, to have an attorney present to advise a witness, in this hearing, is a privilege that is granted. It is not a right.

Mrs. BOUSLOG. I regard the fact that my client has the constitutional right to counsel——

Senator WATKINS. Oh, certainly, but not to be coached as to the testimony he shall give in the proceedings.

Mrs. BOUSLOG. He turned to me and asked me for my advice, and I gave it to him.

Senator WATKINS. I have been watching this very closely, ever since these hearings out here began, and obviously the witnesses have asked for advice in many instances, but obviously the witnesses never have had time to make their requests for legal advice before counsel has begun to give advice. I just warn you. That is all.

Mr. MORRIS. We have information, Mr. Davis—did you answer the last question or did you invoke the privilege of the——

Mr. DAVIS. No; I decline to answer that, on the basis of the fifth amendment.

"Are you a Communist now, Mr. Davis?": When Davis testified before the U.S. Senate in December 1956, he declined to discuss his relationship with the Communist Party, invoking the Fifth Amendment.

Mr. MORRIS. We have information and evidence you were a member of the faculty of the Abraham Lincoln School in Chicago. Is that information accurate, Mr. Davis?

Mr. DAVIS. I decline to answer that, also on the same grounds.

Mr. MORRIS. Mr. Chairman, the Abraham Lincoln School was one of the Communist schools.

Are you a Communist now, Mr. Davis?

Mr. DAVIS. Same answer.

Mr. MORRIS. I have no further questions at this time, Senator. I ask that you order the witness to stand by.

Senator WATKINS. Stand by. That means you will report to the open hearing room.

[End of Davis testimony taken in executive session.]

Mr. MORRIS. That concludes the testimony of Mr. Davis. One other thing, Senator, I would like to point out, because I think it should be abundantly clear from our record, that the last two witnesses who appeared here today were not subpenaed because they represented anybody.

At the very outset these were the first people we subpenaed, and we told them, these particular witnesses, that they were scheduled to be the first witnesses, and they asked that they testify last. They acknowledged that on the public record, and I would like for the record at this point to show that fact.

Senator JOHNSTON. Thank you. Any other questions?

Mr. MORRIS. No, Senator.

Senator JOHNSTON. There are no questions. The witness will be excused at this particular time.

Mrs. BOUSLOG. Thank you, Senator.

Senator JOHNSTON. The committee will adjourn until 9:30 tomorrow morning.

(Whereupon, at 12:30 p. m., the subcommittee adjourned.)

14

Vietnam Dupes:
Protests, Riots, and
the Chaotic Summer of '68

The Cold War took center stage through the remainder of the 1950s, as did rising fears of "the bomb." The horror of nuclear Armageddon cast a pall over the tranquility of the Eisenhower years and the revelry of "Happy Days" and rock 'n' roll; Sputnik loomed over Elvis.

A major conflict consumed the Korean Peninsula from 1950 to 1953, testing both the Truman and the Eisenhower administrations. That first hot war of the Cold War robbed the futures of tens of thousands of American boys, as the Communists in North Korea, backed by Red China and the USSR, invaded the U.S.–backed South Korea.

Quite unforgivably, the likes of Lillian Hellman and Corliss Lamont and Dalton Trumbo and Frank Marshall Davis defended North Korea, assailing the South as the aggressor. Again, they effortlessly parroted the Moscow line, as did CPUSA.

But it was getting harder to dupe others into accepting that Communist regimes were "positive factors for peace." In addition to the North Koreans' aggression, there was the USSR's slaughter of tens of thousands of freedom-seeking Hungarians during the 1956 uprising in Budapest.

Most devastating to Communists was the political earthquake generated by Nikita Khrushchev's February 1956 "Secret Speech." In a marathon address to a closed session of the Twentieth Congress of the Communist Party, Khrushchev, the new Soviet leader, denounced the crimes of predecessor Joseph Stalin, who had made his descent into the next world on March 5, 1953 (thirteen years to the day after he signed the death warrants of more than twenty thousand Polish military officers). Khrushchev unleashed a litany of facts and figures on Uncle Joe's annihilation of millions of human beings.[1] The lengthy text, smuggled out of Moscow by an agent in the Israeli Mossad,[2] was released by the U.S. State Department and ultimately published worldwide, including in a gigantic 24,000-word transcript in the New York Times.[3] Only the blindest Potemkin Progressive could still suffer any delusions about the Soviets' "Great Experiment." Even American Communists not repelled by the Hitler-Stalin Pact now found themselves reeling.

An eyewitness to the despair was David Horowitz, the 1960s radical/Communist who today is a conservative. Horowitz was raised a red-diaper baby in Brooklyn. His father read the New York Times every day from cover to cover. Horowitz recalls when his parents and their friends opened their sacred Times and read the Khrushchev speech: "Their world collapsed—and along with it their will to struggle. If the document was true, almost everything they had said and believed was false."[4]

It was true. Their utopia was a false one. The struggle had been not for good but for evil.

"The last page crumpled in my fist," confessed Peggy Dennis, wife of longtime Communist Party apparatchik Eugene Dennis, upon reading the text of Khrushchev's bombshell. "I lay in the half darkness and I wept." Mrs. Dennis had given everything—mind, body, soul, husband, even her child—to Bolshevism, and now, "a thirty-year life's commitment . . . lay shattered. I lay sobbing low, hiccoughing whimpers."[5]

But never underestimate the zealot's faith. Communism was a religion to its adherents, and many of the laity refused to give up the faith. CPUSA did not saunter off into the night, nor did the Daily Worker. Lenin's altar servers regrouped, keeping the candles lit for another day.

That day arrived in the early 1960s—in Asia. Communists got a gift when the United States began a protracted, unpopular, and costly war in Vietnam. It was a gift in that many American liberals soured on U.S. involvement, especially after the Kennedy years. This meant that American Communists, who naturally opposed America in the conflict, would soon have an entirely new, and extremely effective, propaganda tool to use against Uncle Sam. In fact, this became their best weapon yet.

The grinding Vietnam War, in which the United States was actively engaged from the early 1960s to 1975, spanning four presidents, two Democrats and two Republicans, afforded one of the most fertile periods for dupes in American history. If the Soviets had not been such raving atheists, they might have considered it providential, with fate playing out so fortuitously in favor of Moscow's destructive objectives. Consider: Since the late 1940s the Kremlin had launched a major push to recruit young people from around the world, particularly in its biannual World Youth Festivals, the largest of which was held in Moscow in 1957. The Soviets learned that even when young Americans did not come all the way over to join their cause, or to join America's Communist Party, they could still often be counted on to unwittingly repeat the Soviet line. Youth were some of the best candidates for dupery. And the Vietnam War caused America's university campuses to erupt. As the body count rose—hitting upwards of thirty thousand dead Americans by 1968—and the draft commenced, America's students spilled out into the parks and quads, and behaved in ways never seen in America before or since. The young protesters united in opposition to U.S. policy in Vietnam.

The goal of that policy was to stop a Communist takeover in Vietnam that (policymakers feared) could lead to a "domino effect" throughout Southeast Asia, with nations from Cambodia to Laos potentially falling into the Communist camp. Chiang Kai-shek's China, the most populous nation on the planet, had already fallen to Communism, as had North Korea. The Democratic Kennedy and Johnson administrations, along with most Republicans, feared a wider collapse that would lead these nations to become Soviet allies in the Cold War.

Moscow clearly hoped for Communist ascendancy, even after the Sino-Soviet split in the late 1950s. At the very least, the Kremlin wished for a crushing U.S. defeat. The Soviets did their part to help foster that downfall, through military aid to the Vietcong, diplomatic troublemaking, shamelessly inciting the June 1967 Six-Day War in the Middle East,[6] and launching remarkable "Active Measures" and propaganda campaigns and other forms of mischief and murder.

Morris Childs's Heroic Work

One of the best eyewitnesses to Soviet intentions in Vietnam was Morris Childs. Childs was the number-two man at CPUSA and was plugged into the Soviet leadership. And he was secretly working for the FBI—the greatest of Cold War spies.

Childs, known by only a handful of U.S. government officials as "Agent 58," was born June 10, 1902, outside Kiev. His real name was Moishe Chilovsky. His family, like many Russian Jews, was a victim of the czars' pogroms. Childs's parents fled for America, arriving in Chicago on December 11, 1911.

Nurtured by Chicago's progressives, especially at the Chicago Institute of Art and at Jane Addams's Hull House, Childs quickly became a political radical. At age nineteen he joined the United Communist Party of America (a forerunner to CPUSA), joining so early that he was a charter member. The party insisted on absolute fealty, and he obeyed the master's voice: as biographer John Barron recorded, "Whatever the party asked, Morris did."[7]

Childs became close to Earl Browder, the future general secretary of CPUSA. He was sent to Moscow in January 1929 to attend the Lenin School, which trained leaders for the worldwide revolution. There, he learned violent, clandestine techniques to advance the revolution: explosives, robbery, sabotage, firearms, urban guerrilla warfare. He was also recruited into the OGPU (Soviet secret political police) as an informant. Childs rose steadily within CPUSA, and by the 1960s he had become the second-highest-ranked person in the party hierarchy, behind only Gus Hall, who was named CPUSA general secretary in 1959. From the 1960s until 1980 Childs was the most trusted American in Moscow. He became especially close to Leonid Brezhnev and his regime. The Soviets eventually bestowed on him the prestigious Soviet Order of the Red Banner.

Morris Childs, however, hoodwinked CPUSA and the Soviets. The revelations of the late 1930s—Stalin's purges and mass terror, the famine, the Hitler-Stalin Pact—had been a wake-up call for him. Over time he had become a stalwart anti-Communist, and in the mid-1950s he went to work as an undercover FBI agent against Moscow. The fact that he got so close to the Soviet regime at the very highest levels was a stunning accomplishment for an American agent.

Unaware that they were dealing with a mole, Soviet leaders were fully candid with Childs, including on the subject that dominated American headlines: Vietnam. Brezhnev, Boris Ponomarev, Mikhail Suslov—the latter two were the top dogs in the International Department, the successor organization to the Comintern—and other Politburo members used facts and figures to reassure Childs (and thus CPUSA) that they were doing all they could to assist Communist North Vietnam militarily and politically in order to hasten America's defeat.

For example, during the Twenty-third Congress of the Communist Party, held March–April 1966, the Soviets briefed Childs in great detail on the extent of their military aid to North Vietnam, as well as their plans to enlist leftist Western intellectuals in a propaganda campaign to undermine U.S. forces in Vietnam and to try to prompt an American withdrawal.[8] Central to the Soviet disinformation campaign was a canard that the Left reflexively repeated any time a Communist movement popped up: Vietnam was simply another uprising of "nationalism" by an indigenous force and was in no way a serious Communist threat to American ("imperial") interests.

Between October 1967 and June 1968, Childs journeyed into the Soviet bloc four times, where he met with Soviet officials as well as Communist leaders from

Hungary, Czechoslovakia, and North Vietnam itself. He saw firsthand the Soviet commitment to coordinate all Western Communist parties. The Soviet party dictated to the other parties the position to take on events ranging from the 1967 Six-Day War in the Middle East to the 1968 Prague Spring in Czechoslovakia. (When Soviet tanks rolled into Czechoslovakia, American comrades loyally supported their Soviet masters, defending the indefensible by claiming that Moscow had somehow come to the rescue of Czechs against "imperialist aggression.")[9] Childs also brought home Soviet directives on Vietnam in which the USSR urged Communist parties worldwide to engage in "anti-war actions" against America.[10]

The FBI agent turned the directives over to American officials, from the FBI to certain members of Congress. Those officials must have been jolted by the realization that the Soviets were dumping whatever resources they could into Vietnam, seeking to amplify their military aid. This was a time when the Soviets were financially destitute, unable to spend the money they wanted in the Middle East, Latin America, Cuba, and even at home, and when the USSR was concerned that relations with the United States could deteriorate to the point of nuclear war, not to mention that relations with Red China were seriously worsening. So why would Moscow invest so heavily in Vietnam? Because the Soviet leadership was certain that nothing could better advance its interests than an American defeat in Vietnam. The Kremlin resolved to keep up the support for the North Vietnamese at whatever financial cost.[11]

No doubt, then, Moscow was elated as antiwar sentiment exploded in the United States in the late 1960s. More than that, the Soviets, and the Communist movement generally, particularly CPUSA, sought to infiltrate, support, and manipulate American antiwar sentiment wherever and whenever possible, but always with the most careful concealment.

This is most certainly not to say that the American antiwar movement was a Soviet or Communist movement. The vast majority of students participating in the demonstrations were in no way connected to the Communist Party or the international Communist movement. But the truth is that many of the planners and organizers of antiwar demonstrations did have those sympathies and links. In other words, the Communists and their supporters found many dupes among sincere American antiwar protesters.

Of course, many of the antiwar organizers with Communist sympathies were smart enough never to join the party and to deny any membership when asked—including when asked by congressional committees.

Congressional Investigations—by Democrats

As valuable a source as Morris Childs was, the information he produced was nothing compared to what congressional investigators were learning at the time. Once again on the case was the House Committee on Un-American Activities—or, as it became known in 1969, the House Committee on Internal Security.

Given the common dismissal of congressional investigations into Communism as the product of "right-wing Republicans," it is important to understand that these committees were controlled by *Democrats*. From 1965 to 1969 the Committee on Un-American Activities was chaired by Democratic congressman Edwin E. Willis, a twenty-year veteran of the House from Louisiana. Joining Willis on the committee were such Democrats as John Culver of Iowa and William Tuck of Virginia (who had been governor before entering Congress). The newly renamed House Committee on Internal Security was chaired by Democrat Richard Ichord of Missouri beginning in 1969, and it included such prominent Democrats as Edwin Edwards of Louisiana (a future governor), Richardson Preyer of North Carolina, the very liberal Louis Stokes of Ohio, and no less an authority on Communism than Claude "Red" Pepper of Florida, who was no longer a senator. Ichord, a crusading anti-Communist Democrat, dominated the most heated hearings exploring the associations between the American antiwar movement and the global Communist movement, which took place from 1967 to 1969. The only Republican who received even a portion of Ichord's camera time was the well-known conservative John Ashbrook of Ohio.

In short, the House committee was not some right-wing kangaroo court.

Nor were their hearings a travesty of justice or a black mark on the history of Congress, as the conventional treatment would have it. In truth, as any objective observer can see from the formal resolutions issued by the committee, as well as the transcripts of the hearings, congressmen and their investigators took great care to make the crucial distinctions between Communists and non-Communists, between threats and non-threats, between the guilty and the innocent. The goal was not to toss into jail any eighteen-year-old in Berkeley who hoisted a bong and a banner alongside a hammer and sickle. Quite the contrary: the purpose was to ascertain whether certain Americans were formally cooperating with foreign Communist governments with which the United States was engaged in either hot war or cold war. The House committees took the time to articulate this distinction again and again. Congressman Ichord, in particular, did so repeatedly, with both vigilance and sensitivity.

To see this requires pausing to actually read the transcripts, as scholars should. Too often historians have relied on secondhand accounts from their colleagues in the academy—some of whom were themselves '60s protesters.

The "New Mobe" Committee

One of the organizations that came to the attention of congressional investigators was "New Mobe": the New Mobilization Committee to End the War in Vietnam.

New Mobe was the successor to the National Mobilization Committee to End the War in Vietnam, or "Mobe." Mobe was launched September 10–11, 1966, in Cleveland, while New Mobe was formed the patriotic weekend of July 4, 1969, also in Cleveland. Together these organizations were the driving force behind several major subversive activities and domestic disturbances in the 1960s, such as the November 5, 1966, rally in New York City and the massive April 15, 1967, antiwar marches in New York City and San Francisco. Those were soon followed by a National Antiwar Conference in Washington, D.C., on May 20–21, 1967, which began laying the groundwork for the October 21, 1967, march on the Pentagon. There followed other activities: the August 1968 uprising at the Democratic National Convention in Chicago; the violence at the January 1969 "counter-inaugural" demonstrations in Washington, which protested the swearing-in ceremony of incoming president Richard Nixon; and the huge protests in San Francisco and Washington on November 15, 1969, which were part of the Mobilization Committee's 1969 "Fall Offensive."[12]

From the beginning Mobe and New Mobe were infiltrated by Communists. The organizations grew out of several conferences staged by radicals in Cleveland. There Communists mixed in among socialists, Communist sympathizers, as well as non-Communist liberals and peaceniks. According to a major congressional report, "a large percentage" of the several hundred delegates at the conferences came from front groups and openly Communist groups such as CPUSA, the Trotskyist Socialist Workers Party, and the Young Socialist Alliance.[13] Other entities participating in Mobe and New Mobe included the DuBois Clubs of America, the Workers World Party (a dissident Trotskyist group formed in 1959), Youth Against War and Fascism (a front group that was a youth arm of the Workers World Party), Harry Bridges's usual suspects at the ILWU, the pro-Hanoi Women Strike for Peace, Veterans for Peace in Vietnam (begun in Chicago in 1966 by CPUSA member Leroy Wolins), the Black Panther Party, and Students for a Democratic Society (SDS).[14] Among the fellow travelers, groups like the

Black Panthers and SDS brought together Communists and non-Communists, the dupers and the duped. Overall, Mobe and New Mobe endeavored to reach beyond these groups into a wider swath of American youth, all united against American policy in Southeast Asia. Many of the young people who signed onto Mobe and New Mobe events were non-Communist peace activists utterly unaware of the true intentions of some of the organizers.

New Mobe caught the attention of the House Committee on Internal Security. The congressional committee eventually produced a formal staff study that reflected its careful approach. The foreword to the study, by Congressman Ichord, the Democratic chair, shows that the committee did not blindly assume that commies were under every New Mobe bed:

> This study reveals how the New Mobe has operated from its inception with significant domestic and international communist support, and it details for the interested reader "the basic pattern of communist participation that has remained a characteristic of all Mobe activity." . . .
>
> One additional aspect must be emphasized. The New Mobe is a coalition of organizations, *both communist and noncommunist* [emphasis original]. Its basic organizational principle is nonexclusion. Were it not for this "umbrella" nature of New Mobe, providing association with many sincerely motivated noncommunists, the communists and other subversives within the group would have little effectiveness. All too often such "umbrella" coalitions are cynically exploited by the communists and thereby serve to promote international communism's objectives. This has traditionally been the pattern when communists have coalesced with noncommunists in united front operations.[15]

As this opening to the House study demonstrates, the Committee on Internal Security discovered the crucial role of the dupe in the antiwar fray. The committee recognized that New Mobe would have been dead without the dupes. The Communists within New Mobe needed a big tent, a wide "umbrella," to bring in the non-Communists who gave them surface legitimacy. The dupes were being used—"cynically exploited," as Congressman Ichord put it—by the Communists in order "to promote international communism's objectives." It was an old pattern of exploitation, as old as the Communist movement itself.

We're for Peace

The final sentence of the foreword to Congress's report exculpates New Mobe's dupes from any real guilt, since they were unaware that they were being used. "While the staff study focuses on subversive involvement in New Mobe," Congressman Ichord wrote, "I would caution readers that mere mention of an individual or organization should not necessarily be construed as a finding of subversive intent." Most of those who aided and abetted had no clue that they were aiding and abetting.

The congressional report also noted that New Mobe's mission statement was broad enough to attract thousands of non-Communist liberals under the guise of "peace." New Mobe described itself as "a broad coalition of organizations and individuals whose purpose is to gain an immediate end to the war in Vietnam through immediate and total withdrawal of American men and materiel."[16] Of course, the statement was also, to the letter, the goal of the USSR and the Communist movement, since American withdrawal would allow Vietnam to become a single Communist state and Marxism to spread deeper into Asia, and would represent a massive failure for America. But from that artfully worded mission statement, non-Communist dupes would not be able to detect the Communists' other, overriding objectives.

The dupes cannot be wholly absolved of blame, however. They willingly signed on to an organization whose words became viciously anti-American. New Mobe's ringleaders escalated their rhetoric, deeming U.S. proposals for peace as fraudulent, the insincere demands of an "imperialist," "warmongering" nation supporting "fascism." This was the same language that the American Peace Mobilization had used a generation earlier, and that was now being printed on the front pages of *Pravda* and newspapers up and down the Communist bloc.[17]

New Mobe also insisted on a "unilateral decision for withdrawal," or that Americans immediately begin paying reparations to the people of Vietnam. The language, as Congress noted in its official report, was "militantly pro-Hanoi and anti–United States." The group acted as if there was no South Vietnam at all, nor anyone, anywhere, in all of Vietnam, who was against the Communist Vietcong. In Vietnam, New Mobe saw only naked, brutal aggression, and therein from only one source: America.

For instance, Professor Sidney M. Peck, one of several national cochairs of New Mobe, issued such militant (and childish) demands. "We want the complete and total withdrawal of American forces from Vietnam," stated Peck, a sociology professor at Case Western Reserve University in Cleveland, Ohio. "If that results in a victory of the National Liberation Front, we are pleased with that result because that would in effect be the wishes of the Vietnamese people."[18]

That "pleasing" result also just happened to be the wishes of CPUSA, of the Soviet Union, of the USSR's International Department, of the Communist bloc, of Mao's Red China, of Kim's North Korea, of the fledgling Khmer Rouge movement in Cambodia, of Castro's Cuba, and, of course, of the Vietcong. As it happens, Peck was a former member of the Wisconsin State Committee of CPUSA. He was one of many CPUSA associates explicitly identified among the New Mobe hierarchy.[19]

As Peck's statement shows—and again, the professor was national cochair of New Mobe—ringleaders of American "peace movements" genuinely hoped for a defeat of the United States and a Communist takeover in Vietnam. They wanted America not only to leave but also to *lose*. That is not an exaggeration or misrepresentation.

Another professor and national cochair of New Mobe, Douglas Dowd of Cornell University, waxed wistful about a world where he and his young comrades joined the enemy. Said Dowd: "One of the tensions that we've had to work out within the New Mobilization Committee is that the people who do the organizing for this kind of thing, almost all of them, really feel that not only the war should end but that, that, if there had to be a side in that war, I think most of us feel we would be on the other side."[20]

Note that Dowd, an expert on Karl Marx and the "evolutionary economist" Thorstein Veblen, here referred to "almost all" of the organizers.

Not that many of the marchers were much better than the organizers. Some of them actually preferred to see American boys killed rather than the Vietcong. Those who thought that way were not isolated nutcases who were never heard from again. Consider the case of Arthur "Pinch" Sulzberger Jr., who in the 1960s was such a committed antiwar activist that he was twice arrested during protests. He was asked by his father, Arthur "Punch" Sulzberger Sr., a simple question: "If a young American soldier comes upon a young North Vietnamese soldier, which one do you want to see get shot?" Pinch responded without hesitation, saying this was "the dumbest question I ever heard in my life." He answered: "I would want to see the American get shot. It's the other guy's country."[21]

Today, young Pinch serves as publisher of the *New York Times,* which from 2003 to 2008 led an unrelenting campaign against President George W. Bush's policy in Iraq.

All of this raises the question of just how many of the thousands of young Americans who joined the protests—many simply for the sex and drugs—had

any idea of the views and intentions of organizers and some of their fellow protesters. How many knew they were marching arm-in-arm with comrades whose
sympathies lay on "the other side"?

How many knew they were being used?

Both the Communist and defeatist sympathies at Mobe and New Mobe rallies were transparent from the outset, making it difficult to excuse the dupes.
For instance, the November 5, 1966, protest in New York City, which attracted
twenty thousand people—including members of CPUSA, the Trotskyist Socialist
Workers Party, and the Workers World Party—featured signs that read: "Defeat
the U.S. Imperialists—Victory for NLF [National Liberation Front (the Vietcong)]."[22] That kind of truth in advertising was blatant to anyone but the blind.

Mobe and New Mobe were about more than marches, too. The groups began
targeting local Selective Service and IRS offices. Professor Peck, a sponsor of the
Communist-manipulated Vietnam Week (April 8–15, 1967), was one of the adult
professionals who spearheaded the group RESIST, which specialized in instructing young people in how to avoid being drafted into military service.

The Communist Party always sought a strong presence at conferences organized by Mobe and New Mobe. Consider just one example (among many revealed
in congressional reports): on December 28–30, 1966, antiwar organizers gathered for a conference at the University of Chicago to discuss a nationwide student
strike and other demonstrations for the explicit purpose of demanding U.S. withdrawal from Vietnam. Among the 257 attendees were representatives of CPUSA,
the Trotskyist Socialist Workers Party, and at least four other identified Communist organizations. Three Communist organizations, the DuBois Clubs of America,
the ultra-radical Progressive Labor Party, and the Young Socialist Alliance, set up
tables and handed out literature in the lobby of the university's Kent Hall, where
plenary sessions were held. The Communist presence was open and undeniable.[23]

The main speakers on the first day of the conference included Fred Kushner,
SDS leader and son of Sam Kushner, a longtime CPUSA leader and editor of the
Los Angeles–based *People's World;* and Dan Styron of the Young Socialist Alliance,
a contributor to *The Militant,* the weekly newspaper of the Trotskyist Socialist
Workers Party. Also addressing the delegates was Professor Peck, who told them
openly, "We hope to energize and consolidate opposition movements throughout
the world."[24]

The level of Communist infiltration in Mobe and New Mobe activities was so
extensive that the House Committee on Internal Security's final staff study report
ran to roughly one hundred small-print pages and included more than four hundred endnotes. This was a major operation, with serious infiltration.

Summer of '68

But all of that was merely a warm-up. Mobe played a special role in the unforget-table chaos that enflamed the summer of 1968. That season was a glorious one for Communist radicals in the United States. It was truly their heyday.

The intentions of the radicals that summer—particularly the SDS contin-gent—was made clear in a June 4, 1968, letter from the SDS cofounder Tom Hayden to a North Vietnamese Communist official addressed as "Colonel Lao" (the correct spelling was "Lau"). The letter, which was entered into the official con-gressional record (see page 292), is one of many pieces of evidence which counter the common claim that 1960s antiwar organizers were merely seeking "peace." As the letter makes clear, the goal for many was victory by North Vietnam:

June 4, 1968

Dear Col. Lao;

This note is to introduce you to Mr. Robert Greenblatt, the coordinator of the National Mobilization to End the War in Vietnam. He works closely with myself and Dave Dellinger, and has just returned from Hanoi.

    If there are any pressing questions you wish to discuss, Mr. Greenblatt will be in Paris for a few days.

    We hope that the current Paris discussions go well for you. The news from South Vietnam seems very good indeed.

    We hope to see you this summer in Paris or at a later time.

Good fortune!
Victory!
/s/ Tom Hayden
Tom Hayden

Hayden's valediction would seem to speak for itself: he hoped for "Victory!" by the Vietcong—that is, victory *against* Hayden's own country, the United States.[25]

    David Dellinger, referenced in Hayden's letter, had helped organize Mobe and became its chairman. So active was Dellinger that, the *Washington Post* reported, he organized a September 1968 antiwar meeting in the heart of the Soviet bloc, in Budapest, Hungary. According to the *Post* article, which carried the eye-grabbing

12

The conference also selected a three-man interim committee to serve until such time as various national and regional student and anti-war organizations could choose their own representatives to serve on a national committee to organize the demonstrations. This interim committee consisted of Rennie Davis, active in SDS community organizing projects and the head of National Mobe's 1968 Summer of Support program, an operation aimed at servicemen disaffected with the war in Vietnam; Dave Dellinger; and Vernon Grizzard, who, in addition to having been active in SDS, has traveled to Budapest, Hungary, to consult with representatives of the National Liberation Front and the North Vietnamese forces. Grizzard also traveled to Hanoi in 1968 as part of a three-man National Mobe group invited by the North Vietnamese to participate in the release of three captured American pilots.[173]

The program announced after the Chicago conference of March 22-24 was reiterated in an August mailing from the Mobe's New York national office, following a July 20 Cleveland meeting of the Mobilization's administrative committee:

Our activities will be issue oriented and will not focus on candidates. We will call for an end to the bombing (so that negotiations can take place) and for American military withdrawal - from Vietnam and the black communities. We will call for self determination in Vietnam and in the black and other poor communities.

This letter announced that there was already a staff of 25 persons in Chicago preparing for the projected massive demonstrations. This staff was led by project directors Rennie Davis and Tom Hayden "and is greatly aided by the Chicago Peace Council which is actively committed to the program." The letter was signed by Dave Dellinger, chairman of the National Mobilization Committee, and Robert Greenblatt, Mobe's national coordinator, about whom the following document, written to a North Vietnamese official, is of interest:[174]

June 4, 1968

Dear Col. Lao;

This note is to introduce you to Mr. Robert Greenblatt, the coordinator of the National Mobilization to End the War in Vietnam. He works closely with myself and Dave Dellinger, and has just returned from Hanoi.

If there are any pressing questions you wish to discuss, Mr. Greenblatt will be in Paris for a few days.

We hope that the current Paris discussions go well for you. The news from South Vietnam seems very good indeed.

We hope to see you this summer in Paris or at a later time.

Good fortune!
Victory!

/s/ Tom Hayden

Tom Hayden

On August 4, 1968, another meeting of the National Mobe administrative committee was held in Chicago. Chairman of the session was David Dellinger. Others present at the meeting included:[175]

(1) Tom Bickler, Radical Organizing Committee;[176]
(2) Irving Beinin, Guardian;
(3) Richard D. Conrad, Radical Organizing Committee;[177]
(4) Rennie Davis, National Mobe;
(5) Dave Dellinger, National Mobe;
(6) Ted Dostal, Workers World Party;[178]
(7) Helen Gurewitz, Washington Mobilization for Peace representative and identified member of the Communist Party, U.S.A.;[179]
(8) Richard Hill, Student Mobilization Committee, SWP;
(9) Bob Greenblatt, National Mobe;

"Victory!": Congress reproduced this letter from SDS cofounder Tom Hayden to a North Vietnamese Communist official in which Hayden expresses his hope for a Vietcong victory over the United States.

headline "U.S. War Foes Met with Hanoi Group," the meeting included representatives of North Vietnam and the National Liberation Front, for the purpose of reviewing the war and discussing antiwar strategy for American campuses.[26]

Any reasonable observer who read Hayden's letter, and who knew the publicly available background on him and his fellow antiwar organizers, would not fail to understand that Congress needed to look into this matter immediately. But when the House Committee on Un-American Activities and its successor, the Committee on Internal Security, did so, the American Left responded with howls of "fascism!"

The desire for Communist victory over America in Vietnam was also the position at *The Militant,* a popular publication for New Mobe leaders. *The Militant* candidly explained that "representatives of the [Trotskyist] Socialist Workers Party and Young Socialist Alliance" regarded themselves as "partisans of the Vietnamese liberation struggle." These Communists, *The Militant* explained, had an "obligation to build a broad mass movement in opposition to the war from the viewpoint of aiding the Vietnamese revolution."[27]

War opposition was not so much about American withdrawal as it was about Communist victory.

Blowing up the Democratic Convention

The Communists were emboldened as American public opinion shifted dramatically against the Vietnam War in that brutal year of 1968. The radicals' capstone would come in late August, in the very city where the American Communist Party had taken root in 1919: Chicago. The Windy City was hosting the national convention for the party that controlled the White House and Congress—the Democrats. For many months Communists and their fellow radical peaceniks plotted to turn the Democratic National Convention into a fiasco, an international humiliation for the Democrats. They wanted to provoke shocking images that would show America under siege, a kind of warzone at home.

The other message the radicals wanted to convey to those millions watching on television was that these students, this next generation, were primarily concerned about "peace"—for America and for Vietnam. They would demonstrate for an end to the war in Vietnam so people there, too, could live in peace. Most run-of-the-mill marchers desired just that, but certain antiwar organizers had other goals—goals they carefully concealed in order to dupe their fellow protesters.

U.S. officials understood that radicals were planning an uprising at the Democratic National Convention. In fact, so much evidence surfaced early on that

Congressman Ichord warned fellow members of Congress on two occasions, May 13 and June 26, 1968, that radicals were planning to throw the August convention into chaos.[28] What Ichord had warned about came to fruition.

A congressional investigator sent to Chicago, James L. Gallagher, concluded that "the basic purpose of the Chicago demonstration can perhaps best be summed up in one word, 'Vietnam.'" By this, Gallagher meant that demonstrators were not only antiwar but also *pro*-Vietcong—that is, they supported the objectives of worldwide Communism. "Many placards, projects, and pieces of propaganda," he reported, "indicated that the proposals advocated by the demonstrators were clearly compatible with the policies of Hanoi, Havana, Peking, and Moscow."[29]

That was no surprise: many of the ringleaders in Mobe and among the radicals had been to those very places, interacting with Communist officials there. More than that, they deeply admired those cities and their systems.

How many groups were involved in this mass demonstration in Chicago? The news media estimated anywhere from one hundred to three hundred. Gallagher and his team of investigators pegged eighty-two specific organizations that made plans to attend or were there in Chicago. In addition to all the Communist groups, ranging from CPUSA to the Trotskyists, were a large array of duped groups, some infiltrated and being used by Communists as fronts, particularly the various regional "peace committees," such as the Chicago Peace Council, the Cincinnati Action for Peace, and the Connecticut Peace Coalition. Also in Chicago were such organizations as the High School Union, the National Unity for Peace, the National Welfare Rights Organization, the Parent School, People Against Racism, Teachers for Peace in Vietnam, and the Wisconsin Draft Resistance Union. As usual, the Religious Left was in force as well, with organizations like the American Friends Service Committee, the Catholic Peace Fellowship, Concerned Clergy and Laymen, and the Episcopal Peace Fellowship. Likewise providing a strong presence was the colorful Youth International Party (the "Yippies"), formed earlier that year at a New Year's Eve party in Greenwich Village by Abbie Hoffman, Jerry Rubin, Paul Krassner, and crew. Finally, of course, SDS, the massive group that was quickly becoming (if not already) the dominant student-radical organization in America, was a major factor there.[30]

Upwards of a dozen of the key organizations readying for Chicago were explicitly Communist or well-known front groups for Communists. This was no accident, for CPUSA had been sending out directives since at least 1964 giving detailed marching orders on precisely how, where, and when to protest the U.S. presence in Vietnam. Some of these directives were issued in coordination with (or following the lead of) SDS in particular, as the Communist Party often promoted various strikes and other activities organized by SDS.[31] (See page 296.) Many SDS chieftains were dedicated Communists—a volatile mix of Maoists, Stalinists, and followers of Che Guevara and Fidel Castro.[32]

Roots: Columbia University

Radicals' plans to subvert the Democratic convention were set in motion as early as October 1967, right after the Democrats announced that their convention would be held in Chicago.[33] On October 17 the New York chapter of the Communist-infiltrated National Conference for New Politics held a meeting at Schermerhorn Hall at Columbia University.[34] Columbia, a hotbed of radicalism since before the days of John Dewey, was becoming even more unhinged, especially its SDS contingent. That a New York faction would be organizing a massive demonstration in Chicago was fitting. No two cities had deeper Communist roots, dating back to September 1919.

Dominating the Columbia meeting was the prominent Communist John J. Abt, a member of the national committee of the National Conference for New Politics. Abt was so well-known within those circles that Lee Harvey Oswald, the assassin of President John F. Kennedy—and a Communist—had publicly called for Abt's assistance after his arrest. Other speakers at that meeting included Seymour Copstein and Laird Cummings, both in the past either identified as Communists or linked to various Communist organizations and fronts.[35]

The dupes subsequently suckered into the Chicago effort could not so easily claim ignorance of the protest's radical origins. The Columbia meeting at which Communists and their fellow travelers began planning the convention demonstration had been reported in two columns in the fall of 1967 by popular syndicated columnist Alice Widener. Not long after, the very same National Conference for New Politics placed a seven-column ad in the December 10, 1967, *New York Times* flat out stating that the agitators were preparing "the largest demonstration this country has ever seen. It would descend upon the National Democratic Convention in Chicago." In that huge ad, the group made abundantly clear that it would do everything within its means not only to "help mobilize" this mass demonstration but also to "stop" Lyndon Johnson from again receiving the Democratic Party's presidential nomination.[36]

It was hard to miss the ad in the *Times,* or Widener's warnings.

And yet these items did not awaken the dupes. Two factors aided the Communists and other radicals looking to enlist non-Communist supporters: (1) the

2268 DISRUPTION OF 1968 DEMOCRATIC NATIONAL CONVENTION

COMMITTEE EXHIBIT NO. 2—Continued

January 8, 1968

To All Districts & Leading Youth

Re: International Student Strike _1/

Just a reminder that a conference is being held in Chicago sponsored by
the Student Mobilization to discuss an international student strike. This Conference will take place on January 27-29 at the University of Chicago, in Chicago.
All indications are that it will be one of the most significant conferences in the
student movement. Thousands of invitations have been sent out including more
than 300 to Black student groups.

At the recent SDS Convention it was decided that while national SDS did
not really "like" the idea of the strike, if one took place it would not oppose it
as SDS has on previous national mobilizations. Instead SDS would try to find
some way to integrate it into their Call for ten days of resistance in April.

SDS representatives will be attending the conference to argue their approach.
This development has resolved a number of problems but important questions still
remain.

Still unresolved are the basic questions of:

1. Whether in addition to "disruptive type" actions involving the more left,
    there will be a militant action which can reach out to hundreds of thous-
    ands (such as a student strike).

2. Whether such a movement will work for an alliance with Black students.
    And in general whether some attempts will be made by the Peace move-
    ment to deal with the racist attacks against itself and the whole move-
    ment.

At this point the possibilities for winning these points look good. But they are
still unresolved and will require a lot of debate.

We urge all young Communists to build this conference, to organize as
many students to go as possible and to guarantee Black student attendance.

The Du Bois Clubs has called a meeting of interested young people to discuss approaches to this conference. Their meeting will be held January 27-29
in Chicago.

In a previous memo we requested that you send us information on what you
are doing to mobilize for this conference and also a list of students from your
area to be proposed for a new Continuations Committee of the Student Mobilization.

If you haven't already answered, please rush this information to us immediately.

Black Youth Conference

There will be a Black Youth Conference in Chicago. This Conference is
an outgrowth of a series of regional conferences organized from the Newark Black
Power Conference.

The dates are: February 3-5 in Chicago, at the University of Chicago.

Specific issues in question are not known, but as soon as more information
is received it will be sent out.

Mike Zagarell
for National Youth Commission

_____
1 [Committee Note: The International Student Strike, which is the subject of this Communist Party directive, was
proposed by Bettina Aptheker, a member of the Communist Party's National Committee for the purpose of protesting
the Vietnam War (see Committee Report, *Communist Origin and Manipulation of Vietnam Week*, April 8-15, 1967).]

CPUSA and SDS: The Communist Party frequently sent out detailed directives on how to protest the Vietnam War. In this January 1968 directive, the CPUSA's National Youth Commission promotes SDS antiwar efforts.

DISRUPTION OF 1968 DEMOCRATIC NATIONAL CONVENTION **2277**

GRUBISIC EXHIBIT NO. 1

NATIONAL LAWYERS GUILD
5 BEEKMAN STREET
NEW YORK, N. Y. 10038
(212) - 227-1078

PRESIDENT
VICTOR RABINOWITZ
NEW YORK

EXECUTIVE SECRETARY
KENNETH CLOKE

ADMINISTRATIVE SECRETARY
JOAN LEVENSON

VICE PRESIDENTS
HON. GEORGE B. CROCKETT, JR
DETROIT

OSMOND K. FRAENKEL
NEW YORK

ARTHUR KINOY
NEW YORK

JOHN T. McTERNAN
LOS ANGELES

STANLEY FAULKNER
NEW YORK

BENJAMIN SMITH
NEW ORLEANS

HERMAN WRIGHT
HOUSTON

MAX DEAN
FLINT

ANN FAGAN GINGER
BERKELEY

DORIS BRIN WALKER
OAKLAND

FATHER ROBERT F. DRINAN, S. J.
BOSTON

SECRETARY
HERMAN B. GERRINGER
NEW YORK

TREASURER
DAVID SCRIBNER
NEW YORK

ADVISORY BOARD
JOHN M. COE
PENSACOLA

EARL B. DICKERSON
CHICAGO

BENJAMIN DREYFUS
SAN FRANCISCO

HON. ROBERT W. KENNY
LOS ANGELES

MALCOLM SHARP
CHICAGO

THOMAS I. EMERSON
NEW HAVEN

ERNEST GOODMAN
DETROIT

January 19, 1968

Dear Friend:

A meeting will be held at the office of the National Lawyers Guild, 5 Beekman St., Room 610 at 7:30 on Friday, January 26th to discuss the establishment of a nationwide legal defense apparatus to deal with the projected legal problems arising out of the political protest planned for the Democratic National Convention to be held in Chicago this summer.

The meeting will be attended by the planners of the political protest and by lawyers and law students nationally who wish to be of some help in sorting out the complex legal problems posed by the possibilities of injunctive suits to stop the convention procedings, mass arrests, civil disobedience, coordinated nationwide protest, civil suits for police brutality, and numerous other legal problems we must begin to face now. We will prepare forms, affidavits, research memoranda, and a handbook on mass arrests. We desperately need your help, ideas, criticisms and suggestions.

Please attend the meeting, but if you are unable, send us your name and address and any written suggestions you may have, and we will forward information to you.

Sincerely,

Ken Cloke
Executive Secretary

KC:ak

Preparing for the uprising: In this January 1968 letter, the National Lawyers Guild warns of a litany of "legal problems arising out of the political protest planned for the Democratic National Convention."

benign name, the National Conference for New Politics, and (2) the veneer of legitimacy provided by some of the endorsers. For example, one of the two signers of the *Times* ad was the cochairman of the National Conference for New Politics, whom the ringleaders had shrewdly brought into the fold: the spectacular dupe Dr. Benjamin Spock.[37]

The *New York Times* ran an article on the ad in its news section, titled "Leftists Ponder Convention Move." Reporter John Leo began the story with this lead: "Leaders of the New Left are contemplating a massive anti-Johnson demonstration at next summer's Democratic National Convention in Chicago." He noted that the National Conference for New Politics was made up of "liberals and radicals."[38]

Among the liberals, Leo quoted Dr. Spock saying that the group expected to draw "100,000 adults and 100,000 teenagers" to the Chicago amphitheater in August 1968. Amazingly, Spock dismissed any possibility of riots amid such a gigantic, volatile crowd. "I can't think of a reason why we would be inflammatory," was the doctor's prognosis. "Our demonstration would involve no violence or civil disobedience."

Leo cast doubt on Spock's naïve assurance in the next line of his story, where he quoted Paul Booth, a former SDS official and former board member of the National Conference for New Politics. SDS was on board for the protests in Chicago as well. Asked whether the demonstration would be a passive one, Booth said, "That's one of the topics under discussion." Apparently, it was a discussion that excluded the good doctor.

Not surprisingly, SDS had not been mentioned in the large ad placed in the newspaper that day.

Things were moving rapidly. The Left was lining up for the Chicago blast.

Among those at the front of the line was the legal arm of CPUSA, the National Lawyers Guild. As it said in a prophetic January 19, 1968, letter to certain "friends," the guild foresaw a litany of "legal problems arising out of the political protest planned for the Democratic National Convention." These ranged from "mass arrests" and "civil disobedience" to "civil suits for police brutality." In the letter, the guild invited a small group of associates to a January 26 meeting at its New York offices to discuss "ideas, criticisms and suggestions."[39] (See page 297.)

Target: Democratic Party

The plan to spoil the Democrats' 1968 convention had several motives, including one that has somehow eluded historical accounts: as Congress reported, there was a driving impetus to "break down" America's two-party system and to "bring about the creation of a third party, an independent movement of the left."[40]

That was indeed the case. It was a goal irrespective of whether Lyndon Johnson was the Democratic nominee for president (he ended up not running). The reason the far Left targeted the *Democratic* convention as opposed to the Republican convention is that the Communists and other radicals understood they could engender more support—for a third party and for the their beliefs generally—from people who shared the left side of the political spectrum (the Democrats) than they could from the party of the Right (the Republicans).

It is common for contemporary academics to portray the battles of the 1960s as matters of Left versus Right. In fact, fierce battles thundered from within the Left itself. As we have seen, anti-Communists *within the Democratic Party* investigated Communists diligently. But the radical uprising at the 1968 Democratic convention provides an even more vivid—and destructive—example of Left versus Left. The far Left was looking to undermine the Democratic Party as a way to fracture America's two-party system. Such a claim may seem far-fetched today, but it is true, as a majority-Democratic congressional panel determined at the time. Radical people seek radical ends. Remember, too, that the summer of 1968 was a turbulent time, when the word "revolution" was in the air—and was certainly on the minds of Marxists, as always.

The Aftermath: Congress Investigates

After so many months of planning, the radical organizers got what they wanted in Chicago in August 1968: a zoo. Television viewers all over America—and the world—witnessed the violent, chaotic scene outside the Democratic National Convention: hoses, cages, water cannons, arrests, beatings, club-wielding policemen. The situation was disastrous not only for Democrats but for the entire nation. The whole world was watching. Moscow was watching.

Congress, naturally, was appalled, and demanded explanations. Just a couple of weeks later, on September 12, the Democrat-led House Committee on Internal Security adopted a formal resolution ordering hearings into the matter. The hearings were held soon thereafter, on October 1, 3, and 4. As the resolution noted, the House committee sought, among other things, to uncover "the extent, character, and objectives" of the Communist influence, from home and possibly abroad, among the convention protesters—and especially the organizers.

Many radicals objected to the very notion of investigation, but the committee was clearly operating within its purview: internal security. As the committee's formal resolution observed, the "incidents and acts of force and violence" alone at Chicago merited an investigation. Add to the equation the possibility that foreign elements may have been behind the uprising—that the *Soviets,* through a Kremlin "Active Measures" campaign inside the United States, may have played some role in disrupting the national convention of the political party of the sitting president and congressional majority. For Congress *not* to investigate such a possibility would have been a dereliction of duty.

In short order the Committee on Internal Security was publishing evidence. As Congressman Ichord's prescient warnings had indicated, evidence had been amassing for months leading up to the convention demonstration. The committee's official resolution reported that Congress had received evidence that "communist, pro-communist, and other cooperating subversive elements within the National Mobilization Committee to End the War in Vietnam [Mobe], Students for a Democratic Society, Youth International Party, and various other organizations, were planning disruptive acts and violence in the City of Chicago, Illinois, during the week of August 25, 1968."[41]

The committee's formal resolution added that many of the same "subversive elements" who organized the Chicago uprising had also helped plan the Vietnam Week protests held a year earlier, in April 1967. The committee had published a previous report documenting similar Communist and radical influence at those 1967 events, "Communist Origin and Manipulation of Vietnam Week." It was not difficult for Congress to connect these dots.

Dr. Quentin Young at the Stand

The congressional hearings during those three days in October 1968 made for political theater. Of the six men who testified before the House Committee on Internal Security, none produced as many transcribed pages, or hoots and hollers, as Dr. Quentin Young.[42]

Dr. Young was a physician with offices at East Fifty-fifth Street in Chicago. He headed up something called the Medical Committee for Human Rights, providing special missionary service to SDSers. He was described as the "SDS doctor," the "movement doctor," as one who was always there to take care of the radicals, their friends, and their families for everything from blood poisoning to a head bandage to an abortion.[43]

The forty-three-year-old Young, who had been subpoenaed to testify, began his statement by contesting the validity of the subpoena. He denounced this "Un-American Committee" for its "unconstitutionality" and its thirty-year "ignoble existence," and proclaimed various rights to say nothing to the congressmen. He also lambasted Chicago police and city officials, as well as members of the armed forces, for their "brutality that shamed Chicago" during the Democratic convention. It was his "exceptionally courageous and humane" Medical Committee for Human Rights, said Young, which stepped in to alleviate "so much of the human suffering inflicted on citizens that week." Throughout his extended extemporaneous statement, Young squared off with Congressman Ichord, who gaveled the remarks as in violation of the rules for his testimony.

Once Young completed his statement, the committee members got to the hard questions.

General Counsel Chester D. Smith, after establishing Young's identity and profession, grew tired of the beating around the bush and asked candidly: "Dr. Young, are you a member of the Communist Party?" Congress already felt it had that answer; it had listed Young as an "identified CPUSA member" in its staff study of New Mobe.[44] While anti-anti-Communists regard such a question as the totem of the witch-hunter, recall that Congress was trying to ascertain whether there was international/Soviet involvement in the political disturbance. This was an important line of inquiry.

But the usually loquacious doctor refused to answer the question, disputing its constitutionality and relevance. In response, Congressman Ichord explained that "the legislative purpose of this investigation is to determine the extent of Communist and subversive activities, the part they played in the planning, in the organizations, of the disturbances in Chicago. The committee does have information that you played a part."

Ichord further pushed Dr. Young to answer the question. Young refused. The jousting began in earnest.

Counsel Smith informed Young that the committee had information showing that Young was a member of the Communist Party, and specifically of the "doctor's club of the party of the North Side of Chicago."

That specific question likewise got the committee nowhere. As it became clear that Young would not answer whether he was a party member, Smith got to a more important question: had Young served on the Medical Committee for Human Rights "pursuant to a plan or directive of the Communist Party?" After Young insisted on his rights not to answer that question, he conferred with his attorney and, surprisingly, answered with a direct "No."

Counsel Smith quickly explained that the "doctor's club" to which Young belonged was formally known as the Bethune Club, named for a Canadian surgeon, Norman Bethune, who was a Communist but had always tried to conceal his Communist identity. As Smith immediately proceeded to back up the point, "He [Bethune] served with the Communist—," Young's attorney, William Cousins Jr., objected to the relevance of Smith's information.

Counsel Smith's information then got extremely relevant: He presented a personal check signed by Quentin Young for $1,000, which went to pay the rent of New Mobe's office at 407 South Dearborn in Chicago. Young disputed that the check had been for that purpose, acknowledging only that it had gone to "somebody" in particular. Asked the identity of that somebody, Young conferred with counsel and named Rennie Davis, to whom he said it was a "loan" to be repaid within forty-eight hours.

Rennie Davis was a prominent radical, himself called to testify because of his activities. He had been to Hanoi, where he was welcomed with open arms by the Communists, and was identified by Congress as a "Vietcong supporter."[45] Davis had been a leading figure in New Mobe; he, along with Tom Hayden, had been a "project director" for the Democratic convention protests.[46] Thus, this check from Young to Davis, produced by the committee's legal staff, suggested Young's close connection to the leading organizers of the Chicago uprising.

But Dr. Young simply kept dodging, turning the hearing into a circus. During the course of questioning he launched into musings on the meaning of words like "affiliated," or whether he had indeed "indulged in haranguing," or his awareness (or lack thereof) of what was meant by "lawyers' techniques," or why on earth he would invoke the First Amendment instead of the Fifth Amendment to the Constitution, and on and on. Young and his counsel conferred on elementary points. Supporters inside the hearing room constantly interrupted the proceedings: the wild attorney William Kunstler repeatedly yelled from his seat in the audience; Abbie Hoffman was paraded into the room because of what Young's lawyer deemed an "emergency situation that has just arisen"; Dave Dellinger, Soviet bloc traveler and Mobe chairman, shouted from the floor, as did Jerry Rubin; Rennie Davis suddenly announced that he was present and could explain a matter raised in association with his name; Young's counsel asked the committee counsel, "When did you last beat your wife, sir?"; and on and on. The congressmen and the witnesses and their lawyers issued back-and-forth demands that various people—on the committee itself even—be expelled from the room. An exasperated Congressman Ichord repeatedly pounded his gavel to try to restore order.

The filibustering of Young, his counsel, and his fellow radicals in the hearing room forced the doctor to stay on to testify for another day. Young's attorney objected to going into a second day, but of course the doctor and his legal team had left Congress no other choice but to need more time, since they had avoided answering even the simplest questions.

At one point Congressman Ichord told Dr. Young that previous testimony had yielded the names of twenty-one Communists who were involved in the disturbances at the Democratic convention. Not only did Young not confirm any Communists, including whether he was one himself, but he even acted as if he had never before heard the word "Communist." Ichord had to remind Young: "Let me advise the doctor there have also been threats made to not only disrupt the convention processes in the future, but the Federal election process." The congressman also noted that more than thirty thousand Americans had been killed during the Vietnam War. "Let's not handle this with levity," Ichord concluded.[47]

Remarkably, Young was able to escape without ever addressing the pertinent questions of the hearing. It is understandable that he would not want to answer whether he was a Communist, but with his dissembling and digressions he made a mockery of a significant inquiry into whether foreign Communist powers were involved in the disruptions of the American political process—disruptions designed to force the U.S. government to change its policy on a crucial matter of national security. As Congressman Ichord rightly observed, this was not a matter to be treated with levity—though the men in Moscow were no doubt amused by the whole spectacle.

A reminder of how none of this was funny came from Robert Greenblatt, who also testified during the hearings.

Recall that Greenblatt, another New Mobe cochair, was the person mentioned in Tom Hayden's June 1968 letter to Colonel Lau, in which Hayden wished "Good fortune!" and "Victory!" to the Vietcong. On the stand, Greenblatt was cantankerous but much more open than Dr. Young. From his testimony, Congress learned that the New Mobe leader had met with Colonel Lau and also traveled to Czechoslovakia, Hungary, Cyprus, Paris, Hanoi, and a number of other significant places.[48] Here was clear evidence of *international* Communist involvement in a destructive domestic protest of the Vietnam War.

If Dr. Quentin Young was not in fact a Communist, then he was certainly used by the Communists and unwittingly aided them in their intentions. He and others intimately involved in the August 1968 Chicago uprising were dealing with things that they either did not fully understand or, worse, understood and concealed. Dr. Young was either duped or doing the duping.

Paul Douglas Says Goodbye

Not part of the carnival, but very much caught up in the times, was Senator Paul H. Douglas. Douglas serves as a fascinating case study of the complexity of this period as well as the Left's twists and turns dating back to the 1920s.

By the late 1960s, Senator Douglas was one liberal Democrat from Chicago who was not primed for duping. It had been forty years since Douglas's regrettable Potemkin village tour and tea with Uncle Joe. Now serving his third term in the Senate, the Ph.D. economist, Quaker turned Unitarian, and World War II hero was one of several Democrats in the Senate who were chastened Cold Warriors and supportive of LBJ's policies in Vietnam. He took that position while remaining a social liberal of impeccable credentials, staunchly supporting civil rights and social activism and opposing government abuse and corruption.[49]

The Democrat Douglas caused considerable angst among many of his liberal colleagues with his battle-hardened anti-Communism. He regretted having lobbied for diplomatic recognition of the Soviet Union so many years before, and he now opposed recognition of Mao's China as well as its admission to the United Nations. Duped once into supporting a massive Communist killing field, he was on guard against doing so again.

Douglas's strong anti-Communism and support for President Johnson's war policies ended up costing him politically. In 1966, two years before the 1968 blow-up, he was upset in his bid for a fourth Senate term.[50] The Democrat Douglas lost to a liberal Republican who was inclined to negotiations with the Vietcong. How things had changed.

The colorful life—Columbia doctorate, CPUSA target, SS *Useful Idiot* passenger, luncheon companion of Uncle Joe, University of Chicago professor, labor economist, New Dealer turned Cold Warrior, Okinawa Marine, Purple Heart recipient, U.S. senator, father and husband—would end only a few years later, as Douglas died in 1976. Following a private funeral at the Quaker Meeting House in Washington, D.C., Douglas's ashes were taken to Chicago, where the remains of the veteran of the Pacific theater were scattered at the Japanese gardens in Jackson Park. Douglas's final resting place was a vast distance from the smashed church bells long ago silenced in Stalin's Soviet Union.

The Forgotten Story

Perhaps it was Providence that spared Paul Douglas the ignominy of representing Illinois as its senator during the travesty at the Democratic National Convention in Chicago in August 1968. His embarrassment at the hands of Joseph Stalin forty years earlier had been enough.

Douglas wised up, but too many others did not. The protests at the 1968 Democratic convention offered numerous cases of dupery. Many of the protesters were non-Communist liberal students who did not know they were being used by the Communist movement. The duping continues today, as plenty of liberals, from the media to academia, fail to research the antiwar movement's links to the international Communist movement, or even to recall the evidence of such links that were publicly available at the time. The typical "flashback" news story portrays the 1968 convention as a hope-filled moment gone wrong, of nonviolent "peace" protesters running into the iron fist of the Chicago police and the National Guard. But ample evidence indicates that the Chicago uprising was an insidious Communist-supported (if not Communist-prodded) national-security showdown—a battle waged against Chicago's police and America's troops. Congressional Democrats uncovered this troubling evidence at the time and recognized that thousands of American dupes had unwittingly served Communist intentions.

Some of the characters who played prominent roles in the 1968 Chicago protests—dupes and non-dupes, non-Communists and Communists—are alive and well in America today, where they remain active in politics and enjoy cushy Ivory Tower jobs, seemingly exempt from criticism for their militant actions in 1968. With tenure, they tell their students a decidedly different tale of what happened in the late 1960s.

Nor are these figures found only in the halls of academia. Their influence extends much farther. Some high-profile characters from the October 1968 congressional hearings, such as Dr. Quentin Young, as well as names raised in connection with some of the most remarkable charges of cooperation with North Vietnam, such as Tom Hayden, would later help launch the political career of the current president of the United States, Barack Obama. And as we shall see again and again in the pages ahead, they were not the only radicals to play such an important role in our current political scene.

15

GROWN-UP VIETNAM DUPES:

DR. SPOCK, CORLISS LAMONT, AND FRIENDS

Scattered among the student radicals of the Vietnam era were some questionable grown-ups worthy of extensive discussion.[1] Onetime Potemkin Progressives like Paul Douglas had learned their lessons. They were no longer so easily misled. But others were.

The children of the 1960s quipped that they couldn't trust anyone over the age of thirty. That was not quite true. To the contrary, they not only trusted but embraced older folks who shared their radical-left worldview. There were new friends like Dr. Quentin Young. There were crusty old theoretical Marxists like Herbert Aptheker. There were CPUSA hacks like Gus Hall. There were longtime anti-anti-Communists like Lillian Hellman. And there were Old Left mainstays, leftovers from Soviet pilgrimages past. Some of them had bounced around Russia when Quentin Young was still bouncing on his grandfather's knee: fellow travelers like Corliss Lamont.

Lamont: Still Carrying the Flag

Corliss Lamont was one old codger the students of the '60s could trust. His politics was theirs.

Since the publication of *Russia Day by Day* in 1933, Lamont had continued his strident activism, and was just as far to the left as ever. He did a long stint as a director of the ACLU, from 1932 to 1954. As he stumped for "civil liberties" in America, he also continued to stump for the totalitarian state headquartered in Moscow. In 1939 he followed *Russia Day by Day* with the aptly titled *You Might Like Socialism,* released the same year as the Hitler-Stalin Pact and just after Stalin exterminated tens of millions of people. Then came other Lamont odes to the Motherland: in 1946, *The People of the Soviet Union*; in 1952, *Soviet Civilization.*

Aside from books, the prolific Lamont helped found and subsidize the publication *Marxist Quarterly* in 1936, smack in the middle of Stalin's Great Purge. He also wrote many pamphlets, such as an indefensible 1952 Stalinist apologia, *The Myth of Soviet Aggression,* which blasted the Truman administration.

Not surprisingly, Lamont's continued affinity for the USSR had made him no friendlier to an Almighty. He had written another "humanist" classic, *The Philosophy of Humanism* (1949), and had cobbled together additional atheist screeds like *A Humanist Wedding Service* and *A Humanist Funeral Service.* He would become president of the American Humanist Association.[2]

The beneficiaries of Corliss Lamont's worldview were his students at Columbia, Cornell, and the New School of Social Research, which were now erupting into antiwar protests, billows of pot smoke, and wildly left-wing politics. John Dewey's star pupil seemed to inhale much of it.

In its obituary of Lamont, the *New York Times* described the good professor as being dedicated to "civil liberties and international understanding."[3] The *Times* neglected to note that this included convincing the international community to "understand" why the Soviet Union had "gotten tough" (Lamont's words) in places like Hungary, Poland, Czechoslovakia, and the rest of Eastern Europe "in order to bolster its own self-defense."[4] Sometimes, as in the Soviet invasion of Hungary in 1956, the Red Army would need to "bolster its own self-defense" by murdering tens of thousands of civilians.

The *Times* obituary announced that Lamont, dedicated civil libertarian, had been forced to weather "false accusations of Communist affiliations" by "redbaiters on Capitol Hill in the 1950s"—the *real* bad guys, in the eyes of the *Times* and Lamont. (The headline on the obituary hailed Lamont as a man who had "Battled McCarthy.")[5]

The *Times* noted that Lamont had served as the longtime chairman of the National Emergency Civil Liberties Committee. This is a group still celebrated by liberals as having fought the good fight against *paranoid* anti-Communism. The obituary did not mention that Lamont was cofounder of the committee along with Marxist I. F. Stone—who, it now seems clear, was a paid Soviet agent.[6]

Lamont had started the National Emergency Civil Liberties Committee, in 1954, because by that point he had moved to the left of the ACLU.[7] ACLU founder

Roger Baldwin, a onetime gushing advocate of the Soviet state, as exemplified in his embarrassing 1928 book, *Liberty under the Soviets,* had learned hard lessons about Communism. Perhaps tired of being misled and lied to—duped—by his own officers and "liberal" "friends," by the early 1950s he was insisting that the ACLU's officers take a non-Communist oath.[8] Baldwin came to see that any ACLU member who held allegiance to a totalitarian dictatorship could not truly be serious about civil liberties. But Lamont and others—including I. F. Stone, several editors at *The Nation,* and several professors from Columbia[9]—publicly objected to this attempted "purge" by the ACLU.[10] (*Here* was a purge that Lamont could condemn.) Lamont ended up resigning from the ACLU and starting the National Emergency Civil Liberties Committee.[11]

In 1953, testifying before Congress, Lamont told his questioners that he was not a Communist.[12] At the time, that response may have been correct; the same year he wrote a widely read pamphlet titled *Why I Am Not a Communist*—this coming twenty years after his mentor, John Dewey, wrote a piece by the same name. Of course, not being a member of CPUSA never stopped Corliss Lamont from being at least a pro-Soviet socialist—and a dupe.

Into the 1960s he was supporting various other left-wing endeavors. He fired away at the Kennedy administration for trying to stop a Communist takeover of Cuba; he continued to deny Soviet culpability in the Katyn Wood massacre (as had FDR); he endured a public legal fight with the CIA and State Department over mail sent to him from Red China; and he bitterly battled the U.S. government for refusing to grant him a passport to fly off to more faraway pilgrimages to Communist lands.

The decade also brought Lamont a new life—he and his fellow-traveling wife, Margaret, divorced after more than thirty years of marriage—and a new cause: the Vietnam War. The antiwar effort seemed to invigorate Lamont. He supported seemingly every antiwar group under the Sun. Once again, Dr. Lamont found himself on the side of the Soviet Union. Some things never change.

America's Doctor: Benjamin Spock

Another grown-up that the flower children found they could trust was the doctor whose advice had been a bible for their parents: Dr. Benjamin Spock.

Spock's case is particularly interesting. It has been permitted to fall through the cracks of history. The doctor's role in the 1960s seems to have even escaped some of the better anthologies of the era.[13] Spock is typically remembered simply as the most famous and influential pediatrician of his time. His 1946 book *The Common Sense Book of Baby and Child Care* is one of the all-time bestsellers, selling an estimated fifty million copies worldwide, and translated into upwards of forty languages. His philosophy of parenting, emphasizing the need for affection, provided a much-needed corrective to the cold, austere disciplinary techniques of many parents, though some critics felt he went overboard into permissiveness— leaving a legacy of "brats." An entire generation of young mothers did their parenting under the governing principle *what does Dr. Spock say?*

Born in New Haven, Connecticut, in May 1903, Benjamin M. Spock attended Yale as an undergraduate, where he was a champion rower; he even won a gold medal at the 1924 Olympics in Paris. In the late 1920s he headed off to Columbia University to attend medical school, where he ingested the radical left-wing politics that pervaded the campus.

Spock's first public foray into politics came in 1962, when he joined the anti-nuclear-bomb group Committee for a Sane Nuclear Policy, commonly known as SANE. His political involvement would soon spike up, mirroring the trajectory of rising body bags and protests relating to the Vietnam War.

The Care and Nurturing (and Recruiting) of Dr. Spock

It is difficult to say when, exactly, Dr. Spock got involved in Vietnam War protests, though there is evidence that CPUSA targeted him for manipulation as early as September 1966, and that he had links to Communist front groups possibly as far back as 1963.

Indisputably, longtime Communist Bettina Aptheker singled out Spock for Vietnam Week in April 1967. Organizers planned a week of antiwar demonstrations on campuses and in major cities across the United States, culminating in huge rallies in San Francisco and New York City on April 15. The plans included a national Student Strike for Peace—a brilliant tactic sure to enlist the participation of not merely intensely political students but also apathetic, nonpolitical students simply anxious to skip a few classes.

So blatant was the Communist agitation in this effort that Congress's report on the matter, "Communist Origin and Manipulation of Vietnam Week," was released on March 31, 1967, a week *before* the protests were to be launched.[14] Congressman Edwin E. Willis, Louisiana Democrat, said in the preface to the report, and in an even earlier press release (January 28, 1967), that Vietnam Week was a "crash program" to "undermine and sabotage U.S. resistance to Communist military aggression in Vietnam." Willis wisely warned that "the cry will be raised" that Congress, "in releasing this report, is trying to stifle honest and legitimate dissent. Nothing could be farther from the truth." Liberals cried exactly that. Willis understood how too many in his own party often behaved. He knew the suckers would drift toward the bait.

Congressional Democrats and Republicans alike saw how the objectives of the Vietnam Week organizers were a direct extension of the goals of CPUSA and Moscow. Congressman Willis and his colleagues understood that the organizers were not practicing "honest dissent" but rather were using "deliberate deception" to lure dupes—Dr. Spock among them. Willis stated: "We must not permit Communist propaganda [and] trickery to obscure the difference between legitimate dissent and planned betrayal."[15]

The congressional report on Vietnam Week pointed to Bettina Aptheker as a key ringleader. Unlike many other radicals, the University of California–Berkeley student, who gained notoriety as a leader of the nationally known Free Speech Movement, was quite open about her membership in CPUSA. She wrote an open letter "To my fellow students" in the November 9, 1965, issue of the Berkeley student newspaper, the *Daily Californian,* in which she stated categorically: "I have been for a number of years, I am now, and I propose to remain a member of the Communist Party of the United States."[16]

Aptheker—who today is a professor and chair of Women's Studies at the University of California at Santa Cruz—was the red-diaper daughter of two Brooklyn Communists.[17] Her father, Herbert Aptheker, who had earned his bachelor's and master's degrees as well as his doctorate from Columbia University, signed up for the Communist Party in 1939, the year of the Hitler-Stalin Pact—when Communists were bolting rather than joining the party. Her mother had joined the party well before that. Herb Aptheker became a well-known figure in the Communist movement, and its leading theoretician. In 1957 he published *The Truth about Hungary,* a loathsome defense of the Soviet slaughter of tens of thousands of freedom-loving Hungarians in the Budapest uprising of October–November 1956.[18] (Curiously, years later, the *New York Times* did not mention this book in its obituary of Aptheker, instead highlighting his books on "civil rights.")[19] He also edited the party's monthly theoretical journal, *Political Affairs* (which still exists today), and was a member of the Communist Party's National Committee. In 1964 he founded the American Institute of Marxist Studies near Columbia in New York City.

In the 1960s both father and daughter became radical antiwar activists. In January 1966 Herb Aptheker made a trip to Hanoi with SDS's Tom Hayden and

Staughton Lynd, a Yale history professor.[20] A few months after that trip Bettina Aptheker issued a call for a "nation-wide student-faculty strike" in the Spring 1966 issue of *Dimensions,* a "discussion journal" of the DuBois Clubs, a Communist front group begun under the mandate of new CPUSA chief Gus Hall. Hall desired what the FBI called a "Marxist-oriented youth organization to attract non-Communists as the first step toward their eventual recruitment into the party."[21] Bettina Aptheker and the DuBois Clubs were helping the Communist movement do precisely that. The DuBois Clubs were at the least a duping mechanism, and they could serve as a way station on the road to full party membership.

Bettina Aptheker followed up her *Dimensions* piece with a September 1966 letter titled "Proposal for a National Student Strike for Peace"—a copy of which was obtained by government investigators and published by Congress. The letter called for a meeting in Chicago in late December 1966 to plan a strike. (See pages 314–15.) It declared that "the primary object" of the demonstrations was "to develop a *militant, effective* and *broad united* demonstration against the war" (emphasis in the original).

Aptheker developed a list of thirty-three "initial sponsors" for the strike, which included Berkeley professor Donald Kalish, who described himself as "far to the left" of even CPUSA;[22] SDS leader Carl Oglesby; Brian O'Brian, president of the Berkeley chapter of the American Federation of Teachers; Linda Baughn of the Methodist Student Movement; Clyde Grubbs of the national group Student Religious Liberals; SDS chairman Alex Stein; Episcopal minister Allan Dale; and New York University's Leslie Cagan, among others.[23]

Aptheker also listed Dr. Howard Zinn, a Boston University professor.[24] Zinn is an interesting case. He had been a World War II bombardier, a patriot, who went on to attend Columbia University for graduate school on the GI Bill, where he earned a master's degree and doctorate. With Columbia's training, Zinn was primed for another kind of service. His work found a captive audience in POW camps in Hanoi, where the Vietcong so admired his arguments that it provided his material to detained American airmen (that is, downed bombardiers). Specifically, the Vietcong stocked the prison library with Zinn's book *Vietnam: The Logic of Withdrawal.*[25] He eventually became a runaway bestselling historian, with his leftist work *A People's History of the United States* a staple for many high-school history teachers and devoured by liberal college students.[26]

Zinn and friends made for a strong list of initial sponsors, but Aptheker needed more supporters, especially from unsuspecting non-Communists. Her letter listed potential targets under the subhead "SPONSORSHIP, ENDORSE-MENT, PARTICIPATION." The list included "the Young Democrats," "religious student organizations," "churches, the civil rights movement, trade unionists for peace (and in some local areas perhaps even some unions), Women for Peace, [and] American Friends Service Committee." Aptheker also detailed "prominent individuals" who should be targets, including civil rights activist Julian Bond; "Scheer," probably referring to antiwar activist Robert Scheer, who today is a popular liberal columnist; and "King (as a Nobel Peace Prize Winner)"—that is, Dr. Martin Luther King Jr.[27] As Congress later reported, King ended up signing on for the effort, agreeing to "play a leading role in the April 15 demonstrations in New York City." Landing King, a genuine man of peace, was a coup for the Communists; it showed their success in assembling a "united front" that went well beyond CPUSA hacks.[28]

Aptheker's letter identified another target, "Spock"—Dr. Benjamin Spock. And with that, the co-opting of the good doctor began in earnest. Spock's shop, at 541 Madison Avenue in New York, was just around the corner from the National Conference for New Politics—easily approachable. Soon he was enlisted as cochairman of the organization, in which capacity he put his signature to the huge December 10, 1967, *New York Times* ad that heralded preparations for "the largest demonstration this country has ever seen" at the 1968 Democratic convention in Chicago. This was the protest where Spock predicted no chance of "violence or civil disobedience."[29]

Dr. Spock was now on board as a formal war protester, ready for frequent use.

The college comrades, from Columbia to Berkeley, had done yeoman's work in recruiting the pediatrician to their cause. The radical organizers knew they needed a prominent non-Communist to be the face of the Vietnam Week rallies. Spock was a superb pick, since parents would think to themselves, *If Dr. Spock is so passionately against the war, maybe it really is a bad thing.*

Chairman Spock

A huge crowd of 100,000 to 125,000 participated in the march in New York that closed Vietnam Week on April 15, 1967. Spock served as cochair for the rally along with Dave Dellinger, the cochair of New Mobe, who organized trips to Hanoi for members of the "peace movement," and whose name surfaced more than any other in Congress's October 1968 hearings on the disruption of the 1968 Democratic National Convention.[30] The speakers in New York included several well-known Communists, plus non-Communist radicals like black militant Stokely Carmichael and SDS president Nick Egleson. Also, well-known Communist/far-left musicians performed at the rally, including Pete Seeger (who had performed at American Peace Mobilization rallies in 1941).[31]

It seems unfathomable that the intelligent Dr. Spock could have been oblivious to the Communist orchestration at this parade. In a lengthy report Congress listed sixty-two key participants in the spring offensive, operating on both coasts. The list included some big CPUSA names, such as Bettina Aptheker, Robert Treuhaft, Jessica Mitford, and a wide assortment of representatives from the National Lawyers Guild. Another name on the list was the Reverend William Howard Melish, the Episcopal minister and friend of Arthur Miller and Frank Marshall Davis, whom Davis portrayed in his columns as a lovable liberal persecuted by anti-Communist Torquemadas, but whom the U.S. government now unhesitatingly described in its reports as an "identified member, CPUSA." Also involved, according to Congress's report, was renowned scientist and eventual Nobel Prize winner Linus Pauling, a radical leftist whom Congress called an "identified" CPUSA member.[32]

And, of course, not missing the protest was Corliss Lamont.

Spock had to have noticed the strong Communist presence. If not, then he was duped even worse than we can imagine.

In sponsoring these antiwar activities, Dr. Spock lent legitimacy to the effort. He fulfilled the hope that the West Coast organ of the Communist Party, *People's World,* had expressed four months earlier, on January 21, 1967: that the "national sponsors" of the march would generate "possibilities of unprecedented breadth."[33]

After Vietnam Week, Spock's Red friends were not about to let this big fish slip away. Six months later the doctor was tasked with participating in chaotic demonstrations in Washington, D.C. The rallies, held on October 21, 1967, involved thirty thousand to sixty thousand participants, and included the uprising outside the Pentagon, where as many as a thousand protesters were arrested. Spock joined seven other speakers at the Lincoln Memorial, including Dave Dellinger; Dagmar Wilson, a New Mobe cochair; John Wilson, who made a plea for a moment of silence in memory of the late Che Guevara; and Lincoln Lynch, who urged American soldiers in Vietnam to "lay down their arms by the thousands and come on home and fight." A host of Communist organizations and front groups were present, such as the pro-Chinese Marxist-Leninist Revolutionary Action Movement.[34]

It was no coincidence that companion demonstrations were held the same day in Moscow, Paris, Tokyo, Stockholm, Munich, and five major cities in Canada. There was even a companion Vietnam Week staged behind the Iron Curtain (October 15–21), as the Hungarian Peace Council showed solidarity with the

10   COMMUNIST ORIGIN AND MANIPULATION OF VIETNAM WEEK

EXHIBIT I–B

(Copy)

PROPOSAL FOR A NATIONAL STUDENT STRIKE FOR PEACE

Over the past two years tens of thousands of students have engaged in some form of anti-war activity. With a good deal of consistency efforts to organize student opposition to the war in Vietnam have met with success. Sentiment against the war, against university cooperation with the Selective Service system, and/or university participation in war-research projects is strong and growing. All too often we have underestimated the opposition, and underestimated the numbers of students willing to do something against the war. We have also underestimated the depth of the sentiment and the militant if not radical actions students are willing to take against the war.

There are many campuses with only fledgling peace groups, and others where no organized peace forces exist. We have built large movements on a number of very important campuses. One of the major problems facing the student movement today is how to give new direction and strength to the student movement where it already exists, and how to begin the process of organizing on campuses where the movement is weak or non-existent. We need them to both broaden and deepen the student anti-war movement. There are at least two things required to achieve this: (1) to talk to students about the war, and the effects of the war on their lives - i.e. the draft, the corruption of education when universities are used to research new and refined techniques for killing; the degeneracy and destruction of ideals by a war such as the one being waged against the people of Vietnam. (2) We need a nationally co-ordinated student action to give focus and direction to the movement, as well as making it possible for students who are organizing on campuses with a small movement to feel a part of a national action, and less isolated. The primary object is to develop a militant, effective and broad united demonstration against the war commensurate with the escalation, cruelty and aggressive character of American foreign policy.

It is from such an estimate of student sentiment and confidence in students to respond, a general analysis of the present campus state of affairs, and the desire to mobilize the academic community against the war that the proposal for a National Student Strike for Peace is made.

Many of the left student organizations are now discussing fall campus activity. SDS has several ideas for organizing a national student referendum on the war, and actions against the draft. Some people have suggested making all of November a Month of Protest. None of the proposals for either local actions, or for a number of nationally co-ordinated efforts, seem to me to be mutually exclusive. In fact, each would help to build and strengthen the others. The strike is proposed for the Spring, 1967.

NATURE OF A STUDENT STRIKE

The measure of success for a strike would be the cumulative effect of students (and faculty) all over the country responding on the same day to ACT against the war. Therefore, the success of the strike is not the absence of people from the university, but the active and positive actions of students and others in the academic community. If 'only' 10% of the students participated in the strike - i.e. 550,000, it would be, I think, a tremendous success. When was the last time that anything approaching that number of people from one community nationally has been moved to act in unison? The tactics for each area and/or college should be devised by the local coalition planning the action, and tactics would be as varied as the level of political development differs nationally. We could expect to run the gamut of tactics from a teach-in, to a referendum to a picket-line etc. A group of colleges close to each other might decide to have one joint protest. There are many possibly combinations. The strike should allow for maximum flexibility and initiative by local groups.

"Militant" antiwar demonstrations: Berkeley Communist Bettina Aptheker lays out plans for a "National Student Strike for Peace." Dr. Benjamin Spock is among the prominent liberals targeted as an endorser for the strike.

COMMUNIST ORIGIN AND MANIPULATION OF VIETNAM WEEK   11

EXHIBIT No. 1–B—Continued

The emphasis of the political content of the strike should be on the war as it affects the university and education which of course goes to a dialogue on the nature of this particular war. This is merely a suggestion, and demands and programs should be formulated by a meeting representative of all endorsing and sponsoring organizations. However, the strong feeling it seems to me on a whole number of campuses is on questions of war research projects, CIA undercover operation and projects, military recruiting, ROTC training, the draft, and the general militarization of educational institutions.

SPONSORHIP, ENDORSEMENT, PARTICIPATION

Sponsorship should come from any and all organizations from the university community. In addition to national groupings which now comprise the main section of the present student anti-war movement, we should seek sponsorship from religious student organizations (or the formation of an AD HOC Committee of religious student groups), from faculty peace committees, local student governments, etc. Approaches in local areas could be made to all political and social groups into which students are organized -- the Young Democrats, the glee club, the hiking club, ski clubs, the Sierra clubs, forcing them to confront the war and as a group make a decision for or against the strike. We should make approaches to living groups -- perhaps on a given campus this or that dormitory or co-op would support the strike. In the very organizing process the dialogue on the war could involve groups we have never before approached.

Endorsements for the strike (and possible supporting actions) should come from every conceivable corner of the non-academic community, e.g. churches, the civil rights movement, trade unionists for peace (and if some local areas perhaps even some unions), Women for Peace, American Friends Service Committee, independent election campaigns, e.g. Scheer for Congress now called the Community for New Politics, and prominent individuals, e.g. Scheer, Ted Weiss, Don Duncan, Keating, Spock, Deutcher, Muste, King (as a Nobel Peace Prize winner), Julian Bond, etc.

In terms of participation, then, what is desired is the widest possibly sponsorship and endorsement with a great many national organizations participating in the building of the strike. To achieve a strike what is required is the united cooperative strength of the student organization, and the movement's support. Of great importance as well, is the ability of each organization to be able to maintain itself, its own program and identity while joining in the strike effort. One might add here that the strike is not necessarily limited to Junior College, college and university students. It is conceivable that large numbers of high school students could participate, specifically on issues with which they have special concern. But as the main discussion so far has been on the college level, the possibility of high school participation is mentioned, but not developed. Ideas on this would have to come from the high school students themselves.

Very briefly I sketched some thoughts on the student strike. A copy of the brochure calling for a meeting to plan the strike is enclosed. If, within the next few weeks a number of people from various sections of the academic community will sign the call for a meeting in Chicago during the Christmas recess, the call will be printed, with the signatures,and mailed and distributed as widely as possible. As of now the call has not been printed. I wish to emphasize that these ideas represent a personal conception of a student strike, and by no means are definitive. I sought to fulfill the request of a number of people in the N.C.C. and SDS, and I set down my ideas on the strike to further discussions on it, throughout these organizations and among many other groups and individuals. It is in that spirit that this position paper was written.

                                        Submitted by
                        Bettina Aptheker, University of California, Berkeley

comrades in the United States. The Soviet-controlled World Peace Council had issued a call: "The organizations and groups working for peace in Vietnam should mark October 21 . . . by demonstrations in many countries and towns."[35]

Whether Spock knew it or not, he was part of—actually, a central figure in—a concerted international Marxist campaign to undermine America in Vietnam. The Communists had drummed up a stellar global protest against America, and Dr. Benjamin Spock was there as a poster boy.

Dr. Spock on Vietnam

Dr. Spock was suddenly the toast of the American Communist movement, which now offered him all kinds of awards, honors, and, most assuredly, platforms. One group that commended and joined him at the dais was the National Emergency Civil Liberties Committee, the creation of Corliss Lamont and I. F. Stone. The "civil liberties" committee marketed itself to non-Communist liberals as a gallant fighter for First Amendment freedoms against the tyranny of McCarthyism; the group sponsored the National Committee to Abolish HUAC.[36]

Dr. Spock would soon pay back his new friends on the far Left with a gem of a gift: a major screed against the war in Vietnam, which was published in 1968, and titled simply *Dr. Spock on Vietnam*.[37] The cover of the short book (less than a hundred small pages, with large print) was an eye-grabber, appropriate for the great childcare advocate: a photo of a small Vietnamese girl, a toddler, abandoned on a sidewalk strewn with debris, crying—an unmistakable victim of war. The banner across the front cover cried out, "THE FAMOUS DOCTOR SPEAKS OUT!"

The book began with a foreword by Dr. Spock in which he stated, "I have never been a pacifist," noting that he favored going to war against Hitler "long before we actually did." Though an astute anti-Communist reader might deduce that Spock was merely mimicking the Communist Party line in late June 1941, the doctor quickly quelled that thought by noting that he also supported the Marshall Plan, the creation of NATO, and defending South Korea against Communist North Korea—none of which the likes of Frank Marshall Davis advocated. Turning to the subject of the book, Spock condemned President Lyndon B. Johnson for escalating the conflict in Vietnam "when he promised not to escalate." Vietnam was different, he explained—poorly prosecuted by a bad president, illegally pursued, and not in America's national interest.

These were reasonable objections. The doctor had established credibility with readers.

From there, Spock and his coauthor, Mitchell Zimmerman (identified on the book jacket only as "a twenty-five year old New Yorker who has studied political science at The City College of New York and at Princeton University, where he received his Master's degree"),[38] dove straight into the book's first and shortest chapter, titled "Babies and Vietnam." It played right into the doctor's strength, and to the hearts of his readers. Spock and Zimmerman had adopted an emotionally effective writing approach.

The book, however, began to unravel at the end of that opening chapter—fittingly, the first time it quoted the *New York Times,* which was the dominant source of information the authors tapped to argue against the war. Their slight book quoted the *Times* at least thirteen times, while wisely avoiding quoting any of Spock's new comrades from the Communist movement: no Bettina or Herb Aptheker, no Dave Dellinger, no Corliss Lamont.[39]

Spock and Zimmerman cited a quote from the *New York Times* that made for an odd, off-theme conclusion to the first chapter—which was on "Babies and Vietnam," remember. The *Times* had quoted an American infantryman in Vietnam as saying: "If you put it up [the war] to a vote among the G.I.'s, we would all vote to chuck this whole place. They say we're stopping communism here, but that's just politics, just words."[40]

Of course, it wasn't just politics and words; it was the objective. Perhaps the objective was being poorly pursued, but it was the objective nonetheless. And, of course, there was no way that "all" American GIs would vote to "chuck" the whole of Vietnam. This was nonsense, and a destructive assessment of the war. Spock and Zimmerman, however, took no pause to make such distinctions, allowing the quote to stand without comment. This was symptomatic of the overreach and simplistic analysis of the entire book.

The authors consistently likened the Vietcong—"communist patriots"[41]—to the American revolutionaries of 1776, even as the North Vietnamese battled for the antithesis of the American republic. "The Vietnamese people declared their independence from France," Spock and Zimmerman wrote, "much as we declared our independence from England in 1776." More so, "Their war of independence was fought by a united front of various political groups and was led by the communist patriot Ho Chi Minh. . . . Ho is sometimes called the George Washington of Vietnam."[42]

Upon reading this book, moms who nursed their babies with copies of Spock's earlier books on their lap were probably wondering why America was not fighting *with,* rather than against, Ho Chi Minh and the Communists. *Why would Uncle Sam be at war with George Washington?*

Spock and his coauthor also maintained that the Vietnamese Communists were really *nationalists*—which, of course, was a refrain of the American Left each time a Communist movement sprang up in Asia, Africa, or Latin America, from the 1920s to the 1980s. These modern incarnations of Washington, Jefferson, and Franklin had earned the support of the population (though they were never elected). To drive home this point the authors marshaled "evidence" from a number of sources, including popular liberal columnist Joseph Alsop, Professor Howard Zinn, and *New York Times* reporter James "Scotty" Reston. They quoted Alsop, for example, saying that "it was difficult for me, as it was for any Westerner, to . . . imagine a communist government that was also a popular government and almost a democratic government."[43] But, lo and behold, argued Alsop, and Spock and Zimmerman, the North Vietnamese Communists had planned to take their country in that very direction—until America began blowing it up. *Where was the true spirit of 1776?*

Worse, argued Spock and Zimmerman, was America's *true* agenda in Vietnam: capitalist greed. "We first got involved in Vietnam," the authors explained, "for the same reasons nations have always interfered in business of other peoples: they had something and we wanted it. . . . We feared that, if they [the Communists] won, our businessmen might not be allowed to get what they wanted from that part of the world."[44]

It was as if Ho and his boys had fired their shot at Lexington and Concord, and Uncle Sam responded with napalm—solely because of greed, a lust for territory and money.

If that was not offensive enough to the American cause, Spock and Zimmerman claimed that America's South Vietnamese allies were akin to Nazi storm troopers—corrupt, degenerate village burners. As evidence, the authors predictably went back to the *New York Times*. Yet they also culled a new source: a young senator from Massachusetts named Edward "Ted" Kennedy.

Kennedy had just returned (January 1968) from a fact-finding trip to the refugee camps in South Vietnam.[45] As Spock and Zimmerman noted, the senator had discerned that "half of the 30 million dollars a year the United States has given South Vietnam for refugee relief was finding its way into the pockets of government officials and province chiefs."[46] Kennedy complained of rampant corruption, the kind that was apparently absent—or at least not mentioned—among North Vietnamese officials.[47]

The authors described the South Vietnamese as moral reprobates who "extorted" and "executed," who committed routine "acts of terror," who "looted villages," and who ran not refugee camps but "concentration camps," as they cruised around in Mercedes Benzes and as their wives wore the most expensive clothes and jewelry.[48]

Not that American soldiers were any better. Spock and Zimmerman cited a letter to Senator William J. Fulbright by a GI who claimed that "90 percent" of U.S. military attacks were waged against the people of South Vietnam. Basically, the authors argued, American soldiers were locking up the countryside of South Vietnam. Here again, for backing, the authors went to the *New York Times* and Ted Kennedy. Of the South Vietnamese who were now refugees, reported Senator Kennedy, "the vast majority—I would say over 80 percent—claimed that they were either deposited in camps by the Americans or fled to camps in fear of American airplanes and artillery. Only a handful claimed they were driven from their homes by the Viet Cong."[49]

All of this the authors described in a section titled "Their Terror and Ours." Spock and Zimmerman, drawing from Senator Kennedy, the *New York Times,* and other choice sources, portrayed South Vietnam as virtually one enlarged terror/concentration camp, thanks to America and its soldiers. Millions had been forced into captivity, compliments of the Red, White, and Blue. At best, "only a handful" of South Vietnamese people (according to Kennedy) were refugees because of anything done by the Communists of North Vietnam. Everything was the fault of the anti-Communists, from the United States to South Vietnam.

The authors next sliced at the Domino Theory. They dismissed the crucial Soviet and Chinese involvement in the Vietnam War as unimportant by saying, "Today neither of the two major communist powers, Russia or China, is advancing toward our shores. Neither has any troops stationed in North or South Vietnam at the present time."[50] Besides, Spock and Zimmerman suggested. even if China were somehow involved in Vietnam. why would this be a bad thing? After all, Mao Tse-tung, like Ho Chi Minh, and like Fidel Castro, was a "revolutionary." In Vietnam and China and Cuba, "The motivation for revolution is the same today as it was in 1776: the desire for justice and a better life."[51]

In the very next sentence came perhaps the most tragic false prophecy in the book. Again dismissing fears of a spread of Communism in Asia, Spock and Zimmerman maintained that "Cambodia, right next door to Vietnam, is in no danger of revolution."[52]

In fact, within only a few years of the publication of this book, the criminally insane Pol Pot and his vicious Communist Khmer Rouge would seize Cambodia and turn it into arguably the worst killing field in human history, with upwards of two to three million people slaughtered out of a population of only five to seven million over the course of barely four years.

Highly Recommended Reading—by the Vietcong

Dr. Spock's book was a smash among the political Left. The good doctor had joined the side of the antiwar "progressives." And whether he knew it or not, he had also joined the same team as America's Communists, who could not have dreamed up a better teammate.

The book had another audience—a set of admirers much farther away. An eyewitness to this new Benjamin Spock book club was Lieutenant Robert Frishman, U.S. Navy, a twenty-eight-year-old former dental student turned Vietnam fighter pilot. Frishman, who received the Distinguished Flying Cross, nine Air Medals, two Navy Commendation Medals, and a Purple Heart, was shot down over hostile territory on October 24, 1967. He ended up being held in captivity for twenty-one months, until August 4, 1969.[53]

Once detained, Frishman and his fellow American soldiers were granted only antiwar information and propaganda permitted by their captors. Around 6 A.M. each day, they were awakened to a voice they called "Hanoi Hannah," the Vietnamese equivalent of Japan's "Tokyo Rose" during World War II. They would end the day to the dulcet tones of Hanoi Hannah at 8 P.M. That was the routine.[54]

In between these voices of Vietnam, Frishman and his friends got intermittent doses of misinformation. Much of this material came courtesy of liberal Americans. "We would also get other information about the events in the United States," Frishman later told Congress. "We would hear about the moratoriums, the peace marches." The former POW politely expressed frustration at the ignorance of the "peace" activists as to how America's enemies exploited their presence at antiwar rallies: "I have people come to me and say, 'I think I will go to one of those moratoriums because I am for peace.' I say, 'What does your participation in a moratorium mean?'"[55] These "young, impressionable youth [get] swallowed up" by the ringleaders in these movements, said Frishman. Even the "well-educated," the lieutenant said, were susceptible to being used, again and again.[56]

Lieutenant Frishman learned in captivity about New Mobe and SDS, and recalled reading an American magazine with a sparkling profile of Dave Dellinger, Dr. Spock's new best friend. Frishman and the other inmates suffered the news about the riots at the 1968 Democratic convention, which had greatly impressed the North Vietnamese; the convention blow-up became a handy propaganda tool to use against the soldiers. Frishman and the POWs also heard "quite a bit" about the Black Panther Party, Stokely Carmichael, and the assassination of Dr. King— all for the purpose of conveying to them the Frank Marshall Davis image of the "repressive" and "racist" American state.[57]

This negative information from the United States, explained Frishman, was used not only to try to demoralize the POWs but also to inspire the North Vietnamese. He said, "They use these statements . . . to gain support for their people, for their cause, to try to rally their troops—they say, 'Look, this is the way the American people believe.'" He noted how his interrogators pulled antiwar material from the American press and "they shoved it down our throat." The enemy had its favorite congressmen: Frishman most often heard the Vietcong quoting the remarks of Democratic senators William Fulbright, George McGovern, Eugene McCarthy, and Bobby Kennedy.[58]

The enemy also fed the POWs books. Originally the North Vietnamese gave them books published in Russia, Albania, China, North Korea, and other Communist countries, but Frishman told his captors that "all that stuff" was mere "propaganda" from the Communist world. So the Vietcong got smart, reaching for a better form of information: they gave the POWs selective readings from back home. Frishman recalled the authors most popular among the Vietcong prison guards, including Bertrand Russell, author of *War Crimes in Vietnam,* who started an "International War Crimes Tribunal," which received funding from Ho Chi Minh's North Vietnamese regime;[59] Wilfred Burchett, later identified as a Soviet agent;[60] and a certain extremely popular book by Benjamin Spock—namely, *Dr. Spock on Vietnam.*[61]

Apparently, the doctor's antiwar work was a mainstay at the POW camp, used for regular drilling and anti-American indoctrination. Said Frishman: "*Dr. Spock on Vietnam,* I got to read that four or five times."[62]

"The Progressive, True American People"

Nearly identical testimony came from another former POW, Doug Hegdahl. Hegdahl was a U.S. Navy petty officer from Clark, South Dakota, who received a number of ribbons and commendations during the war, including the National Defense Medal. On the night of April 6, 1967, he came to the deck of his ship, the USS *Canberra,* which was engaged in a firing mission off the coast of North Vietnam. (Contrary to the military expertise of Dr. Spock and Senators Kennedy and Fulbright, Hegdahl's ship was engaging enemy combatants, not children in villages.) "I came up on the deck and the next thing I remember I was in the water," recalled Hegdahl, "and I can't tell you how I fell from my ship."[63]

Hegdahl managed to regain his senses, kept afloat, and then swam for about five hours before he was picked up by a North Vietnamese fishing boat. The fishermen treated him "reasonably well," but when they brought him to shore, hostile North Vietnamese villagers turned him over to the village militia. He did not know the name of the village, though he did recognize the material he was handed: it was a "pamphlet on the Bertrand Russell War Crimes Tribunal and some cartoon clippings from the American papers."[64]

Hegdahl was held in captivity for more than two years in multiple detention centers, including the infamous "Hanoi Hilton," where men like future U.S. senator John McCain were brutally tortured and permanently disabled. Like Lieutenant Frishman, Hegdahl learned all about groups like New Mobe and antiwar activists like Dave Dellinger from his Communist captors. He was saturated with the thinking of individuals who were a virtual "who's who" of the April 1967 New York City antiwar rally headed up by Dr. Spock, including SDS leaders like Nick Egleson and Black Panther Stokely Carmichael.[65]

Carmichael, in fact, joined Hanoi Hannah in being broadcast over the airwaves in Vietnam, his voice used to demoralize Americans there. Hegdahl explained:

> Stokely Carmichael's voice actually came over the radio at times to broadcast to the GIs in the South. At one time he was pleading with his brother, who was a soldier in South Vietnam, "What are you fighting for? Why are you fighting for the imperialists, the white imperialist power structure?" Then he went on to say, "Can you vote in Tennessee? Can you vote in Texas? No, you can't, so why are you fighting?"[66]

Asked explicitly whether it seemed that Carmichael had been "giving aid and comfort to the enemy," Hegdahl did not hesitate to respond: "Definitely, yes."[67]

The North Vietnamese who tortured and attempted to deprogram Doug Hegdahl and other POWs were big advocates of America's progressives. Hegdahl's captors told him "we want you to be loyal to the progressive, true American people."[68] The Vietcong looked earnestly for reading material from the progressives, to be furnished for the edification of America's boys in captivity. Two American newspapers were particular favorites of the Vietcong, Hegdahl said: "They quoted American papers such as, well, the *New York Times* and the *Washington Post*." There was plenty of negative material in the *Times* and *Post* for the Vietcong to excerpt.

Hegdahl also recalled a series of pamphlets by Helen Boyden Lamb. A word on Lamb: Born Helen Elizabeth Boyden in Cambridge, Massachusetts, in May 1906,[69] she attended Radcliffe College, where she received a bachelor's degree in 1928 and a Ph.D. in 1943. Her first husband, Robert Keen Lamb, died from cancer in 1952. Ten years later, she remarried and moved to New York City.

At that point there was a clear upsurge in Lamb's left-wing activities—evident in her private papers, which are housed at the Arthur M. Schlesinger (Sr.) Library at Harvard.[70] Starting around the time of her remarriage, Lamb's name began to appear frequently in newsletters from the American Humanist Association, in works distributed by the National Emergency Civil Liberties Committee, in correspondence and even greeting cards with Vietnamese officials as high up as Ho Chi Minh himself, in letters to and from Owen Lattimore (one of the most duplicitous Communist suspects and sympathizers of the entire Cold War), through involvement with Religious Left clergy protesting the war, in dealings with numerous Communist front groups, and via her many speeches to student groups and civics clubs, ranging from the Columbia Student Union (October 3, 1963), to the Liberal Club at Rutgers University (April 22, 1964), to the Columbia University Humanist Society (November 12, 1964), to Americans for Democratic Action (November 18, 1964), to the New York City YWCA (May 14, 1965).

By 1964 Dr. Lamb was speaking out against the war at colleges, to civic organizations, on radio shows, and in published articles, pamphlets, and books. Her popular pamphlets, "The Tragedy of Vietnam," started publishing in May 1964. In these and in her later book *Vietnam's Will to Live* (1972), she gloried in Vietnam's "steadfastness and resolve" against "America's frightful capacity and willingness to destroy." As Doug Hegdahl attested, the Communist Vietcong so valued her work that they handed out her pamphlets to American POWs to attempt to convince U.S. soldiers of the injustice of their cause.[71]

One wonders whether Helen Lamb and other favored authors of the Vietcong were troubled when they heard the congressional testimony of former POWs like Doug Hegdahl and Robert Frishman and learned how their materials were being used to brainwash tortured American soldiers. More likely, the testimony reinforced their view that they were making a *positive* impact, far and wide, from the Heartland to Havana to Hanoi.

And no doubt, Dr. Helen Lamb could count on the encouragement of her spouse: Dr. Corliss Lamont.

Lamont surely assured his new wife that she was on the right track if the Vietcong enjoyed her work. After all, the Soviets had once enjoyed the work of Corliss and his ex-wife, Margaret.

Aside from Lamb's pamphlets and the articles from the *New York Times* and *Washington Post,* did the Vietcong prison guards provide Doug Hegdahl with any choice books? Oh, yes: There was Dave Dellinger's *In the Teeth of War,* as well as such antiwar books as *I Protest* and *Vietnam! Vietnam!* There was also, of course, the must-read, *Dr. Spock on Vietnam.*[72]

America's Doctor, and Hanoi's

As usual, the likes of Dr. Benjamin Spock could not imagine the full ramifications of their actions. Spock and his comrades likely had no clue of the extent to which they and their work were exploited by Communists at home and abroad, from New York City to Hanoi.

Spock's manifesto against the war in Vietnam—a Vietcong favorite—was far from the pediatrician's swan song. He found himself atop invite lists for every new and exciting Communist "offensive" against the war, frequently offered the chance to be a headline speaker.[73] By 1972 he had veered so far to the left that he ran for president as the People's Party candidate, through which the children's doctor campaigned for legalization of abortion (pre–*Roe v. Wade*), gay rights, decriminalization of marijuana, socialized medicine, minimum- and maximum-wage caps, and other measures consistent with the permissive, libertine lifestyle of the flower children. Of course, his People's Party platform was also marked by staunch opposition to the Vietnam War.

To current knowledge, Dr. Spock was not a Communist or even a small "c" communist, even though he moved about as far left as one could at the time. Generally, he was a non-Communist liberal who came to adamantly oppose the war in Vietnam. Opposition to the war was not in itself troubling. Some of America's leading generals, such as Matthew Ridgway and Douglas MacArthur, had long warned of the peril of getting involved in a land war in Asia, and some of the nation's sharpest anti-Communists, including the theologian Bishop Fulton Sheen, were steadfast critics of the war.[74] These and many other Americans practiced honorable dissent, reasonably questioning the Johnson administration's handling of the war as well as the immorality of total war.

Countless Americans achieved the task of protesting the war without being co-opted and humiliated by the Reds. Dr. Benjamin Spock was not among them. He was a dupe—over and over and over and over.

Dr. Spock was taken in in part because legions of students, duped and dupers, were there to aid and abuse him. Among the worst culprits was a hodgepodge of the oblivious and the insidious known as Students for a Democratic Society.

16

RADICALS:
BILL AYERS, BERNARDINE DOHRN,
SDS, AND THE WEATHERMEN

As grown-ups like Dr. Spock misbehaved like political bad boys, some of the '60s kiddies reveled in their big opportunity to defy authority. For many of them, it was a thrill to go to battle on manicured campus quads and take to city streets to denounce the "pigs" keeping people safe at home and the "fascist" military trudging through swamps, jungles, and landmines in Southeast Asia. Among the student movement's rank and file, surely at least some were more interested in the rush of the protests—in the accompanying sex, drugs, and psychedelic music—than in the actual matters being protested.

That said, the 1960s student movement was motivated by some genuine concerns. This youth culture raised legitimate questions about a war that seemed to have no end but produced a definitive list of names of the dead in the local paper. These young people also recognized that the outrageous treatment of black Americans for two centuries was overdue for redress.

The leadership of the student antiwar movement, in particular, was keenly interested in the issues. But their objectives, which the former student leaders will candidly discuss even today, were different from—and far more militant than—those of the young non-Communist liberals they enlisted for their rallies and protests. Those objectives were colored Red rather than the sunny rainbow of peace placards. The dedicated comrades leading the way really did want a revolution all right—and many still do. And they found their dupes among the rank-and-file protesters.

One of the most prominent of these student movements was Students for a Democratic Society (SDS). Categorizing SDS's melting pot of antiwar activists is no easy task, but the leadership of this group—and especially of the contingent that splintered into Weatherman—makes for a fascinating case study of how the anti–Vietnam War movement morphed dramatically from "peace" marches into something far more sinister.

After the 1967 spring uprising, and especially following the student strikes during Vietnam Week, SDS was invigorated. By the time of its annual national convention in June 1968, where it prepared to storm the Democratic National Convention in August, SDS boasted thirty thousand members and three hundred chapters across the United States, making it the largest radical student organization in the nation. It was ready for big things.

Socialist Origins

Though a '60s group, SDS could trace its origins back much earlier. Initially the group was known as the Student League for Industrial Democracy. Started in the early 1930s, it was the youth arm of the socialist League for Industrial Democracy, an organization founded early in the century by such high-profile socialists as politician Norman Thomas and authors Jack London and Upton Sinclair. In 1959 the Student League for Industrial Democracy changed its name to Students for a Democratic Society. The new SDS lifted the previous ban on Communists as members, and, in fact, welcomed Marxists with open arms. This was no surprise: many of the leaders were Marxists.[1]

SDS began attracting a variety of different types of Communists and Communist groups, such as the Maoist Progressive Labor Party. The SDS kids picked a curious time to lie with the Maoists: tens of millions of Chinese perished at the hands of Chairman Mao during his disastrous collectivization known as the Great Leap Forward (1957–60) and, later, during the human insanity known as the Cultural Revolution (1966–69). In September 1965 the League for Industrial Democracy severed all ties with SDS.

The most important player in the early SDS was Tom Hayden, born December 1939 in Detroit, Michigan. Hayden, unlike most of the SDS leadership, was not a red-diaper baby. His close friend David Horowitz, who was a red-diaper baby, notes that Hayden harbored what Irving Howe once described as an "obscure personal rage," possibly from his upbringing by an alcoholic father with whom he was not on speaking terms. "Tom was indeed an angry man," records Horowitz, "who seemed in perpetual search of enemies."[2]

Hayden began his activism as a student at the University of Michigan, eventually an SDS hotbed. He served as SDS president in 1962 and 1963, drafting the organization's founding charter, the Port Huron Statement. This manifesto contained a historically neglected but crucial section on a perceived plague facing America, a "major social problem"—*anti*-Communism. This section of the statement was written by Hayden's mentor, Richard Flacks, whose parents were Communist schoolteachers.[3]

Hayden's fame and impact would spike up in 1968. He was a ringleader of the demonstrations at the Democratic National Convention that summer, and his activities in Chicago were nothing short of scandalous, especially his deceptive provocations.[4] He was arrested at the convention, becoming one of the "Chicago Eight" charged with inciting the uprising, along with such radicals as Jerry Rubin and Abbie Hoffman.

Also in 1968, Hayden and an SDS delegation traveled to the Communist bloc, where, according to observer Sol Stern, who was there as a privileged correspondent for the radical *Ramparts,* "The SDSers held a seminar with the Communists on how to conduct their psychological warfare campaign against the United States."[5] Hayden's notoriety surged when he took one of his controversial trips to Cambodia and Vietnam with the young actress Jane Fonda, daughter of liberal actor Henry Fonda, who, along with Humphrey Bogart, had been one of the members of the 1947 Committee for the First Amendment, which protested the work of the House Committee on Un-American Activities.

Of course, Jane Fonda is herself a huge story. The wealthy young actress was a go-go girl for Communism, regularly telling student audiences: "If you would understand what Communism was, you would pray on your knees that we would someday be Communist."[6] Once arriving in Hanoi, she became a cheerleader for the Vietcong.[7] The trip was arranged (in part) by Wilfred Burchett, who was later identified by KGB defector Yuri Krotkov as a Soviet agent; Burchett also reportedly helped script Fonda's talks.[8] The actress became the toast of the Communist world for her "heroics" on behalf of "anti-imperialism" and anti-Americanism. Her face was splashed across media everywhere—especially by an ecstatic Communist press. As pretty Jane Fonda flirted and cavorted with the Communist enemy, tight clothes, wavy hair, curvaceous figure, fist in the air, grinning aboard and aside Vietcong weaponry, the Soviets and North Vietnamese were smitten.

And so was Tom Hayden. His first marriage was finished; shortly after Fonda's theatrics in Southeast Asia, he married the actress.

By that point, SDS was finished as well. It had splintered into rival factions, the most infamous being a domestic Communist-terrorist group called Weatherman. The key leadership figures who made the transition from SDS to Weatherman were Bernardine Dohrn, Bill Ayers, Jeff Jones, Michael Klonsky, Carl Davidson, John Jacobs, Kathy Boudin, and Mark Rudd. Some of them remained with Weatherman, going underground, in some cases as fugitives from the law, and forming the Weather Underground, whereas others fell away from the faith and the movement—but never completely.

The Ringleaders

Among the ringleaders in the transition from SDS to Weatherman was Bernardine Dohrn, born Bernardine Ohrnstein in Milwaukee, Wisconsin, in January 1942.[9] The young Dohrn was raised in an upper-middle-class suburb. She led a normal life—high-school cheerleader, member of the dance club and honor society, editor of the student newspaper. She left Milwaukee to attend college and law school at the University of Chicago, graduating with bachelor's and law degrees in 1963 and 1967.

It was Dohrn's early work in law that brought her into contact with Communist radicals, as she began working for the National Lawyers Guild, the legal bulwark for CPUSA. In 1967 she headed to New York to work with the guild. Through that association she began to emerge on the national scene.

In 1968 Dohrn was an active participant at the January meeting of the National Lawyers Guild, along with comrades Tom Hayden and Rennie Davis, plus about a dozen others. So close was Dohrn to the guild that the minutes for the group's January 26, 1968, meeting actually listed her address as 5 Beekman, New York, NY 10038—the address of the guild offices.[10] It was as if she and the National Lawyers Guild were one and the same, though the former Milwaukee schoolgirl managed to drift even to the left of her comrade counselors.

A few months later, at the June 1968 annual SDS convention, Dohrn and Michael Klonsky—two of the organization's three newly elected national secretaries—announced in a public session that they were Communists.[11] By August, Dohrn was front and center in Chicago, playing her part in igniting the city and undermining the Democratic convention.

She was present, too, at the October 1968 congressional hearings on the Democratic convention. Her name was raised several times, to the point that counsel in the audience interjected to ask committee chairman Richard Ichord if the young lady could step forward to "respond to her name."[12]

The Midwest girl had a couple of steadies in the movement. Her first beau

was Jeff Jones, an SDS leader five years her junior. As the New York regional organizer for SDS, Jones coordinated the rabid chapters at Columbia and Cornell, the
heirs of the 1920s radicals in New York City and Ithaca. He was one of three SDS
organizers invited to Hanoi in December 1967 by the Vietnamese Student Union.
Jones, too, was on hand to disrupt the 1968 Democratic convention in Chicago.[13]
By the fall of 1969 he had joined Bernardine in at least one incident that Congress
categorized as a "SDS-initiated act of violence or demonstration advocating violence." Also that fall, Jones was involved in (without Dohrn) what Congress called
an "SDS invasion" of several Pittsburgh high schools.[14]

Another younger man to Dohrn's liking was Bill Ayers, who took Bernardine's hand from Jeff Jones. A Chicago native, Ayers was, like Corliss Lamont,
like Fred Field, a champion of the proletariat who was born with a silver spoon
in his mouth. His father, Thomas Ayers, was CEO of Commonwealth Edison of
Chicago and a big shot in the corporate world who served on the boards of companies, foundations, and universities. His well-born son would demand that others
(under force of government fiat) give up their possessions while not surrendering
his own. In fact, as author Daniel J. Flynn reports, Bill Ayers "still accepted his
allowance [from his father] despite engaging in parricidal rhetoric, rationalizing
that it was fine by him if his dad bankrolled the revolution."[15]

Like Tom Hayden and Arthur Miller before him, Ayers was a student at the
University of Michigan, preparing for a life of revolution and education.[16] The
University of Michigan was the right place for Ayers's budding interest in educational development. During this period, the University of Michigan, which had
proudly hosted John Dewey's first academic appointment, produced influential
textbooks for the field of education with titles like *Training for Change Agents: A
Guide to the Design of Training Programs in Education and Other Fields.*[17]

Ayers would spend the rest of his life seeking to be a "change agent" and
working to advance the political careers of "change agents."

Initially, however, that change was not coming quickly enough for him—or
for his comrades over at Columbia.

The Columbia Cell

As in the 1920s, Columbia University had itself quite a crew in the 1960s. The
roster was so loaded that it is difficult to condense it to a short list.

Among others, there was Howard Machtinger, who earned bachelor's degrees
in sociology and English from Columbia in 1966 before moving on to do graduate

work in sociology at the University of Chicago, where he would be on-site for the SDS-Weatherman eruptions.

Also at Columbia was John Jacobs. Born in September 1947, Jacobs was raised in a far-left family where he imbibed the readings of Karl Marx. His father, Douglas, was a well-known leftist journalist. Young John enrolled at Columbia in 1965.

Arriving at the university that same semester was Mark Rudd, who became Jacobs's best friend, and would become the most influential of the entire Columbia apparatus.

Rudd was born Mark William Rudnitsky in Irvington, New Jersey, in June 1947. His mother and father were non-Marxist Jewish immigrants from Poland and Lithuania. His parents, hardworking and more blue-collar, had a very different worldview from the Jacobses and other parents of radical Columbia children.

After struggling to find his place in the world as an uneasy youth, and spending many hours on a couch talking to his psychiatrist, Rudd found his calling at Columbia University, where he ended up heading the school's SDS chapter. He practically set the college on fire. Columbia was the perfect place for Rudd, given its history, its far-left activism, and its reinforcement of Communists.

Drawn to Rudd and the boys were several female comrades, particularly Kathy Boudin, another founding member of SDS and Weatherman. Boudin was born May 19, 1943, to a family of prominent Jewish Marxists and progressives in New York City. This included an uncle, Louis Boudin, who was a well-known theoretician, and her father, Leonard Boudin, who was a Harvard constitutional law professor and National Lawyers Guild attorney whose clients included Paul Robeson, the Socialist Workers Party, the National Emergency Civil Liberties Committee (for which he served as general counsel), Fidel Castro, and Benjamin Spock. Leonard's brother-in-law was I. F. Stone.[18]

Of course, the Boudins' identification with the workingman went only so far. They lived in an opulent New York brownstone that the hit 1980s sitcom *The Cosby Show* later used as the façade for the wealthy TV family's home.[19] Such, of course, has always been the arrangement between the Left's leaders and the masses they purport to represent: the apparatchiks get their dachas; the serfs get their ghettoes.

When Kathy Boudin was a little girl, her parents sent her to primary school at the Downtown Community School, a supplement to the Little Red School House, which was founded in the early 1920s by New York Communists and progressives. There, Kathy met musical talents like Pete Seeger, who regularly played and taught at the school, and who performed at the summer "Commie camps" where the New York faithful sent their children (the Red version of Vacation Bible School).[20]

Other New York comrades placed their children in the Downtown Community School, including Franklin Folsom, a writer for TASS, the official Soviet news agency; Simon Gerson, editor of the *Daily Worker;* and V. J. Jerome, editor of the Communist Party's theoretical journal *Political Affairs.* Famed anthropologist Margaret Mead (a liberal, with graduate degrees from Columbia), also sent her daughter there, and Lillian Hellman was on the school's board of trustees.[21]

The leftist parents and the administrators at the school frequently bickered: Stalinists versus Trotskyites, progressives versus Communists, liberal Christians versus secular liberals, observant Jews versus nonobservant Jews. The only theories they universally adhered to were those of John Dewey, their unifying force. The director of the Downtown Community School was Norman Studer, a Ph.D. student of Dewey at Columbia. While a teacher at the Little Red School House, he had taken his pupils on field trips to Communist May Day parades. He also wrote for *New Masses.*[22]

As Kathy Boudin matured, she entered radical circles of her own. She dated one of the sons of convicted Soviet atomic spies Julius and Ethel Rosenberg (the Soviets' code name for Julius was "Liberal").[23] When she went to college at Bryn Mawr, her academic "role model," according to Boudin family biographer Susan Braudy, was Corliss Lamont, a close friend of her father.[24] She was already to the left of her father when Mr. Boudin decided to send her to the Soviet Union for fifteen months of study in 1965. There she held forth on a Soviet collective, endeavoring to enlighten the young Soviet masses about how American fascists responded to Communism with hysteria. She was taken aback, however—not only by the poverty of the Soviet youngsters but also by their insistence that the Soviet system was far worse than anything Joe McCarthy had done in America. "How many of your friends, for all their protests, are in jail now?" they asked her. Boudin's answer: none.[25]

Returning to the United States, Boudin knew where to go to find youth who actually believed in Communism: Columbia University. While organizing protests from New York City to Chicago, she hooked up with the Columbia contingent to drink in the bountiful opportunities for campus Communist politics that only this radical university afforded.

Who Are We Fighting? Liberal Democrats

All of these young activists were against the Vietnam War, of course. But they were also against the Democratic Party, and against liberals.

As a freshman at Columbia, Mark Rudd learned this quickly from his senior classmates. "The liberals say the war in Vietnam is a well-intentioned mistake," a classmate lectured Rudd from a platform in March 1966, in one of the earliest campus protests of the war. "Bullsh-t! It was the liberals who started it."[26]

These youngsters did not like Lyndon Johnson. They had not liked John F. Kennedy. They were against the war well before Republican Richard Nixon was its commander in chief. "Hey, hey, LBJ, how many kids did you kill today?" Columbia's comrades chanted as they marched down Fifth Avenue from Ninety-first Street to Seventy-second Street.

In his 2009 memoir, *Underground: My Life with SDS and the Weathermen*—a depraved but commendably honest tell-all—Mark Rudd made plain that he and his fellow apparatchiks were fighting against liberal Democrats. "It was the liberal enemy [that was] trying to destroy our movement," wrote Rudd. "Liberals, including Robert Kennedy, his martyred brother John, and LBJ had given us Vietnam in the first place."[27] Again, this is a point that many of today's liberals seem not to grasp.

If the young radicals were fighting against liberals, who were they fighting *for?* Like so many others in the antiwar movement's upper echelons, plenty of the ringleaders favored the enemy; they were for the North Vietnamese, and for Communism. They were pro-Mao, pro-Castro, pro-Che, pro-Lenin, and some were even pro-Stalin. Very few were working-class kids. Most, in fact, had been pampered rich kids, red-diaper babies from well-off, highly educated families in New York and the Northeast.[28] Rudd made this clear in his memoir, in which he acknowledged that he and his fellow Ivy League Marxists made frequent trips into blue-collar neighborhoods around the country, especially in Chicago, to preach to the proletariat, only to get beaten up by the "greasers." This saddened the enlightened apparatchiks: the unwashed, ignorant masses did not know what was good for them; the brave new world would need to be imposed upon them.

But they were reinvigorated when they got back to the anointed halls of Columbia. There, said Rudd, he would listen in rapt attention at SDS meetings, captivated by "passionate debates by upper-classmen and graduate students about China's Cultural Revolution, the Cuban revolution, the nature of American class society. . . . They all agreed on one solution, Marxist revolution."[29] In addition to the writings of Mao, Lenin, and Marx, the young Reds gobbled up the writings of secret Soviet agent Wilfred Burchett, which the Vietcong were simultaneously force-feeding to American POWs at the Hanoi Hilton.[30]

Speaking of those POWs, in 1967 Rudd got himself a cherished gift: a titanium ring hammered from the debris of a downed U.S. aircraft in Vietnam. He couldn't wait to put it around his finger. "I wore mine proudly for years after-ward," said Rudd.[31]

Crass as that sounds, it was not unusual. Another New Jersey kid at Colum-bia, Michael Lerner—later editor of the Jewish spiritual magazine *Tikkun* and (in the 1990s) celebrated "Politics of Meaning" guru to First Lady Hillary Rodham Clinton—exchanged such rings with his bride during their wedding ceremony. His wife had brought them back from North Vietnam, with the metal from the downed fuselage to be an eternal symbol of their love, the consummation of a rad-ical marriage.[32] Such rings were a badge of honor to certain Columbia faithful.[33]

Rudd also found inspiration in Che Guevara's dispatch of "undying militancy" just before he was killed in Bolivia: "Our every action is a battle cry against imperi-alism and a battle hymn for the people's unity against the great enemy of mankind: the United States of America. Wherever death may surprise us, let it be welcome."[34]

Mark Rudd and his Communist friends mourned the death of their beloved Che. Now they would elevate him as their "revolutionary martyr and saint" (Rudd's words) at the funeral of the United States of America, the great enemy of mankind.[35] They would fight for Che, Fidel, Cuba, and the USSR, and against LBJ, JFK, and the United States.

This was their religion, their faith. Che was their Jesus Christ: "Like a Chris-tian seeking to emulate the life of Christ," Rudd remembered, "I passionately wanted to be a revolutionary like Che, no matter what the cost."[36]

Blowing Up Columbia

To that end, Rudd led riots on the Columbia campus. Most infamously, he spear-headed the shocking Columbia student revolt of 1968. Rudd and the other youth protesters shouted obscenities at the administration through bullhorns, smashed windows, broke down doors, pillaged and seized the offices of the president, occupied university buildings, and shut down the entire campus. At long last at Columbia, it was October 1917; the revolution had finally commenced. As Rudd wrote in his SDS pamphlet, titled simply "Columbia," "It was no accident that we hung up pictures of Karl Marx and Malcolm X and Che Guevara and flew red flags from the tops of two buildings."[37]

Columbia, declared the agitators, was "liberated." But in reality the scene was a tragedy. It is a shame that the Potemkin Progressive professors who forty years earlier had sown the seeds for this destruction were not there to witness the bitter fruits of their political indoctrination. John Dewey had long since passed away.

Even the once duped who had come to their senses about the Communists, like Whittaker Chambers, had died. Thomas Merton, devoutly focused on transcending this fallen existence and rising above its inanities—he was now a Trappist monk—unexpectedly perished that year at the age of fifty-three.

Of course, Corliss Lamont probably enjoyed every minute. He likely strolled to the scene from his New York apartment to bask in the images of Lenin, as he and his wife had once done in Moscow. Likewise, Columbia's Religious Left clergy was inspired by the violent revolt. The Protestant pastors were invigorated with a heightened sense of "social justice." As Diana Trilling described the clergy reaction to the student occupation, they "threw themselves with hearts bleeding and souls aflame into this newest movement of youthful idealism."[38]

As usual, the Religious Left was there as sucker. This time, however, the academic Left was not so willing. College presidents shuddered in fear at the student takeover. Well, not *all* college presidents: The University of Chicago's Robert Maynard Hutchins, a favorite of Frank Marshall Davis because of his scathing attacks on "Red-baiting," "witch-hunting" anti-Communism, was impressed by the student coup. The former chancellor suggested that the plotters "not only should be granted full amnesty for taking over five college buildings for six days, but should be honored at special graduation ceremonies for forcing open the door to university reform."[39] Heretofore, Columbia had not been far enough to the left for Dr. Hutchins.

Hutchins had one thing right: the doors certainly had been forced open; most, in fact, had been kicked down. As a *Newsweek* cover attested, Rudd and the children were in charge.[40] Student strikes ensued, and a general rage enveloped Columbia for weeks. It was sheer madness. It was violence—what Rudd himself dubbed "total war" on campus.[41] It had been orchestrated, from the top, by Communists—American Communists. And there to supply marchers for the young Bolsheviks were the liberal innocents, likewise protesting "the war."

Again, the ringleaders knew much more than the dupes who offered the bodies to fill the streets. One can only hope that some of the naïve at least raised an eyebrow at the sight of Red flags hoisted atop Columbia University's seized buildings at the moment of "victory."

To the SDS radicals, Columbia had now richly earned the mantle of Che Guevara. The comrades envisioned it as their own version of Moscow State University. More than that, they saw the uprising as just a start. The goal was to remake campuses across the country in Columbia's image. SDS national secretary Carl Davidson said that the "Columbia rebellion" had provided a model for the nation. Likewise, in *Ramparts* magazine, edited by young Communists David Horowitz and Peter Collier, who today are prominent anti-Communist conservatives, Tom

Hayden employed a new battle cry, a paraphrase of Saint Che's mantra for Vietnam: "Create two, three, many Columbias!"[42]

And Mark Rudd and the Columbia militants had much more in store. Within a year of the student revolt, Rudd writes, "Columbia would give birth to the 'revolutionary' faction known as Weatherman."[43]

From SDS to Weatherman

Not surprisingly, the political harlot that was Columbia University spawned a wretched child in Weatherman.

Rudd succinctly sums up the bastard son that he, more than any other figure, created: "My friends and I formed an underground revolutionary guerrilla band called Weatherman which had as its goal the violent overthrow of the United States government."[44]

That was the stated objective of the Weathermen: *the violent overthrow of the United States government.* The '60s Communists were not much different from CPUSA; both sides shared the same end goal, differing only in means, and candor and maturity.

The shift toward Weatherman was the culmination of a deep split within SDS. The hardcore Marxists among the SDS leadership had balkanized into different factions, from Maoists to followers of Che and Fidel and even to Stalinists. One Stalinist was Mike Klonsky, the SDS national secretary based in Chicago. Klonsky had Communism in his bloodline, particularly from his father, who, according to liberal lore, was another of those innocent practitioners of civil liberties hounded by the evil Joe McCarthy. Rudd recalls a meeting in 1969 when Klonsky "several times" told Rudd and Howard Machtinger that "Stalin is the cutting edge." This "adulation of Joseph Stalin" (Rudd's description) made no sense to Rudd and Machtinger.[45] Such internal differences drove a wedge between SDS principals, which led Rudd and others to break off with Weatherman.

Another critical area of separation involved the divergent feelings about violence. The typical rank-and-file SDSer was an antiwar, pro-peace, nonviolent liberal, whereas certain leaders—Rudd among them—openly expressed their commitment to violence in order to hasten the revolution. Mercifully, endorsements of violence woke up some of the duped non-Communist liberals in SDS. Eventually the more violent among the SDSers formed Weatherman. In addition to Rudd, Weatherman would include such bomb-setting fanatics as Bernardine Dohrn and Bill Ayers.

Two events in Chicago in 1969 precipitated the formation of Weatherman. First, there was the final SDS national convention. It opened June 18, 1969, at the Chicago Coliseum on South Wabash, just down the street from the Chicago police headquarters, home of the "pigs" with whom Rudd and his violent cohorts prepared for war. With America and its policemen and servicemen as the identified enemy, Che's partisans were ready for action. It was at this convention that Rudd and his fellow militants began publicly referring to themselves as "Weathermen."

Next, with Rudd, Ayers, Dohrn, John Jacobs, and Jeff Jones taking the lead, the cadre came together in the protest they called the National Action, held in Chicago October 8–11, 1969. The group gathered under the banner "BRING THE WAR HOME!"—Jacobs is credited as the author of that slogan—and issued battle cries like "Ho, Ho, Ho Chi Minh, NLF is going to win!"[46]

The National Action had been planned a year earlier in Boulder, Colorado. Jacobs had drafted the resolution, which was titled "The Elections Don't Mean Sh-t—Vote Where the Power Is—Our Power Is in the Street." Jacobs declared an "all-out civil war over Vietnam" and against "fascist U.S. imperialism."[47]

Rudd affirmed the plan of action: "In Chicago the pigs have to be wiped out. We're going to fight with violence and wipe out Chicago." SDS planned to have fifteen thousand student demonstrators on hand for the event, which coincided with the trial of the Chicago Eight.[48] Joining Rudd and Jacobs for the festivities were Ayers, Dohrn, Tom Hayden—on hand for an inspiring pep talk—Michael Klonsky, David Gilbert, Kathy Boudin, and the other usual suspects. What ensued was an organized riot, commenced on October 5, when the "flower children" dynamited the statue commemorating the Chicago police who had been killed in the 1886 Haymarket Riot. As far as the "students" were concerned, these men were not Chicago's finest but jackbooted swine. In the ensuing upheaval the protesters violently clashed with more than a thousand policemen.

Mayor Daley's police won the battle, but it was not a total loss for the student revolutionaries. They found solace in the roughly thirty "pigs" they injured and in the city official who was paralyzed.[49]

The day after that initial rampage, with the student Reds bruised and cut and beaten, or locked in jail, Bernardine Dohrn, the former cheerleader, tried to boost the spirits of the protesters at a rally in Grant Park. She was anointed the commissar to spearhead the Women's Militia.

Coincidentally, that fall of 1969 marked the fiftieth anniversary of the founding of the American Communist Party in that same city. These young Reds were the heirs of those Marxist forebears. They walked the same streets where Charles

Ruthenberg, long since buried at the Kremlin, excitedly reported to the Comintern back in the fall of 1919. At the Kremlin, Ruthenberg's corpse now rested close to Lenin in body; at Chicago, the comrades from Columbia and the University of Michigan and elsewhere were close to Lenin in spirit.

Men of God, Days of Rage

The National Action had become the "Days of Rage." This was one of the ugliest incidents in the history of Chicago.

The radicals who orchestrated this violence had the help of dupes, of course. Naïve non-Communist liberals helped the protesters deal with a sticky issue: where would this large radical contingent, upwards of six hundred organizers, find housing? There was no easy solution, especially since many were already wanted by the law for violent activities.

The Religious Left stepped up to help. The liberal mainline denominations in Chicago and nearby Evanston established a special group to find housing for the young folks.[50] As Mark Rudd put it, many of the protesters stayed in "churches loaned to us by sympathetic clergy."[51]

According to the official congressional investigator tasked to probe the incident, the revolutionaries stayed at University Disciple Church in Chicago and, in Evanston, at St. Luke's Lutheran Church, Covenant Methodist Church, and Garrett Theological Seminary. At Garrett a police officer was beaten.[52]

The clergy had laid down one condition for the dope-smoking, weapons-toting militants: no dope or weapons in the churches. That simple rule, naturally, was violated. The Vietcong had used "sanctuaries" in Cambodia to launch attacks on American troops inside Vietnam, and now the young radicals used literal sanctuaries to stage assaults on their domestic enemies: the "pigs" that had always protected these churches and their congregations.

Of course, the folks in the pews were not thrilled when they caught wind of this news. Members of the congregations and people from the surrounding community soon demanded that the duped preachers expel the extremists from their houses of worship. Fighting the fight for "social justice," the good reverends sided with the marijuana smokers.

In one case, the police were forced to enter the Covenant Methodist Church with warrants to arrest those who had engaged in violent action. There, reportedly, the Methodist minister complained that the police broke down the door. But as the congressional investigator calmly explained during hearings, "They broke the door down because the Weathermen had barricaded the door of the church and had refused to let the police serve the warrants."[53]

The pastor was shocked at what was happening in his church—shocked, that is, by the behavior of the police.

War Council

As so often happens with extremist movements, the increasing violence among the revolutionaries was descending into a bloodlust.

Just a couple of months after the Days of Rage, the newly launched Weatherman organized an appropriately titled "War Council" meeting in Flint, Michigan. On December 27, 1969, some four hundred student troops attended the gathering, which the jocular activists described in the pamphlets as a "Wargasm."

John Jacobs, with his knack for bombast, conjured up another fitting slogan: "We're against everything that's good and decent."[54]

That vulgar certainty was made manifest when Bernardine Dohrn grabbed the microphone. True to form, the militant Milwaukee maiden went on a scorching rant. She described the group's mission thusly: "We're about being crazy motherf—ers and scaring the sh-t out of honky America!"[55]

As if at a radical revival meeting, Mark Rudd got caught up in the fervor. He found himself uttering words he later regretted: "It's a wonderful feeling to hit a pig. It must be a really wonderful feeling to kill a pig or blow up something."[56]

Likewise moved by the spirit, Kathy Boudin declared all mothers of white children to be "pig mothers." Invoking the unity of the Christmas season, she led the faithful in a new rendition of Bing Crosby's "White Christmas": "I'm dreaming of a white riot . . . ," she sang. Boudin then shouted about "doing some sh-t like political assassinations."[57]

Bernardine Dohrn wanted to do even more. Much as Lenin was always adding to his list of "harmful insects"—the people destined for death or the gulag—Dohrn's category of "pigs" was rapidly expanding. In the very recent past, the pigs had been America's police and boys in Vietnam. Now Dohrn applied the "pigs" label to the innocent people whom the Charles Manson "family" had brutally murdered earlier that year. The future children's rights advocate expressed no sympathy for the victims of the satanic Manson brood, who broke into homes and mutilated a host of innocent people—including a married couple, the LaBiancas; the actress Sharon Tate, eight and a half months pregnant; three of Tate's friends; and a teenager named Steven Parent. Instead, Dohrn gleefully described the demonic spectacle produced by the Manson "revolutionaries"—including their horrifying act of ripping open Tate's belly, slashing her unborn child. Dohrn thrilled: "Dig it! First they killed those pigs. Then they ate dinner in the same room with them. Then they even shoved a fork into the victim's stomach! Wild!"[58]

One would like to say that this moment of gory madness shocked even the hardcore in the room, but that would not be accurate. The faithful, from Dohrn's sweetheart, Bill Ayers, to everyone else in the hall, knew that she was serious[59]— and they dug it. As Mark Rudd reported, the assembled "instantly adopted as Weather's salute four fingers held up in the air, invoking the fork left in Sharon Tate's belly."[60]

Rudd translated this message for the wider world: "The message was that we sh-t on all your conventional values, you murderers of black revolutionaries and Vietnamese babies. There were no limits to our politics of transgression."[61]

No, there were not. This is not quite the flowery image of the children dancing with daisies captured by modern hagiographers and '60s documentarians.

A line had been crossed—the first steps into a dark world. As with the Jacobins after the first drop of the guillotine, the blood began to flow, rushing from the altar where Bishop Dohrn exhorted the faithful. A "new decade now dawned," judged Rudd, as "the New Red Army marched out from Flint, exhilarated and terrified."[62]

Exhilarated to commit terror.

Terrorism

The New Red Army that Rudd described was the Weather Underground. This was itself an offshoot of Weatherman, as the revolutionaries most committed to destructive action decided that "peace" marches must be replaced by domestic terror cells and bomb-making units. In time the Weather Underground would proudly take credit for upwards of a dozen bombings. Mark Rudd, Bernardine Dohrn, Bill Ayers, Kathy Boudin, David Gilbert, and Jeff Jones were among the violent founders of Weatherman who went underground. For at least some the decision to hide out was not a choice: they were wanted by the law for criminal acts and refusals to appear before courts to testify.

Violence was not the only reason to go underground: many of the comrades were inspired by, and even interacting with, foreign adversaries of the United States.

Ayers, for example, had been inspired by the Cuban revolution, by Fidel and Che. That is no small thing. At the time that Ayers dedicated himself to *la revolucion,* insurgent Marxist guerrillas had penetrated countries throughout the Western hemisphere, and always with guns blazing—from Cuba to Peru, from Brazil to Colombia, from El Salvador to Nicaragua. Ayers and his youthful revolutionaries would not let the Communist groundswell miss the most important country: America.

The young American revolutionaries were embraced by Castro's Cuba, which sponsored Marxist subversion throughout the Western hemisphere. When the Weathermen went underground, Castro and his forces offered training and asylum in Cuba—including training by the KGB. Here the Weathermen continued the long and dishonorable tradition of American radicals traveling abroad to meet with representatives all over the Communist world, from Havana to Hanoi to Prague to Bratislava. To this day, the old comrades have not dared divulge details of such highly disturbing trips. Even Mark Rudd, in his otherwise tell-all memoir, did not address claims that he visited Castro's Cuba and that the uprisings he initiated at Columbia were in some way planned in Cuba.

Nevertheless, it seems clear—based on congressional reports, the recollections of ex-Communists, testimony by FBI informants, FBI investigations, and other sources[63]—that at least some of the Weathermen interacted with the Cubans. Weathermen looking to join the Cubans could be fed through the Cuban embassy in Canada. They could operate in clandestine cells, fronts, and "collectives," so careful about secrecy that they would not carry cards or register in formal membership rolls. Such secrecy would be necessary because the group's activities were dangerous and illegal.

Consider, for example, the pipe-bomb attack on a San Francisco police station on February 16, 1970. The bomb, which detonated at Park Police Station at roughly 10:30 P.M., took the life of a young police sergeant named Brian V. McConnell, severely injured another officer, and hurt seven more.

The young Red storm troopers who organized this assassination never did a day in jail for it. Law-enforcement officials have long suspected that Ayers and Dohrn not only were involved in but actually orchestrated the attack, with Dohrn herself allegedly placing the bomb in the window.

FBI informant Larry Grathwohl pointed to Dohrn's hand in the operation. A Vietnam vet who penetrated SDS and the Weather Underground, Grathwohl implicated both Dohrn and Ayers in sworn testimony in the 1970s and in his 1976 book, plus numerous times since.[64] He testified before the Democrat-controlled Senate Judiciary Committee on October 18, 1974, where he spoke at length, and under oath, about his relationship with Ayers and Dohrn, including how Dohrn personally (in Grathwohl's words) "had to plan, develop, and carry out the bombing of the police station in San Francisco."[65]

Even as this book was being written, the San Francisco Police Officers Association was still implicating Dohrn and Ayers, and demanding justice. In March 2009, for example, the police association issued public statements maintaining that "irrefutable and compelling reasons" established Dohrn and Ayers as responsible for the bombing.[66]

Of course, the San Francisco bombing was just the start of the violence for the Weather Underground.

On the other side of the country, Weather Underground troops began producing nail bombs to detonate at a military dance in Fort Dix, New Jersey, where the revolutionaries hoped to murder young Vietnam vets reunited for an evening of happiness with their wives.[67] The plan backfired.

On March 6, 1970, in a borrowed apartment in the wealthy Greenwich Village section of New York City, three members of the Weather Underground were killed when a bomb they were manufacturing accidentally exploded. The dead revolutionaries were Diana Oughton, Terry Robbins, and Ted Gold, all dear friends of Rudd, Ayers, Dohrn, Boudin, Gilbert, Jones, Jacobs, and crew. Robbins and Gold had been Columbia comrades, with Gold having served as vice chairman of the school's SDS chapter. Oughton, meanwhile, had attended Bryn Mawr along with Kathy Boudin.

Oughton was another tragic case. Her upbringing stood apart from that of her red-diaper-baby friends. Her father was a Republican, a bank and restaurant owner, and her great grandfather reportedly founded the Boy Scouts of America. The happy debutante was radicalized in college, particularly after an all-night browbeating by Boudin, in which the SDS activist overwhelmed the innocent Illinois native with feelings of white guilt and indifference to injustice. With her new "social justice" conscience and sudden spurning of "bourgeois" values, Oughton rejected a marriage offer from a handsome quarterback at Princeton, trading in the life that would have spared her from violent death.[68] The radicalization process continued once Oughton got to the University of Michigan, where she pursued a master's degree in education. She met Bill Ayers and Tom Hayden at the UM chapter of SDS.

Oughton's parents had already agonized over their "lost" little girl; now, on March 6, 1970, they would receive a phone call from hell.[69]

Two female Weathermen escaped the blast in the Greenwich Village apartment. One, who had been reclining in a cedar-lined sauna at the time of the explosion, fled naked from the scene. As the likes of actor Dustin Hoffman (who lived next door) looked on, the two survivors were helped by a neighbor, who happened to be the ex-wife of Henry Fonda, before they disappeared. The naked woman was Kathy Boudin, who had led Diana Oughton down her tragic path.[70]

One might think that this tragedy would have quelled the desire for destruction by America's Red revolutionaries. Not at all. There was little time or desire for remorse. Boudin was undeterred, living to play a part in another crime, with more dead victims, another day. When David Gilbert got the news (he was heading to target practice at the time), he immediately blamed the "pigs" for killing Gold, a friend from Columbia days. As Mark Rudd put it, the young Reds had three "brand-new martyrs, Diana, Ted, and Terry"—in addition to their beloved Che.[71]

The young revolutionaries could also count on adults to defend them. The "liberal" I. F. Stone—Corliss Lamont's "civil liberties" pal and Kathy Boudin's uncle—published a defense of the bombers, titled "Where the Fuse on That Dynamite Leads."[72]

Prairie Fire

Although the former SDSers stayed underground, they continued to draw attention to their cause, and not just with bombings. The Weather Underground crafted a manifesto to address the masses. In 1974 the devoted radicals released *Prairie Fire: The Politics of Revolutionary Anti-Imperialism,* published as the "political statement of the Weather Underground." It was signed by four members of the Weather Underground: Bill Ayers, Bernardine Dohrn, Jeff Jones, and Celia Sojourn.

"We are a guerrilla organization," the authors explained. "We are communist women and men, underground in the United States for more than four years."They went on: "We need a revolutionary communist party in order to lead the struggle, give coherence and direction to the fight, seize power and build the new society."

"We have only begun," continued the fanatical four. They vowed that "the only possibilities are victory or death." This "revolutionary program" was one of "an urgent and pressing strategic necessity." "Our intention," they wrote, was "to disrupt the empire" of "U.S. imperialism," "to incapacitate it." "The only path to the final defeat of imperialism and the building of socialism is revolutionary war." That "war," the authors promised, "will be complicated and protracted. It includes mass struggle and clandestine struggle, peaceful and violent. . . . Without armed struggle there can be no victory."

Che Guevara was the poster boy for *Prairie Fire.* Full pages inside the book featured loving illustrations of the godlike Communist revolutionary. "In our own hemisphere," the authors wrote, "Che Guevara urged that we 'create two, three, many Vietnams,' to destroy U.S. imperialism . . . and opening another front within the US itself." The Weather Underground had opened that front. The "war" to defeat imperialism was being conducted under "THE BANNER OF CHE," the authors said.

And if Democrats still, by now, could not discern that these Communists were not their friends, the four authors dedicated their manifesto to, among others, Sirhan Sirhan, the assassin of Robert F. Kennedy.

What's Twenty-five Million Dead Americans?

The same year that the Weather Underground announced its violent intentions in *Prairie Fire,* Larry Grathwohl gave even more alarming testimony about the terrorists. Grathwohl, the FBI informant, testified against SDS and the Weathermen before the Senate Judiciary Committee on October 18, 1974. In doing so he infuriated his erstwhile comrades, especially as he implicated Dohrn and Ayers in the San Francisco Park Police bombing. When they learned that Grathwohl was an informant, the Ivy League apparatchiks turned on him with a vengeance, posting his face on "WANTED" posters and labeling him a "pig infiltrator" who had committed "crimes against the people." (See page 344.)

Before the Senate and in his book, Grathwohl bravely testified to the comrades' willingness to kill innocents. He explained how Bill Ayers, discussing a planned bombing of the Detroit Police Officers Association building, told him and other plotters: "We blast that f—ing building to hell. And we do it when the place is crowded. We wait for them to have a meeting, or a social event. Then we strike." Grathwohl noted to Ayers that a Red Barn restaurant nearby would get blown up in the process. Ayers, he said, was unconcerned, responding: "We can't protect all the innocent people in the world. Some will get killed."[73]

Grathwohl offered an utterly chilling account in a videotaped interview he gave for the 1982 documentary *No Place to Hide: The Strategy and Tactics of Terrorism.*[74] In it he spoke of a meeting he attended with twenty-five leaders of the Weather Underground.[75] He pressed his comrades for some specifics as to how they planned to manage the massive social-political American reengineering project they all desired. Grathwohl recalled:

> I brought up the subject of what's going to happen after we take over the government. You know, [once] we become responsible for administering, you know, 250 million people. And there was no answer. No one had given any thought to economics. How are you going to clothe and feed these people?

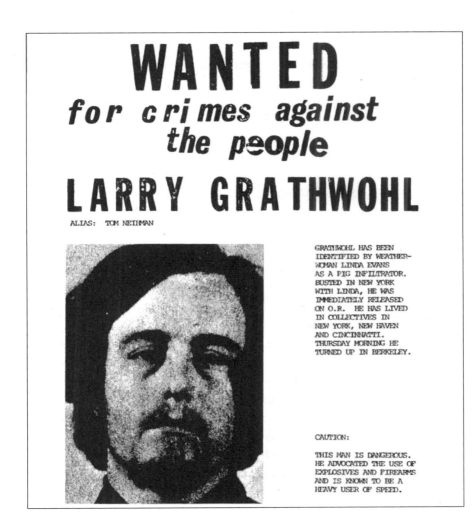

"Pig infiltrator": The Weather Underground distributed this "WANTED" poster when the radical organization discovered that Larry Grathwohl was an FBI informant.

The only thing that I could get was that they expected that the Cubans, the North Vietnamese, the Chinese, and the Russians would all want to occupy different portions of the United States.

They also believed that their immediate responsibility would be to protect against what they called the "counterrevolution." And they felt that this counterrevolution could best be guarded against by creating and establishing *reeducation* in the [American] Southwest, where we would take all of the people who needed to be reeducated into the new way of thinking and teach them how things were going to be.

I asked, "Well, what is going to happen to those people that we can't reeducate, that are diehard capitalists?" And the reply was that they'd have to be eliminated. And when I pursued this further, they estimated that they'd have to eliminate 25 million people in these reeducation centers. And when I say "eliminate," I mean *kill* 25 million people.

I want you to imagine sitting in a room with 25 people, most of whom have graduate degrees from Columbia and other well-known educational centers, and hear them figuring out the logistics for the elimination of 25 million people.

And they were dead serious.[76]

Grathwohl's account may shock observers today, but no one should be surprised. Bear in mind that these young revolutionaries, educated at America's leading universities—and many of whom today teach at universities—were diehard Communists and moral relativists. They accepted that millions would need to die to usher in the "better world," as Lenin, Stalin, Mao, Pol Pot, Che, and on and on and on, had always said.

Even milder Marxist murderers like Leon Trotsky, exiled by Stalin and thus deprived of adequate killing power, preached the necessity of eliminating innocents. As Trotsky famously said, the Bolsheviks would not arrive at the kingdom of socialism on a polished floor with white gloves. Blood would need to be spilled. The blood of innocents would consecrate the Communist ground.

Remember, too, that the Weather Underground gaggle was largely Maoist. Compared to Mao's death toll, twenty-five million was actually quite small— barely a third of the lives that the Chinese Communist tyrant took. Like Mao, and Stalin and Lenin and the others, the young revolutionaries professed no higher authority than their own, and were willing to do whatever suited their purposes.

The Weatherman's talk of reeducation centers should not come as a surprise either. It was fully in keeping with the group's Maoist model. This was Mao's

"Sinification" of Marxism, stripped bare. The American Maoists were planning to carry out precisely what they had long advocated. Such 1960s discussions among the SDSers at Columbia University had not been mere dorm-room "bull sessions." They were serious—*deadly* serious.

Mark Rudd Bolts

The situation got so bad at the Weather Underground that some, like Mark Rudd, finally had enough.

Rudd was taken aback at the behavior of his companions, especially Bernardine Dohrn. He was struck by their paranoia. He saw a Stalinist purge mentality beginning to consume Dohrn and crowding in on the whole group, almost as if it were possessed. "The effort had degenerated into mindless Stalinism," said Rudd.[77]

Rudd came to see that his and the others' hopes and dreams had deteriorated into reckless madness. Now the demons haunted him. He plunged into despair, considering suicide. He later admitted that he had gone almost "crazy."[78]

By 1976 Rudd was ready to leave the Weather Underground. He continued a life on the run as a fugitive for a while, but he finally turned himself over to authorities in New York in October 1977. He would never do jail time.

It was left to Bernardine Dohrn, Bill Ayers, and the remaining true believers to carry on the unholy crusade.

The Brinks Job

The Weather Underground was never able to match its heroes' murder of millions, lacking the absolute power that mentors like Mao Tse-tung and Vladimir Lenin had achieved. Nonetheless, the group's hellions ruined more than a few lives.

In October 1981 the faithful pulled off an armed robbery of a Brinks security truck in Nanuet, New York, in which two more "pigs," plus a Brinks guard, were murdered. One of the policemen was the only black officer on the force. This was ironic given that the perpetrators had done the job to finance a Communist war against racism in America, the apotheosis of which would be the establishment of a "New Afrika" in America's southern states.[79]

The Brinks attackers included Weathermen Judy Clark, David Gilbert, and Kathy Boudin. The conspirators were arrested. Boudin would do long-term prison time, with her father, counsel to other Communists, from Paul Robeson to Fidel Castro, unable to save his client-daughter from jail. Clark and Gilbert received even longer sentences. Boudin and Clark would now teach their inmates about "social justice."[80] Gilbert is still in the penitentiary.[81]

Mark Rudd, who had been classmates with Gilbert at Columbia—together they had orchestrated the Columbia student revolt—described Gilbert as sensitive and brilliant. If not for the path he chose that led to a life in prison, Gilbert probably would have had "a career as a respected professor" in sociology, according to Rudd.[82] No doubt, that is a fair estimation. Gilbert's story is yet another cautionary tale from a group whose radicalism and destructiveness are often sugarcoated today.

When he went to jail, Gilbert left behind a young son, Chesa, who was only fourteen months old at the time of the Brinks robbery. Chesa also lost his mother, who was none other than Kathy Boudin. With Chesa's parents both off to prison, Bill Ayers and Bernardine Dohrn offered to raise the orphaned child.

Boudin happily agreed. She turned over the nurturing of her son to the author of the four-finger salute that glorified the fork that had gashed the baby in Sharon Tate's womb.

From Terrorists to Tenured Radicals

Much more could be said about the Weathermen's destructive ambitions and terrorist activities, but even this brief synopsis conveys the human carnage they left in their wake. Of course, even then, Bill Ayers feels that he and his cohorts "showed remarkable restraint" in their activities—in light, that is, of American bombings in Vietnam.[83]

The radicals justified their own bombings as necessary to advance the revolution. They considered their depths of cruelty "appropriate" given what American "authorities" had done at home and were doing internationally. And generally, as Communists had always preached, they believed a measure of violence was necessary to create the better world.

One good thing did come from the radicals' open advocacy of violent revolution: it finally awakened the duped liberals who supported them and (inadvertently) their goals. The ringleaders of the Weather Underground—people like Dohrn, Ayers, Jones, and Rudd—had been way too aggressive for the non-Communist liberals who truly wanted peace and not an "American Vietnam." Rudd later acknowledged that he and his fellow militants had "made such disastrous mistakes on such a big level" and "played into the hands of the FBI—our sworn enemies. We might as well have been on their payroll."[84]

Really, the old salts at CPUSA had done a much better job of duping than these amateurish revolutionaries of the '60s. With the Weathermen trumpeting their plans for violent revolution, even the most delusional LSD droppers could recognize that the leaders' objectives were far different from their own.

Many of the Weathermen, however, would not end up paying for their mistakes—or for their crimes. Aside from Kathy Boudin, David Gilbert, and Judy Clark, most of the comrades eluded prison time. Ultimately, Bernardine Dohrn and Bill Ayers avoided jail because of charges dropped due to prosecutorial problems. That escape from due justice has since prompted Ayers to celebrate: "Guilty as hell, free as a bird! America is a great country!"[85]

Free as a bird to pursue what? Ayers and others may have received the answer to that question as early as 1967, at a pre-Weatherman SDS conference held in Ann Arbor, Michigan, Ayers's academic home. The conference, held July 14–16, 1967, was staged by SDS's Radical Education Project and titled "Radicals in the Professions."[86] Dr. Quentin Young, the "SDS doctor" who would turn congressional hearings into a circus the following year, spoke on the importance of radicals entering the field of health care. But at the conference, the student radicals paid particular attention to the American educational establishment, especially higher education—and specifically departments of education, where they could train the future teachers of America.

Bill Ayers would eventually follow the Deweyan tradition of ushering in social and political change through education rather than politics—the latter of which had failed him and his fellow Marxist-Leninists. He and Dohrn both sought out the ivory tower again. They believed they had a lot to impart to America's youth and its future. Rudd, too, eventually ended up in education, teaching and lecturing at colleges.[87] Basically, almost all of them would take that path.

And the contacts they would make in that capacity are nothing short of awe-inspiring. One of them, yet another product of Columbia University, would—forty years after that conference in Ann Arbor—become a political rallying point for the suddenly reborn SDS and Weather Underground "progressives." He was a beacon for Ayers, Dohrn, Rudd, Hayden, Klonsky, Machtinger, Jones, and more. They would again come to Chicago, this time with a very different take on the man the Democrats were looking to send to the presidency. In 2008 they would organize yet again, this time working *within* the system, to help make this man— Barack Obama—president of the United States of America.

To achieve that goal, they would need to be very careful in publicly expressing their true feelings and motivations. Otherwise they would risk driving away the masses, especially traditional Democrats, moderates, and crossover voters. They had made that mistake in the initial SDS split, losing the support of a huge number of non-Communists. In 2008 they would be vigilant not to repeat the error.

But that was still decades down the road. For now, they would need to wait. The twentieth century was far from finished.

17

JOHN KERRY—AND GENGHIS KHAN

Lest anyone doubt that the USSR and its satellites manipulated the anti–Vietnam War movement in the United States, consider the testimony of one of the Soviet bloc's highest-ranking propagandists, Lieutenant General Ion Mihai Pacepa, a top Romanian intelligence official who worked closely with the KGB.

"During the Vietnam War," said Pacepa (who, as noted, ultimately defected to the United States), "we spread vitriolic stories around the world, pretending that America's presidents sent Genghis Khan–style barbarian soldiers to Vietnam who raped at random, taped electrical wires to human genitals, cut off limbs, blew up bodies and razed entire villages. Those weren't facts. They were our tales." Nonetheless, said Pacepa, millions of Americans "ended up being convinced their own president, not communism, was the enemy."[1]

According to Pacepa, it was the odious Yuri Andropov, then head of the KGB (and later the Soviet supreme leader), who conceived this *dezinformatsiya* war—disinformation campaign—against the United States. The Soviets devoted exorbitant spending to the cause. Andropov told Pacepa that "people are more willing to believe smut than holiness." Certainly that was often the case for the emotional Left.

"As far as I'm concerned," Pacepa said elsewhere, "the KGB gave birth to the antiwar movement in America."[2]

Pacepa probably gave too much credit to the KGB and not enough to LBJ. The Johnson administration's mismanagement of the war (and, of course, the draft) was what sent those college kids into the streets in the first place. That said, the

KGB exacerbated the discontent as much as possible, and received a helping hand from American Communists.

What the Soviet propagandists needed was American suckers, and they got them in spades from the non-Communist left—from those peace-loving liberals who yet again were far more suspicious of the anti-Communists than of the Communists.

Most of the Vietnam War protesters recoiled at the thought of donning a military uniform for their country at the time. Some of them came to hate America as much as they hated the war, literally spitting on returning men in uniform. Others, like the Weathermen, went further, hatching plans to kill GIs.

But one of America's most famous war protesters actually put on the uniform and stood for America in Vietnam. Because of that, his denunciations of the war carried far more credibility than did those of the pampered radicals at Columbia.

His comments, offered during well-publicized hearings in the U.S. Senate, must have thrilled Moscow—for in condemning the U.S. handling of the war, the Vietnam veteran inadvertently repeated the Soviets' disinformation line. He used language strikingly similar to Pacepa's.

This Vietnam vet and headlining war protester was, oddly enough, another twenty-first-century Democratic Party presidential nominee. Like Barack Obama, this figure—John Kerry—provides a fascinating link between the past and present.

John Kerry Testifies

On April 22, 1971, John Kerry, who had returned from his tour of duty in Vietnam the previous year, testified before the Senate Foreign Relations Committee. Helping to arrange the testimony was Senator Ted Kennedy, whose 1962 campaign had included a young volunteer named John Kerry. Kennedy introduced Kerry to Democratic senator J. William Fulbright at a private fundraising event at the home of antiwar Democratic senator Philip A. Hart of Michigan.[3] Fulbright was chair of the Senate Foreign Relations Committee.

Kerry's appearance came at a pivotal moment in the war. At the time, Congress was considering at least seven legislative proposals relating to Vietnam.[4] In other words, continued funding for the war hung in the balance. Whether that funding was increased or decreased would signal whether the United States tried to win or opted for withdrawal, and whether the troops in the field got more or fewer weapons to fight the enemy and defend themselves.

The day Kerry testified, the Senate hearing room was packed with report-ers and clicking cameras. The lieutenant, who was still in the U.S. Navy Reserve at the time, went before Fulbright's committee and dumped a flaming supply of verbal napalm on American troops.

Presenting himself as a representative of a small organization known as Viet-nam Veterans Against the War—and "of a very much larger group of veterans in this country"—Kerry stated:

> I would like to talk, representing all those veterans, and say that several months ago in Detroit, we had an investigation at which over 150 honorably discharged and many very highly decorated veterans testified to war crimes committed in Southeast Asia, not isolated incidents but crimes committed on a day-to-day basis with the full awareness of officers at all levels of com-mand. . . .
>
> They told stories [of how] they had personally raped, cut off ears, cut off heads, taped wires from portable telephones to human genitals and turned up the power, cut off limbs, blown up bodies, randomly shot at civil-ians, razed villages in fashion reminiscent of Genghis Khan, shot cattle and dogs for fun, poisoned food stocks, and generally ravaged the countryside of South Vietnam in addition to the normal ravage of war, and the normal and very particular ravaging which is done by the applied bombing power of this country.[5]

Kerry's testimony hit Vietnam vets like carpet bombing. He had claimed that some American soldiers had acted as brutally as Genghis Khan—widely consid-ered one of the worst beasts in all of history, the very embodiment of tyrants. It was a damning indictment of U.S. troops and what they were fighting against in Southeast Asia.

Kerry's blistering claims made headlines across America and throughout the world. Overnight, his face was everywhere. He was inundated with media requests, which he unhesitatingly accepted, speaking to the likes of *Meet the Press* and being profiled by *60 Minutes*.[6] He was an instant celebrity, discussed at NBC, CBS, the *Washington Post*—and even the White House.

President Richard Nixon was soon discussing Kerry with aides, as we now know from the released "Nixon Tapes." In a meeting with Chief of Staff H. R. Haldeman and National Security Adviser Henry Kissinger, Nixon gave Kerry a backhanded compliment, distinguishing him from the other "bearded weirdos" in the antiwar movement, and conceding that he had been "extremely effective" in his Senate appearance.[7] At the same time, the president doubted not only Kerry's medals for his service but the very war crimes that Kerry alleged. When Haldeman spoke of "shoot[ing] babies out of women's arms," Nixon, a Navy veteran himself, said dismissively, "Oh, stop that. People in the Navy don't do things [like that]." Also, in a telephone call with aide Charles Colson, the president called Kerry a "phony."[8]

The young John Kerry had made a huge impact. When the long-haired, grungy hippies leveled such nasty accusations against American boys, it had little effect on Joe Sixpack and Mom and Pop; they expected the radicals to make radical statements. But to hear an actual veteran say such things? A *decorated* veteran? This was a serious wake-up call.

Undeniably, Kerry's reports upset America's troops abroad. His words badly hurt their morale and mission. And the testimony must have delighted the enemy, from Ho Chi Minh City to Moscow.

Had John Kerry spoken the truth—or, more precisely, what he *thought* was truth? That was the rub, as Kerry's claims were immediately disputed.

Firing Back

One of the most dramatic challenges to Kerry's testimony came two months later, during the nationally televised *Dick Cavett Show* on June 30, 1971. The high-profile veteran appeared on the program against John E. O'Neill, who had taken command of Swift Boat PCF-94 after Kerry. O'Neill vigorously countered his predecessor's allegations—and has never stopped.

So incensed was O'Neill that more than thirty years later he and roughly two hundred other Swift Boat veterans organized to publicly challenge Kerry's claims. The Swift Boat Veterans for Truth, as the group called itself, held a press conference in Washington, D.C., on May 4, 2004. That summer, while Kerry campaigned as the Democratic presidential nominee, O'Neill wrote a best-selling book laying out at great length where he and the other Swift Boat veterans judged that Kerry had erred. In fact, the book, *Unfit for Command,* called Kerry "a liar and a fraud, unfit to be the commander in chief of the United States of America."[9] These "swifties" believed that a grave injustice had been made against their honor, that Kerry had impugned the very character and humanity of American troops with vicious falsehoods.

The goal here is not to try to resolve whether, and if so where, John Kerry lied or manufactured abuses by fellow soldiers; whether he was simply mistaken on certain points, reporting false claims by others without knowing they were false; or the merits of John O'Neill's counterclaims. Rather, the interest here is in dupery. Was John Kerry duped, unwittingly repeating disinformation from the Communist propaganda machine?

According to General Pacepa, the high-level Soviet-bloc intelligence official, Kerry probably was a dupe. Pacepa, of course, affirmed that the Soviets created malicious lies intended to dishonor American servicemen and undermine the U.S. position in Vietnam. But he went deeper, zeroing in on Kerry's "Genghis Khan" claim:

> The exact sources of that assertion should be tracked down. Kerry also ought to be asked who, exactly, told him any such thing, and what it was, exactly, that they said they did in Vietnam. Statutes of limitation now protect these individuals from prosecution for any such admissions. Or did Senator Kerry merely hear allegations of that sort as hearsay bandied about by members of antiwar groups (much of which has since been discredited)?
>
> To me, this assertion sounds exactly like the disinformation line that the Soviets were sowing worldwide throughout the Vietnam era. KGB priority number one at that time was to damage American power, judgment, and credibility. One of its favorite tools was the fabrication of such evidence as photographs and "news reports" about invented American war atrocities. These tales were purveyed in KGB-operated magazines that would then flack them to reputable news organizations. Often enough, they would be picked up. News organizations are notoriously sloppy about verifying their sources. All in all, it was amazingly easy for Soviet-bloc spy organizations to fake many such reports and spread them around the free world.
>
> As a spy chief and a general in the former Soviet satellite of Romania, I produced the very same vitriol Kerry repeated to the U.S. Congress almost word for word and planted it in leftist movements throughout Europe.[10]

Pointing to some of the international "peace" organizations that the KGB loaded with mendacious anti-American propaganda on the Vietnam War, Pacepa stated: "The quote from Senator Kerry is unmistakable Soviet-style sloganeering from this period. I believe it is very likely a direct quote from one of these organizations' propaganda sheets."

The Usual Suspects

General Pacepa rightly suggested that the sources of John Kerry's 1971 assertions should be tracked down. But in fact, Kerry cited a source in his testimony: a 1971 gathering in Detroit by Vietnam Veterans Against the War.

As Pacepa suggested, this antiwar veterans' group has been discredited. Vietnam Veterans Against the War became notorious in part for an event known as Dewey Canyon III, held shortly before Kerry's Senate testimony. Representatives of the group, including Kerry himself, marched all the way to the White House and Congress to deliver petitions. This display included the striking scene of veterans tossing their medals over a fence outside the Capitol building. Kerry, too, hurled medals, although controversy has since ensued over whether they were his own.[11]

The group's Detroit gathering had been held three months earlier, in January 1971. The organizers of this antiwar event included actress Jane Fonda (Kerry attended at least one antiwar rally with Fonda),[12] comedian Dick Gregory, and Mark Lane, the JFK-assassination conspiracy theorist.[13] The Winter Soldier Investigation, as it was called, claimed precisely the crimes that Kerry would later share with the Senate. And of course, Kerry, at the outset of his Senate statement, cited the Detroit gathering as the basis for his remarks.

And that, in essence, was the fatal flaw of the testimony.

Mackubin Thomas Owens, a professor at the Naval War College who led a Marine infantry platoon in Vietnam in 1968–69, puts it bluntly: "In fact, the entire Winter Soldiers Investigation was a lie."[14]

The investigation had been inspired by Mark Lane's 1970 book *Conversations with Americans,* which claimed to relate atrocities committed by Vietnam soldiers.[15] Owens notes that the book was panned by no less than James Reston Jr. and Neil Sheehan, both ultra-liberals who were not exactly known as supporters of the war. Sheehan was especially hard on Lane's book, maintaining that many of Lane's "eye witnesses" had not actually served in Vietnam or not in the capacity they had claimed.

That did not prevent Senator Mark Hatfield of Oregon—the most commonly duped Republican of his era—from inserting the transcript of the Winter Soldier testimonies into the *Congressional Record.* Hatfield also requested that the Marine Corps commandant investigate the alleged war crimes.[16]

But investigations did not produce the results that Hatfield probably expected. The Naval Investigative Service tried to interview the supposed witnesses but discovered, as Owens reports, "that some of the most grisly testimony was given by fake witnesses who had appropriated the names of real Vietnam veterans."[17]

Owens, like Pacepa, notes that John Kerry's 1971 testimony included "every left-wing cliché about Vietnam and the men who served there. It is part of the reason that even today, people who are too young to remember Vietnam are predisposed to believe the worst about the Vietnam War and those who fought it."

Unfortunately, the American press, already decidedly against American policy in Vietnam, was predisposed to believe people like John Kerry. When Kerry alleged savagery, liberal journalists jumped for the bait.

Honoring John Kerry as a "Hero"—in Vietnam

Even with knowledgeable sources like General Pacepa and Professor Owens raising doubts about the sources and legitimacy of Kerry's testimony, one can debate where and when Kerry got his information, and the validity of his claims. What is undeniable, however, is the *value* of his testimony to the Vietcong. Indeed, to understand how it outraged American soldiers, one need only consider this question: how valuable was John Kerry's testimony to the Vietnamese enemy?

In *Unfit for Command*, John O'Neill recalls the sad experience of Bill Lupetti, a Navy corpsman who was stationed in Vietnam in 1969–70 and treated injured Swift Boat soldiers.[18] Lupetti had served at An Thoi, the small base and unit where both O'Neill and Kerry had served. For Memorial Day 2004, Lupetti returned to Vietnam, visiting Ho Chi Minh City, wandering through the streets trying to piece together a period of his life that he had once tried hard to forget, and looking earnestly to find out whether certain Vietnamese friends had survived the merciless Communist takeover that Ayers, Dohrn, Rudd, Boudin, Gilbert, Gold, Jacobs, Jones, Hayden, Fonda, and friends had hailed.

Lupetti happened upon the War Remnants Museum. Inside, he came to an exhibit dedicated to "heroes" around the world who had helped the Vietnamese Communists win the war. A wall plaque at the head of the exhibit, written in both Vietnamese and English, offered a note of appreciation from Vietnam's Communist authorities: "We would like to thank the communist parties and working class countries of the world."

Among those whom the Vietcong wished to thank for their "strong encouragement to our people's patriotic resistance against the U.S." were "progressive human beings for their wholehearted support."[19] That included, of course, America's "progressives."

Lupetti was not surprised to see photographs of China's Communists and American radicals from the 1960s. He was staggered, however, by a picture of John Kerry.

The photo showed Kerry in 1993, by which point he was a celebrated Democratic senator, in conversation with a former general secretary of the Communist Party of Vietnam, Do Muoi. There he was, John Kerry, in a special exhibit honoring those whose "heroic" contributions had helped the Vietcong defeat the United States.

The Vietnamese Communists never forgot Kerry's Senate testimony in 1971. It had been a great help to their efforts.

"Our Most Significant Success"

Ion Mihai Pacepa, noting that KGB chairman Yuri Andropov had managed the Kremlin's Vietnam operation, said that Andropov "often bragged about having damaged the U.S. foreign-policy consensus, poisoned domestic debate in the U.S., and built a credibility gap between America and European public opinion through our disinformation operations."

"Vietnam," Andropov once told Pacepa, had been "our most significant success."[20]

Yes, it had. And it could not have succeeded without the unwitting, unsuspecting American accomplices who bought and then sold some of the worst Soviet slanders of American boys fighting for their lives and for others' freedom abroad.

John Kerry served his country in Vietnam, but he seems to have misserved many of his countrymen with his ill-advised testimony on Vietnam. Whatever the ultimate sources for his claims against his brothers-in-arms, his assertions were enormously damaging and personally hurtful. His erstwhile band of brothers has not forgiven him.

18

A KISS FOR BREZHNEV:
JIMMY CARTER

From 1974 to 1980, the Soviet Union incorporated at least ten nations into its orbit—new Communist allies from the Third World, including some countries that had been traditional anti-Communist American allies.[1] These changes represented big losses for the United States in its ongoing Cold War against the USSR.

This dramatic swing was no accident. Under the regime of Leonid Brezhnev and the doctrine that bore his name, the Soviets were suddenly expanding Communism with alarming haste. They did so as they trumpeted an "easing" of East-West frictions and talked of "peaceful coexistence."

The Brezhnev Doctrine would not have been so successful had Moscow not found the U.S. leadership so easy to exploit with talk of peaceful coexistence. The Soviet gains took place during an era when the United States was following a policy of détente. This was a bipartisan policy, carried out both by Republican presidents, Richard Nixon and Gerald Ford, and by a Democratic president, Jimmy Carter. Throughout, presidential candidates like Ronald Reagan warned—consistently, during both Republican and Democratic administrations—that détente amounted to a "one-way street" benefiting the expansionary ambitions of Soviet Communism.[2]

Reagan, it turns out, was exactly right. After the Cold War, Genrikh Trofimenko, the colorful director of the prestigious Institute for U.S.A. and Canada Studies of the Russian Academy of Sciences, candidly summed up the Soviet government's take on détente: "There could not be a peaceful coexistence between wicked warmongering imperialists [America] and honorable and peace-loving communists caring for the well-being of all progressive humanity."[3]

Détente facilitated the Brezhnev Doctrine of advancing Communist "national liberation movements" around the world. Occasionally, even the anti-anti-Communist American press managed to get the story right. In a revealing January 1976 article in the *Washington Post,* Peter Osnos reported: "Soviet commentators have been saying almost daily that the 'policy of relaxation of tensions [détente] between states with different social systems [U.S. and USSR] cannot be interpreted as a ban on the national liberation struggle of peoples who come out against colonial oppression or as a ban on class struggle.'"[4]

Chairman Brezhnev himself said as much. In February 1976, addressing the Twenty-fifth Congress of the Soviet Communist Party in Moscow, he frankly conceded: "We make no secret of the fact that we see détente as the way to create more favorable conditions for peaceful socialist and communist construction."[5]

Brezhnev was even more candid in a secret speech he delivered to fellow Communist leaders in Prague in 1973: "We are achieving with détente what our predecessors have been unable to achieve using the mailed fist. . . . We have been able to accomplish more in a short time with détente than was done for years pursuing a confrontation policy. . . . Trust us, comrades. For by 1985, as a consequence of what we are now achieving with détente, we will have achieved most of our objectives."[6]

This bold enunciation was downplayed by most of the American media when it became public four years later. When Ronald Reagan learned about it, he devoted a number of his syndicated daily radio commentaries to the speech, insisting that it "should have been front page [news] in every major paper in the land."[7]

Such was the sorry state of affairs for America by the latter 1970s. Uncle Sam suffered a painful setback in Vietnam, withdrawing in the spring of 1975. The country was experiencing terrible domestic problems like Watergate and President Carter's economic "malaise." Added to all that, the Soviets were surging in their global competition with the United States. In short, America was losing the Cold War, and Americans knew it.

"Inordinate Fear of Communism"

The USSR's dramatic global expansion should have been enough to convince President Carter to be suspicious of Comrade Brezhnev and his Marxist-Leninist ambitions. Instead, Carter continued to trust the Soviets, even in the face of advice from shrewd anti-Soviet aides like National Security Adviser Zbigniew Brzezinski. Carter's naïveté was so pervasive, so deep, that his gullibility seemed to come from the very marrow of his bones.

Carter trusted the Communists to an unhealthy degree. The first week of his presidency, on January 27, 1977, Carter told high-school students in West Chester, Pennsylvania: "My own hope as president is to explore every possible way to work with the Soviet Union and with other potential enemies of ours, who at this point seem to be our friends."[8] Two months later, at a March 24 news conference, when asked how he might help political dissidents suffering in the Soviet Union, Carter magnanimously reassured his Soviet friends: "I have tried to make sure that the world knows that we are not singling out the Soviet Union for abuse or criticism."[9] Besides, Carter added on June 23, 1978, "We want to get along with the Soviet Union."[10] Three days later, during a June 26 press conference, he said, "We want to be friends with the Soviets."[11] But Carter did not just want to be friends; he saw the Soviets as partners. On July 11 he said, "We are deeply committed to détente, both we and, I believe, the Soviet Union leaders."[12]

In Jimmy Carter's mind, that partnership was paying dividends, especially in places like Vietnam, where the Soviets—by Carter's estimation—were suddenly inactive. How did he know that? Leonid Brezhnev had told him so: "I discussed the South Vietnamese question with President Brezhnev this week," Carter told Japanese reporters on June 20, 1979, "and particularly the Soviet presence there, both ships and airplanes. He assured me personally that there would be no establishment of Soviet bases in South Vietnam and that the present ship and plane use of the ports and airports is of a routine nature."[13]

It was clear to Carter that "the Communist nations who sometimes we look upon as adversaries want to avoid war and to have peace just as much as we do."[14]

By Carter's thinking, so much of America's previous misunderstanding was based on a poisonous anti-Communism. The president lamented America's "inordinate fear of Communism," from which he hoped to unshackle the nation.[15] Pushing the idea of peaceful coexistence that the Soviets so effectively exploited, Carter promised the world, "We are not trying to bring the Soviets to their knees."[16]

Here, as in so many other instances, Jimmy Carter stood in stark contrast to the man who ultimately defeated him for the presidency, Ronald Reagan. As president, Reagan would be committed to doing whatever he could to end the Cold War—end it, that is, with the United States and its free allies victorious over Soviet Communism. For Reagan, the real objective was, in his words, to "bring it [the USSR] to its knees"—the polar opposite of Carter's position.[17]

Carter and Reagan also parted ways on the Berlin Wall, that cold, gray tomb-stone to human freedom. In 1987 President Reagan would famously stand aside the wall and exhort Mikhail Gorbachev to tear it down. But many years before that landmark speech it was already clear that he and Carter took fundamentally different approaches to the barrier that divided the free and democratic West from the Communist East.

In July 1978, during Carter's visit to Germany, a West Berlin woman asked him, "For how long, Mr. President, do you think we've got to live with the Wall?" A help-less Carter responded, "I don't know. I hope that it will be removed in the future, but I have no idea when it might be. I'm sorry I can't give you a better answer, but that's the truth." Onlookers actually laughed at the American president.[18]

Of course, Carter made this comment when the Cold War was raging and the Soviets seemed to be gaining the upper hand. Perhaps he could be excused for failing to foresee an end to Communism. But just four months later, in November 1978, Ronald Reagan went to Berlin as a private citizen and had no difficulty envi-sioning an endgame. In a moment witnessed by only a handful of friends, Reagan stared at the Berlin Wall with a mixture of pity, contempt, and anger. With teeth and fists clenched, he told his two friends and colleagues, Richard V. Allen and Peter Hannaford, "We have got to find a way to knock this thing down."[19]

Reagan, by this point in his life and career, had no illusions about Commu-nism or the Soviet leadership. Two years earlier he had nearly defeated sitting president Gerald Ford in the Republican primaries. After he fell short at the 1976 Republican National Convention, Reagan privately told his son Michael that his only regret was that he would not be able to lean over and whisper "nyet" in the ear of General Secretary Brezhnev.[20]

But the man who won the White House that year, Jimmy Carter, apparently did not make "nyet" part of his vocabulary. The president who decried America's "inordinate fear of Communism," who disdained desires to "bring the Soviets to their knees" in favor of seeking "peaceful coexistence" with the USSR, wanted to accommodate his Soviet counterpart, not tell him no.

The entire world got a chance to see Carter's approach to the Soviets on June 18, 1979. During the signing of the SALT II Treaty in Vienna, President Carter leaned over toward Brezhnev not to whisper "nyet" in his ear but rather to plant a kiss on his cheek. Photographers on hand captured the embrace, preserving the moment forever on film (in the photo that graces the cover of this book).

That visual of Carter kissing Brezhnev is a most instructive metaphor. It truly says it all.

In the Cold War, it would be the difference between winning and losing.

Carter's Belated Wake-up Call

Late in his presidency, Jimmy Carter finally woke up—sort of. On Christmas Day 1979 the Red Army poured into Afghanistan in the first Soviet invasion of a nation outside the Warsaw Pact since World War II. This blatant act of aggression put the final nail in the coffin of détente.

Days after the Soviet invasion, President Carter expressed his shock: "My opinion of the Russians has changed most dramatically in the last week. . . . This action of the Soviets has made a more dramatic change in my own opinion of what the Soviets' ultimate goals are than anything they've done in the previous time I've been in office."[21]

Those words were streamed across front pages all over the world, from Manhattan to Moscow.[22] Among those reading them, probably in his *Los Angeles Times,* was Ronald Reagan, who would be Carter's presidential challenger in the fall. The former California governor was beside himself at the thirty-ninth president's assessment, though he did his best to keep his disbelief and disappointment to himself. In one private letter he wrote that Carter's assessment "would be laughable, I think, if it were not so tragic."[23] Reagan added, in another private letter to a friend, "It is frightening to hear a man in the office of the presidency who has just discovered that the Soviets can't be trusted, that they've lied to him."[24]

Reagan knew what it was liked to be duped, having been duped by Communists himself decades earlier in Hollywood. But then, Reagan had been a mere actor. Carter was the sitting president of the United States of America. The country was not damaged when an actor said something stupid. For a president to be so misled, however, was downright dangerous.

A week after those remarks, Carter remained perplexed. "It's difficult to understand why the Soviets took this action," he told members of Congress in a White House briefing. "I think they probably underestimated the adverse reaction from around the world."[25]

Even then, while pledging to "oppose this Soviet invasion with the means at our disposal," as both a "moral imperative and a strategic imperative," the president hoped that détente could be salvaged. It was a tune that Carter did not change. Speaking at the Venice Economic Summit in June 1980, he reassured the world: "We also know that by resisting Soviet militarism and aggression in the present that we can reopen the paths of peace, détente, accommodation in the future."[26]

For Carter, the fatal misplaced trust, the sorry surprise, was an outgrowth of his liberal worldview. As with so many liberals of his day, what was to be denounced and feared was not Communism but anti-Communism.

There was a toxic moral equivalency at work here as well. Carter reflected the common liberal tendency to insist that neither the United States nor the USSR could claim moral superiority over the other—that both sides were equally culpable for the Cold War and its sins, and neither system was much (if at all) better than the other. As president he publicly expressed this sentiment. "We've got our own problems in this country," Carter stressed. To his fellow Americans, he called attention to what Soviet ambassador Anatoly Dobrynin instructed him: "He said to me, 'At least in the Soviet Union, our women have equal rights.'"[27]

This was a view that Ronald Reagan attacked as rubbish. "Don't let anyone tell you we're morally equivalent with the Soviet Union," he insisted. "I have heard that term used in places. . . . We are morally superior, not equivalent, to any totalitarian regime, and we should be darn proud of it."[28]

As these comments suggest, Jimmy Carter had been soft on the Soviets. Only the most peculiar observer would think otherwise. One such observer was Senator Ted Kennedy.

According to Vasiliy Mitrokhin, a KGB official and senior Soviet archivist who defected in 1992 (bringing with him a huge cache of documents), Kennedy privately relayed a message to Leonid Brezhnev on March 5, 1980. Kennedy had his trusted friend John Tunney personally deliver the message in Moscow. Tunney, himself a former U.S. senator (a Democrat representing California), had been close with Kennedy since they were roommates during law school. According to Mitrokhin, Tunney was there "to relay [Kennedy's] ideas on ways to lessen international tension to the Soviet leadership." Amazingly, Kennedy blamed the escalation in Cold War tensions not on the Soviets but on Jimmy Carter. In Mitrokhin's words, Kennedy felt that "the Carter administration was trying to distort the peace-loving ideas behind Brezhnev's proposals," and that "the atmosphere of tension and hostility" was "being fuelled by Carter." Tunney said that the great Massachusetts liberal was approaching the Soviet leader because he saw it as (in Mitrokhin's words) "his duty to take action himself."[29]

In other words, Mitrokhin's report indicates that Ted Kennedy was undercutting the American commander in chief by attempting secret conversations with the Kremlin. It is important to note, of course, that in March 1980 the Massachusetts senator was campaigning against Carter, a member of his own party, for the presidency; he was trying to take the 1980 Democratic nomination from the sitting president. Kennedy apparently felt that President Carter was guilty of belligerence but that the Soviet dictator was committed to peace, including to a peaceful settlement in Afghanistan—which the Red Army had just invaded and would bomb mercilessly for a decade.

Hugs and Kisses from the Ayatollah

The year 1979 brought two foreign-policy disasters—not only the Soviets' invasion of Afghanistan but also the fall of the shah in Iran, which led to the overnight radical Islamization of Iran and the seizing of more than fifty Americans as hostages. The United States suddenly went from being Iran's best friend to Iran's "Great Satan." It was another horrible embarrassment for America, and for Jimmy Carter.

It hadn't started that way. On December 31, 1977, President Carter stood aside the shah, a close and dependable American ally, and raised his glass to give a toast: "Iran, because of the great leadership of the shah, is an island of stability in one of the more troubled areas of the world."[30]

One year later, that island of stability erupted into a volcano. Militant demonstrations exploded throughout Iran, as a fanatical Shiite cleric named Ayatollah Khomeini led an Islamist uprising against the shah. The shah turned to the U.S. government for assistance in this crisis. But on December 7, 1978, when a reporter asked Carter whether he thought the shah "could survive," the president gave a waffling, weak response that deserves infamy:

> I don't know. I hope so. This is something that is in the hands of the people of Iran. We have never had any intention and don't have any intention of trying to intercede in the internal political affairs of Iran. . . . We personally prefer that the shah maintain a major role in the government, but that's a decision for the Iranian people to make.[31]

To say this was a sudden sea change in American policy toward Iran is insufficient. Carter had casually delivered a jaw-dropper. And no one was as surprised as the Iranian extremists, who read Carter's words—properly so—as a sign that Uncle Sam would not, this time around, save the shah.

Within only weeks of that Carter statement, by February 1979, the shah was gone, the ayatollah was in, and the birth of modern Islamic terror had begun—more than twenty years before the catastrophe of September 11, 2001.

Thus, Jimmy Carter's record is marred not only by the fact that he did nothing to facilitate the collapse of Communism but also by the reality that the eventual successor to Communism as an international menace—radical Islam—was largely set in motion during his presidency.

Carter's dubious connections to both militant Communism and militant Islamism were not confined to his presidency. As we shall see, even well after he left the White House he would continue to be duped by these destructive "isms." In this sense Carter would serve as a twisted bridge between America's two chief foes of the past hundred years.

19

Defending the "Evil Empire": Stopping Ronald Reagan's "Errors" and "Distortions"

The foreign-policy fiascoes of the late 1970s, from Afghanistan to Iran, were major reasons for Jimmy Carter's crushing defeat at the hands of anti-Communist crusader Ronald Reagan in the November 1980 presidential election (Reagan claimed forty-four of fifty states, winning the Electoral College by a vote of 489 to 49). Indeed, it is hard to imagine the nation electing Ronald Reagan without the mess—foreign and domestic—left by Carter.

With Reagan triumphant, and supremely confident, he now had a chance to carry out a plan he had outlined to his foreign-policy adviser Richard V. Allen four years earlier. During a private lunch together in Los Angeles in January 1977, at the start of the Carter presidency, Reagan told Allen: "Dick, my idea of American policy toward the Soviet Union is simple, and some would say simplistic. It is this: We win and they lose. What do you think of that?"[1]

This was a stunning (and in retrospect prophetic) statement—an impossibility to the vast majority of experts and analysts at the time. For years as a private citizen and candidate, Reagan had fiercely opposed the accommodationist policy of détente and spoken frankly about the true nature of Soviet Communism. In the White House he would do the same. He continued an unrelenting rhetorical-moral assault against the foundations of Marxism-Leninism—an assault invigorating to those languishing inside the Iron Curtain.[2] And now, as president, he had the power of policy to put behind his rhetoric. He had the power to try to end—and win—the Cold War, especially through his "peace through strength" military-technological challenge to the USSR via efforts like the Strategic Defense Initiative (SDI).

For taking this stance, Reagan earned the undying enmity of the American Left—from the media to academia to Congress. Liberals demeaned Reagan from the very first weeks of his presidency, castigating him as a "nuclear warmonger," a primitive anti-Communist, a simpleton, a babbling buffoon, one lacking any semblance of intellectual fiber—lazy, senile, preferring old movies to books. The Left's caricature of Reagan was so vicious that anyone born after the 1980s would be astonished to go back in time and see the appraisals of a man who is now regularly ranked as one of America's top presidents,[3] and who, in one extensive poll of 2.4 million participants, was voted "the greatest American of all time."[4]

Even the most rudimentary historical knowledge of Marx, Lenin, the USSR, and the Cold War showed that Reagan rightly understood Communism as expansionary, cruel, and militantly atheistic. These were precisely the points that Democratic predecessors in the Oval Office, including Woodrow Wilson and John F. Kennedy, had made. But apparently the American Left no longer had an appetite for such pronouncements. So when Reagan made his now historic, prophetic predictions that Communism would end up on the "ash heap of history," many liberals judged him out of his mind—literally bordering on senility.

Even when Reagan was shot and nearly killed just two months into his presidency, the most radical quarters of the Left responded not with outrage over an attack on the American president, but rather with delight.

Wayne Allyn Root, who today is a prominent Libertarian Party politician, was then a (rare) Republican student stumping for Reagan at Columbia University. Root recalls sitting in a political-science course on March 30, 1981, when a breathless student ran into the room yelling, "President Reagan has been shot! They've assassinated Reagan!" Not knowing that Reagan was still alive, Root's Columbia classmates erupted into applause. They were "cheering," says Root, "celebrating." There were "high-fives all around," "hugging and screaming with glee, 'Yes! Reagan is dead!'" As he recounts, these classmates literally "rooted for the death of a conservative president."[5]

Columbia University was as unhinged as it had been in the days of John Dewey and Corliss Lamont, and in the '60s, when Mark Rudd, David Gilbert, John Jacobs, Ted Gold, and comrades took over the campus. Though Dewey had long since passed on, his prize student, an aging Corliss Lamont, was still around. Indeed, he was still chair of the National Emergency Civil Liberties Committee, where he publicly condemned the "shocking hypocrisy" of Reagan foreign policy.[6]

The Soviets would have been as delighted by Lamont's swipes at the new American president as they were by his work decades earlier. And in the 1980s, of course, plenty of liberal voices joined the chorus.

The USSR's state-run media made sure the Soviet people heard the Americans' attacks.

The Soviet Side

In the 1980s Americans could catch the Left's attacks on Reagan any time they opened newspapers and news weeklies or watched the evening news. What Americans did not see were Soviet newspapers and news weeklies and television. If they had, they would have been intrigued by what they saw: there was a bracing similarity between what the American Left and Soviet propagandists were stating about President Reagan.

This is not to suggest that the two sides coordinated. It is simply that both sides were moving along leftward tracks, and both looked to alternately ridicule and demonize their common political adversary—a conservative Republican and vocal anti-Communist. They jointly portrayed Reagan as a trigger-happy troglodyte who should not be trusted and most assuredly ought not to be president.

In the course of research for this book and several previous books on Ronald Reagan, I have read thousands of transcripts from Soviet media archives—from *Pravda, Izvestia,* TASS, *Studio 9* TV broadcasts (once the leading "news" program in the USSR), and dozens of lesser-known Soviet government publications. These broadsides were often filled with encomiums to American liberals who excoriated Reagan.

Here are only some of the liberals whose statements against Reagan and his policies the Soviets frequently quoted: *Washington Post* columnist Mary McGrory; *New York Times* columnist James "Scotty" Reston; *New York Times* columnist Anthony Lewis; Senator Howard Metzenbaum, Ohio Democrat; Democratic presidential candidate and civil-rights activist Jesse Jackson; nuclear-freeze activist Dr. Helen Caldicott; President Reagan's daughter, Patti Davis; Dr. Carl Sagan; Phil Donahue; Senators Ted Kennedy and John Kerry, both Massachusetts Democrats; reporter Helen Thomas; CBS News anchor Dan Rather; Senator Patrick Leahy, Vermont Democrat; Congressman Edward Boland, Massachusetts Democrat; 1984 Democratic Party vice-presidential nominee Geraldine Ferraro; 1972 Democratic presidential nominee George McGovern; House Speaker Tip O'Neill, Massachusetts Democrat; Senator Alan Cranston, California Democrat; Madeleine Albright, a leading foreign-policy voice among Democrats, having served on President Carter's National Security Council; and 1984 Democratic presidential nominee Walter Mondale.

The Soviets also looked to leading American newspapers, which were dominated by liberals who typically opposed Reagan's policies and did not respect the
president's mind. Among the Soviets' commonly cited sources were the *New York
Times,* the *Washington Post,* the *Toronto Star,* the Associated Press, UPI, Reuters, and
the *Los Angeles Times.* Over and over, *Pravda* and other Soviet publications would go
to these sources, typically employing a tack that went something like this: *If only
the imperialists in the Reagan White House would listen to the wisdom of this enlightened
American. . . . .* It was not surprising for TASS in the 1980s to take, say, a *Washington Post* op-ed from editor Robert Kaiser—such as Kaiser's lengthy November 1, 1983, op-ed blasting the Reagan administration's invasion of Grenada—
and excerpt it into basically a press release disseminated throughout the Soviet
empire.[7] Indeed, an examination of these old media clips shows that it was probably a daily occurrence for a Soviet commentator or "reporter" to authoritatively
cite a liberal columnist or politician to buttress the case *du jour* against Reagan.

When I first began researching these archived transcripts of Soviet media, I
was amazed to see the similarity between what the Soviet state-run media were
reporting about Ronald Reagan and what American liberals were saying. I truly
felt at times like I was reading talking points from the 1984 Democratic National
Convention. This remarkable overlap has never been fully acknowledged or
appreciated.

To be fair, these liberal Americans did not intend for their material to become
handy propaganda for the Kremlin, and they probably had no idea that they were
feeding the ever-churning Soviet propaganda machine. Most of them were (quite
properly) engaged in political criticism or dissent. They were playing their part
in a free political system that allows open discourse. In that sense, their actions
could not have been more quintessentially American.

Nonetheless, these individuals often unwittingly aided Soviet purposes. Some
American reporters helped the Kremlin even more by crossing the line between
news reporting and opinion writing, which only strengthened Moscow's talking
points. Moreover, the journalists, academics, and policymakers who condemned
Reagan's anti-Communism as primitive and simplistic were themselves display-
ing ignorance, for, as noted, even a cursory examination of the proclamations of
Marx and Lenin, or of the bloody record of the Soviet Union and other Communist regimes, should have revealed that the threat of Communism was nothing to
dismiss. But in the 1980s many American liberals were simply duped by the Communists—just as a young actor named Ronald Reagan had been decades earlier.

Certainly not all liberals or Democrats were snagged in the Communists'
net. Millions of of Democrats crossed over to vote for this conservative Repub-

lican, becoming known as "Reagan Democrats." And some conservative Democrats in Congress, such as Senator Henry "Scoop" Jackson, joined Reagan in blasting détente.

But in the 1980s the Soviets did find fertile ground for dupery, as the Democratic Party, on the heels of Vietnam and Watergate, had drifted notably leftward. The crop of extremely liberal Democrats that had come to Congress just prior to Reagan's election was bold and aggressive. Likewise, the campus protesters of the 1960s had gone into journalism and academia; they knew how to be rebellious. By the 1980s the Democratic Party was producing presidential front-runners like Walter Mondale, Ted Kennedy, and Jesse Jackson; these were not Cold Warriors in the mold of Harry Truman and JFK. As President Reagan's United Nations ambassador, Jeane Kirkpatrick, herself a former Democrat, had put it, this was now the party of the "San Francisco Democrats." It was a party, said former Democrat Ronald Reagan, which he didn't leave, but which had left him.

Ronald Reagan and other former Democrats may not have been pleased with the party's leftward direction, but the Soviets were nothing short of enchanted with the liberals who provided grist for the Kremlin propaganda mill.

The Duped: The American Press

So who, then, was duped in the 1980s? In which areas did the duping occur?

The examples from the Reagan years could fill this book. It was difficult—due to space constraints—to exclude some of the more delectable areas, like the nuclear-freeze campaign, which depended on dupes to a shocking extent. In this book I will focus on just a few examples, mainly involving the American media. That is a fitting place to start, as the nation's most celebrated liberal journalists—highly condescending in their take on Ronald Reagan—had no idea that Reagan was right and they were wrong about the nature of Soviet Communism. Moscow was more than happy to tap their arrogant ignorance.

Given that liberals, including in the press, had long viewed strident anti-Communists as unsophisticated, it drove them nearly mad to watch one get elected to the Oval Office—especially a former actor not seen as an intellectual. Worse, the new president spoke unapologetically about the dangers of the USSR, its inherent "evil" and expansionary tendencies—rooted, so he said, in Marxist-Leninist doctrine—while also predicting its demise.

Reagan had strategic reasons for doing so.[3] He wanted to declare a just war against the very foundations of Marxism-Leninism, which formed the basis of the

Communist state and the underlying rationale for Moscow's successful expansion of a dehumanizing, destructive ideology. Reagan, despite the Left's demeaning portrayal of him as a lightweight, understood Communism because he had studied it since the 1940s and had engaged in "hand-to-hand combat" (his words) with Communists when he headed the Screen Actors Guild. The new president wanted Americans to have a better grasp of precisely what they were facing a continent away, so he pounded the point that the Soviets were committed to a one-world Communist state,[9] as he had done on the campaign trail in the 1970s.[10]

Reagan's warnings about Soviet expansionism jolted the sensibilities of the American Left, including liberal journalists. Imagine the astonishment felt by liberals who had been educated in American universities where uncompromising anti-Communism was depicted as a greater threat than uncompromising Communism, where Joe McCarthy was a bigger demon than Joe Stalin. Liberals in the press went after Ronald Reagan every time he dared to negatively quote Vladimir Lenin or insist that the USSR was pursing something as brazen as global Communism.

They Lie, They Cheat, They Steal . . .

Left-leaning journalists began their attacks on President Reagan as early as his first press conference, held on January 29, 1981, barely a week after he took office. When the new president was asked about Soviet aims and intentions, he calmly explained to the Washington press corps that the Soviet leadership had "openly and publicly declared that the only morality they recognize is what will further their cause, meaning they reserve unto themselves the right to commit any crime, to lie, to cheat."

The assembled press responded with what one observer, National Security Adviser Richard V. Allen, described as "an audible gasp."[11] Reagan had left no doubt that Jimmy Carter was out of the White House.

And the president was not finished. He explained that the Soviets considered their relativistic behavior "moral, not immoral," and that this was something the United States needed to "keep . . . in mind" when doing "business" with Moscow.[12]

Of course, what Reagan said was no different from what many Cold War Democrats had always said, from Woodrow Wilson to Harry Truman to JFK and even to liberals like Adlai Stevenson.[13] In fact, it may have been mild by comparison. His words read almost verbatim like the text of the esteemed George F. Kennan's most famous of writings, his 1947 "Sources of Soviet Conduct," which became the cornerstone for the launching of containment.[14] But many liberals either were unaware of this history or blissfully cast it aside for partisan reasons. Reagan's remarks sent reporters "rushing to their telephones" the moment the press conference ended, Allen remembered.[15]

Somehow, the fact that Ronald Reagan made such observations about Soviet Communism made them unpalatable and unbelievable. *Surely Reagan could not have meant what he said,* an astonished press corps reported. The lead story on the front page of the *New York Times* the next day insisted that Reagan's description of Soviet intentions was "historically debatable."[16] In the *Washington Post* the lead headline declared, "Reagan Voices a Tone on Relations Far Harsher Than His Predecessors."[17] In an editorial the *Post* lamented the "indiscriminate quality of some of the things being said." The new president was "moving roughly, perhaps too roughly." The *Post* warned that "approaching international political relations strictly on the basis of a nation's supposed moral character invites a crusade in place of the Carter administration's approach." Worst of all, this sudden "good-vs.-evil approach risks missing what legitimate opportunity for honorable accommodation there may be."[18] Even George Kennan would become a staunch Reagan critic, with the sort of harsh language he once aimed at the Kremlin now being directed toward the Oval Office. Kennan said that the Soviet leadership expected nothing but a "total, blind, and almost deadly hostility" from Reagan and his administration.[19]

In the ensuing weeks, America's leading journalists—perplexed and offended—repeatedly pressed the new president for clarification. And so Reagan would make the simple point again and again, saying of the Soviet leadership: "They don't subscribe to our sense of morality. They don't believe in an afterlife; they don't believe in a God or a religion. And the only morality they recognize, therefore, is what will advance the cause of socialism."[20]

This was too much for Walter Cronkite, the grand old anchor at CBS. Cronkite got the opportunity to confront Reagan during a March 3 interview. He told Reagan that the president's views seemed too "hard line toward the Soviet Union," adding that "there are some who . . . feel that you might have overdone the rhetoric a little bit in laying into the Soviet leadership as being liars and thieves, et cetera."[21]

Reagan did not back down. He explained himself again, telling Cronkite, in a gentle manner: "Well, now, let's recap." The president noted that he had merely responded truthfully to a question from a reporter about "Soviet aims." On that, said Reagan, "I don't have to offer my opinion. They [the Soviets] have told us where they're going again and again. They have told us their goal is the Marxian philosophy of world revolution and a single, one-world Communist state, and that they're dedicated to that." The president harkened back to the Soviet version of morality: "Remember their ideology is without God, without our idea of morality in a religious sense." The onetime dupe told Cronkite that Americans would be "naïve" not to understand this.

The president then repeated almost verbatim what he had said at the press conference, reaffirming his view that the Soviets "resort to lying or stealing or cheating or even murder if it furthers their cause. . . . We have to keep that in mind when we deal with them."

Cronkite, however, seemed befuddled and bothered. He described Reagan's words against the Kremlin as "name-calling," and expressed concern that this would make "it more difficult" to sit down with Leonid Brezhnev and the Soviet leadership. Reagan disagreed, saying that, to the contrary, Brezhnev had already "suggested having a summit meeting since I said that."

That response from Reagan is very telling: he understood that certain words, uttered from the bully pulpit of the American presidency, could have an immeasurable impact. He pursued a "peace through strength" approach to bring the Soviet Union to the negotiating table. For Reagan, that strength included the power of rhetoric; he used *words* as weapons, quite apart from missiles and tanks and rifles. So, for Reagan, Brezhnev's (perceived) positive response to his harsh language was early vindication of the constructive effect of strong words. Reagan's many critics never appreciated or even understood this tactic during his presidency.

While countless journalists at the time were vigorously disputing Reagan's descriptions of Soviet thinking, a few oddball members of the mainstream media did pause to investigate the merits of his claims. *Time* magazine, for instance, did a little homework on Lenin and determined that Reagan had accurately characterized the Soviet understanding of morality. *Time* cited Lenin's famous 1920 speech before the All-Russia Congress of the Russian Young Communist League, in which the Bolshevik leader said: "We repudiate all morality that proceeds from supernatural ideas that are outside class conceptions. Morality is entirely subordinate to the interests of class war. Everything is moral that is necessary for the annihilation of the old exploiting social order and for uniting the proletariat."[22]

Pravda Erupts

Still, the vast majority of American journalists were not so charitably inclined to the new president. Nor were the Soviets, who sensed a major propaganda opportunity with Reagan's unapologetic statements about Soviet expansionism and immorality.

As is evident from Soviet media archives, the USSR fired back in full force: in TASS, which was the official state news agency, and the twin newspapers *Pravda* and *Izvestia*. The USSR, of course, had no free press, meaning that "news sources" were instead propaganda arms of the Communist state. Many if not most of the "reporters" were either KGB staff or completely loyal to the dictatorial arm of the state.

Pravda returned Reagan's salvo with a five-hundred-word analysis of the president's first press conference.[23] *Pravda,* which in Russian means "Truth," lambasted Reagan's "deliberate distortions" of Soviet policy and accused the new president of wanting to launch a "new Cold War." Moscow commonly leveled this accusation at Reagan, insisting that there was no longer a Cold War—thanks to détente—but instead only aggressive attempts to rekindle one by a saber-rattling Reagan.

Pravda also accused Reagan of speaking in an "unseemly manner about some kind of 'insidiousness' in the Soviet Union's policy, which allegedly has the goal of 'creating a one-world socialist or communist state.'" Like the American Left, the Soviet media acted incredulous, refusing to concede this penchant for expansionism. *Pravda* criticized Reagan for an "inability to understand the meaning of the changes that are taking place in the world"—that is, the changes born of détente and the Soviet Union's successful exporting of its "liberating" ideology into the Third World. "These changes," said *Pravda,* "spring from the striving of the peoples for national liberation, independence and economic social progress." Such had been the "liberating" spirit thriving in Nicaragua, Afghanistan, Cambodia, Vietnam, Laos, North Korea, Cuba, and other Soviet-friendly nations.

A companion statement was published in *Izvestia.*[24] *Izvestia,* which in Russian means "News," decried Reagan's "relapse into the Cold War" during his first press conference, particularly his "blatantly" absurd "allegation" of a Soviet desire for world revolution. Vladimir Lenin, *Izvestia* informed readers, had been an apostle of *peace:* "Is there any need to recall that Lenin, back at the dawn of Soviet power, advanced the principle of peaceful coexistence as a fundamental principle of Soviet policy?" Moreover, insisted *Izvestia,* this Leninist peace principle had been "repeatedly and resolutely" reaffirmed at "the CPSU's Congresses, which have come out in favor of détente and of the improvement—in particular—of Soviet-American relations." Sadly, it was Reagan who was poisoning this well of good intentions by advancing "a completely absurd anti-Soviet cock-and-bull story."

The Soviet spin was now clear, in bold print—of which these are only two of several examples[25]—merely days after Reagan's first press conference. And as the Soviet media gleefully reported, the American press was already taking the same angle in opposing Reagan. The *Izvestia* piece highlighted reactions from the *Washington Post* and Reuters: "After the new president's press conference, the *Washing-*

ton Post carried a story saying that, with respect to the Soviet Union, Reagan 'set a tone that was very much different from that of the Republican and Democratic administrations of the 1960s and 1970s.' Reuters reported that it has been 25 years since Washington has heard such candid cold-war statements."

There was hope in the Soviet media—hope that the non-Communist liberal press would likewise hammer Reagan.

Here again, for the Communists, dupes would be imperative. For victory in this latest propaganda campaign, the non-Communists needed to be brought along. And as usual, the American Left provided Moscow with a target-rich environment for dupes.

An American Counter-response

Fortunately for the Kremlin, liberal American journalists seemed to relish the opportunity to contest Reagan's anti-Communist claims. They were not Communists, of course, but they shared the Soviets' revulsion of expressive anti-Communism. More than that, Reagan was a Republican who stood between the Democrats and the White House. Thus, many journalists shared the Soviets' desire to embarrass the president.

Consequently, some members of the Reagan administration created an internal counter-response team to deal with the double assault from Soviet Communists and liberal American journalists. An unofficial team within the Reagan administration tasked itself with verifying Soviet quotations cited by Reagan, in order to be able to defend the president against charges leveled by the American media and by Soviet propagandists. This group worked primarily out of the United States Information Agency (USIA).

USIA ended up working a form of "public diplomacy" for the Reagan administration that has been neglected in histories of the Reagan administration and the Cold War.[26] The agency was headed by old Reagan friend Charlie Wick, who worked closely with Ambassador Gil Robinson, among others. The unofficial front man for handling the Soviet quotes Reagan cited was Herb Romerstein, America's top expert on everything Communist. As a former Communist himself, Romerstein knew his Marxism-Leninism and could be called upon at any moment to certify the authenticity of certain quotes.

Other members of the Reagan administration outside of USIA helped support the president's strategic use of strong rhetoric against the USSR. One of those figures was top Reagan aide and confidant Bill Clark, who headed the National

Security Council in 1982 and 1983, and was the single most important Reagan adviser in the effort to take down the Soviet Union.[27] Clark worked closely with Ambassador Robinson at USIA. Another Reagan administration official, Assistant Secretary of State Elliott Abrams, reached out to Clark. A fascinating letter from Abrams to Clark, which today sits in Clark's private boxes at his ranch in Paso Robles, California, illustrates the degree to which Reagan officials came to the president's defense when he was attacked for revealing the true nature of Soviet Communism.

Abrams, who dealt with Latin American affairs at the State Department, was a Harvard J.D. who was long accustomed to confronting vicious, and often specious, charges from the Left. In a typed letter dated March 10, 1983—not coincidentally, two days after President Reagan called the USSR an "evil empire," for which he was being derided—Abrams began, "Dear Bill: Press people may well ask on what basis the President says that the communists have no morality, so herewith are two useful quotes from Lenin which can be used as backing for the President's statements."[28] With full citations from the *Selected Works* of Lenin, Abrams passed along the source for the most commonly contested Lenin quote used by Reagan, "We repudiate all morality . . . ," as well as a Lenin gem that Reagan had not yet employed: "We have never rejected terror on principle, nor can we do so. Terror is a form of military operation that may be usefully applied."[29]

Abrams, who had worked for Clark at the State Department, knew that Clark was closer to Reagan than any other White House figure, including in terms of shared perception of the Communist threat. Abrams knew that Bill Clark would hold on to the letter, which he did.[30]

In short, the president's defenders were arming themselves behind the scenes. They were forced to do so, as the American and Soviet media were lining up the cannons, with the same anti-Communist target in their sights.

"Nikolai" Lenin

One such cannon bore Lenin's name—or at least a variation on his name. Early in the Reagan administration the American media ripped into the president over his alleged misuse of Lenin's first name: Reagan occasionally (not regularly) called Vladimir Lenin "Nikolai" Lenin. The very top liberal newspapers rushed to accord this supposed mistake the status of grave infraction and comical dimwittedness.

For example, on January 22, 1983, the *Washington Post,* one of the two leading newspapers in America, took Reagan to task for his supposedly embarrassing ignorance of things Soviet in a piece titled "Pseudo-Nym and Pseudo-History."[31] The news story was prompted by Reagan's press conference two days earlier, in which the president had again cited nasty comments made by Lenin.[32] The piece called out Reagan for making two (alleged) errors: referring to the Bolshevik godfather as "Nikolai" Lenin, and claiming that Lenin "said that promises 'are like pie crust, made to be broken.'"

In fact, neither was an error.

First, the question of Lenin's first name: "Nikolai" was, in point of fact, a name that Lenin used. He sometimes wrote under the pseudonym "Nikolai Lenin." The American Communist press frequently published the Bolshevik as "Nikolai" (or "Nicolai") Lenin. This was certainly the case in the early 1920s with organs of the American Communist Party, such as *Communist Labor*, published by the Communist Labor Party of America.[33] The same went in other Western countries. The Communist Party of Great Britain published some of Lenin's most famous works under the name "Nikolai Lenin." The British Communists listed "Nikolai Lenin" as the author of, for example, *"Left Wing" Communism: An Infantile Disorder;* this was the case in both the first and second editions, in 1920 and 1928, respectively.[34] (See pages 380–81.)

Apparently, this elementary fact—known to the supposedly ill-informed Ronald Reagan—was unknown to the *Washington Post*. The *Post* reporter wrote that according to "the Soviet embassy and several Soviet scholars, to use 'Nikolai' as Lenin's first name is a recurrent error, common to conservatives, that annoys the Soviets to no end. In fact, the Nikolai problem was 'the biggest complaint' from the Soviets during a U.S.-Soviet project that for more than two years tried to remove some of the more glaring errors and propaganda from textbooks of the two countries."[35] The article quoted Dr. Stuart D. Goldman, Soviet affairs analyst at the Congressional Research Service, who maintained, "It's an error which seemed to appear frequently, although not invariably, in the rhetoric and writings of people hostile to Lenin. Historically, it's generally been found in the writings on the right."

The *Washington Post*'s questioning of the "pie crust" remark was even more off the mark. The remark was indeed real—taken from Lenin's *Collected Works*, the standard, go-to guide for such quotations.[36] Reagan had cited Lenin to underscore the fact that Lenin brazenly lied about many things, especially diplomatic agreements. The Bolshevik leader was notorious for trampling on agreements, and even boasted about it. Many old-time Democrats had condemned Lenin for this behavior, from Woodrow Wilson and his State Department to Harry Truman.[37] Reagan's feelings about the Bolsheviks were mild compared to those of a

young Winston Churchill, who (long before he was prime minister) described the
Bolsheviks as "ferocious baboons" who had created a "most destructive" and "most
degrading" tyranny. Churchill told the cabinet of Prime Minister David Lloyd
George that Lenin and Trotsky should be captured and hanged, and that the prime
minister "might as well legalize sodomy as recognize the Bolsheviks."[38]

The *Washington Post* article wrapped up by criticizing the general thrust of
Reagan's understanding of Lenin. To buttress the point, the *Post* offered a quote
from a dubious confirming source: a member of the Soviet embassy. This would
seem an odd choice for attestation. Certainly, the Soviet embassy had as much bias
on the issue as did the president.

The *Post*'s skepticism of Reagan's understanding of Marxism-Leninism was
not confined to this one story or even this reporter. The *Post*'s White House correspondent, Lou Cannon, who became effectively the first major Reagan biographer, also derided Reagan for supposedly misidentifying Lenin. Generally,
summed up Cannon, "I reached the conclusion that Reagan was wonderful about
Jack Benny and worthless on the subject of Lenin."[39]

Cannon's conclusion fit the mainstream press's caricature of Reagan: the
"B-movie actor"–turned–conservative president was fine commenting on movies
like *Bedtime for Bonzo* but useless on historical knowledge.

Gorbachev on Lenin

While the American media frequently attacked President Reagan for supposedly
inaccurate claims about Lenin, the same press exhibited a total lack of alarm over
the truly outrageous remarks on Lenin by Mikhail Gorbachev. The Soviet leader,
a darling of the American media in the 1980s, did not make a mistake or two;
he was responsible for a litany of errors and dangerous misunderstandings. Of
course, the American press, which generally portrayed Gorbachev as intellectually superior to Reagan, never deigned to doubt the Soviet leader.

Gorbachev idolized Lenin, an adoration he made embarrassingly clear. He
considered Lenin his ideological mentor and hero, invoking him with reverence
in his public statements and writings, including in his bestselling 1987 book *Perestroika,* the definitive Gorbachev statement to the world. In one of his prayerful
ruminations on Lenin in *Perestroika,* Gorbachev gushed:

> The works of Lenin and his ideals of socialism remained for us an inexhaust-
> ible source of dialectal creative thought, theoretical wealth and political

sagacity. His very image is an undying example of lofty moral strength, all-round spiritual culture and selfless devotion to the cause of the people and to socialism. Lenin lives on in the minds and hearts of millions of people. . . . Turning to Lenin has greatly stimulated the Party and society in their search to find explanations and answers to the questions that have arisen.

Gorbachev wrote that he had not only an "interest in Lenin's legacy" but a "thirst to know him." The leader of the Soviet Union, sounding like Billy Graham talking about the redemptive sacrifice of Jesus Christ, explained that he and the rest of the Soviet leadership "draw inspiration from Lenin. Turning to him, and 'reading' his works each time in a new way. . . . Lenin could see further."[40] Gorbachev perceived in Lenin a source of almost infallible wisdom: "We have always learned, and continue to learn, from Lenin's creative approach."[41]

Ronald Reagan was often accused of not having read Lenin's works. But Gorbachev's statements make one wonder: did *Gorbachev* really read Lenin? For Reagan undoubtedly understood Lenin better than did Gorbachev.

Take this example: "In the West," protested Gorbachev, "Lenin is often portrayed as an advocate of authoritarian methods of administration. This is a sign of total ignorance of Lenin's ideas and of their deliberate distortion. In effect, according to Lenin, socialism and democracy are indivisible."[42]

No, *Gorbachev* was guilty of distortion. He somehow transmogrified Vladimir Lenin into a liberal Democrat, a composite of Thomas Jefferson and Franklin Delano Roosevelt.

In reality, Gorbachev had learned wrong, and was teaching wrongly. This is seen in another embarrassing statement he made in *Perestroika,* when he maintained, "More than once he [Lenin] spoke about the priority of interests common to all humanity over class interests."[43]

No, that was not true, as can be seen from Lenin's famous 1920 remark, repeated often by Ronald Reagan, including in that first press conference.[44]

In sum, Gorbachev's remarks on Lenin were nonsense from start to finish. Lenin was a ruthless human being, not a saintly font of eternal wisdom.

Ronald Reagan had Lenin right. Gorbachev had Lenin wrong. But the media protested only the former, not the latter. Once again, the American Left had found its target for ridicule and condemnation in the anti-Communist, not in the Leninist.

"Nikolai" Lenin: Though Reagan was mocked for supposedly getting Vladimir Lenin's first name wrong, the Bolshevik leader actually published under the name "Nikolai," as seen in these two British editions of his book *"Left Wing" Communism.*

The Soviets Sense an Opening—
and the *New York Times* Steps In

Well into Reagan's presidency the Soviet Communists continued to use Reagan's forceful rhetoric as a propaganda opportunity—and they continued to count on American liberals to help them make political hay against the president.

Moscow's ongoing propaganda strategy is evident from a secret 1985 document issued by the Central Committee of the Communist Party of the Soviet Union. The committee's secret memorandum, marked "Not for Publication," was dated September 25, 1985, and titled "On the Hostile Speeches of the President of the U.S.A."[45] (See page 384).

Signed by the chief of the Propaganda Department and the chief of the Department of Foreign Political Propaganda, the memorandum claimed that Reagan had "frequently resorted to falsified quotes, attributing them to V.I. Lenin." The American president had already "done this in the past, but now this is becoming standard practice." The Soviet press had often "rebuffed strongly the slanderous attacks of R. Reagan, but nevertheless, this line [of speech] by the head of the White House continues."

The two propaganda chiefs instructed the Soviet Foreign Ministry, via the Soviet embassy in Washington, "to categorically protest to the U.S. Department of State the falsifying of the works of the founder of the Communist Party of the Soviet Union and the Soviet state, V.I. Lenin." The propagandists angrily insisted: "We demand the American administration end such antagonistic attacks against the Soviet Union and the gross falsification of Lenin's works."

Interestingly, the Communist memo did not mention Reagan's use of "Nikolai Lenin."[46] Instead, it took aim at a statement in which the president attributed to Lenin plans to spread Communism to Eastern Europe, Asia, Latin America, and finally the United States—the last of which, according to Reagan, Lenin had said would fall into Soviet hands like "overripe fruit." Reagan had said this more than once, and at least twice in September 1985 alone.[47]

Two weeks after the Moscow propaganda chiefs sent orders to the Foreign Ministry and the Soviet embassy to contest the quote in the United States, the most influential newspaper in the English-speaking world, the *New York Times*, took Reagan to task for his latest Lenin comments. The *Times* ran an editorial on the subject on October 8, 1985. It is, of course, impossible to say how and where the *Times* got the cue to respond as it did. Had the paper simply reacted to what Reagan had said about Lenin? Or had it swallowed the bait that the Soviets had dropped into the water in that September 25 memo? For example, had the *Times* been prompted by a leak from a friendly source at the U.S. State Department, which Moscow had ordered the Soviet embassy to target? Whatever the case, the Soviets got what they wanted: a high-profile denunciation of Reagan for "falsifying" Lenin's arguments.

The October 8 *New York Times* editorial was unusual in that it carried a byline; the *Times* usually runs unsigned editorials. The author was Karl E. Meyer, one of the members of the *Times*'s editorial board.[48] He found it incredible that Vladimir Lenin might have said that after the Bolsheviks took Europe and Asia, America would be next.

Meyer set out to verify the alleged Lenin quote Reagan had used, that America would "fall into our outstretched hands like overripe fruit." The first source the editorial cited was the Soviet propagandist Georgi Arbatov, who, Meyer informed readers, denounced the "overripe fruit" line, saying that Reagan had picked it up from no less than Hitler and his Nazis. Meyer described Arbatov only as a "Soviet official," mentioning nothing about the fact that this was a full-time, paid propagandist for the Kremlin—and hence patently unreliable.

More respectably, Meyer considered television commentator Alistair Cooke, who suggested that the president may have gotten the line "from an old movie script."[49] Next the *Times* editorialist went to "researchers" at the Library of Congress, who apparently had no luck confirming Reagan's fanciful musing.

Then Meyer said that a *Times* colleague recalled having heard the line employed by "right-wing generals in Pretoria"—in other words, by white, racist apartheid leaders in South Africa. These racists had reportedly exhumed the fictitious phrase from a 1971 conspiracy tract "avidly read by members of the John Birch Society."

With that, Meyer was on a roll. He dug some more, he told readers, until he found "what seems to have been President Reagan's source," *The Blue Book of the John Birch Society*, published in 1958 by Robert Welch, the founder of that far-right organization known for its wild anti-Communism.

"So there it is," Meyer concluded, "an undocumentable Birchite 'paraphrase' offered . . . as a live quotation by a President of the United States."[50]

It was a damning piece. Unfortunately for the *New York Times*, Meyer was guilty of precisely what he was accusing Reagan of doing: making assumptions without documentation. Reagan had indeed used a questionable quote, which is no small matter; an American president is—and should be—held to a high standard of accuracy. That said, what Meyer alleged was, overall, less accurate than what Reagan said.

Not for Publication   <u>Secret</u>
                                   TsK KPSS, 2nd Sector
                                   September 25, 1985   25374
                                   Return to General Department
                                   of the TsK KPSS

     Central Committee of the Communist Party of the Soviet Union

        <u>On the Hostile Speeches of the President of the U.S.A.</u>

        Recently, the president of the U.S.A., in his official
speeches, has more frequently resorted to falsified quotes,
attributing them to V.I. Lenin.

        Reagan has done this in the past, but now this is becoming
standard practice. During one of his recent statements (September
18, 1985), Reagan attributed to Lenin plans to seize Eastern
Europe, China, Latin America, and the United States.

        The Soviet press often has rebuffed strongly the slanderous
attacks of R. Reagan, but nevertheless, this line [of speech] by
the head of the White House continues.

        The propaganda and external political propaganda departments
of the Central Committee of the Communist Party advise instructing
the USSR Ministry of Foreign Affairs (MID SSSR), via the Soviet
Embassy in Washington, to categorically protest to the U.S.
Department of State the falsifying of the works of the founder of
the Communist Party of the Soviet Union and the Soviet state, V.I.
Lenin, emphasizing that this practice is not acceptable, insults
the Soviet people, and causes justifiable indignation among the
Soviet people. We demand the American administration end such
antagonistic attacks against the Soviet Union and the gross
falsification of Lenin's works.

        The text of the protest to the State Department is to be
published in the Soviet Press.

        Draft instructions to Soviet embassy in the U.S.A. enclosed.
Request concurrence.

        Chief of the Propaganda   Chief of the Department of
        Department of the TsK KPSS   Foreign Political
                                           Propaganda of the TsK KPSS

             /s/ A. IAkovlev   /s/ L. Zamiatin

        "25" September 1985   Communicate concurrence
             19-03-134   1 October 1985 /s/ [illegible]
....

                                               B.18.5

Moscow's propaganda strategy: The USSR's propaganda chiefs secretly instruct the Soviet Foreign Ministry, via the Soviet embassy in Washington, "to categorically protest" President Reagan's "falsifying of the works of" Lenin.

Lenin's use of the phrase "overripe fruit" has not been fully substantiated, though it had been in circulation for decades, sometimes linked to other Soviet figures.[51] Most notably, the "overripe fruit" quotation has been attributed, credibly, to one of Lenin's successors, Nikita Khrushchev. During the Soviet leader's historic September 1959 visit to the United States, President Dwight Eisenhower's secretary of agriculture, Ezra Taft Benson, hosted Khrushchev for a half day. Benson later recalled of his time with Khrushchev: "As we talked face-to-face, he indicated that my grandchildren would live under Communism . . . [and] arrogantly declared, in substance: You Americans are so gullible. . . . We won't have to fight you. We'll so weaken your economy until you fall like overripe fruit into our hands."[52]

Khrushchev's comment—which went unmentioned in the *New York Times* editorial—was entirely consistent with Marxist-Leninist doctrine. And that is the more important point regarding Reagan's comment: the thrust of what the president was claiming—namely, that Lenin outlined Communism's global ambitions, and that he wanted America to be Communist as well—was completely accurate, as any honest observer with the slightest bit of knowledge on Lenin would have known.

Recall Lenin's August 1918 open letter to American workers, published in *Pravda*. In it he spoke of "the inevitability of world revolution" and said that in such a revolution American workers "will be with us, for civil war against the bourgeoisie." The Bolsheviks, Lenin said, "are in a besieged fortress until other armies of the world socialist revolution come to our aid"—and as his letter made clear, an American army would most certainly join the "invincible" proletarian revolution.[53]

Likewise, in November 1918, Lenin emphasized that "Anglo-French and American imperialism" stood in the way of "world-wide Bolshevism" and "worldwide socialist revolution." The Soviet system, he vowed, must "conquer" in "every advanced country in the world," especially the United States, since "Anglo-American imperialism" threatened to "strangle" the great Russian experiment.[54]

These comments were typical of Lenin's militaristic language. His blunt calls for revolution in America, for the American proletariat to rise up against the "capitalist sharks" and "bloodsuckers' and "modern slave-owners," were actually far more militant than what Reagan had attributed to him with the "overripe fruit" line. The Soviet propagandists may have insisted that Reagan was guilty of "gross falsification" of Lenin's views—and the *New York Times* may have scoffed at the idea that the Soviets had such expansionary aims—but Reagan was quite correct that from the outset, the Soviets had trumpeted their global objectives.

The *New York Times*'s Karl Meyer was seemingly unaware of this background, or else he chose to omit it from his editorial. Instead he concluded that Reagan had culled the "overripe fruit" quote from a John Birch Society publication, a contention for which he had no proof. An examination of Reagan's conservative background should have raised serious doubts that he would read, let alone favorably cite, Birch literature. Reagan was an avid reader of conservative sources who stood firmly against the Birch Society, such as William F. Buckley Jr.'s *National Review*, which had sought to purge Birchers from the conservative movement.[55] Reagan's anti-Communism was informed by sophisticated anti-Communist writers such as Frank Meyer, James Burnham, and Whittaker Chambers—all ex-Communists—plus Malcolm Muggeridge, Aleksandr Solzhenitsyn, Wilhelm Röpke, Milton Friedman, Friedrich Hayek, Ludwig von Mises, Henry Hazlitt, Frederic Bastiat, Russell Kirk, and lesser-known authors like Laurence Beilenson,[56] the Harvard-educated student of Harold Laski and Felix Frankfurter, whom Reagan read closely and corresponded with frequently.[57]

For liberals in the press, however, the caricature of Reagan as an ignorant anti-Communist was apparently irresistible. Thus the *New York Times* could cite, uncritically, a Soviet hatchet man like Georgi Arbatov pointing to Nazis as the source for the president's statement.

Had Meyer and the expert researchers dug a little deeper, perhaps in the archives of the *Times*'s chief competitor, the *Washington Post*, they might have found a June 26, 1955, article in which another leader, South Korean president Syngman Rhee, also invoked the "overripe fruit" quote. Rhee had seen international Communism divide his homeland with a horrendous war, and now he warned that the Communists were ready to attack the United States. As the *Post* reported, "The President [Rhee] pointed out that Lenin had laid down the following master plan for world conquest: 'First we will take eastern Europe, then the masses of Asia. After that we shall surround and undermine the United States, the last citadel of capitalism, which will fall into our lap like an overripe fruit, without a struggle.'"[58]

That warning, in a major American newspaper, came three years before the publication of the obscure John Birch tract Meyer cited as the source of Reagan's quote.

Calling the Soviets' Bluff

For the Soviets, the *New York Times* editorial was quite a coup. The Gray Lady served as a feeder service to newspapers and news broadcasts all over America and across the world. The *Times* article, on the heels of others like the *Washington*

Post piece, must have reinforced Kremlin hopes that the American media could aid the USSR in its campaign to discredit the president who was committed to undermining Marxist-Leninist ideology.

In 1987 the Soviet regime continued its efforts to discredit Reagan, this time working behind the scenes to try to pressure the U.S. government. That spring, Valentin Falin, another dedicated Soviet government propagandist, came to Washington with a Soviet delegation to meet with American officials, including Charlie Wick of USIA. Wick also brought along his top researcher, Herb Romerstein, expecting that Falin might pull some kind of stunt. The Soviet propagandist did not disappoint.

Falin came armed with the same material that the *New York Times* and *Washington Post* had been using against Reagan. He started in on the American president's use of "Nikolai" and the "promises are like pie crust, made to be broken" quotation. Like Georgi Arbatov before him, Falin said that Reagan was citing not Lenin but the Nazis. The inauthentic quote, he said, originated in German wartime propaganda circulated by Joseph Goebbels.

Unfortunately for Falin, he was not sitting across the table from sympathetic American journalists who held Ronald Reagan in equal disregard. As Falin began railing against the supposedly spurious "pie crust" quote, Wick turned to Romerstein and ordered, "Answer him." Romerstein was ready, opening a large copy of Lenin's *Collected Works,* where the quote resided. Romerstein read the quote aloud.[59]

The Soviets' bluff had been called. A stammering Falin turned red, and leaned on one of his cronies for a stammering response. It was not a good moment for the masters of agitprop. That was especially so because Romerstein had put Falin and his comrades in their place in front of an audience of government officials and specialists from both sides. It was a small victory for the USIA and the Reagan administration in general.

Of course, Falin and his team's setback had occurred behind closed doors, without journalists there to report it. The Soviets would continue their propaganda campaign against Ronald Reagan, and America's monolithic media would continue to unwittingly support the effort.[60]

Cashing In: Zorin and the Soviets Confront Reagan

After Falin faltered in charging the Reagan administration with "misquoting" Lenin and making "vulgar" accusations of Soviet expansionism,[61] the Kremlin dispatched another propagandist to the United States, this time to confront President Reagan directly.

Valentin Zorin was the Soviet "journalist" called on for this task. Zorin was a regular on *Studio 9,* the Soviet Union's premier "news" show, and he wrote for both *Pravda* and *Izvestia.* He displayed religious-like devotion to totalitarian Communism. Fellow Soviet official Genrikh Trofimenko, the director of the influential Institute for U.S.A. and Canada Studies of the Russian Academy of Sciences, later described Zorin as a "faithful follower of Lenin's dictum regarding morality" who would happily contrive "any" information necessary—including "slander"—to discredit what Zorin termed "American warmongers." Trofimenko condemned Zorin as a "mini-Goebbels" who had spent his "whole life . . . devoted to piling on the United States heap upon heap of unspeakable dirt and, pardon me, dung."[62]

From his perch on *Studio 9,* Zorin—along with other propagandists like Vitaly Kobysh, Yevgeny Velikhov, Falin, and Arbatov—nightly took aim at President Reagan. Zorin had been trashing Reagan ever since the American had emerged as a serious presidential candidate in the 1970s. For example, in a February 16, 1976, statement issued by the Moscow Domestic Service, Zorin attacked Reagan for criticizing détente, saying that the candidate had demonstrated "complete irresponsibility" and was seeking to "poison the atmosphere."[63] Once Reagan was in the White House, Zorin ridiculed the American president as a lazy, dimwitted, addled, aged ex-actor, as a "blockhead" who "does not care to think."[64]

Zorin was especially outraged by President Reagan's June 1987 call to tear down the Berlin Wall. On *Studio 9,* he, Arbatov, and Falin teed off on the president, accusing the "American cowboy" of "slander," "blackmail," and "vulgar demagoguery."[65] Zorin often denounced Reagan for supporting those struggling for human freedom. He blamed Reagan for developments toward democracy in Poland, and he angrily attacked the American president when Reagan prevented Grenada from becoming a Cuban-Soviet proxy dictatorship. In fact, he assailed the invasion of Grenada in mocking language strikingly similar to that used by Senator Patrick Leahy, Senator John Kerry, Jesse Jackson, Walter Mondale, Madeleine Albright, and the editorial pages of the *New York Times.*[66]

On May 20, 1988, shortly before Reagan's summit with Mikhail Gorbachev in Moscow, Zorin got his big opportunity: he and fellow "journalist" Boris Kalyagin went to the White House to interview the president for Soviet television.[67]

Sure enough, Zorin and Kalygin took Reagan to task for his "allegation" that Lenin and Soviet Communists had "expansionistic aims." They challenged Reagan on the sources, saying that "Soviet specialists," the "U.S. press," and "people who work in the Library of Congress" had "studied all of the compositions of Lenin's" but hadn't "found one similar quotation or anything that's even close to some of those quotations." No doubt by "U.S. press" they meant, among other outlets, the *Washington Post* and *New York Times,* whose aforementioned articles had cited a generic category of Soviet specialists and, in the case of Karl Meyer's *Times* editorial, researchers from the Library of Congress. Notably, Zorin and his partner did not argue whether Lenin ever said anything expansionary. Instead, the well-prepared apparatchiks said only that people in the U.S. media and at the Library of Congress had searched for such quotes but could not find them. Zorin was a prodigious reader of American newspapers; it is clear that the U.S. media had supplied the Soviets with the sources they needed to indict Reagan.[68]

The impish Zorin then put Reagan on the spot by asking: "So, I would like to ask you what works of Lenin did you read, and where were those quotations that you used taken from?" Reagan held his ground. Though he was not forthcoming about specific sources, he wisely turned the discussion to the gist of Marxist-Leninist ideology, where he was dead-on:

> Karl Marx said your system, Communism, could only succeed when the whole world had become Communist. And so, the goal had to be the one-world Communist state.
>
> Now, as I say, I can't recall all of the sources from which I gleaned this, and maybe some things have been interpreted differently as in modern versions, but I know that Lenin expounded on that and said that must be the goal. But I also know—and this didn't require reading Lenin—that every leader, every General Secretary but the present one had, in appearances before the Soviet Congress, reiterated their allegiance to that Marxian theory that the goal was a one-world Communist state. So, I wasn't making anything up; these were the things we were told. For example, here in our government, we knew that Lenin had expressed a part of the plan that involved Latin America and so forth. And the one line that sounded very ominous to us was when he said that the last bastion of capitalism, the United States, would not have to be taken; it would fall into their out-stretched hand like overripe fruit.[69]

Reagan felt no need to list sources, because this material was second nature to him. His explanation to his Soviet interrogators could have come straight out of one of his GE speeches in the 1950s, right down to the use of the older colloquial "Marxian" instead of "Marxist."

Zorin may have been eager to trip up Ronald Reagan on the eve of his pivotal summit meeting, but the president would not be disturbed so easily.

When Fiction Becomes History

In time, the Soviet propaganda push against Reagan acquired not only sympathetic liberal American journalists but liberal American academics as well. Not surprisingly, given the New York Times's sacred status among American liberals, pieces like the one by Karl Meyer live on in the works of liberal academics, especially those who upbraid Reagan for his "reactionary" views on the Cold War and Soviet Communism.

Many academics still use the Meyer piece as a catch-all to demonstrate that Reagan employed a vast reservoir of Soviet "quotes of uncertain origin." For instance, Garry Wills, in his book Reagan's America, accepts Meyer's verdict as ironclad, concluding that Reagan "used a fake quote from Lenin, taken from Welch's" book.[70]

Going much further than Wills is Raymond Garthoff, whose work The Great Transition: American-Soviet Relations and the End of the Cold War credits Gorbachev, not Reagan, with ending the Cold War. Published by Brookings Institution Press, the book received the Left's imprimatur as one of the most authoritative works on the end of the Cold War. It became required reading in graduate schools across America in the 1990s, billed by some as the definitive judgment on how the Cold War ended.[71]

Garthoff depicts Reagan as both a simpleton and a political zealot, and he cites Meyer's New York Times piece to substantiate his claim that Reagan displayed a "notorious disregard for concrete facts."[72] Garthoff points readers to an outside source that is supposedly an authoritative guide to Reagan's many "egregious errors of fact in public statements"—a 1984 book called Ronald Reagan's Reign of Error, coauthored by the liberal activist Mark Green.[73]

Where might America's fortieth president have gotten such inaccurate ideas? "Apparently," Garthoff explains, without providing evidence, "their origin was a Nazi propaganda fabrication that had made its way by professional anticommunists into right-wing publications of the kind read by Ronald Reagan." This "odious" reality, notes the historian, is quite an "insult." Just imagine that such could be "part of the personal intellectual baggage of the president of the United States."

With Garthoff's historical explication, bad reporting on Reagan in the 1980s has become bad history.

Most puzzling about Garthoff's swipe at Reagan is that the historian's explanatory notes at times actually back up Reagan. For example, in the main text of his book, Garthoff writes that Reagan's use of the name "Nikolai" for Lenin "presumably" originates from the Bolshevik's "early writing under the pseudonym 'N. Lenin.'" The text does not mention that Lenin published not solely under "N. Lenin" but also under "Nikolai Lenin." In his notes, however, Garthoff explains that, yes, Lenin published under the pseudonym "Nikolai." And yet the historian, like the *New York Times* before him, leaves readers with an image of a president who employed Nazi misinformation in his press conferences.

Many liberal scholars and journalists maintained that the conservative Reagan was misled, when it's possible that they themselves had been misled by Soviet disinformation.

What "Evil" Empire?

Nothing so outraged the Soviets and the American Left as the president's description of the USSR as an "evil" empire.

President Reagan first used this description during a speech in Orlando, Florida, on March 8, 1983. In it he called the Soviet Union the "focus of evil in the modern world" and an "evil empire."

This blunt language was a major departure from the discourse used by President Jimmy Carter and even by his Republican predecessor, Gerald Ford. Such frank talk was, of course, part of Reagan's larger strategy to include strong rhetoric as a weapon against the USSR. Reagan's description also happened to be accurate.

An honest observer could hardly disagree that the Soviet empire was a pernicious place. Since the Bolshevik Revolution the Communist regime had a horrifying record of human carnage, killing anywhere from twenty million to seventy million innocents. The USSR refused to allow citizens to leave the Communist empire, and even erected walls to keep them captive. It suppressed the most basic civil liberties. The atheist regime carried out a comprehensive "war on religion," in Gorbachev's apt description. And from the beginning, Communist leaders had spoken openly of "crushing" and "conquering" the "disgusting" bourgeoisie in a worldwide revolution. Again, Reagan was simply acknowledging what Democrats like Woodrow Wilson had noted from the very start.

Nevertheless, many Americans were aghast at Reagan's statement of the obvious.[74]

The first line of resistance came from "pragmatists" within the Reagan White House. These establishment Republicans repeatedly crossed out the "evil empire" section when the speech was in draft form. Particularly upset was aide David Gergen, who would go on to work for the Clinton White House. Gergen, much like Colin Powell later with the "tear down this wall" line in the Brandenburg Gate speech,[75] was troubled by what he called the "outrageous statements" in the speech and tried to tone it down.[76]

But the speech survived the White House pragmatists. Speechwriters Tony Dolan and Aram Bakshian knew the address was a winner. They also knew that this was exactly what Reagan wanted to say; the president had written nearly half the speech himself.[77] Dolan refused to make the cuts Gergen and others were pushing. He called for the president to make the final decision. Reagan rejected the advice of the pragmatists and chose to leave in the language. Reagan adviser Ed Meese remembered, "He really insisted on it and kept it in."

When Reagan delivered the address as is on March 8, America's progressives responded with righteous indignation, even before *Pravda* got its chance to torch the speech.

Over at the *New York Times,* columnist Anthony Lewis dashed to his typewriter to denounce the speech as "dangerous" and "outrageous." To Lewis, the speech was "sectarian" and "simplistic." More than that, he said, it was simply "primitive—the only word for it."[78]

Washington Post columnist Richard Cohen began his response with this odd Q & A: "Question: What does Ronald Reagan have in common with my grandmother? Answer: They are both religious bigots."[79] Reagan, said Cohen, lacked "tolerance," dividing the United States and USSR into categories of "us" versus "them" over matters of religion.

This was a strange criticism. In reality, the Soviet government was the divisive force on religion. Starting with the Bolsheviks, the regime had long attacked belief, shutting down churches, erecting museums to atheism, and deriding religion through such organizations as the League of the Militant Godless. Reagan merely spoke candidly about the incontrovertible atheism of the Soviet system—just as John F. Kennedy, among other Democrats, had done in the past. The president pointed out the distinctions between the U.S. and Soviet systems—one promising religious liberty; the other, antireligious tyranny.

Cohen insisted that Reagan "likes to see things in black and white." He did not mention that in the Orlando speech, Reagan paused to carefully underscore that America was far from perfect, with its own legacy of sins and evil, from slavery to racism.

In truth, Cohen's analysis of Reagan's speech—and Lewis's analysis, for that matter—was more black and white, more simplistic, than what the president said. What Reagan said was factual. What Cohen said was a stereotype.

Over at *The New Republic,* which more than fifty years earlier had published John Dewey's "impressions" of the USSR as a utopian empire, the editors were scandalized by Reagan's depiction. In the April 4, 1983, issue, *TNR* ran an editorial titled "Reverend Reagan."[80] It claimed that the president had "left friends and foes around the world with the impression that the President of the United States was contemplating holy war."

The editors were particularly offended at Reagan's story of a friend who said he would rather see his little girls die in America now, still believing in God—and thus able to go to heaven—than watch the girls grow up under Communism not believing in God. Although the folks at *TNR* probably did not know this, it is interesting that TASS likewise took special offense at this anecdote, blasting away (in English) in its March 11 response to the speech.[81] The editors at *The New Republic* were in lockstep with the editors over at TASS.

Here, *TNR*'s editors complained that in the area of foreign policy, this anecdote about God was hardly the "question at issue."

Actually, in Ronald Reagan's mind, this *was* the question at issue. That the Soviet state could become so intrusive that it would actively deny the right to faith was an outrage that should concern every person and every nation. Yes, this was a theological concern to the Christian Reagan, but it was also a matter of basic human liberty.

To *TNR,* however, it seemed that Reagan "profoundly misunderstands" the "nature of secularism." Overall, the editorial declared, the speech was a "deeply divisive" "orgy of cheap shots," and "very poor history" to boot.

Like the magazine that published Dewey's pro-Soviet writings, Dewey's alma mater was disturbed by Reagan's speech, as was the professoriate as a whole. Renowned Columbia University/Amherst College historian Henry Steele Commager judged that Reagan's address "was the worst presidential speech in American history, and I've read them all." Why? Because, said Commager, of Reagan's "gross appeal to religious prejudice."[82]

Liberal politicians expressed outrage as well. The leader of the Democrats and the Congress, Speaker of the House Tip O'Neill, was so incensed at Reagan's display of anti-Communism that a year and a half later, at the 1984 Democratic National Convention, he declared that the evil did not truly reside with the Communists in the Kremlin: "The evil is in the White House at the present time. And that evil is a man who has no care and no concern for the working class of America and the future generations of America. . . . He's cold. He's mean. He's got ice water for blood."[83]

Kindred Spirits

The Soviet Union's Marxist-Leninists certainly appreciated the American Left's analysis, which they echoed in their own speeches and writings.

The day after the "evil empire" speech, Soviet despot Yuri Andropov, who compared Reagan to Hitler[84]—eliciting no outpouring of protest from the American Left—called Reagan's remarks deliberately "provocative." The comments, Andropov said, revealed that Reagan and his administration "can think only in terms of confrontation and bellicose, lunatic anti-Communism."[85]

Reagan clearly had touched a nerve in Moscow, as TASS attacked the president's speech in multiple press releases.[86] In one statement, TASS bristled at the president's "McCarthyism." The Soviet "news" agency said that "the White House boss" was "quite prepared to sacrifice [American children] in the name of his rabid anti-Communism and militarism."[87]

Pravda condemned Reagan's "latest provocative speech," saying that it betrayed his administration's "extreme militarism," and confirmed that the president could "only think in terms of confrontation and militant, unbridled anti-communism." Worse, the Soviet paper said, Reagan had offered no "evidence" of any misdeeds by the USSR.

Typical of Soviet propaganda techniques, Pravda cited the negative reaction among American liberals as proof of the universal outrage over Reagan's "bellicose" and "hysterical" anti-Communism. The paper reported that "UPI called attention to Reagan's pathological hatred of socialism and communism, noting that his statements resurrected the worst rhetoric of the cold war era."[88] (Also underscoring the UPI statement was the Red Army flagship, Krasnaya Zvezda.)[89] Pravda cited the three American TV networks for support as well, including an ABC News commentary that, said the Soviet government newspaper, "made special note of the fact that [Reagan's speech] had an 'openly militaristic bias.'"[90]

On Soviet TV, reporter Gennady Gerasimov reiterated a common complaint of American liberals when he blasted Reagan's religious references and alleged laziness of the mind. It sounded, said Gerasimov, as if the president thought "he were God's vicar on earth." Of course, added the Soviet reporter, this was "not the first time the President has used similar moral categorizations: on the one side good, which naturally means him and America, which is the embodiment of this good, and on the other side evil." Gerasimov said this was "an easy scheme of things for those too lazy to think."[91]

Georgi Arbatov was put on the case a few days later, writing a typical hatchet piece in *Pravda*. Arbatov leveled many of the same criticisms employed by *The New Republic*: "[This is] outright medievalism," he opined. "And all this is covered up by hypocritical talk about faith and God, about morality, eternal good and eternal evil."[92]

Moscow saw another propaganda opportunity here, surely at least in part because the liberals that dominated the American media were excoriating the speech.

On Reagan's Side

This was quite a cacophony. Did President Reagan have any defenders?

Yes: those who resided within the evil empire, under the jackboot of Communist totalitarianism. Only years later, however, once these captives were free, could they respond to their captors and to American liberals.

One of them, Natan Sharansky, had a chance to do just that near the end of Reagan's presidency. He had been an inmate of Permanent Labor Camp 35, a Jewish dissident jailed for his beliefs. Once released, he told the president and his staff of how his prison guards had informed him of Reagan's "warmongering" statement about the evil empire, underscoring what a dangerous, unstable man occupied the White House. They flashed him *Truth* itself, *Pravda*'s front page, which derided Reagan's speech.

This "truth" alert, however, backfired on Sharansky's tormentors. Once they left, Sharansky leapt for joy in his cell. Someone—indeed, the American president, the leader of the free world—had finally spoken the truth about this undeniably evil empire. Sharansky tapped the news in Morse code to a fellow prisoner on the other side of the wall, who received it with equal elation and in turn tapped the message along to his neighbor, and so on. Reagan had spoken for those in the gulag, who now rang out the words "evil empire."[93]

When a freed Sharansky—let out of prison with Reagan's help—eventually met the president, he thanked him. "I told him that his speech about the evil empire was a great encourager for us," Sharansky said of himself and his inmates. Reagan had "understood the nature of the Soviet Union" and had called "a spade a spade."[94]

That sentiment was shared by Vladimir Bukovsky, who spent twelve years in the Soviet gulag. Bukovsky said the Reagan speech had been a "major event" to political prisoners and dissidents, who "greeted" it warmly. The phrase "evil empire" had the worst possible effect on those running the USSR, noted Bukovsky: it became "incredibly popular" behind the Iron Curtain.[95]

Similar testimony came from Jan Winiecki, who was an economic adviser to Poland's Solidarity underground. Once able to travel to America, Winiecki said of Reagan's colorful description of the Soviet empire: "To us, it was, of course, true. The leftist intellectuals in the West thumbed their noses at it, but we said 'What's the big deal?' What he said was a statement of the obvious. This was not [a] mystery."[96]

Even former Soviet political officials testify to the liberating nature of Reagan's piercing pronouncement.[97] Andrei Kozyrev, a longtime Soviet official who ultimately became Boris Yeltsin's foreign minister, said it had been a mistake to have called the USSR "the Union of Soviet Socialist Republics." No, said Kozyrev, Ronald Reagan had come up with a better title: "It was, rather, [an] Evil Empire, as it was put."[98]

Sergei Tarasenko, a high-level official in the Soviet Foreign Ministry under Mikhail Gorbachev, commented: "So the president said, 'It is an Evil Empire!' Okay. Well, we are an Evil Empire."[99]

Arkady Murashev, a young leader who emerged during the days of *Perestroika* and eventually became leader of Democratic Russia, a political party that took root after the USSR disintegrated, likewise defended Reagan: "He called us the 'Evil Empire.' So why did you in the West laugh at him? It's true!"[100]

A slightly dissenting view came from Genrikh Trofimenko, head of the USSR's top think tank, who had a minor complaint. In retrospect, said Trofimenko, Reagan's "evil empire" description "was probably too mild."[101]

Overdue Truths

When Ronald Reagan spoke of expansionary, evil Soviet Communism, he spoke the truth. That truth was long overdue after the 1970s, which began with détente and ended with Soviet gains and American losses all over the world, and with Jimmy Carter's kiss of Brezhnev. The millions held captive inside the evil empire—those "captive people," those "freedom fighters," as Reagan saw them—certainly appreciated that Reagan had spoken the truth. These people lacked in the most basic liberties, including the right to say how much they hated living under the regimes that repressed them and kept them confined within barbed-wire borders.

Amazingly, however, the American Left—like the Soviet regime—judged Reagan not just wrong but idiotically, belligerently wrong. Many journalists, academics, and politicians in the United States failed to acknowledge the desperately needed truths that the president was speaking.

And the Left's ridiculing of Reagan—with Soviet appreciation and backing—was only beginning. Merely two weeks after roasting Reagan for his speech in Orlando, many liberal Americans were about to unwittingly join sides again with Soviet Communist officials, this time in lampooning a major Reagan policy initiative.

Reagan's new policy, which America's Left and the Soviet regime did their best to derail, would ultimately prove as devastating to the USSR as the president's declaration of evil.

20

"STAR WARS":
THE SDI SABOTAGE

Another troubling case of American liberals in the 1980s inadvertently providing a tremendous boost to the Soviets was their ridiculing of President Reagan's Strategic Defense Initiative (SDI), which liberals—starting with Senator Ted Kennedy—immediately trivialized as "Star Wars." In so doing, they nearly sabotaged SDI, and perhaps would have if not for Reagan's extraordinary personal commitment to the program, evident from its origins in March 1983, through the Reykjavik summit in October 1986, and beyond.

If liberals had been successful in mocking SDI into oblivion, it would have been to the great detriment of America, of those living under Soviet Communism, and of peace worldwide. It is no exaggeration to say that if SDI had been nixed, the United States would have been robbed of what turned out to be one of the most effective tools in bringing the Soviets to the negotiating table and ending the Cold War without a shot fired. Soviet officials themselves testify to that impact of SDI.

Privately, we now know, the Kremlin was terrified by SDI and what it could mean to the USSR's ability to compete—militarily, technologically, economically, and politically—with the United States in the Cold War. Publicly, however, the Soviets joined the American Left in lampooning SDI. They seized on the "Star Wars" label that Kennedy first applied and that a partisan American press corps picked up right away, converting the pejorative into a major propaganda tool. More than that, Moscow manipulated Kennedy's term in a way that neither the Massachusetts senator nor his liberal allies in the American media could have imagined, or even recognize today. Certainly, journalists have never offered any self-critical analysis exposing how this manifestation of their political bias caused notable damage.

In all, it is a disturbing but fascinating story that Americans did not witness in the 1980s. For the first time, here is that story.

March 1983: The Kremlin's Really Bad Month

Ronald Reagan made a series of bold moves in March 1983, at a time when the USSR was on the ropes.

The Kremlin had been deeply concerned ever since Reagan's inauguration in January 1981, a total turnabout from its confident surge in the latter 1970s. The Soviet leadership was taken aback by Reagan's bravado in his very first press conference. Its fears only heightened throughout 1981 and 1982, as the president repeatedly pronounced that Communism and the Soviet Union itself were doomed, such as in his May 1981 speech at the University of Notre Dame and his June 1982 address to Britain's Parliament, to name only two examples. The Soviets stirred over what they suspected Reagan was pursuing in Poland, in Afghanistan, in Nicaragua, and via relationships with the likes of Margaret Thatcher and Pope John Paul II. Moscow understood that Ronald Reagan was committed to trying to undermine the USSR.[1]

Still, the Kremlin could not have imagined what was about to happen next. Reagan's first big move in March 1983 was a devastating rhetorical blow: his March 8 speech in which he called the Soviet Union an "evil empire."

A week later came the disclosure of one of the Reagan administration's most significant National Security Decision Directives (NSDD). On March 16 Robert Toth of the *Los Angeles Times* broke the story on NSDD-75, in which the administration resolved to pursue victory in the Cold War by peacefully liberating Eastern Europe and bringing political "pluralism" to the USSR.[2]

Just a week before Toth's story on NSDD-75, TASS had issued a press release warning that Reagan's evil empire speech symbolized the reality that it was now "official state policy" for the Reagan team to make its "crusade against communism . . . the fatal denouement to which Mr. Reagan is nudging the world." Now, with the disclosure about NSDD-75 (which Reagan had privately signed a few weeks earlier), the Moscow Domestic Service released two statements, dubbing the directive a "subversive" attempt "to try to influence the internal situation" within the USSR. The Reagan administration, Moscow said, had set out "to exhaust the

Soviet economy . . . to undermine the socioeconomic system and international position of the Soviet state." A piece by Grigori Dadyants in the Soviet publication *Sotsialisticheskaya Industriya* stated, "Directive 75 speaks of changing the Soviet Union's domestic policy. In other words, the powers that be in Washington are threatening the course of world history, neither more nor less."[3]

Fortunately for the Soviets, certain liberal editorial boards in the West were there to reassure them. For instance, Dadyants cast doubt on Reagan's ability to change the USSR by citing editorials from the *Los Angeles Times,* the *Toronto Star,* and the *San Francisco Chronicle.* Dadyants quoted the *Los Angeles Times* as saying, "Our country simply has no means of exerting pressure of this sort [on the Soviet Union], and it was staggering to hear that the Reagan administration thinks otherwise." The *Star* accused Reagan of "simply the purest stupidity," and of needing a "new cold war."[4]

Nevertheless, Moscow remained very nervous about what the U.S. government was doing. The Soviets knew that their system was, as Reagan put it, held together by bailing wire.[5] Reagan had rightly sensed Communism's perilous condition, and now he was making Moscow's life even more difficult.

And the USSR's really bad month was about to get worse.

On the evening of March 23, 1983, Ronald Reagan disclosed to the world a secret he had shared with only a handful of his most trusted advisers: "My fellow Americans, tonight we're launching an effort which holds the promise of changing the course of human history," declared the president in a nationally televised address. He announced his Strategic Defense Initiative, a vision for a space-based missile-defense system.

Coming only two weeks after the evil empire speech, and one week after the revelation about NSDD-75—not to mention other audacious military initiatives then under way, including the deployment of the MX Missile and the Pershing IIs—Reagan's remarks left Moscow shell-shocked.

The Immediate Soviet Reaction

The response from the Soviet side was instant. Both behind the scenes and in official news coverage, Moscow betrayed its panic.

The CIA learned right away that the Soviet officials were shaken by the SDI announcement. Herb Meyer, CIA Director Bill Casey's right-hand man and one of the most important under-the-radar players in the Reagan administration's "takedown" strategy against the USSR,[6] spent much of his time conducting Soviet vulnerability assessments. Today he recalls: "The intelligence coming in the morning of March 24—literally hours after the president's SDI speech—was different from anything we'd seen before. The Soviet Union's top military officials had understood instantly that President Reagan had found a way to win the Cold War." Reagan had referred to SDI as a "shield over the United States," but, Meyer says, the Soviets understood that SDI "was really a lid over the Soviet Union. It meant their missiles would be worthless."[7]

Meyer's point is especially intriguing given that many critics of SDI focused on the fact that such a missile shield was technologically difficult if not impossible to build, at least in the immediate term. (Top American scientists like Carl Sagan mocked SDI as a "pipe dream.") While technological feasibility was a real issue, Meyer points out that such an argument ignores a more critical issue: the Soviets grasped right away that even if SDI could not shoot down all of their missiles, it introduced a "devastating" uncertainty that sent their nuclear strategy into a tailspin. "Even if [the Soviets] were able to hit New York City, Los Angeles, Washington," Meyer explains, "they didn't know which, if any, of our missile sites, silos, Minutemen, that they could hit."[8] In other words, the question of retaliation was thrown into chaos. "They knew right away, when Reagan made that speech, that this was the bullet between the eyes," Meyer says. He adds that it is "crucial to understand" that SDI would never need to shoot down 100 percent of Soviet missiles: "The critics didn't get this. The *New York Times* didn't get it."[9]

In any case, the Soviets were not so blithely confident that the SDI technology was impossible to build. The reason for this, as Meyer notes, was that years earlier Soviet physicists had begun studying the concept of missile defense—specifically, of using weapons to knock down a missile. They knew the technology could be done (as America's Patriot missiles would demonstrate against Saddam Hussein's Scuds over the skies of Israel less than ten years after Reagan's SDI speech). Soviet technical and academic journals, which Meyer and analysts at Langley studied, were filled with articles on the subject. Realizing the potential of missile defense, the Soviets had launched a comprehensive project to research such a system. Wanting to keep the military research project secret, they pulled the scientific journals from circulation. The CIA, however, had copies of the journals.[10]

Ronald Reagan knew all this from his briefings—the same Reagan that the American Left derided as an uninformed idiot. After his SDI announcement, the president tried to get the American press to take notice of the Soviets' own missile-defense project, openly talking about the "Red Shield," or the "Soviet SDI."[11] In short, Reagan's argument to his detractors was that with SDI, America was finally pursuing what the USSR had already been pursuing on a massive scale.

But the liberal press dismissed the president's arguments, just as it dismissed the very notion of missile defense.

The Soviets may have had a head start on missile defense, but they went into panic mode the moment Reagan gave his SDI speech. Why? Because, from their own research, they knew SDI could work (at least to some degree), and they knew that the United States not only was far more technologically advanced than they were but also had far more money to invest in the project.

Says Herb Meyer: "Once Reagan said we could do it, they [the Soviets] knew they were finished. . . . The intel began hitting my desk on March 24, and you could see the shift. You could see the shift immediately—*immediately.* Overnight. Just like that."[12]

The Long-Term Soviet Reaction

Mikhail Gorbachev knew better than anyone the technological and financial advantages the United States had over the Soviet Union. As a result, SDI became his single greatest obsession during U.S.-USSR summit meetings. The testimonies to this are voluminous.[13]

According to Foreign Minister Alexander Bessmertnykh, the Soviets were "enormously frightened" by Reagan's announcement of SDI.[14] Bessmertnykh said the initiative was "something very dangerous" that "made us realize we were in a very dangerous spot." He called SDI Gorbachev's "number-one preoccupation": "When we were talking about SDI, just the feeling that if we get involved in this SDI arms race, trying to do something like the U.S. was going to do with space-based programs, looked like a horror to Gorbachev." Bessmertnykh said flatly that programs like SDI "accelerated the decline of the Soviet Union."[15]

Similarly, Genrikh Trofimenko said that SDI "was the most effective single act to bring [Gorbachev] to his senses—to the understanding that he could not win." Here, of course, Trofimenko echoed Herb Meyer's statement that with SDI, the Soviets "knew they were finished." Trofimenko added that Gorbachev "had to cry 'uncle' and to vie for a peaceful interlude."[16] (Interestingly, Reagan, when devising his strategy to undermine the Soviets economically, used the phrase "yell 'Uncle.'"[17])

The power of SDI was evident in the Reagan-Gorbachev summits. Soviet ambassador Anatoly Dobrynin later confirmed that Gorbachev's "principal goal" at the 1985 Geneva summit was to halt SDI.[18] The same was true for the Reykjavik summit in October 1986, where Reagan chief of staff Donald Regan said that Gorbachev was worried about SDI to the point of fixation.[19] Gorbachev was so concerned about SDI at Reykjavik that he actually proposed to eliminate *all* nuclear missiles if Reagan gave up missile defense. Likewise, at the third summit, in Washington in December 1987, Secretary of Defense Frank Carlucci made special note of Gorbachev's "usual tirade about SDI."[20]

In short, the Soviet government at the very highest levels was genuinely concerned about—even fearful of—SDI, and not just in the immediate aftermath of Reagan's March 1983 announcement.

Americans could have never imagined the extent of Soviet trepidation from listening to the counsel of Democratic politicians. Former Vietnam figure John Kerry, who became the junior senator from Massachusetts in 1985 and would later be the Democrats' 2004 presidential nominee, sponsored a bill to slash President Reagan's request for SDI funding. Senator Al Gore Jr., who would later be the Democrats' 2000 presidential nominee, dismissed SDI as "not feasible," and insisted it was "madness" to think that SDI could "pressure the Soviets economically to induce a radical change in their system."[21]

The Democrats' words were like salve on the Soviets' wounds. The strong anti-SDI movement among American liberals offered Moscow hope: if the Kremlin hung in there and did not let its worries be known, SDI might fall apart before Ronald Reagan could ever get the program going.

Moscow's master propagandists would do their part to try to derail SDI. They just needed an angle on SDI, a way to belittle it in the eyes of their countrymen, of Americans, of the citizens of the world. They got the spin they needed just hours after Reagan's SDI speech.

The spin was provided by the senior senator from Massachusetts.

Senator Kennedy to the Rescue

As the intelligence streaming across Herb Meyer's desk at Langley showed, Reagan's SDI speech sent the Soviets into a panic. But then the president's liberal critics—and more specifically, Senator Ted Kennedy—unwittingly handed Moscow a glistening pearl of propaganda with which to publicly attack the new proposal.

Not even twenty-four hours after Reagan's speech, Senator Kennedy rushed to the Senate floor to rebuke the president for "misleading Red-scare tactics and reckless Star Wars schemes."[22] Kennedy's ridicule proved masterful, as it reinforced the liberal caricature of Ronald Reagan in two important ways. First, Kennedy's accusation of "misleading Red-scare tactics" raised the specter of Joe

McCarthy, feeding into the liberal view that Reagan was guilty of that worst of sins: strident anti-Communism. Second, by referencing the hugely popular film *Star Wars,* the Massachusetts senator played off the image of Reagan as an addled ex-actor who got all his ideas from movies—even SDI. (Some liberals make this ad hominem accusation even today, despite having no reasonable evidence for the claim.)[23]

The "Star Wars" term of derision immediately struck a chord. The *New York Times* included it in headlines typed the same day Kennedy gave his anti-SDI speech.[24]

Kennedy inspired other Democratic politicians, as well as liberal columnists, to run with the imagery and sensationalize it even more. Senator Daniel Inouye of Hawaii followed Kennedy by charging that Reagan was trying to distract the American public with talk of "Buck Rogers" weapons, a reference to a popular space-age television hero of the day. "Mr. President," Inouye solemnly intoned, "our scientists, our engineers, our generals, are not dunces."[25]

Mary McGrory of the *Washington Post,* who was frequently quoted in the Soviet press, boarded the "Buck Rogers" battleship right away. She called SDI "lunacy" and scoffed that the president had presented "a Buck Rogers plan to transfer the arms race to outer space."[26] The claim about an arms race in space was no small accusation, as we shall see.

Representative Barbara Boxer, today a U.S. senator from California, mocked SDI as the president's "astrological dream." The zany ex-actor, Boxer said, envisioned "'garages' in orbit."[27]

This line of derision trickled up to liberals in the scientific community, including astronomer Carl Sagan, bestselling author of *Cosmos,* which became a popular documentary series on PBS. Sagan mocked Reagan at scientific gatherings, typically to howls of laughter among assembled kindred spirits. "In the foreground comes a very attractive *laser battle station,*" Sagan said condescendingly, "which then makes a noise like *bzzzt . . . bzzzt . . . bzzzt.*"[28]

The intelligentsia was having a terrific laugh at the expense of Reagan's so-called Tinseltown fantasy. This was exactly what Moscow needed to attack Reagan's powerful idea.

Herb Meyer was in the rarest of positions, able to observe simultaneously the Soviets' private response to SDI and the Democrats' public denouncements. He recalls the jarring contrast between the Kremlin's frightened reaction and Kennedy's dismissive caricature. "I had Kennedy saying that on my radio," says Meyer, "and on my desk [I had] the report from Moscow showing the Soviet leadership saying, effectively, 'Oh, no, it's over.'"[29]

Although the Soviets' behind-the-scenes response was spot-on, Kennedy's assessment would dominate discussion of missile defense throughout the Reagan administration. "Star Wars" became the epithet of choice to ridicule SDI, to the delight of the Kremlin.

Ted Kennedy's Russian Romance

Before considering the full impact of the gift that Ted Kennedy had unwittingly bestowed on the USSR, we must consider the larger context of what Kennedy was doing. For whatever reason, Senator Kennedy liked the Soviets, and he thought they liked him—when, in fact, they used him, wining and dining and duping him.

An eyewitness to this was Yuri Bezmenov, a journalist and editor for Novosti, the Soviet press agency (where he also worked for the KGB), before he defected to the West in the 1970s.[30] Among Bezmenov's chief duties was to handle Western visitors through propaganda and misinformation. This entailed other responsibilities. "One of my functions," recalled Bezmenov in a 1984 television interview, "was to keep foreign guests permanently intoxicated from the moment they landed at Moscow airport." He would "accompany groups of so-called 'progressive intellectuals'—writers, journalists, publishers, teachers, professors of colleges. . . . For us, they were just a bunch of political prostitutes to be taken advantage of."[31]

Bezmenov had come to see the rotten totalitarianism of the Soviet system, and was quite bothered that these Western progressives could not discern the obvious. "I did my job," he lamented, but "deep inside I still hoped that at least some of these useful idiots [would catch on]."

Among the worst of them, said Bezmenov, was Senator Ted Kennedy.[32]

Pointing to a photo that he said showed Ted Kennedy dancing at a wedding at Moscow's Palace of Marriages (see page 406), Bezmenov stated, "Another greatest example of *monumental idiocy* [among] American politicians: Edward Kennedy was in Moscow, and he thought that he's a popular, charismatic American politician, who is easygoing, who can smile, [who can] dance at a wedding at Russian Palace of Marriages. What he did not understand—or maybe he pretended not to understand—is that actually he was being taken for a ride." Bezmenov noted that Kennedy, in this particular instance, was participating in a "staged wedding used to impress foreign media—or useful idiots like Ed Kennedy. Most of the guests there [had] security clearance and were instructed what to say to foreigners."[33] Bezmenov himself worked these weddings. He noted that Kennedy "thinks he's very smart," but "from the viewpoint of Russian citizens who observed this

Ted Kennedy's "monumental idiocy": Former Soviet propagandist Yuri Bezmenov said Moscow took Senator Ted Kennedy "for a ride." According to Bezmenov, this photo shows Kennedy dancing at a Soviet wedding that was really staged as a "propaganda function."

idiocy," he was "an idiot," a "useful idiot," participating in "propaganda functions like this"—a so-called wedding that was really a "farce," a "circus performance."

The Soviets saw Ted Kennedy as someone they could entertain and manipulate. And for the senator from Massachusetts, the Russian romance was ongoing.[34] In March 1983 he reciprocated whatever wedding prize Soviet handlers gave him with a gift of his own: ridicule of Ronald Reagan's self-described "dream" of missile defense. Around this same time the Massachusetts senator also made an extraordinary private bequest to the Kremlin—and he did so quite consciously.

As we now know from a highly sensitive KGB document, the liberal icon, arguably the most important Democrat in the country at the time, so opposed Ronald Reagan and his policies that the senator approached Soviet dictator Yuri Andropov, proposing to work together to undercut the American president.

This episode was stunning—indeed, truly "misleading" and "reckless," which is how Kennedy had described Reagan's SDI. Had Americans known of Kennedy's overture to the Soviets at the time, it would have been a scandal. To this day it has not received the attention it demands.

I first reported on this KGB document, which was pulled from the Soviet archives in early 1992 before the file was resealed, in my 2006 book, *The Crusader: Ronald Reagan and the Fall of Communism,* where I discussed it at length in the text and endnotes. The document is republished here in its entirety. (See Appendix A, pages 497–505.)

The KGB report is dated May 14, 1983, less than two months after Kennedy first ridiculed SDI. KGB head Viktor Chebrikov sent the memo with "Special Importance," under the highest classification, directly to General Secretary Andropov. The subject line read: "Regarding Senator Kennedy's request to the General Secretary of the Communist Party Y. V. Andropov." It concerned a "confidential" Kennedy offer to Andropov.

According to the KGB memo, Senator Kennedy had conveyed his message to the Soviets through his "close friend and trusted confidant" John Tunney—the same go-between he had used in approaching the Kremlin in March 1980, according to Vasiliy Mitrokhin. Chebrikov said that Kennedy was "very troubled" by "the current state of Soviet-American relations," which the senator attributed not to Andropov and the Kremlin but to "Reagan's belligerence," especially his defense policies. "According to Kennedy," reported Chebrikov, "the current threat is due to the President's refusal to engage any modification to his politics." Reagan's political success, said the letter, had made the president more dangerous, since it led him to be even surer of his course, and more obstinate—and reelectable.

Chebrikov said that the Democratic senator held out hope that Reagan's 1984 reelection bid could be thwarted, "which would benefit the Democratic party." This seemed unlikely, of course, given Reagan's undeniable political successes and popularity. Where was the popular president vulnerable? Kennedy provided an answer for his Soviet friends. In Chebrikov's words, "The only real threats to Reagan are problems of war and peace and Soviet-American relations. These issues, according to the senator [Kennedy], will without a doubt become the most important of the election campaign."

These threats were very fresh in Soviet memory, given the Reagan salvos fired back in March: first the evil empire remark, then the news of NSDD-75, and finally the SDI announcement. Such "problems of war and peace and Soviet-American relations" seemed to be the chink in the president's armor.

At this point in the memo, Chebrikov conveyed the U.S. senator's precise offer to the USSR's general secretary: "Kennedy believes that, given the state of current affairs, and in the interest of peace, it would be prudent and timely to undertake the following steps to counter the militaristic politics of Reagan." Step number one, according to the document, would be for Andropov to invite the good senator to Moscow for a personal meeting. Said Chebrikov: "The main purpose of the meeting, according to the senator, would be to arm Soviet officials with explanations regarding problems of nuclear disarmament so they would be better prepared and more convincing during appearances in the USA."

Kennedy recommended that he bring along Senator Mark Hatfield of Oregon, probably the most liberal Republican in the Senate, and a surefire target for duping. It seems the Democrat felt that the appearance of bipartisanship would "have a strong impact on Americans and political circles in the USA."

The second step of Kennedy's plan, the KGB head informed Andropov, was a strategy to help the Soviets "influence Americans." Chebrikov explained: "Kennedy believes that in order to influence Americans it would be important to organize in August–September of this year [1983], televised interviews with Y. V. Andropov in the USA." The media-savvy Massachusetts senator proposed to the Soviet dictator that he seek a "direct appeal" to the American people. "Kennedy and his friends," explained Chebrikov, were willing to help, and even named television reporters Walter Cronkite and Barbara Walters as good candidates for sit-down interviews with the dictator.

Cronkite in particular would have been a choice suitable to both sides. Frequently hailed as "the most trusted man in America," Cronkite actually had some critics, including many conservatives who suggested that his on-air editorializing against the Vietnam War undermined the American war effort. Recall, too, that in March 1981 Cronkite openly questioned Reagan about his "hard-line" anti-Soviet statements and Kremlin "name-calling." Privately, the CBS anchor also questioned Reagan's policies. On that, an FBI document originally classified "secret" has just emerged that suggests the Communists targeted Cronkite— along with four other journalists, including Phil Donahue and Bill Moyers[35]—as a potential member of a U.S. delegation that would sign the pro-Soviet "People's Peace Treaty." This Moscow propaganda campaign was pushed by the Communist front group the National Council of American-Soviet Friendship, which CPUSA founded in 1943 as an offshoot of Corliss Lamont's old Friends of the Soviet Union.[36] The newly declassified June 25, 1986, FBI report listing Cronkite was obtained via a Freedom of Information Act (FOIA) request by journalist Cliff Kincaid.[37] (See page 410.) The document does not indicate Cronkite's response to the attempt to enlist him on this occasion, just as the May 1983 document does not indicate his response to the attempt by the Soviets and Senator Kennedy to enlist him to interview Yuri Andropov.

And Ted Kennedy wanted more than just Andropov to conduct a PR campaign through the American media. According to the KGB memo, the senator also urged "lower level Soviet officials, particularly from the military," to do interviews with the press in the United States. Kennedy indicated that he could help organize this media blitz, since he wanted Soviet military and government officials to "have an opportunity to appeal directly to the American people about the peaceful intentions of the USSR."

Apparently, Ted Kennedy viewed Yuri Andropov, that notorious KGB disinformation master who had become arguably the Soviet Union's dirtiest leader since Stalin, as an honest broker, a potential partner against the supposedly dangerous anti-Communist Ronald Reagan. As Chebrikov noted, "Kennedy is very impressed with the activities of Y. V. Andropov and other Soviet leaders," admiring "their commitment to heal international affairs" and to "improve mutual understandings between peoples." Senator Kennedy was approaching the Soviets with this proposal because they could "root out the threat of nuclear war," "improve Soviet-American relations," and "define the safety for the world."

The memo concluded with a discussion of Ted Kennedy's political prospects, mentioning that the senator "wants to run for president in 1988" but also "does not discount that during the 1984 campaign, the Democratic party may officially turn to him to lead the fight against the Republicans." Chebrikov also reported that Kennedy "underscored that he eagerly awaits a reply to his appeal."

So according to this confidential memo from the head of the KGB to the leader of the Soviet Union, Senator Ted Kennedy had secretly approached a

CAMPAIGN FOR A PEOPLE'S PEACE TREATY
162 Madison Avenue; New York, NY 10016

The Campaign Committee met at 1140 Broadway Sunday, May 18th. 15 persons were present.

The Committee received and considered three alternative redraftings of the Treaty. A committee of three will produce a new draft by the end of the week which Alan Thomson will take to the Soviet Peace Committee in Moscow next week.

It was AGREED that the Campaign will seek both individual signatures and organizational endorsements to the treaty.

Several alternative locations for an office were considered. A decision will be made at the next meeting. Members are asked to suggest possible staff people.

Roger Powers agreed to report on the Treaty to the meeting of peace organizations in Philadelphia May 21st.

The new Treaty draft will be available with a covering letter to be sent to potential endorsers.

O/S

Possible members of the US delegation to sign the Treaty were discussed:

1.   Military person - from Center for Defense Information
2.   Scientist -
3.   Clergy -

4.   Medical
5.   Education
6.   Youth - Winner of PEP contest
7.   Veteran - someone from Veterans for Peace
8.   Labor -   ACTWU
9.   Artist
10. Homemaker
11. Athlete
12. Elected official -
13. Industry - Armand
14. Senior -
15. Media -   , Walter Cronkite, Harrison Salisbury, David Brinkley,
         Bill Moyers

b6
b7C

The final group should have thirteen members. Committee members have agreed to seek out people on the above list after the final treaty text is available.

The next meeting will be held on Sunday, June 15th at 1140 Broadway, Rm. 401 at 2:00 p.m.

O/S

8

SECRET

Targeting Cronkite: This declassified 1986 FBI report says that longtime CBS anchor Walter Cronkite was among the prominent liberals targeted by the Communist front group the National Council of American-Soviet Friendship.

foreign government—an abusive regime with which the United States had been engaged in a Cold War for nearly forty years—in an effort to "counter" the policies of the president of the United States and to weaken that president's political standing. This is shocking.

It is not clear what happened after Andropov digested the memo. Sadly, reporters never attempted to fill in the blanks by asking some basic questions of Kennedy. American journalists flatly refused to cover the story in the two decades since the *Times* of London first mentioned the KGB document in February 1992,[38] in the several years since the entire document was published in my 2006 book, and in the period since Kennedy's death in 2009. That remained the case even though Kennedy's office never denied the legitimacy of the document.[39] That remained so even though, as we saw in Chapter 18, it appears this was not the first time Kennedy approached Moscow making such an offer.[40] The partisan American press chose not to report on an episode that would embarrass a politician frequently hailed as "the Senate's last lion."[41]

As for Andropov's ability to respond, the despot was slowed later that year by his health—he died only months after receiving this memo—and by his attempts to cover up the shooting down of KAL 007, the South Korean commercial airliner. That dirty deed, which Andropov and his cronies initially denied, claimed the lives of 269 civilians, including 61 Americans. It is unlikely that this activity "impressed" Senator Kennedy.

The "Star Wars" Effect

After making his private effort to undermine Reagan, Ted Kennedy continued his public campaign against the president's policies. In March 1984—the year Reagan was up for reelection—Kennedy wrote an article for *Rolling Stone* magazine in which he again denounced Reagan's "Star Wars schemes," which was now standard rhetoric for Kennedy. He dubbed Reagan "the best pretender as president that we have had in modern history." As if those criticisms were too mild, Kennedy then charged—not for the first time[42]—that Reagan and his advisers were "talking peace in 1984 as a prelude to making war in 1985." What kind of war? The most inconceivable and worst of all: "winnable nuclear conflict."[43]

Ironically, as that edition of *Rolling Stone* hit newsstands, the Senate Armed Services Committee conducted a hearing on Soviet treaty violations. The hearing provided still more confirmation of the Soviets' ongoing mendacity. Senator Kennedy was a member of the committee, but unfortunately he was absent that day.[44]

Of course, Kennedy was focused on warning the world not about the USSR but about the hazard that was Ronald Reagan. By this point he had a lot of allies in his campaign—many of whom had adopted his "Star Wars" phrase to portray an actor-turned-president whose make-believe world had been fabricated by Hollywood.

The *New York Times* is a good example. As noted, the paper immediately used the phrase in a March 25 headline. Then on March 31, a week after Reagan's announcement, the *Times* claimed that the SDI proposal was "Mr. Reagan's answer to the film 'Star Wars.'"[45] This line was in a news story, not an opinion piece. A term of ridicule seemed to have become an item of (unsubstantiated) fact at the offices of the vaunted Gray Lady.

The rest of the media joined in, too. White House reporters like Helen Thomas happily embraced the new name for Reagan's initiative. Incredibly, when the president asked reporters to call SDI by its actual name rather than by the politically motivated slang term, they responded as if the very thought were outrageous. In one such exchange, at a press conference, Thomas asked: "Mr. President, if you are flexible, are you willing to trade off research on Star Wars . . . or are you against any negotiations on Star Wars?" Reagan replied, "Well, let me say, what has been called 'Star Wars'—and, Helen, I wish whoever coined that expression would take it back again, because it gives a false impression of what it is we're talking about."[46] Despite Reagan's plea, Thomas continued: "May I ask you, then, if 'Star Wars'—even if you don't like the term, it's quite popular. . . ."

Of course, the term was "quite popular" because journalists like her, who shaped public perception and opinion, used the term; they were making it popular.[47]

Other members of the White House press corps ignored the president's request as well, opting for the term of mockery. At the same press conference where Reagan and Thomas went back and forth on "Star Wars," reporter Chris Wallace followed up by saying, "I'm a little confused by your original answer on, if you'll forgive me, 'Star Wars'—if we can continue to use that term."[48]

"False Impression": War amid the Stars

Reagan was concerned about the "Star Wars" label not because it suggested he was a dimwit or a delusional actor: he was accustomed to the sniping at his intellect and had an extraordinary ability to shrug it off.[49] What troubled Reagan was what the term "Star Wars" seemed to imply to the USSR—or at least how the Soviets publicly interpreted the term. It was here that American liberals created serious damage—quite obliviously.

The Soviets ditched the formal "SDI" and used the term of derision in almost every reference to the Reagan administration's missile-defense plan. But to Moscow the nickname was more than just a swipe at Reagan's allegedly addled mind; the Soviets used it to suggest that the president had grim motives with the program. Specifically, whereas liberal journalists capitalized "Star Wars" to laugh off the idea as pure Hollywood, the Kremlin keyboards struck a lower-case "s" and "w" to suggest that SDI was Reagan's new vehicle to launch an actual war in space. This was perfect for the Soviets: another tool to portray Reagan as a nuclear warmonger, or, in Senator Kennedy's words, a man itching for a "winnable nuclear conflict."

This was a constant angle in the Soviet media. Moscow was obsessed with SDI. Ken Adelman, Reagan's director of the Arms Control and Disarmament Agency, conducted a study in 1984 which showed that 80 percent of Soviet-funded propaganda was being directed solely at SDI.[50] Here are merely a few of innumerable examples of the USSR's public ridicule of Reagan's plans for missile defense.[51]

During a June 30, 1984, *Studio 9* TV news broadcast, Valentin Zorin said: "You know that Reagan is now possessed of dreams of star wars and the militarization of space. This has been his fixation."[52]

Added Viktor Olin in a December 18, 1984, Moscow World Service statement: "Preparations for star wars are under way in the United States."[53]

TASS fired off multiple such statements, sometimes two in one day. In 1985, in the lead-up to the first U.S.-Soviet summit under Reagan—the November 1985 Geneva summit—TASS and other Soviet outlets began driving home the message that the American president was ruining the chance for arms-reduction treaties between the two superpowers. For example, a TASS statement on February 1, 1985, started and ended with the words "star wars," noting that Reagan's "plan" to build "space weapons" would scuttle all negotiations on missile cuts. A second TASS statement that same day, carrying the byline of a Soviet academician-scientist, lamented that Reagan's "militarization of space" would "put an end" to any viable chance of missile treaties between the USSR and United States.[54]

The March 8 edition of *Krasnaya Zvezda,* the flagship publication of the Red Army, made the same point in a lengthy, foreboding analysis instructively titled "How the 'Star Wars' Are Being Prepared."[55]

Later that month, the March 25 *Studio 9* broadcast offered a particularly disgraceful example of the Soviets' anti-Reagan propaganda. Zorin, Falin, and Vitaly

Kobysh unloaded on Reagan's "plans" "to fill the space around the entire planet with battle stations"—this despite the fact that SDI was explicitly a *defensive* system. During that broadcast, Kobysh approvingly cited Senator Kennedy and other liberal critics of SDI. To demonstrate the awful ambitions Reagan had for the program, Kobysh explained that "U.S. politicians call it [SDI] the greatest deception of our time."[56]

During the same broadcast, Falin castigated Reagan's idea by referring to a *Washington Post* editorial that, in his words, perceived Reagan and SDI as "cuckoo," "evil," and a "prospect of fabulous new riches for the [U.S.] military-industrial complex."[57]

The Soviets often made use of the *Washington Post* in criticizing SDI. To cite just one other case, TASS, on October 28, 1985, used a *Post* editorial as the basis for a press release. TASS began: "In recent weeks the president of the United States has dismayed even supporters by an insistence on the most simplistic variations of the most complicated issues of his presidency, the *Washington Post* writes today. . . . Reagan's simplistic approach to one of the most complex issues of our times, the *Washington Post* emphasizes, enables him to make the mental leap from fantasy to reality."[58]

In September 1985, Moscow's *New Times,* which was printed in English, likewise used material from the American press to make the case against SDI. The *New Times* piece sarcastically noted that the American president felt "hurt" by this application of "star wars" to his pet project and had expressed a wish that the individual who coined the term would retract it. (This was clearly a reference to Reagan's plea to Helen Thomas.) But, the article noted, the president's protests were illegitimate. To support the claim that Reagan had aggressive rather that defensive intentions, the *New Times* pointed to an op-ed in the *Los Angeles Times,* which it quoted as saying: "The secret of 'star wars' is that it is intended to defend weapons, not people. The purpose is not to keep the Soviets from threatening us, but to make sure we can threaten them."[59]

The Soviet Communist press used this particular *Los Angeles Times* piece repeatedly, over a period of weeks rather than days. TASS, for instance, cited the op-ed in a press release that claimed Reagan's assertions about SDI's being a peaceful system for defensive purposes were simply "clever tricks." "There is nothing defensive about SDI," TASS declared. It was an "offensive system."[60]

A week after that shot from TASS, with the Geneva summit quickly approaching, the Moscow Domestic Service fired off another bullet at SDI. In this salvo, TASS commended the likes of Ted Kennedy and Helen Thomas—though not citing them by name—for getting it right on SDI:

They christened it ["star wars"] with full justification, since this initiative envisages deploying strike weapons systems in space aimed at targets not only in earth orbit, but also on the ground. All the while, the White House has convinced itself that they have been misunderstood, that they have good-will toward all mankind. . . . [The White House believes that] certain forces, it seems, have distorted the essence of the Strategic Defense Initiative by labeling it the "star wars" program. . . . However, Washington is resorting to mediocre verbal balancing acts in vain. There is nothing defensive about it.[61]

The Soviets were fortunate to be able to call on so many Americans to prop up their arguments against Ronald Reagan and SDI. From the start, said Moscow, these wise liberals had understood Reagan's *real* intentions.

Of course, Moscow's public pronouncements about SDI were very different from its private concerns about the American missile shield, as Herb Meyer had learned. But they kept those fears hidden for the most part, instead adopting the spin of Ted Kennedy and his friends in the American press. It was a classic case of dupery: American liberals were unwittingly helping Moscow advance its interests.

Reagan Protests in Vain, and Gets Cornered Again

While Reagan's critics were oblivious to how the USSR's anti-SDI propaganda campaign worked, the president figured out what Moscow was doing. But because of the American media's inadvertent complicity in the Soviets' propagandistic spin, Reagan struggled to develop an effective counter-response to the liberal lampooning and Soviet onslaught about "Star Wars"/"star wars." When he protested that he desired a peaceful *defensive* system, not an *offensive* war in space— SDI "isn't about war, it's about peace," he said[62]—the Kremlin could easily dismiss his claims, as we have seen.

Reagan understood that the American press ran with "Star Wars" to make fun of him and "to denigrate the whole idea,"[63] whereas the Soviets embraced it to suggest a much more aggressive purpose. He got a good idea of just how Moscow was exploiting the term during an interview with Soviet media personalities shortly before the Geneva summit.

The Soviet "journalists" quickly ripped into Reagan on "star wars": *Why was he looking to deploy offensive missiles in space?*

The president explained the unfortunate origins of the term "Star Wars" (though he charitably did not cite Ted Kennedy by name), and then he noted that "our press picked it up." This was all rather regrettable, averred the president, because of the subsequent "misconception" it conveyed. Reagan attempted to set the record straight for the Soviets: "We're not talking about star wars at all. We're talking about seeing if there isn't a defensive weapon that does not kill people."[64]

This was a tough box for the president, and one that he had not constructed. But even after witnessing how the Soviet media were attacking Reagan for a system he had clearly identified as defensive, the White House press corps did not back away from using the term "Star Wars."

On November 6, one week after Reagan's interview with the Soviets, Helen Thomas showed her continued preference for the "quite popular" phrase. With the historic summit now only days away, and the U.S. president hoping to arrive at Geneva with confidence and in a position of negotiating strength, Thomas asked Reagan: "Will you negotiate Star Wars at all?"[65]

SDI Survives, and Works Magic

Like Reagan, the president's advisers struggled to deal with this double-barreled assault on SDI. They wondered whether the president could withstand the barbs from both the American press and the Soviet state-run media. How would he hold up under the criticisms and mischaracterizations when in negotiations with Gorbachev in Geneva?

Former national security adviser Bill Clark conceded that the barrage of propaganda against Reagan was fierce. But he continued to urge the administration's pragmatists—David Gergen, Jim Baker, Dick Darman, Mike Deaver, and Nancy Reagan, all of whom had wanted Clark fired when he was national security adviser—to "let Reagan be Reagan," meaning that the president would be fine, especially in one-on-one interaction with Gorbachev.[66]

At the Pentagon, Secretary of Defense Caspar Weinberger likewise marveled at how Reagan had to battle the politics of his own press corps and liberal politicians as much as he had to combat the Soviet press and Communist apparatchiks.

One who was especially irritated was Reagan's science adviser, George Keyworth, one of the central figures in formulating SDI. Keyworth would later lament that "the greatest criticism" of SDI came from "leftist elements" in the U.S. press and intellectual establishment. He saw firsthand, daily, how these bedfellows fueled the Soviet assault. "These have been the amplifier for Soviet propaganda more than *Pravda* has," he asserted. "Pardon my polarization, but that's the truth."[67]

But when Reagan arrived at Geneva, he immediately learned why the Soviets had been so eager to disparage SDI. Mikhail Gorbachev made abundantly clear at the time (and later in his memoirs) that stopping SDI was his chief priority at Geneva; it would be even more so at the next summit, at Reykjavik a year later. Sensing that the missile-defense program gave him major leverage in negotiations, Reagan carried on in the face of the ongoing attacks. Because of his ability to persevere, SDI persevered.

And because it did, the Reagan administration thrust deep into the underbelly of the Soviet system. SDI was devastating to Moscow. The Soviets themselves saw it as a core cause in the undermining of their system.

Vladimir Lukhim, a high-ranking Soviet official, later maintained: "It's clear that SDI accelerated our catastrophe by at least five years."[68] Genrikh Trofimenko added: "99 percent of all Russians believe that Reagan won the Cold War because of his insistence on SDI."[69]

That post–Cold War appraisal from high-ranking Soviet officials is all that one needs to know. Yet even some liberal scholars in the United States today acknowledge SDI's impact on Gorbachev and the Soviets, especially as a bargaining chip that brought them to the table. Strobe Talbott of the Brookings Institution, who was deputy secretary of state under Bill Clinton, has said just that. So has Raymond Garthoff, whose book *The Great Transition*, as noted, largely credits Gorbachev, not Reagan, with ending the Cold War. Top Reagan biographers like Edmund Morris and Lou Cannon, as well as the most respected of Cold War historians, such as John Lewis Gaddis, cite Reagan's SDI as a major factor in eventual missile cuts with Moscow.[70]

Reagan secretary of state George Shultz has also highlighted the vital role of SDI. Shultz is the Reagan cabinet official whom liberal historians routinely cite as the most crucial in securing an end to the Cold War, in spite of (in their view) hardliners like Caspar Weinberger. Shultz was initially an SDI skeptic, but he later wrote: "The Strategic Defense Initiative in fact proved to be the ultimate bargaining chip. And we played it for all it was worth."[71]

For the record, too, SDI did not prevent the United States from achieving limitations on nuclear arms. Many liberals had warned that "Star Wars" would backfire when it came to arms-limitation negotiations. Ted Kennedy had used heated rhetoric to make this case, while more measured counsel came from authorities like Harold Brown, secretary of defense under President Jimmy Carter; Robert McNamara, LBJ's defense secretary; and diplomat George Kennan—all of whom Moscow quoted in support of the Soviet position.[72] But in fact, Reagan achieved much more than missile *limitations;* he got actual missile *reductions* (the START treaties) and even eliminated an entire class of nuclear weapons via the 1987 Intermediate-range Nuclear Forces (INF) Treaty.

Those stupendous achievements likely would not have happened had American liberals—and the Soviet propagandists—succeeded in their relentless campaign to get the Reagan administration to abandon SDI.

"We're Going to Win the Cold War"

In November 1983, Herb Meyer—the CIA official who, on the morning of March 24, 1983, caught a glimpse of the Soviet apoplexy generated by Reagan's SDI announcement—wrote a prophetic secret memo. The USSR, Meyer wrote, was entering a "terminal phase." "If present trends continue," he predicted, "we're going to win the Cold War."[73]

Reagan, too, foresaw that scenario. He grasped the inherent, fatal flaws of the Soviet system, and the potential for America to help collapse the whole house of cards. It was a prescient understanding that stood in marked contrast to that expressed by "expert" Sovietologists at esteemed Ivy League institutions. "The Soviet Union is not now, nor will it be during the next decade, in the throes of a true systemic crisis," predicted Columbia professor Seweryn Bialer in the elite journal *Foreign Affairs* in 1982. "The Soviet economy, like any gigantic economy administered by intelligent and trained professionals, will not go bankrupt. . . . Like the political system, it will not collapse." For the Reagan administration to think it had "the capacity seriously to affect" the Soviet system, was, by Bialer's expert estimation, "simply fallacious and . . . unrealistic."[74]

Columbia University was wrong and Ronald Reagan was right.[75] That's the blessed lesson of the twentieth century.

And Ronald Reagan's SDI was crucial to securing victory against Soviet Communism, despite attempts by American liberals to make it the laughingstock of the universe.

With weapons like SDI, and much more, President Reagan plotted a course to win the Cold War. The likes of Senator Ted Kennedy and the nation's leading media outlets did little to help, and too often did everything to hurt.

In 1989, Ronald Reagan's final year in the White House, Communism crashed in the evil empire, beginning with free and fair elections in Poland in June, continuing with the fall of the Berlin Wall in November, and ending with the eradication of Romanian dictator Nicolae Ceauçescu in December. It was the close of more than just a war; it was, as historian John Lukacs has noted, the end of the twentieth century. The Communist menace born in Russia in October 1917 would not survive the century.

And as the twentieth century ended in 1989, the twenty-first century arguably did not begin until September 11, 2001.

21

SEPTEMBER 11, 2001

On September 11, 2001, the Cold War was relegated to distant memory by a burning image. On that new day of infamy, a group of suicidal Islamic fanatics, backed by a homicidal Islamic extremist with billions of dollars, pulled off the worst attack ever on American territory. Osama bin Laden and his al-Qaeda terrorist network pulverized thousands of Americans, blowing to pieces innocent human beings in New York City; in Washington, D.C.; and across a farmer's field in western Pennsylvania.

"Today our nation saw evil, the very worst of human nature," the president of the United States, George W. Bush, plainly told a sickened nation.[1]

In New York City a breathtaking historical coincidence was being played out on September 11. At least some of the victims in the World Trade Center towers, and other New Yorkers forced to flee for their lives in ash-strewn streets, would have read that morning's *New York Times* and noted an incendiary article. The *Times* piece was titled "No Regrets for a Love of Explosives: In a Memoir of Sorts, a War Protester Talks of Life with the Weathermen." The article opened with these chilling words, so ominous in light of what was happening in New York that morning: "I don't regret setting bombs," said an unrepentant Bill Ayers. "I feel we didn't do enough."[2]

The former SDS member and fugitive of the Weather Underground had spoken to *Times* reporter Dinitia Smith from his tony nineteenth-century stone house in the Hyde Park district of Chicago. Still visible was the tattoo on his neck of the rainbow-and-lightning Weatherman logo that appeared on the letters that took responsibility for bombings in the 1970s. The *Times* reporter was not exactly appalled; she admitted being taken by Ayers's "ebullient, ingratiating manner" as he discussed his newly released memoir, the aptly titled *Fugitive Days*.

In those *New York Times* pages of September 11, 2001, as New York City and Washington, D.C., smoked and bled from the strikes by foreign terrorists, Ayers boasted of how he had participated in bombings in New York City and Washington, D.C. He and his network of domestic terrorists in 1970 had bombed New York City Police Headquarters—the "pigs" who, the very day this article appeared, were risking, and in some cases sacrificing, their lives to rescue innocents inside the World Trade Center. Like the 9/11 attackers, Ayers and friends had also hit Washington: in 1971, the U.S. Capitol, where Bernardine Dohrn and Kathy Boudin planted a bomb in the ladies room;[3] and in 1972, the Pentagon.[4]

Yes, the Pentagon had been bombed twice: in 1972, by Bill Ayers, Bernardine Dohrn, and their network of Communist-terrorist crazies, and now on September 11, 2001, the day of the *Times* article, by Osama bin Laden and his Islamist terrorist crazies.

The day of the 1972 Pentagon strike was idyllic in Ayers's memory. "Everything was absolutely ideal on the day I bombed the Pentagon," he wrote wistfully in his memoir, in a line the *Times* quoted. It had been a lovely day—just as September 11, 2001, had started. It had been a perfect day to bomb the Pentagon.

Would Ayers do it all again?

"I don't want to discount the possibility," he told the *Times* reporter. He confessed that he found "a certain eloquence to bombs," admiring their "poetry and pattern." Ayers, explained the *Times,* could still wax poetic about "the wild displays of noise and color, the flares, the surprising candle bombs," and especially for "the Big Ones, the loud concussions."

There had never been a Big One, a loud concussion, on American soil quite like that on September 11, 2001.

A Career in Education

When Bill Ayers thus expounded in the September 11, 2001, edition of the *New York Times,* no one could claim he was a misled, crazy "kid." He was fifty-six years old. He was now a "distinguished professor"—in the field of education, no less. He trained America's future teachers.

To gain such a position at an institution of higher learning, specifically the University of Illinois at Chicago, required an advanced degree. But what institution would have allowed Ayers into its educational program? This, after all, was a man that many—perhaps including Ayers himself—figured should have been in prison rather than graduate school. He had spent a decade and a half on the run, living in fifteen different states. During that time Ayers had used the names of dead babies in cemeteries as aliases.[5] Would any graduate school even begin to consider his application?

Oh, yes. In fact, Ayers did not have to hunt for a backwater school. He could turn to a prestigious institution right in New York City: Columbia University. John Dewey's celebrated home was there to roll out the red carpet for Bill Ayers. He entered the doctoral program at Columbia Teachers College, eventually earning his doctorate in 1987. One wonders whether Ayers's application to Columbia included his previously authored works, such as *Prairie Fire,* or his infamous credo for the Weathermen: "Kill all the rich people. Break up their cars and apartments. Bring the revolution home, kill your parents, that's where it's really at."[6]

In heading into higher education, Ayers followed the pattern of nearly every single one of the SDS-Weatherman fanatics. His bride, Bernardine Dohrn, also entered the academy.

As Dohrn had joined her husband as a fugitive in the 1970s, she had also joined the FBI's Ten Most Wanted list. (See page 423.) FBI director J. Edgar Hoover had dubbed her "the most dangerous woman in America" and "La Pasionaria of the Lunatic Left."[7]

By September 11, 2001, however, Dohrn had set down her bombing plans in preference for lesson plans: she had taken her unique training in law, beginning with the National Lawyers Guild in the 1960s, to Northwestern University School of Law, which made her a faculty member in 1991.[8] Professor Dohrn began specializing in children at the law school's Family Justice Center.

To most observers, this would seem a poor match—an injustice at the Justice Center—for a person who once openly celebrated the mutilation of a pregnant woman by cheering, "Dig it! . . . They even shoved a fork into the victim's stomach! Wild!" Apparently, however, the deans and provost at Northwestern judged that the former Weather Underground terrorist had much to impart to their students.

A Bridge to Nowhere

In a perverse way, Bill Ayers and Bernardine Dohrn offer a bridge between America's twentieth-century foe—Communism—and its successor, the malevolent enemy that attacked the United States on September 11, 2001: Islamic totali-

"The most dangerous woman in America": Weather Underground leader Bernardine Dohrn was on the FBI's Ten Most Wanted List. She never went to jail, and today is a prominent lawyer and academic.

tarianism. Just as in the Cold War, America's efforts to counter the adversary today are complicated by a range of people on the domestic front—not just true believers but also, far more numerous, left-leaning dupes, who fail to recognize the enemy, or who see the enemy only to the right.

Ayers, Dohrn, and other homegrown Communist terrorists went to violent extremes that most dupes did not during the Cold War, but still they were part of a larger contingent who repeatedly excused the other side. A similar phenomenon is occurring in the current confrontation against Islamic radicalism. Today we encounter plenty of dupes—including some of the same individuals from the Cold War—who chastise not the evil motivations of the violent extremists but, too often, the noble intentions of the Americans doing their best to stop the terror.

The tragic destiny of the dupe is to consistently, unwittingly defend the bad people on the bad side—the wrong people on the wrong side of history.

"Why Do They Hate Us?"

One way in which the political Left has apologized for Islamic fundamentalists/terrorists has been to argue that Islamic militancy is a product of the policies of America, of the West, of Israel, or, even more generally, a result of poverty or inadequate education in the Muslim world. There is no shortage of blame to shovel at everyone and everything—except, too often, the fanatics themselves.

One wonders how Corliss Lamont might have explained September 11, 2001. Lamont, a lifetime New Yorker, was spared that horror. The atheist-humanist had departed this world six years earlier, in April 1995, at the ripe old age of ninety-two, leaving behind an endowed chair in civil liberties at Columbia Law School as well as his private papers and a Corliss Lamont Rare Book Reading Room named in his honor at the university. Nonetheless, until the day he died, even after the Cold War ended, Lamont was still blaming America for the faults of the totalitarian world, as he did during a June 1993 trip to Cuba—one of the final remaining bastions of Communist true believers.[9]

Lamont and his cohorts often blamed America for the latest Soviet action, or for Fidel Castro's woes, or for starting the Cold War. Recall how Lamont's mentor, John Dewey, wrapped up his final article in his 1928 series for *The New Republic* by arguing that Britain's withdrawal of recognition for Russia "had done more than any other one thing to stimulate the extremists and fanatics of the Bolshevist faith, and to encourage militarism and hatred of bourgeois nations."[10] In this astounding assertion, Dr. Dewey charged Britain with fueling Communist hatred, militarism, and extremism—rather than placing the guilt on Lenin and Stalin, who had unleashed a campaign that would kill tens of millions of Russians.

Lamont's "progressive" heirs similarly blamed America into the War on Terror. After September 11, 2001, and particularly after the Bush administration's 2003 invasion of Iraq, it became all too common to hear warnings from the Left that America was "stirring up a hornet's nest" in the Middle East, or that Uncle Sam had better be careful not to "anger" the "Muslim street." *We will only spawn terrorism and extremism,* was a common refrain.

This line of argument did not take account of the fact that America and the West had been attacked by Islamic fanatics beginning long before September 11, 2001. The attacks went back more than thirty years at least, and included the Black September hijackings of 1970; the 1979–80 Iranian hostage crisis; the killing of 241 U.S. Marines in Beirut in October 1983; the torture of Americans abroad like William Buckley, the CIA station chief in Lebanon, who was kidnapped in 1984 and eventually executed; the 1985 hijacking of the *Achille Lauro;* the 1988 bombing of Pan Am Flight 103; the 1993 World Trade Center attack; the suicide attack on the USS *Cole* in 2000; and on and on and on.

Somehow, though, *Why do they hate us?* became the question the handwringing Left so often asked—suggesting that *America* must be to blame for inciting such violence and extremism. And when the United States finally took action to defend itself against these repeated attacks, many on the Left suggested that America was fueling the hatred.

Curiously, the U.S. government was blamed even for inciting the hatred of the theocratic-terrorist state of Iran, since President Bush in 2002 declared the rogue regime part of an "axis of evil." It didn't seem to matter that Iran had called America "the Great Satan" ever since the Shiite revolution in 1979. Nor did it matter that the ayatollah's theocracy had been among the world's leading sponsors of terrorism for the past thirty years—as the Clinton State Department had detailed throughout the 1990s in lengthy, formal reports to Congress. (The Clinton administration also identified Iraq as one of the chief sponsors of international terrorism.)[11] This terrorism was well established years before September 11, 2001.

The terrorists who attacked America on 9/11 did so because they were terrorists. Those terrorists precipitated the War on Terror.

Bush Hatred

One way to inadvertently help the adversary is to eviscerate the man trying to stop that adversary. That is precisely what happened to President George W. Bush when he was commander in chief during the War on Terror.

Many American liberals were vitriolic in their condemnations of Bush and his policies. This is not to suggest that Bush should have been exempt from criticism; legitimate questions were raised about the president's handling of certain issues. Too often, however, the criticisms seemed to go beyond the usual dissent or a genuine articulation of policy differences. With Bush, it truly was an evisceration.

The far Left despised Bush more than any president since Richard Nixon. Many (but not all) of the most egregious statements regarding the War on Terror, the wars in Afghanistan and Iraq, and even post-9/11 policy toward Iran were more anti-Bush than pro-Iraq, pro-Saddam, pro-Iran, or pro-Islamist. In other words, some of the worst criticisms stemmed not from genuine conviction about the Islamist enemy but from political jockeying and an intense personal dislike for Bush.[12]

This represented a departure from the Cold War, when many critics of American presidents spoke out of sympathy or admiration for, if not loyalty to, Soviet Communism. Equally important, during the Cold War, Communists, whether stationed in Moscow or New York City, Prague or Chicago, deliberately sought to manipulate liberals through carefully crafted propaganda. By and large this has not been the case during the War on Terror; neither terrorist organizations like al-Qaeda nor terror-sponsoring regimes like Iran have undertaken international propaganda campaigns as widespread or precisely plotted as the Soviet Union's. Thus, whereas ridiculous statements by American liberals in, say, the 1930s were often prompted by Communist propaganda, ridiculous statements by American liberals in the War on Terror usually have not been the result of manipulation by the enemy.

It is crucial to understand this distinction. Wildly criticizing the American government does not by itself make a person a dupe; typically, a dupe is someone whose unthoughtful statements are deliberately prompted by the enemy.

That said, the bile aimed at Bush no doubt served the interests of America's adversaries. Example after example of that hostility could be cited from blogs or rants by everyday hard-left Americans. Unfortunately, some of the nation's top politicians joined in the reckless attacks. Former vice president Al Gore, for example, became positively unhinged. Perhaps not coincidentally, soon after losing the presidency to Bush in the bitterly contested 2000 election, Gore accepted a teaching position at Columbia University's Graduate School of Journalism—not a place to go for political healing or to learn political moderation. By February 2004 he seemed consumed by fury against Bush. No longer did it appear that he was simply critiquing Bush policy. Condemning President Bush during a speech in his native Tennessee, Gore shouted at the top of his lungs: "HE BETRAYED THIS COUNTRY!!! HE PLAYED ON OUR FEARS!!!"[13]

It was a frightening display by a former vice president who had won the popular vote for president. Saddam Hussein would have relished the attack, not because it was pro-Saddam but because it was so vigorously anti-Bush. It served anti-Bush interests everywhere, including the Islamists who wanted Bush to withdraw American troops from Iraq.

Senate Democratic leader Harry Reid also gave the Islamists what they hoped for when he publicly called the president of the United States "a loser" and later declared that the Iraq war was "lost."[14] What the enemy in the Middle East needed was for enough Americans and members of Congress to join Reid in his defeatism.

Reid insisted the war was lost even as President Bush's "surge" of troops was turning around the very difficult postwar reconstruction of Iraq. Despite Reid's vocal defeatism—which was backed by such Democratic colleagues as House Speaker Nancy Pelosi—the surge worked. Even Bush's harshest critics, from Hillary Clinton to the *New York Times,* conceded as much.

Reid conceded little, however. The Democratic leader seemed eager to denounce the commander in chief. He declared flatly: "President Bush is a liar." Echoing Al Gore, Reid added of Bush: "He betrayed the country." Reid refused to apologize for these statements even when NBC's Tim Russert asked him whether such incivility was appropriate in a congressional leader. The senator replied, "I don't back off one bit."[15]

And why would he? It became commonplace for liberal Democrats in Congress to publicly blast Bush as a liar. For example, a trio of California liberals—Representatives Maxine Waters, Barbara Lee, and Pete Stark—all called the president a liar. "The president is a liar," declared Waters flatly, in remarks quickly published by *People's World,* formerly the *People's Weekly World,* the Communist organ and offshoot of the *Daily Worker.*[16] Congressman Stark probably made the ugliest charges. Speaking from the House floor in October 2007, Stark—who earlier had called the U.S. action an "act of extreme terrorism" and a "terrorist act"[17]—not only called the president a liar but also ripped America's troops for allegedly "blow[ing] up innocent people." Then he said Bush wanted to send more American boys "to Iraq to get their heads blown off for the president's amusement."[18] (Stark had made similar accusations against President Reagan regarding the Grenada invasion in 1983.)[19]

Some Democrats in Congress spoke as if they wanted to get rid of George W. Bush seemingly as much as (if not more than) they wanted Saddam Hussein gone. Just weeks into the Iraq war in the spring of 2003, John Kerry, the Vietnam-vet-turned-protester-turned-senator, said: "What we need now is not just a regime change in Saddam Hussein and Iraq, but we need a regime change in the United States."[20] At the time, Kerry was angling to become the Democratic Party's next nominee for president.

A year later Kerry was even more blunt. "These guys" in the Bush administration, Kerry said, "are the most crooked . . . lying group I've ever seen. It's scary."[21]

Our Troops Are Barbarians and Nazis

What was scary was the degree to which many American liberals reacted to the War on Terror by lambasting and undermining the Americans waging battle against terrorists.

Pete Stark's unfounded charge that U.S. troops were "blow[ing] up innocent people" was outrageous, but the congressman was hardly alone among elected Democrats in making irresponsible accusations. During the Vietnam War elected members of Congress like Senator Ted Kennedy, future senators like John Kerry, antiwar radicals like the SDS leaders, and dupes like Benjamin Spock had alleged the most terrible things about American soldiers. Now the Left was back—sometimes the exact same voices—deriding the American troops who were fighting the terrorists as terrorists themselves.

Probably the worst offender was Senator Dick Durbin, Illinois Democrat, who compared the thankless work of U.S. military interrogators at the Guantanamo Bay facility to the work of "Nazis, Soviets in their gulags, or some mad regime—Pol Pot or others—that had no concern for human beings."[22] This was not a flip comment. Durbin said it on the floor of the U.S. Senate, reading from a text, on June 14, 2005, amid the single worst stretch of killings of American soldiers by terrorists inside Iraq. The terrorists' goal was to subvert support for America's mission in Iraq and the War on Terror. Durbin had helped the cause.

The senator obviously knew nothing about Nazis, Soviets, or Pol Pot and his Khmer Rouge. It was absurd, and offensive, to compare the nonlethal interrogation of Islamist POWs to these skull-laden killing fields. The senator's analogy was so grossly unfair that Durbin should have immediately apologized not only to U.S. troops but also to victims of the Nazis, of the Soviets, and of Pol Pot.

Blasting U.S. military personnel, whether at Guantanamo or in Iraq or in Afghanistan, was all too common among Democrats—again, much as during the Vietnam War. George W. Bush may have been the ultimate target, but in the process of attacking the president's handling of the war they accused U.S. troops of various atrocities.

Senator Barack Obama put it this way in August 2007: "We've got to get the job done there [Iraq]. And that requires us to have enough troops so that we're not just air-raiding villages and killing civilians, which is causing enormous pressure over there."[23]

Even Vietnam vets, now in Congress, were making such baseless allegations, reminiscent of John Kerry after Vietnam. Most egregiously, Congressman John Murtha accused U.S. Marines of killing "innocent" Iraqi civilians "in cold blood." The Pennsylvania Democrat said that Marines from the Third Battalion were "cold-blooded killers" who "murdered innocent civilians."

The exonerated and acquitted Marines found Murtha's comments so inaccurate that they sued the congressman for slander. They wanted to clear their good names. Even after that lawsuit was filed, and after Murtha denounced his own constituents as "racists" and "rednecks," the congressman cruised to easy reelection a few weeks later. Only a few months later the U.S. Navy gave Murtha the Distinguished Public Service Award.[24]

After all that, Murtha must have stunned his constituents by announcing that he would be happy to have the Islamist terrorists detained at Guantanamo Bay relocated to his district of "rednecks" in Johnstown, Pennsylvania. "Sure, I'd take 'em," said Murtha. "They're no more dangerous in my district than in Guantanamo."[25]

Even Murtha's fellow Democrats raised an eyebrow at that one. Well, maybe not all Democrats. Dick Durbin was on board with the idea, too. When President Obama considered new locations for Guantanamo within the United States, he called Durbin, his former Illinois colleague. Sure enough, Durbin professed the Heartland as the ideal place to house the world's most dangerous terrorists. "Make no mistake about it," said a grateful Senator Durbin, "this is a once-in-a-lifetime opportunity. We have a chance to bring more than two thousand good-paying jobs with benefits to this region."[26]

When it came to trashing the troops, Murtha and Durbin were newcomers. An old hand at such rhetoric was John Kerry. Almost thirty-five years after he testified to "war crimes" allegedly committed by his fellow troops, Kerry was back, in a new war, once again to blister American soldiers abroad.

In December 2005, on CBS's *Face the Nation,* Senator Kerry insisted to Bob Schieffer: "And there is no reason, Bob, that young American soldiers need to be going into the homes of Iraqis in the dead of night, terrorizing kids and children, you know, women, breaking sort of the customs of the—of—the historical customs, religious customs."[27] Kerry had suddenly reversed the terms in the War on Terror: it was the American troops fighting the war against terrorism who were now guilty of terror.

Just imagine how Kerry's assessment had served the interests of the true terrorists wreaking havoc inside Iraq. No doubt, al-Qaeda wished it could print his words on fliers.

Senator Kerry's statement, made against an American military fully committed to avoiding civilian casualties, was inexcusable. His assessment was remarkably similar to his 1971 Senate testimony, with Kerry merely leaving out the words "genitals" and "Genghis Khan."

Much milder, but still hurtful, was Kerry's degrading statement in October 2006, when the junior senator from Massachusetts cracked this joke to a group of California college students: "You know, education, if you make the most of it and you study hard and you do your homework and you make an effort to be smart, you can do well. If you don't, you get stuck in Iraq."[28]

It is almost unbelievable that such a crack came from a veteran, and a highly educated one at that.

Kennedy and Columbia

Many of the same figures who made outrageous statements during the Cold War were still making outrageous statements during the War on Terror. It seemed as if they never learned from past mistakes. Most never even saw their statements as mistakes.

Senator Ted Kennedy—who in the 1960s had made terrible accusations against U.S. troops in Vietnam, and who in the 1980s had ridiculed President Reagan and his ideas, and had made an extraordinarily improper confidential "offer" to Soviet leader Yuri Andropov—emerged during the War on Terror as a cruel critic of the American president and of the troops under the president's command.

On May 10, 2004, Kennedy went to the Senate floor and declared: "On March 19, 2004, President Bush asked: 'Who would prefer that Saddam's torture chambers still be open?' Shamefully, we now learn that Saddam's torture chambers reopened under new management—U.S. management."[29]

Though Kennedy's hyperbolic condemnation of the Abu Ghraib scandal was intended to rip President Bush, it was an arrow at the heart of the U.S. military personnel who ran the detainee camps. It was also an absurd analogy, as practically any member of Congress with even rudimentary knowledge of Saddam Hussein's "Republic of Fear" would have known. The single worst case of unauthorized abuse by U.S. military personnel after 9/11 does not begin to compare to the daily terror that Saddam employed against Iraqi women, children, Shiites, Marsh Arabs, army deserters, dissidents, and on and on.

Just as he had targeted Ronald Reagan in the 1980s, Senator Kennedy focused his ire on the conservative president in the White House during the War on Terror. The senior senator from Massachusetts had sought to undermine the moral legitimacy of the Bush case for war even before the postwar occupation/reconstruction of Iraq went sour, and before body bags piled up.

For instance, in September 2003 Kennedy made the unsupportable claim that George W. Bush had pursued the Iraq war strictly for political purposes, not for strategic or foreign-policy purposes. Kennedy said that the decision to go to war had been a "fraud" that was "made up in Texas." The president and his political advisers had "announced . . . to the Republican leadership that war was going to take place and was going to be good politically."[30]

The problem with this very serious allegation was that it was not remotely logical. In fact, at the moment that Bush decided to pursue a risky path to war in Iraq, he was still surfing an unprecedented wave of popularity. Bush *gave up* that popularity to do what he thought was right in Iraq, which he saw (correctly or incorrectly) as central to a wider victory in the War on Terror. Bush can be accused of many things, even a bad war policy, but he cannot be accused of going to war to help his popularity, which was already sky-high.

Although Kennedy was roundly criticized for his nonsensical argument against the Iraq war, he persisted in this line of attack. He went to the Senate floor a few weeks later, in October 2003, to assert that the president's alleged "trumped-up reasons for going to war have collapsed" under the weight of "lie after lie after lie." The Bush administration, said the senator, "still refuses to face the truth or tell the truth."[31]

In January 2007, when the Bush mission in Iraq had finally begun to turn around thanks to the surge, Kennedy invoked Vietnam, that national "quagmire." "Iraq is George Bush's Vietnam," the Massachusetts senator declared.[32]

Ted Kennedy's high-profile criticisms did not serve truth. They did not serve the American mission in Iraq. They served only the aims of the enemy that the Bush policy hoped to vanquish.

Leftists in media and academia joined politicians like Kennedy in attacking the White House. Walter Cronkite, another voice from the Cold War, who had long since retired as CBS news anchor, decried President Bush's "arrogance" and forecast a "very, very dark" future for the country—again like Vietnam.[33] From the academic ranks, a notable example was well-known history professor Eric Foner. The onetime president of the American Historical Association was a professor at—you guessed it—Columbia University.

Foner had George W. Bush in mind when he claimed: "I'm not sure which is more frightening: the horror that engulfed New York City or the apocalyptic rhetoric emanating daily from the White House."[34]

Professor Foner's statement was one of remarkable hyperbole, especially from a decorated historian who lives and teaches in New York City, site of the 9/11 apocalypse. When criticized for this remark, specifically in a report by the American Council of Trustees and Alumni, Foner knew what to do: he blamed Joe McCarthy. The criticism smacked of "McCarthyism," cried Foner in a cover story in *The Progressive;* it smelled of "blacklisting." It was "disturbing," and "loyalty oaths" were possibly right around the corner.[35] Foner seemed to sense yet another apocalypse, this one with Joe McCarthy as lead horseman.

When it came to apocalyptic rhetoric, another leader far outdid anything George W. Bush ever said. That leader was Iranian despot Mahmoud Ahmadinejad, who hopes to engulf the nation of Israel in an unholy nuclear inferno. At a December 12, 2006, gathering of Holocaust deniers—a group of which he is a vocal member— Ahmadinejad pledged that "the Zionist regime soon [will] be wiped out and humanity will be free." The Iranian madman replaced the executed Saddam Hussein as the world's leading anti-Semite, terrorist sponsor, and desirer of nuclear weapons.[36]

Eric Foner complained little about Ahmadinejad's truly murderous rhetoric and dangerous objectives. In fact, he defended the Iranian hatemonger against his own university's president when Columbia offered Ahmadinejad a platform in September 2007.

Yes, the same university that invited Bill Ayers to enter its doctoral program in education lent its Ivy League imprimatur to another preacher of violence. Columbia invited Ahmadinejad to speak when the Iranian despot came to New York to address the United Nations. John Dewey's university again broke new ground in higher education.

The day of the event, Columbia president Lee Bollinger—perhaps to defuse the national outrage over his invitation to Ahmadinejad—harshly criticized the Iranian leader in his introductory remarks. Foner later took Bollinger to task for not rolling out the red carpet for Ahmadinejad. He was one of more than a hundred Columbia professors who signed a "statement of concern" about Bollinger's leadership, which cited, among other issues, the "strident tone" of the university president's introductory comments. Bollinger had committed a cardinal sin at Columbia: as Foner and his fellow faculty wrote in their statement, Bollinger's Ahmadinejad introduction "allied the University with the Bush administration's war in Iraq, a position anathema to many in the University community."[37] Foner went further in a follow-up faculty meeting, criticizing Bollinger for having used "the language of warfare at a time when the administration of our country is trying to whip up Iran, and to my mind is completely inaccurate."[38]

Many of those in the Columbia audience for Ahmadinejad's speech apparently shared Foner's deference to the Iranian antidemocrat. The crowd applauded lustily when the leader of Tehran's repressive regime chastised Bollinger by saying that in Iran they allow people "to make their own judgment." No doubt, too, the Columbia faithful were pleased to hear him bash George W. Bush and U.S. foreign policy. Those attacks on the United States came amid his insistence that Iran should have a nuclear program and amid a series of denials—that Iran was a longtime sponsor of terrorism, that the Holocaust happened, and that homosexuals existed in Iran.[39]

Remarkably, the Ahmadinejad episode may not have been Columbia University's most ignominious moment in the War on Terror. That honor may belong to a faculty-led "teach-in" against the Iraq war held at Columbia on March 26, 2003—and organized by Professor Foner. At the antiwar rally, Professor Nicholas De Genova wished "a million Mogadishus" upon U.S. soldiers in Iraq, a reference to the Somalia tragedy a few years earlier, when the corpses of American boys were mutilated and dragged through the streets—captured on film for their families (and the world) to see.[40]

Columbia University made a seamless transition from Cold War inanity to War on Terror inanity.

Jimmy Carter Returns

Jimmy Carter may have lost forty-four of fifty states to Ronald Reagan in 1980, but his work was far from finished. He reemerged to play a very active role in world affairs as ex-president, accommodating both post–Cold War Communist despots and post-9/11 Islamic despots. Regarding the former, one particular case merits special mention: Carter's June 1994 visit to the world's most repressive state, North Korea.

Carter's account of the trip defies imagination. Kim Il Sung was a tyrant, one who died mere weeks after Carter's visit.[41] But the impressionable ex-president found Kim "vigorous, alert, intelligent," and a man who engaged in "very free discussions with his ministers."

Kim spearheaded a militantly atheistic regime. But Carter, a born-again Baptist, found Kim "very friendly toward Christianity."[42]

Kim took the former American president on a Potemkin-village tour of Communist North Korea. Carter was impressed, reporting home to his fellow Americans:

> We found Pyongyang to be a bustling city. The only difference is that during working hours there are very few people on the street. They all have jobs or go to school. And after working hours, they pack the department stores, which Rosalynn visited. I went in one of them. It's like Wal-Mart in American stores on a Saturday afternoon. They all walk around in there, and they seem in fairly good spirits. Pyongyang at night looks like Times Square. They are really heavily into bright neon lights and pictures and things like that.[43]

In truth, North Korea is a literal sea of darkness. As satellite imagery shows, at night the northern half of the Korean Peninsula is draped in black—that is, when the lights are not ablaze to hoodwink America's most naïve ex-president— in contrast to the southern half, which is awash in the glow of freedom.[44]

Most tragic, within one year of Carter's enthusiastic appraisal, two to three million North Koreans (out of a population of twenty million) would starve to death in this Communist dungeon of a country.[45]

A few years after that, the North Korean regime announced that it was a nuclear state, a direct violation of the Agreed Framework that Carter had brokered with Kim in 1994. Back then, Carter had stood outside the Clinton White House and triumphantly assured reporters that "the crisis is over"—words headlined by both the *New York Times* and the *Washington Post*. Even many Democrats were wary of that grand declaration.[46]

Carter continued offering such unbelievable appraisals into the War on Terror, shifting almost seamlessly from the likes of Kim to Saddam. As President George W. Bush prepared for war in Iraq, Carter urged a return of UN weapons inspectors to Iraq—the same inspectors whom Saddam had repeatedly expelled as they had closed in on suspected weapons sites.[47]

Throughout the debate over war in Iraq, Carter smashed the time-honored tradition that ex-presidents refrain from public criticism of sitting presidents, especially in wartime. Carter penned an op-ed for the *Washington Post* titled "The

Troubling New Face of America," in which he lamented the "belligerent and divisive" Bush administration and its lack of "comprehensible" Middle East policy.[48]

His criticism grew even more personal in an op-ed for the *New York Times*. On March 9, 2003—exactly one month before ecstatic Iraqis pounced on a fallen statue of Saddam at Baghdad's Firdos Square—Carter fired a salvo titled "Just War—or a Just War?"[49] In this article the former president charged not only that the current president was shattering two centuries of "consistent bipartisan commitments" in foreign policy but also that Bush—self-professing Christian—was in "violation" of sixteen centuries of "just war" doctrine. "As a Christian" who was "thoroughly familiar with the principles of a just war," Carter judged himself fit to decide that Bush's "substantially unilateral attack" on Iraq "does not meet" just-war standards[50]—especially as the president's Pentagon (allegedly) fired upon a "defenseless Iraqi population."

The *New York Times* typically did not look kindly upon presidents integrating their faith into policy.[5] This time, however, was different. The editorial board suspended its usual objections, offering the Georgia Baptist a platform to employ his Christianity—at least in service against George W. Bush.

Unfortunately for Saddam, Carter was not able to spare him from U.S. tanks, just as the ex-president was not able to rescue him during the first Persian Gulf War in January 1991.[52] Later, however, Carter made his way to the Middle East to engage another terrorist leadership: Hamas. There, the ex-president blasted Bush and his State Department for daring to call the terrorist group "terrorist." "After they [Hamas] got elected to head their government," said an angry Carter, "they were declared to be terrorists."[53]

Even many of Carter's admirers in the press were taken aback by this one. Asked by an incredulous reporter whether he trusted Hamas, Carter objected: "It's not a matter of trusting them. It's a matter of what . . . they've pledged to do. They've gone on record as being amenable to a number of the proposals I've made."[54]

Carter has not expressed regret for such remarks about the evil men running Iraq, Iran, North Korea, and their terrorist allies. Rather, he regrets George W. Bush's January 2002 remark in which he labeled as "evil" the men running Iraq, Iran, North Korea, and their terrorist allies.[55] "I think it will take years before we can repair the damage done by that statement," sniffed Carter.[56]

Duped by Saddam: "Baghdad Jim" and Friends

Troubling as these post-9/11 examples are, most of them are not classic cases of dupery, wherein the liberals were carefully manipulated by the enemy. But the

War on Terror has produced clear incidents of dupery in the strict sense—that is, cases of America's enemies seeking out liberals for assistance. Hollywood stars such as Sean Penn and Annette Bening have been flown to places like Baghdad and Tehran, where their hosts hoped they would return to America singing the praises of some of the most illiberal and intolerant men on the planet—and denouncing the man in the White House.[57]

More disturbing are the elected officials who have been targeted as dupes. In one outrageous instance, three congressmen traveled to Saddam Hussein's Iraq months before a single American troop was dispatched to take down Saddam's regime. Congressmen Jim McDermott of Washington, David Bonior of Michigan, and Mike Thompson of California made the trip in September 2002, as the Bush administration was trying to persuade Congress to authorize military action in Iraq.

All three men had served in the military during Vietnam, with Thompson seeing combat through the 173rd Airborne. But these liberal Democrats were all predictable antiwar, anti-Bush votes. If Saddam was fishing for suckers, McDermott and Bonior in particular would be among the very best candidates in the U.S. Congress. Of course, Saddam knew that, which is why he wanted them in Iraq for potential exploitation.

Right on cue, McDermott, the most liberal of the three, mouthed the Iraqi Baathist Party line. He said that President Bush "will lie to the American people in order to get us into this war."[58]

Naturally, Saddam's aides could not wait to get a microphone in front of McDermott. More than that, they had a studio ready. On September 29, 2002, the Iraqi government eagerly positioned McDermott and Bonior there for an interview with ABC News's *This Week with George Stephanopoulos.*[59]

When Stephanopoulos asked McDermott whether he stood by his claim that the president would intentionally lie to drag the nation into war, the congressman held firm: "I think the president would mislead the American people." The Seattle congressman deduced that Bush and the administration would "give out misinformation . . . information that is not provable." When Stephanopoulos asked for evidence of Bush's lying, McDermott did not proffer any, simply reaffirming his conviction that the president was a deceiver.[60]

Stephanopoulos, a Democrat and a former top aide to Bill and Hillary Clinton, was surprised, perhaps shocked, when McDermott said he did not harbor the same suspicion toward his endearing hosts in Iraq. Whereas the congressman alleged that the president of the United States operated on duplicity, McDermott said of Saddam and his regime: "I think you have to take the Iraqis on their face value."[61] He wanted the United States to take the Iraqi dictator at his word even though Saddam had spent more than a decade obstructing UN weapons inspectors and murdering hundreds of thousands of innocents. The Iraqis, Americans were supposed to believe, suddenly supported "unfettered inspections"; Baghdad had given the trusting politicians "assurances" of that, McDermott said in a press conference.[62] The congressman was doing yeoman's work for the Republic of Fear.

The Baghdad Three were a hit in Iraq. Saddam's Ministry of Information published the itinerary of their goodwill tour in the regime's government-controlled newspapers, television, and radio, and on the ministry's website in both Arabic and English. These stories were headlined on newspaper front pages and on news broadcasts; they ran aside other celebratory Iraqi news items, including stories on the "criminal Bush," or U.S. "war crimes" against Iraqi children, on how the "U.S. embargo" starved Iraqi infants and killed seniors in hospitals, on nonstop U.S. military "war waging" around the world, on Palestinian suicide bombers who gave their lives as "intrepid martyrs," and on how Jews had been responsible for 9/11.[63]

Even friendly liberal news sources in America seemed embarrassed by the Baghdad Three. A CNN reporter asked Congressman McDermott whether he minded being exploited for propaganda by Saddam's tyrannical regime. "If being used means that we're highlighting the suffering of Iraqi children, or any children," replied the congressman, "then, yes, we don't mind being used."[64]

Didn't mind being used. This was worse than John Dewey and Corliss Lamont in the USSR. At least the Columbia professors had convinced themselves that they weren't being used.

McDermott's fellow Democrats—from the head of the Democratic National Committee, to former president Bill Clinton, to John Kerry, to leading members of Congress like Nancy Pelosi, Dick Gephardt, and Barney Frank—were stunned, some of them into complete silence, others into brief replies of "no comment."[65]

And McDermott was not finished. He continued to carry water for Saddam upon his return from Iraq. In an appearance on PBS's *NewsHour with Jim Lehrer,* McDermott said that Congress was faced with a war authorization that was really about whether "the United States can decide to wipe out another country's leader whenever we don't like them." Interviewer Gwen Ifill was compelled to ask McDermott to respond to the charge that he had returned from Iraq as "an apologist for Saddam Hussein." McDermott said that the people making such accusations were "stupid."[66]

So blatant and successful had been Saddam's manipulation of Jim McDermott that conservatives began derisively calling the congressman "Baghdad Jim." But even they could not have known just how badly McDermott and his friends had been exploited.

As the Associated Press reported six years later, in a March 2008 story, federal prosecutors found that Saddam Hussein's intelligence agency had "secretly financed" (AP's words) the trip to Iraq by the three U.S. lawmakers. The prosecutors determined that the trip had been arranged by a Middle Easterner in Detroit, Michigan, named Muthanna Al-Hanooti, who was charged with setting up the trip "at the behest of Saddam's regime." Iraqi intelligence officials, prosecutors learned, reportedly paid for the trip through an intermediary, and rewarded Al-Hanooti with two million barrels of Iraqi oil.[67]

Prosecutors said they had "no information whatsoever" that the three congressmen were aware that Saddam's henchmen had underwritten the trip. "Obviously, we didn't know it at the time," explained McDermott. "The trip was to see the plight of the Iraqi children. That's the only reason we went."[68] (Actually, McDermott's remarks had gone well beyond the plight of Iraqi children.)

Representative McDermott's spokesman, Michael DeCesare, said the congressman had been invited to Iraq by a Seattle "church group" and had been unaware of Iraqi funding for the trip. Congressman Thompson likewise said he had no "question at all regarding the sponsor of the trip or the funding."[69] The Baghdad Three had been oblivious.

Congressmen Jim McDermott, David Bonior, and Mike Thompson had been duped by Saddam Hussein. It was a snow job in the Iraqi desert.

Dupes, Yesterday and Today

As the "Baghdad Jim" example shows, each case of suspected dupery in the War on Terror needs to be evaluated on its own merits. McDermott and crew had been duped, whereas, say, Ted Kennedy—who had not been flown to Baghdad for special handling by Saddam—had served the Iraqi dictator's interests more indirectly, through outrageous statements that the senator aimed at George W. Bush, not at Saddam. Again, Senator Kennedy had *inadvertently* helped the adversary. That is also true for degrading remarks about American troops uttered by the other Massachusetts senator, John Kerry, or by Dick Durbin, or by Barack Obama, or by Pete Stark, or by other post-9/11 Democrats.

Kennedy's and Kerry's remarks were more typical of the sort of suspected dupery we have seen in the War on Terror, which is quite different from the textbook dupery of the Cold War. When John Kerry accused the troops of war atrocities in Vietnam in April 1971, a Communist intelligence chief like Ion Pacepa could claim that Kerry had been taken by Soviet propaganda. But when Kerry did the same to troops in Iraq in December 2005, there was no al-Qaeda operative claiming to have signaled the senator.

To be sure, in both the Cold War and the War on Terror, certain ill-advised statements by leftist Americans inadvertently helped U.S. opponents. But the statements in the latter have not usually been cued or coordinated as they were so often in the former. It is a big difference, with a notably different kind of adversary.

Soviet Communism, of course, has been long since dispatched to the ash heap of history. But this doesn't mean that all battles from the Cold War past have gone away. As we shall see next, debates still rage over some of the most disturbing cases of dupery, with many Communists from the Cold War continuing to find their greatest protectors in liberals.

22

STILL DUPES FOR THE COMMUNISTS

W hile the great international battle facing America has shifted from the Cold War to the War on Terror, from militant Communism to radical Islamic terrorism, certain skirmishes from the former remain. FDR's actions at Yalta, John Kerry's quarrel with the Swift Boat Veterans, the political relevance of top former members of SDS and the Weather Underground—all these are still debated today. The jury also remains out on many of those accused of having been Communists or of secretly working with the Kremlin, and on those who were just plain duped.

What was Ted Kennedy up to in May 1983 with that offer to Yuri Andropov via the KGB? Why was a grimacing Lillian Hellman so consistently, vindictively wrong? What was Corliss Lamont truly thinking? Is there more we need to know about Humphrey Bogart in the early 1930s (see Postscript)? Did FDR really treat George Earle that badly over the Katyn Wood massacre?

Those are ongoing debates, often between anti-Communist Cold Warriors and liberals who continue to cover for Communists—including Communists who looked to use them, who excoriated their favorite presidents and party leaders and policy initiatives, who viewed them contemptuously as dupes, and who counted on them to help conceal the Communists' identity and agenda. Whether in Hollywood, journalism, or the academy, many liberals even today provide cover for the Communists—and, more pointedly, deride the anti-Communists.

Films depicting every Hollywood Red as an innocent victim and every anti-Communist as a paranoid witch-hunter remains a cottage industry, including such movies as Tim Robbins's *Cradle Will Rock* (1999), which depicts the House Committee on Un-American Activities in the 1930s persecuting Federal Theater Project (a group that, in fact, was dominated by Communists); *Good Night and Good Luck* (2005), based on the 1954 confrontation between Joe McCarthy and TV journalist Edward R. Murrow; and *Trumbo* (2008), a paean to Communist screenwriter Dalton Trumbo. Only in Hollywood could Lillian Hellman, an unrepentant Stalin apologist, be beatified in a film like *Julia* (1977)—an Oscar-winning movie that starred Vietcong cover girl Jane Fonda—while Elia Kazan, a man of conscience and a liberal throughout his life, remains forever demonized for committing the unforgivable sin of anti-Communism.

Many contemporary liberals display the strangest naïveté as they rally around their suspected heroes. Recall what *The Nation* wrote of Arthur Miller at the time of his death: "He certainly wasn't a communist, and he wasn't a socialist," eulogized fellow playwright Tony Kushner in the pages of that leftist mainstay.[2]

Despite Kushner's assurances, we cannot be so certain about Miller's political views. Was he really *never* a communist, or even a socialist? The evidence makes that claim difficult to believe.

Claims such as Kushner's are hardly uncommon. When alleged Soviet agent I. F. Stone died in 1989, just as Poland was having free and fair elections, and shortly before the fall of the Berlin Wall, he was praised to no end. The *New York Times* hailed him as a "pugnacious advocate of civil liberties, peace, and truth." The *Los Angeles Times* saw Stone as the "conscience of investigative journalism." CNN's Larry King dubbed him a "genuine hero." To the deans of journalism, from James Reston of the *New York Times* to Fred Friendly of Columbia's School of Journalism, I. F. Stone, the "liberal" journalist, had become the epitome of virtue: Saint Stone. A political cartoon by Pat Oliphant showed Stone outside the Pearly Gates, with St. Peter telephoning God to say, "Yes, *that* I. F. Stone, sir. He says he doesn't want to come in—he'd rather hang around out here, and keep things honest."[3]

I. F. Stone deluded them all—if not quite to the Pearly Gates, then at least until his last breath.

One might expect that the momentous declassification of Communist archives in both the United States and Russia would prompt scholars to reevaluate the story of the supposedly innocent victims of anti-Communists. But even in the face of ample new evidence indicting Communists whom the liberal community long defended, many academics have refused to concede that the conventional anti-anti-Communist narrative may have been wrong.

Alger Hiss's Dupes

A case in point was the grand opening of New York University's Center for the United States and the Cold War, a joint project of the school's Faculty of Arts and Sciences and its Tamiment Library. Tamiment now houses portions of CPUSA's vast reservoir of records (materials that were consulted for this book). Here, at last, was an opportunity to dispassionately reach some firm conclusions about a cloudy past. This voluminous record could resolve some long-standing debates, including by showing who was and was not a CPUSA member.

Or maybe not. At its public debut in 2007, the new center announced that it would host a regular series of seminars "to encourage research on how the Cold War and the *red scares* shaped domestic political culture and foreign policy" (emphasis added). The center sought proposals from scholars dealing with the "political repression and resistance" of the times.

Historian Ronald Radosh, himself a former Communist who now reports carefully on the most mendacious characters of the Cold War, highlighted the bias in the NYU-Tamiment project. In a piece for *The New Republic*,[4] Radosh wrote that the NYU-Tamiment project had clearly implied that "no proposal . . . would be welcome that took as its starting point the belief that, in the 1930s and 1940s, American communists just may have posed an actual threat to America's national security, and that does not view the question of how to deal with this problem as anything but repression."[5]

The Center for the United States and the Cold War reinforced this impression with its inaugural conference, titled "Alger Hiss and History."

And what of the history of Alger Hiss? It has been long settled. Though Hiss's conviction for perjury in his famous spy trial wasn't enough to convince his most ardent defenders of his guilt, mountains of evidence have emerged since then to prove that Hiss was a Communist spy. Sam Tanenhaus's masterful 1997 biography of Whittaker Chambers and Allen Weinstein's definitive 1978 account of the Hiss-Chambers case showed beyond doubt that Hiss was a Soviet agent. Even before that, way back in 1962, there was an authoritative book demonstrating Hiss's guilt by a former vice president named Richard Nixon.[6] And the Venona transcripts made public in the 1990s discussed a Soviet spy code-named "Ales" who was almost certainly Hiss. As Christopher Hitchens, a brutally frank man of the Left, put it, the thoroughly discredited claim that Hiss was somehow innocent remains "one of the most persistent (and repelling) myths of the fellow-travelling Left." Arthur M. Schlesinger Jr., who knew Hiss, noted that even "Alger's friends" knew he was guilty.[7] This history on Hiss is indisputable, and extremely well established (which is why he is mentioned little in this book).

But to the Center for the United States and the Cold War, the Hiss story was not nearly so clear-cut. The tone of the center's comments were favorable toward Hiss, reporting, for example, that he "embodied the reformist vision that linked FDR's domestic agenda to an internationalist foreign policy." Instead of noting the evidence proving that Hiss was a Soviet agent, the NYU-Tamiment center wrote simply that he had been "accused of spying." The center said that the Hiss-Chambers trial, rather than exposing Hiss as a spy, had helped "discredit the New Deal, legitimize the red scare, and set the stage for Joseph McCarthy." It was as if nasty Republicans pursued Hiss solely for partisan purposes. Mark Kramer, the meticulously fair director of the Harvard Project on Cold War Studies, said that the NYU-Tamiment conference consisted of "diehard supporters of Hiss whose attempts to explain away all the new available evidence are thoroughly unconvincing."[8]

Contemporary examples like this are numerous. They have prompted eminent Cold War historians such as Harvey Klehr and John Earl Haynes to plead with their colleagues to do their job as scholars—to actually do the research and evaluate based on facts.[9]

Sadly, after all of these years, and all the new evidence now available, some things never change. The Left's anti-anti-Communism is one such thing.[10]

Comintern? What Comintern?

Alger Hiss is a high-profile case involving obvious guilt. The pattern persists with less-known cases as well, with many academics reacting to newly declassified documents not as long-awaited evidence that can finally resolve historical puzzles but instead as unfortunate opportunities for "demonization" by anti-Communists. In a December 2007 article in *The American Historical Review*, three academics lamented that "newly released documents of the Communist International (Comintern) in Moscow" are being "frequently deployed . . . to provide support for a renewed demonizing of the Comintern and its activists."[11]

A renewed demonizing of the Comintern and its activists?

I submit here that the Comintern and its activists, from their tutelage under Lenin to Stalin, to their homage to Lenin and Stalin, did an adequate job demonizing itself.

Communist activity and penetration was very real and very deep. It should not be shrugged off.

Frank Marshall Davis's Ghost

Illustrative of the enduring impact of many of these Cold War characters is the suddenly reemergent case of Frank Marshall Davis. Whereas so many comrades and their fellow travelers abandoned ship once the crimes of Stalin were exposed, Davis kept the faith, even as he publicly denied his membership in the party.

Davis died in 1987, but his influence it still felt today, and extends far beyond what he wrote for the *Chicago Star* and the *Honolulu Record.* His impact is profound because he mentored a young man who made it all the way to the White House, and is now leader of the free world: Barack Obama.

That Davis-Obama relationship was kindled by Obama's maternal grandfather, Stanley Dunham, who in many ways saw eye-to-eye with Davis. Dunham saw in Davis a potential role model and father figure to his grandson, whose biological father had abandoned him. (Obama's Kenyan father was likewise a man of the Left.)[12] Davis and Dunham were "closest friends," according to Davis biographer Dr. Kathryn Takara, a University of Hawaii professor.[13]

Not a lot is known about Stanley Dunham. Occasionally, some mainstream media sources have cast flickers of light on the man through their stories about his famous grandson. For instance, *Newsweek,* in an insightful article on Barack Obama's religious faith, described Dunham and his wife as "two lapsed Christians" from the Midwest, who, in turn, raised a "Christian-turned-secular mother," the single mom who raised Obama. All were people of the Left, the article noted.[14] According to the *Chicago Tribune,* the grandparents attended, for a period, the East Shore Unitarian Church, known among locals as the "Little Red Church on the Hill." (The *Tribune* article attributes this moniker not to the far-left political sympathies of the congregation but, instead, to the "McCarthyism" infecting the period.)[15] Like their later grandson, who would attend the church of Jeremiah Wright, the radical, ranting, raving, racist reverend, this was a very political church.

In other words, the media will at times shed light on Obama's grandfather's political radicalism, but they do so almost accidentally, via articles on other subjects, such as Obama's religious faith. It is left to conservative sources, like Glenn Beck, to raise such questions—legitimate and important questions that nonetheless invite the wrath of the progressive choir.

Barack Obama was close with Frank Marshall Davis in the 1970s, during the formative years of his adolescence. At the time Obama was attending prep school and readying to leave Hawaii for college.[16] Obama admits to learning from Davis, knowledge which surely was nothing like the "midwestern values" that former Kansas governor Kathleen Sebelius (now President Obama's secretary of health and human services) maintained that Obama had learned in her state.

In his pre-presidential memoir, *Dreams from My Father,* Obama was very affectionate toward Davis, and clearly proud of him. We see there that Davis constantly offered advice to the young man: on women, on race, on college, on life. The adolescent listened in awe as Davis passed the time with his grandfather drinking whiskey and swapping stories, and even enlisting the boy into his composition of dirty limericks. "I was intrigued by old Frank," writes Obama, "with his books and whiskey breath and the hint of hard-earned knowledge behind the hooded eyes."[17]

How much of that hard-earned knowledge, about the world, its events, and the dialectic of history, did Davis pass along to the current president of the United States during these crucial formative years? That remains a riddle. Sadly, an uncritical press has never bothered to ask such simple questions that are usually standard fare for any president.

They are important questions in many respects. Consider, for instance, that most Americans by the late 1970s and early 1980s were at last convinced that détente with the Soviets was a sham, and that the USSR needed to be dissolved—the emerging view that propelled Ronald Reagan to win forty-four states in 1980. Obama, however, would have learned nothing like that from Davis. Frank Marshall Davis swam against what Ronald Reagan described as the "tide of history," a "freedom tide" that would "leave Marxism-Leninism on the ash heap of history."

Instead, as Obama wrote in *Dreams from My Father,* he was prepping for a college career of hanging out with the "Marxist professors," attending "socialist conferences," and "discuss[ing] neocolonialism."[18] The mentor Davis would not have been telling the young Obama about the American exceptionalism that would soon bring freedom to the USSR and Eastern Europe. After all, this was the man who had written that American democracy had become "synonymous with oppression instead of freedom." Instead, he almost certainly would have instructed Obama in the glory of the Bolshevik experiment—the party line he adhered to in his columns. This was the wrong side of history, but it was the side of Frank Marshall Davis.

Defining this Davis influence would fill in some gaps. It might lend credence, for instance, to assertions by Dr. John Drew, who was a contemporary of Obama at Occidental College, and who met Obama as a fellow Marxist. Drew was a well-known campus Communist when Obama was introduced to him as "one of us." "Obama was already an ardent Marxist when I met in the fall of 1980," said Drew in an interview for this book. Drew is certainly cognizant of the gravity of his statement: "I know it's incendiary to say this," he added in a separate inter-view with television journalist Scott Baker, but Obama "was basically a Marxist-Leninist." He noted how Obama, in *Dreams from My Father,* wrote that he had "hung out" with Marxist professors, but what Obama did not explain in that book, or clarify, said Dr. Drew, is that Obama "was in 100 percent, total agreement with these Marxist professors."[19]

If Obama was indeed a Marxist when he arrived at Occidental, Frank Mar-shall Davis likely would have been a prime reason.

It is fitting that after Occidental, a young Barack Obama transferred to Colum-bia University. It was 1981, as Ronald Reagan was beginning his crusade to under-mine atheistic Communism, and Obama found himself at the home of the extreme Left that wasted the twentieth century wallowing in error upon error regarding Communism and the Cold War. In his memoir, Obama recalls at length the college advice he got from Davis.[20] Did Frank Marshall Davis also support his application to Columbia, possibly with a letter of recommendation? We have no idea, since Colum-bia—contacted for this book, as was Occidental[21]—has not made those records available, and as the dominant press has not demanded even a glimpse at the files.

"Frank"

Not surprisingly, Barack Obama shaded the identity of Frank Marshall Davis in his book. He referred to Davis as simply a "poet" and called him only "Frank," conspicuously avoiding his full name (yet more reason for the press to ask ques-tions).[22] That said, Obama's memoirs make it clear that "Frank" is Frank Marshall Davis. Likewise, scholars of Davis, plus others with intimate knowledge of the relationship, have attested to the identity.

Those testimonies are worthy of quoting, because they illuminate so much more. Among the observers is Gerald Horne, who spoke at the reception for the opening of the CPUSA archives at NYU's Tamiment Library. A transcript of Horne's speech is posted at the website of *Political Affairs Magazine,* the Herb Aptheker publication published by CPUSA, which today carries the subhead "Marxist Thought Online." Horne began his remarks on a sour note, bemoan-ing how the history of CPUSA and the global Communist movement "has been distorted grievously by the infestation of anti-Sovietism and anticommunism." He hoped that "the opening of these wonderful archives should not only lead to a reassessment of the party but help to push back the right-wing which has profited so handsomely from anti-Sovietism and anticommunism."[23]

Horne was optimistic that future generations would not be "seized" with such a jaded view of the former USSR, which "was a supposed 'Evil Empire.'" Future generations, said Horne, would instead see the *wisdom* and *vision* of CPUSA, of the USSR, and of those American Communists who supported the Soviet state. If those future generations looked at the situation rationally, Horne averred, they would "tend to agree" with him and former KGB-thug-turned-Russian-leader Vladimir Putin that "the fall of the USSR was the greatest geo-political catastrophe of the 20th century." Horne greatly regretted American victory in the Cold War and predicted that rather than asking "who lost China?" future historians may well be asking "who lost the US?"

Horne finished his lengthy, bitter oration with an unexpected burst of optimism, as he closed with effusive words of praise for Frank Marshall Davis, plus a note of clarification on the then-rising star in the Democratic Party. Taking his comrades back to Hawaii, Horne noted how Davis, "who was certainly in the orbit of the CP—if not a member," had decamped to Honolulu in 1948 at the suggestion of good friend Paul Robeson, where he "befriended another family." That family included a young man "who goes by the name of Barack Obama, who, retracing the steps of Davis, eventually decamped to Chicago." Horne highlighted the fact that in his memoir, Obama "speaks warmly" of Davis and identifies the older man "as being a decisive influence in helping him to find his present identity."

Horne recommended that professors have their students read Obama's memoirs "alongside Frank Marshall Davis's equally affecting memoir, 'Living the Blues.'" "When that day comes," he confidently predicted, "I'm sure a future student will not only examine critically the Frankenstein monsters that US imperialism created in order to subdue Communist parties but will also be moved to come to this historic and wonderful [CPUSA] archive in order to gain insight on what has befallen this complex and intriguing planet on which we reside."

Frank Marshall Davis's Modern Dupes

As with his association with the Reverend Jeremiah Wright at the Trinity United Church of Christ in Chicago, Barack Obama has since sought safe distance from Davis, no doubt fearful of how the relationship might have damaged his presidential pursuits.

Would the Davis link be a liability? In a rational world, yes. Once again, however, the answer hinged on a battle between Communists and anti-Communists, between liberals and conservatives, between Left and Right, with the dupes in the middle playing the decisive role.

Though Davis's Communist sympathies were undeniable, some still try to deny them. Dr. Kathryn Takara of the University of Hawaii describes Davis today as a "loving man," who "did not have a hateful bone in his body," who studied, knew, and valued "democracy," and who handed on to Obama "a sense of believing that change can happen" through "living in a diverse world." Takara told Cliff Kincaid, a conservative who was one of the first to diligently trace the influences of the likes of Davis, that she did not think that Davis's CPUSA membership had been proven.[24] "Proven" is the key word in that statement, as it depends on who or what was seeking to do the proving. Davis publicly tried to deny his Communist affiliations, and even pleaded the Fifth Amendment in 1956 before the Senate Internal Security Subcommittee.

Yet other Davis scholars disagree, including the leading authority. "Sometime during the middle of the war [World War II], he [Davis] joined the Communist Party," recorded John Edgar Tidwell, the University of Kansas professor and Davis biographer, who is the reigning expert on Davis's writing and career.[25]

Tidwell has authored or edited several works on Davis. In one volume, he provides the smoking gun, quoting Davis himself admitting in writing that he joined CPUSA. Specifically, in the introduction to the edited volume *Frank Marshall Davis: Black Moods, Collected Poems,* Tidwell produces a letter by Davis to a Kansas friend named Irma Wassall. Davis was trying to recruit Wassall to CPUSA, in a much more direct way than he typically had done in the open forum of his *Honolulu Record* column. In that letter, Davis wrote: "I've never discussed this with you and don't know whether you share the typical American uninformed concepts of Marxism or not, but I am risking such a reaction by saying that I have recently joined the Communist party."[26]

Davis then explained his reasoning, noting that Communism was "the only movement that is actually conscious of social evolution and the meaning of various forces at play in the world today." He added, as a "matter of fact," that he had "leanings in that direction since I was in college." It was a "risk" for Davis to finally admit this in writing, but here he did so—in a private letter.

Thus, Tidwell notes that "despite Davis's public denial of his [Communist] activities," the "historical record" indicates that the FBI's suspicions of Davis were not based "solely on supposition."

That is indeed certain. In fact, the entire six-hundred-plus-page FBI file on Frank Marshall Davis has been released, thanks to a Freedom of Information Act (FOIA) request by Cliff Kincaid.[27] Kincaid immediately posted the entire file—

reflecting some nineteen years of FBI investigation—at his website, where anyone has been able to view the records since 2008.[28] Among the links on the website is a select compendium of thirty-four documents, which cover forty pages.[29] These pages in particular make it clear—based on repeated witness testimonies—that Frank Marshall Davis was a Communist; they indicate that Davis had CPUSA affiliations going back to 193? and was an actual member of CPUSA starting in 1943, if not earlier.[30] (See Appendix B, pages 506–15.) As one report demonstrates, the FBI even knew Davis's Communist Party card number: 47544.[31] Numerous informants and former party members spoke of Davis's membership in the party, in front groups, as a leader of an underground cell group, and as a dues-paying member; they also spoke of the party membership of Davis's wife, Helen (card number 62109).[32] Again, these FBI reports have been available on the Web since 2008.

But none of this has stopped modern-day liberals and Davis defenders from falling to the usual lines of retreat—that is, suspecting the *anti*-Communists of a Red-baiting witch hunt.

Professor Takara has adopted a line on Davis that could have been written by Davis himself: "Any group that was progressive was considered communist," she said.[33] As we have seen, Davis adopted precisely this argument, repeatedly, in his *Honolulu Record* column.

Takara's statement reflects a standard exaggeration from the Left. Speaking of allegations against other "progressives" handily diverts from the central question of whether Davis himself was a Communist.

Even in death, then, Frank Marshall Davis can still count on non-Communist liberals to help dismiss the charges of anti-Communists. And that is especially the case given that Davis's star pupil has risen to the level of Democratic Party icon and forty-fourth president of the United States.

As Hillary Clinton learned during the 2008 Democratic primary, and as was parodied on *Saturday Night Live* at the time, the American mainstream media adored Barack Obama. That made it difficult for legitimate investigations into Obama's record and his past to get any pickup in the press—and if the mainstream media did pick up a story, it was usually to dismiss it. Herb Romerstein and Cliff Kincaid learned this when they held a May 22, 2008, press conference on Capitol Hill to announce the release of two new reports the veteran investigators had produced on presidential candidate Obama's association with extremist elements from the American Left, from Davis to domestic terrorist Communists Bill Ayers and Bernardine Dohrn.

At the press conference, Romerstein discussed the report on Davis, who he correctly noted was an influential figure in Obama's early life. Romerstein added that

Davis had been a member of CPUSA. He developed that fact very carefully in his report, which contained more than a half-dozen primary-source exhibits and other forms of reliable documentation. More than that, he showed that (as we have seen in this book) Davis and his comrades worked to undermine the dearest liberal causes because of their lockstep subservience to the Comintern and the USSR, including flip-flopping on issues as grave as Nazism and World War II based entirely on Stalin's position. Romerstein highlighted another unsavory aspect of Davis's career, demonstrating (again as we have seen) how Davis exploited and subverted the NAACP and the larger civil-rights movement. Laying out this case at length, Romerstein quoted letters from NAACP members like Roy Wilkins and Edward Berman. Berman, recall, wrote Wilkins to warn that "Comrade Davis" and his cohorts were out to "destroy the local branch of the NAACP" after having done the same at another branch, where they "recently 'sneaked' into the organization with the avowed intent and purpose of converting it into a front for the Stalinist line."

Romerstein, in short, laid out a well-documented and legitimate case. As noted, too, he was an extremely credible source, probably the single most respected authority on American Communism. He was such an authority that the Library of Congress had tasked him to produce an analysis of the Venona papers when the U.S. government finally declassified them in the 1990s. One reason he had earned such a strong reputation as an expert on Communism is that he was fair, precise, nuanced, and knowledgeable, constantly exhorting other researchers to distinguish between "good guys and bad guys," between mere suspects and the genuinely guilty, between anti-Communist liberals and gullible liberals, between small "c" communists and party members, between practicing Communists and former Communists who cooperated with the FBI.[34]

None of that seemed to matter to Dana Milbank, the popular columnist for the *Washington Post*. Milbank was one of the few high-profile mainstream journalists who bothered to attend the Romerstein-Kincaid press conference on Capitol Hill. Unfortunately, it quickly became apparent that he was there to mock the event.[35] Milbank did not disappoint. He described the press conference as a new Vast Right-Wing Conspiracy, as the 2008 version of the Swift Boat veterans, and cruelly described Romerstein as "a living relic from the House Committee on Un-American Activities." The whole thing, reported Milbank, sounded "like a UFO convention." He pooh-poohed the legitimate, quite compelling contention, raised by Romerstein and Kincaid, that Barack Obama's past affiliations were so "dodgy" (Milbank's word) that Obama would have difficulty getting a government security clearance.[36]

At the press conference, Milbank asked whether Romerstein and Kincaid were trying to argue that Barack Obama was a communist.[37] In other words, what was the point of this hoopla if Obama was not a communist?

Of course, no one claimed that Obama had been a member of CPUSA. That was not the issue. The larger point was that Obama's associations were revealing, as was his struggle to distance himself from those associations once some researchers began investigating them. The facts were that many of Obama's friends had been dedicated Marxists, Maoists, and Stalinists; he was party to a long-running personal and professional association with people from the most extreme Left; and he cited some of these people—such as Frank Marshall Davis—as no less than mentors. For any person, such influences from the past are formative. This is why biographers do not hesitate to look at their subjects' mentors.[38] These influential figures are, in fact, the first go-to figures in any historical-biographical narrative. They are never irrelevant or to be completely ignored. The fact that the current president happens to be a liberal Democrat, and his mentor a closet Communist, does not suddenly push the inquiry out of bounds.

Another way to consider the question of a political leader's formative influences is to imagine how the mainstream media would react were Barack Obama a conservative Republican who had these sorts of long-running associations with the far Right. What would Dana Milbank think of, say, a John McCain mentor who carried water for Hitler, as Davis had for Stalin? No liberal journalist would laugh at that question.

Enter More Liberals

Dana Milbank was far from alone. The more that conservatives like Cliff Kincaid sounded the alarm on Frank Marshall Davis, the harder it became for liberal journalists to ignore the matter. But even when compelled to address Obama's connections to Davis, they went to great lengths to downplay the issue.

A case in point was the Associated Press, which in 2008 ran two articles on Barack Obama's life in Hawaii, including one specifically on Frank Marshall Davis. Both of these articles were nothing short of astounding in their ability to ignore the obvious. The slight was so bad that a frustrated Cliff Kincaid denounced the articles as "blatant fraud and deception," especially in light of the fact that the AP had contacted Kincaid and Romerstein, and had received reports, documentation, and follow-up phone calls.[39]

One of the AP stories, published on August 2, 2008, did confirm the tight relationship between Obama and Davis.[40] It called Davis "a constant figure in his

[Obama's] early life," and an "important influence," who Obama "looked to," like a "father," like a "mentor," for "advice on living."

From there, however, the article was scandalous in its omissions. Of all the articles that Davis filed for the *Honolulu Record* in 1949—which form a lengthy chapter in this book—the AP managed to quote only one: "I refuse to settle for anything less than all the rights which are due me under the constitution." The AP placed this quote strictly in the context of Davis's "advocating civil rights amid segregation."

This quotation is hardly representative of where David stood at the time. To call it cherry-picking is insufficient. To rely on this line was shamelessly misleading to AP readers. In AP's account, the Frank Marshall Davis of 1949 was a civil-rights defender and crusader for the U.S. Constitution, suffering the jackboot of segregation. There was no sign of the Stalinist, of the unyielding trasher of Harry Truman, of the bomb thrower targeting the Democratic president's alleged attempts at a neocolonial state, a fascist-imperialist state, a racist state, a third world war.

The word "communism"—which had been the central force in Davis's life, the very reason for his column and arrival in Hawaii in the first place—was never mentioned in the AP article. Worse than that, the article said dismissively that the charges of Davis's "allegedly anti-American views" were soundly rejected by "those who knew Davis and his work," who maintained that "his activism was aimed squarely at social injustice."

Harry Truman and the Democrats of the 1940s would beg to differ. That piece of reportage by the AP was tremendously ill-informed.

The article noted that Davis worked for "a wire service for black newspapers" but not did mention the *Chicago Star* or the *Honolulu Record*. It listed his close African-American contemporaries, except for Paul Robeson. And while the article made no mention of Joe Stalin, it did mention Joe McCarthy. The article quoted John Edgar Tidwell, the University of Kansas professor who has confirmed Davis's CPUSA affiliation. The AP, however, quoted Tidwell calling Davis a victim of a "McCarthy-era strategy of smear tactics and condemnation by association."

The AP story also quoted Tidwell waxing poetic of Davis as "a beacon, a light shedding understanding and enlightenment on the problems that denied people, regardless of race, national origin or economic status." Frank Marshall Davis was, according to the Associated Press, not a slash-and-burn agitator for the Communist movement who unrelentingly attacked an honorable American (Democratic) president and opposed everything from the Marshall Plan to the Truman Doctrine to America's attempt to save West Germany; he was, instead, a uniter, a healer, a champion of fairness and the underprivileged.

The Honolulu Community Media Council took the same tack. This local civic group issued a press release exposing the disreputable work not of Communists past but, rather, of today's anti-Communists, specifically Cliff Kincaid, Herb Romerstein, and Bill Steigerwald, a Pittsburgh reporter who had dared to report on the inappropriateness of Dana Milbank's behavior at the May 22, 2008, press conference. It was the anti-Communists, not Davis, who were guilty of "shoddy journalism and smear tactics," said the council, which, incidentally, found "no substance" to the claims that Davis was "a lifelong communist and mentor to Mr. Obama." No, said the council, Davis had moved to Hawaii in 1948 "in part to seek a climate more favorable to his mixed-race marriage."[41]

Later that August, the *Washington Post* ran an in-depth profile of Obama's life in Hawaii. The lengthy article, which ran to an incredible ten thousand words, was the work of Pulitzer Prize–journalist David Maraniss, who did superb reporting on a young Bill Clinton a decade earlier. Amazingly, this extraordinarily comprehensive article, the most in-depth piece on Obama in Hawaii by any major newspaper, neglected to mention Frank Marshall Davis even one time.[42] That was something that Obama himself could not avoid.

When called on this shocking omission by Kincaid's watchdog group, Maraniss, who, characteristically, was courteous enough to respond, explained, "My reporting conclusion was the role of 'Frank' had been hyped out of all proportion, both by Obama himself in his book and some others later."[43]

As Kincaid noted, Maraniss did not explain how he arrived at that conclusion, and he failed to let readers decide on the importance of a figure whom Obama himself and other sources had identified as a key influence. Perhaps, like Conrad Black refusing to believe a credible account of FDR's admiration for Stalin, David Maraniss simply did not want to take the word even of the subject himself when that word hurts the subject's image.

One day after Maraniss's piece appeared in the *Post*, *Newsweek*'s Jon Meacham heralded Frank Marshall Davis as a "strong voice for racial justice," whose commendable "writings on civil-rights and labor issues" had wrought the unholy wrath of the anti-Communists. "His political activism," Meacham wrote of Davis, "especially his writings on civil-rights and labor issues, prompted a McCarthyite denunciation by the House Un-American Activities Committee."[44]

Examples continue to roll in from leading journalists. To cite just one, *New Yorker* editor David Remnick, author of excellent works on Soviet Russia, including the acclaimed *Lenin's Tomb*, took little account of Davis in his major book on

Obama released in April 2010. The book, *The Bridge,* runs more than six hundred pages long but mentions Davis only a handful of times. Remnick dismisses the "attacks" of the "right-wing blogosphere" as "loud and unrelenting," and even scoffs at claims that Davis was a "card-carrying Communist."[45]

Perhaps Remnick should have consulted Davis's FBI files, which are available to any interested reader or researcher.

An Anointing from Ayers

Unlike Frank Marshall Davis, Bill Ayers was very much alive during the 2008 presidential campaign. His influence on Barack Obama was not confined to Obama's youth; he was a friend and colleague of an adult Obama. Because of that, and because he was unrepentant about his past in the Weather Underground— a past recent enough and shocking enough that many Americans were aware of him—Ayers became a bigger issue in the 2008 campaign. But once again, liberals rallied to defend Obama over his radical connections.

After getting his doctorate from Columbia Teachers College, Ayers had moved to Chicago, where he not only got a job in academia but also became active in politics. In 1995 he and his wife, Bernardine Dohrn—still self-proclaimed small "c" communists—hosted a political christening of sorts for the individual hand-chosen by radical Illinois state senator Alice Palmer as her successor.

That very small gathering at the Ayers-Dohrn home included only several people. Among them was Dr. Quentin Young, who had testified before the House Committee on Internal Security in 1968.[46] Young, who once refused to say whether he was a member of the Communist Party, was now, in the post–Cold War era, a member of the Democratic Socialists of America, a group that on May Day 1992 honored Young with its highest prize: its annual Debs Award—named for Eugene Debs, the four-time Socialist Party presidential candidate.[47] The doctor was a staunch proponent of "single-payer" (government-run) health care.[48]

Alice Palmer, the state senator, was there as well. In the 1980s Palmer had served on the executive board of the FBI-identified Communist front group the U.S. Peace Council, an affiliate of the Soviet stooge World Peace Council. Also on that board was future Democratic congresswoman Barbara Lee. (See pages 456–57.) Palmer had begun serving the Illinois State Senate in 1991. Now, like Barbara Lee, she had her eyes on a run for the U.S. Congress. She chose this function at the Ayers-Dohrn home to anoint her preferred successor—an aspiring politician in his mid-thirties named Barack Obama.[49] Yes, Obama was there, with Palmer, with Quentin Young, to get the political blessing of Ayers and Dohrn.

Is it an exaggeration to make a lot of this moment? Did Alice Palmer make this gesture only at the Ayers-Dohrn gathering? Or did she repeat it elsewhere?

The difficulty in answering those questions is compounded by the fact that the mainstream press has not pushed Obama for any details, even when the subject was broached by the one source that liberal Obama supporters would trust: the *New York Times*. The *Times* flagged the meeting in a page-one story on Obama and Ayers on October 4, 2008.[50]

That story was somewhat noncommittal on the incident in question, although not silent. The *Times* confirmed the "gathering" at the Ayers-Dohrn home, and quoted a local rabbi named A. J. Wolf, an Obama supporter, as calling it a "coffee" and "one of several such neighborhood events as Mr. Obama prepared to run."[51] The rabbi was the only source the *Times* quoted. Everyone else was tight-lipped, including Ayers and Dohrn, who, said the *Times* reporter, refused "multiple requests" to be interviewed.[52]

That said, the article conveyed the import of the meeting. The *Times* conceded that it was there, at the Ayers-Dohrn home, where "State Senator Alice J. Palmer, who planned to run for Congress, introduced Mr. Obama to a few Democratic friends as her chosen successor."[53]

A few weeks after receiving that political blessing, on September 19, 1995, this emergent political dynamo announced his candidacy for Palmer's seat to a packed room of two hundred supporters at the Ramada Inn Lakeshore in Hyde Park.[54] Barack Obama was setting sail toward a truly vast political horizon.

Bill and Barack

There was, undoubtedly, a symbolism to the political christening that occurred at the Ayers-Dohrn home that day in 1995. There, in that living room, Bill Ayers, lifelong revolutionary and educational "change agent" from the University of Michigan and Columbia, would, along with the infamous Bernardine Dohrn, lay hands upon the king of all "change agents," Barack Obama.

Ayers and Obama had already known each other prior to that kickoff party. Precisely when they first met remains a mystery. The *New York Times,* in its October 2008 story on Ayers and Obama, said that the two men had met in 1995 at a "meeting about school reform." But the *Times* reported this based on the claim of an Obama "campaign spokesman." Many conservatives expressed doubts about

**US PEACE COUNCIL OFFICERS AND EXECUTIVE BOARD
1983-1985**

Co-Chairpersons:
Rep. Saundra Graham, *Massachusetts State Legislature*
Eugene "Gus" Newport, *Mayor of Berkeley, CA*
Frank Rosen, *President, District 11, United Electrical
   Workers Union*
Mark Solomon, *Professor, Simmons College, Boston, MA*
Sara Staggs, *Executive Director, Chicago Peace Council*

Vice-Chairpersons:
Sentwall Aiyetoro, *National Conference of Black Lawyers*
Anan Jabara, *President, Palestine Aid Society*
Rob Prince, *Vice President, Colorado CC Federation of Teachers*
Mary Ruth Robinson, *Mid-South Peace and Justice Center,
   Memphis TN*
Marlo Vazquez, *Attorney, Los Angeles, CA*

Palmer and Lee: Alice Palmer, who anointed Barack Obama as her successor in the Illinois State Senate, and Congresswoman Barbara Lee both served on the board of the FBI-identified Communist front group the U.S. Peace Council in the 1980s.

Executive Director:
Michael Myerson

Executive Board:
Bill Archer, *Bristol Peace Coalition, Bristol, CT*
Barbara Armentrout, *Chicago Peace Council*
Mark Belkin, *Denver, CO*
Dwight Bowman, *American Federation of Government Employees, Washington, DC,*
Arnold Braithwaite, *New York Peace Council, NYC*
Owen Brookes, *Delta Ministry, Greenville, MS*
Frank Chapman, *National Alliance Against Racist and Political Repression, NYC*
Doug Collins, *Clinton, IA*
Linda Coronado, *Chicago Peace Council*
Otis Cunningham, *Chicago Peace Council*
Shirley Douglas, *Niagara Democratic Club, Oakland, CA*
Dana Fisher, *Houston, TX*
Matilda Gibbs, *New Haven, CT*
Jack Hart, *Philadelphia, PA*
Alex Hurder, *Southern Organizing Committee for Economic and Social Justice, Nashville, TN*
James Jackson, *Communist Party USA, NYC*
Kathryn Kasch, *Boston Peace Council*
Mike Kelly, *West Va. Peace News, Charleston, WV*
Kamal Khouri, *Iraqi Democratic Union, Detroit, MI*
Werner Lange, *Rainbow Coalition, Warren, OH*
Barbara Lee, *Oakland, CA*
Kevin Lynch, *NYC*
Atiba Mbiwan, *Providence, RI*
Antonio Medrano, *San Francisco, CA*
Joseph Miller, *SANE, Philadelphia, PA*
Anne Mitchell, *Women's International League for Peace and Freedom, Philadelphia, PA*
Frank Paige, *Birmingham Peace Council, AL*
Alice Palmer, *Black Press Institute, Chicago, IL*
Steve Pietsch, *Chicago Peace Council*
Connie Pohl, *Brooklyn Peace Council, NY*
Arlene Prigoff, *San Francisco Bay Area Peace Council, CA*
Pauline Rosen, *Women Strike for Peace, NY*
Cathy Schuster,, *Colorado Peace Council, Denver*
Jose Soler, *Puerto Rican Socialist Party, New Brunswick, NJ*
Michele Stone, *Michigan Peace Council, Detroit*
Ken Wilson, *Quad Cities Peace Council, Davenport, IA*
Denise Young, *Metro-Act, Rochester, NY*

that official story. Some have presented evidence that Obama and Ayers may have worked together as early as 1988, on a project involving Chicago schools.[55] And Ayers and Obama could have met even earlier. Specifically, it seems feasible to consider that they met in New York City around 1983.

Obama attended Columbia from 1981 to 1983, a transfer student from Occidental College. Ayers got his master's degree from Bank Street College, just blocks from Columbia, in 1984, which suggests he began graduate studies in 1982.[56] We know that Ayers was living in the city, working as a teacher at a nursery school in Manhattan, in 1982.[57] Also, Ayers received his doctorate from Columbia in 1987, and Obama may have lived in New York City and around Columbia well after he graduated in 1983. The overlap between Ayers and Obama is there. Of course, New York is a huge city, but there is a possibility that the two were introduced, particularly if they had mutual friends and ran in similar circles.

Unfortunately, the media's unwillingness to ask these basic biographical questions of the man holding the most influential position on the planet has created unnecessary confusion. Exacerbating the situation is Columbia's refusal to release Obama's college records—an unusual reticence for this self-anointed bastion of open inquiry. Worse, Obama has been extremely reticent about this period in his life, which is odd for a man who had already written two memoirs by his mid-forties.[58]

Either way, Obama and Bill Ayers would both leave New York for Chicago, where they would interact and work together on many occasions and in varied capacities. They jointly served as board members at the Woods Fund in Chicago; they worked on "school reform" through the Chicago Annenberg Challenge; they served on a juvenile-justice panel (organized by Michelle Obama); they appeared together as speakers or panel participants at Chicago events; they had many mutual associations, including with troubling figures like Rashid Khalidi, the Columbia University Middle East studies professor known for his controversial views; they acknowledged one another in books and reviews and even endorsed the other's books; and they had a relationship as neighbors (three blocks apart). These are just some of the numerous reported associations. The relationship was both professional and personal. Some have speculated that Barack Obama met his wife, Michelle, at the Sidley & Austin law firm where Bernardine Dohrn worked.[59]

Of course, this came after Bill Ayers stopped detonating bombs, as Obama was quick to note as a presidential candidate in 2008—although Ayers had told the September 11, 2001, *New York Times* that he still loved the "eloquence" and "poetry" of explosives. Obama also frequently noted that he "was only eight years old" when Ayers, Dohrn, and the Weathermen were killing police. That, too, is correct. Yet it is also correct that Obama was forty years old when Ayers told the *Times* that he had no regrets about bombing the Pentagon.

By then, Ayers and Obama had known each other for at least six years, including the political blessing that transpired at the Ayers-Dohrn home. Obama was a respected Chicago professional, serving in prominent positions in the community, working with Ayers, all while Ayers remained unrepentant about his past. The Ayers-Obama relationship went up to and continued through Ayers's comments to the *New York Times* in 2001.

Consider: The longest period that Obama and Ayers formally worked together—on the board of the Chicago Annenberg Challenge—appears to have run from 1995 through 2000, with Obama the chair. As the *New York Times* reported, archives from the project show that the two attended at least six meetings together, with Ayers providing briefings on educational issues.[60] As chair, Obama could have easily rejected Ayers's contributions and even participation. He most certainly did not.

Not only did Obama not distance himself from the onetime bomber, but he even personally accepted money from Ayers. According to the *New York Times,* in 2001, the same period when Ayers openly lamented that he had not done enough damage to the Pentagon, Ayers donated $200 to Obama's reelection campaign for the Illinois State Senate, which Obama happily accepted.[61] To my knowledge, no one in the mainstream media has asked Obama to repudiate that donation.

From 1999 to 2002, again stretching over the September 2001 period, the pair also served together on the board of the Woods Fund, a tight board of only seven members. Officials from the fund refuse to release minutes from these meetings, but confirmed to the *Times* that the board met quarterly during this four-year period, which would equate to sixteen meetings.[62]

Obama and Ayers also spoke at the same conferences. For example, in November 1997 the *University of Chicago Chronicle* reported that Ayers "is one of four panelists who will speak on juvenile justice at 6 P.M. Thursday, Nov. 20." One of the other panelists, the *Chronicle* noted, would be "Sen. Barack Obama, Senior Lecturer in the Law School, who is working to combat legislation that would put more juvenile offenders into the adult system." The story also quoted a key university administrator responsible for "bringing issues like this to campus": the associate dean of student services and director of the University Community Service Center—a woman named Michelle Obama.[63]

Seven months after Ayers's September 2001 comments, both Barack Obama and Bill Ayers spoke on another panel together. This time they appeared together at a conference on "intellectuals" held April 19–20, 2002, at the Chicago Illini Union at Ayers's school, the University of Illinois at Chicago. (See page 461.) The speakers included Obama, Ayers, Bernadine Dohrn, Columbia University's Patricia Williams, and Richard Rorty. (The late Rorty was a pragmatist, a Dewey disciple, and an angry atheist who wrote that the goal of college educators must be to help "bigoted, homophobic religious" students "escape the grip of their frightening, vicious, dangerous parents," so those students will "leave college with views more like our own.")[64]

Naturally, these formal meetings involved additional encounters and exchanges, especially given that Obama and Ayers were friends, colleagues, and neighbors, and given that Ayers and Dohrn sponsored Obama politically with their own money and home.

Not surprisingly, then, Ayers and Obama were intimately familiar with one another's work. In fact, Obama gave a glowing endorsement for his friend's book *A Kind and Just Parent: The Children of Juvenile Court* that was published in the *Chicago Tribune*. In the December 21, 1997, issue of the *Tribune*, the state senator was featured in a section called "Mark My Words," which quoted local figures on what they were reading. Obama praised Ayers's book, calling *A Kind and Just Parent* "a searing and timely account of the juvenile court system, and the courageous individuals who rescue hope from despair."[65] (See page 462.)

Obama's defenders would dismiss the endorsement by saying that it related to Ayers's *educational* work rather than political work. In fact, Ayers's educational work *is* political, and is radical. And this particular Ayers book is quite political, including very controversial sections regarding the American prison system and American foreign policy.

Of course, why would that surprise anyone?

No Big Deal

During the 2008 presidential campaign, the Obama-Ayers connection raised eyebrows, from those of debate moderators like George Stephanopoulos, to Democratic presidential contender Hillary Clinton, to Republican presidential nominee John McCain.

Conservatives believed that Barack Obama's relationship with Bill Ayers was a legitimate statement on Obama's judgment and his far-left political views. The relationship, they said, suggested not that Obama shared Ayers's fondness for bombs but reflected Obama's radicalism on issues from abortion to "spreading the wealth." After all, reputable, nonpartisan sources like *National Journal* ranked Obama the most liberal member of the most liberal U.S. Senate in history.[66]

Conference Schedule

April 19th

2:00-3:30 p.m., Chicago Illini Union, 828 S. Wolcott
Conference Registration

3:30-5:00 p.m.
I. Why Do Ideas Matter? (a keynote panel)
We introduce the "meta" theme of the conference by hearing "success stories" from diverse voices discussing their experiences intervening intellectually.

> Timuel Black, Chicago activist; Prof. Emeritus, City Colleges of Chicago
> Lonnie Bunch, President, Chicago Historical Society
> Bernardine Dohrn, Northwestern University Law School, Children and Family Justice Center
> Gerald Graff, UIC, College of Liberal Arts & Sciences
> Richard Rorty, Stanford University, Philosophy

6:00 p.m. Patricia Williams (Columbia University Law School) Harold Washington Library Center

7:30 p.m. Dinner for Patricia Williams and Conference Presenters

Saturday, April 20th 9:00-11:00 a.m.
I. Working Breakfast
This session brings together people taking on important social problems in theory and in practice. They will gather according to interest, such as "housing," "poverty," "human rights," and "education," to teach each other to create new collaborative networks. All are invited to participate.

> Guest participants will include:
> Arvis Averette (housing issues)
> Jim Duignan (DePaul, Stockyard Institute)
> Stevan Weine (UIC Psychiatry, refugees and survivors of terrorism)
> and others

11:15-2:00 p.m.
III. Lunch and Public Encounters
Alternative breakout tours led by Chicago activists. Tours of Bronzeville and other communities, and visits to organizations that are working on partnering theorists with activists.

2:15-3:45 p.m.
IV. Intellectuals in Times of Crisis
Experiences and applications of intellectual work in urgent situations.

> William Ayers, UIC, College of Education; author of *Fugitive Days*
> Douglass Cassel, Northwestern University, Center for International Human Rights
> Cathy Cohen, University of Chicago, Political Science
> Salim Muwakkil, Chicago Tribune; In These Times
> Barack Obama, Illinois State Senator

Obama and Ayers: Barack Obama knew Bill Ayers, serving on boards with and speaking at the same conferences as the former Weatherman. This April 2002 conference program shows Obama and Ayers speaking on the same panel.

Obama's praise for Ayers: In the December 21, 1997, issue of the *Chicago Tribune*, Barack Obama warmly praises Bill Ayers's book.

It was not only conservatives who raised the Ayers issue. Senator Hillary Clinton brought it up during the Democratic primary. She did so in a clever way, saying that Republicans would be raising it, and thus Obama should be prepared with a good explanation for the association.

Clinton had understandable reasons for bringing up Ayers. As a native of the Chicago area and a child of the '60s herself, she knew about Ayers and Dohrn. Hillary Rodham had been a liberal in the 1960s—but not a radical; she had never advocated violence. Moreover, as a senator from New York, she noted to Obama that Ayers's comments about not regretting his past bombings were "deeply hurtful to people in New York."[57] Her point was spot-on.

By this point conservatives had been investigating Obama's Ayers association for months. Television and radio host Sean Hannity, for example, had been calling attention to this underexplored issue since early 2007. Finally the mainstream media could no longer ignore it entirely. A fair liberal journalist, George Stephanopoulos, directly asked Obama during a Democratic debate, "Can you explain that relationship [with Ayers] for the voters and explain to Democrats why it won't be a problem?" Many on the Left viciously criticized Stephanopoulos for asking this question.[68]

After Obama won the Democratic nomination against Senator Clinton, the *New York Times* did a story, signaling to other mainstream media sources that it was permissible to follow suit. Like Hillary Clinton before him, John McCain raised the subject in presidential debates. McCain was rightly unsettled, as he had been brutally tortured and permanently crippled by the very Vietcong soldiers that Ayers, Dohrn, Rudd, Klonsky, Hayden, Fonda, and all the SDSers and Weathermen had hailed as heroes to be emulated. Why wouldn't he want answers on Obama and Ayers?

In the end, though, it did not matter. On November 4, 2008, the majority of the American public showed that they did not care enough about Obama's personal and political relationship with Bill Ayers to hold it against him at the ballot box. He was handily elected president of the United States.

And with the election over, a triumphant Bill Ayers, ever the bad boy, seemed to relish in his unwillingness to repent or pay a price for his past. Defiantly, almost snidely, he spoke to the nation in an interview with ABC's *Good Morning America,* where he asserted: "I've been quoted again and again as saying, 'I don't regret it,' and saying, 'I don't think we did enough.' And I don't think we did enough."[69]

A "Communist"? Who Cares . . .

Most relevant to the focus of this book is the fact that while Bill Ayers was derided throughout the campaign as an "unrepentant terrorist"—a phrase employed especially by Sean Hannity—his past as a communist got far less attention. Although Ayers professed communism at far greater length than he did terrorism, that part of the equation seemed to have no impact at all.

Once again, Cliff Kincaid and Herb Romerstein and crew were there to shed light on that aspect of Ayers, much as they had with Frank Marshall Davis. They again presented a volume of research and printed and posted materials. They again held a press conference—this time at the National Press Club, on March 12, 2009. But again they were ridiculed, mocked, or ignored.

The dominant media culture in America, which, sadly, serves as educator-in-chief to millions of citizens, even in this incredibly diverse new media age, continued to be unconcerned with Communism. That was the case even when the *contemporary* Communist Party was the issue.

In 2008 current Communists were quite open in their support of Obama's presidential bid. In an article titled "Communist Party Backs Obama," Cliff Kincaid quoted Joelle Fishman, chair of CPUSA's Political Action Commission, and CPUSA member, and blogger, Alan Maki.[70] In a truly shocking display, Maki, who maintained a blog called "Communist Manifesto," announced a "Frank Marshall Davis roundtable for change" on no less than the official Obama '08 website. There, Maki explained his enthusiasm: "Reading Barack Obama's book I learned about his mentor, Frank Marshall Davis. Of course, *as we all know* [emphasis added], Frank Marshall Davis was a communist and . . . understood through his thorough studies of the situation that socialism provided the only workable alternative to capitalism." Maki thanked Obama for bringing Davis to his attention: "Now I can say that Frank Marshall Davis is in many ways my mentor, too."[71]

Non-Communist liberals did not want this kind of information to get circulated to the wider public, and especially to the moderates and Reagan Democrats that Obama needed to win the election. Every story on Davis, or whiff of a CPUSA endorsement, or photo of a Che Guevara poster at an Obama campaign office, was political dynamite that had to be snuffed out.[72]

When the *People's Weekly World,* the modern official newspaper of CPUSA, wrote an editorial endorsing Obama's "transformative candidacy," calling it a "thrilling opportunity to end 30 years of ultra-right rule and move the nation forward with a progressive movement," it was left solely to far-right websites to post the piece.[73] Other Marxist sources gave speeches and wrote editorials hailing what they hoped would be the start of a new era, celebrating Obama's planned "change," and insisting that at long last their "time has come."[74]

Likewise telling, and ever-present here, was the bogeyman of anti-Communism: Cliff Kincaid rightly noted that not even conventional conservative news outlets would touch the Frank Marshall Davis story. Kincaid's group tried to run paid ads on the Davis-Obama connection on conservative websites, which fled from them as "too controversial."[75] No doubt that is because of the backlash that would crash upon those sources; the howls of "McCarthyism" would again resound.

An Unchanging Theme

For many non-Communist liberals, it seems, there is always a reason to provide cover for Communists. At the opening of the CPUSA archives at NYU-Tamiment, the liberals had their reasons: to expose the alleged malevolent doings of anti-Communists' past. At the gatherings hosted by Cliff Kincaid and Herb Romerstein, where the targets were Frank Marshall Davis, Bill Ayers, and Bernardine Dohrn, the liberals had their reasons: to protect the 2008 Democratic presidential nominee.

Either way, it is always the anti-Communists who emerge as the liberals' bad guys. This has been a consistent, indeed unchanging, theme for nearly a century. Even while mocking, manipulating, and trashing non-Communist liberals, Communists—Stalinists and Leninists and Maoists, followers of Che and Fidel and Trotsky, supporters of Katyn and the Hungarian massacre—have happily observed many of those same liberals attacking their critics, and unwittingly doing their bidding.

There is truly nothing new under the sun.

23

2008: A "Progressive" Victory

The Marxist radicals of the 1960s had fought to "disrupt" and "incapacitate" the American "empire." They aimed to "seize power and build the new society." But they had lost the fight; America had won.

Then, just when it seemed they had been defeated for good, with their dreams crumbled like the Berlin Wall razed by Ronald Reagan, Pope John Paul II, Margaret Thatcher, Mikhail Gorbachev, Vaclav Havel, Lech Walesa, and millions of freedom-starved Eastern Europeans, those Marxist radicals found inspiration and direction in the presidential candidacy of Barack Obama. They suddenly had new life.

Whether Obama knew it or not, he was the man on whom they projected their ideals and vision for America and the world—a vision that had long ago been exposed as false utopianism. They felt they could graft their program upon his. He was the first Democrat whose politics approached theirs.

Hillary Clinton had not been far enough to the left for them. Bill Clinton had been too *conservative* for them, as had Jimmy Carter, who, in their view, was a "born-again" buffoon. And going back further still, the Democratic presidents of their day, LBJ and JFK, had been "sellouts" they despised, especially for opposing such heroes as Ho Chi Minh in Vietnam and Fidel Castro in Cuba.

It was Barack Obama alone; he was nearer them and their dreams.

Progressives for Obama

Most notable among these radicals were those who reunited in a group called Progressives for Obama. Whereas Bill Ayers was thrust into the national spotlight by conservative commentators like Sean Hannity, Progressives for Obama flew under the radar, largely unnoticed even by the Right.

Spearheading Progressives for Obama was the man who had spearheaded SDS: Tom Hayden. Hayden was one of the four "initiators" of Progressives for Obama, along with author Barbara Ehrenreich, activist Bill Fletcher Jr., and actor Danny Glover.[1] Hayden's lead role was appropriate, since the list of Progressives for Obama read like a Who's Who of the 1960s SDS crowd. Among the group's ninety-four formal "signers" were Mark Rudd, Carl Davidson, Thorne Dreyer, Richard Flacks, John McAuliff, and Jay Schaffner—all names that appear throughout the index of the transcripts from Congress's December 1969 investigation of SDS—plus former SDS education secretary Bob Pardun and Paul Buhle, a professor who had recently sought to revive SDS.[2] Another signer was former SDS president Todd Gitlin, who now was a prominent professor at Columbia University. Still other SDSers, some of whom became Weathermen, were not formal signers for Progressives for Obama but signed online petitions backing Obama's candidacy, including Howard Machtinger, Jeff Jones, and Steve Tappis.[3]

Progressives for Obama also included high-profile names such as Daniel Ellsberg, best known for publishing the *Pentagon Papers,* and Tom Hayden's former wife, Jane Fonda. The endorsement of Fonda, Vietcong cover girl, prompted *Los Angeles Times* blogger Andrew Malcolm to opine, "There goes his [Obama's] crossover vote."[4]

That crossover vote would be more crucial than ever in the 2008 election. Which way would the independent/moderate voter lean? That was the million-dollar question the morning of November 4, 2008. The verdict arrived, and as it turned out, Obama had nothing to worry about: this huge group of swing voters went for Obama over John McCain by eight points, 52 to 44 percent, and thereby decided the election (since McCain got 90 percent of the Republican vote and Obama got 89 percent of Democrats).[5] These crossover voters, unaffected by any of the outrageous Obama associations and endorsements, won the day for the Democrat.

Hayden's Thinking

Among the Progressives for Obama, the testimony of leader Tom Hayden is worth considering carefully. It is telling.

After his early life establishing SDS, meeting with the Vietcong, wishing "Good fortune!" and "Victory!" to North Vietnamese colonels who killed American soldiers, and vigorously protesting the American system, Hayden went into politics, professional activism, and education. Like Mark Rudd, like Bill Ayers, like Bernardine Dohrn, like Michael Klonsky, Hayden came to view a quick "revolution" of the system as too daunting, if not impossible. He has become much more patient, instead advocating a "progressive" *evolution* of slower, measured change.

Hayden now advances the "progressive" cause within the Democratic Party establishment. Of course, he once helped blow up the Democratic Party's national convention in 1968. No matter: the party has warmly accepted him. Hayden believes that the masses, including traditional Democrats, and some independents and crossover voters, might support his causes and candidates, whom he endorses more subtly.

Hayden was ecstatic over Obama's presidential campaign. He looked to assist wherever he could, with a rush of enthusiasm not seen since his days undermining America in Vietnam. Not one to tinker around, Hayden got to work on a formal organization, as he had done with SDS. The man who drafted SDS's pivotal Port Huron statement began drafting mission statements for Progressives for Obama.

During the 2008 campaign Hayden was moved to verse over the emergence of Obama. In one piece, "Obama and the Open and Unexpected Future," written for CommonDreams.org, which describes itself as a website for "Breaking News & Views for the Progressive Community," Hayden mused:

> I didn't see him coming. When I read of the young state senator with a background in community organizing who wanted to be president, I was at least sentient enough to be interested. When I read *Dreams of My Father* [sic], I was taken aback by its depth. This young man apparently gave his first public speech, against South African apartheid, at an Occidental College rally organized by Students for Economic Democracy, the student branch of the Campaign for Economic Democracy which I chaired in 1979–82. The buds of curiosity quickened.[6]

Hayden saw in Obama a long-awaited vehicle for "economic democracy," an instrument to channel an equal distribution of wealth—"economic justice," or "redistributive change," as Obama himself once put it.[7] Hayden said that, "win or lose, the Obama movement will shape progressive politics . . . for a generation to come." He also expressed his hope that the progressive movement "might transform" Obama as well. Each could reinforce and shape the other.

Hayden wrote this in June 2008. When Obama was elected in November, the former SDS leader was beside himself with joy, surely shocked that the American electorate had finally voted for a candidate that he saw as his kind of president. Those traditional Democrats who had shaken their heads in disgust at what Hayden and friends did at their party's convention in Chicago in 1968, at what they did during the Days of Rage the next year, at what they did at Columbia during the student strike, and on and on, had at long last—in the view of Hayden and friends—done the right thing.

Hayden became particularly vocal in his praise for Obama once the election was over. During the election, the goal was to organize, raise money, but not speak too loudly, out of fear of driving away the moderates and traditional Democrat moms and pops who had worked in the mines and the mills, who owned guns, who prayed rosaries and filled churches—who might perceive the young Obama as "another Jack Kennedy." With the presidency now secured, Hayden opened up (just as Bill Ayers waited to speak out until after Obama had been elected). Joined by his former comrades at the take-no-prisoners website of Progressives for Obama, he now regularly sounds off against Obama's critics—those opposing "single payer" or the "public option" in "healthcare reform," or government "management" of General Motors—with the subtlety of a howitzer.

With the presidency won, Hayden and his allies are free to express themselves, to demonize health-insurance companies, the financial-services industry, AIG, the Big Three automakers, or whatever other capitalist "reptile" (Lenin's term) stands in the way of President Obama's desire for "reform" and mandate for "change."

The Good Professors

In switching his goal from *revolution* to *evolution,* Tom Hayden embraced not only politics but also higher education. Like many of his SDS brethren, he now teaches college students. He has been a professor at Pitzer College and, coincidentally, at Obama's Occidental College.

Education is now the common refuge of the '60s radical Left, which searches always for a new generation of disciples. Among the Progressives for Obama, no other field appears in their bios as prominently as teaching.

That is the case for Mark Rudd, who today teaches at a college in New Mexico. When he is not behind his regular lectern, Rudd travels the country speaking at universities, where the tenured radicals of the '60s welcome him with open arms to inspire their students. He specializes in teaching social activism.

Along with Ayers and Dohrn, Rudd serves on the board of Movement for a Democratic Society (MDS), which he and others envisage as a "new SDS," and which he longs to resurrect with his talks in college classrooms. The group was founded in Chicago in August 2006, and includes board members ranging from Jeff Jones to Barbara Ehrenreich. Its chair is Columbia University professor Manning Marable.[8]

Rudd remains a stalwart for Communist Vietnam and Cuba, whose systems he still touts. He also touts Barack Obama, whose election he celebrates as a major "advance" and "opening."[9] Rudd did not like any of the Cold War Democrats of his era. He despised Kennedy and Johnson. He views Obama as much closer politically.

Rudd appreciates that it was moderates and independents who made the difference in electing Obama. He noted the crucial importance of Obama's gaining those votes, and doing so by not openly conceding his far-left views:

> Obama is a very strategic thinker. He knew precisely what it would take to get elected and didn't blow it. . . . But he also knew that what he said had to basically play to the center to not be run over by the press, the Republicans, scare centrist and cross-over voters away. He made it. . . . And I agree with this strategy. . . . Any other strategy invites sure defeat. It would be stupid to do otherwise in this environment.[10]

It seems fair to say that Rudd basically stated that Obama fooled—duped— "centrist" and "cross-over" voters. As he put it, Obama could not be candid about his true intentions in "this environment." Rudd is exactly right.

That environment is an America whose citizens, in poll after poll, year after year, have described themselves as "conservative" over "liberal" by a margin of roughly two to one, by approximately 40 percent to 20 percent. Remarkably, those numbers were unchanged even on November 4, 2008, when Obama— the antithesis of a conservative—easily won the presidential election. They held through the start of Obama's presidency and through the peak of his popularity. For instance, a major Gallup poll conducted from January to May 2009, at the height of "Obama mania," found more self-described conservatives than liberals by a margin of 40 percent to 21 percent.[11]

In other words, as Rudd and Hayden and friends recognize, the American political "environment" is a conservative country, not a liberal or socialist or far-left one. Thus, a political candidate as far to the left as Barack Obama, not to mention his advocates, can succeed only by pushing his agenda guardedly. Obama ran for president as a centrist, not as *National Journal*'s most liberal member of the Senate.[12] It worked. As Rudd put it, Obama "didn't blow it."

Now, with Obama having secured victory, Rudd can, like Hayden, be less circumspect in how he "organizes." He states: "Here's my mantra: 'Let's put this country on our shoulders and get to work.'"[13]

In 2008 Mark Rudd, Tom Hayden, and many of their old comrades came back from the '60s dead, from their past sojourns to Hanoi and Havana, from their work for and with Che, Fidel, the Vietcong, and even the KGB, to do their part for Obama in 2008. They must have been stunned by the result: victory.

Other SDSers

Another SDSer to reemerge from the shadows in connection to Obama was Michael Klonsky. Klonsky, recall, was the one whom Mark Rudd described as a Stalinist, too far to the Left even for Rudd and company.

Klonsky had been raised a radical. In the 1960s he walked in lockstep with his far-left parents. Eventually, Klonsky, like Mao Tse-tung, bolted from the USSR and Stalin, but not from Communism. Klonsky became head of the New Communist Movement in the United States. He found CPUSA too reactionary for his tastes. The former SDS national secretary followed the Maoist path all the way to Red China, where he became one of the first Western visitors. In 1977 the Chinese Communist leadership hailed the young pioneer as representative of the "aspirations of the proletariat and working people."[14]

Klonsky, however, was reportedly disappointed with the booming free-market reforms pursued in the 1980s by Mao's milder successor, Deng Xiaoping, prompting a permanent split with his Chinese friends.[15] He went home to get a Ph.D. in education (University of South Florida) and began looking to the American classroom as the best platform for Marxist dogma. He landed in Chicago—on the same faculty as Bill Ayers.

Like Ayers, Klonsky became a professor in the University of Illinois at Chicago's College of Education. Klonsky and Ayers have been described as joint "pioneers in small school development." These "small school" projects were funded to the tune of almost $2 million in grants from the Chicago Annenberg Challenge, where Barack Obama was chairman of the board, and from the Joyce Foundation and Woods Fund, where Obama also served on the boards.[16]

Klonsky and Ayers have been especially successful in packaging their ideas as furthering "social justice," a handy cliché they use as a substitute for their socialism, even authoring books on the subject—published, naturally, through Columbia Teachers College.[17] The language has worked brilliantly in enlisting gullible left-leaning Christians, especially at liberal Catholic and Protestant colleges.[18]

Klonsky and Ayers have coauthored articles on education, including in sources like *Phi Delta Kappan,* a professional journal of education. In one of them, the two SDSers raved about Arne Duncan, longtime head of Chicago public schools, whom the pair described as "the brightest and most dedicated schools leader Chicago has had in memory."[1] Today, Arne Duncan is President Obama's secretary of education.

As for Klonsky's work with and for Barack Obama, not only did Obama approve multimillion-grants to fund Klonsky's educational work in Chicago, especially his "social justice" educational work, but he even hosted a "social justice" blog for Klonsky at the official Obama '08 campaign website.[20]

Klonsky, too, was surely astounded that the American public in 2008 finally agreed with him on a presidential candidate. Forty years earlier, in 1968, he had said that the SDS motto was to "Vote in the Streets" rather than at the ballot box.

Significantly, Klonsky, Rudd, Ayers, Dohrn, Hayden and the other '60s radicals have not suddenly supported the Democratic Party's presidential nominee because they have moved to the center. They retain basically the same core political philosophy. "My own support for Obama is not a reflection of a radically changed attitude toward the Democratic Party," Klonsky told author Daniel J. Flynn.[21] What has changed is not their ideology but their tactics.

Klonsky remains on the far left. This time, in 2008, the Democratic Party moved toward him. He found a kindred soul in the party's nominee. He saw the Obama campaign as a "rallying point" for activists old and young alike.[22]

Also there for Obama was Carl Davidson, another SDS stalwart—a national officer from the class of 1968—another longtime Castro enthusiast, and another who forty years earlier ecstatically watched the Democratic Party descend into national disgrace in Chicago. Now, in 2008, Davidson found a Chicagoan running on the Democratic ticket whom he, too, could at long last promote for president. He had helped organize the first public rally where Obama denounced the Iraq war, and now he became webmaster for Progressives for Obama.[23]

Today, with Obama as president, Davidson blasts "the rightwing blogo-sphere" for its attempts to "cripple and take down Obama" and "the progres-sive left" through "more and more sham 'connections,' such as with me"—and with Van Jones. Van Jones was the avowed communist that President Obama had named as his so-called green-jobs czar, until conservatives like Glenn Beck exposed Jones's political extremism. (For this, Beck was smeared by the Left.) After pooh-poohing these "sham 'connections' to Obama," Davidson instructed readers to "lend a hand" against the political Right by clicking the PayPal button at Progressives for Obama, which he conveniently made available via a hyper-link.[24]

Another of the born-again SDS faithful stumping for Obama was Jeff Jones. Jones, who was Bernardine Dohrn's beau during the days of the four-finger fork salute in Flint, was one of the four Weathermen who signed the violent Marxist manifesto *Prairie Fire,* along with Ayers, Dohrn, and Celia Sojourn. After a life as a fugitive, taking credit for various bombings aimed at "pigs,"[25] he had settled down for a life as a reporter and an environmental activist. Prior to Obama's meteoric rise, his name occasionally came up in connection with his Weather Underground days, as when his son published a memoir of their life on the run.[26] Like Ayers, Jones, as recently as 2004, was quoted saying that he did not regret his past: "To this day, we still, lots of us, including me, still think it was the right thing to do."[27]

Jones was not a signer of Progressives for Obama; no doubt, the group was smart enough to exclude the *Prairie Fire* authors from among its signers. Nonethe-less, Jones was there for Obama—playing an especially active role after Obama entered the White House.

In September 2009 the *New York Post* reported that Jones's consulting firm, the Apollo Alliance—Jones serves as director of the New York affiliate and a consultant to the national organization—helped write President Obama's budget-bursting $800 billion "stimulus" bill passed by Congress shortly into the Obama presidency.[28] The *Post* described the Apollo Alliance as "a coalition of left-wing interest groups unified around the green-jobs concept." Van Jones, the green-jobs czar himself, had helped build the alliance—which received taxpayer funding, according to the *Post.* As the *New York Post* reported—and the Apollo Alliance trumpeted on its own website—Senate Majority Leader Harry Reid personally credited Apollo with helping to write the stimulus bill and getting it passed.[29]

If this is accurate, it is an astonishing behind-the-scenes policy function played by one of the four central figures in the Weather Underground. For Jones, it would constitute a powerful role in crafting what to that point was the single biggest spending binge in the history of the United States—one that exploded

President George W. Bush's record $400 billion budget deficit to an unsustainable $1.2 trillion.[30]

Thus, it appears that a former domestic terrorist who was intimately involved with Dohrn and Ayers contributed to the first major policy development of the Obama presidency, and certainly one of the most costly. It shows that Obama's radical "associations" do seem to matter.

"Education Is the Motor-Force of Revolution"

Though so many SDSers have entered the ivory tower, they have not given up politics for education. Tom Hayden keeps organizing his comrades; Jeff Jones lobbies for green jobs; Carl Davidson puts together antiwar rallies; Mark Rudd calls for his fellow radicals to "put this country on our shoulders and get to work"; and Bill Ayers helps nurture the political careers of promising candidates like Barack Obama.

Such political activism, again, undermines the claim that Obama's endorsement of Ayers's educational work was no big deal. In fact, Ayers's educational work is a handmaiden to his political work.

That is true for all the comrades. They did not enter education to teach nonpolitical subjects like math. They went into education to inculcate the nation's youth into their worldview. They are John Dewey's disciples to an extreme degree.

For many of them, including Ayers, there is little to no separation between their educational work and the Marxism they have long espoused. Consider the syllabus for a graduate course Ayers teaches at the University of Illinois at Chicago. The course, CIE 576, is titled "Conceptions of Teaching and Schooling." The good professor's syllabus begins with a reference to the Weather Underground's *Prairie Fire*. "A single spark can start a prairie fire—an ancient saying."[31]

Ayers has taken this vision global, to the kind of Marxist dictators who welcome his message. This is evident in his own account of his work for Venezuela's Miranda International Center. Ayers has sat on the board of this Venezuelan government think tank, which is a direct extension of Marxist leader Hugo Chavez and is, in the words of *Investor's Business Daily*, "focused on bringing Cuba-style education to Venezuelan school children."[32] Ayers's work in support of what he has praised as Chavez's "profound educational reforms" led him to make at least four pilgrimages to Venezuela during the time that he and Obama served together on the Woods Fund and Annenberg Challenge.[33]

During one of those trips, in November 2006, Ayers addressed the World Education Forum in Caracas. During the speech he spoke of how Chavez and the Venezuelans "continue to overcome the failings of capitalist education." He concluded his address with words of solidarity for Chavez and Venezuela's Marxist regime:

Viva Presidente Chavez!
Viva La Revolucion Bolivariana!
Hasta La Victoria Siempre![34]

Here Ayers showed that his ardor for revolution remains strong. In this case it is the "Bolivarian Revolution," the name that Hugo Chavez himself has given to his destructive Marxist agenda. Ayers's final line, "Hasta La Victoria Siempre!" (Forever, until victory), paid homage to Che Guevara, who famously used the line in his last letter to Fidel Castro.[35] Che, the animating spirit behind Ayers's *Prairie Fire,* remains a strong influence on Ayers decades later.

The Bill Ayers–Hugo Chavez connection is about policy, politics, communism, and education, all of which, in Ayers's universe, are inextricably related. As Ayers put it in his World Education Forum speech: "Education is the motor-force of revolution."

Ayers and Chavez also share a strong affection for Barack Obama. In an extraordinary September 2009 statement at the United Nations, Chavez sniffed and said with a grin: "It doesn't smell of sulfur here anymore." This was a swipe at former president George W. Bush, whom Chavez had denounced as "the devil" in UN remarks in 2006. There was freshness in the air this time, said Chavez. Now, the dictator said, "It smells of something else. It smells of hope."[36]

There is even a personal component to the Ayers-Chavez connection. Chesa Boudin is the adopted son of Ayers and Dohrn, whom the couple raised once the boy's biological parents, Weather Underground radicals David Gilbert and Kathy Boudin, were jailed for the Brinks murder in 1981. Chesa Boudin now describes himself as a "foreign policy adviser to President Hugo Chavez."[37] He has picked up the mantle of his adoptive parents and his biological parents.

Kathy Boudin herself has not put down that mantle. After she was sent to prison for her work in the Brinks murders, Boudin studied education, publishing articles in journals like the *Harvard Educational Review.* Her liberal friends fought for her parole. When it was delayed, they blamed not her past affinity for evil men like Mao and Che but, curiously, the current "evil" they perceived in the White House: George W. Bush.[38] Despite Bush's presence in the world, Boudin was paroled in 2003.

What path did she take once she was let out of prison? Higher education, of course. Having earned her doctorate in education from Columbia Teachers College, she has become adjunct assistant professor at the Columbia University School of Social Work. As her bio states at the university's website, Boudin's work focuses on "Mother-child relationships," "criminal justice," "restorative justice," "health care," and "working within communities with limited resources to solve social problems."[39]

Education Was the Motor-Force for Obama's Election

By choosing education, the students of the '60s chose smart. They knew where to instill the influence they needed to stoke the embers of political change.

Those embers caught fire on November 4, 2008. Aside from moderates who went for Obama, it was America's youth, particularly the college crowd, who made Obama president. According to exit polls, those aged eighteen to twenty-nine, who made up nearly one in five voters—or about twenty-five million ballots—went for Obama by more than two to one: 66 to 32 percent.[40]

This was an enormous cache of ballots, far surpassing Obama's overall popular advantage. Even wider was the margin in a related category: first-time voters. They went for Obama by 69 to 30 percent. A third related category, single (unmarried) voters, who accounted for one in three voters, went for Obama by 65 to 33 percent.

Together, these categories capture the youth vote

Many of these people were instructed by their college professors to vote for Obama, or were at least influenced by the socialistic, humanistic milieu of the modern secular-left campus. To many of the "progressive" ideologues who teach in college, Obama represented what they had preached for decades. They celebrated his message of "hope" and "change" to their young and often impressionable students.

The Chicago Coronation

Imagine the joy the comrades must have felt as they watched their TV screens announce Barack Obama as the nation's president-elect late in the evening of November 4, 2008. Imagine the thoughts of those on-site in Chicago's Grant Park, where a victorious Barack Obama greeted legions of his devoted and delirious followers.

The symbolism was too extraordinary for words—a powerful reminder that Cold War battles were still very much with us. Obama ascended the platform after a gracious John McCain, a Vietnam veteran whom the comrades had once grouped into a category of "fascist pigs," conceded the election. The revolutionaries once proudly wore rings hammered out of the downed aircraft of McCain's imprisoned band of brothers, who were suffering unspeakable hell in places like the Hanoi Hilton. McCain's own aircraft had been shot down; one of the radicals may well have worn debris from his plane. The defeated Republican represented what they had always fought against.

Obama, meanwhile, was the political godchild of those shadowy Marxists who had despised the likes of McCain and fought to defeat the forces of American "imperialism." Now the comrades and thousands of other Obama devotees assembled on hallowed ground for the radicals: where the SDSers and the Weathermen some forty years earlier had rallied for the Democratic convention blow-up and the Days of Rage. It was a scene almost beyond belief.[41]

Under Democrats and Republicans alike, America's comrades had failed to defeat the forces responsible for fighting the Communists, from Ho Chi Minh City to Peking to Pyongyang to Prague to Havana to Managua to Moscow. Now, their chosen vehicle—Barack Obama—had defeated a representative of those anti-Communist forces, John McCain. They had finally won—and with the legitimate support of Americans voters. Obama was the first Democratic presidential candidate to secure more than 50 percent of the popular vote since Jimmy Carter in 1976 (and Carter barely cleared 50 percent).

Americans had finally chosen *their* guy. America's comrades had lost the Cold War, but they won this time.

Dr. Quentin Young was one of the old comrades around to enjoy the victory. At eighty-five years old, he was still active as head of a group of physicians urging socialized medicine. Young stepped forward to hail the "remarkable and historic victory of Barack Obama and the mandate for change." He was quoted at length by the late Herb Aptheker's surviving *Political Affairs* magazine, which wasted no time running articles on Young and his organization's call upon President-elect Obama "to establish a single, publicly financed [health care] system." Young noted that Obama, as a state senator in Illinois, had supported a "single-payer universal healthcare system," and that Obama had remarked. "First we have to take back the White House, we have to take back the Senate, we have to take back the House." Now, said Young, "Tuesday's election has made all of these conditions happen." Obama just needed to "do the right thing."[42]

Dr. Young was basking in the possibilities. He had helped launch this young man's political career thirteen years earlier in the living room of Bill Ayers and Bernardine Dohrn. Back then, the focus was on a mere seat in the Illinois State Senate. Now, behold, the young man was president of the United States.

America had come a long way in the forty years since Young had testified before Congress about the radical uprising at the 1968 Democratic National Convention. Now, in 2008, thanks to the election of Chicago's Obama, Young felt that socialism—certainly the socialization of America's health-care system—was at his fingertips. Young's eyes must have moistened as he observed the massive Obama victory rally in his own city. Americans had finally voted Quentin Young's way.

In fact, Americans had voted CPUSA's way: the party could not contain its excitement over Obama's victory. The election of Barack Obama was the chance for a wish list to come true—a potential host of nationalizations, from the auto industry to financial services to health care, beginning with more modest steps like establishing the "public option" in health-care reform, plus massive government "stimulus" packages, more public-sector unionization and control, more redistribution of wealth, more collectivization. "All these—and many other things—are within our reach now!" celebrated Sam Webb in his keynote speech for the New York City banquet of *People's Weekly World,* the official newspaper of CPUSA, which reprinted the speech under the headline "A New Era Begins." With the election of Obama, said Webb, "the impossible" had become "possible."

Speaking for his comrades at CPUSA, Webb thrilled that under President Obama, "We can dream again."[43]

"Hapless Sheep"?

While CPUSA rejoiced in Obama's election, some former Soviet Communists, oddly enough, feared that America would experience a monumental shift to the left under the new president. No less than *Pravda,* the former Bolshevik mouthpiece, ran an article lamenting the death of American capitalism under President Obama. "It must be said," regretted *Pravda's* Stanislav Mishin, "that like the breaking of a great dam, the American descent into Marxism is happening with breathtaking speed, against the backdrop of a passive, hapless sheep." That "final collapse," said the pages of the chief party organ of the former USSR, "has come with the election of Barack Obama."[44]

A more measured assessment came from a surprising source: Manning Marable, the socialist professor from Columbia University who chairs Mark Rudd's new MDS, the adult successor organization to SDS. In December 2008 Marable wrote an astute analysis of the "four-legged stool" that elected Obama as president. Writing in the *Socialist Review,* Marable conceded that "a lot of the people working with him [Obama] are, indeed, socialists with backgrounds in the

Communist Party or as independent Marxists." Yet, he cautioned fellow leftists, "Obama is not a Marxist. . . . He is a progressive liberal." Marable said Obama was not even a socialist, but rather a Keynesian.[45]

Many Americans, both moderates and conservatives, have been disturbed by the leftward course President Obama has set for America in the early years of his presidency. But that leftward shift, no matter how alarming to a broad sector of Americans—and to the former Soviet Union—is, indisputably, less radical than the violent "revolution" that the extremist Left was angling for some forty years ago. The fact that the old radicals have accepted Obama's "progressive" course shows that these comrades have learned the virtue of patience and the necessity of incrementalism—or "creeping socialism," as Ronald Reagan called it.

The American far Left seems to have taken to heart the observation attributed to the storied socialist Norman Thomas, who allegedly maintained that Americans would never "knowingly adopt" socialism, but "under the name of liberalism" would adopt every bit of the socialist program until the nation was one day socialist. Americans would arrive at that point "without ever knowing how it happened."[46]

A Century of Dupery

The radical Left may have adopted a new, incrementalist approach, but that strategy does not diminish the critical role of the dupe. Quite the contrary: the extreme Left can never succeed in America, even incrementally, without nonextremists helping to spread and implement its far-left goals. Most liberals, traditional Democrats, and moderates and independents do not support the end goal of the communist or even socialist Left. But they can be prodded and persuaded to accept—sometimes unwittingly—many or most of the pivotal steps along the way to the socialist program.

The trillion-dollar question with President Barack Obama is what he personally believes, where he really stands, and how much he is leading, or being led. Could he be manipulated by a narrow hard-left constituency that hopes to move him in a certain, centralized direction? We know his past associations. We know his voting record, which was further to the left than that of anyone else in the U.S. Senate.

The vexing uncertainty for Americans is that if Obama is as far left as a group like Progressives for Obama, he cannot say so, just as those progressives could not advertise their true objectives during the 2008 election, because doing so would have been Obama's political undoing. Sadly, the American press corps simply did not care to ascertain the crucial answers during the 2008 campaign, and to this day hasn't shown interest in doing so. As we have seen, on the rare occasions when mainstream media outlets did bring up Obama's radical associations, it was usually to mock or attack the so-called McCarthyite fanatics who had the nerve to ask the uncomfortable questions.

In the end, the actions of such liberals have the effect—again unwittingly—of continuing to cover for the goals of the extreme Left. Yet again, the soft Left is helping to conceal the hard Left, whether it realizes it or not. This is a familiar pattern, one we have witnessed in this country for close to a century. Whatever the reason for this protection—this time it is to shield Barack Obama's presidency—the result is the same: the Communists toiling behind the scenes never need to apologize, and often escape the exposure they merit.

It is always the anti-Communists whom the liberals despise. The effect is that the bad guys on the Communist Left—who, again, were as bad to liberals as to conservatives—repeatedly get a pass, even long after they have departed this world. Even in death, many of them remain protected, their dirty work covered up—by a liberal press, by a liberal academia, by a liberal Hollywood, or by some other liberal group that refuses to acknowledge the obvious lessons of Cold War history.

The most mordant irony for the liberals who lend this cover is that while they laugh at the anti-Communists, they seem to have no idea that the loudest howls have always emanated from the Communists who take them as dupes: gullible fools to be used to advance the Communist cause. It is a time-honored tradition, and many genuine liberals have failed liberalism by filling the role of dupe again and again. It is always important to know who your friends are and who they are not.

If liberals take just one message from this book, I hope it will be this: *the Communists were never your friends*. Until that lesson is learned, many well-intentioned liberals will continue to be used. And the long underappreciated role of the dupe will remain much more than a mere sideshow in history.

Postscript

BOGART AT THE WORKERS SCHOOL?

his book was born as a response to the massive volume of documents
recently declassified from archives in Moscow, throughout the former
Communist bloc countries, and within the United States. To take only
one notable example from among the treasure trove of information newly available to researchers, the Library of Congress's files from the Comintern Archives
on CPUSA proved an essential source for this project. These archives—which
represent only a portion of the full collection in Moscow—contain hundreds of
reels of microfiche. Each reel I consulted took me a full day to read through. That
is to say nothing of the lengthier rabbit trails of investigation to which these files
led. Unexpected findings within the Library of Congress files took me to other
archives, from FBI files to archives housed at New York University's Tamiment
Library and beyond.

One such surprise came as I was reviewing Reel 273, Delo 3512 of the Comintern Archives on CPUSA. While reviewing this material on microfiche, I came
across an eye-opening series of 1934 documents apparently missed or dismissed by
others. I, too, initially chose to bypass these documents, and revisited them only
later as one particular name on one particular page haunted me: "Bogart."

This series of documents related to CPUSA's National Training School, more
commonly known as the Workers School. These schools operated in a few large
cities, such as Chicago—where the Communist-turned-conservative-intellectual
Frank Meyer had directed a Workers School from 1938 to 1941—and New York
City.[1] The New York operation was the most active.

As the lead sentence of the New York school's mission statement explained, the CPUSA Central Committee ran the Workers School to ensure that "the Party carry on its work for the winning of the majority of the American working class, for the overthrow of capitalism and the establishment of the Proletarian Dictatorship in the U.S.A." The school endeavored to become "a permanent institution for training cadres for our Party."

Clearly, this was no small thing. The Workers School's letterhead, which listed the address as 35 East Twelfth Street—CPUSA's headquarters—boasted the very top names in the party: William Z. Foster, Max Bedacht, and Abe Markoff, among others. Earl Browder was invited to speak at the school. (See page 483.)

The curriculum underscored the seriousness of the school's training. It required an intense 430 hours of preparation and featured courses ranging from "Study of the *Communist Manifesto*" to "Soviet Economy" to "War and Revolution" to "Strategy and Tactics." One attendee, who testified before Congress in July 1953, said that at the Workers School, which he described as notably secretive, he was "trained to become a professional revolutionist."[2]

Reel 273, Delo 3512 in the Comintern Archives includes materials on the New York Workers School session that ran from January 9 to March 15, 1934. The summary report for the ten-week session stated that it was attended by thirty-six students, "90% of [whom] were native born, five of which were women and seven Negro comrades." The students hailed from districts all over the country, but the vast majority lived in New York.

Among those New Yorkers was someone called "Bogart."

Even in these internal documents, which were not to be published or distributed, the Workers School carefully concealed the identity of those who wanted to be concealed, or those deemed wise to conceal. Only about one-third of the names were given in full. Bogart's full name was concealed.

The name appeared twice in the documents: on the district page and on an evaluation page. On the district page it appeared as "Bogart (E) Westinghouse (college) Sec. Org." (See page 484.)

Importantly, the "(E)" is not an initial for a first name. This we know because these parenthetical letters do not match the first names of the students when the full names appear in the evaluation section.

The words "Westinghouse (college)" come in the space where each comrade's occupation is shown. (Other attendees included a metal worker, a miner, and a waitress.) This listing, then, implies that Bogart worked in some capacity at the Westinghouse company and also attended college. It is possible that "college" was a general category for Workers School students who were in and out of college.

"Without revolutionary theory
there can be no revolutionary
practice."   LENIN.

WORKERS SCHOOL
35 EAST 12th STREET
NEW YORK CITY
ALgonquin 4-1199

A. MARKOFF, Director

"Training for th
Class S

EXECUTIVE
COMMITTEE
I. Amter
M. Bedacht
Wm. Z. Foster
S. Don
A. Markoff
M. James
G. Siskind
A. Trachtenberg

COURSES IN
Communist Theory
Trade Unionism
Political Economy
History
Marxism
Leninism
Public Speaking
Revolutionary Jour
English
Russian
Etc.

February 8, 1934

Earl Browder.

Dear Comrade Browder:

This is to confirm the arrangement made this morning with your
secretary, Comrade Maul, for you to speak for the benefit of
the National Training School, Friday, March 9th, at 8:30 P.M.,
at the Irving Plaza.

We would appreciate it if you would write us a note acknowledging
this engagement, so that we can go ahead with the printing and
advertising.

In a day or two we will communicate with you about the subject.
In the meantime, if you have any preference or any suggestions
as to what you want to speak on, please let us know.

Yours with comradely greetings,

Judith Knight

Judith Knight
Secretary

JK

CPUSA's Workers School: The New York Workers School, which "Bogart" attended, was located
at CPUSA headquarters. Top CPUSA officials served on the school's executive committee,
and the party's general secretary, Earl Browder, spoke at the Workers School.

```
                STUDENTS OF THE NATIONAL TRAINING SCHOOL
                        January to March 1934

District 2 - Lewis (B)      marine worker    Port Org.
             Little (F)      chauffeur        ILD Org.
             Miller (S)      factory worker   YCL Sec. Org.

District 3 - Freed (E)       textile worker
             *Crowell (W)    worked in factory   Sec. Org.
                             (college graduate)

District 4 - Strong (W)      metal worker        Sec. Org.

District 5 - *McGoran (E)    worker           T.U. Org.
             *Brunt (K)      miner            Sec. Org.
             *Bogart (E)     Westinghouse (college) Sec. Org.
             Whitney (S)     miner's wife     Women's Auxiliary Org.

District 6 - Evans (R)       Member D.C.      T.U. Org.
             *Cory (O)          "             Unemployed Org.
             Duke (D)        worker           Unemployed

District 7 - Carpenter (S)   auto mech.          D. C.
             Williams (B)    "   working in factory - T.U.
             Cocek (Joe)     "       "       "    "    YCL Org.

District 8 - Fulton (M)      transport. Unemployed - Sec. Org.
             Raynolds (Ch)   waitress         YCL - Sec. Org.

District 9 - Steckes (A)     longshoreman        T. U.

District 14 *Reeder (Ch)     unemployed       Unemployed Org.

District 15 *Nelson (C)      college          Section Org.

District 16  Patterson (M)   laborer             ---

District 17 *Philips (W)     college          Section Org.
             Landry (S)      marine           Distr. Org. Sec.
             Thornton (M)    foundry          Negro Org.
             *Rolls (T)      lineman          Unemployed Org.
             *Hill (M)       sharecropper     YCL Org.

District 18  Masen (T)       farmhand (college)   Org.

St. Louis   *Stock (S)       draftsman (college) Org.
             Burt (RB)       office worker       S. O.

Florida      Smith (B)       farmer              O.
             Tasher (N)      farm laborer
             Randolph (R)    clerk               YCL.
```

Bogart: Among the students who attended the winter 1934 session of the New York Workers School was a "Bogart," listed under District 5.

In fact, the intensity of the Workers School surely would have forced a currently enrolled college student to withdraw from the winter/spring semester.

Finally, the abbreviation "Sec. Org." means a section organizer for CPUSA.

The only additional information on Bogart in these documents—which exist in microfiche at the Library of Congress's Comintern Archives and in original hard copy at Tamiment Library in New York (both of which I've examined)—is the evaluation section, titled "Characteristics of comrades N.T.S." There, Bogart is described as "persistent," "hard working," and adhering to the "Party line."

That is all the Workers School records offer on this student.

This, of course, begs the question: who was "Bogart"?

Other Bogarts

First let's consider the evidence that could perhaps disqualify Humphrey Bogart as the Bogart at the Workers School.

I searched the New York City residence directory for 1933–34, as well as the New York City telephone directory for that same period. The residence directory is much longer, since many or even most residents did not have a telephone. "Bogart" was a fairly common name among New York City residents; the smaller phone directory lists thirty Bogarts, and the residence directory lists nearly a hundred. That is a lot of Bogarts, throwing wide open (it would seem) the possibilities for the Bogart at the Workers School.

This is the best evidence against pinpointing Humphrey Bogart as the prime suspect. Further, I found a "J. Bogart" who appeared in the Communist *Daily Worker* the same year (1934) as the Bogart at the Communist Workers School, and who was, according to that *Daily Worker* listing, from New York City. On page 6 of the November 3, 1934, edition of the *Daily Worker*, J. Bogart is listed as a financial contributor to the Communist newspaper (making a very small donation, as in cents, not dollars). This Bogart also seems to be identified as a Communist Party member.[3] Specifically, the person is shown as a member of "District 2 (New York City)," which is described as one of twenty-six districts from around the country.[4]

The 1933–34 New York City residence directory lists six Bogarts with the first initial "J": a Jacob Bogart, a Jennie, three Johns, and a Joseph. The shorter New York City telephone directory for that period lists only one "J." Bogart: John Bogart, a lawyer who lived at 1450 Broadway.

Who was this John Bogart? It might be the same John Bogart whose obituary ran in the *New York Times* on October 12, 1992. That Bogart, who lived in Manhat-

tan until his final days, was, as the *Times* described him, a "longtime labor relations executive at New York City newspapers," including at the *Times*. The obituary noted that he "began his career in 1934 at *The New York Herald Tribune,* where
he was a reporter and editor and later promoted into management."[5] In other
words, John Bogart began his career as a young reporter (he turned twenty-two
in 1934) the same year that "J. Bogart" enrolled in the New York Workers School.

More information based on media archives reveals the full name of this John
Bogart to be John Abendroth Bogart. In April 1937 John Abendroth Bogart married Marjorie Goodell.[6] After Marjorie's death in 1974, he married again, in
October 1976.[7] His new wife, Jacqueline Branaman, a widow, was a 1947 graduate of Barnard, sister college to Columbia University, and in 1950–51 she served
in Moscow as the secretary to the U.S. ambassador. She died in January 2008.[8]

This John Bogart might, by a reasonable guess, be the same "J. Bogart" in the
Daily Worker from November 3, 1934, although we cannot say for certain based on
the information available.

How About Humphrey Bogart?

All of that is, to some degree, disconfirming evidence against claims that the Bogart at the Workers School was Humphrey Bogart.

But can a case be made that the future Hollywood icon was the Bogart at
the Workers School? Where was Humphrey Bogart in this period, and what was
he doing?

We know for certain that Bogart lived in New York City in early 1934, the
time of the Workers School session. This is clear from many biographical accounts
of Bogart's life, as well as from rare eyewitnesses who remain among the living.[9]
It turns out that the actor was struggling terribly at this point in his life, so much
so that he and his wife, Mary, had moved in with his father, Dr. Belmont Bogart,
who lived at 25 Prospect Place.

Humphrey Bogart had actually made ten films before 1934: four in 1930,
three in 1931, and three in 1932. But none was significant, and certainly none
was of the caliber (or achieved the success) of the movies he made later. Moreover, he had made *no* movies in 1933, would make only one in 1934, and none
again in 1935.[10] Similarly, he had performed in four plays between October 1932
and May 1933 but made none during the period when the Workers School was
in session.[11] His first major success, the film *The Petrified Forest,* would not be
released until 1936.[12]

In short, the January–March 1934 period was a down time for Bogart. His prospects seemed dim. As biographer Gerald Duchovnay described these days, "Hard times set in, and Bogart was reduced to playing chess, a favorite hobby he learned from his father, for up to a dollar a game to help support himself and his wife." Bogart was, wrote Duchovnay, "bringing home barely enough money to eat."[13]

Worse, his talented, respected father collapsed both physically and financially during this time. In 1934—when the Workers School was in session—Dr. Bogart separated from his wife and racked up huge debts. Later that year the well-regarded physician endured a miserable death in New York's Hospital for the Ruptured and Crippled, having accumulating some $10,000 in debt—an enormous sum during the Great Depression, all of which his penniless son vowed to pay back.[14] It seemed that America and its free-enterprise system had horribly failed Bogart's father.

Overall, the Great Depression was hitting Bogart harder than most Americans. Had he turned to Communism in this period, few would blame him. If Humphrey Bogart had ever considered the philosophy of Marxism-Leninism, it seems that 1934 would have been ideal.

Miserable about his life, and his father's life, Bogart continued to fight with his overbearing but highly accomplished mother, Maud. He always had a tense relationship with his mother, as had his father. Dr. Bogart's battles with his wife wore on the son. This, too, only added to Bogart's turmoil. He drank heavily, and looked for answers

Further adding to his woes, Bogart was battling for his own marriage—his second, to fellow actress Mary Philips, whom he had married in April 1928.

Philips herself adds to the potential intrigue at the Workers School.

Listed directly above "Bogart" in the evaluation section of the Workers School for January–March 1934 is no less than a "Phillips." On the district page the name is spelled "Philips," meaning there is a misspelling in one of the two spots (which is not uncommon with the name "Philips"/"Phillips"). Like "Bogart," Philips is described as "college," as a "Section Organizer," and as from a New York district. The evaluation section characterizes Philips as "sentimental," but as holding the potential to "make a rapid advance toward becoming an effective Party worker." (See page 488.)

Could this Philips be Humphrey Bogart's wife? Mary had retained her maiden name, personally and professionally. Also, it appears that she was available to attend the Workers School at that time: though she had roles in three plays in New York between December 5, 1933, and June 1934,[15] none of the plays ran in that ten-week window when the Workers School was in session.

```
√ Smith:                                                        √2

      √ Petty-bourgeois ideology.  Non-Party approach to many
      √ problems.   rejected criticism and reluctant to offer
        self-criticism.  Should not be given any responsible
        work.


  / Phillips:

        Individualistic and sentimental approach to problems,
      / which is explained by desire to do a great deal of
        literary work.  Made a good effort to acquire political
        knowledge and orientate on taks of the Party.  When given
        opportunity to work in industrial center together with
        other Party members will make a rapid advance toward
        becoming an effective Party worker.

  √ Bogart:

        Slow and lack of critical approach towards the solution
        of problems and in orientating in given situation,
      √ but when once the problem is solved and line laid down,
        will be persistent in carrying the same out.  Hard working-
        good Party line.


  / Thornton:

        Made marked advance in theoretical development - especially
        taking into consideration lack of previous training.
        A proletarian approach towards Party tasks.  With proper
        guidance for a short period, xxxx will make very effective
        worker in his District.


  | Strong:

      / Did not put in sufficient effort in study - resistance
        to self-criticism.  Tendencies towards individualism -
        due to remnants to petty-bourgeois idology, which he will
        have to overcome in his work in the Party.


  / Williams:

        Lack of previous training and Party experience made it
```

Bogart and Philips: Listed directly above "Bogart" in the Workers School's evaluation section is a "Phillips"—spelled "Philips" on the district page.

I was unable to learn anything more about Mary Philips, including her politics. She and Bogart divorced in 1937. She married again to another actor, and, to my knowledge, never had children. She died in April 1975.

The "College" and "Westinghouse" Questions

From all of that evidence, one might reasonably speculate that the Bogart at the Workers School was Humphrey Bogart. But there remain sticky items that make confirmation elusive, if not unlikely.

Among them is the note on "college," though, again, this designation might have been a broader category not necessarily implying current enrollment in a college. Humphrey Bogart never earned a college degree, but college certainly dominated his and his family's thoughts. Bogart had attended a prestigious prep school: the esteemed Philips Academy in Andover, Massachusetts. College was the expected next step. His parents (who were well educated) wanted him to attend Yale. Nonetheless, again, he never earned a college degree, nor, to my knowledge, attended college on a consistent basis.[16]

Likewise unclear is the "Westinghouse" reference listed next to Bogart's name at the Workers School. I was unable to link the Westinghouse reference to any Bogart from this period, Humphrey or John or any other, whether through Web searches or phone calls and e-mails to archivists/record keepers at Westinghouse or historical societies with records on Westinghouse. A simple piece of paper with some sort of illustration of Westinghouse employment by a New York–based Bogart in 1933 or 1934 might have easily settled this case, but my research never produced such evidence. (Perhaps now, after the fact, some source from Westinghouse or elsewhere will contact me with the answer.) Apparently, Westinghouse does not have such records from that long ago; this was an era not only before computers and digitalization but even before Social Security.

That said, a few noteworthy items might link Humphrey Bogart to Westinghouse. First, remember that Bogart's financial prospects at the time were bleak. He needed work, and Westinghouse was very active in the New York area, in the business of electricity, manufacturing, broadcasting, radio, and more. Westinghouse at different points owned RCA and was also part of NBC. Located at 150 Broadway in New York City, Westinghouse was not far from where Bogart lived and was even closer to where he performed on Broadway.[17] Among the major Westinghouse projects from the era was installation of the many elevators popping up throughout New York's booming skyscrapers, which provided lots of employment for locals.[18] So it is not inconceivable that Bogart might have done some work for the company, whether to earn a paycheck as a common laborer working on elevators or through something in broadcasting, media, theater, or the entertainment industry.

On the latter, it is entirely plausible that Westinghouse might have sponsored some form of entertainment work by Bogart, given that from the outset the company's most influential activity was broadcasting, especially radio broadcasting. Consider how Ronald Reagan was a spokesman for General Electric, which for years ran *GE Theater* as one of the top shows on television. In fact, at the height of Bogart's acting career, Westinghouse was drawing celebrities of his caliber for its *Best of Broadway* drama airing on CBS.[19] Thus, a Westinghouse connection to Humphrey Bogart in the early 1930s is not impossible, although, again, I found nothing conclusive in Bogart's biography that would identify him with Westinghouse at this period.

John Leech's Testimony

With all of that said, here is the most critical question: was there ever a suggestion that Humphrey Bogart was a Communist (or even a small "c" communist) in this period? We know of the suspicions raised over the duping he received from his comrade "friends" in 1947—John Howard Lawson, Dalton Trumbo, Alvah Bessie, and the rest—but what about the early 1930s?

Actually, yes, there was a major allegation. It was a significant testimony made under oath, more than once and in great depth, in 1940. And it is what makes all of this so intriguing.

Specifically, in August 1940, a man named John L. Leech shared a list of suspected Communists with a Los Angeles County grand jury. When that testimony hit the press, it was a national scandal overnight. Among the accused were some high-profile Hollywood names, including Jimmy Cagney, Frederic March, Franchot Tone, Jean Muir, and Humphrey Bogart, though Bogart at that point was not nearly the headliner that the others were or that he later became.

Leech testified during the first two weeks of August 1940 in an "extraordinary session" of the Los Angeles County grand jury; his lengthy testimony produced a 192-page transcript. Leech was no flake found wandering Venice Beach. He had been at the top echelon of the Los Angeles area Communist Party, for which he had served as organizer and executive secretary. He joined the party in 1931. From 1934 to 1936 he served as a paid organizer and recruiter.[20] He even appears to be the same John L. Leech who, according to congressional records, ran for Congress (in California's Seventeenth District) on the Communist Party ticket in 1932. (He earned a dismal 1.8 percent of the vote, putting him well behind the Democrat's 71.9 percent and the Republican's 26.3 percent.)

For reasons not entirely clear, Leech soured on the party and the movement, and they on him. He was eventually expelled from CPUSA in 1937. His disillusionment with the party only grew after the 1939 Hitler-Stalin Pact.[21] Prior to his grand jury testimony in 1940, Leech had been a prominent witness at the deportation hearings against Frank Marshall Davis's friend Harry Bridges.

Now, in August 1940, Leech named forty-three Hollywood personages as, variously, dues-paying party members, financial contributors, or very close associates. He claimed that everyone he named was, in some form, intimately related to the local party. These were people involved much deeper than some front-group capacity. By and large, these were not dupes; these were dupers.

Leech cited Bogart as a notable financial contributor to the Communist Party.[22] He also told the grand jury that Bogart was among those who participated in a "study club" where Leech and Hollywood luminaries "came and read the doctrines of Karl Marx and other writers," whom "they would read for hours and then talk it all over." Those who attended the study club were members of the Communist Party, said Leech; he knew this "because they contributed their dues and donations to me personally." He added that the celebrities adopted a "Party name" in order to conceal their identity.[23]

Adding credibility to Leech's charge was the meeting place he cited for the "study club": Budd Schulberg's estate at Malibu Beach.[24] We now know definitively that Budd Schulberg was a Communist during that period. This was not public knowledge in 1940. (Years later, in 1951, Schulberg admitted in testimony before Congress his involvement in the Communist Party; he also explained that he had been involved in "a Marxist study group" at that time.)[25]

Bogart, for the record, vehemently denied Leech's accusations, immediately issuing a statement to the press. "I dare the men who are attempting this investigation to call me to the stand," he retorted. "I want to face them myself."[26] As for the charge of attending a "study club," Bogart responded: "Furthermore, I have never attended the school mentioned nor do I know what school that may be."[27]

This was an interesting choice of words. Leech had not mentioned a *school,* but a *club.*

Leech v. Bogart

The fracas had just begun.

Congressman Martin Dies, the Texas Democrat who chaired the House Committee on Un-American Activities, wasted no time in investigating the issue. Congressman Dies and the committee's chief investigator, Robert Stripling, immediately hopped on a plane for the West Coast. On August 16—just one day after Bogart's denial was published in the press—both Leech and Bogart were testifying before a special congressional session in Los Angeles.

There, under oath, Leech again made his charges, including against Bogart. He repeated his claims that Bogart had paid contributions to the party and had attended the study club. When Congressman Dies asked point blank, "Are you contending that Mr. Bogart was a member of the Communist Party?" Leech immediately answered, "Yes I am."[28] On the study club, Leech also told Dies: "I do definitely recall Mr. Bogart's association with these study groups."[29] He added that Bogart had been present at a party meeting in honor of Earl Browder in Los Angeles in August 1936.

Bogart, also under oath, emphatically denied all of these charges. He disputed not only the specific charges but also having ever known John Leech. He told Dies that "Hollywood people are dupes in the most part"—that is, liberals who tend to get hoodwinked by Communists, but not Communists themselves.[30]

Here again, despite the Left's caricature of the House Committee on Un-American Activities as full of hysterical Red-baiters, Chairman Dies could not have gone easier on Bogart and the other Hollywood figures. Almost instantly, Dies cleared Bogart, as well as Cagney, Frederic March, and writer Philip Dunne—the big names under heated dispute—of charges of being Communists. Dunne was so grateful to Dies and Stripling that he paused in his testimony to express warm appreciation for the honest treatment they had given him.[31] The newspapers immediately flashed headlines declaring that Dies had absolved the stars.[32]

In truth, Dies may not have done enough homework. Had he had access to the Workers School roster for January–March 1934, which listed a "Bogart," he surely would have posed a question to the actor along those lines, especially given what Leech had added to the picture. Consider that Leech's charges against Bogart applied to the 1934–36 period, when Leech was chief organizer of the Hollywood Communist community.[33] In his testimony, Leech remarked on exactly the time that Bogart would have returned to Hollywood (permanently) after his very difficult year (1934) in New York, a year that began with the Workers School session in question and ended with the sad death of his father. Moreover, throughout this period, Bogart shuttled back and forth between New York and Hollywood in search of work. In other words, the timeline fits, as does the geography.

One more critical point on Leech: Many of the names that Leech presented in 1940 proved to be high-profile, significant Communists, including actual party members. Amazingly, Leech had managed to name among his short list seven men who would be implicated among the Hollywood Ten—*fully seven years later*: Lester Cole, Herb Biberman, Dalton Trumbo, Albert Maltz, John Howard Lawson, Alvah Bessie, and Sam Ornitz.[34] He had also named the likes of Budd Schulberg, later confirmed as a Communist at the time.

How would Leech have known all of this if he was not who he claimed to be? He was a legitimate, credible source on Communism in Hollywood, as Communist Party records confirm his role as an official and organizer for the party.

Bear in mind, too, that Leech made these allegations well before the Cold War began; America at the time was worried about Hitler and fascism, not Stalin and Communism.

Might Leech simply have been mistaken about Humphrey Bogart? It is possible, but that would be an odd mistake, given that Bogart was an established Hollywood actor by this time. But it is equally difficult to argue that Bogart was fingered because of his star power; at this point in his career he had some success in Hollywood but was far from being a household name across the country. Most of the newspaper coverage of Leech's accused—which was sensational—focused not on Bogart but on bigger stars like Cagney, March, Muir, and Tone. True, Bogart had recently made a splash with *The Petrified Forest* (1936), based on the popular play by Robert Sherwood, who later became Harry Hopkins's privileged biographer, and with *Dead End* (1937), a grim, class-based Depression-era film—written by Lillian Hellman. But major Bogart films like *Casablanca* and *The Maltese Falcon*, the latter written by Communist and Hellman lover Dashiell Hammett, were still down the road.

Although some of the accused angrily denounced Leech as a liar, he had little to gain by falsely implicating—under oath to a grand jury and then to the chairman of a congressional committee—Bogart or the others. Actually, he gained nothing, material or otherwise; there was no book deal, no personal celebrity. He seemed to disappear from the face of the earth, in fact. Research into what happened to him produced no hard information; I could not even confirm the date of his death (though a John L. Leech did die in Inglewood, California, in August 1972). A post on Leech at the respected Hollywood biographical website imdb.com maintains that Leech had been "a police agent who had infiltrated the Communist Party before being expelled in 1937."[35] Other websites similarly claim that he was a "spy" of some sort. On the other hand, archival documents from the Communist Party claim, among other things, that he was expelled from the party out of fear of blackmail because of sexual indiscretions.[36] Either way, he did work as an organizer, secretary, and recruiter for the party in Los Angeles from 1931 to 1937.

Whatever the final verdict on Leech, his charges remained part of the background in later government investigations of Bogart. This is evident today in Bogart's partially declassified FBI file, which I obtained as part of a Freedom of Information Act (FOIA) request and consulted at length for this book. Though the file remains partly redacted, the documents that have been released do not clearly link Bogart to the Communist Party. To the contrary, many of the documents, including an FBI "Summary Memorandum" from November 24, 1947, and a December 7, 1943, War Department "Loyalty and Character Report," conclude that Bogart, despite certain flaws like a "violent temper," was of overall "excellent character" and a loyal American, with no track record of "financial contributions" to the Communist Party. The reports say there was no factual substance to allegations that Bogart had been "connected with the Communist Party."[37]

The fact remains, however, that John L. Leech was a credible witness, some of whose charges were confirmed many years after the fact. Even today his allegations hardly seem outlandish.

Humphrey Bogart: *Daily Worker* "Hero"

Whether or not Humphrey Bogart was a contributor to the Communist Party, he did run in some of the same circles as Communists and Communist sympathizers. That was not difficult to do in Hollywood, given the party's pervasiveness in the film industry, especially among screenwriters. Still, it must be noted that Bogart was celebrated by the Communist press, which the Communists rarely did for someone whose politics they did not approve of. For example, the October 15, 1944, *Daily Worker* toasted Bogart with the glowing headline "Bogart: Anti-Fascist Film Hero."[38] In that article, *Daily Worker* reporter David Platt (who also wrote about the actor in 1951)[39] praised Bogart's on-screen portrayals against fascism as well as his "off-screen performances," which were, according to Platt, just as "thrilling." Specifically, the article highlighted the Bogart films *Across the Pacific* (1942), *Action in the North Atlantic* (1943), and *Sahara* (1943). The CPUSA organ neglected to mention the screenwriter of the latter two films: the angry apparatchik John Howard Lawson.

The *Daily Worker* especially liked Bogart's (and Lawson's) *Action in the North Atlantic,* which the newspaper called "magnificent." But as another reviewer of the film, Bernard Dick, pointed out, Lawson had borrowed the structural outline for the movie, and many of the action scenes, from the 1925 Bolshevik propaganda film *The Battleship Potemkin.* Dick described *Action in the North Atlantic* as "Soviet propaganda at its most artful."[40]

Of course, that was because its writer, Lawson, was a master of Soviet propaganda, dedicated to Stalin. Bogart, in that sense, had been used. This wouldn't be the last time that Bogart was Lawson's dupe; a much more infamous episode would follow in October 1947, with the Committee for the First Amendment.

The other Lawson-penned film that the *Daily Worker* recommended in its gushing profile of Bogart was *Sahara.* Here, too, Bernard Dick pointed out what the *Daily Worker* failed to inform readers: that Lawson borrowed from the Russian film *The Thirteen,* cobbling together "dialectic rendered as narrative."[41]

Now there was a movie that a Marxist-Leninist could enjoy.

In sum, the *Daily Worker* hailed Humphrey Bogart for offering America a real movie "hero," unlike previous "phonies" like Rudolph Valentino. Reporter David Platt finished his puff piece with this summation: "It is actors like Humphrey Bogart, in thoughtful films like *Action in the North Atlantic* and *Sahara,* who catch the public eye. After years of idolizing matinee idols with nothing more to offer than an interesting profile, it is gratifying to see the nation's filmgoers at last take to a movie hero, who has something important to say. It is a sign of America's awakening."

There he was: Humphrey Bogart, *Daily Worker* "hero," "awakening" America with "something important to say."

Bogart's Moment of Truth

So what does all of this ultimately mean about Humphrey Bogart's politics?

First and foremost, I cannot report that Bogart was a supporter (or member) of the Communist Party or even a small "c" communist. Yet it would have been scholarly negligence not to investigate the issue and consider the question after encountering the winter 1934 Workers School records in the Comintern Archives on CPUSA.

If Bogart had been a Communist or Communist sympathizer, it would shed entirely new light on his behavior in October 1947 as a member of the Committee for the First Amendment, particularly his public expressions of rage over being duped. It would also raise questions about his denial in 1940. That said, it would not necessarily mean that Bogart was lying to America when he said, in 1947, "I am not a Communist." By that point in time, it seems safe to assume that he was not.

Perhaps Bogart became involved in the Communist movement, and considered joining (or actually did join) the Communist Party, during the depths of the Great Depression, when he hit rock bottom—with his father bankrupt and dying, and his own career, marriage, and finances foundering. But even if that were the case, he clearly seems to have changed his politics over time, moving away from the far Left as he developed a fuller understanding of Communism. Such a political sojourn was not uncommon, as we have seen. It was a path traversed by many characters in this book, from William Bullitt and Paul Douglas to fellow actor Ronald Reagan.[42]

If Humphrey Bogart had been an eager pupil at the Workers School in New York City in January 1934, he was no longer on the extreme Left by the late 1940s when he declared, "I detest Communism." Like so many others, Bogart was on a journey in search of truth, which is a path that—for every human being—leads a world away from the Communist Party.

Appendix A

TED KENNEDY'S SECRET OVERTURE
TO THE SOVIET UNION

One former Soviet propaganda minister tasked with influencing Western visitors called Senator Ted Kennedy a "useful idiot"—indeed, an example of "monumental idiocy." And the highly sensitive KGB document shown on the following pages (together with English translation) indicates just how useful Senator Kennedy could be to the Soviets in their campaign against Ronald Reagan and the United States.

This May 14, 1983, memorandum, which the head of the KGB sent with "Special Importance" to Soviet leader Yuri Andropov, discloses Kennedy's "confidential" offer to work together with the Kremlin to overcome President Reagan's "belligerence."

In other words, the Massachusetts senator—probably the leading Democratic politician in America at the time—proposed to work secretly with the Soviet dictator to undercut the president of the United States. Had Americans known of Kennedy's overture to the Soviets at the time, it would have been a scandal.

К О М И Т Е Т
ГОСУДАРСТВЕННОЙ БЕЗОПАСНОСТИ СССР

14.05.83.   № 1029-Ч/ОВ

Москва

ЦК КПСС
1490
19 МАЯ 1983
Особой важности

Товарищу Ю.В.Андропову

Об обращении сенатора Кеннеди к
Генеральному секретарю ЦК КПСС
Ю.В.Андропову.

9-10 мая с.г. в Москве находился близкий друг и доверенное
лицо сенатора США Эдварда Кеннеди Д.Танни, которому сенатор поручил, используя конфиденциальные контакты, довести до сведения Генерального секретаря ЦК КПСС Ю.В.Андропова следующее.

Нынешнее состояние советско-американских отношений не может
не вызывать у него, Кеннеди, как и у всех здравомыслящих людей
серьезного беспокойства. События развиваются так, что эти отношения и обстановка в мире в целом могут еще больше обостриться.
Главная тому причина - воинственный внешнеполитический курс Рейгана и прежде всего его твердое намерение разместить в Западной
Европе новые американские ядерные ракеты средней дальности.

Опасность ситуации, по оценке Кеннеди, заключается в том,
что президент не желает вносить какие-либо разумные коррективы в
свою политику. Он чувствует, что его позиции внутри страны в последнее время несколько упрочились в результате известного улучшения экономического положения в США: существенно снизился уровень
инфляции, наблюдается рост производства и деловой активности,
имеются предпосылки для дальнейшего снижения банковских процентных ставок. Все это всячески раздувается Белым домом и средствами
массовой информации как "успех рейганомики".

Конечно, в данной области у Рейгана не все идет так гладко,
как ему хотелось бы. Многие крупные экономисты, представители финансовых кругов, особенно северо-восточных штатов, видят некото-

рые скрытые тенденции, которые способны привести к новому серьез-
ному осложнению экономического положения в США. Произойти это может в самый разгар президентской избирательной кампании 1984 года,
что было бы на руку демократической партии. Однако твердой уверен-
ности в таком развитии событий пока нет.

Пожалуй, единственным потенциально опасным для Рейгана вопро-
сом становятся проблемы войны и мира и советско-американских отношений. Этот вопрос, как считает сенатор, несомненно будет важным
фактором в избирательной кампании. В Соединенных Штатах ширится
движение за замораживание ядерных арсеналов обеих стран, предпри-
нимаются, в том числе и им, Кеннеди, меры к его дальнейшей активи-
зации. В политических, деловых кругах страны, в конгрессе возрас-
тает сопротивление непомерному наращиванию военных расходов.

И все же, по мнению Кеннеди, оппозиция Рейгану еще слаба.
Выступления противников президента разрозненны и недостаточно эф-
фективны, а Рейган обладает возможностями вести успешную контр-
пропаганду. С целью нейтрализовать критику в свой адрес по поводу
неконструктивности линии США на переговорах с СССР, Рейган готов
и дальше выдвигать внешне броские, но по существу лишь пропаган-
дистские инициативы. В то же время инициативы и выступления советских руководителей в области ограничения вооружений часто искажа-
ются, замалчиваются или просто огульно отвергаются под любым наду-
манным предлогом. Самим американцам в сути этих сложных вопросов
разобраться трудно, да и аргументы советской стороны до них иног-
да не доходят. Хотя изложение выступлений руководителей СССР и
помещают в прессе, нельзя не учитывать, что большинство американцев не читает серьезных газет и журналов.

Кеннеди полагает, что в данной обстановке в интересах дела
мира было бы полезным и своевременным предпринять некоторые допол-
нительные шаги по противодействию милитаристской политике Рейгана

к его кампании психологического давления на американское населе-
ние. В этой связи он хотел бы обратиться к Генеральному секретарю
ЦК КПСС Ю.В.Андропову со следующими предложениями:

I. Кеннеди просил бы Ю.В.Андропова рассмотреть вопрос о воз-
можности принять его в Москве для личной беседы в июле с.г. Глав-
ную цель встречи сенатор видит в том, чтобы вооружиться разъясне-
ниями советского руководителя по проблемам ограничения ядерных
вооружений и использовать их в последующем для более убедительных
выступлений в США. В этой связи он хотел бы проинформировать, что
им также запланирована поездка в Западную Европу, где, в частности, предусмотрены встречи с премьер-министром Англии Тэтчер и президентом Франции Миттераном, с которыми он намерен обменяться мне-
ниями по тем же проблемам.

Если просьба о приеме его Ю.В.Андроповым будет сочтена в
принципе приемлемой, Кеннеди направит в Москву своего представи-
теля для решения вопросов, связанных с организацией поездки.

Кеннеди считает, что позитивное влияние беседы с Ю.В.Андро-
повым на общественность и политические круги США может оказаться
еще большим, если он пригласит с собой кого-либо из видных сена-
торов-республиканцев, например Марка Хэтфилда. (Хэтфилд совместно
с Кеннеди в марте 1982 года выдвинул проект резолюции о заморажи-
вании ядерных арсеналов США и СССР и опубликовал книгу на ту же
тему).

2. Кеннеди полагает, что с точки зрения воздействия на умо-
настроения американцев было бы желательным организовать в августе-
сентябре с.г. интервью Ю.В.Андропова для телевидения США. Такое
непосредственное обращение Генерального секретаря ЦК КПСС к амери-
канскому народу несомненно вызовет огромное внимание и интерес в
стране. Сенатор убежден, что оно получит максимальный резонанс,
ибо телевидение в США — наиболее эффективное средство массовой

информации.

Если это предложение будет сочтено заслуживающим внимания,
то Кеннеди и его друзья предпримут соответствующие шаги, чтобы
кто-либо из представителей крупнейших телекомпаний США обратился
к Ю.В.Андропову с просьбой принять его в Москве и дать интервью.
В Москву, в частности, могли бы прибыть председатель совета дирек-
торов телевизионной компании "Эй-Би-Си" Элтон Рул, обозреватели
Уолтер Кронкайт или Барбара Уолтерс. Важно, подчеркнул сенатор,
что инициатива при этом будет исходить от американской стороны.

Затем в тех же целях можно организовать серию интервью для
телевидения США ряда советских деятелей, в том числе военных. Они
также получили бы возможность непосредственно обратиться к амери-
канскому народу с разъяснением мирных инициатив СССР, со своей ар-
гументацией относительно того, каков же истинный баланс сил СССР
и США в военной области. А этот вопрос особенно грубо искажается
администрацией Рейгана.

Кеннеди просил передать, что это обращение к Генеральному
секретарю ЦК КПСС объясняется его стремлением внести посильный
вклад в дело устранения угрозы ядерной войны, улучшения советско-
американских отношений, которые он считает определяющими для сох-
ранения мира. На него, Кеннеди, производит большое впечатление
активная деятельность Ю.В.Андропова вместе с другими советскими
руководителями, направленная на оздоровление международной обста-
новки, улучшение взаимопонимания между народами.

Сенатор подчеркнул, что будет с нетерпением ждать ответа на
свое обращение, который можно довести до него через Танни.

Изложив обращение Кеннеди к Генеральному секретарю ЦК КПСС
Ю.В.Андропову, Танни рассказал, что сенатор Кеннеди в последнее
время активизирует выступления в пользу устранения угрозы войны.
Формальный отказ от участия в избирательной кампании 1984 года

пособствовал тому, что высказывания сенатора воспринимаются в

ША не предвзято, так как они не связаны с предвыборными сообра-

:ениями. Танни отметил, что сенатор нацелен на то, чтобы добиться

:збрания на пост президента США в 1988 году. К тому времени ему

:сполнится 56 лет, будут устранены проблемы личного плана, кото-

:не ослабляли его положение (Кеннеди без излишней шумихи закончил

:ракоразводный процесс и вскоре планирует повторно вступить в

:рак). Вместе с тем Кеннеди не исключает, что в избирательной кам-

:ании 1984 года может возникнуть ситуация, когда демократическая

:артия официально обратится к нему с просьбой возглавить ее в

:орьбе против республиканцев и добиваться избрания президентом.

:то объясняется тем, что ни один из нынешних претендентов от демо-

:ратов не имеет реальных шансов на победу над Рейганом.

    Просим указаний.

:редседатель Комитета   В.Чебриков

Special Importance

Committee on State Security of the USSR
14.05.1983 No. 1029 Ch/OV
Moscow

Regarding Senator Kennedy's request to the General Secretary of the Communist Party Y. V.
Andropov

Comrade Y. V. Andropov

On 9-10 May of this year, Senator Edward Kennedy's close friend and trusted confidant J.
Tunney was in Moscow. The senator charged Tunney to convey the following message, through
confidential contacts, to the General Secretary of the Central Committee of the Communist Party
of the Soviet Union, Y. Andropov:

Senator Kennedy, like other rational people, is very troubled by the current state of Soviet-
American relations. Events are developing such that this relationship coupled with the general
state of global affairs will make the situation even more dangerous. The main reason for this is
Reagan's belligerence, and his firm commitment to deploy new American middle range nuclear
weapons within Western Europe.

According to Kennedy, the current threat is due to the President's refusal to engage any
modification to his politics. He feels that his domestic standing has been strengthened because of
the well publicized improvement of the economy: inflation has been greatly reduced, production
levels are increasing as is overall business activity. For these reasons, interest rates will continue
to decline. The White House has portrayed this in the media as the "success of Reaganomics."

Naturally, not everything in the province of economics has gone according to Reagan's plan. A
few well known economists and members of financial circles, particularly from the north-eastern
states, foresee certain hidden tendencies that may bring about a new economic crisis in the USA.
This could bring about the fall of the presidential campaign of 1984, which would benefit the
Democratic party. Nevertheless, there are no secure assurances this will indeed develop.

The only real potential threats to Reagan are problems of war and peace and Soviet-American
relations. These issues, according to the senator, will without a doubt become the most important
of the election campaign. The movement advocating a freeze on nuclear arsenals of both
countries continues to gain strength in the United States. The movement is also willing to accept
preparations, particularly from Kennedy, for its continued growth. In political and influential
circles of the country, including within Congress, the resistance to growing military expenditures
is gaining strength.

However, according to Kennedy, the opposition to Reagan is still very weak. Reagan's
adversaries are divided and the presentations they make are not fully effective. Meanwhile,
Reagan has the capabilities to effectively counter any propaganda. In order to neutralize criticism
that the talks between the USA and USSR are non-constructive, Reagan will be grandiose, but
subjectively propagandistic. At the same time, Soviet officials who speak about disarmament
will be quoted out of context, silenced or groundlessly and whimsically discounted. Although
arguments and statements by officials of the USSR do appear in the press, it is important to note
the majority of Americans do not read serious newspapers or periodicals.

Kennedy believes that, given the current state of affairs, and in the interest of peace, it would be prudent and timely to undertake the following steps to counter the militaristic politics of Reagan and his campaign to psychologically burden the American people. In this regard, he offers the following proposals to the General Secretary of the Central Committee of the Communist Party of the Soviet Union Y. V. Andropov:

1. Kennedy asks Y. V. Andropov to consider inviting the senator to Moscow for a personal meeting in July of this year. The main purpose of the meeting, according to the senator, would be to arm Soviet officials with explanations regarding problems of nuclear disarmament so they may be better prepared and more convincing during appearances in the USA. He would also like to inform you that he has planned a trip through Western Europe, where he anticipates meeting England's Prime Minister Margaret Thatcher and French President Mitterand in which he will exchange similar ideas regarding the same issues.

If his proposals would be accepted in principle, Kennedy would send his representative to Moscow to resolve questions regarding organizing such a visit.

Kennedy thinks the benefit of a meeting with Y. V. Andropov will be enhanced if he could also invite one of the well known Republican senators, for example, Mark Hatfield. Such a meeting will have a strong impact on Americans and political circles in the USA. (In March of 1982, Hatfield and Kennedy proposed a project resolution to freeze the nuclear arsenals of the USA and the USSR and published a book on this theme as well).

2. Kennedy believes that in order to influence Americans it would be important to organize in August-September of this year, televised interviews with Y. V. Andropov in the USA. A direct appeal by the General Secretary of the Central Committee of the Communist Party of the Soviet Union to the American people will, without a doubt, attract a great deal of attention and interest in the country. The senator is convinced this would receive the maximum resonance in so far as television is the most effective method of mass media and information.

If the proposal is recognized as worthy, then Kennedy and his friends will bring about suitable steps to have representatives of the largest television companies in the USA contact Y. V. Andropov for an invitation to Moscow for the interview. Specifically, the president of the board of directors of ABC, Elton Raul and television columnists Walter Conkrite or Barbara Walters could visit Moscow. The senator underlined the importance that this initiative should be seen as coming from the American side.

Furthermore, with the same purpose in mind, a series of televised interviews in the USA with lower level Soviet officials, particularly from the military would be organized. They would also have an opportunity to appeal directly to the American people about the peaceful intentions of the USSR, with their own arguments about maintaining a true balance of power between the USSR and the USA in military terms. This issue is quickly being distorted by Reagan's administration.

Kennedy asked to convey, that this appeal to the General Secretary of the Central Committee of the Communist Party of the Soviet Union is his effort to contribute a strong proposal that would root out the threat of nuclear war, and to improve Soviet-American relations, so that they define the safety for the world. Kennedy is very impressed with the activities of Y. V. Andropov and other Soviet leaders, who expressed their commitment to heal international affairs, and improve mutual understandings between peoples.

The senator underscored that he eagerly awaits a reply to his appeal, the answer to which may be delivered through Tunney.

Having conveyed Kennedy's appeal to the General Secretary of the Central Committee of the Communist Party of the Soviet Union, Tunney also explained that Senator Kennedy has in the last few years actively made appearances to reduce the threat of war. Because he formally refused to partake in the election campaign of 1984, his speeches would be taken without prejudice as they are not tied to any campaign promises. Tunney remarked that the senator wants to run for president in 1988. At that time, he will be 56 and his personal problems, which could hinder his standing, will be resolved (Kennedy has just completed a divorce and plans to re-marry in the near future). Taken together, Kennedy does not discount that during the 1984 campaign, the Democratic party may officially turn to him to lead the fight against the Republicans and elect their candidate president. This would explain why he is convinced that none of the candidates today have a real chance at defeating Reagan.

We await instructions.

President of the committee   V. Chebrikov

Appendix B

FRANK MARSHALL DAVIS'S FBI FILE

Those who defend Frank Marshall Davis, mentor to a young Barack Obama in Hawaii, against charges of Communist sympathies typically do not take account of the documentary record. That record includes his regular column for the Communist newspaper the *Honolulu Record,* in which Davis unfailingly echoed the Moscow party line (see Chapter 13). It also includes Davis's FBI file, which runs more than six hundred pages and covers some nineteen years.

Selections from that FBI file shown on the pages that follow indicate that Davis had Communist Party affiliations going back to 1931 and even joined the party.

~~SECRET~~

BIOGRAPHICAL DATA

FRANK⊙DAVIS

FRANK M.⊙DAVIS
MARSHALL⊙DAVIS
F.M.⊙DAVIS

Name: Frank Marshall Davis

Born: 12/31/05, Arkansas City, Kansas

Description: Race: Negro
Height: 6'1"
Weight: 230
Eyes: Brown
Hair: Black
Complexion: Light Brown

Communist Party No: 1946 CP #47544

Social Security No: 337-16-3459

Addresses: 1923-1924: 1014 North Summit, Arkansas City, Kansas.

1944- : 3539 South Vincennes Avenue, Chicago, Illinois.

1944- : 3507 South Parkway, Chicago.

-1948: 3852 South Lake Park Avenue, Chicago.

1948-1950: 1830 Waiola, Apt. #1, Honolulu, T.H.

1950-1953: Punaluu, Kapaka District, Windward Oahu, T.H., c/o Post Office at Hauula, Oahu, T.H.

Marital Status: Wife - Thelma B. Davis, born 5/8/03, place not stated. Married on 7/12/31 at Atlanta, Georgia.

b6
b7C
Wife - [   ] a member of the white race, born [   ] at [   ] Date of marriage not stated.

~~SECRET~~

-3-

"CP #47544": In this secret document, only recently declassified, the FBI matter-of-factly reports Frank Marshall Davis's membership number in the Communist Party USA: 47544.

HN 100-5082   b6
                                                                                          b7C
Employment:

        Owner, Oahu Papers, 867 Akua Street, Honolulu, and columnist
for the Honolulu Record Publishing Company, Ltd., 811 Sheridan Street,
Honolulu, which has been described by [   ] self-admitted   I.H.
former member of the Communist Party of Hawaii from 1937-1949 and a
member of the Executive Board of the Communist Party in Hawaii for
several years, as publishers of the English-language weekly "Honolulu
Record", whose editorial policies and slanting of the news were
controlled by the Executive Board of the Communist Party in Hawaii.

            II. CONNECTIONS WITH THE COMMUNIST PARTY

        [   ] self-admitted former member of the
Communist Party in Hawaii from 1947 to June 1962, made the following   I.H.
signed statement to SA LEO S. BRENNEISEN on November 10, 1953:

                                                                                          b6
                                                                                          b7C
                                        November 10, 1953
                                        Honolulu, T. H.

        "I, [   ] am going to make the following
voluntary statement to LEO S. BRENNEISEN, known to me as a
Special Agent of the Federal Bureau of Investigation. I am
willing to appear in court and testify to the following facts
to be cross-examined by Counsel and faced by FRANK MARSHALL
DAVIS.

        "I believe it was in 1949 in Honolulu, T. H. when I first met
FRANK MARSHALL DAVIS at a social function sponsored by the
Hawaii Civil Liberties Committee. I had previously joined the
Communist Party in San Francisco in 1946 and transferred my
membership in January, 1947 to the Communist Party of Hawaii.
In 1950 after the Communist Party had conducted a series of   I.H.   b6
control interviews [   ] known to me as a   b7C
Communist Party Organizer, told me that the Party was being
reorganized and was going underground. [   ] explained to me
that the Party was being broken down into "Groups of 3's" and
that I was being made chairman of Group #6 and in addition given
the assignment of being contact man for my own group and four

                                - 2 -

"Chairman of Group #10": In this FBI report (two pages), a former member of the Communist Party names Frank Marshall Davis as the chairman of an underground Communist group.

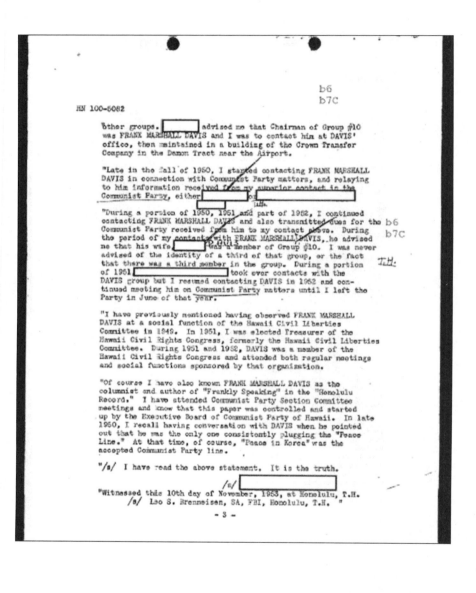

b6
b7C

HN 100-5082

"Other groups. [   ] advised me that Chairman of Group #10 was FRANK MARSHALL DAVIS and I was to contact him at DAVIS' office, then maintained in a building of the Crown Transfer Company in the Damon Tract near the Airport.

"Late in the fall of 1950, I started contacting FRANK MARSHALL DAVIS in connection with Communist Party matters, and relaying to him information received from my superior contact in the Communist Party, either [   ] or [   ].

"During a portion of 1950, 1951 and part of 1952, I continued contacting FRANK MARSHALL DAVIS and also transmitted dues for the Communist Party received from him to my contact above. During the period of my contacts with FRANK MARSHALL DAVIS, he advised me that his wife [   ] was a member of Group #10. I was never advised of the identity of a third of that group, or the fact that there was a third member in the group. During a portion of 1951 [   ] took over contacts with the DAVIS group but I resumed contacting DAVIS in 1952 and continued meeting him on Communist Party matters until I left the Party in June of that year.

"I have previously mentioned having observed FRANK MARSHALL DAVIS at a social function of the Hawaii Civil Liberties Committee in 1949. In 1951, I was elected Treasurer of the Hawaii Civil Rights Congress, formerly the Hawaii Civil Liberties Committee. During 1951 and 1952, DAVIS was a member of the Hawaii Civil Rights Congress and attended both regular meetings and social functions sponsored by that organization.

"Of course I have also known FRANK MARSHALL DAVIS as the columnist and author of 'Frankly Speaking' in the 'Honolulu Record.' I have attended Communist Party Section Committee meetings and know that this paper was controlled and started up by the Executive Board of Communist Party of Hawaii. In late 1950, I recall having conversation with DAVIS when he pointed out that he was the only one consistently plugging the 'Peace Line.' At that time, of course, 'Peace in Korea' was the accepted Communist Party line.

"/s/ I have read the above statement. It is the truth.

/s/
/s/ [   ]

"Witnessed this 10th day of November, 1953, at Honolulu, T.H.
/s/ Leo S. Brenneisen, SA, FBI, Honolulu, T.H. "

- 3 -

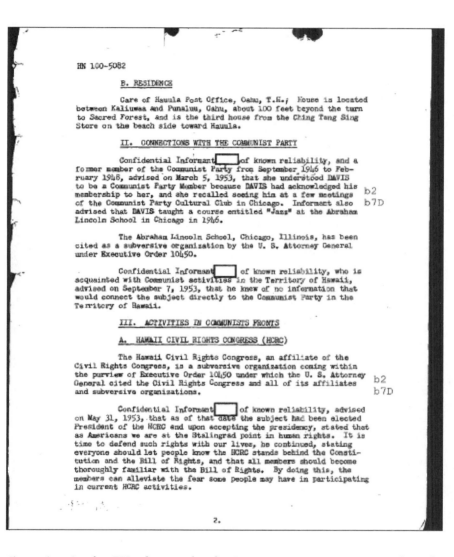

HN 100-5082

B. RESIDENCE

Care of Hauula Post Office, Oahu, T.H.; House is located
between Kaliuwaa and Punaluu, Oahu, about 100 feet beyond the turn
to Sacred Forest, and is the third house from the Ching Tang Sing
Store on the beach side toward Hauula.

II. CONNECTIONS WITH THE COMMUNIST PARTY

Confidential Informant[   ]of known reliability, and a
former member of the Communist Party from September 1946 to February 1948, advised on March 5, 1953, that she understood DAVIS
to be a Communist Party Member because DAVIS had acknowledged his
membership to her, and she recalled seeing him at a few meetings
of the Communist Party Cultural Club in Chicago. Informant also
advised that DAVIS taught a course entitled "Jazz" at the Abraham
Lincoln School in Chicago in 1946.

b2
b7D

The Abraham Lincoln School, Chicago, Illinois, has been
cited as a subversive organization by the U. S. Attorney General
under Executive Order 10450.

Confidential Informant[   ] of known reliability, who is
acquainted with Communist activities in the Territory of Hawaii,
advised on September 7, 1953, that he knew of no information that
would connect the subject directly to the Communist Party in the
Territory of Hawaii.

III. ACTIVITIES IN COMMUNISTS FRONTS

A. HAWAII CIVIL RIGHTS CONGRESS (HCRC)

The Hawaii Civil Rights Congress, an affiliate of the
Civil Rights Congress, is a subversive organization coming within
the purview of Executive Order 10450 under which the U. S. Attorney
General cited the Civil Rights Congress and all of its affiliates
and subversive organizations.

b2
b7D

Confidential Informant[   ] of known reliability, advised
on May 31, 1953, that as of that date the subject had been elected
President of the HCRC and upon accepting the presidency, stated that
as Americans we are at the Stalingrad point in human rights. It is
time to defend such rights with our lives, he continued, stating
everyone should let people know the HCRC stands behind the Constitution and the Bill of Rights, and that all members should become
thoroughly familiar with the Bill of Rights. By doing this, the
members can alleviate the fear some people may have in participating
in current HCRC activities.

2.

Chicago days: Another FBI informant identifies Davis as a Communist Party member. The
informant attests that Davis admitted his membership to her and that she saw him "at a few
meetings" in Chicago.

FEDERAL BUREAU OF INVESTIGATION

Form No. 1 THIS CASE ORIGINATED AT	HONOLULU, T. H.		FILE NO.	
REPORT MADE AT	DATE WHEN MADE	PERIOD FOR WHICH MADE	REPORT MADE BY	
HONOLULU, T. H.	11-13-50	11/2-6/50	KNAPP	LPS
TITLE			CHARACTER OF CASE	
FRANK MARSHALL DAVIS			INTERNAL SECURITY - C	

SYNOPSIS OF FACTS: Subject's business address is now 405 F Road, Honolulu. He admitted to an informant he became interested in the Communist Party in 1931 and urged informant to join the Communist Party. However, he claimed Communist Party of Hawaii was built around a group of white chauvinists who do not fully understand the basic principles underlying the Communist Party. In recent months he has sent two checks to the International Workers Order. Subject has been active in affairs of the Hawaii Civil Liberties, a Communist front, and occupies the position of Chairman of the Legal Action Committee of this organization. On June 29, 1950, he issued a $500.00 check to the Honolulu Record. He continues to write a weekly column for this publication and in recent months has condemned the conviction of HARRY BRIDGES, the House Committee on Un-American Activities, United States intervention in Korea, and the Communist Control Bill. Subject is Assistant Secretary of his Democratic Party Precinct Club and was a Delegate to the Territorial Democratic Convention.

COPIES OF THIS REPORT
5 - Bureau (100-328955)
5 - Honolulu
COPY IN FILE

Drawn to CPUSA early on: According to this FBI document, Davis "became interested in the Communist Party in 1931."

Honolulu File 100-5082   b6
                                                                    b7C

recruits for the Communist Party among members of the International Workes
Order. This informant stated that [   ] said she had been
charged by the Chicago Executive Board of the Communist Party with the
responsibility of organizing negroes throughout the nation into an
autonomist national group society and that subject was working with her in   b2
this connection.   b6

                Confidential Informant [   ] of Chicago, reported on   b7C
March 6, 1945 that [   ] organizer for the South Side Council, b7D
Communist Political Association, told this informant that DAVIS was at
that time a member of the Communist Political Association in Chicago.

                On May 22, 1945, Confidential Informant [   ] furnished informa-
tion that subject was at that time a member of the Carver Second Ward,
West, Communist Political Association Club of Chicago, Illinois. Information was received from the Kansas City Office, as furnished to that office   b2
by Confidential Informant [ ] in May, 1949. According to this informant,   b7D
WALTER S. STEELE, Editor of the National Republican, had testified before
the Un-American Activities Committee, that FRANK MARSHALL DAVIS was a
faculty member of the Abraham Lincoln School, a Communist Front organization
where Communist philosophy is taught, in Chicago, Illinois. STEELE was
said to have described DAVIS as the leader of the American Negro Congress,
which he said is alleged to have become chiefly financed by the Communist
Party. He further testified that DAVIS at one time was a member of the
Board of Directors of the Chicago Star which he described as a left-wing
publication, backed by the Communist Party.

                Confidential Informant [   ] reported that [   ]   b2
[   ] subject's wife, was a member of the Paul Robeson Communist Party   b6
Club in Chicago, Illinois and her membership number for 1947 was 62109.   b7C

        17. ADMISSIONS OF MEMBERSHIP IN FRONT ORGANIZATIONS

                On December 11, 1948, DAVIS admitted to [   ] previously
referred to, that he was on the "Washington Subversive List" because of his
affiliation with the Abraham Lincoln School of Chicago, the American Youth
for Democracy and the Civil Rights Congress. DAVIS stated that he has   b2
taught art classes at the Abraham Lincoln School, said he is an officer in   b7D
the American Youth for Democracy and is a functionary of the Civil Rights
Congress.

                                -4-

Communist fronts: In Chicago, Davis reportedly participated in a number of Communist front groups, including the Abraham Lincoln School, the *Chicago Star,* and the American Negro Congress.

Chicago File 100-15799

b2
b7D

On December 4, 1946 [redacted] advised that DAVIS was giving up his apartment number 301 at 3852 South Lake Park Avenue, Chicago, Illinois.

Employment

On March 23, 1945 [redacted] of the Honolulu office advised that DAVIS had under consideration an offer to take some unspecified position with the International Long Shoremen and Warehousemen Union – CIO in Honolulu which would put him "on easy street" if he succeeded in obtaining this position.

b2
b7D

On November 13, 1949 [redacted] advised that FRANK MARSHALL DAVIS and his wife were going to leave for Honolulu where DAVIS would be employed by the International Long Shoremen and Warehousemen Union – CIO.

b2
b7D

II. ACTIVITIES AND AFFILIATIONS

Communist Political Association Membership

On May 22, 1945 Chicago [redacted] furnished information that FRANK M. DAVIS of 3559 Vincennes Avenue, was a member of the Carver Second Ward West Communist Political Association Club. FRANK M. DAVIS gave his occupation as a newspaper man.

[redacted] now deceased, advised that FRANK MARSHALL DAVIS at this time resided at 3559 Vincennes Avenue, Chicago, Illinois.

b2

Communist Party Activities

b2
b6

On May 26, 1944 Chicago [redacted] advised that FRANK MARSHALL DAVIS on April 1, 1944 recruited [redacted] to the Second Ward Branch of the Communist Party.

b7C
b7D

On June 23, 1946 [redacted] furnished a report of a meeting of the Carver Communist Party Club held at 4241 Michigan Avenue, Chicago, Illinois. He advised that FRANK MARSHALL DAVIS was present at this meeting.

On July 8, 1946 [redacted] furnished a printed financial bulletin issued by the South Side Section of the Communist Party. This bulletin listed a group of persons active in the Communist Party financial campaign to raise funds. The name of F. DAVIS appears on the list. [redacted] was unable to furnish any additional identifying information regarding the F. DAVIS listed.

b2
b7D

On April 16, 1947 [redacted] advised that a meeting of the Negro Commission of the Communist Party, District No. 8, Chicago, Illinois, was held on this date

- 2 -

Off to Hawaii: After engaging extensively in "Communist Party activities" in Chicago, according to this FBI file, Davis went to Hawaii for a job with the Communist-controlled International Longshoremen's and Warehousemen's Union (ILWU).

UNITED STATES GOVERNMENT

Memorandum

TO : DIRECTOR, FBI (100-328955)   DATE: JUL 30 1962

FROM : SA HONOLULU (100-5082)

SUBJECT: FRANK MARSHALL DAVIS
SM-C

     Included as enclosures, 4 copies of report of SA
LEO S. BRENNEISEN, concerning above captioned subject.

     Review of instant file reflects FRANK MARSHALL DAVIS,
a Negro male, was active in the CP in Chicago prior to coming
to Hawaii in 1948. Shortly after his arrival in Hawaii, both
he and his wife [ ] became active in the CP and continued
that membership until at least 1952. Thereafter, the Party
in Hawaii ceased operations. DAVIS, during the late 1940s
and early 1950s, was active in several CP front groups and
was the columnist in the old communist line "Honolulu Record",
a weekly newspaper of Honolulu, which ceased existence in
1957. Since that time, there has been little pertinent
activity on the part of DAVIS. The last front group to
operate in Hawaii ceased existence in the fall of 1956.
In late 1956, DAVIS refused to testify before the Senate
Internal Security Sub-Committee holding hearings in Honolulu.
In December, 1960, his name was listed on material distributed
on the Mainland as one of the sponsors for the American Committee
for Protection of Foreign Born. However, this organization
has not been active in Hawaii and there is no indication that
DAVIS has done other than lend his name to that organization.

b6
b7C

     Due to the inactivity of DAVIS over a lengthy
period of time, it is felt he does not presently fit the
criteria for the Security Index. It is therefore recommended
that he be deleted from the Security Index of the Honolulu
Division. In the event, he is deleted, he will be placed on
the Reserve Index B.

EX 101   160-328955-58

2 - Bureau (Enels) (RAM)
1 - Honolulu   REG-8
ISB:jem
(3)   ALL INFORMATION CONTAINED
HEREIN IS UNCLASSIFIED

SUBV. CONTROL

"Active in the CP": This 1962 memo to FBI director J. Edgar Hoover summarizes Davis's involvement in the Communist Party and various front groups.

SAC, Honolulu (100-5082)   August 15, 1962
               REC-135
Director, FBI (100-328955) — 58

                                             1 - Mr. Pettit

FRANK MARSHALL DAVIS
SECURITY MATTER - C

        Reurlet 7-30-62.

            Subject is a Negro male, 56 years of age, who
has been employed most of his life as a reporter. He was
a Communist Party (CP) member in Chicago from 1945 until
1948 when he moved to Hawaii. He was very active in the
Party there until Party activity as such ceased in 1952.
He was active in front groups in a leadership capacity
until such front groups became inactive in 1956. When
questioned before the Senate Internal Security Subcommittee
in 1956, Davis took the Fifth Amendment.

            He wrote a column which constantly followed the
CP line in the now defunct "Honolulu Record" until 1957.
In 1958 he frequented the premises of this newspaper. He
contributed to "The Worker" prior to 1956.

            He was listed as a sponsor for the 27th National
Conference of the American Committee for Protection of
Foreign Born in December, 1960.

            In 1957 he championed the policies of Soviet
Russia.

            His name is being retained on the Security Index
at this time.

                                ALL INFORMATION CONTAINED

NOTE ON YELLOW:

                Relet recommended deletion from SI.

BGLP:bmt
   (4)

"He championed the policies of Soviet Russia": Another 1962 FBI document traces the Communist
Party activity and pro-Soviet work of Frank Marshall Davis.

Notes

Introduction: The Overlooked Role of the Dupe

1. *The Oxford English Dictionary* (2nd edition, 1989) defines a dupe as a "deluded person," one "who allows himself to be deceived or deluded; one who is misled by false representations or notions; a victim of deception." *Merriam-Webster*'s online dictionary (retrieved January 2010) defines a dupe as "one that is easily deceived or cheated."

2. In his Farewell Address (September 19, 1796), Washington stated, "Real Patriots, who may resist the intrigues of the favorite, are liable to become suspected and odious; while its tools and dupes usurp the applause and confidence of the people, to surrender their interests." See W. B. Allen, ed., *George Washington: A Collection* (Indianapolis, Indiana: Liberty Fund, 1988), 524. Another example from the period was provided by Adam Smith, a Scottish "pen pal," so to speak, of some of the founders (especially Benjamin Franklin); in his classic work *The Theory of Moral Sentiments*, Smith used the phrase "dupes of their own sophistry." See Adam Smith, *The Theory of Moral Sentiments*, introduction by E. G. West (New Rochelle, NY: Arlington House, 1969), 79.

3. There remains dispute over whether Lenin actually used the famous phrase "useful idiots," though he often employed language and expressions very similar—as will be seen later in this chapter. A number of sources challenge the authenticity of the "useful idiots" quotation. One of the better summaries can be found in William Safire, "On Language: Useful Idiots of the West," *New York Times*, April 12, 1987. See also Paul F. Boller Jr. and John George, *They Never Said It: A Book of Fake Quotes, Misquotes, and Misleading Attributions* (New York: Oxford University Press, 1989), 76–77.

4. A search for previous books on the subject of "dupes" yielded almost nothing. A February 2009 search of Amazon.com, Google Books, and Library of Congress for any books with the title or subject "Dupes" produced only two titles: one, a foreign book titled *Dupes*, was published in 1901 and obviously is unrelated to the focus here; another, titled *9 Spies, Traitors, and Dupes*, was published in 1941, also pre–Cold War, and dealt with France. Later, I came across a 1952 book by Ralph de Toledano, titled *Spies, Dupes, and Diplomats*, which I reference later in this book.

5. For any doubters, I can show this through email documentation. Of course, anyone familiar with the long, arduous process of writing a book of this length will know that this project clearly began long before the January 2009 inauguration of Obama. I turned in my initial draft manuscript to the publisher in November 2009.

6. This is certainly the case for the cast of characters from the 1960s, such as Bill Ayers and Tom Hayden.

Of course, others, like Frank Marshall Davis, got far more attention than I otherwise would have given them because of their clear relevance both to the theme of the book and to the life of Obama, the latter of which I learned as the project evolved.

7. Even when those current political figures are not themselves Marxists, or are no longer radicals, their influence during the Vietnam era is undeniable, was sometimes lasting, and, at the very least, is historically notable. They provide a contemporary link to some of the shadowy figures of the Cold War past. Each and every one of them is a different case, and I certainly do not want to paint them with a broad brush, as close study reveals major differences. One case not addressed in this book is that of Secretary of State Hillary Rodham Clinton. As a young woman she worked with several Marxists at a law firm in San Francisco and closely studied the writings of non-Marxist radicals like Saul Alinsky, who offered the young Hillary a job, and who was the subject of Hillary's thesis as a college student at Wellesley. Secretary of State Clinton is precisely the kind of figure I'm referring to in the text. On these associations in Clinton's early life, see Paul Kengor, *God and Hillary Clinton* (New York: HarperCollins, 2007), 18–19, 37–47.

8. For more on this, see the Author's Note for a comment on motivations.

9. Mona Charen, *Useful Idiots* (Washington, DC: Regnery, 2003). See the acknowledgments for a note on Mona Charen.

10. Using the words "liberal" and "progressive" synonymously is problematic, though they usually refer to the same thing—certainly by those applying the terms. The distinctions have been blurred further with the recent reemergence of the word "progressive," especially since the election of President Obama. Suddenly, liberals who have always called themselves "liberals" are now calling themselves "progressives," and, likewise, their opponents are calling them such. Again, it is a complex matter. In this book, I tend to use the two words synonymously, fully cognizant of the risks.

11. James Burnham, *Suicide of the West: An Essay on the Meaning and Destiny of Liberalism* (New York: John Day Co., 1964), 208, 216.

12. See V. I. Lenin, *Collected Works, Vol. 31: April–December 1920* (Moscow: Progress Publishers, 1977), 291.

13. See, among others, Stéphane Courtois et al., *The Black Book of Communism: Crimes, Terror, Repression* (Cambridge, MA: Harvard University Press, 1999). Courtois et al. put the figure at sixty-five million. The latest figure of more than seventy million deaths is recorded in Jung Chang and Jon Halliday, *Mao: The Unknown Story* (New York: Knopf, 2005).

14. This is evident, for instance, in existing transcripts of meeting notes from CPUSA's central coordinating commission—basically, the personnel office—which reviewed applications for admission and readmission into the party. One might think that this desperate, ever-shrinking political party would take anyone willing to join. Not at all. I've read the minutes of these meeting notes, which are housed in the Comintern Archives on CPUSA at the Library of Congress. They are almost comical in their childish nastiness. A run-of-the-mill meeting would see every single application denied, with the final action in each case being to "expose" the applicant as, say, a "liar" or a "stool pigeon" in the next edition of the *Daily Worker.* These were generally not nice people. And they did not look nicely on liberals.

15. I do not discuss Trilling in this book, but he is an excellent case in point. For an insightful analysis, see Michael Kimmage, *The Conservative Turn: Lionel Trilling, Whittaker Chambers, and the Lessons of Anti-Communism* (Cambridge, MA: Harvard University Press, 2009).

16. Here I'm talking about political resemblance relating to the Soviet/Communist threat; obviously there are similarities on a host of other issues.

17. These words are taken from the *Public Presidential Papers* of Kennedy, specifically the volumes for the years 1961 (page 341) and 1962 (page 723n). See also Martin Walker, *The Cold War and the Making of the Modern World* (London: Fourth Estate, 1993), 132; and Eric Hobsbawm, *The Age of Extremes: A History of the World, 1914–1991* (New York: Pantheon Books, 1994), 231n.

18. "The Confusion of the West: An Analysis of Certain Aspects of Communist Political Warfare," Remarks of Senator Thomas J. Dodd at the Conference on Soviet Political Warfare, Paris, France, December 1, 1960 (Washington, DC: GPO, 1961).

19. M. Stanton Evans, *Blacklisted by History: The Untold Story of Senator Joe McCarthy and His Fight Against America's Enemies* (New York: Crown Forum, 2007), 9.

20. This applies to the modern incarnation of *The New Republic,* given that *TNR* in the 1920s, for instance, was a disastrous example of the theme of this book.

21. Harvard University Press, for example, published the seminal work *The Black Book of Communism.*

22. See John J. Miller, "The Annals of Jonathan Brent," *National Review,* May 22, 2006, 43–45.

23. Courtois et al., *The Black Book of Communism,* 3–4.

24. Malia in Courtois et al., *The Black Book of Communism,* xvii–xviii.

25. Ibid., x.

26. Ibid., x.

27. The *Black Book* estimated 20 million deaths in the USSR, which is one of the lowest usually cited. Most accounts exceed 33 million, some twice that. Lee Edwards, citing the epic work on "democide" by political scientist R. J. Rummel, who draws on the research and accounts of the likes of Robert Conquest and Aleksandr Solzhenitsyn, estimates that Soviet governments were responsible for the death of 61.9 million of their own from 1917 to 1987. See, among others, Lee Edwards, ed., *The Collapse of Communism* (Stanford, CA: Hoover Institution Press, 1999), xiii. Moreover, the North Korea numbers in the *Black Book* total do not include the 2 to 3 million who died in the famine from 1995 to 1999, directly resulting from Communist policies. See the figures cited in Barbara Crossette, "Korean Famine Toll: More Than 2 Million," *New York Times,* August 20, 1999.

28. Yakovlev recorded the gruesome details in his work *A Century of Violence in Soviet Russia* (New Haven: Yale University Press, 2002). This book should be required reading for anyone interested in the history of the period. Yakovlev's numbers are among the highest yet, but they come from a true authority who should know.

29. The latest figures of more than 70 million deaths under Mao are recorded in Jung Chang and Jon Halliday, *Mao: The Unknown Story* (New York: Knopf, 2005).

30. Crossette, "Korean Famine Toll: More Than 2 Million."

31. Aside from World War II deaths attributed to Hitler, most estimates are that he killed 6 to 10 million Jews, Slavs, gypsies, and various others he dubbed "misfits."

32. Among the worst of these, Pol Pot killed upwards of 2 to 3 million out of a Cambodian population of 5 to 7 million. In terms of percentage of population, Pot occupies the winner's circle as mankind's champion executioner. His Khmer Rouge achieved this over a mere four years. The manpower alone responsible for this enterprise is almost inconceivable. And yet Pot's yearly yield in the Killing Fields—500,000 to 750,000 per year—somehow manages to be *lower* than that of Communism as a whole.

33. Even if one takes the highest estimates for the Spanish Inquisition (1481–1545)—figures that, according to the latest scholarship, are far too high—the total of 31,912 deaths means that fewer people were killed in sixty-four years than were felled in a single year under Lenin, and probably fewer than were killed *weekly* in Stalin's Great Purge of 1934–38. The Spanish Inquisition total factors to roughly 499 killed per year or about 42 per month—a fraction of Communism's 1.4 million yearly or 119,000 monthly during its massacre. Aleksandr Solzhenitsyn cites a lower figure of 10 per month for the Inquisition. The source for 42 per month comes from the early authoritative work on the subject: J. A. Llorente, *A Critical History of the Inquisition of Spain* (1823), 575–83. As noted, the Llorente figures are now judged way too high. Solzhenitsyn's figures are published in his *Alexander Solzhenitsyn Speaks to the West* (London: Bodley Head, 1978), 17.

34. See Kennan's classic "X" article, "The Sources of Soviet Conduct," *Foreign Affairs,* July 1947.

35. An April 2008 Gallup poll found President George W. Bush with the highest disapproval ratings in the history of Gallup's presidential polling. On this, see Paul Kengor, "George 'Truman' Bush," May 9, 2008, posted at the website of the Center for Vision & Values, www.visandvals.org.

Chapter 1: World Revolution, the Comintern, and CPUSA

1. Among other editions, see Karl Marx and Friedrich Engels, *The Communist Manifesto* (New York: Penguin, Signet Classics, 1998), 91. See also Stéphane Courtois and Jean-Louis Panne in Courtois et al., *The Black Book of Communism,* 271–75.

2. Quoted in Barry Lee Woolley, *Adherents of Permanent Revolution: A History of the Fourth (Trotskyist) International* (Lanham, MD: University Press of America, 1999), 12–13.

3. Richard Pipes, *Communism: A History* (New York: A Modern Library Chronicles Book, 2001), 49.

4. Cited in Pipes, *Communism: A History*, 49. Pipes's source is A. G. Latyshev, *Rassekrechennyi Lenin* (Moscow: Mart, 1996), 40.

5. Lenin, "The Activities of the Council of People's Commissars," Report Delivered January 24 [11], 1918, at the Third All-Russian Congress of Soviets, *Lenin's Selected Works* (New York: International Publishers, 1943), vol. 7, 280.

6. The decree was published in "The Gazette of the Temporary Workers and Peasants Government," No. 31, December 13, 1917, translated and published in "Brewing and Liquor Interests and German and Bolshevik Propaganda," Report and Hearing of the Subcommittee on the Judiciary, U.S. Senate (Washington, DC: GPO, 1919), vol. 3, 185.

7. Cited by Pipes, *Communism: A History*, 49. Pipes's source is V. I. Lenin, *Polnoe sobranie sochinenii* (Complete Works), 5th ed. (Moscow: Foreign Languages Publishing House, 1958–65), vol. 42, 1.

8. Quoted by Leon Trotsky, *The History of the Russian Revolution*, translated by Max Eastman (Ann Arbor: University of Michigan Press, 1932), 395. On Trotsky and global communism, see Woolley, *Adherents of Permanent Revolution*, 13, 35, and the works of Richard Pipes.

9. This was commonplace throughout the Cold War, and will be seen especially in the Reagan chapter later in this book. For a telling denial, made by one of the biggest dupes in this book, see the interview with Ambassador Joseph E. Davies in *Life* magazine's famous March 1943 "special issue" on the USSR, which carried Stalin's face on the cover. In the article "The Soviets and the Post-War," Davies was asked whether Russia was "determined to pursue the cause of world revolution"; he said flatly, "No." Source: Joseph E. Davies, "The Soviets and the Post-War," *Life*, March 29, 1943, 49.

10. V. I. Lenin's "Letter to American Workers" was written August 20, 1918, and published in *Pravda*, August 22, 1918. The quotations here are taken from the translated version published in V. I. Lenin, *Collected Works* (Moscow: Progress Publishers, 1965), vol. 28, 62–75.

11. Quoted by Trotsky, *The History of the Russian Revolution*, 395.

12. In the original quote, the word "triumph" is "triumphs"—that is, "the Soviet government triumphs." See Lenin, "Valuable Admissions by Pitirim Sorokin," November 21, 1918, *Lenin's Selected Works* (1943 edition), vol. 8, 148–49.

13. This is published in the English translated edition of *The Capitalist World and the Communist International Manifesto of the Second Congress of the Third Communist International* (Moscow: Publishing Office of the Third Communist International, 1920), 23. This is the "American edition" published by the United Communist Party of America.

14. See Stalin's secret August 1939 speech to the Central Committee, where he urges that a continental war in Europe would be in the best interests of the Bolshevik-communist class struggle and world revolution. The text is published in Brian Crozier, *The Rise and Fall of the Soviet Empire* (Rocklin, CA: Forum, 1999).

15. I quote Stalin's speech at length later in Chapter 12. Among Lenin's missives, see Pipes, *Communism: A History*, 50–51, 93–94.

16. Some translations of this quote finish with "is inevitable," some with "will be inevitable," some with "is unavoidable." See, for instance Trotsky, *The History of the Russian Revolution*, 395; and Lenin, "Report of the Central Committee of the Russian Communist Party (Bolsheviks) at the Eighth Party Congress," March 18, 1919, *Lenin's Selected Works* (1943 edition), vol. 8, 33.

17. Lenin, "Speech Delivered at a Meeting of Nuclei Secretaries of the Moscow Organization of the Russian Communist Party (Bolsheviks)," November 26, 1920, *Lenin's Selected Works* (1943 edition), vol. 8, 297.

18. See Arthur M. Schlesinger Jr., "The Origins of the Cold War," *Foreign Affairs*, vol. 46, no. 1, October 1967, 22–52.

19. George F. Kennan, "The Sources of Soviet Conduct," *Foreign Affairs*, July 1947.

20. These Lenin letters are quoted in Solzhenitsyn, *Alexander Solzhenitsyn Speaks to the West*, 48, 54.

21. See James Bunyan, *Intervention, Civil War, and Communism in Russia, April–December 1918* (Baltimore: Johns Hopkins University Press, 1936), 227.

22. Quote cited by Solzhenitsyn, *Alexander Solzhenitsyn Speaks to the West*, 45, who cites vol. 25, 187, of Marx's collected works.

23. Dmitri Volkogonov, *Lenin: A New Biography* (New York: The Free Press, 1994), 390. On Lenin, world revolution, and the Comintern, see also Volkogonov, *Lenin*, 387–407.

24. Courtois and Panne in Courtois et al., *The Black Book of Communism*, 271–75.

25. Lenin, *Collected Works*, vol. 28, 480.

26. Ibid., 477.

27. The Comintern had notable success in pursuing its goals. The grand total of national communist parties worldwide by the 1960s was ninety-two. This was noteworthy success for a violent system that scarcely worked. The earliest party was founded in Chile in 1912. By 1924, there were thirty-seven parties in the world. Among other sources, see Crozier, *The Rise and Fall of the Soviet Empire*, 38–40, and Courtois et al., *The Black Book of Communism*, 275–76.

28. Discussion with Herb Romerstein, July 9, 2007.

29. Richard Pipes, "The Cold War: CNN's Version," in Arnold Beichman, ed., *CNN's Cold War Documentary: Issues and Controversy* (Stanford, CA: Hoover Institution Press, 2000), 45–46. These guidelines are consistent with the goals of Leninism, outlined in Lenin's 1920 work *Left-Wing Communism: An Infantile Disorder*. See Crozier, *The Rise and Fall of the Soviet Empire*, 3, 38–40.

30. See Pipes, *Communism: A History*, 93.

31. Ibid., 94–95.

32. This was point fourteen among the Comintern's twenty-one requirements of admission. See Jane Degras, ed., *The Communist International, 1919–1943: Documents*, (London: Oxford University Press, 1956), vol. 1, 166–72; and "The Communist Party of the United States of America: What It Is, How It Works," Committee on the Judiciary, U.S. Senate, 84th Congress, 2nd Session, April 23, 1956 (Washington, DC: GPO, 1956), 1–2.

33. See Pipes, *Communism: A History*, 95.

34. See Degras, *The Communist International, 1919–1943*, vol. 1, 166–72.

35. The full quotes from this program are published by Crozier, *The Rise and Fall of the Soviet Empire*, 38–40.

36. Among them, Richard Pipes told me this without hesitation when I asked him to pick a start date for the Cold War. Source: Interview with Richard Pipes, September 9, 2002. From the outset, write Courtois and Panne in *The Black Book of Communism*, Lenin regarded the Comintern as one of several instruments for international subversion. The world's many communist parties, Courtois and Panne note, "rapidly became more and more subordinate, before surrendering completely to the Comintern." This subordination was "both political and organizational," as the Comintern came to "make all major decisions for these parties and ultimately decided all questions of policy." At Moscow's instigation, the Comintern installed an armed group within each Communist Party to prepare for revolution and civil war against the reigning powers. Regardless, then, of where communism next appeared, Moscow was always the source. "Soviet Russia was the first communist regime," Courtois writes. "The Leninist and Stalinist U.S.S.R. was the cradle of all modern communism." The Soviet leadership took great pride in this fact. And the Bolsheviks' confidence that communism would expand from the Russian Civil War to Europe and the world would serve as the justification for Soviet terror for decades to come. See Courtois and Panne in Courtois et al., *The Black Book of Communism*, 271–75, 727, and 742.

37. See Degras, ed., *The Communist International, 1919–1943: Documents*, vol. 1, 166–72; and O. Piatnitsky, *The Twenty One Conditions of Admission Into the Communist International* (New York: Workers Library Publishers, February 1934), 29–31.

38. On August 8, 1920, the Comintern sent a dispatch ordering that all Communist parties in America were "immediately obliged to amalgamate and form one party." This was decided, said the Comintern, "on the basis of the decisions of the 2nd World Congress of Communist International." The Comintern also issued a deadline: "This union should be finally completed in 2 months, i.e. not later than October 1920." See Communist Party USA in the Comintern Archives, Library of Congress, Reel 1, Delo 17, Fond 515. Harvey Klehr, in his opening to the Library of Congress reference book *Files of the Communist Party of the United States of America in the Comintern Archives*, an internal source used for researchers, describes the longer series of mergers and name changes that occurred in the 1920s. The Communist Labor Party and a faction of the Communist Party of America merged in 1920 to form the United Communist Party. Later, the Communist Party of America and the United Communist Party merged under

the name of the former. In 1921 his group changed its name to the Workers Party of America, which changed again in 1925 to Workers (Communist) Party of America. The name was changed once more in 1929 to Communist Party USA (CPUSA).

39. A typical example was William Schneiderman, who in the 1930s was an agent of the NKVD, code-named "Nat" (Venona transcripts), with an alias of "Sherman," and was later made head of the Communist Party of California, where he would come into contact with individuals as significant as J. Robert Oppenheimer, the chief scientist at the Manhattan Project. Information provided by Herb Romerstein. The best source for this is Herbert Romerstein and Eric Breindel, *The Venona Secrets: Exposing Soviet Espionage and America's Traitors* (Washington, DC: Regnery, 2000), 258–68.

40. See Theodore Draper, *American Communism and Soviet Russia: The Formative Period* (New York: Viking, 1960), 162.

41. Printed in "The Communist Party of the United States of America: What It Is, How It Works," 2.

42. In the 1920s, CPUSA leaders were surprisingly open about publishing Moscow's instructions to them, which remain via the many pamphlets from the period. By 1947, U.S. government officials began to collect the pamphlets as evidence of Moscow's control, some of which they gathered from defectors but others of which were handily available as published party documents. E-mail correspondence with Herb Romerstein, April 16, 2007. Romerstein discusses these in his *Venona Secrets* and also his *KGB Against the Main Enemy*. This, too, is an obvious fact that could be demonstrated *ad nauseam,* and, for those interested, should be pursued in other sources, such as former Communist Party member Ben Gitlow's 1940 book, *I Confess. The Truth About American Communism* (New York: E. P. Dutton, 1940), which demonstrates unequivocally Moscow's control of the American party during its first ten years.

43. Any scholar interested in examining the ironclad relationship between the Comintern and CPUSA should consult these reels. Among the reels *not* referenced in this book, but likewise containing very rich material, are reels 2, 3, 10, 16, 17, 18, 20, 36, 37, 68, 70, 72, 101, 200, 201, 202, 230, 243, 247, and 287. The material in these reels is not discussed here simply because there is a limit to how much of the material can be incorporated into this book.

44. This document does not contain a date, though it clearly was produced in the summer of 1919. Communist Party USA in the Comintern Archives, Library of Congress, Fond 515, Opis 1, Delo 1.

45. Communist Party USA in the Comintern Archives, Library of Congress, Fond 515, Opis 1, Delo 1.

46. On quote, see Safire, "On Language: Useful Idiots of the West."

47. Herb Romerstein states that "only a handful" of comrades were present in Chicago "in these activities" relating to the American Communist Party's entrance into the Comintern. Source: E-mail correspondence with Herb Romerstein, November 26, 2009.

48. Communist Party USA in the Comintern Archives, Library of Congress, Fond 515, Opis 1, Delo 9.

49. Corliss and Margaret Lamont, *Russia Day by Day: A Travel Diary* (New York: Covici-Friede Publishers, 1933), 121–22.

50. Communist Party USA in the Comintern Archives, Library of Congress, Fond 515, Opis 1, Delo 9.

51. "Guide to Subversive Organizations and Publication (and Appendices), revised and published December 1, 1961, to supersede Guide published on January 2, 1957 (including Index)," prepared and released by the Committee on Un-American Activities, U.S. House of Representatives, 87th Congress, 2nd Session, House Document No 398 (Washington, DC: GPO), 198.

52. Fraina laid this out at great length in the August 23, 1919, edition of *Revolutionary Age,* reprinted in its entirety in: "Organized Communism in the United States," Committee on Un-American Activities, U.S. House of Representatives, 85th Congress, 2nd Session, August 19, 1953 (Washington, DC: GPO, 1958), 25–29. In this same report, see pages 4, 10, 29, and 141 for more on Fraina.

53. See subhead "Communist Party, USA, as a Puppet," in "The Communist Party of the United States of America: What It Is, How It Works," 64.

54. E-mail correspondence with Herb Romerstein, April 16, 2007.

55. Communist Party USA in the Comintern Archives, Library of Congress, Reel 1, Delo 17, Fond 515.

56. Communist Party USA in the Comintern Archives, Library of Congress, Fond 515, Opis 1, Delo 16.

57. The document is not dated, but clearly would have been written in May 1920. Communist Party USA in the Comintern Archives, Library of Congress, Reel 1, Delo 17, Fond 515.

58. Communist Party USA in the Comintern Archives, Library of Congress, Reel 1, Delo 25, Fond 515.

59. The speculation on churches is mine. As for the sources on the funding, there are several. The Library of Congress went public with documentation on the funding in *Revelations from the Russian Archives: A Report from the Library of Congress* (Washington, DC: Library of Congress, 1993), 29. Other sources on the funding include two articles by John E. Haynes and Harvey Klehr, "'Moscow Gold,' Confirmed at Last?" *Labor History,* vol. 33, no. 2, Spring 1992, 279–93, and vol. 33, no. 4, Fall 1992, 576–78. Haynes and Klehr actually published receipts signed by Gus Hall, head of CPUSA. See also Harvey Klehr, John E. Haynes, and Fridrikh Igorevich Firsov, *The Secret World of American Communism* (New Haven: Yale University Press, 1996), 24, and Harvey Klehr, John E. Haynes, and Kirill Mikhailovich Anderson, *The Soviet World of American Communism* (New Haven: Yale University Press, 1998), 150.

Congress has also heard testimony on this. In July 1982, FBI official Ed O'Malley testified on Soviet active measures before the House Permanent Select Committee on Intelligence. The relevant testimony appears on pages 202–3 of the bound transcript of the hearings that day, July 14, 1982, second session, 97th Congress. O'Malley testified that the KGB itself clandestinely transferred funds to CPUSA on behalf of the CPSU. He noted that CPUSA was one of the most loyal, pro-Soviet branches in the world.

The most intriguing source documenting the funding from 1953 to 1980, told through a remarkable story, is revealed in John Barron, *Operation Solo: The FBI's Man in the Kremlin* (Washington, DC: Regnery, 1996), xv, 339–40. This is the biography of Morris Childs, who is discussed later in this book, along with more details on the funding of CPUSA by the USSR. Herb Romerstein has also reported on the funding in a number of publications.

60. Among others, see Sam Tanenhaus, *Whittaker Chambers: A Biography* (New York: Random House, 1998), 58.

61. "Guide to Subversive Organizations and Publications (and Appendices), revised and published December 1, 1961, to supersede Guide published on January 2, 1957 (including Index)," 180.

62. On Childs, see Barron, *Operation Solo.* On Freeman, see Tanenhaus, *Whittaker Chambers,* 57.

63. Krafsur and Burns served in the International Brigades in the Spanish Civil War and show up often in the Comintern Archives and Venona transcripts. Heiman, whose father had been a Soviet intelligence agent, worked for the Soviet embassy and TASS, and became a spy against the U.S. government. Source: E-mail correspondence with Herb Romerstein, April 9, 2007; Romerstein and Breindel, *The Venona Secrets,* 411, 429; and John Earl Haynes and Harvey Klehr, *Venona: Decoding Soviet Espionage in America* (New Haven and London: Yale University Press, 1999), 344.

64. Interestingly, the remainder of the quote (usually not noted) reads: "That is my belief. But I don't want to live there." Among others, see the discussion in Paul Hollander, *Political Pilgrims* (New York: Harper & Row, 1983), 64.

65. E-mail correspondence with Herb Romerstein, April 16, 2007, and June 23, 2007.

66. E-mail correspondence with Herb Romerstein, April 16, 2007.

67. This quote is generally considered reliable. The quote was recorded by Yuri Annenkov from Lenin's own papers, which Annenkov gathered at the Lenin Institute. It has been published in Eduard Radzinsky, *Stalin* (New York: Doubleday, 1996), 209, among several other sources.

68. Among Lenin's deaf-mutes, including those he is apparently referring to in this quote, were the Western capitalists, of whom he is also reputed to have said (in another disputed Lenin quote) that he and his Bolsheviks would sell the capitalists the rope to hang themselves.

69. Lenin said this in a December 6, 1920, speech to the Moscow Organization of the Revolutionary Communist Party of Britain (RCPB), a transcript of which is published in Lenin, *Collected Works,* 449.

70. Karl Marx and Friedrich Engels, *The Communist Manifesto* (New York: Penguin Signet Classics, 1998), 67.

71. See Solzhenitsyn, *Alexander Solzhenitsyn Speaks to the West,* 17.

72. Courtois et al., *The Black Book of Communism,* 15.

73. Nicolas Werth, "The Dirty War," in Courtois et al., *The Black Book of Communism,* 103–4.

74. See Douglas Brown, *Doomsday 1917: The Destruction of Russia's Ruling Class* (London: Sidgwick and Jackson, 1975), 174; and George Leggett, *The Cheka: Lenin's Political Police* (Oxford: Clarendon Press, 1981), 463–68.

75. See Robert Conquest's Congressional testimony, "The Human Cost of Soviet Communism," in

Document No. 92–36, 92nd Congress, 1st session, U.S. Senate, Judiciary Committee, Subcommittee to Investigate the Administration of the Internal Security Act and Other Internal Security Laws, July 16, 1971, 5–33.

76. For only one example on Lenin specifically preaching the words "mass terror" (to Zinoviev), see Lenin, "To G. Zinoviev," June 20. 1918, *Sochineniya (Works)*, 4th ed., (Moscow: State Publishing House for Political Literature, 1951), 275.

77. Leggett, *The Cheka,* 103.

78. For transcripts of Lenin directives, see Richard Pipes, ed., *The Unknown Lenin* (New Haven: Yale University Press, 1996), 1, 3, 8–11, 13–16, 46, 50, 55–56, 61, 63, 69, 71, 116–21, 127–29, and 150–55.

79. In *The Red Terror in Russia,* published in Berlin in 1924. the Russian historian and socialist Sergei Melgunov cited Latsis, one of the first leaders of the Cheka, as giving this order to his thugs on November 1, 1918. This quote has been cited by a number of sources. Most recently, see Courtois et al., *The Black Book of Communism,* 8. Among other sources that cite this quote, see Brown, *Doomsday 1917,* 173; and Leggett, *The Cheka,* 463–68.

80. I have written a very brief summary of this view: Paul Kengor, "A Manifesto on the *Communist Manifesto,*" April 2010, posted at the website of the Center for Vision & Values, www.visandvals.org.

81. See Jean Wagner, *Black Poets of the United States: From Paul Laurence Dunbar to Langston Hughes* (Chicago and Urbana: University of Illinois Press, 1973), 435; and Faith Berry, *Langston Hughes: Before and Beyond Harlem* (New York: Citadel Press, 1992), 296–97.

82. Ibid. This famous Hughes poem is titled "Goodbye Christ."

Chapter 2: Woodrow Wilson: "Utter Simpleton"

1. Among others, see John Milton Cooper, *Reconsidering Woodrow Wilson* (Baltimore, MD: The Johns Hopkins University Press, 2008), 9.

2. A recent scathing conservative indictment is the best-selling book by Jonah Goldberg, *Liberal Fascism* (New York: Doubleday, 2008), 78–120. Goldberg makes his best case on pages 106–18.

3. Arthur S. Link, director of the Wilson papers at Princeton, said that throughout his life Wilson, a Presbyterian elder with a superb command of Reformed theology, "drew his greatest strength from the sources of Christian faith." He read the Bible daily. "It was no accident," said Link, that Wilson "never thought about public matters, as well as private ones, without first trying to decide what faith and Christian love commanded in the circumstances."

4. See the *Public Presidential Papers of Woodrow Wilson,* including: "Address to Congress," delivered to Joint Session, December 4, 1917, vol. 17, 8403; *Cablegrams,* January 13, 1919, vol. 17, 8685; "Statements on Russia," vol. 17, 8589–92; "Remarks to Democratic Committee," February 28, 1919, vol. 55, 320; "Seventh Annual Message to Congress," read (not delivered because of illness) to Congress, December 2, 1919, vol. 18, 8819; Secretary of State Bainbridge Colby, "Note of State Department on Polish Situation," August 10, 1920, vol. 18, 8864–66; and Acting Secretary of State Norman H. Davis, "Note to League of Nations" (Urging International Neutrality Towards Soviet Russia), January 18, 1921, vol. 18, 8910.

5. Wilson, "A Report of an Interview by William Waller Hawkins," *Public Papers of President Woodrow Wilson.* September 27, 1920, vol. 66, 154.

6. Wilson, "Remarks to Democratic Committee," *Public Papers of President Woodrow Wilson,* February 28, 1919, vol. 55, 320.

7. Colby, "Note of State Department on Polish Situation," 8866.

8. Wilson, "An Address in Kansas City," *Public Papers of President Woodrow Wilson,* September 6, 1919, vol. 63, 73.

9. Ibid.

10. This is recorded by Dr. Cary Grayson in his diary entry for Sunday, March 10, 1919, which is published in the *Public Papers of President Woodrow Wilson,* vol. 55, 471. The diary is held in the Grayson Collection at the Woodrow Wilson Presidential Library.

11. Wilson's 1886 piece for the prestigious *Political Science Quarterly,* titled "The Study of Administration," is credited with launching an entire subfield of political science: public administration. When I

taught public administration, this was the first reading in the course; it is often the lead article in readers used in public administration courses. Wilson's dissertation, *Congressional Government*, was for more than a century a landmark work in the field.

12. I've seen numbers ranging as high as twenty thousand U.S. troops. For two modern sources that cite roughly ten thousand, which is a conservative estimate, see Nicholas V. Riasanovsky and Mark D. Steinberg, *A History of Russia* (New York: Oxford University Press, 2005). Seventh Edition; and Walter G. Moss, *A History of Russia,* vol. 2 (New York: McGraw Hill, 1997).

13. Robert J. Maddox, *The Unknown War with Russia* (New York: Presidio Press, 1978).

14. Another gem is Lenin's March 12, 1922, "On the Significance of Militant Materialism," published in *Lenin's Collected Works,* vol. 33 (Moscow: Progress Publishers, 1972), 227–36.

15. Here I'm quoting from the translation of the speech published in the October 1919 issue of *Communist Labor,* published on page 2 as "The Tactics of the Communists, By Nicolai Lenin." It is housed in the Comintern Archives on CPUSA, Reel 1, Delo 24, Fond 515.

16. Quoted by Trotsky, *The History of the Russian Revolution,* 395.

17. Lenin said this in a December 6, 1920, speech to the Moscow Organization of the Revolutionary Communist Party of Britain (RCPB), a transcript of which is published in Lenin, *Collected Works,* Fourth Edition, translated from Russian (Moscow: Progress Publishers, 1966), 449.

18. "Guide to Subversive Organizations and Publication (and Appendices), revised and published December 1, 1961, to supersede Guide published on January 2, 1957 (including Index)," Washington, DC, 198.

19. Flier contained in Comintern Archives on CPUSA, Reel 1, Delo 26, Fond 515.

20. Ibid.

21. Conrad Cherry, *God's New Israel: Religious Interpretations of American Destiny* (Englewood Cliffs, NJ: Prentice-Hall, 1972), 288.

22. Anton Pannekork, "Bolshevism and Democracy," *Communist Labor,* May 15, 1920. This article is housed in the Comintern Archives on CPUSA, Reel 1, Delo 24, Fond 515.

23. Flier contained in Comintern Archives on CPUSA, Reel 1, Delo 26, Fond 515.

24. James W. Loewen, *Lies My Teacher Told Me* (New York: Touchstone Books, 1995), 29.

25. See Comintern Archives on CPUSA, Reel 1, Delo 24, Fond 515. The February 25, 1920, issue was vol. 2, no. 3.

26. "Alexander Mitchell Palmer," *Encyclopedia of World Biography* ([City?]: Thomson Gale, 2004). Listing at Encyclopedia.com was retrieved on September 11, 2009.

27. The article is reprinted in its entirety in "Investigation of Communist Activities in the New York City Area—Part 5," Committee on Un-American Activities, U.S. House of Representatives, 83rd Congress, 1st Session, July 6, 1953 (Washington, DC: GPO, 1953), 2240–42.

Chapter 3: Potemkin Progressives

1. On the archives, see, in particular, Pipes, *The Unknown Lenin.*

2. The investigation was done in the 1950s and was published in December 1961. It is referenced many times in the course of this book.

3. For discussion and some examples, see Hollander, *Political Pilgrims,* 18, 108, 153, 354, 388–89, 395, and 399. The example on pages 388–89 is particularly good. *Political Pilgrims* is a seminal work on the phenomenon of Western intellectuals who traveled to, and bought into the myths peddled by, the Soviet Union and other Communist states.

4. H. G. Wells, *An Experiment in Autobiography: Discoveries and Conclusions of a Very Ordinary Brain (Since 1866)* (New York: Little, Brown & Co., 1984), 215, 667, 687–89. Wells made several trips to the USSR in the 1920s and 1930s. See H. G. Wells, *Russia in the Shadows* (New York: George H. Doran Company, 1921), 160–62.

5. This meeting took place in July 1931. Shaw, who by then was in his seventies, visited the USSR for ten days. See George Bernard Shaw, *The Rationalization of Russia* (Bloomington, IN: Indiana University Press, 1964), 112. This book (134 pages in length) resulted from Shaw's lectures and interviews upon his return from the USSR and from an unfinished manuscript that he intended to complete. Harry M. Geduld picked up the manuscript and published it along with an introduction. The book was also published in 1977 by Greenview Press.

6. We know this not because Shaw admitted it in his book, but because Lady Astor, who was also present at the meeting with Stalin, asked the dictator how long he was going to continue killing people. Stalin's response was precisely along the lines of Shaw's explanation.

7. Shaw, *The Rationalization of Russia*, 73, 80–81, 109, 132n.

8. Ibid., 76.

9. Shaw wrote this in a letter to the editor of the *Manchester Guardian*, published March 2, 1933. He was the author and lead signatory of the letter, followed by twenty other signers. As the letter stated, Shaw and the other twenty had all been "recent visitors to the USSR."

10. Shaw, *The Rationalization of Russia*, 80.

11. Malcolm Muggeridge, *Chronicles of Wasted Time, Chronicle 1: The Green Stick* (New York: Quill, 1982), 244.

12. Malcolm Muggeridge, *The Sun Never Sets* (New York: Random House, 1940), 79.

13. Ibid.

14. Muggeridge, *Chronicles of Wasted Time*, 211–13.

15. Communist Party USA in the Comintern Archives, Library of Congress, Reel 302, Delo 3968, Fond 515.

16. Some accounts say that he graduated in 1913.

17. See Will Brownell and Richard N. Billings, *So Close to Greatness: A Biography of William C. Bullitt* (New York: Macmillan, 1987); and Francis P. Sempa, "William C. Bullitt: Diplomat and Prophet," *American Diplomacy*, February 2003.

18. Brownell and Billings, *So Close to Greatness*, 63.

19. Ibid., 69.

20. Ibid., 87–88.

21. Sempa, "William C. Bullitt: Diplomat and Prophet."

22. This is from a very strange, often contradictory, editorial titled "For and Against the Bolsheviki," *The New Republic*, April 6, 1918, 230–82.

23. Townsend Hoopes and Douglas Brinkley, *Driven Patriot: The Life and Times of James Forrestal* (Annapolis, MD: Naval Institute Press, 2000), 261.

24. Brownell and Billings, *So Close to Greatness*, 142–44.

25. Douglas was profiled in Amity Shlaes's bestselling book *The Forgotten Man: A New History of the Great Depression* (New York: HarperCollins, 2007). His name also appears in newly opened Soviet Comintern archives on CPUSA.

26. Communist Party USA in the Comintern Archives, Library of Congress, Reel 1, Delo 25, Fond 515.

27. "Latimer" also appears in the same Comintern collection as "J Latimer." I was able to narrow down "Latimer" to three or four most likely candidates, but was unable to confirm the precise identity. It would not be right, of course, to speculate or share those names.

28. E-mail correspondence with Herb Romerstein, November 26, 2009.

29. CPUSA in the Comintern Archives, Reel 1, Delo 25, Fond 515.

30. This is precisely how the listing reads in the document. I should, of course, state simply, "University of Iowa."

31. In the 1920s Roger Baldwin was pro-Soviet and worked closely with the Communist Party and its members, but didn't join the party. The Hitler-Stalin Pact in 1939 was his wake-up call, as it was for many liberals. He began purging Communists from the ACLU national board. After World War II, Baldwin became very anti-Communist and even shared information with the FBI. He, too, is a remarkable story of political redemption when it came to Communism.

32. In a July 1953 report by the House Committee on Un-American Activities regarding Communist activities in the New York City area, there are more references to Harry Ward than any other figure— twice as many as the next most-cited figure, CPUSA leader Earl Browder. "Investigation of Communist Activities in the New York City Area—Part 5," Committee on Un-American Activities, U.S. House of Representatives, 83rd Congress, 1st Session, July 6, 1953 (Washington, DC: GPO, 1953), 2284, 2291.

33. Kennedy wrote this in a July 3, 1945, letter while working as a young postwar journalist in Europe. See Deirdre Henderson, ed., *Prelude to Leadership: The European Diary of John F. Kennedy, Summer 1945* (Washington, DC: Regnery, 1995), 23–24, 96.

34. Most of the biographical information on Douglas cited here can be found in two books: Paul H. Douglas, *In the Fullness of Time* (New York: Harcourt and Brace, 1971); and Roger Biles, *Crusading Liberal: Paul H. Douglas of Illinois* (DeKalb, IL: Northern Illinois University Press, 2002). Also helpful is a biographical essay by John Keohane, which is available online at the library database of the University of Chicago. See also *The Biographical Directory of the U.S. Congress: 1774–Present* (available online).

35. Shlaes, *The Forgotten Man*, 47–73.

36. On this, see my paper "Red Herring: The Great Depression and the American Communist Party," October 2008, posted at the website of the Center for Vision and Values.

37. Shlaes, *The Forgotten Man*, 76.

38. Sylvia R. Margulies, *Pilgrimage to Russia* (Madison: University of Wisconsin, 1968); and Shlaes, *The Forgotten Man*, 399.

39. Shlaes, *The Forgotten Man*, 76.

40. Ibid., 77.

41. Documents available in "Archives of the Communist Party and Soviet State," collection in the Hoover Institution Archives, FOND 89, "Communist Party of the Soviet Union on Trial," compiled by Lora Soroka. These letters are coded as Reel 1.1006, opis 49, (21) (22) (23).

42. Shlaes, *The Forgotten Man*, 77.

43. Ibid.

44. Ibid., 78.

45. Ibid., 77.

46. Ralph de Toledano, *Spies, Dupes, and Diplomats* (New York: Duell, Sloan, and Pearce, 1952), 190.

47. See Corliss Lamont, *The Illusion of Immortality* (New York: Continuum, 1990), vii–xiii. This is the fifth edition of the work, originally published in 1935. The book was his dissertation at Columbia, finished in 1932.

48. Corliss Lamont's precise title and role with Friends of the Soviet Union is difficult to determine. Various sources list different titles. For instance, an obituary published by the *Independent* (London) called Lamont "a sometime chairman of the Friends of the Soviet Union." (John Gregory, "Obituary: Corliss Lamont," *Independent*, May 12, 1995.) The titles are complicated by the fact that the name of the organization itself, and its related organizations and even apparent umbrella organization, were constantly changing. For example, the *New York Times* obituary on Lamont described him as "head" of the National Council of American-Soviet Friendship, whereas others sources (including the Web-based politicalgraveyard.com) list him as "president" of the council. (Robert D. McFadden, "Corliss Lamont Dies at 93," *New York Times*, April 28, 1995.) A July 23, 1938, edition of the *Daily Worker*, excerpted as "Exhibit No. 1" in a 1944 congressional report, called Lamont "head of the American Friends of the Soviet Union," whereas "Exhibit No. 2," which was a simple listing of the officers and national board of the "American Council on Soviet Relations," listed him as "national chairman." ("Investigation of Un-American Propaganda Activities in the United States," prepared and released by the Committee on Un-American Activities, U.S. House of Representatives, Washington, DC, 82nd Congress, 2nd Session, 1944, 365–66.) All of these titles for Lamont varied along with the ever-shifting titles of the organizations themselves, the names of which always seemed to change ever so slightly (and suspiciously). Either way, Lamont was one of the principal leaders of Friends of the Soviet Union.

49. "Guide to Subversive Organizations and Publications (and Appendices), revised and published December 1, 1961, to supersede Guide published on January 2, 1957 (including Index)," 77.

50. William Z. Foster, *Toward Soviet America* (New York: International Publishers, 1932), 272–73.

51. The copy of the magazine that I'm citing is the January 1932 edition. The degree to which Sinclair was duped is quite remarkable. I intend to detail Sinclair's dupery in another work.

52. Countless examples of those letters are today available for reading in the Comintern Archives on CPUSA.

53. CPUSA in the Comintern Archives, Reel 259, Delo 3366, Fond 515.

54. Corliss and Margaret Lamont, *Russia Day by Day: A Travel Diary* (New York: Covici-Friede Publishers, 1933).

55. The Lamonts mentioned a travel agency called "Open Road," on which I was unable to find informa-

tion. The interpreters are identified as "Mrs. Lydia Diederichs" and "Mrs. Frankel." Likewise, I could not find any information on these two people.

56. Muggeridge wrote about this experience many times, including in a personal, detailed March 1983 letter to President Ronald Reagan. This letter is quoted and cited in my *God and Ronald Reagan: A Spiritual Life* (New York: ReganBooks, 2004), 253.

Chapter 4: John Dewey: The Kremlin's Favorite Educator

1. "Ten Most Harmful Books of the 19th and 20th Centuries," *Human Events,* November 19, 2007, 10. This was a republication of the list, which actually first appeared in the May 30, 2005, issue.

2. Henry T. Edmondson III, *John Dewey and the Decline of American Education* (Wilmington, DE: ISI Books, 2006), xiv.

3. This quote is taken from Carey's endorsement on the back cover of Edmondson's book.

4. Pragmatism, developed by Charles Pierce and William James, is the theory that the meaning of a course of action or proposition lies in its observable consequences; it is the sum of those consequences that constitute the meaning of the action or proposition. This is considered a practical way of addressing problems. It can be applied—as it was by Dewey—to the classroom in the form of a desire to experiment in search of the best methods of learning.

5. To cite merely some recent buzzwords that spring from this mindset, there are "whole language," "outcomes-based education," "self-esteem," and "values clarification."

6. Michael L. Peterson sheds light on these various shades of Dewey's thinking: "Experimentalism rejects any concept of a transcendent, ultimate, fixed reality (such as the idealist's realm of ideas and supreme mind, the Aristotelian's pure form, and the Thomist's absolute being). According to experimentalism, all traditional, otherworldly views rest on the unfounded metaphysical presumption. Experience—common human experience—is the only basis for philosophy. Since experience is constantly changing, experimentalists think about how we can adapt to as well as control changes in our environment. This approach has far-reaching implications for education, whether conceived narrowly as curriculum reform and teacher training or broadly as the basis for the adjustment process of the individual in the social and physical environment." Michael L. Peterson, *With All Your Mind: A Christian Philosophy of Education* (Notre Dame, IN: University of Notre Dame Press, 2001), 51–52.

7. Edmondson, *John Dewey and the Decline of American Education,* 13, 25–27, 40, 97–114.

8. Peterson, *With All Your Mind,* 53.

9. Edmondson, *John Dewey and the Decline of American Education,* 6.

10. Ibid., 6–7.

11. Sources vary on whether she was staunchly Congregationalist, a strict five-point Calvinist, or, as one biographer put it, possessive of "a comparatively cool, urbane Universalism." Neil Coughlan, *Young John Dewey* (Chicago, University of Chicago Press, 1975), 3–4.

12. Generally speaking, Mrs. Dewey, as a young woman, became a devout person, which she brought into her marriage and her parenting. John Dewey never forgot how his mother often asked him and his brothers if they were "right with Jesus." She ordered her sons not to drink, smoke, dance, gamble, play cards, shoot billiards, and so on. A number of leading leftist intellectuals of the day, some of them prominent converts who left the "clutches of the God that failed"—as Communism had been famously referred to in those days—wrote about this aspect of Dewey, from Sidney Hook to Max Eastman, both of whom knew Dewey very well.

13. Too few scholars have delved into spiritual biography of Dewey. An article by Jared Stallones provides valuable historical detail. Jared Stallones, "Struggle for the Soul of John Dewey," *American Educational History Journal,* vol. 33, no. 1, 2006.

14. Stallones, "Struggle for the Soul of John Dewey," 21–23.

15. Ibid.

16. Ibid., 23.

17. Ibid., 24.

18. When Dewey moved to Chicago in 1894, he withdrew as a member of the First Congregational Church in Ann Arbor without requesting a transfer to another church. Ibid., 25.

19. Alan Ryan, *John Dewey and the High Tide of American Liberalism* (New York: W. W. Norton, 1997), 186.

20. Specifically, Dewey said that it was the "belief in immortality more than of any other element of historic religions" that made him believe that "religion is the opium of peoples." Dewey's review of Lamont's book *The Illusion of Immortality,* ran in the April 24, 1935, issue of *The New Republic.* See Lamont, *The Illusion of Immortality,* vii–xiii. This is the fifth edition of the work, originally published in 1935.

21. Edmondson, *John Dewey and the Decline of American Education,* 19.

22. Ibid., 19–20.

23. Ibid.

24. The alleged Dewey quote states, "There is no god and there is no soul." This is cited, for instance, at the sites for Accuracy in Media (AIM.org) and AllAboutPhilosophy.org.

25. Dewey was one of thirty-four signers. The manifesto, which lists fifteen principles for which humanists stand, is available at the website of the American Humanist Association: http://www.americanhumanist.org/who_we_are/about_humanism/Humanist_Manifesto_I.

26. Lamont, *The Illusion of Immortality,* 254.

27. Dewey judged Lamont's work "an extraordinarily complete and well-informed discussion."

28. Lamont, *The Illusion of Immortality,* vii–xiii.

29. Merton downplayed his own short-term infatuation with Communism as youthful silliness, which, for him, seemed the case. Still, his chronology of this period reveals him to have been duped repeatedly by Communists. He and others mouthed the party line, whatever it was, including the convenient preaching for peace—proffered only when it served Moscow's interests. Merton came to his senses much quicker than many other dupes—with the aid of a firm intellectual grounding in Roman Catholicism, which was intensely anti-Communist—and developed a mature understanding of the "virulence" of Soviet Communism.

30. Thomas Merton, *The Seven Storey Mountain* (New York: Harcourt Brace, 1948), 153–57.

31. Ibid., 153–56. Merton was an admirer of Mark Van Doren, another *New Republic* writer who was on the left and suspected (by some) of being on the Marxist left. Merton credits Van Doren's presence at Columbia for saving him from Communism: "It was a very good thing for me that I ran into someone like Mark Van Doren at that particular time, because in my new reverence for Communism, I was in danger of docilely accepting any kind of stupidity."

32. Ibid., 194.

33. Columbia philosophy professor John Herman Randall was a prominent member of the American Philosophical Association. He was a Columbia man through and through, receiving his own education there (undergraduate and graduate school) as well as being an educator at the university. Ibid.

34. Kimmage, *The Conservative Turn,* 26.

35. Edmondson, *John Dewey and the Decline of American Education,* 10–11.

36. William Brooks, "Was Dewey a Marxist?" *Discourse: The Journal of the St. Lawrence Institute,* vol. 13, Winter 1994, available at the website for St. Lawrence Institute for the Advancement of Learning, http://stlawrenceinstitute.org/vol13brk.html.

37. For a discussion of Dewey's reported membership in the Socialist Party, see, among others, an insightful analysis by Tiffany Jones Miller, "John Dewey and the Philosophical Refounding of America," *National Review,* December 31, 2009, 37–40.

38. Sometimes, after a number of lessons learned, Dewey and other socialists parted ways with the Communists—in some cases angrily expelling their comrades. This was the case, for instance, with the League for Industrial Democracy, the socialist group of which Dewey was a member in the 1930s. At the same time, even with such repudiations, Dewey worked arm-in-arm with the Trotskyites, the anti-Stalin wing of the international Communist movement. This raised suspicions that Dewey was anti-Stalin (which he was, adamantly) but not anti-Trotsky, and, hence, not really anti-Communist. As was so often the case with Dewey, ambiguity prevailed when trying to get a handle on what the philosopher-educator truly believed.

39. William W. Brickman, ed., *John Dewey's Impressions of Soviet Russia and the Revolutionary World, Mexico-China-Turkey 1929* (New York: Bureau of Publications, Teachers College, Columbia University, 1964), 17.

40. Ibid., 17–18.

41. Ibid., 18.

42. W. Bruce Lincoln, *Red Victory: A History of the Russian Civil War* (New York: Simon & Schuster, 1989), 11–12.

43. Brickman, ed., *John Dewey's Impressions*, 18.

44. Edmondson, *John Dewey and the Decline of American Education*, 10–11.

45. Strong's trip took place in either 1922 or 1923.

46. "Investigation of Communist Activities in the New York City Area—Part 5," Committee on Un-American Activities, U.S. House of Representatives, 83rd Congress, 1st Session, July 6, 1953 (Washington, DC: GPO, 1953), 2250.

47. For example, Strong wrote a letter to the editor published in the October–November 1941 issue of *The Protestant* (pages 105–6) in which she claimed that the Vatican was pushing for religious freedom in the USSR not because religious freedom was lacking there—she suggested such freedom was flourishing—but because the Catholic Church was seeking political and religious control, and especially over the Russian Orthodox Church. This was just what liberal Protestants wanted to hear, and many swallowed it hook, line, and sinker. The letter is republished in "Investigation of Communist Activities in the New York City Area—Part 5," Committee on Un-American Activities, 2250–51.

48. Corliss and Margaret Lamont, *Russia Day by Day*, 82, 118.

49. Tanenhaus, *Whittaker Chambers*, 33.

50. Brickman, ed., *John Dewey's Impressions*, 19.

51. Albert P. Pinkevich, *The New Education in the Soviet Republic* (New York: John Day, 1929), vi.

52. Thomas Woody, *New Minds, New Men?* (New York: Macmillan, 1932), 47–48.

53. Brickman, ed., *John Dewey's Impressions*, 19.

54. During his trip to the USSR in the summer of 1928, Dewey attended an educational conference organized by Professor Kalashnikov. They apparently hit it off quite well. It was ten days after the conference that Kalashnikov sent Dewey the two-volume encyclopedia.

55. Quoted in Jay Martin, *The Education of John Dewey: A Biography* (New York: Columbia University Press, 2002), 354.

Chapter 5: John Dewey's Long, Strange Trip

1. Brickman, ed., *John Dewey's Impressions*, 19–20, 58n.

2. Ibid., 55.

3. Ibid.

4. Ibid., 55–56.

5. The collection of essays was published in 1929 by The New Republic, Inc., as well as in subsequent Dewey writings and a later (1964) volume edited by William W. Brickman, produced and published by the Teachers College at Columbia University. The quotes cited herein are taken from the Brickman edition.

6. Brickman, ed., *John Dewey's Impressions*, 44.

7. Ibid.

8. Ibid., 44–45.

9. Ibid., 45.

10. Ibid., 46.

11. Ibid., 47.

12. Ibid.

13. Ibid., 48.

14. Ibid., 50.

15. Ibid., 54–55.

16. Ibid.

17. Ibid., 63.

18. Ibid.

19. Ibid., 65.

20. Ibid., 65n.

21. For one striking source on this, see Alexander Solzhenitsyn, *The Gulag Archipelago, 1918–1956* (New York: Harper and Row, 1974), 29, 37–38, 325–27, 345–51.

22. Brickman, ed., *John Dewey's Impressions*, 65n.

23. Brickman, ed., *John Dewey's Impressions*, 65.

24. "A Restored Look for the Long-Ignored Churches of Russia," Associated Press, July 23, 1976, B3.

25. Brickman, ed., *John Dewey's Impressions*, 65.

26. In a blessed moment for Russia's beleaguered believers, neither seen or appreciated in the West, First Lady Nancy Reagan, during the June 1988 Moscow summit, threw a fit over what had happened to these cherished items of Russian religious and cultural history—specifically the holy classics in the reserve collection of the Tretyakov Gallery. The Communists had removed these lovely, sacred works from public view. The Russian authorities, very sensitive to PR, acceded to the request of their high-profile guest and momentarily displayed the images. It was maybe Nancy Reagan's finest hour. I write about this in *God and Ronald Reagan*, 308. Also, Nancy Reagan's trip was briefly but cautiously reported by *Pravda*. See "Nancy Reagan Visits Moscow Art Gallery," *Pravda*, June 2, 1988, 5, translated text from Soviet media printed in Foreign Broadcast Information Service (hereafter FBIS), June 6, 1988, 24.

27. Mikhail Gorbachev, *Memoirs* (New York: Doubleday, 1996), 328.

28. Mikhail Gorbachev, *On My Country and the World* (New York: Columbia University Press, 2000), 20–21.

29. Brickman, ed., *John Dewey's Impressions*, 72.

30. Ibid., 74, 89.

31. Ibid., 47, 74–75, 99.

32. Ibid., 74–75.

33. Ibid., 75–76.

34. Ibid., 75n.

35. Ibid., 78–80.

36. Ibid.

37. Ibid., 79.

38. Ibid., 29.

39. Ibid., 110–11.

40. See Ibid., 29; and Jane M. Dewey, "Biography of John Dewey," in Paul A. Schilpp, ed., *The Philosophy of John Dewey* (Evanston, IL: Northwestern University Press, 1939), 43.

41. Shlaes, *The Forgotten Man*, 47–48, 50, 144.

42. Ibid., 144–45.

43. Many of those of similar mind saw the collectivization as enormously promising. Dewey saw it as potentially promising, and (predictably) was more in favor of (and impressed by) the Soviet willingness to "experiment" in the realm of economic "collectivism." See ibid., 144–45; and Brickman, ed., *John Dewey's Impressions*, 102–3.

44. I will address this in more detail later in the book. "He [Dewey] was very left," notes Herb Romerstein, "but not under the control of the Communist Party." Interview with Herb Romerstein, August 9, 2007.

Chapter 6: The Redemption of Professor Dewey

1. The article was John Dewey, "Why I Am Not a Communist," *Modern Monthly*, vol. 8, April 1934, 135–37. It was reprinted in Sidney Hook, ed., *The Meaning of Marx: A Symposium by Bertrand Russell, John Dewey, Morris Cohen, Sidney Hook, and Sherwood Eddy* (New York: Farrar & Rinehart, 1934).

2. Steven C. Rockefeller, *John Dewey: Religious Faith and Democratic Humanism* (New York: Columbia University Press, 1991), 439. See also John Patrick Diggins, *The Promise of Pragmatism* (Chicago: University of Chicago Press, 1995), 399; and Robert B. Westbrook, *John Dewey and American Democracy* (Ithaca, NY: Cornell University Press, 1993), 468–69.

3. Ronald Reagan, News Conference, January 29, 1981, available at http://www.presidency.ucsb.edu/ws/index.php?pid=44101.

4. Brickman, ed., *John Dewey's Impressions*, 19–20.

5. This committee has also been called the Committee for the Defense of Leon Trotsky, as well as numerous other names. It is sometimes said that there was a Committee of Inquiry, of which the Committee for the Defense of Leon Trotsky was an offshoot. It is impossible to find a single common name used by historians. The one I've chosen to use is taken from the early edited book by William W. Brickman (*John Dewey's Impressions*, p. 7), who seemed meticulous in trying to get these names exactly right. See also Tanenhaus, *Whittaker Chambers*, 140–41.

6. Herb Romerstein offers this insight: "Dewey was not a Trotskyite sympathizer. In fact, most of the people on the Dewey Commission were opposed to Trotsky because they quite properly blamed him for a lot of the persecution of non-Communist leftists when Trotsky was Lenin's partner in ruling Russia. The Trotskyites, of course, supported the commission and had a front organization—the American Committee for the Defense of Leon Trotsky. Even that group had a lot of other leftists in it. While they disliked Trotsky, they were even more opposed to Stalin." Interview with Herb Romerstein, August 9, 2007.

7. Tanenhaus, *Whittaker Chambers,* 118, 140–44.

8. For details on this, see Romerstein and Breindel, *The Venona Secrets,* 329–31.

9. Historians will alternately refer to these as both "reports" and "books," sometimes in quotation marks, sometimes italicized. In fact, both were published by Harper & Row, and are basically reports published as books.

10. See Romerstein and Breindel, *The Venona Secrets,* 331; Brickman, ed., *John Dewey's Impressions,* 20; and Klehr, Haynes, and Anderson, *The Soviet World of American Communism,* 301.

11. Bloomfield regretted that Duranty "cannot conceal more or less sympathy for the concerned," which included a number of his persecuted Communist "friends," such as Karl Radek, Grigori Sokolnikov, and Trotsky.

12. CPUSA in the Comintern Archives, Fond 515, Opis 1, Delo 4076.

13. CPUSA in the Comintern Archives, Fond 495, Opis 20, Delo 536.

14. Shlaes, *The Forgotten Man,* 326.

15. Brickman, ed., *John Dewey's Impressions,* 20–21.

16. Ibid., 21–22.

Chapter 7: Smearing Another Liberal Icon: CPUSA's Assault on "Fascist" FDR and the New Deal

1. It would seem especially obvious that Communists would prefer the liberal FDR to Herbert Hoover if we believe the standard historical narrative about Hoover. Many historians have painted Herbert Hoover as a president who recklessly pursued laissez-faire economic policies. In fact, this is wrong: Herbert Hoover was not a laissez-faire conservative; he intervened extensively in the economy. See, for example, the work of economist and economic historian Lawrence Reed of the Mackinac Center and Foundation for Economic Education, specifically: Lawrence W. Reed, "Great Myths of the Great Depression," *The Freeman,* August 1998.

2. This is evident particularly in reels 230 to 236.

3. CPUSA in the Comintern Archives, Fond 515, Opis 1, Reel 230, Delos 2967–2979.

4. Ibid.

5. CPUSA in the Comintern Archives, Fond 515, Opis 1, Reel 260, Delo 3371.

6. Ibid.

7. Ibid.

8. This flier is not dated by year. My best estimate is that it referred to January 21, 1934, which is the timeframe where it was located in the Comintern Archives on CPUSA. (Other documents in that particular reel featured dates from December 1933 to January 1934.) It could not have been prior to 1934, and was almost certainly part of the tenth-anniversary celebrations (for Lenin) that year. CPUSA in the Comintern Archives, Fond 515, Opis 1, Reel 259, Delo 3364.

9. This is filed in the Comintern Archives on CPUSA under Fond 515, Opis 1, Reel 273, Delo 3484.

10. There were many accusations that Perkins, who was very liberal, was a Communist. To my knowledge, no such proof ever materialized. Indeed, Perkins's FBI file, now available for examination, says she was not a Communist. The file is posted and available for viewing at http://foia.fbi.gov/alpha.htm.

11. This was the assessment in the article by Grace Hutchins, "You're Telling Me," *The Working Woman,* May 31, 1934, 3. Hutchins was a well-known party member. See "Investigation of Communist Activities in the New York City Area—Part 5," Committee on Un-American Activities, U.S. House of Representatives, 83rd Congress, 1st Session, July 6, 1953 (Washington, DC: GPO, 1953), 2097, 2106.

12. Tanenhaus, *Whittaker Chambers,* 91–94.

13. On Ware, see also "The Shameful Years: Thirty Years of Soviet Espionage in the United States," prepared and released by the Committee on Un-American Activities, U.S. House of Representatives,

82nd Congress, 2nd Session, (Washington, DC: GPO, December 30, 1957) 55–58; and Tanenhaus, *Whittaker Chambers,* 91–94.

14. On Abt, see "The Shameful Years," 55–58; Tanenhaus, *Whittaker Chambers,* 91–94.

15. Editorial, *The New Republic,* February 6, 1935.

16. Tanenhaus, *Whittaker Chambers,* 91–94.

17. Ibid.

18. Ibid.

19. On Pressman, see "The Shameful Years," 58. On Hopkins, see Romerstein and Breindel, *The Venona Secrets,* 215–16. The authors write, "One of the members of the group was Harry Hopkins."

20. Romerstein and Breindel, *The Venona Secrets,* 215.

21. Christopher Andrew and Oleg Gordievsky, *K.G.B.: The Inside Story* (New York: HarperCollins, 1992). For a contemporaneous counter to Gordievsky, see Verne W. Newton, "A Soviet Agent? Harry Hopkins?" *New York Times,* October 28, 1990. This counterpoint is not well done, but Newton does raise (but not resolve) Gordievsky's confusing phrase "unconscious agent."

22. Romerstein and Breindel, *The Venona Secrets,* 212.

23. Military historian Eduard Mark has broken this down in careful detail. See Eduard Mark, "Venona's Source 19 and the 'Trident' Conference of May 1943: Diplomacy or Espionage?" *Intelligence and National Security,* Summer 1998, 1–31. See also Romerstein and Breindel, *The Venona Secrets,* 214, 473. A photocopy of the transcript is published on page 473 of *The Venona Secrets.*

24. Interview with Herb Romerstein, via e-mail, February 13, 2009.

25. FDR said this in a January 19, 1941, meeting with Wendell Wilkie. See, among others, Conrad Black, *Franklin Delano Roosevelt: Champion of Freedom* (New York: Public Affairs, 2003), 610.

26. Earl Browder, *Report to the 8th Convention, Communist Party* (New York: Workers Library Publishers, 1934), 104.

27. "Conditions of Admission to the Communist International," *Party Organizer,* February 1931, 31.

28. Quoted in "Structure and Function of Party Units," *Party Organizer,* February 1931, 2. As further evidence of such thinking, M. J. Olgin, Communist and Browder colleague, said during FDR's first year in power: "The Communist Party of the U.S.A. is thus part of a worldwide organization which gives it guidance and enhances its fighting power. Under the leadership of the Communist Party the workers of the U.S.A. will proceed from struggle to struggle, from victory to victory, until, rising in a revolution, they will crush the capitalist State, establish a Soviet State, abolish the cruel and bloody system of capitalism and proceed to the upbuilding of Socialism." M. J. Olgin, *Why Communism?* (New York: Workers Library Publishers, 1933), 95.

29. On Browder's work, see, among others, Jerrold L. Schecter and Leona Schecter, *Sacred Secrets: How Soviet Intelligence Operations Changed American History* (Dulles, VA: Brassey's, 2002), 35, 50; Allen Weinstein and Alexander Vassiliev, *The Haunted Wood: Soviet Espionage in America* (New York: Random House, 1999), 302–3; and Haynes and Klehr, *Venona,* 211.

30. Sources differ on the exact date of the pardon, with a lot of very sloppy scholarship all over the Internet. My best estimate is that the pardon took place in May 1942. One would think that this would be an easy thing to confirm. Yet even the most reliable historians use different dates.

31. Dimitroff had been head of the Comintern from 1934 until well after Stalin claimed to have dissolved the organization. Some sources claim that Dimitroff took over the Comintern in 1933 or 1935. He remained in office until the organization's alleged dissolution by Stalin in 1943. After the war, he would leave the Comintern to go back to his native Bulgaria, where he became the beleaguered nation's Communist despot after its "liberation" by the Red Army. It was largely in 1946 that Dimitroff took the reins of power in Bulgaria. He died in 1949. Like Lenin, his body was embalmed and put on display. When the Cold War ended, his body was buried (in 1990).

32. On Dimitroff to Browder, radio message, received June 12, 1943, see Comintern Archives, Fond 495, Opis 184, Delo 19, 28. For letters, see Roosevelt Library, Franklin Roosevelt correspondence, Earl Browder to President Roosevelt, June 14, 1943; President Roosevelt to Browder, June 23, 1943; President Roosevelt to Browder, June 26, 1943; and Browder to President Roosevelt, July 12, 1943. On the domestic politics dealings, see the early work by John T. Flynn, *The Roosevelt Myth* (New York: Devin-Adair, 1948), 371–74.

33. See Sheldon B. Liss, *Marxist Thought in Latin America* (Berkeley, CA: University of California Press, 1984), 56–57.

34. This is all clear from the letters. See also Romerstein and Brendel, *The Venona Secrets,* 179.

35. James G. Ryan, *Earl Browder: The Failure of American Communism* (Tuscaloosa, AL: The University of Alabama Press, 1997), 108.

36. Romerstein and Breindel, *The Venona Secrets,* 178–79; and Ryan, *Earl Browder: The Failure of American Communism,* 129.

37. Haynes and Klehr, *Venona,* 212–13.

38. The Comintern was eventually morphed into the "International Department," which existed until the Soviet implosion in the 1980s.

39. Ibid., 213–15.

40. Robert E. Sherwood, *Roosevelt and Hopkins: An Intimate History* (New York: Harper, 1948), 313.

41. George N. Crocker, *Roosevelt's Road to Russia* (Chicago: Regnery, 1959), 18, 211.

42. Crocker here cites Cordell Hull, *The Memoirs of Cordell Hull* (New York: Macmillan, 1948), 974.

43. Crocker, *Roosevelt's Road to Russia,* 18, 211.

44. In addition to viewing these letters in or by other sources, some published, others not, I've corresponded (via e-mail) with Robert Clark, supervisory archivist at the FDR Presidential Library at Hyde Park, New York, July 3 and 8, 2008.

45. In addition to the material cited hereafter, see also Harvey Klehr, "The Strange Case of Roosevelt's 'Secret Agent': Frauds, Fools, and Fantasies," *Encounter* [Great Britain] 59, no. 6 (1982), 84–91; and Joseph P. Lash, *Eleanor and Franklin: The Story of Their Relationship, Based on Eleanor Roosevelt's Private Papers* (New York: Norton, 1971), 702–4.

46. Ryan, *Earl Browder: The Failure of American Communism,* 212–13. Ryan's sources include the *Philadelphia Inquirer,* May 23, 1941, as well as interviews and private papers of Theodore Draper, housed at Emory University, Atlanta, Georgia.

47. Ibid.

48. Ryan, *Earl Browder: The Failure of American Communism,* 212–14. Ryan cites correspondence (four letters from December 1941 to April 1942) between Eleanor and Adams, as well as a Theodore Draper interview with Eleanor.

49. Romerstein and Breindel, *The Venona Secrets,* 178–79, 181. The authors cite Comintern Archives, Fond 495, Opis 74, Delo 485, 21 (in Russian), and July 4 and 12, 1944, letters between Josephine Adams and Eleanor Roosevelt, July 4, 1944, and Secretary Earl G. Harrison.

50. Ryan, *Earl Browder: The Failure of American Communism,* 212–13.

51. Ibid., 214–15.

52. These letters were from Adams to Eleanor Roosevelt, January 1944, and from Eleanor Roosevelt to Adams, July 13, 1944, which are housed in the Eleanor Roosevelt papers, Franklin D. Roosevelt Library, Hyde Park, NY. Haynes and Klehr write about this and even produce the letters in their works, including their *Venona* (213–17) and *The Secret World of American Communism* (249–58), which are the go-to sources for detailed examination of this matter.

53. Haynes and Klehr, *Venona,* 213–17

54. Ryan, *Earl Browder: The Failure of American Communism,* 214.

55. Haynes and Klehr, *Venona,* 213–17.

Chapter 8: War Communism: Hating FDR, Loving FDR

1. Comintern Archives on CPUSA, Library of Congress, Reel 302, Delo 3973.

2. "Guide to Subversive Organizations and Publications (and Appendices), revised and published December 1, 1961, to supersede Guide published on January 2, 1957 (including Index)," No. 398, 22–23.

3. Comintern Archives on CPUSA, Library of Congress, Fond 515, Opis 1, Delo 4082.

4. "Investigation of Un-American Propaganda Activities in the United States," Special Committee on Un-American Activities, House of Representatives, 78th Congress, Second Session, on H. Res. 282, App. part IX, vol. 1 (Washington, DC: GPO, 1944), 431; and "Guide to Subversive Organizations and Publications (and Appendices), revised and published December 1, 1961, to supersede Guide published on January 2, 1957 (including Index)," 26–28.

5. Comintern Archives on CPUSA, Library of Congress, Fond 515, Opis 1, Delo 4091.

6. See the biography of Eugene Dennis by his wife, Peggy Dennis, *The Autobiography of an American Communist: A Personal View of a Political Life, 1925–1975* (Westport, CT: Greenwood Press, 1977).

7. Judy Kaplan and Linn Shapiro, eds., *Red Diapers: Growing Up in the Communist Left* (Urbana and Chicago: University of Illinois Press, 1998), 317–18.

8. The House Committee on Un-American Activities said that the American Peace Mobilization began in the summer of 1940 under the auspices of CPUSA and the Young Communist League. Ryan/Dennis's date of September 1940 simply refers to the launch of the national meeting.

9. "Peace Group Assails Roosevelt," *Washington Post,* October 11, 1940.

10. A flier on this event was provided by Herb Romerstein.

11. See David H. Anthony, "Max Yergan," *Encyclopedia of the American Left,* 2nd ed., eds. Mary Jo Buhle, Paul Buhle, and Dan Georgakas (New York: Oxford University Press, 1998), 912.

12. Wallace D. Best, *Passionately Human, No Less Divine: Religion and Culture in Black Chicago, 1915–1952* (Princeton, NJ: Princeton University Press, 2005); and R. Marie Griffith and Barbara Dianne Savage, eds., *Women and Religion in the African Diaspora: Knowledge, Power, and Performance* (Baltimore: Johns Hopkins University Press, 2006).

13. Archibald Roosevelt et al., "A Compilation of Public Records, 20.5%, 1411 Protestant Episcopal Rectors," March 1958 (Cincinnati, OH: Publishing Committee). This document was self-published, and received a lot of attention in its day.

14. "Clergymen Group Charges War Aim," *New York Times,* January 10, 1941.

15. Edward T. Folliard, "A.P.M. Head 'Welcomes' Aid of Communists," *Washington Post,* January 26, 1941.

16. Ibid.

17. Toledano, *Spies, Dupes, and Diplomats,* 182–85; and Evans, *Blacklisted by History,* 375.

18. Senate Judiciary Committee, Senate Report 2050, on the Institute of Pacific Relations (July 2, 1952), 223, 225; and "Guide to Subversive Organizations and Publications (and Appendices), revised and published December 1, 1961, to supersede Guide published on January 2, 1957 (including Index)," 87.

19. Toledano, *Spies, Dupes, and Diplomats,* 189–90.

20. Evans, *Blacklisted by History,* 406–7.

21. Edward T. Folliard, "Peace Mobilizers Deny Communism," *Washington Post,* May 17, 1941.

22. Of the six *New York Times* articles that I consulted on this period, only one (published May 13, 1941) noted that the American Peace Mobilization "has been charged with being a Communist Front group." See "'Peace' Pickets Routed at White House Gates," *New York Times,* May 13, 1941.

23. "Call, American People's Meeting," New York City, April 5–6, 1941.

24. Romerstein and Breindel, *The Venona Secrets,* 114.

25. Among the Columbia professors frequently found at American Peace Mobilization gatherings, sometimes as officers, sponsors, or endorsers, were Franz Boaz and Walter Rautenstrauch. See "Investigation of Un-American Propaganda Activities in the United States," Special Committee on Un-American Activities, House of Representatives, 432, 446.

26. Seventeen of the eighteen listed as "Rev." were Protestants. The lone Catholic was the Reverend F. Hastings Smyth.

27. Interview with Herb Romerstein, June 27, 2007.

28. As noted, Olgin had vowed in his 1933 book that "the workers of the U.S.A. will proceed from struggle to struggle, from victory to victory, until, rising in a revolution, they will crush the capitalist State, establish a Soviet State, abolish the cruel and bloody system of capitalism and proceed to the upbuilding of Socialism." See M. J. Olgin, *Why Communism?,* 95.

29. Some of these individuals were more open about their party membership, even if only later in life. Pete Seeger, interviewed for a 2008 episode of the PBS series *American Masters,* and by then an old man, conceded that he had been a Communist. He first joined the Young Communist League as a student at Harvard in the mid-1930s and then in the early 1940s joined CPUSA as a card-carrying member. Ronald and Allis Radosh refer to the Almanacs as "the Communist folk-singing group." See Ronald Radosh and Allis Radosh, *Red Star Over Hollywood: The Film Colony's Long Romance with the Left* (San Francisco:

Encounter Books, 2005), 78. See also Paul C. Mishler, *Raising Reds* (New York: Columbia University Press. 1999), 7, 101, 105–6.

30. Comintern Archives on CPUSA, Library of Congress, Fond 495, Opis 184, Delo 3.

31. A number of sources confirm this. Aside from the documents themselves, located in the Comintern archives on CPUSA, there is also the published account in Georgi Dimitroff's diary, published in German, specifically on page 364. (The title of the book is *Georgi Dimitroff Tagebucher 1933–1943*, published by Aufbau-Verlag.) I also confirmed this in various conversations with Herb Romerstein, including several emails in June 2007.

32. Many documents like this now exist. There are transcripts of secret radio messages from Moscow to CPUSA in 1939 ordering American Communists to toe the Soviet line and shape their propaganda accordingly. Likewise, transcripts from 1941 order a complete reversal in the party line after Hitler betrayed Stalin and invaded the Soviet Union.

33. "Protest Against War Staged by Women," *New York Times*, May 11, 1941.

34. "'Peace' Pickets Routed at White House Gates"; "2,000 Attend Peace Rally," *New York Times*, May 17, 1941; and "Pickets Picketed," *Time*, June 2, 1941.

35. "White House Pickets Quit," *New York Times*, June 22, 1941.

36. Ibid.

37. The Germans invaded Russia in the very early morning hours of June 22, local time; in Washington it was still June 21, which was the dateline for the *Times* piece that ran in the June 22 edition.

38. Border troops inside the USSR were alerted as early as 00:30 Moscow time on June 22, 1941, which would have been late afternoon June 21 in Washington. German pilots were bombing Soviet cities by 3:00 A.M. Moscow time on June 22.

39. Henry Winston, "Our Tasks Today," report to the national committee of the Young Communist League, July 19, 1941. The text was published in *Clarity*. the self-described "Theoretical Organ of the Young Communist League, U.S.A.," Summer 1941, vol. 2, no. 2, 30–40.

40. The emergency meeting would be held July 19–20, 1941.

41. I cited this same document earlier. It is from Wilkins in a November 22, 1949, letter to Communist William L. Patterson, who headed the front group the Civil Rights Congress. Wilkins and the NAACP made it available to the media in a November 23, 1949, press release.

Chapter 9: Duping FDR: "Uncle Joe" and "Buddies"

1. David McCullough, *Truman* (New York: Simon & Schuster, 1992), 262.

2. James MacGregor Burns, *Roosevelt: The Soldier of Freedom* (New York: Harvest Books, 2002), 114.

3. Black, *Franklin Delano Roosevelt: Champion of Freedom*, 642–44. Hopkins sent the cable to FDR from the U.S. embassy in Moscow on August 1.

4. Flynn, *The Roosevelt Myth*, 340.

5. Among others directly citing this quote, see Flynn, *The Roosevelt Myth*, 340; John T. Flynn, *While You Slept* (New York: Devin-Adair, 1951), 38; Frazier Hunt, *The Untold Story of Douglas MacArthur* (New York: Devin-Adair, 1954), 191; and Tim Tzouliadis, *The Forsaken: An American Tragedy in Stalin's Russia* (New York: Penguin, 2008), 204. On Hopkins and Stalin's "nationalism," see also Donald W. Treadgold and Herbert J. Ellison, *Twentieth-Century Russia*, ninth edition (Boulder, CO: Westview Press, 2000), 296.

6. Jan Ciechanowski, *Defeat in Victory* (New York: Doubleday, 1947), 231; and Flynn, *The Roosevelt Myth*, 340–41.

7. John R. Deane, *Strange Alliance* (New York: Viking, 1947), 43.

8. The harshest critics of Stalin's vicious idiocy were the Soviets themselves, including Stalin's eventual successor, Nikita Khrushchev.

9. Some of the best recent work in this area has been done by Ronald Radosh. See, for instance Ronald Radosh and Joyce Milton, *The Rosenberg File* (New Haven, CT: Yale University Press, 1997).

10. Romerstein and Breindel, *The Venona Secrets*, 210–11.

11. A copy of the receipt is published in ibid., 210–11, 468.

12. Ibid., 210–11.

13. FDR said this on January 8, 1934, in his welcome of the Soviet ambassador. The full quote reads: "I trust that you will inform His Excellency, the President of the Central Executive Committee, the Gov-

ernments, and the people of the Soviet Union of the Soviet Socialist Republics that their kind messages of good-will are deeply appreciated and that I send in return sincere wishes for their peaceful progress and happiness." Source: *The Public Papers and Addresses of Franklin D. Roosevelt*, vol. 3, 24–25.

14. The quote attributed to FDR (in an alleged statement to Joe Davies, of all people) is: "I can't take communism, nor can you, but to cross this bridge I would hold hands with the Devil." See, among others, John Lewis Gaddis, *Strategies of Containment* (New York: Oxford University Press, 2005), 6; John Lewis Gaddis, *The Cold War: A New History* (New York: Penguin, 2006), 93; and Stephen M. Walt, *The Origins of Alliances* (Ithaca, NY: Cornell University Press, 1990), 38n. Conrad Black records that "Roosevelt was much more cautious" than Churchill about supporting the Communists after they were attacked by Nazi Germany. Black cautions that FDR "was no admirer of the Soviet regime, as he had often made clear." Black, *Franklin Delano Roosevelt*, 640.

15. A case where FDR was openly critical of the Soviet system, referring not to Stalin (by name) but to the "dictatorship" of "Russia," was his February 10, 1940, address to delegates from the American Youth Congress in Washington, DC.

16. Published in Warren Kimball, ed., *Churchill and Roosevelt: The Complete Correspondence*, vol. I (Princeton, NJ: Princeton University Press, 1984), 421.

17. Jan Ciechanowski, *Defeat in Victory* (New York: Doubleday, 1947), 231; and Flynn, *The Roosevelt Myth*, 340–41.

18. Wilson D. Miscamble, *From Roosevelt to Truman* (New York: Cambridge University Press, 2007), 52.

19. Will Brownell and Richard N. Billings, *So Close to Greatness: A Biography of William C. Bullitt* (New York: Macmillan, 1987); and Francis Sempa, "William C. Bullitt: Diplomat and Prophet," *American Diplomacy*, February 2003.

20. Brownell and Billings, *So Close to Greatness*, 278.

21. The quote has been published in a number of sources. Bullitt's original August 10, 1943, memo, as well as his accounting of FDR's response, is published in Orville H. Bullitt, ed., *For the President—Personal and Secret: Correspondence Between Franklin Delano Roosevelt and William C. Bullitt* (Boston: Houghton Mifflin, 1972), 595–99. It is also published in William C. Bullitt, "How We Won the War and Lost the Peace," *Life*, August 30, 1948, 94.

22. Bullitt made the comments on "factual evidence" and "wishful thinking" in a memo to FDR earlier in the year, on January 29, 1943.

23. I first encountered the Hopkins portion in a book by conservative author Thomas Woods, and was simply shocked by it. Source: Thomas E. Woods Jr., *The Politically Incorrect Guide to American History* (Washington, DC: Regnery, 2004), 184. It took me time to track down the original quotation, but I found that Woods had it right. Wilson Miscamble includes the Hopkins portion in his account, *From Roosevelt to Truman* (page 52). A book by Townsend Hoopes and Douglas Brinkley, two fair historians, does not include it, inserting, instead, an ellipsis. See Townsend Hoopes and Douglas Brinkley, *Driven Patriot: The Life and Times of James Forrestal* (Annapolis, MD: Naval Institute Press, 2000), 261. Historian Martin McCauley uses part of the quote, but leaves out the Hopkins portion. See Martin McCauley, *The Soviet Union: 1917–1991* (London: Longman, 1993), 170. The worst offender is Conrad Black, who not only breaks up the quote, eliminating the Harry Hopkins portion, but then maligns William Bullitt's credibility, writing: "It is inconceivable that Roosevelt would have said anything so foolish as Bullitt claims." Black writes: "William Bullitt became more erratic than ever following his loss of influence after forcing Sumner Welles out of government. He fathered the claim that Roosevelt had a hunch that if he gave Stalin 'everything I possibly can and ask for nothing in return . . . he won't try to annex anything and will work with me for a world of democracy and peace.'" Black, *Franklin Delano Roosevelt*, 1076–77. Additional examples of Roosevelt biographies that do not include the Bullitt quote, either in part or full (with or without Hopkins), include: Nathan Miller, *F.D.R.: An Intimate History* (New York: William Morrow, 1992); and Frank Freidel, *Franklin D. Roosevelt: A Rendezvous with Destiny* (New York: Little Brown, 1990). An acclaimed and extremely sympathetic biographer of Roosevelt who does not cite the quote is William Leuchtenburg. See William Edward Leuchtenburg, *In the Shadow of FDR: From Harry S. Truman to George W. Bush* (Ithaca, NY: Cornell University Press, 2001); and William Edward Leuchtenburg, *The FDR Years: On Roosevelt and His Legacy* (New York: Columbia University Press, 1995).

24. These numbers are easy to find today. For a fairly contemporary and very widely read analysis that

includes precisely these numbers, see Fulton Sheen, *Communism and the Conscience of the West* (New York: Bobbs-Merrill, 1948).

25. Samuel I. Rosenman, ed., *The Public Papers and Addresses of Franklin D. Roosevelt, The Tide Turns 1943*, vol. 12 (New York: Random House, 1950), 558.

26. FDR used this term of endearment, for instance, in an August 26, 1944, note to Churchill. For the full text, see Kimball, *Churchill and Roosevelt: The Complete Correspondence*, vol. 3.

27. As relayed by FDR to Frances Perkins. See Perkins's full account: Frances Perkins, *The Roosevelt I Knew* (New York: The Viking Press, 1946), 83–85.

28. Ibid.

29. Ibid.

30. Ibid., 85.

31. Black, *Franklin Delano Roosevelt*, 882.

32. Perkins, *The Roosevelt I Knew*, 83.

33. For the record, I was one of the sixty-five presidential scholars included in C-SPAN's survey of the presidents published for Presidents' Day 2009. Although I did lower my score on FDR in the category of foreign policy because of his dealings with Stalin and the USSR, overall I ranked him very high, among the top four or five of presidents. So what I've described here is not a reflection of my overall evaluation of Roosevelt and his presidency.

34. Published in Kimball, *Churchill and Roosevelt, The Complete Correspondence*, vol. 3.

35. FDR referring to Stalin as "UJ" in correspondence dated June 28, 1943, which is the earliest existing reference, to my knowledge. See Kimball, *Churchill and Roosevelt, The Complete Correspondence*, vol. 2.

36. As an example, Biddle noted of FDR: "He said that for a year and a half he had been trying to persuade 'Winnie'—as he always calls Churchill—to agree to return Hong Kong to the Chinese after the war. Winnie's response had always been a grunt." Quoted, among others, in Freidel, 493. Freidel cites Biddle's notes from December 17, 1943, held at the Library of Congress. Freidel also cites Harold Ickes's diary notes from December 19, 1943, also held at the Library of Congress. See also John M. Blum, ed., *The Price of Vision: Diary of Henry A. Wallace 1942–1946* (Boston: Houghton Mifflin, 1973), 279–84.

37. Perkins, *The Roosevelt I Knew*, 83.

38. Ibid., 83–84.

39. Miscamble, *From Roosevelt to Truman*, 53.

40. Among others, see Benjamin B. Fischer, "The Katyn Controversy: Stalin's Killing Field," *Studies in Intelligence*, Winter 1999–2000, available online at the CIA website, www.cia.gov; and Laurence Rees, *World War II Behind Closed Doors: Stalin, the Nazis, and the West* (New York: Pantheon, 2008), 52–55.

41. There are several sources on the Earle episode, including Fischer, "The Katyn Controversy"; Allen Paul, *Katyn: The Untold Story of Stalin's Polish Massacre* (New York: MacMillan, 1991), 314–15; and Rees, *World War II Behind Closed Doors*, 247–50. The most interesting recent account is the 2009 PBS documentary to which Rees's book was a companion volume, both by the same name. The documentary includes filmed footage of interviews with Earle's son. Earle himself died in 1974. The Earle account was first publicly exposed when Congress held hearings on Katyn in 1951 and 1952, though FDR's hagiographers were quick to let it drop.

42. See Evans, *Blacklisted by History*, 87–93.

43. Klehr, Haynes, and Firsov, *The Secret World of American Communism*, 281–83.

44. Ciechanowski, *Defeat in Victory*, 30–32; and Remarks of Congressman John Lesinski, *Congressional Record*, June 17, 1943, 6000. See also Evans, *Blacklisted by History*, 90–91.

45. Romerstein and Breindel, *The Venona Secrets*, 403.

46. Corliss and Margaret Lamont, *Russia Day by Day*, 249.

47. U.S. Congress, House of Representatives, Select Committee on the Katyn Forest Massacre. *The Katyn Forest Massacre: Hearings Before the Select Committee on Conduct and Investigation of the Facts, Evidence, and Circumstances of the Katyn Forest Massacre*, 82nd Congress, 1st and 2nd Session, 1951–1952 (Washington, DC: GPO, 1952), 2197.

48. Ibid.

49. Ibid., 2204–7; Rees, *World War II Behind Closed Doors*, 248–49; and Rees's PBS documentary, part 2 of a three-part series.

50. *The Katyn Forest Massacre: Hearings Before the Select Committee on Conduct and Investigation of the Facts, Evidence, and Circumstances of the Katyn Forest Massacre,* 2204–7; Rees, *World War II Behind Closed Doors,* 248–49; and Rees's PBS documentary, part 2 of a three-part series.

51. Eugen Kovacs, "East Poland Reported Starving Because Russia Is Taking Food: Refugees Say Many Have Been Deported to Interior of Soviet Union," *New York Times,* April 15, 1940, A5.

52. *The Katyn Forest Massacre: Hearings Before the Select Committee on Conduct and Investigation of the Facts, Evidence, and Circumstances of the Katyn Forest Massacre,* 2204–7; Rees, *World War II Behind Closed Doors,* 248–49; and Rees's PBS documentary, part 2 of a three-part series.

53. *The Katyn Forest Massacre: Hearings Before the Select Committee on Conduct and Investigation of the Facts, Evidence, and Circumstances of the Katyn Forest Massacre,* 2204–7; Rees, *World War II Behind Closed Doors,* 248–49; and Rees's PBS documentary, part 2 of a three-part series.

54. Rees, *World War II Behind Closed Doors,* 249, 423n; and Rees's PBS documentary, part 2 of a three-part series. Rees cites a facsimile of the March 24, 1945, letter published by George Earle in his article "FDR's Tragic Mistake," *Confidential,* August 1958 (vol. 6, no. 3).

55. Rees, *World War II Behind Closed Doors,* 249–50; and Rees's PBS documentary, part 2 of a three-part series. See also Fischer, "The Katyn Controversy," which also reports the dispatching to Samoa.

56. Ibid.

57. Rees, *World War II Behind Closed Doors,* 38–39.

58. In a major speech in Latvia in May 2005, Bush condemned Yalta as following in "the unjust tradition of Munich and the Molotov-Ribbentrop Pact [the Hitler-Stalin Pact]." On Reagan and Yalta, see Kengor, *The Crusader,* 42–43, 87, 106.

59. Jacob Heilbrunn, "Once Again, the Big Yalta Lie," *Los Angeles Times,* May 10, 2005. Heilbrunn's op-ed piece was in response to Bush's comments on Yalta in Latvia in May 2005. For responses to both, from the Right, see Editorial, "Yalta Regrets," *National Review Online,* May 11, 2005; and Arnold Beichman, "FDR's Failure Not Forgotten," *Human Events,* May 13, 2005.

60. Black, *Franklin Delano Roosevelt,* 1080.

61. Ibid.

62. Hiss at Yalta is a subject currently receiving attention in the research of M. Stanton Evans and Herb Romerstein, who are investigating the subject, and take a very different view than Black.

63. Robert E. Sherwood, *Roosevelt and Hopkins: An Intimate History* (New York: Harper, 1948), 869–70.

64. Ibid.

65. Ibid.

66. Though his language is more restrained than mine here, Wilson Miscamble expresses a similar view. He uses the phrase "single moment of surrender or betrayal." See Miscamble, *From Roosevelt to Truman,* 61.

67. Gary Kern, "How 'Uncle Joe' Bugged FDR: The Lesson of History," *Studies in Intelligence,* vol. 47, no. 1, 2003, available online at the CIA website, www.cia.gov.

68. Black, *Franklin Delano Roosevelt,* 1080.

69. Ibid.

70. Ibid.

71. Ibid., 1081.

72. Beichman, "FDR's Failure Not Forgotten"; and Susan Butler, ed., *My Dear Mr. Stalin: The Complete Correspondence of Franklin D. Roosevelt and Joseph V. Stalin* (New Haven, CT: Yale University Press, 2005), 27.

73. *Foreign Relations of the United States, Diplomatic Papers, The Conferences of Malta and Yalta, 1945* (Washington, DC: GPO, 1960), vol. 5, 194–96.

74. I detail this at length in Paul Kengor, *Wreath Layer or Policy Player? The Vice President's Role in Foreign Policy* (Lanham, MD: Lexington Books, 2000), 22–25.

75. For this and similar quotations, including from Ambassador Robert Murphy, see ibid., 23. The original source for the quote is Vaughan's oral-history testimony at the Truman Library. Many historians, especially scholars of Harry Truman and the vice presidency, have made use of the quotation, the latter particularly including Marie Natoli, who has done excellent work on this subject.

76. Ibid.

77. Sherwood, *Roosevelt and Hopkins*, 851–55.

78. Ibid.

79. Rees, *World War II Behind Closed Doors*, 362–66.

80. *Foreign Relations of the United States, Diplomatic Papers, The Conference of Berlin, 1945* (Washington, DC: GPO, 1960), vol. 1, 28.

81. Rees, *World War II Behind Closed Doors*, 351–52.

82. Many conservatives, however, did not like Bohlen at all. On this, see Evans, *Blacklisted by History*, 481–89.

83. Charles E. Bohlen, *Witness to History, 1929–1969* (New York: Oxford University Press, 1998), 211.

84. Ibid., 211.

Chapter 10: The Hollywood Front

1. Other versions of the quote, based on slightly differing translations, have Lenin saying, "Of all the arts, the motion picture is for us the most important." That version was widely quoted in the Communist press. To cite one instance, this quotation appears on page 502 of the September 1925 edition of *The Workers Monthly*. Another commonly quoted variation is: "You must remember that of all the arts, for us the most important is cinema." For sources on this version, see Anna M. Lawton, *The Red Screen* (London: Routledge, 2002), 58; and Ian Christie, ed., *The Film Factory: Russian and Soviet Cinema in Documents, 1896–1939* (London: Routledge, 1994), 56–57.

2. "Special Magazine Supplement," *Daily Worker*, August 15, 1925 7.

3. Lawton, *The Red Screen*, 58

4. Peter Hanson, *Dalton Trumbo, Hollywood Rebel: A Critical Survey and Filmography* (Jefferson, NC: McFarland, 2001), 79.

5. John Howard Lawson, *Film in the Battle of Ideas* (New York: Masses & Mainstream, 1953).

6. Ibid.

7. Kenneth Lloyd Billingsley, *Hollywood Party: How Communism Seduced the American Film Industry in the 1930s and 1940s* (Rocklin, CA: Prima Forum, 1998), 258.

8. Ibid., 205.

9. In a "FAQ" section on its website, under the heading, 'Who are some of the people who have been members of the CPUSA?" CPUSA lists Dashiell Hammett among a short list of fourteen members. See http://www.cpusa.org/article/static/511/#question12 (retrieved from website December 12, 2009). Hammett joined the party in the latter 1930s (most accounts claim 1937) and also supported the "anti-war" platform of the American Peace Mobilization, meaning he, too, flip-flopped on Hitler based on where Stalin stood.

10. Billingsley, *Hollywood Party*, 179, 267.

11. Ibid., 196.

12. Robeson, too, is today proudly proclaimed by CPUSA (on its website) as one of its members.

13. If true, this would have likely meant she did not join the party, meaning she was not technically or officially a "Communist."

14. The suit never went to trial because of Hellman's death. See Stephen Buckley, "Literary Critic and Novelist Mary McCarthy Dies at 77," *Washington Post*, October 26, 1989, B11.

15. Paul Johnson, *Intellectuals* (New York: HarperCollins, 1990), 288.

16. Hellman was one of the infamous signers of an "Open Letter to American Liberals" that attacked the Dewey Commission. See Alan M. Wald, *The New York Intellectuals: The Rise and Decline of the Anti-Stalinist Left* (Chapel Hill, NC: The University of North Carolina Press, 1987), 132; and Radosh and Radosh, *Red Star Over Hollywood*, 80, 182, 188, 204–6.

17. Alan M. Wald, *Trinity of Passion: The Literary Left and the Antifascist Crusade* (Chapel Hill, NC: The University of North Carolina Press, 2007), 182, 210–35.

18. Ibid., 297–98. Among others, Wald cites: Isidor Schneider, "All My Sons," *New Masses*, February 18, 1947, 28–29; Isidor Schneider, "Death of a Salesman," and Samuel Siller, "Another Viewpoint," *Masses & Mainstream*, April 1949, 88–96; Mike Phillips, "Letter on Arthur Miller," *Daily Worker*, March 1, 1949, 12; Lee Newton, "Arthur Miller's Hit Play," *Daily Worker*, February 14, 1949, 11.

19. Wald says that "circumstantial evidence is overwhelming" that Miller wrote for *New Masses* under

the name of Matt Wayne. Wald cites the testimony of two editors of *New Masses*. Wald, *Trinity of Passion*, 212, 294n.

20. Arthur Miller, "Should Ezra Pound Be Shot?" *New Masses*, December 25, 1945, 4.

21. The *Daily Worker* interview was done by Beth McHenry, who carried the byline for the article. Beth McHenry, "*Focus* Author Hopes to Make Anti-Semitism Understood," *Daily Worker*, April 17, 1946, 13.

22. Wald, *Trinity of Passion*, 228.

23. McHenry, "*Focus* Author Hopes to Make Anti-Semitism Understood," 13.

24. This meeting took place on October 14, 1947. See Wald, *Trinity of Passion*, 227.

25. Fast's nonfiction *The Incredible Tito* was published in 1944 by the New York–based Magazine House.

26. Wald, *Trinity of Passion*, 228.

27. Tony Kushner, "Kushner on Miller," *The Nation*, June 13, 2005, 6.

28. For instance, much later, in his memoir *Timebends*, Miller at long last acknowledged the failure to discern "the clear parallels between the social institutions of the fascist and Nazi regimes and those of the Soviet Union." Arthur Miller, *Timebends: A Life* (New York: Grove Press, 1987), 86.

29. Harry Raymond, "*The Crucible*: Arthur Miller's Best Play," *Daily Worker*, January 28, 1953, 7.

30. Allen Drury, "Arthur Miller Admits Helping Communist-Front Groups in '40s," *New York Times*, June 22, 1956.

31. Ibid.; and "Investigation of the Unauthorized Use of United States Passports—Part 4," Hearings before the Committee on Un-American Activities, House of Representatives, June 21, 1956, 4655–89.

32. This was done as an exhibit presented during the testimony of Sue Warren, who had been "educational director" for the Communist Party. See "Investigation of the Unauthorized Use of United States Passports—Part 5," Hearings before the Committee on Un-American Activities, House of Representatives, July 26, 1957, 1352–61.

33. "Investigation of the Unauthorized Use of United States Passports—Part 4," Hearings before the Committee on Un-American Activities, House of Representatives, June 21, 1956, 4689.

34. Miller's refusal to openly discuss his motivations has long caused much confusion. I personally know of two cases from completely different ideological perspectives, both within western Pennsylvania, where I reside. One is a liberal high-school history teacher who, for decades before Miller's admission in the *Guardian* in June 2000, taught his students that *The Crucible* was a parable of McCarthyism. The other, a conservative, is a stage director at a university who was asked to stage *The Crucible*; she did her research and could not find attestation from Miller admitting that the play was a lesson against McCarthyism.

35. Arthur Miller, "Are You Now or Were You Ever . . . ?" *Guardian*, June 17, 2000.

36. Ibid.

37. "Arthur Miller, Moral Voice of American Stage, Dies at 89," *New York Times*, February 12, 2005. Also, on Miller's admission, see Roger Kimball, "Arthur Miller, Communist Stooge," *The New Criterion*, February 12, 2005.

38. Miller, "Are You Now or Were You Ever . . . ?"

39. See Miller, *Timebends*, 81, 116, 183–84, 192, 308–9, 516–18; Drury, "Arthur Miller Admits Helping Communist-Front Groups in '40s"; Wald, *Trinity of Passion*, 216; Joanna E. Rapf, *On the Waterfront* (New York: Cambridge University Press, 2003), 42; and Martin Gottfried, *Arthur Miller: His Life and Work* (Cambridge, MA: Da Capo Press, 2003), 157–58.

40. Billingsley, *Hollywood Party*, 220.

41. Ibid., 242.

42. It has been widely reported that Geer was not only a communist but also a Communist Party member. Online encyclopedia sources (including Wikipedia, retrieved December 11, 2009) go so far as to claim that Geer joined CPUSA in 1934. I cannot verify that, but clearly he was quite far to the left, and very likely a communist (ideologically) at some point.

43. See, among others, Ron and Allis Radosh, *Red Star Over Hollywood*, 183–84.

44. Billingsley, *Hollywood Party*, 222–24.

45. Ibid., 55.

46. Katharine Hepburn's mother, also named Katharine, was a suffragette, birth-control advocate, and friend of Margaret Sanger. In the 1920s Katharine's mother served on the board of directors of

Sanger's American Birth Control League. Sanger preached "race improvement" and desired widespread use of birth control in part for that purpose. She hoped to rid the American population of what she termed "human weeds." Among others, see Margaret Sanger, "The Pope's Position on Birth Control," *The Nation*, January 27, 1932, 103; and Margaret Sanger, *The Pivot of Civilization* (New York: Brentano's, 1922), 80–104.

47. See Ronald Reagan and Richard G. Hubler, *Where's the Rest of Me?* (New York: Duell, Sloan & Pearce, 1965), 183; and Radosh and Radosh, *Red Star Over Hollywood*, 113.

48. See Billingsley, *Hollywood Party*, 177–78.

49. Even then, there are other claims, and rumors, swirling around this controversy. Readers can read these files online at the FBI's database http://foia.fbi.gov/alpha.htm.

50. This, too, is a claim reported by sources in the FBI file; the bureau investigated the claim. It seemed to be the main source of evidence that Lucille Ball was possibly still involved in the party.

51. Ronald Reagan talks warmly of Robinson and how he was a gentle soul frequently exploited. See Reagan, *Where's the Rest of Me?* 183 and Billingsley, *Hollywood Party*, 230.

52. Radosh and Radosh, *Red Star Over Hollywood*, 169–70.

53. See, for instance Billingsley, *Hollywood Party*, 180.

54. California Legislature, "Fourth Report of the Senate Fact-Finding Committee on Un-American Activities, 1948, Communist Front Organizations," California Senate, Senate Committee on Un-American Activities, 236–40.

55. Radosh and Radosh, *Red Star Over Hollywood*, 165.

56. For a fair discussion, see ibid., 33–35.

57. Patrick McGilligan and Paul Buhle, eds., *Tender Comrades: A History of the Hollywood Blacklist* (New York: St. Martin's Press, 1997), 143. Also, on Bright, see Radosh and Radosh, *Red Star Over Hollywood*, 33–34.

58. McGilligan and Buhle, *Tender Comrades*, 143.

59. Billingsley, *Hollywood Party*, 86.

60. Ibid., 86.

61. Luce's instruction into the Catholic Church by Bishop Fulton Sheen, a staunch anti-Communist, played a major role in her informed anti-Communism.

62. Clayton R. Koppes and Gregory D. Black, *Hollywood Goes to War: How Politics, Profits, and Propaganda Shaped World War II Movies* (Berkeley: University of California Press, 1937), 190.

63. David H. Culbert, *Mission to Moscow* (Madison, WI: University of Wisconsin Press, 1980), 17.

64. The movie is available for purchase. It is occasionally broadcast on Turner Classic Movies. One recent broadcast, which I watched, was on February 8, 2009.

65. Examples of this are given by the Radoshes. See Radosh and Radosh, *Red Star Over Hollywood*, 98, 271.

66. Koppes and Black, *Hollywood Goes to War*, 198.

67. Historian Steven Casey writes that "Roosevelt was instrumental in getting this [Davies's] book turned into a full-length movie." Steven Casey, *Cautious Crusade: Franklin D. Roosevelt, American Public Opinion, and the War Against Nazi Germany* (New York: Oxford University Press, 2001), 62.

68. Todd Bennett, "Culture, Power, and Mission to Moscow," *Journal of American History*, vol. 88, no. 2, September 2001, 495.

69. Ibid.

70. Ibid.

71. Ibid.

72. Culbert, *Mission to Moscow*, 253–55; and Radosh and Radosh, *Red Star Over Hollywood*, 97.

73. Ibid.

74. Ibid.

75. Bosley Crowther, "Mission to Moscow, Based on Ex-Ambassador Davies' Book," *New York Times*, April 30, 1943.

76. Radosh and Radosh, *Red Star Over Hollywood*, 92–97.

77. Letter to the editor, John Dewey and Suzanne La Follette, "Several Faults Are Found in 'Mission to Moscow' Film," *New York Times*, May 9, 1943.

78. The Nazis were not appalled at all, and, either way, did not mind the Soviet greed because they planned to break their pact with Stalin.

79. Radosh and Radosh, *Red Star Over Hollywood,* 92–97.

80. See Woolley, *Adherents of Permanent Revolution,* 22–27.

81. Reagan, *Where's the Rest of Me?* 141. This may have been a historically unappreciated factor in Reagan's later writing his own speeches, including many while he was president.

82. Ibid., 164–65; Anne Edwards, *Early Reagan* (New York: William Morrow, 1987), 246, 300; and Billingsley, *Hollywood Party,* 123.

83. Reagan, *Where's the Rest of Me?* 141, 164–65; and Edwards, *Early Reagan,* 300.

84. This has been described in many accounts, including Reagan's own autobiographies, *An American Life* (New York: Simon & Schuster, 1990) and *Where's the Rest of Me?* (pages 164–70). Among the better accounts are those by Anne Edwards in her *Early Reagan* and the excellent research of Stephen Vaughn in his *Ronald Reagan in Hollywood: Movies and Politics* (New York: Cambridge University Press, 1994), 124–26. See also Billingsley, *Hollywood Party,* 123; and Radosh and Radosh, *Red Star Over Hollywood,* 115.

85. Reagan, *Where's the Rest of Me?,* 164–70; Billingsley, *Hollywood Party,* 123; Radosh and Radosh, *Red Star Over Hollywood,* 115.

86. Radosh and Radosh, *Red Star Over Hollywood,* 114–15.

87. Ibid.

88. Billingsley, *Hollywood Party,* 123–24.

89. On this, see Reagan, *An American Life,* 106–7.

90. Quote taken from Reagan, *An American Life,* 106–7. There Reagan's version of Kleihauer's quote is slightly different from the version used in *Where's the Rest of Me?* (pages 141–42), where he records Kleihauer as saying: "I agree with most of what you said, but don't you think, while you're denouncing Fascism, it would be fair to speak out equally strongly against the tyranny of Communism?" I write about this episode in *God and Ronald Reagan,* 51–53.

91. For just two examples of Reagan being called a "fascist," by his own account, see Reagan, *Where's the Rest of Me?* 167, 175.

92. I have noticed repeatedly in my research on Reagan how he went from being the darling of liberals and progressives—feted as brilliant, caring, sensitive—to being a loathsome, reactionary "moron" as he nudged more and more to the right, and especially as he became politically active on the right. Likewise, he quickly morphed (in the eyes of the Left) from being a respected actor who did good work to a "B-movie actor" who ranked only slightly more intelligent than a chimpanzee. He went from being a civil-rights champion—who indeed had always treated black Americans with great kindness and no prejudice whatsoever (since he was a boy in Dixon, Illinois)—to being a "racist." This is what happened when Reagan went to the "other side"; the Left savaged him. Other Reagan researchers have told me or reported that they discerned a similar pattern, including (in their books and articles) Hollywood observers Anne Edwards and John Meroney. See Kengor, *The Crusader,* 11–12, 326–27.

93. Hayden would ultimately cooperate with the House Committee on Un-American Activities, naming names and confessing his past Communist ties. But he later strongly regretted doing so.

94. The exact period of Hayden's membership in the Communist Party is unclear, though he seems to have joined (for certain) by some point in 1946 and remained in the party for a fairly short time, leaving no later than 1947. See Hayden's memoirs, Sterling Hayden, *Wanderer* (New York: Knopf, 1963), 371; and also his bio at the website of Turner Classic Movies (TCM), http://www.tcm.com/tcmdb/participant.jsp?spid=83248.

95. Reagan, *Where's the Rest of Me?* 173.

96. Radosh and Radosh, *Red Star Over Hollywood,* 117–22.

97. See Peggy Noonan, *When Character Was King: A Story of Ronald Reagan* (New York: Viking-Penguin, 2001), 56–57; and Peter Schweizer, *Reagan's War* (New York: Doubleday, 2002), 11–12.

98. See "Threatened in '46 Strike, Ronald Reagan Testifies," *Los Angeles Times,* January 14, 1954, 3. Reagan subsequently wrote and talked about this a number of times. See also Billingsley, *Hollywood Party,* 153; and Reagan, *Where's the Rest of Me?* 148–58, 174.

99. See Reagan, *Where's the Rest of Me?* 159–62, 171–75; and Radosh and Radosh, *Red Star Over Hollywood,* 120–22.

100. The strike was jurisdictional, meaning that it centered over which union would represent the workforce.

101. See Reagan, *Where's the Rest of Me?* 159–62, 172; and Radosh and Radosh, *Red Star Over Hollywood,* 120–22.

102. Hayden talked about this in his April 10, 1951, testimony before the House Committee on Un-American Activities.

103. See Radosh and Radosh, *Red Star Over Hollywood,* 121–22.

104. Stalin's remarks were published in the March 13, 1946, edition of *Pravda.* For a number of analyses of Stalin's reaction, see Martin Gilbert, *Churchill: A Life* (New York: Macmillan, 1991), 868–69; Michael H. Hunt, *Crises in U.S. Foreign Policy* (New Haven: Yale University Press, 1996), 123; and Alfred F. Havighurst, *Britain in Transition* (Chicago: University of Chicago Press 1985), 392.

105. One almost humorous but telling account is found in the March 26, 1946, and April 2, 1946, issues of *New Masses,* which reported how the faithful gathered for lunch at a New York City restaurant to develop proposals for a strategy to pillory and counteract Churchill. This was reported in both issues in the "Between Ourselves" column, published on page 2.

106. Author James Humes claims that Mrs. Roosevelt went so far as to denounce Churchill as a "warmonger." See James Humes, *Eisenhower and Churchill: The Partnership That Saved the World* (New York: Prima, 2001), 216. I have not been able to confirm that Mrs. Roosevelt used that exact term.

107. Mrs. Roosevelt was quoted by Drew Pearson in his "Washington Merry-Go-Round" column, syndicated in newspapers throughout the country, including the *Post Standard* (Syracuse, NY) and the *Washington Post,* March 23–24, 1946. Mrs. Roosevelt herself wrote: "After my husband's death, I was lunching one day with Mr. and Mrs. Churchill at their home in London and sitting by me he suddenly turned to me and said: 'You have never really approved of me, have you?' I was a little taken aback because it would have never occurred to me to say I had not approved of Mr. Churchill. . . . I hesitated a moment and finally said: 'I don't think I ever disapproved, Sir.' But I think he remained convinced that there were things he and I did not agree upon, and perhaps there were a number!" Of course, the Iron Curtain speech was one of those. See the "Eleanor Roosevelt Speech and Article File," specifically, "Winston Churchill Articles, 1960," held among the Eleanor Roosevelt Papers at the Roosevelt Library.

108. Pearson, "Washington Merry-Go-Round."

109. "The Refugees Still Wait," *New York Times,* October 5, 1947, E8.

110. The camps were also located in Britain, Canada, Belgium, and Latin America. See "Marshall Says DP Exit Would Ease U.S.-Russian Friction in Europe," *New York Times,* July 17, 1947, A6.

111. "U.S. Opposes Soviet on the Displaced," *New York Times,* November 4, 1947, A5.

112. "Marshall Says DP Exit Would Ease U.S.-Russian Friction in Europe," *New York Times,* July 17, 1947, A6.

113. "Rosenwald Urges U.S. to Take DP's," *New York Times,* May 13, 1947, A8.

114. "Bill on Displaced Faces Stiff Fight," *New York Times,* May 18, 1947, A29.

115. "Reagan Backs Bill for DP's," *New York Times,* May 8, 1947, A5.

116. I discuss this in my book *The Crusader,* 14–15.

Chapter 11: October 1947: Hollywood v. "HUAC"

1. McCarthy was a senator and thus not a member of the *House* Committee on Un-American Activities. It is a common mistake to think otherwise.

2. "Threaten Film Folk with Jail Terms in 'Red' Hunt," *Chicago Star,* November 1, 1947.

3. "Star Witnesses," *Newsweek,* November 3, 1947, 23–25.

4. Reagan, "Testimony before the House Un-American Activities Committee," October 25, 1947.

5. Quoted by Vaughn, *Ronald Reagan in Hollywood,* 166.

6. "Film Stars' Lawyer Hits Kangaroo Court," *Daily Worker,* October 24, 1947, 3. (Note: the date may have been misprinted.)

7. "I certainly do believe that the Communist Party should be outlawed," said Taylor. See, among others, Billingsley, *Hollywood Party,* p. 186.

8. Reagan, *An American Life,* 115. Reagan's campaign against Communism in Hollywood has been written about at length in other sources. For my own account, see Kengor, *The Crusader,* 10–20.

9. Anne Edwards gives two excellent examples of Reagan (as an actor in Hollywood) warning others about being duped. In February 1947 Reagan warned a progressive Jesuit priest, Father George H. Dunne of Loyola University in Chicago, about "being a dupe for communists." In 1950 Reagan wrote a guest column for Victor Riesel, the labor columnist, where he warned a much larger audience. See Edwards, *Early Reagan,* 315–17 and 404n; and Reagan, *Where's the Rest of Me?* 181. Reagan himself gave examples, writing about handling "innocent dupes" in Hollywood, which he also referred to as those in the "sucker group." See Reagan, *Where's the Rest of Me?* 158–59.

10. Reagan, *Where's the Rest of Me?* 162.

11. On this, Reagan cited not his own speculation but the congressional testimony of Communist director Edward Dmytryk. Reagan, *Where's the Rest of Me?* 163.

12. Reagan played in two movies with Bogart in 1938 and one in 1939. See Reagan letter published in Kiron Skinner, Annelise Anderson, and Martin Anderson, eds., *Reagan: A Life in Letters* (New York: Free Press, 2003), 128. See also Doug McClelland, ed., *Hollywood on Ronald Reagan: Friends and Enemies Discuss Our President, the Actor* (Winchester, MA: Faber and Faber, 1983), 182

13. This was widely reported at the time, and reaffirmed to me many times in discussions I've had with Michael Reagan. On the other hand, some claim that reports of both Reagan and Ann Sheridan costarring in *Casablanca* was merely a studio PR trick to promote *King's Row,* and that, in fact, Reagan had not been offered the role. Nonetheless, reports at the time stated that the role of "Rick" was first offered to Reagan. For additional information, see Gerald Duchovnay, *Humphrey Bogart: A Bio-Bibliography* (Westport, CT: Greenwood Press, 1999), 177, 184.

14. Duchovnay, *Humphrey Bogart: A Bio-Bibliography,* 177–18.

15. Of course, these things were arranged in part through the studios. It did not mean that Bogart was a Reagan "fan" in the sense of a run-of-the-mill fan, obviously. Nonetheless, Bogart's place in Reagan's "Fan Club" is reflective of their friendship and support of each other's careers.

16. This information is printed on an official Reagan Fan Club document that lists honorary members, chapters from around the country, various departments within the club, and associated groups. I received this information from Ron Werntz of Freeport, Illinois, who owns an impressive collection of original Reagan memorabilia and materials from Hollywood and Dixon, Illinois. As another sign of their friendship, Reagan was present at Bogart's funeral. See Duchovnay, *Humphrey Bogart: A Bio-Bibliography,* 36–37.

17. Gerald Cook, "Stars Arrive at LaGuardia on Bill-of-Rights Tour," *Daily Worker,* October 30, 1947.

18. I say there were "roughly two dozen" people who flew to Hollywood. For whatever reason, historians have differed on this point, saying anywhere from nineteen to twenty-nine people. Billingsley says nineteen. The Radoshes say twenty-nine. The *Daily Worker,* at the time, reported twenty-six.

19. Radosh and Radosh, *Red Star Over Hollywood,* 152.

20. Quoted in, among others: Billingsley, *Hollywood Party,* 191; and Stephen Humphrey Bogart, *Bogart: In Search of My Father* (New York: Penguin, 1995), 147.

21. Among the better summations of Bogart's character were those by Alistair Cooke and Bosley Crowther, both quoted in Duchovnay, *Humphrey Bogart: A Bio-Bibliography,* 22, 121–22, and 131–32.

22. Billingsley, *Hollywood Party,* 192.

23. See Lauren Bacall, *By Myself* (New York: Ballantine Books, 1990), 212–16. This is also the name reported by the Radoshes in *Red Star Over Hollywood.* Other accounts have the name listed as *Star of the Red Sea,* which may have been shorthanded "Red Star." The *Daily Worker* reported "Star of the Red Sea." See Cook, "Stars Arrive at LaGuardia on Bill-of-Rights Tour."

24. "Bogart, Bacall Lead 26 Notables," *Daily Worker,* October 27, 1947.

25. Quoted in Bacall, *By Myself,* 212.

26. The Hollywood Ten included: Alvah Bessie, Herbert Biberman, Lester Cole, Edward Dmytryk, Ring Lardner Jr., John Howard Lawson, Albert Maltz, Samuel Ornitz, Adrian Scott, and Dalton Trumbo.

27. See Paul Kengor, "Buchenwald and the Totalitarian Century," posted at the website of the Center for Vision & Values, March 2010.

28. "Jail for Kenny, Cite 3 Writers," *Daily Worker,* October 29, 1947.

29. Ralph Izard, "Contempt Proceedings Launched Against Lawson," *Daily Worker,* October 28, 1947; and Billingsley, *Hollywood Party,* 193.

30. Billingsley, *Hollywood Party*, 193–94, 271–79; and "Leading Books Put on Probers' Purge List," *Daily Worker*, October 29, 1947.

31. "Jail for Kenny, Cite 3 Writers."

32. This has been widely reported. Among others, see Rees, *World War II Behind Closed Doors*, 32.

33. "Jail for Kenny, Cite 3 Writers." On Maltz, and, for that matter, Lawson, Trumbo, and Bessie, see Radosh and Radosh, *Red Star Over Hollywood*, 123–35.

34. See Wald, *Trinity of Passion*, 18–19.

35. "Jail for Kenny, Cite 3 Writers."

36. The play was released in 1957. See Wald, *Trinity of Passion*, 19–20.

37. As Ron and Allis Radosh record, "Communists were not satisfied by a defense of their political rights as American citizens; they wanted their defenders to join forces with them in the campaign against 'incipient fascism.'" Radosh, *Red Star Over Hollywood*, 152.

38. Quoted in Edwards, *Early Reagan*, 404.

39. For instance, the quote was carried (among others) in the October 27 and 30, 1947, editions of the *Daily Worker*.

40. Jim Kepner, "Hollywood Fights Back," *Daily Worker*, November 9, 1947.

41. "Bogart, Bacall Lead 26 Notables," *Daily Worker*, October 27, 1947.

42. Ibid.

43. Ibid.

44. Ibid.

45. "Stars Fly to Fight Probe," *Daily Worker*, October 27, 1947.

46. Ibid.

47. Kelly said this in an interview done and broadcast by radio station WIP in Philadelphia at 10:00 PM on October 29, 1947. This was one of the stops by the traveling stars of the Committee for the First Amendment. A transcript of the broadcast was created by the Philadelphia office of the FBI, which in turn was sent to FBI headquarters in Washington. I found the transcript in the FBI file of Humphrey Bogart. Several stars were interviewed, including Bogart, Danny Kaye, Sterling Hayden, and others.

48. Quoted in Gladwin Hill, "Stars Fly to Fight Inquiry into Films," *New York Times*, October 27, 1947.

49. "Sen. Pepper Urges Film Stars Defy House Probe. Says Committee Helps Fascism," *Daily Worker*, October 22, 1947. See also "Hollywood, B'way, Liberals Question Committee's Legality," *Daily Worker*, November 2, 1947.

50. "Sen. Pepper Urges Film Stars Defy House Probe."

51. Jack O'Keefe, "PCA Urges Abolition of Thomas Comm.," *PM Daily*, October 27, 1947.

52. Samuel Sillen and Louise Mitchell, "Film Snoopers Front . . . ," *Daily Worker*, October 27, 1947.

53. Ibid.

54. Quoted in, among others: Jeffrey Meyers, *Bogart: A Life in Hollywood* (New York: Houghton Mifflin, 1997), 209.

55. George Dixon, "Washington Scene," *Washington Times Herald*, October 31, 1947.

56. Also on the editorial board was Howard Fast. See "Fifth Report of the Senate Fact-Finding Committee on Un-American Activities, 1949," California Legislature, published by the California Senate, 545.

57. Mary Spargo, "Lawson Cited in Contempt as Audience Cheers, Boos," *Washington Post*, October 27, 1947; Mary Spargo, "3 More Film Writers Cited for Contempt for Defying House Quiz on Communism," *Washington Post*, October 29, 1947; and "Script Writer Won't Tell If He Joined Commie Party," *Washington Daily News*, October 27, 1947.

58. Biberman was one of the Hollywood Ten.

59. All of these individuals were sponsors of the American Peace Mobilization rally in New York City on April 5, 1941. "Investigation of Un-American Propaganda Activities in the United States," Special Committee on Un-American Activities, House of Representatives, 78th Congress, Second Session, on H. Res. 282, App. part 9, vol. 1 (Washington, DC: GPO, 1944), 432–33, 446.

60. Spargo, "Lawson Cited in Contempt as Audience Cheers, Boos."

61. Billingsley, *Hollywood Party*, 193–94 and 271–79.

62. Bacall, *By Myself*, 212–16.

63. Lauren Bacall speaking in the 1997 documentary *Bogart: The Untold Story*, hosted by Stephen Bogart.

64. Radosh and Radosh, *Red Star Over Hollywood,* 161.

65. Ibid.

66. California Legislature, "Fourth Report of the Senate Fact-Finding Committee on Un-American Activities, 1948, Communist Front Organizations," California Senate, Senate Committee on Un-American Activities, 210–11, 236–38, 252–53.

67. Reagan, *Where's the Rest of Me?* 200.

68. This testimony took place in February 1948. On Gershwin and others, see "Tenney Group Bares Red Front Links Here," *Hollywood Citizen-News,* February 20, 1948; and "Hot Clashes Mark Tenney Red Inquiry," *Los Angeles Times,* February 20, 1948.

69. These remarks from Bogart began circulating in November–December 1947. Ultimately they ran in a piece titled "I'm No Communist," which ran in the March 1948 issue of *Photoplay,* 52–53, 86. Among the articles that carried some or all of these quotes, see "The Playbill: Citizen Bogart in Defense of a Principle," *New York Herald Tribune,* November 23, 1947; "The Movie Hearings," *Life,* November 24, 1947; and "Bogart's Regret," *Newsweek,* December 15, 1947. See also Duchovnay, *Humphrey Bogart: A Bio-Bibliography,* 29.

70. Ibid.

71. Duchovnay, *Humphrey Bogart: A Bio-Bibliography,* 29.

72. "Was Bogart's Face Red?" *News Chronicle,* December 15, 1947. See also "Bogart 'Regrets' His Red Protest," UP, December 3, 1947; and "Bogart Admits He Was Foolish," Associated Press, December 3, 1947.

73. George E. Sokolsky, "Who Foxed Whom?" *New York Sun,* February 6, 1948.

74. Some of Bogart's friends on the left called his recanting "graceless and unnecessary." See Radosh and Radosh, *Red Star Over Hollywood,* 162; and Duchovnay, *Humphrey Bogart: A Bio-Bibliography,* 29.

75. Bogart, *Bogart: In Search of My Father,* 147.

76. Quoted in Radosh and Radosh, *Red Star Over Hollywood,* 162.

77. David Platt, "Sorry Spearfield, Ferrer," *Daily Worker,* September 25, 1951.

78. Editorial, "Apologia," *Washington Post,* December 4, 1947.

79. See Stephen Bogart speaking in his 1997 documentary on his father, *Bogart: The Untold Story.*

80. Platt, "Sorry Spearfield, Ferrer."

81. Dmytryk said this before the House Committee on Un-American Activities on April 25, 1951.

82. "Investigation of Un-American Propaganda Activities in the United States," Special Committee on Un-American Activities, House of Representatives, 78th Congress, Second Session, on H. Res. 282, App. part 9, vol. 3 (Washington, DC: GPO, 1944), 1768–69. The report stated: "When he was a witness before the Special Committee on Un-American Activities, Earl Browder stated categorically that he would attempt to plunge this country into civil war in the event of a war between the United States and the Soviet Union."

83. The 1944 report by the House Committee on Un-American Activities, which quoted Browder, Clarence Hathaway, and William Weinstone, stated that "the foregoing quotations are only a few among hundreds which might be cited from official Communist Party sources." Ibid., 1769.

Chapter 12: Trashing Truman: World Communism and the Cold War

1. The dissolution of the Comintern took place on May 13, 1943, at a meeting of the Presidium of the Executive Committee of the Comintern, held in Moscow. Herb Romerstein has written about this on many occasions. See, for instance, his October 1988 paper for the Bureau of Intelligence and Research, the U.S. Department of State. The report was published as: Herbert Romerstein, "History of the ID [International Department]," in *The International Department of the CC CPSU Under Dobrynin* (U.S. Department of State, Foreign Service Institute, September 1989).

2. On this subject, three excellent scholarly examinations were done by Mark Kramer, Herb Romerstein, and Donald E. Graves. Graves was with the Bureau of Intelligence and Research, the U.S. Department of State. The three papers were presented at a conference hosted by the bureau October 18–19, 1988, and were published in *International Department of the CC CPSU Under Dobrynin.* Graves did the introduction to the proceedings. Kramer's analysis was titled "The New Role of the CPSU International Department in Soviet Foreign Relations and Arms Control." Romerstein's paper was titled "History of the ID [International Department]."

3. Discussion with Herb Romerstein, July 9, 2007.

4. Maria Reiss also went by the names Manya Reiss and Maria Aerova. See Romerstein and Breindel, *The Venona Secrets,* 92–93.

5. Discussion with Herb Romerstein, July 9, 2007.

6. As Donald Graves described it in October 1988, "The International Department . . . is the successor organization to the Comintern." Mark Kramer stated: "The International Department was founded in 1943 at roughly the same time the Comintern was abolished. . . . The International Department . . . remained in charge of relations with all Communist parties in the capitalist world and in developing countries. . . . Much of the economic and military aid that the Soviet Union provided to Third World clients, especially the money transferred to local Communist parties, passed directly through the International Department." As Herb Romerstein put it: "The work of the international Soviet fronts is coordinated by the International Department." The two major forces who spearheaded the International Department were Boris Ponomarev and Mikhail Suslov. Source: Graves Kramer, and Romerstein, in *The International Department of the CC CPSU Under Dobrynin.*

7. E-mail correspondence with Herb Romerstein, April 16, 2007.

8. Morris Childs, the longtime number-two figure in CPUSA, revealed in great depth the extent to which the party took orders from Moscow. We know this because Childs for thirty years was a spy working for the FBI. For the definitive biographical account of Childs's incredible story, see John Barron, *Operation Solo: The FBI's Man in the Kremlin* (Washington, DC: Regnery, 1996).

9. Joseph Stalin was obviously expansionistic. And yet some academics dispute even this matter-of-fact issue. Those on the political Right have argued that Stalin's extension into Eastern Europe was in keeping with his goal (the Bolshevik goal) of achieving global communism. A counterview, not confined solely to Stalin apologists, maintains that Stalin took Eastern Europe because he wanted a "buffer zone" between Russia and the West; after all, the Russians had been invaded multiple times over the centuries, and as recently as the 1940s. The truth is that Stalin *did* want a buffer zone and that was a primary motivation for him seizing Eastern Europe. But he *also* wanted the region for purposes of Communist expansion. Furthermore, if Stalin wanted merely a buffer zone, he wanted a very, very deep buffer zone that also included most of Western Europe. He relished the prospect of France, Germany, and Italy going Communist. The only debate is the extent to which he was willing to use force to take these nations. He preferred they go Communist on their own, not desiring a direct military confrontation with a nuclear-armed United States, which had a monopoly on the bomb until the Soviets successfully tested it in August 1949.

10. There are slight variations in the quote, depending upon the translation. None of the variations are different enough to change or confuse the meaning. Among others, see Milovan Djilas, translated by Michael B. Pterovich, *Conversations with Stalin* (New York: Harcourt, Brace & World, 1962), 114.

11. See John T. Rourke, Ralph G. Carter, and Mark A. Boyer, *Making American Foreign Policy* (New York: McGraw-Hill/Dushkin, 1994), 140.

12. Joseph Stalin, speech to the Central Committee, August 19, 1939. The full text of this speech is reprinted in Crozier, *The Rise and Fall of the Soviet Empire,* 519–21.

13. Ibid.

14. The above-the-fold headline on the front page of the *Washington Post* the next day, February 10, 1946, read, "Stalin Blames Capitalism for 2 Wars."

15. One of the best sources for Nitze and others' views on this was the CNN's 1998 *Cold War,* specifically the early installment, "Iron Curtain: 1945–47."

16. Truman did so when confronted by reporters who were angry with the speech. This was especially troublesome in that Truman had read the speech ahead of time and seemed to have approved. See David McCullough, *Truman* (New York: Simon and Schuster, 1992), 487–90; and Humes, *Eisenhower and Churchill,* 215–16.

17. Antony Beevor, *The Fall of Berlin 1945* (New York: Viking-Penguin, 2002), 32–34, 410–13.

18. See Frank Trippett, "The Marshall Plan: A Memory, a Beacon," *Time,* June 6, 1977.

19. Ion Mihai Pacepa, "Propaganda Redux," *Wall Street Journal,* August 7, 2007.

20. This pamphlet was published in 1951. See Romerstein and Breindel, *The Venona Secrets,* 451–52.

21. Quotes taken from Thomas W. Devine, "The Communists, Henry Wallace, and the Progressive Party of 1948," *Continuity: A Journal of History,* vol. 26, Spring 2003, 43–45, 51–54.

22. Ibid., 69; and Radosh and Radosh, *Red Star Over Hollywood,* 114–16.

23. "Guide to Subversive Organizations and Publications (and Appendices), revised and published December 1, 1961, to supersede Guide published on January 2, 1957 (including Index)," 218.

24. Ibid., 21, 184.

25. Devine, "The Communists, Henry Wallace, and the Progressive Party of 1948," 39.

26. Benjamin Gitlow, *I Confess: The Truth about American Communism* (New York: E. P. Dutton, 1940); and Benjamin Gitlow, *The Whole of Their Lives: Communism in America* (New York: Scribner's, 1948).

27. Gitlow wrote, "Not only does the Communist Party member give every moment of his time to the cause but every dollar he can spare as well, often giving much more than he can afford." Gitlow, *I Confess,* 289.

28. This document is in the Comintern Archives on CPUSA, Fond 515, Opis 1, Delo 4084. See also Romerstein and Breindel, *The Venona Secrets,* 20–21.

29. Arthur M. Schlesinger, Jr., "The Origins of the Cold War," *Foreign Affairs,* vol. 46, no. 1, October 1967, 22–52.

30. Arthur M. Schlesinger, Jr., "The U.S. Communist Party," *Life,* July 29, 1946, vol. 21, 84–96.

31. In his classic 1967 piece on the Cold War's origins, Schlesinger used phrases like "Marxist gospel" and "Moscow's theology," and called the USSR a "messianic state." Schlesinger, "The Origins of the Cold War," 22–52.

32. See Shlaes, *The Forgotten Man,* 330.

Chapter 13: Dreams from Frank Marshall Davis

1. The document that forms the decision brief on this meeting was pulled from the Comintern Archives in Moscow (it is not available in the United States) by Herb Romerstein prior to when the specific archives were reclosed. This document is filed in Fond 495, Opus 72, Delo 277, with Opus 72 reclosed.

2. See Romerstein and Briendel, *The Venona Secrets,* 73–77, 258–68.

3. The document was dated the same day as the meeting—February 17, 1935. This is the document filed as Fond 495, Opus 72, Delo 277.

4. This document, too, was obtained on-site in Moscow by Herb Romerstein.

5. This information is taken from a second document in the Comintern Archives in Moscow (not in the United States), this one filed under Fond 495, Opus 20, Delo 541. It is published as "Exhibit 2" in Herb Romerstein's May 2008 report, "The Communist Assault on Hawaii," which is published at the website of Accuracy in Media. This document was a follow up to both the February 17, 1935 meeting and memo by Schneiderman.

6. Ibid.

7. This document has been published as "Exhibit 1" in Romerstein's May 2008 report, "The Communist Assault on Hawaii."

8. On the *Chicago Star* and Davis, see "Fifth Report of the Senate Fact-Finding Committee on Un-American Activities, 1949," California Legislature, published by the California Senate, 546, 562; and Bill V. Mullen, *Popular Fronts: Chicago and African-American Cultural Politics, 1935–46* (Champagne, IL: University of Illinois Press, 1999).

9. "Reveal Pepper Columnist for Red-Tinged Newspaper," *Logansport* (Indiana) *Pharos-Tribune,* April 21, 1947. This was a syndicated UP piece.

10. See "Hearings Before the Subcommittee to Investigate the Administration of the Internal Security Act and Other Internal Security Laws of the Committee on the Judiciary," United States Senate, 84th Congress, Second Session, on Scope of Soviet Activity in the United States, Part 41-A, Appendix II, 1953 and 1954 Reports of the Commission on Subversive Activities of the Territory of Hawaii (Washington, DC: U.S. GPO, 1957), 2696–98.

11. "Reveal Pepper Columnist for Red-Tinged Newspaper."

12. Credit for this find goes to blogger Trevor Loudon, who posted these materials at his "New Zeal" blogspot in June 2009.

13. See Yvonne Shinhoster Lamb, "Vernon Jarrett, 84; Journalist, Crusader," *Washington Post,* May 25, 2004. In 1983 Valerie married Dr. William Robert Jarrett, son of Vernon Jarrett.

14. Flier provided by Herb Romerstein, and made available in the Romerstein May 2008 report, "The Communist Assault on Hawaii," as Exhibit 8.

15. Robeson's declassified FBI file is now posted and available for viewing at http://foia.fbi.gov/alpha.htm. It is one of the largest files at the site, covering 2,680 pages.

16. Frank Marshall Davis, *Livin' the Blues: Memoirs of a Black Journalist Poet* (Madison, WI: University of Wisconsin Press, 1992), 311.

17. Kawano said this in testimony before the U.S. Senate. Published in "Hearings Before the Subcommittee to Investigate the Administration of the Internal Security Act and Other Internal Security Laws of the Committee on the Judiciary," 2696.

18. Comintern Archives, Fond 495, Opus 74, Delo 467. The document in the Moscow archives is now in a closed section of the archives. Once again, we can thank the diligence of Romerstein for finding this document.

19. One of the CIO reports on Bridges was published in the collection "Communist Domination of Certain Unions" (Washington, DC: Government Printing Office, 1951), 79–96.

20. Davis, *Livin' the Blues,* 311.

21. See "Hearings Before the Subcommittee to Investigate the Administration of the Internal Security Act and Other Internal Security Laws of the Committee on the Judiciary," 2696. Koji Ariyoshi was among seven Honolulu defendants identified as Communists and convicted under the Smith Act in 1953 for "conspiring to teach and advocate the overthrow of the government by force and violence."

22. This is written in the November 15, 1947, preface of Ichiro Izuka's self-published memoir/pamphlet, "The Truth About Communism in Hawaii," made available in the Romerstein May 2008 report, "The Communist Assault on Hawaii," as Exhibit 7.

23. Quote from Edward Berman in a 1949 letter to Roy Wilkins, acting secretary of the national branch of the NAACP. The Berman letter was included as part of his testimony before the House Committee on Un-American Activities in April 1950. "Hearings Regarding Communist Activities in the Territory of Hawaii—Part 3," Hearings before the Committee on Un-American Activities, House of Representatives, 81st Congress, Second Session, April 17, 18, and 19, 1950, Appendix, Index (Washington, DC: U.S. GPO, 1950), 2065–68.

24. Ibid.

25. Ibid.

26. Ibid.

27. See "Hearings Before the Subcommittee to Investigate the Administration of the Internal Security Act and Other Internal Security Laws of the Committee on the Judiciary," 2698.

28. Davis's columns for 1949 and 1950 are available online at two University of Hawaii websites, www.hawaii.edu/uhwo/clear/HonoluluRecord1/frankblog1949.html and www.hawaii.edu/uhwo/clear/HonoluluRecord1/frankblog1950.html. The columns are also available on microfiche at the University of Hawaii Manoa Hamilton Main Library under the call number "Microfilm S90146." One of my researchers, Emily Hughes, confirmed the original hard copy with the editorials reproduced on the Web. We found some minor discrepancies in the dates of the articles. For instance, a column dated September 29, 1949, on the website is actually dated October 6, 1949, in the original hard-copy edition of the newspaper. Importantly, however, the text of the articles is identical, and these small discrepancies do not bear on the content of Davis's work. Overall, the reproduction on the website seems to be generally reliable.

29. Another glowing piece by Davis on Robeson was his August 11 column, in which he held up Robeson and Henry Wallace as the men with the answers for the problems of America and the world. He quoted Robeson, whom he repeatedly called "Paul," and who hoped that the oppressed peoples of the world, from "the Negro workers in the cotton plantations of Alabama, the sugar plantations in Louisiana, the tobacco fields in South Arkansas," to "the workers in the banana plantations or the sugar workers in the West Indies," to "the African farmers who have been dispossessed of their land in the South Africa of Malan," would "fight for peace and collaboration with the Soviet Union and the new democracies."

30. Harten was cited in the *Daily Worker* at least fifteen times from 1942 to 1950. The source for this, which indexes and details each occasion by name and date and title, is the well-known report "A Compilation of Public Records of 658 Clergymen and Laymen connected with the National Council of Churches," published in April 1962 by Circuit Riders, Inc. (Cincinnati, OH), 65–66. The chief investigator was J. B. Matthews. Hereafter cited as "658/NCC."

31. Frank Marshall Davis, "Threaten Film Folk with Jail Terms in 'Red' Hunt," *Chicago Star,* November 1, 1947.

32. According to the website of the University of Chicago, Hutchins's address was delivered in June 1949. A partial transcript of the speech was published (oddly) in the *American Journal of Public Health.* See "The Cause We Serve," *American Journal of Public Health,* September 1949, vol. 39, 1177–78.

33. There are nineteen separate page references to Hutchins in the "Supplement to Cumulative Index to Publications of the Committee on Un-American Activities, 1955 through 1968 (84th through 90th Congresses)," September 1970 (Washington, DC: GPO), 254.

34. He used the "new democracies" phrase in his August 11 column, to cite just one example.

35. See Judy Kaplan and Linn Shapiro, eds., *Red Diapers: Growing Up in the Communist Left* (Urbana and Chicago: University of Illinois Press, 1998), 319; and David Horowitz, *Radical Son* (New York: The Free Press, 1997), 72.

36. For instance, see http://historymatters.gmu.edu/d/6440.

37. "For Freedom and Peace," transcript of address by Paul Robeson at a "Welcome Home Rally" in New York, June 19, 1949. Robeson insisted that it was unjust to go to war with the USSR or "with the people of China and the new democracies."

38. See also Frank Marshall Davis, "Test of Democracy," *Honolulu Record,* November 17, 1949; and Frank Marshall Davis, "Africa Is Next Door," *Honolulu Record,* January 12, 1950.

39. For a concise analysis of Truman on civil rights, see McCullough, *Truman,* 586–90.

40. Frank Marshall Davis, "End of an Era," *Honolulu Record,* November 10, 1949; and Frank Marshall Davis, "Mobilizing for Civil Rights," *Honolulu Record,* January 5, 1950.

41. One such example is Davis's June 22, 1950, op-ed for the *Honolulu Record,* "Christ in 1950."

42. See "658/NCC"; and "A Compilation of Public Records, 20.5%, 1411 Protestant Episcopal Rectors (as of 1955)," published in March 1958 by Circuit Riders, Inc. (Cincinnati, OH). Hereafter cited as "20.5%/Episcopal."

43. Melish took up two pages, whereas his son, William Howard Melish, took up nine pages. Together, they filled pages 102–12 of the "20.5%/Episcopal" compilation.

44. "Guide to Subversive Organizations and Publications (and Appendices), revised and published December 1, 1961, to supersede Guide published on January 2, 1957 (including Index)," 117–18.

45. "20.5%/Episcopal," 104–12.

46. See Wald, *Trinity of Passion,* 297n69.

47. Some groups were unhappy with Pope John Paul II's beatification of Stepinac, as it reignited old rivalries and debates between (among others) Serbs and Croats. But as for the question of whether Stepinac was the victim of Communist persecution, there is no doubt.

48. I was unable to confirm the precise identity of this particular Benjamin Shaw. There was a Benjamin Shaw listed twice in the exhaustive 1944 investigative report by the House Committee on Un-American Activities. That Shaw was a radical clergyman from Birmingham, Alabama, listed as "Benjamin G. Shaw." There, Shaw was among the names on two different Communist fronts, both times falling as the third name after Paul Robeson. The second of these fronts (a not-so-subtle one) was a group of "Negro Citizens" that formed the organization "For the Freedom of Earl Browder." Source: "Investigation of Un-American Propaganda Activities in the United States," Special Committee on Un-American Activities, House of Representatives, 78th Congress, Second Session, on H. Res. 282, App. part 9, vol. 1 (Washington, DC: GPO, 1944), 620–25.

49. Truman and Churchill's recollections are quoted in Robert C. Williams and Philip L. Cantelon, eds., *The American Atom: A Documentary History of Nuclear Policies from the Discovery of Fission to the Present, 1939–1984* (Philadelphia: University of Pennsylvania Press, 1984), 55–56.

50. Though Gorbachev did not stop the Berlin Wall from falling, he was very concerned about a reunified Germany. He made his opposition to a unified Germany clear in face-to-face discussions with Ronald Reagan and Margaret Thatcher. At the May–June 1988 Moscow Summit Reagan directly asked Gorbachev to tear down the wall; Gorbachev said (in the words of his translator, Igor Korchilov) that he "could not agree with the president's view." On this, see Kengor, *The Crusader,* 263–67, 277–78.

51. Transcript: Barack Obama, "A World That Stands as One," Berlin, Germany, July 24, 2008.

52. In the report by the California Senate, Davis's name appears on pages 545 and 562, where he was listed among the lead figures in the *Chicago Star* and American Youth for Democracy, which the Senate was investigating as a Communist front.

53. See "Hearings Before the Subcommittee to Investigate the Administration of the Internal Security Act and Other Internal Security Laws of the Committee on the Judiciary," United States Senate, 84th Congress, Second Session, on "Scope of Soviet Activity in the United States," Part 41-A, Appendix II, 1953 and 1954 Reports of the Commission on Subversive Activities of the Territory of Hawaii (Washington, DC: U.S. GPO, 1957), 2698.

54. See "Hearings Before the Subcommittee to Investigate the Administration of the Internal Security Act and Other Internal Security Laws of the Committee on the Judiciary," United States Senate, 84th Congress, Second Session, on Scope of Soviet Activity in the United States, December 5 and 6, 1956, Part 41 (Washington, DC: U.S. GPO, 1957), 2518.

55. Davis, *Livin' the Blues*, 243.

56. James Edward Smethurst, *The New Red Negro: The Literary Left and African American Poetry, 1930–46* (Oxford: Oxford University Press, 1999).

57. These poems are widely available on the Web today.

Chapter 14: Vietnam Dupes: Protests, Riots, and the Chaotic Summer of '68

1. The speech was delivered in Moscow the night of February 24–25, 1956.

2. Our historical understanding is that the original text received in the United States came via the Mossad and the U.S. State Department, but John Barron makes an interesting case that the first text came via Jack Childs, an FBI spy trusted by the Soviets (and the brother of Morris Childs), who got a text to the FBI. See Barron, *Operation Solo*, 54–55.

3. The *New York Times* published the text in its June 5, 1956, edition. According to the electronic version available from the *Times* online, the text is 24,264 words long.

4. Horowitz, *Radical Son*, 83–84.

5. Quoted in, among others, Billingsley, *Hollywood Party*, 255; and Horowitz, *Radical Son*, 84.

6. I discuss this in my book *The Crusader*, 36–39. It was a stunning, blatant, shameful Soviet incident, one that ultimately would inspire Robert Kennedy's assassin. Anyone who finds this hard to believe—understandably so, as it was incredibly devious, even by Soviet standards—should research the subject. It was one of the most awful examples of Soviet international behavior in the entire history of the Cold War. It has not been given its historical due. I encourage many others to tell this story at greater length. The outstanding 1999 PBS series *The Fifty Years War* offers one of the best presentations on the subject, complete with interviews with the major players in the conflict from the Egyptian, Soviet, and Israel sides (including the late Levi Eshkol's wife).

7. Barron, *Operation Solo*, 19.

8. Ibid., 19, 129.

9. Barron's *Operation Solo* shows how American comrades followed the Moscow-dictated line time and time again. Barron records four particularly notable examples on pages 163–67. Among them, the despicable Soviet behavior that prompted the Six-Day War also prompted the Soviets to try to backtrack on their involvement, including through a planned speech by Premier Alexey Kosygin at the United Nations. Through Morris and Jack Childs, the Soviets gave Gus Hall an advanced copy of the speech so he would understand the position the American party must adopt on the war. This was likewise the case a year later, in 1968, when Soviet tanks rolled into Czechoslovakia: Moscow instructed Hall on how to try to defend the invasion.

10. Barron, *Operation Solo*, 164, 353.

11. Ibid., 173, 200.

12. House Committee on Internal Security, "Subversive Involvement in the Origin, Leadership, and Activities for the New Mobilization Committee to End the War in Vietnam and Its Predecessor Organizations," U.S. House of Representatives, 91st Congress, Second Session, 1970, vii.

13. Ibid.

14. Ibid., ix.

15. Ibid., vi.

16. Ibid., vii.

17. The Soviet press continued to use such language on Vietnam as late as the 1980s. A casual reading of *Pravda, Izvestia*, and numerous other Soviet "news" sources in the 1980s, including transcripts of TV and

radio broadcasts, would lead one to believe that the United States was still fighting in Vietnam, years after the last helicopter left Saigon (1975). The Soviets rarely let go of an excellent propaganda chip.

18. House Committee on Internal Security, "Subversive Involvement in the Origin, Leadership, and Activities for the New Mobilization Committee to End the War in Vietnam and Its Predecessor Organizations," vii.

19. Ibid., x–xi.

20. Ibid., vii.

21. Quoted in Susan E. Tifft and Alex S. Jones, *The Trust: The Private and Powerful Family Behind the New York Times* (New York: Back Bay Books, 1999), 499.

22. House Committee on Internal Security, "Subversive Involvement in the Origin, Leadership, and Activities for the New Mobilization Committee to End the War in Vietnam and Its Predecessor Organizations," 2.

23. House Committee on Un-American Activities, "Communist Origin and Manipulation of Vietnam Week," U.S. House of Representatives, 90th Congress, First Session, March 31, 1967, 22–24.

24. Ibid.

25. House Committee on Internal Security, "Subversive Involvement in the Origin, Leadership, and Activities for the New Mobilization Committee to End the War in Vietnam and Its Predecessor Organizations," 12.

26. "U.S. War Foes Met with Hanoi Group," *Washington Post,* September 21, 1968, A3; House Committee on Internal Security, "Subversive Involvement in the Origin, Leadership, and Activities for the New Mobilization Committee to End the War in Vietnam and Its Predecessor Organizations," x; and "Subversive Involvement in Disruption of 1968 Democratic Party National Convention," Part 1, Hearings Before the Committee on Un-American Activities, House of Representatives, 90th Congress, Second Session, October 1, 3, and 4, 1968, 2324.

27. This statement was printed in a July 18, 1969, article in *The Militant,* cited in House Committee on Internal Security, "Subversive Involvement in the Origin, Leadership, and Activities for the New Mobilization Committee to End the War in Vietnam and Its Predecessor Organizations," 24.

28. In fact, Ichord's warning was so unequivocal that it was included in the committee's formal resolution adopted on September 12, 1968, which established the basis for the investigation of the convention blow-up. "Subversive Involvement in Disruption of 1968 Democratic Party National Convention," Part 1, 2238.

29. Ibid., 2244.

30. Ibid., 2245–62.

31. A number of these directives are published in "Subversive Involvement in Disruption of 1968 Democratic Party National Convention," Part 1, 2262–68.

32. These will be noted in short order, as they ranged from Tom Hayden to Mark Rudd, Bill Ayers, Bernardine Dohrn, Michael Klonsky, and many more.

33. As Congress documented, the evidence suggests that the seeds for the assault on the 1968 Democratic National Convention in Chicago were planted by Communists and their fellow travelers at Columbia in October 1967. See "Subversive Involvement in Disruption of 1968 Democratic Party National Convention," Part 1, 2270–71.

34. "Subversive Involvement in Disruption of 1968 Democratic Party National Convention," Part 1, 2269–72.

35. The committee investigation detailed Copstein's clear links to the Communist Party, dating back to the early 1940s. For Cummings, it listed Communist associations or relationships with Communist fronts or Communist-led activities. Ibid., 2269–71.

36. The ad ran on page E7 of the Sunday, December 10, 1967, edition of the *New York Times,* under the giant banner "Johnson vs. Reagan? God help us." Congress certainly noticed. The ad was cited in "Subversive Involvement in Disruption of 1968 Democratic Party National Convention," Part 1, 2271–72.

37. "Subversive Involvement in Disruption of 1968 Democratic Party National Convention," Part 1, 2271–72.

38. John Leo, "Leftists Ponder Convention Move," *New York Times,* December 10, 1967, A38. Congress also caught this one. See "Subversive Involvement in Disruption of 1968 Democratic Party National Convention," Part 1, 2271–72.

39. A photocopy of the letter is published in "Subversive Involvement in Disruption of 1968 Democratic Party National Convention," Part 1, 2277.

40. James Gallagher reported this. "Subversive Involvement in Disruption of 1968 Democratic Party National Convention," Part 1, 2244.

41. "Subversive Involvement in Disruption of 1968 Democratic Party National Convention," Part 1, 2237–40.

42. The material that follows is taken from Young's testimony and his exchanges with committee members and counsel during the testimony, which is transcribed in this report: "Subversive Involvement in Disruption of 1968 Democratic Party National Convention," Part 1, 2422–74.

43. See, for example, the congressional testimony of Mike Soto, published in "Extent of Subversion in the 'New Left,'" Hearings Before the Subcommittee to Investigate the Administration of the Internal Security Act and Other Internal Security Laws of the Committee of the Judiciary, U.S. Senate, 91st Congress, Second Session, March 31, 1970, 224.

44. "Subversive Involvement in the Origin, Leadership, and Activities for the New Mobilization Committee to End the War in Vietnam and Its Predecessor Organizations," 11.

45. "Hearings on Restraints on Travel to Hostile Areas,' Hearings Before the Committee on Internal Security, House of Representatives, 93rd Congress, First Session, May 9 and 10, 1973, 15–16.

46. "Subversive Involvement in the Origin, Leadership, and Activities for the New Mobilization Committee to End the War in Vietnam and Its Predecessor Organizations." 10–16.

47. "Subversive Involvement in Disruption of 1968 Democratic Party National Convention," Part 1, 2430–31.

48. Ibid., 2412–21, 2475–91.

49. See William Conrad Gibbons, *The U.S. Government and the Vietnam War* (Princeton, NJ: Princeton University Press, 1986), 158.

50. Douglas served in the U.S. Senate from January 1949 to January 1967, losing to Republican Charles H. Percy.

Chapter 15: Grown-up Vietnam Dupes: Dr. Spock, Corliss Lamont, and Friends

1. The cast of grown-up Vietnam dupes is so extensive as to merit a book unto itself. I heartily encourage future researchers to take up the task.

2. Biographical details presented in Lamont, *The Illusion of Immortality.*

3. Robert D. McFadden, "Corliss Lamont Dies at 93; Socialist Battled McCarthy," *New York Times,* April 28, 1995.

4. See Corliss Lamont, *A Lifetime of Dissent* (Buffalo, NY: Prometheus Books, 1988), 187; and Corliss Lamont, *Soviet Civilization* (New York: Philosophical Library USA, 1952), 324.

5. McFadden, "Corliss Lamont Dies at 93; Socialist Battled McCarthy."

6. More evidence is being released on this subject, demonstrating that Stone was as bad as (if not worse than) anti-Communists long suspected. In their 2009 book *Spies: The Rise and Fall of the KGB in America* (Yale University Press), historians John Earl Haynes, Harvey Klehr, and Alexander Vassiliev conclude: "To put it plainly, from 1936 to 1939 I. F. Stone was a Soviet spy." For that quote and an easily accessible summary, see the excerpted article published in April 2009 by the online version of *Commentary* magazine, titled "Special Preview: I.F. Stone, Soviet Agent—Case Closed." See also Haynes and Klehr, *Venona,* 247–49; and Romerstein and Breindel, *The Venona Secrets,* 432–39. On page 436, Romerstein and Breindel write: "It is clear from the evidence that Stone was indeed a Soviet agent." Of course, Stone (in death) has defenders who dispute the allegations (not convincingly, in my view). To see the refutations, visit the I. F. Stone tribute website: http://www.ifstone.org/biography-refuted.php.

7. Some sources state that the committee was formed in 1951.

8. This actually had begun in the 1940s, though most people report it as beginning in the 1950s. See next endnote.

9. Actually, these "others"—seventeen of them—were ahead of Lamont, having signed a letter in 1940 condemning the ACLU's barring of Communists as office holders. In signing, Stone was listed with *The Nation* at the time, as were signers Maxwell Stewart and James Wechsler. Also signing, from Colum-

bia University, were Professors Franz Boas (also cited as "Boaz") and Robert S. Lynd. On this, see "Investigation of Un-American Propaganda Activities in the United States," Special Committee on Un-American Activities, House of Representatives, 78th Congress, Second Session, on H. Res. 282, App. part 9, vol. 2 (Washington, DC: GPO, 1944), 1386–88.

10. For an interesting article that revisits this history while also highlighting one of Lamont's colorful battles during the 1960s, see Sidney E. Zion, "Yelling Match Disrupts Rights Forum," *New York Times,* December 10, 1967, 40. In this article, the reporter (not Lamont) used the word "purge," but did so to imply (correctly) that Lamont and his friends used that word as well. They saw it as a purge.

11. Sources date this period of starting the committee and leaving the ACLU as between 1951 and 1954.

12. McFadden, "Corliss Lamont Dies at 93; Socialist Battled McCarthy."

13. See, for instance: Ann Charters, ed., *The Portable Sixties Reader* (New York: Penguin, 2003).

14. House Committee on Un-American Activities, "Communist Origin and Manipulation of Vietnam Week."

15. Ibid., 1–3.

16. Ibid., 6.

17. See Kaplan and Shapiro, eds., *Red Diapers,* 278–85.

18. Herbert Aptheker, *The Truth About Hungary* (New York: Mainstream Publishers, 1957).

19. See Christopher Lehmann-Haupt, "Herbert Aptheker, 87, Dies; Prolific Marxist Historian," *New York Times,* March 20, 2003. Among those who noticed this curious omission: Frederic U. Dicker, "Lies After Death," *Human Events,* April 7, 2003; and Ronald Radosh, "Herbert Aptheker: Hero or Hack?" *Hudson Institute* (online), March 26, 2003.

20. Lehmann-Haupt, "Herbert Aptheker, 87, Dies; Prolific Marxist Historian."

21. House Committee on Un-American Activities, "Communist Origin and Manipulation of Vietnam Week," 5.

22. House Committee on Internal Security, "Subversive Involvement in the Origin, Leadership, and Activities for the New Mobilization Committee to End the War in Vietnam and Its Predecessor Organizations," 5.

23. House Committee on Un-American Activities, "Communist Origin and Manipulation of Vietnam Week," 12–13.

24. Ibid.

25. Howard Zinn, *Vietnam: The Logic of Withdrawal* (Cambridge, MA: South End Press, 1967). On the book's usage by the Vietcong in POW camps, see Mary Hershberger, *Jane Fonda's War: A Political Biography of an Antiwar Icon* (New York: The New Press, 2005), 96.

26. In 2009 *A People's History of the United States* found incarnation on the History Channel as a documentary called *The People Speak.*

27. Another name on the list was Ted Weiss. Though I cannot say for certain, this was possibly the Ted Weiss who became a prominent liberal congressman from New York (1977–92). From 1962 to 1977 Weiss was a member of the New York City Council and vocal critic of the Vietnam War. He ran for Congress in 1966 on an antiwar platform.

28. House Committee on Un-American Activities, "Communist Origin and Manipulation of Vietnam Week," 10–11, 53. The committee was particularly troubled by the King aspect, a focus of the conclusion of its report: "Dr. Martin Luther King's agreement to play a leading role in the April 15 demonstrations in New York City," concluded the report, was "evidence that the Communists have succeeded, at least partially, in implementing their strategy of fusing the Vietnam and civil rights issues in order to strengthen their chances of bringing about a reversal of U.S. policy in Vietnam."

29. See Leo, "Leftists Ponder Convention Move," 38. "Subversive Involvement in Disruption of 1968 Democratic Party National Convention," Part 1, 22713.

30. Ibid., i–ix.

31. House Committee on Internal Security, "Subversive Involvement in the Origin, Leadership, and Activities for the New Mobilization Committee to End the War in Vietnam and Its Predecessor Organizations," ix.

32. Ibid., 5–6.

33. Quoted in ibid., ix.

34. Quotes taken from the coverage in the *Washington Star*, October 22, 1967, A8. See also House Committee on Internal Security, "Subversive Involvement in the Origin, Leadership, and Activities for the New Mobilization Committee to End the War in Vietnam and Its Predecessor Organizations," 8–9.

35. House Committee on Internal Security, "Subversive Involvement in the Origin, Leadership, and Activities for the New Mobilization Committee to End the War in Vietnam and Its Predecessor Organizations," 9.

36. Ibid., 22.

37. Dr. Benjamin Spock and Mitchell Zimmerman, *Dr. Spock on Vietnam* (New York: Dell, 1968).

38. I was unable to find much information on Zimmerman, then and today. He does not seem to be as active as he was in the 1960s. More recently, he published a very left-leaning article for the far-left Alexander Cockburn publication *Counterpunch*, titled "The Bizarre Legal Philosophy of Justice Janice Rogers Brown: First Amendment Protection for On-the-Job Racism?" which *Counterpunch* carried in a March 31, 2005, issue. The tagline in the piece refers to Zimmerman as "a former SNCC organizer and co-author of *Dr. Spock on Vietnam*" and "a partner at a high-tech firm in Mountain View, California."

39. The *New York Times* is quoted on pages 14, 28, 32, 41, 42 (three times), 44, 45, 49, 71, 77, and 78.

40. Spock and Zimmerman, *Dr. Spock on Vietnam*, 14.

41. Ibid., 18, 42, 54, 57, 71–72.

42. Ibid., 15–7.

43. Ibid., 18.

44. Ibid., 19–20.

45. For more on this trip and Ted Kennedy's reversal on Vietnam, see Adam Clymer, *Edward M. Kennedy: A Biography* (New York: HarperPerennial, 2000), 80–82, 99–103.

46. These are Spock's and Zimmerman's words, and not a direct quote from Kennedy. They wrote that Kennedy "reported" this. They then quoted Kennedy indeed reporting such claims. Spock and Zimmerman, *Dr. Spock on Vietnam*, 45–46.

47. Spock and Zimmerman, *Dr. Spock on Vietnam*, 45–46.

48. Ibid., 46.

49. The Kennedy quote is a direct quote from Kennedy—i.e., Kennedy's words, not Spock's and Zimmerman's. See ibid., 15, 48–49.

50. Spock and Zimmerman, *Dr. Spock on Vietnam*, 52–55.

51. Ibid.

52. Ibid., 54.

53. "Investigations of Students for a Democratic Society," Part 7-A, Hearings Before the Committee on Internal Security, House of Representatives, 91st Congress, First Session, December 9–11 and 16, 1969, 2186–88.

54. Ibid., 2195–96.

55. Ibid., 2256.

56. Ibid.

57. Ibid., 2197–98.

58. Ibid., 2197–98, 2243.

59. In a letter written directly to Ho Chi Minh on August 12, 1966, Russell thanked the Communist leader "for your welcome contribution towards the cost of preparing the War Crimes Tribunal." See Nicholas Griffin, ed., *The Selected Letters of Bertrand Russell: The Public Years, 1914–1970* (New York: Routledge, 2001), 590.

60. KGB defector Yuri Krotkov identified Burchett as a Soviet KGB agent. Himself a KGB agent, and a playwright, Krotkov did this in detailed testimony to a U.S. Senate subcommittee. Among others, see R. C. S. Trahair, *Encyclopedia of Cold War Espionage, Spies, and Secret Operations* (Westport, CT: Greenwood Publishing Group, 2004), 37–38; and Robert Manne, *Left Right Left* (Melbourne, Australia: Black Inc., 2004), 53, 66.

61. "Investigations of Students for a Democratic Society," Part 7-A, 2200, 2208, 2242. Other books held in POW prison "libraries" in Hanoi—not cited by Frishman—included Howard Zinn's *Vietnam: The Logic of Withdrawal*, Townsend Hoopes's *The Limits of Intervention*, James Gavin's *Crisis Now*, and even Daniel Ellsberg's *The Pentagon Papers*. See Hershberger, *Jane Fonda's War*, 96.

62. "Investigations of Students for a Democratic Society," Part 7-A, 2208.

63. Ibid., 2259–60.

64. Ibid., 2261.

65. Ibid., 2261–66, 2279.

66. Ibid., 2280.

67. Ibid.

68. Ibid., 2281.

69. Her mother, Elizabeth B. Boyden, was a supporter of America's role in the Communist World Youth Festivals of the 1940s. See "The Communist International Youth Festival," a monograph prepared for the Subcommittee to Investigate the Administration of the Internal Security Act and other Internal Security Laws, Committee on the Judiciary, U.S. Senate (Washington, DC: GPO, 1963), 45.

70. The material on Lamb in this section is drawn from those papers.

71. "Investigations of Students for a Democratic Society," Part 7-A, 2281.

72. Ibid., xi–xii and 2281.

73. House Committee on Internal Security, "Subversive Involvement in the Origin, Leadership, and Activities for the New Mobilization Committee to End the War in Vietnam and Its Predecessor Organizations," 37, 39, 43, 44, 57, 65, 67, 69.

74. See, for instance, Thomas C. Reeves, *America's Bishop: The Life and Times of Fulton J. Sheen* (San Francisco: Encounter Books, 2001), 284, 287, 308–10, 327, 338.

Chapter 16: Radicals: Bill Ayers, Bernardine Dohrn, SDS, and the Weathermen

1. Different sources vary in some of these dates (even years) and titles. My source is the formal investigation of SDS done by Congress in October 1968. See "Subversive Involvement in Disruption of 1968 Democratic Party National Convention," Part 1, Hearings Before the Committee on Un-American Activities, House of Representatives, 90th Congress, Second Session, October 1, 3, and 4, 1968, 2254.

2. Horowitz, *Radical Son,* 105.

3. Ibid., 106.

4. For more, see Ibid., 165–68.

5. Ibid., 160.

6. Fonda reportedly said this (verbatim) at Michigan State University in November 1970 and also (almost verbatim) at Duke University in December 1970. On the first of these, see Lee Winfrey, "Jane Fonda—an LP Record with a Socialist Sermon," *Detroit Free Press,* November 22, 1970. For an account by someone who is strangely skeptical that Fonda said these things, perhaps at least in part because a young, pre-senatorial Jesse Helms turned them into a TV commentary at the time, see Hershberger, *Jane Fonda's War,* 68–72. In fact, the Fonda quotes (reported almost verbatim here on two separate occasions by separate sources) are completely believable. She had very radical views at the time, fully consistent with those in her intimately shared political circles. Certainly, this was what Tom Hayden—her husband—believed.

7. Jane Fonda was in Vietnam from July 8 to July 22, 1971.

8. See Trahair, *Encyclopedia of Cold War Espionage, Spies, and Secret Operations,* 37–38; and Manne, *Left Right Left,* 53, 66.

9. Bernardine's father reportedly changed the family surname when she was in high school.

10. I doubt that Dohrn lived there. The closeness is symbolic rather than literal. "Subversive Involvement in Disruption of 1968 Democratic Party National Convention," Part 1, 2277–78, 2282–90.

11. "Subversive Involvement in Disruption of 1968 Democratic Party National Convention," Part 1, 2254.

12. Ibid., 2254.

13. Ibid., 2371.

14. See "Investigations of Students for a Democratic Society," Part 7-A, Hearings Before the Committee on Internal Security, House of Representatives, 91st Congress, First Session, December 9–11 and 16, 1969, 2318, 2321; and "Investigations of Students for a Democratic Society," Part 7-B, Hearings Before the Committee on Internal Security, House of Representatives, 91st Congress, First Session, December 17–18, 1969, 2477–80, 2600–1.

15. Daniel J. Flynn, *A Conservative History of the American Left* (New York: Crown Forum, 2008), 313.

16. "Subversive Involvement in Disruption of 1968 Democratic Party National Convention," Part 1, 2360.

17. Ronald G. Havelock and Mary C. Havelock, *Training for Change Agents: A Guide to the Design of Training Programs in Education and Other Fields* (Ann Arbor, MI: University of Michigan Press, 1973). This was a serious, comprehensive, academic work in the field of education, including a list of more than fifty contributing academics. It was done through the University of Michigan's Institute for Social Research.

18. Boudin family biographer Susan Braudy writes, "Unlike nearly all his clients, Leonard never actually joined the party," but did consider doing so at one point in the 1930s. He clearly had Communist sympathies, and at one point ideologically leaned in that direction. See Susan Braudy, *Family Circle: The Boudins and the Aristocracy of the Left* (New York: Knopf, 2003), 81–84, 399–400n. Some conservative sources state that Leonard Boudin was much worse than that, though I have not seen supporting evidence.

19. Braudy, *Family Circle*, 78.

20. Among the more popular camps was the Indian-sounding Wo-Chi-Ca, which was an abbreviation for "Workers Children's Camp." Among those who have written about their time at these camps is David Horowitz in *Radical Son* (pages 63–65).

21. Mishler, *Raising Reds*, 100–2; and Braudy, *Family Circle*, 40–42, 390n.

22. Mishler, *Raising Reds*, 100–2; and Braudy, *Family Circle*, 40–42, 390n.

23. See, among others, Romerstein and Breindel, *The Venona Secrets*, 233.

24. Braudy, *Family Circle*, 118.

25. Ibid., 132–33.

26. Mark Rudd, *Underground: My Life with SDS and the Weathermen* (New York: William Morrow, 2009), 13.

27. Ibid., 43.

28. Ibid., 14–15.

29. Ibid., 21.

30. Ibid., 22.

31. Ibid., 40.

32. Moreover, their wedding cake was inscribed with the Weatherman slogan "Smash monogamy." The marriage lasted less than a year. See Horowitz, *Radical Son*, 175–76.

33. See Barbara Olson, *Hell to Pay* (Washington, DC: Regnery Publishing, Inc., 1999), 312–13; and Joyce Milton, *The First Partner* (New York: William Morrow and Company, Inc., 1999), 283–84.

34. Rudd, *Underground*, 41.

35. Ibid., 41–42.

36. Ibid., 41.

37. Ibid., 61–67.

38. Diana Trilling, *We Must March My Darlings* (New York: Harcourt, 1977), 113–14.

39. Quoted in Hollander, *Political Pilgrims*, 190.

40. The September 30, 1968, *Newsweek* showed a picture of Mark Rudd in a fracas with police on campus, with the short title "Confrontation at Columbia."

41. Rudd, *Underground*, 110.

42. Ibid., 116.

43. Ibid.

44. Ibid., viii.

45. Ibid., 146.

46. Ibid., 154–59.

47. Kevin Gillies, "The Last Radical," *Vancouver Magazine*, November 1998. Jacobs died in Vancouver in 1997, hence the profile (odd at first glance) in *Vancouver Magazine*.

48. Rudd, *Underground*, 154–59.

49. Flynn, *A Conservative History of the American Left*, 313.

50. See "Investigations of Students for a Democratic Society," Part 7-B, 2477–78.

51. Rudd, *Underground*, 175.

52. See "Investigations of Students for a Democratic Society," Part 7-B, 2472, 2477–78.

53. Ibid. This was not uncommon. FBI informant Larry Grathwohl testified on planning meetings for the National Action held not in Chicago but at places like St. John's Unitarian Church in Cincinnati, which was hosted by the "Weatherman collective in Cincinnati." See Testimony of Larry Grathwohl, published in "Terroristic Activity: Inside the Weatherman Movement," Hearings Before the Subcommittee to Investigate the Administration of the Internal Security Act and Other Internal Security Laws of the Committee of the Judiciary, U.S. Senate, 93rd Congress, Second Session, October 18, 1974, 92.

54. See Jeremy Varon, *Bringing the War Home: The Weather Underground, the Red Army Faction, and Revolutionary Violence in the Sixties and Seventies* (Berkeley, CA: University of California Press, 2004), 158–60. Jacobs died of melanoma in October 1997, at the age of fifty. He was another Weather Underground onetime fugitive who never did a day of jail time, absconding to Vancouver, British Columbia. Today, his ashes lie in Cuba on the ground of a mausoleum to Che Guevara. A plaque commemorates Jacobs and his immortal political beloved: "He wanted to live like Che. Let him rest with Che."

55. Varon, *Bringing the War Home,* 160

56. Rudd, *Underground,* 189.

57. Braudy, *Family Circle,* 197–200. Obscene as this may sound, it got much worse.

58. This quote has been reported countless times and is easily available for documentation. As horrible and unimaginable as it may seem, it is not disputed. For an example of it being reported very recently by one of the attendees at the War Council, see Rudd, *Underground,* 189.

59. Ayers has been asked to comment on this episode many times. He cannot escape the numerous testimonies from observers who have always insisted that Ayers's wife was "deadly serious." The best face that Ayers has tried to put on the episode is to claim that his sweetheart was being "ironic" or had employed "rhetorical overkill" or was speaking "partly as a joke" (but never *fully*). Another radical from that period, David Horowitz, said: "In 1980, I taped interviews with thirty members of the Weather Underground who were present at the Flint War Council, including most of its leadership. Not one of them thought Dohrn was anything but deadly serious." Source: David Horowitz, "Allies in War," *FrontPageMagazine.com,* September 17, 2001.

60. Rudd, *Underground,* 189.

61. Ibid.

62. Ibid., 191–92.

63. Among other sources, Larry Grathwohl provided testimony to the U.S. Senate in October 1974, where he listed names of Weatherman radicals who had actually trained in Cuba. See Testimony of Larry Grathwohl, published in "Terroristic Activity: Inside the Weatherman Movement," 108–10. Another source of information on this are FBI reports, some of which are now posted at www.usasurvival.org. These top-secret documents were declassified (with redactions) for use in the trial of FBI officials Mark Felt and Edward S. Miller, who had been charged with breaking the law in their attempts to apprehend Weather Underground fugitives. According to these documents, Mark Rudd and other visitors to Cuba "received specific instruction from Cuban officials," and the Rudd-led uprising at Columbia may have been "planned in Cuba." Cliff Kincaid, who posted these documents at usasurvival. org, says that they were entered into evidence on behalf of the defense in the Felt-Miller trial and were not disputed by the prosecution. (Source: E-mail correspondence with Cliff Kincaid, November 6, 2009.) If this is indeed the case, then the "liberals" who joined Rudd and crew in these demonstrations had yet again been duped by the international Communist movement—by some genuinely bad guys. These documents are posted and available for viewing at www.usasurvival.org/docs/declassified_docs.pdf. One report published by Kincaid's group, written by Herb Romerstein, includes pages (specifically, pages 125 and 126) of one of the FBI reports, which noted that the Cuban government had been "cultivating such groups as the VB [Vencemeros Brigade] and allowing them to travel to Cuba." As Romerstein notes, SDS had been instrumental in creating the Vencemeros Brigade, with certain SDS members working directly with the Cuban government on the effort. Romerstein references a reported November 1969 trip to Cuba that included "numerous" SDSers among the 216 travelers. Based on the FBI's investigation, Romerstein lists Mark Rudd's trip to Cuba (just prior to the Columbia riots) as February 1968. See Herbert Romerstein, "What Was the Weather Underground?" 8–10, 13, posted at the website of www.usasurvival.org. See also Horowitz, *Radical Son,* 160; Ron Radosh's recollections of visits to places like Cuba, told at length in his memoir *Commies;* and "Hearings on

Restraints on Travel to Hostile Areas, H.R. 1594 . . . ," Hearings Before the Committee on Internal Security, House of Representatives, 93rd Congress, First Session, May 9–10, 1973; and Larry Grathwohl, *Bringing Down America: An FBI Informer with the Weathermen* (New Rochelle, NY: Arlington House Publishers, 1976), 108–9, 115–16.

64. See Grathwohl, *Bringing Down America*; *No Place to Hide: The Strategy and Tactics of Terrorism,* a 1982 documentary directed by Dick Quincer and written by G. Edward Griffin; press conferences with Grathwohl available at www.usasurvival.org and available on DVD; Tamara Barak Aparton, "Police Union Targets '60s Radical," *San Francisco Examiner,* March 12, 2009; and Demian Bulwa, "S.F. Police Union Accuses Ayers in 1970 Bombing," *San Francisco Chronicle,* March 12, 2009.

65. Testimony of Larry Grathwohl, published in "Terroristic Activity: Inside the Weatherman Movement," 106–7.

66. The officers came together in March 2009 to issue a statement and talk to the media. For press coverage of the event, see Bulwa, "S.F. Police Union Accuses Ayers in 1970 Bombing"; and Aparton, "Police Union Targets '60s Radical."

67. The targeting of Fort Dix was a major revelation that came through in the classic *Rolling Stone* article by Peter Collier and David Horowitz, "Doing It: The Inside Story of the Rise and Fall of the Weather Underground," which was a seminal early profile of the Weather Underground done shortly after its members were free, published in the September 30, 1982, issue. Horowitz wrote about it again in his memoirs, *Radical Son,* and Rudd himself divulged the Fort Dix revelation ten years later in his own memoirs, *Underground.*

68. Braudy, *Family Circle,* 118–19.

69. Ibid., 205–7.

70. Rudd, *Underground,* 195; and Braudy, *Family Circle,* 205–7.

71. Rudd, *Underground,* 199.

72. Braudy, *Family Circle,* 206–7.

73. See Grathwohl, *Bringing Down America,* 108, 140–41, 167; and Testimony of Larry Grathwohl, published in "Terroristic Activity: Inside the Weatherman Movement," 106–15.

74. *No Place to Hide.* More recently, this interview has been excerpted on YouTube. It was widely viewed during the 2008 presidential race, when Ayers, Dohrn, and the Weathermen reemerged from the shadows. Various transcripts are also posted on the Internet.

75. In the video, Grathwohl does not give the date of the meeting, but it may have been the Weathermen's War Council held in Flint, Michigan, December 26–31, 1969.

76. There are several transcribed versions of this interview available on the Web today. Most I've seen are very good, with almost no variation. The differences are based largely on things like paragraph breaks.

77. Rudd, *Underground,* 214–15, 232, 280.

78. Ibid.

79. Horowitz, *Radical Son,* 334.

80. Braudy, *Family Circle,* 353–55.

81. See Scott Shane, "Obama and '60s Bomber: A Look into Crossed Paths," *New York Times,* October 4, 2008, A1.

82. Rudd, *Underground,* 305–8.

83. See Shane, "Obama and '60s Bomber."

84. Rudd, *Underground,* ix.

85. This, of course, is a very well-known quote. I believe it was probably first sourced by David Horowitz, who interviewed a freed ex-fugitive Ayers early on for the classic September 1982 *Rolling Stone* piece that Horowitz and Peter Collier wrote together. For a full, more recent account by Horowitz, see Horowitz, *Radical Son,* 333–34.

86. An account of this conference was published in the *National Guardian* on August 5, 1967.

87. Rudd said this at an April 22, 2009, press conference on his book release. See Cliff Kincaid, "Terrorists on Tour," Accuracy in Media, www.aim.org, April 23, 2009.

Chapter 17: John Kerry—and Genghis Khan

1. Ion Mihai Pacepa, "Propaganda Redux," *Wall Street Journal,* August 7, 2007.

2. Ion Mihai Pacepa, "Kerry's Soviet Rhetoric," *National Review,* February 26, 2004.

3. See Michael Kranish, Brian C. Mooney, and Nina J. Easton, *John F. Kerry: The Complete Biography by the* Boston Globe *Reporters Who Knew Him Best* (New York: Public Affairs, 2004), 122–23; and O'Neill and Corsi, *Unfit for Command,* 99–100.

4. This is according to Professor Ernest Bolt of the University of Richmond, who posted an analysis of Kerry's testimony at the "facultystaff" portion of the University of Richmond website.

5. "Hearings Before the Committee on Foreign Relations," United States Senate, 92nd Congress, First Session (April–May 1971) (Washington, DC: Government Printing Office, 1971), 180–208.

6. Kerry appeared on NBC's *Meet the Press* on April 18, 1971.

7. See Michael Kranish, "With Antiwar Role, High Visibility," *Boston Globe,* June 17, 2003.

8. Ibid.

9. John E. O'Neill and Jerome R. Corsi, *Unfit for Command* (Washington, DC: Regnery, 2004), 6.

10. Pacepa, "Kerry's Soviet Rhetoric."

11. Whether Kerry threw his own medals or those of other vets was a debate heard throughout the 2004 presidential campaign, and it still persists. For the record, Thomas Oliphant, a *Boston Globe* reporter, was there, and maintains that Kerry tossed his own medals. See Thomas Oliphant, "I Watched Kerry Throw His War Decorations," *Boston Globe,* April 27, 2004.

12. A photo of Kerry and Fonda at the same antiwar rally is included in the photo gallery of O'Neill's *Unfit for Command.*

13. See, among others, Mark Lane, *Plausible Denial: Was the CIA Involved in the Assassination of JFK?* (New York: Thunder's Mouth Press, 1992).

14. Mackubin Thomas Owens, "Vetting the Vet Record," *National Review,* January 27, 2004.

15. Mark Lane, *Conversations with Americans: Testimonies from 32 Vietnam Veterans* (New York: Simon & Schuster, 1970).

16. Owens, "Vetting the Vet Record."

17. Ibid. As Owens notes, Guenter Lewy tells the full story in his book *America in Vietnam* (New York: Oxford University Press, 1978).

18. O'Neill and Corsi, *Unfit for Command,* 7–8.

19. A photo of the plaque is contained in the photo section of O'Neill and Corsi, *Unfit for Command.*

20. Pacepa, "Kerry's Soviet Rhetoric."

Chapter 18: A Kiss for Brezhnev: Jimmy Carter

1. Most observers would agree on at least ten nations, including, among others, Ethiopia, Nicaragua, and Mozambique. Thomas Henriksen of the Hoover Institution, for example, wrote that from 1974 to 1979 the Soviets "incorporated 10 countries into their orbit." Constantine Menges, a member of the Reagan National Security Council, said that between 1975 and 1980, eleven new "pro-Soviet regimes" were established. See Thomas Henriksen, "The Lessons of Afghanistan," *Washington Times,* December 29, 1999; and Constantine C. Menges in 1993 Hofstra University conference on the Reagan presidency, published in Eric J. Schmertz et al., eds., *President Reagan and the World* (Westport, CT: Greenwood Press, 1997), 29–30. Hereafter referred to as "Hofstra Conference (1993)."

2. Reagan blasted Republican president Gerald Ford on détente before Jimmy Carter even became president. Ford was so wedded to détente that he refused to meet with the great dissident Aleksandr Solzhenitsyn out of fear of offending the Soviets. For an extended discussion of this, see Kengor, *The Crusader,* 40–55.

3. Genrikh Aleksandrovich (Henry) Trofimenko, in Hofstra Conference (1993), 136.

4. Peter Osnos, "Angola Stirs Questions on Détente Fine Print," *Washington Post,* January 16, 1976, A12.

5. Quoted by James Reston, "The Mood of the Capital," *New York Times,* February 27, 1976, 31.

6. See "Kissinger Said to Reject Report on Soviet View," *Washington Post,* February 12, 1977, A2. The *Post* piece (among others) followed up the original February 11, 1977, *Boston Globe* article by William Beecher, which was the source for the story. See William Beecher, "Brezhnev Termed Détente a Ruse,

1973 Report Said," *Boston Globe,* February 11, 1977. According to the *Globe* article, in early 1973 British intelligence obtained a speech by Leonid Brezhnev given at a secret meeting of Eastern European Communist rulers in Prague. The Brits rated the speech comparable in importance to Nikita Khrushchev's 1956 "Crimes of Stalin" speech.

7. Reagan delivered this commentary on March 23, 1977. His source was the February 11, 1977, *Boston Globe* article by Beecher, which was reprinted in *National Review* on March 4, 1977, in an article titled "Secret Speech: Did Brezhnev Come Clean?" In the handwritten text of his radio commentary, Reagan complained that "the British informed our government of Brezhnev's speech, but apparently it didn't lessen our desire for 'détente.'" Text located in "Ronald Reagan: Selected Radio Broadcasts, 1975–1979," January 1975 to March 1977, Box 1, RRL. For a full transcript, see Kiron Skinner, Martin Anderson, and Annelise Anderson, eds., *Reagan, In His Own Hand* (New York: Free Press, 2001), 117–19.

8. President Jimmy Carter, "Remarks at Stetson Junior High School in West Chester, PA," *Public Papers of the Presidents of the United States,* 1977, vol. 1, January 27, 1977, 28.

9. President Jimmy Carter, "News Conference," *Public Papers of the Presidents of the United States,* 1977, vol. 1, March 24, 1977, 502.

10. President Jimmy Carter, "Remarks and a Question-and-Answer Session at a Luncheon Sponsored by Fort Worth Civic Organizations in Fort Worth, Texas," *Public Papers of the Presidents of the United States,* 1978, vol. 1, June 23, 1978, 1160.

11. President Jimmy Carter, "News Conference," *Public Papers of the Presidents of the United States,* 1978, vol. 1, June 26, 1978, 1184.

12. President Jimmy Carter, "Question-and-Answer Session with Western European and Japanese Leaders," *Public Papers of the Presidents of the United States,* 1978, vol. 2, July 11, 1978, 1256.

13. President Jimmy Carter, "Question-and-Answer Session with the Japanese Press," *Public Papers of the Presidents of the United States,* 1979, vol. 2, June 20, 1979, 1148.

14. President Jimmy Carter, "Remarks on Arrival at the White House," *Public Papers of the Presidents of the United States,* 1978, vol. 1, January 6, 1978, 40.

15. Among other occasions, Carter said this in his June 1977 commencement speech at the University of Notre Dame and in a press conference on May 25, 1978.

16. President Jimmy Carter, "Meeting with Student Leaders," *Public Papers of the Presidents of the United States,* 1980–1981, vol. 1, February 15, 1980, 330.

17. After one classified briefing on the Soviet economy, on March 26, 1982, Reagan concluded: "The situation was so bad that if Western countries got together and cut off credits to it [the USSR], we could bring it to its knees." See Ronald Reagan, *An American Life* (New York: Simon & Schuster, 1990), 552.

18. In the official transcript of the exchange, published in the *Public Papers of the Presidents of the United States,* this laughter is noted aside Carter's remarks. It reads: "I don't know. [Laughter] I hope that it will be removed." President Jimmy Carter, "Question-and-Answer Session at a Town Meeting in Berlin (west side), Federal Republic of Germany," *Public Papers of the Presidents of the United States,* 1978, vol. 2, July 15, 1978, 1301.

19. Allen remarks, published in Peter Schweizer, ed., *The Fall of the Berlin Wall* (Stanford, CA: Hoover Institution Press, 2000), 55–56.

20. Interview with Michael Reagan, May 9, 2005. Michael Reagan has since told me this story many times. It is one of his favorite anecdotes about his father, and genuinely a telling one.

21. President Carter initially said this in a December 31, 1979, interview with Frank Reynolds of ABC News's *World News Tonight.* See ABC News Transcript, *World News Tonight,* December 31, 1979. See also "Transcript of President's Interview on Soviet Reply," *New York Times,* January 1, 1980, 4.

22. See, for example, "Transcript of President's Interview on Soviet Reply."

23. Reagan wrote this in a January 1980 letter to a "Professor Nikolaev." The letter is published in Skinner, Anderson, and Anderson, eds., *Reagan: A Life in Letters,* 400.

24. Reagan wrote this in a January 1980 letter to a man named Edward Langley. The letter is published in ibid., 433–34.

25. President Jimmy Carter, "Situation in Iran and Soviet Invasion of Afghanistan, Remarks at a White House Briefing for Members of Congress," *Public Papers of the Presidents of the United States,* 1980–81, vol. 1, January 8, 1980, 38–42.

26. President Jimmy Carter, "Venice Economic Summit: Concluding Statements of the Participants," *Public Papers of the Presidents of the United States,* 1980–81, vol. 2, June 23, 1980, 1177–78.

27. President Jimmy Carter, "Remarks to the Democratic National Committee," *Public Papers of the Presidents of the United States,* 1977, vol. 2, October 7, 1977, 1749.

28. Reagan said this constantly. See, for example, President Ronald Reagan, "Remarks at a Fundraising Dinner for Senator Paula Hawkins in Miami, Florida," *Public Papers of the Presidents of the United States,* 1985, vol. 1, May 27, 1985, 674; and President Ronald Reagan, "Remarks at a Fundraising Luncheon for Senator Don Nickles in Oklahoma City, Oklahoma," *Public Papers of the Presidents of the United States,* 1985, vol. 1, June 5, 1985, 718.

29. See Vasiliy Mitrokhin, "The KGB in Afghanistan," Working Paper No. 40, English edition, introduced and edited by Christian F. Ostermann and Odd Arne Westad, Cold War International History Project, Woodrow Wilson International Center for Scholars, Washington, DC, July 2002, 160. Note: a full copy of the working paper, in PDF format, is available at the website of the Wilson Center: http://www.wilsoncenter.org/topics/pubs/ACFAE9.pdf.

30. President Jimmy Carter, "Remarks at a Toast for the President and the Shah," Tehran, Iran, *Public Papers of the Presidents of the United States,"* 1977, vol. 2, December 31, 1977, 2221.

31. President Jimmy Carter, "Remarks at a Question-and-Answer Session at a Breakfast with Members of the White House Correspondents Association," *Public Papers of the Presidents of the United States,* 1978, vol. 2, December 7, 1978, 2172.

Chapter 19: Defending the "Evil Empire": Stopping Ronald Reagan's "Errors" and "Distortions"

1. Allen says this lunch took place the last week of January 1977. Source: Interview with Richard V. Allen, November 12, 2001; and Richard Allen, "An Extraordinary Man in Extraordinary Times: Ronald Reagan's Leadership and the Decision to End the Cold War," Address to the Hoover Institution and the William J. Casey Institute of the Center for Security Policy, Washington, DC, February 22, 1999, text printed in Schweizer, ed., *The Fall of the Berlin Wall,* 52.

2. Natan Sharansky, who was imprisoned in the gulag, has discussed this at length, quite dramatically. Similar testimonies from the Polish Solidarity movement are innumerable. For example, one Solidarity member, Jan Winiecki, said: "It's very important for those underground to know they'll have support diplomatically if they're repressed. They knew they could count on Reagan and his administration for this rhetorical, moral, public support—this political support. It raised their spirits that they could survive." I have published many of these accounts. From the Soviet side, including Sharansky, see Kengor, *God and Ronald Reagan,* 262–69. From the Solidarity side, see Kengor, *The Crusader,* 84–111, 285–92.

3. This is true for rankings both by the general public and by presidential scholars. Reagan consistently ranks extraordinarily high in public rankings, usually among the top three to five presidents, and sometimes number one. For instance, a 2001 Gallup poll showed that Americans rank Reagan the greatest president of all time. As for presidential scholars, C-SPAN released a survey for Presidents Day 2009 that ranked Reagan the tenth best president. Among other citations of these polls and other appraisals, see Lou Cannon and Carl Cannon, *Reagan's Disciple* (New York: Public Affairs, 2008), xii.

4. A June 2005 survey by the Discovery Channel and AOL (2.4 million participants) declared Reagan the "greatest American of all time," beating Lincoln and Washington.

5. Root told this story numerous times in the summer of 2009 during promotion for his latest book. The quotes cited here are taken from his blog entries posted at www.rootforamerica.com/blog as well as a March 7, 2008, interview he did with Glenn Beck, posted at www.glennbeck.com.

6. In particular, Lamont blasted the president's support of groups like "the savage and terrorist [Nicaraguan] Contras." Lamont stated this in a full-page ad by his National Emergency Civil Liberties Committee, for which he provided the lead signature. Among others, the ad was placed in publications like *Mother Jones* magazine, June–July 1987, 61.

7. See Kengor, *The Crusader,* 198.

8. See my discussion in Kengor, *God and Ronald Reagan,* 264–69.

9. See Reagan, "Address at Commencement Exercises at Eureka College in Illinois, May 9, 1982," *Presidential Papers, 1982,* vol. 1, 583. On July 19, 1982, he said that the USSR's "self-proclaimed goal is the domination of every nation on Earth." See Reagan, "Remarks on Signing the Captive Nations Week Proclamation, July 19, 1982," *Presidential Papers, 1982,* vol. 2, 936. Two months earlier, on May 27, he told Western European journalists that the USSR's "worldwide aggression" stemmed from "the Marxist-Leninist theory of world domination." See Reagan, "Interview with Representatives of Western European Publications, May 21, 1982," *Public Papers of the Presidents of the United States, Ronald Reagan, 1982,* vol. 1, 696. He constantly said the USSR was expansionary in nature and committed to a "one-world Communist state." He said this so often—in formal speeches, on the stump, in interviews, wherever—that it's impossible to count all the references. See, for example, Reagan, "Interview with Reporters from the *Los Angeles Times,* January 20, 1982," *Presidential Papers, 1982,* vol. 1, 62; Reagan, "Interview with Morton Kondracke and Richard H. Smith of *Newsweek* Magazine, March 4, 1985," *Presidential Papers,* vol. 1, 1985, 261; Reagan, "Interview with Representatives of College Radio Stations, September 9, 1985," *Presidential Papers, 1985,* vol. 2, 1068–69; Reagan, "Question-and-Answer Session with Students at Fallston High School, Fallston, Maryland, December 4, 1985," *Presidential Papers, 1985,* vol. 2, 1438. He didn't just charge this motive to the leadership generally. He specified each Soviet leader—and top officials like Andrei Gromyko—as hell-bent on expansion and world domination. Importantly, he found one exception—Mikhail Gorbachev—and said so openly. Before Gorbachev, Reagan wrote, every other had vowed to pursue the Marxist commitment to a one-world Communist state. See Reagan, *An American Life,* 641, 706–7.

10. In a 1975 radio broadcast that he wrote, Reagan complained, "The Russians have told us over and over again their goal is to impose their incompetent and ridiculous system on the world." Quoted by Ronnie Dugger, *On Reagan: The Man and His Presidency* (New York: McGraw Hill, 1983), 439. Another example: In May 1977 Reagan wrote that "every Soviet leader," including Brezhnev, "has sworn to carry out to the letter the words of Lenin." This passage is from a May 25, 1977, radio broadcast he wrote, located in "Ronald Reagan: Pre-Presidential Papers: Selected Radio Broadcasts, 1975–1979," April 1977 to September 1977, box 2, RRL. For a transcript, see Skinner, Anderson, and Anderson, eds., *Reagan, In His Own Hand,* 33–35. This was common for Reagan in his 1970s pronouncements. See also "Keng Piao," radio broadcast written by Reagan, May 4, 1977, located in "Ronald Reagan: Pre-Presidential Papers: Selected Radio Broadcasts, 1975–1979," April 1977 to September 1977, box 2, RRL. A transcript is in Skinner, Anderson, and Anderson, eds., *Reagan, In His Own Hand,* 35–36; and "Reagan: 'It Isn't Only Washington . . . ,'" *National Journal,* March 8, 1980, 391.

11. Allen interviewed in Stephen F. Knott and Jeffrey L. Chidester, *At Reagan's Side* (Lanham, MD: Rowman & Littlefield, 2009), 94.

12. Reagan, "The President's News Conference," January 29, 1981.

13. In a speech to the American Legion Convention at New York's Madison Square Garden on August 27, 1952, Adlai Stevenson, a liberal's liberal, an intellectual, and twice the Democratic Party's standard-bearer in the 1950s, spoke approvingly of America's "healthy apprehension about the Communist menace within our country." Sounding mild compared to Reagan, Stevenson declared: "Communism is abhorrent. It is strangulation of the individual; it is death for the soul. Americans who have surrendered to this misbegotten idol have surrendered their right to our trust. And there can be no secure place for them in our public life."

14. Among other points in his classic Long Telegram, Kennan warned *caveat emptor*—that America must recognize that when the Soviets put their signature to a document, it is for strategic purposes only, and should not be trusted. George F. Kennan, "The Sources of Soviet Conduct," *Foreign Affairs,* July 1947.

15. Allen interviewed in Knott and Chidester, *At Reagan's Side,* 94.

16. Bernard Gwertzman, "President Sharply Assails Kremlin," *New York Times,* January 30, 1981, A1.

17. Lee Lescaze, "Reagan Voices a Tone for Relations Far Harsher Than His Predecessors," *Washington Post,* January 30, 1981, A1.

18. "Sizing Up the Kremlin," *Washington Post,* February 1, 1981.

19. See Lee Congdon, *George Kennan: A Writing Life* (Wilmington, DE: ISI Books, 2008), 114.

20. "On Soviet Morality," *Time,* February 16, 1981, 17.

21. Reagan, "Excerpts from an Interview with Walter Cronkite of CBS News," March 3, 1981.

22. "On Soviet Morality," 17. This version of the quotation doesn't match *Time*'s to the exact letter, but is nearly identical, differing only because of translations. For this version of the quote, see V. I. Lenin, *Collected Works, Vol. 31: April–December 1920* (Moscow: Progress Publishers, 1977), 291. Another reporter who came to see that Reagan's statements on Lenin were correct was *Washington Post* White House correspondent Lou Cannon, who affirmed the accuracy of Reagan's account in his first biography of the fortieth president. See Lou Cannon, *President Reagan: The Role of a Lifetime* (New York: Public Affairs, 2000), 241–42.

23. "R. Reagan's Press Conference," *Pravda,* January 31, 1981, 5.

24. S. Kondrashov, "This Is a New Beginning?" *Izvestia,* February 1, 1981, 5.

25. Among others strictly from Soviet print media, there was a TASS statement carried on page 4 of both *Izvestia* and *Pravda* on February 3, 1981, plus columns such as: N. Prokofiev, "Rejoinder to the Point," *Pravda,* February 5, 1981, 5; and Yuri Rudnev, "Washington's Dishonorable Game," *Sovetskaya Rossia,* February 5, 1981, 1.

26. I've written about this in Paul Kengor, *The Judge: William P. Clark, Ronald Reagan's Top Hand* (San Francisco: Ignatius Press, 2007), 194–95.

27. I know this well, as Clark's biographer. See Kengor, *The Judge.*

28. Letter, Elliott Abrams to Bill Clark, March 10, 1983. A photocopy of the letter is in my possession.

29. Abrams cited the source as "V. I. Lenin, 1901. From the essay: 'Where to Begin' *Selected Works,* vol. 2 page 17."

30. In fact, Clark put a copy in his own files for delivering his own speeches. He scribbled in the upper right corner of the letter, "Save (speech file materials)."

31. Joanne Omang, "Pseudo-Nym and Pseudo-History," *Washington Post,* January 22, 1983.

32. Reagan, "Remarks and a Question-and-Answer Session with Reporters on the Second Anniversary of the Inauguration of the President," January 20, 1983, *Presidential Documents.*

33. For example: Nicolai Lenin, "The Tactics of the Communists," *Communist Labor,* February 25, 1920, vol. 2, no. 3, 2.

34. For both, the publisher was the London-based Communist Party of Great Britain.

35. Omang, "Pseudo-Nym and Pseudo-History."

36. V. I. Lenin, *Collected Works, Vol. 19* (Moscow: Progress Publishers, 1977), 439–42. Lenin stated this in a piece published in *Za Pravdu,* No. 8, October 12, 1913. (*Za Pravdu* was, in effect, an early version of *Pravda,* as Lenin was attempting to transition the paper from its Vienna roots into Bolshevik Russia during the revolution.) Lenin apparently said it in regard to David Lloyd George's Labour Government in Britain. Lenin wrote: "And the promises of reform . . . does not the English proverb say that promises are like pie-crusts, made to be broken?" If there was a valid criticism of Reagan, or anyone, using this quote, it was that Lenin applied it to British thinking. Of course, that point was not raised at all; the criticism of Reagan was that Lenin allegedly never made the statement. The criticism was not that Reagan had quoted Lenin out of context, but that he had cited a "Lenin quote" that was not actually a Lenin quote. Over time, after 1913, the quote came to be applied to Lenin's thinking, given Lenin's penchant for happily, candidly breaking agreements. The quote is Lenin's quote, and it was an accurate representation of both his thinking and his behavior.

37. This is common knowledge regarding Lenin, Stalin, and the Bolsheviks generally. Woodrow Wilson's State Department complained that the Bolshevik "spokesmen say that they sign agreements with no intention of keeping them." See Secretary of State Bainbridge Colby, "Note of State Department on Polish Situation," *Public Papers of President Woodrow Wilson,* August 10, 1920, vol. 18, 8866. George Kennan focused on the Soviet tendency to break signed agreements in his 1947 "Long Telegram," where, as noted, Kennan said that Bolshevik betrayal was so common that any document with a Soviet signature should be interpreted in the spirit of *caveat emptor.* President Harry Truman complained about this tendency openly and colorfully, as has been well recorded. Reagan would have begun hearing and learning about it in the 1940s, when he (as a Truman Democrat) took a strong interest in the Cold War that was erupting all around him. I can say with absolute certainty that Reagan learned more about it in the late 1960s when he read a book by Laurence W. Beilenson called *The Treaty Trap: A History of the Performance of Political Treaties by the United States and European Nations* (Washington, DC: Public Affairs Press, 1969), which was a historical analysis of the Soviets' penchant for breaking diplomatic agreements. The book greatly influenced Reagan, who remarked on and recommended it quite often, including in print. The

book sat in Reagan's personal library. He and Beilenson became friends and corresponded very frequently—including in the 1980s—as attested by the letters on file at the Reagan Library.

38. Quoted in Paul Johnson, *Modern Times* (New York: HarperPerennial, 1992), 73–74.

39. Cannon, *President Reagan: The Role of a Lifetime*, 110.

40. Mikhail Gorbachev, *Perestroika* (New York: Harper & Row, 1987), 25, 45, 145.

41. Ibid.

42. Ibid., 32, 48–49.

43. Ibid., 145.

44. See V. I. Lenin, *Collected Works, Vol. 31: April–December 1920* (Moscow: Progress Publishers, 1977), 291. See also "On Soviet Morality," 17.

45. The document is today located in the Central Committee Archives of the Soviet Union. After the Cold War, it was featured as one of several interesting documents presented in an Archives Exhibit at the Library of Congress.

46. Nor did it mention another disputed phrase where Reagan attacked the "Ten Commandments" of Lenin. This is one that seemed vulnerable, and indeed questionable. Perhaps the lack of mention meant that it was not so vulnerable or questionable. I cannot resolve this phrase or the reason the Soviets did not mention it.

47. The exact dates of when Reagan said this in September 1985 were contested by Raymond Garthoff in the footnotes of his book *The Great Transition*, specifically footnote 8 on page 9. I will not argue with Garthoff here, but it appears that Reagan made the "overripe fruit" statement twice between roughly September 9 (to a group of college students) and also on September 18 to ABC's Ted Koppel. See David Hoffman, "Inside the White House: Lessons from the President," *Washington Post*, September 12, 1985, A21.

48. Karl E. Meyer, "The Elusive Lenin: Where Ronald Reagan Read of the Plot to Conquer America," *New York Times*, October 8, 1985, A30.

49. The way this was handled in Meyer's piece is odd. Meyer traced the Nazi link to both Arbatov and Cooke, since Cooke was discussing the "overripe fruit" line with Arbatov on Arbatov's TV show. Meyer said that Cooke had once exposed the line as Nazi propaganda. It is impossible for me to say whether Cooke or the Soviets first exposed the line as a Nazi plant. I would expect the Soviets to have attempted that connection, given their long history of tracing their own vicious deeds to the Nazis, including the Katyn Wood massacre. Either way, the Soviets claimed throughout the 1980s that the line was begun by the Nazis.

50. Meyer, "The Elusive Lenin."

51. Herb Romerstein says that the quote has been traced to Trotsky's collection of Lenin remarks. Source: Discussions and e-mails with Herb Romerstein, who in the 1980s checked this quote, along with many others.

52. Benson recalled this in a speech at Brigham Young University in October 1966. Audio clips of the speech, including this passage, can be found on several websites and appear on YouTube. The correct citation for the Benson speech (which is cited incorrectly on many websites) is "Our Immediate Responsibility," October 25, 1966, a "Devotional Address" at Brigham Young University, posted at the BYU website. Khrushchev's memoirs confirm the time he spent with Benson on September 16, 1959. See Sergei Khrushchev, ed., *Memoirs of Nikita Khrushchev: Statesman, 1953–64*, vol. 3 (University Park, PA: Penn State University Press, 2007), 187.

53. Again, as referenced earlier in this book, V. I. Lenin's "Letter to American Workers" was written August 20, 1918, and published in *Pravda*, August 22, 1918. See V. I. Lenin, *Collected Works*, vol. 28 (Moscow: Progress Publishers, 1965), 62–75.

54. Lenin in November 1918: "The facts of world history have shown that the conversion of our Russian revolution into a socialist revolution was not an adventure but a necessity, for there was no other choice. Anglo-French and American imperialism will inevitably strangle the independence and freedom of Russia unless world-wide socialist revolution, unless world-wide Bolshevism, conquers." Quoted in Trotsky, *The History of the Russian Revolution*, 395.

55. This is a well-known fact regarding Buckley and *National Review*. For a current source, see Lee Edwards, *William F. Buckley Jr.: The Maker of a Movement* (Wilmington, DE: ISI Books, 2010), 56, 80–82.

56. Of all of these authors, Beilenson in particular detailed these many Soviet quotes and how they reflected the USSR's and its leaders' poor character and inability to be trusted in things like diplomatic agreements. Reagan was a big fan of Beilenson's book, referencing it and recommending it very frequently, maybe more than any other book on the Soviets. See Beilenson, *The Treaty Trap.*

57. On this, see Kengor, *God and Ronald Reagan,* 75–77. Also, I wrote the content for the Reagan Ranch museum exhibit that lists the authors that Reagan read, based on the books that rested on the shelves (marked up with annotations) of the Reagan ranch home. I have not only seen but even handled and turned the pages of the books Reagan kept at the ranch; titles by these authors were among those on those shelves. Yet more books sat on the shelves at the Reagan home in Bel Air, California, which my colleague Lee Edwards observed during an interview with Reagan in the 1960s. Edwards, too, saw these and other authors.

58. "Rhee Cautions On Reds' Aims," *Washington Post,* June 26, 1955, A8

59. This story was relayed to me several times by Herb Romerstein, who also confirmed this print version.

60. On the monolithic media: This was an era before conservative talk radio, FoxNews, and the Internet, when the political Left almost completely dominated the American media.

61. "Vulgar" was a common adjective used by the Soviet media against Reagan. For a quoted example, see endnote 65 below referring to the June 18, 1987, broadcast of the *Studio 9* program.

62. Trofimenko in Hofstra Conference, 144.

63. Commentary by Valentin Zorin, Moscow Domestic Service, February 16, 1976, printed as "Reagan Making Détente a 'Football Game,'" in FBIS, February 27, 1976, B5–6.

64. Valentin Falin, "Interview? No, a Program," *Izvestia,* June 21, 1985, 4, printed as "Falin Sees Reagan's Words, Deeds at Variance," in FBIS, June 27, 1985, A5–6.

65. *Studio 9,* June 18, 1987, transcript printed as "*Studio 9* Participants Discuss Reagan's Recent Speeches," in FBIS, June 19, 1987, A1–10. "What Reagan is saying is simply political vulgarity," yelled Arbatov. "Political vulgarity!" Falin derided Reagan's request as "frantic demagoguery" and "plain blackmail, blackmail by an American cowboy." To Zorin and the boys, the wall was a "strictly defensive" measure, an overture of peace, intended to preserve prosperity and tranquility in Europe.

66. On Zorin on Reagan and Poland, see Valentin Zorin, "Moscow Viewpoint," December 27, 1981, published as "Zorin Commentary," in FBIS, December 30, 1981, F3–5. On Zorin on Reagan and Grenada, see Valentin Zorin speaking through Moscow Domestic Service, January 13, 1984, transcript printed as "'International Situation: Questions & Answers,'" in FBIS, January 16, 1984, CC8–9. See also Kengor, *The Crusader,* 194.

67. The transcript is available at the official online repository for the Reagan *Presidential Documents,* http://www.reagan.utexas.edu/archives/speeches/1988/052088j.htm.

68. Meyer, "The Elusive Lenin."

69. Reagan, "Interview with Soviet Television Journalists Valentin Zorin and Boris Kalyagin, May 20, 1988," *Presidential Papers,* 1988, 667. In general, Reagan performed extremely effectively in this interview. Anyone who believes he was a dummy who couldn't hold his own without a script or teleprompter should turn to pages 665–70 of the 1988 *Presidential Papers* and read more from the transcript of this interview.

70. Garry Wills, *Reagan's America: Innocents at Home* (Garden City, NY: Doubleday, 1987), 342, 523n.

71. I was required to read the book in two different courses in graduate school, and found it among suggested readings on the syllabus of several additional courses.

72. Raymond L. Garthoff, *The Great Transition: American-Soviet Relations and the End of the Cold War* (Washington, DC: Brookings Institution Press, 1994), 9n.

73. Mark Green and Gail MacColl, *Ronald Reagan's Reign of Error* (New York: Pantheon Books, 1984).

74. I cover these in Kengor, *God and Ronald Reagan,* 249–62. Most of the quotes that follow in this section were used in that treatment.

75. See Peter Robinson, *How Ronald Reagan Changed My Life* (New York: ReganBooks, 2003). Robinson was the Reagan speechwriter who wrote the Brandenburg Gate speech.

76. Dolan said that among the items that most bothered staff were passages on abortion, another issue from which Reagan never backed down. See Cannon, *President Reagan: The Role of a Lifetime,* 274.

77. See Kengor, *God and Ronald Reagan,* x–xi, 244–49.

78. Anthony Lewis, "Onward Christian Soldiers," *New York Times,* March 10, 1983.

79. Richard Cohen, "Convictions," *Washington Post,* May 26, 1983, C1.

80. Editorial, "Reverend Reagan," *The New Republic,* April 4, 1933.

81. March 11, 1983, statement from TASS in English, "TASS Criticism," printed in FBIS, March 14, 1983, A2–3.

82. The Commager quote has been widely quoted. Among recent sources, see Charles Krauthammer, "Reluctant Cold Warriors," *Washington Post,* November 12, 1999, A35; and Edmund Morris, *Dutch: A Memoir of Ronald Reagan* (New York: Random House, 1999), 475.

83. Tip O'Neill, July 1984 Democratic National Convention. A LexisNexis search yielded only one reference to the quote—a June 8, 1998, column in *Jewish World Review* by columnist Don Feder of the *Boston Herald.* Source for quote: Don Phillips, "O'Neill: Mondale Must Attack 'Cold, Mean' Reagan," UPI, July 19, 1984.

84. Through TASS, Andropov and the Soviet leadership compared Reagan to Hitler. They did this often in their propaganda. See Cannon, *The Role of a Lifetime,* 275, 666; and "Men of the Year: Ronald Reagan and Yuri Andropov," *Time,* January 2, 1984.

85. "Moscow Terms Speech 'Bellicose,'" *Facts on File,* March 1983, 164.

86. March 9, 1983, statement from TASS in English. "Reagan Orlando Speech Reflects U.S. 'Militarism,'" printed in FBIS, March 10, 1983, A1–2.

87. "TASS Criticism," FBIS, March 14, 1983.

88. "Rhetoric from the Cold War Era," *Pravda,* March 10, 1983, 5. Printed in *The Current Digest of the Soviet Press,* April 6, 1983, 19–20).

89. Manki Ponomarev, "The United States: Policy with No Future," *Krasnaya Zvezda,* March 8, 1987, 3, reprinted as "Army Paper on Links Between Reagan, 'Truman Doctrine,'" in FBIS, March 13, 1987, A6–8.

90. "Rhetoric from the Cold War Era."

91. March 13, 1983, transcript from Moscow Domestic Television Service, "Geramisov Denunciation," printed in FBIS, March 14, 1983, A2.

92. Georgi Arbatov, "The U.S.—Will There Be Changes?" *Pravda,* March 17, 1983. Printed in "Arbatov Assails US 'Propaganda Tricks,'" *The Current Digest of the Soviet Press* vol. 35, no. 11, April 13, 1983, 4.

93. Sharansky, *Fear No Evil* (New York: PublicAffairs, 1998), 245, 334, 341, 362.

94. Sharansky is quoted in Noonan, *When Character Was King,* 213–14.

95. By the time of the March 1983 speech, Bukovsky had been released to the West. He was frequently consulted by Reagan speechwriters, including Dolan, Mark Palmer (State Department), and John Lenczowski (National Security Council). Interview with Vladimir Bukovsky, March 5, 2003.

96. Jan Winiecki, "Poland Under Communism," presentation at Grove City College, March 6, 2002.

97. This is a very brief sample of the millions languishing behind the Iron Curtain who heartily endorsed Reagan's phrase, and are free to say so only today, from everyday Soviet citizens to politicians, available and eager to talk to any scholar or journalist willing to consult them. For more examples, see Kengor, *God and Ronald Reagan,* 259–69.

98. Kozyrev on ABC News, *This Week with David Brinkley,* August 25, 1991. From ABC News, Brinkley transcript no. 513, 7.

99. Tarasenko said this during a February 25–27, 1993, conference at Princeton University. See William C. Wohlforth, ed., *Witnesses to the End of the Cold War* (Baltimore: Johns Hopkins University Press, 1996), 20.

100. David Remnick, "Dead Souls," *New York Review of Books,* December 19, 1991, 79.

101. Trofimenko in Hofstra Conference, 136.

Chapter 20: "Star Wars": The SDI Sabotage

1. This is the subject of my book *The Crusader.* In particular, see parts 2 and 3.

2. The three crucial NSDDs that solidified this effort between May 1982 and March 1983 were NSDDs 32, 66, and 75.

3. G. Dadyants, "Pipes Threatens History," *Sotsialisticheskaya Industriya,* March 26, 1983, 3, published

as "New Directive on USSR Trade 'Threatens History,'" in FBIS, March 29, 1983, A6–7. Also: Two releases from the Moscow Domestic Service were released at 1940 and 2015 GMT on March 17, 1983. Transcripts are published as "'Economic, Military Blackmail'" and "Directive 75 'Subversive' Anti-Soviet Plan" in FBIS, March 18, 1983, A8–9.

4. Dadyants, "Pipes Threatens History."

5. Reagan, An American Life, 237–38.

6. Meyer was special assistant to the CIA director from 1981 to 1987 and vice chair of the National Intelligence Council, a prestigious seat at the CIA, where he observed the full scope of the Reagan strategy against the USSR. I would list Meyer along with Roger Robinson at the National Security Council as the top behind-the-scenes players, with the major out-in-front figures being Bill Clark, Caspar Weinberger, Ed Meese, and Bill Casey. Robinson often used the phrase "take-down," as did Clark. I write about this in both The Judge and The Crusader.

7. Interview with Herb Meyer, February 29, 2008.

8. Ibid.

9. Ibid.

10. Ibid.

11. See, for example, Reagan, "Remarks to Administration Supporters at a White House Briefing on Arms Control, Central America, and the Supreme Court," November 23, 1987; Reagan, "Remarks at a Luncheon Hosted by the Heritage Foundation," November 30, 1987; and Reagan, "Remarks to the Institute for Foreign Policy Analysis at a Conference on the Strategic Defense Initiative, March 14, 1988," Presidential Papers, 1988, 331.

12. Interview with Meyer, February 29, 2008.

13. For a sample of testimonies, see Kengor, The Crusader, 300–2.

14. Alexander Bessmertnykh speaking on "Reagan," The American Experience, PBS, 1998. Note: This book could be filled with such testimonies, from the Russian in the street, to military officials, to apparatchiks, to the Soviet ministry, to Gorbachev. I cut twenty pages of testimonies from this chapter.

15. See Princeton University, Woodrow Wilson School of Public and International Affairs, "Retrospective on the End of the Cold War," A Conference Sponsored by the John Foster Dulles Program for the Study of Leadership in International Affairs, Princeton, NJ, February 25–27, 1993; and Bruce Olson, "SDI, Chernobyl Said to Break Cycle of Nuclear Buildup," Executive News Service, February 26, 1993. His remarks are also published in Wohlforth, ed., Witnesses to the End of the Cold War, 31–32.

16. Trofimenko in Hofstra Conference, 138.

17. "They are in very bad shape," wrote Reagan in his diary on March 26, 1982, "and if we can cut off their credit they'll have to yell 'Uncle' or starve." Reagan, An American Life, 316.

18. Anatoly Dobrynin, In Confidence (New York: Random House, 1995), 591.

19. Donald Regan, For the Record (San Diego, CA: Harcourt Brace Jovanovich, 1988), 297.

20. Kenneth W. Thompson, ed., Leadership in the Reagan Presidency, Pt II: Eleven Intimate Perspectives (Lanham, MD: United Press of America, 1993), 52.

21. George Wilson, "Senate Refuses to Slash 'Star Wars' Funding," Washington Post, June 5, 1988, A30; and Tom Burgess, "Differing Viewpoints on SDI," San Diego Union-Tribune, October 22, 1986, A10.

22. See Lou Cannon, "President Seeks Futuristic Defense Against Missiles," Washington Post, March 24, 1983, A1; Hedrick Smith, "Would a Space-Age Defense Ease Tensions or Create Them?" New York Times, March 27, 1983; Francis X. Clines, "Democrats Assert Reagan Is Using 'Star Wars' Scare to Hide Blunders," New York Times, March 25, 1983; David B. Wilson, "How Reagan's 'Star Wars' Got Its Name," Boston Globe, January 27, 1985; and Morris, Dutch, 477. For further documentation on Kennedy's statement, see Congressional Quarterly: "Reagan on Defense in Space," Historic Documents of 1983 (Washington, DC: CQ Press, 1984), 306. Among these, David B. Wilson, a columnist for the Globe's op-ed page, claimed credit for coining the term "Star Wars" in an earlier application (March 1982) he made to missile defense. He speculated whether the phrase may have been "consciously or unconsciously borrowed" by Kennedy or his staff, though he could not confirm it. (Wilson, unlike Kennedy, didn't use the phrase as a pejorative.) Either way, it was Kennedy who first used the term in response to Reagan's proposal.

23. Lou Cannon, almost certainly with some measure of regret, once advanced this unsustainable argument, which at best is pure speculation, with no documentable attestation either from Reagan's writings

or statements or from any of those who worked with or advised Reagan on SDI. See Cannon, *President Reagan: The Role of a Lifetime*, 251. Another book that makes reference to Reagan, Brass Bancroft, and their "Inertia Projector" was *Way Out There in the Blue* by the *New York Times*'s Frances FitzGerald. See Frances FitzGerald, *Way Out There in the Blue: Reagan, Star Wars, and the End of the Cold War* (New York: Simon & Schuster, 2000), 22–23, 40, 47–49. The FitzGerald book is of the genre that saw Reagan as a dunce not to be taken seriously. In fact, Reagan's thinking on SDI is clearly rooted in other sources, particularly a 1967 meeting with physicist Edward Teller at Lawrence Livermore National Laboratory and a 1979 visit to NORAD, among others. See Kengor, *The Crusader*, 177–80.

24. See Clines, "Democrats Assert Reagan Is Using 'Star Wars' Scare to Hide Blunders." The dateline on the story is listed as "Washington, March 24." The hardcopy version ran March 25. The reporter wrote and filed the story on March 24, as did the editor who submitted the headline. This was the same day as Kennedy's comment.

25. Quoted in Clines, "Democrats Assert Reagan Is Using 'Star Wars' Scare to Hide Blunders."

26. McGrory wrote this in her syndicated column that followed the Reagan speech. It was distributed in most newspapers on March 27–28, 1983. See also Mary McGrory, "The Stars Spoke on Capitol Hill," *Washington Post,* May 5, 1988.

27. Quoted in McGrory, "The Stars Spoke on Capitol Hill."

28. Sagan said this publicly at a scientific colloquium, speaking as part of a panel discussion. The laughter in the middle and end of his quote was loud. This is captured on film in the documentary *In the Face of Evil: Reagan's War in Word and Deed,* done in 2005 by American Vantage Media in association with Capital Films, produced by Tim Watkins and Stephen K. Bannon, based on Peter Schweizer's book *Reagan's War.*

29. Herb Meyer speaking at the Third Annual Ronald Reagan Lecture, Grove City College, Grove City, PA, February 5, 2009.

30. In 1970 the CIA helped Bezmenov leave India, where he had been stationed on diplomatic assignment. He eventually made his way to Canada and by the mid-1980s was working as a writer and political analyst in Los Angeles under the name Tomas D. Schuman. See Jay Mathews, "Group Sets Safety Net to Snatch Defectors at Olympic Games," *Washington Post,* April 14, 1984, A1. Bezmenov was born in 1939. According to online sources, he died in 1997.

31. Interview by G. Edward Griffin, *Soviet Subversion of the Free Press: A Conversation with Yuri Bezmenov* (Westlake Village, CA: American Media, 1984). The entire hour-plus video is available online at http://video.google.com/videoplay?docid=-2307456730142665916#.

32. Bezmenov discusses Kennedy approximately forty-five minutes into the interview.

33. Bezmenov did not give the date of the wedding or the photo. It isn't completely clear from his comments whether Bezmenov arranged or was present for this particular wedding. The Soviets staged weddings throughout the Cold War. See "Comrades Have Lovely Soviet Wedding; But Irked Party Finds It Was a Fraud," *New York Times*, March 10, 1958.

34. Tracking down Kennedy's visits to Moscow is difficult. Articles from the *New York Times* during this period show that he was in the Soviet Union in 1974, 1978, and 1986: Clyde Haberman, "After Six Years, the Soviets Set Exit Date for Leviches," *New York Times*, November 24, 1978; Wayne King and Warren Weaver Jr., "Travels with Kennedy," *New York Times*, February 1, 1986; and Bernard Gwertzman, "Kennedy Starts Soviet Visit Looking for a Resolution of Emigration Cases," *New York Times*, February 5, 1986.

35. The other two journalists were Harrison Salisbury and David Brinkley, with Brinkley being the odd man among an otherwise very left-of-center group.

36. "Guide to Subversive Organizations and Publications (and Appendices), revised and published December 1, 1961, to supersede Guide published on January 2, 1957 (including Index)," 117–18.

37. Kincaid has posted the document at his website, along with supporting background material. See "Cronkite Named as Soviet Target by FBI in 'Active Measures' Document," May 17, 2010, posted at www.usasurvival.org, specifically: http://www.usasurvival.org/docs/cronkite.pdf.

38. "Teddy, the KGB and the Top Secret File," *Sunday Times* (London), February 2, 1992.

39. The only sources that talked about the revelation were conservative talk-radio outlets. No matter how much we tried, from my own efforts to those of publicists, we could not get mainstream news outlets to touch the story, even in a critical way. The sole exception was the CN8 cable news outlet,

based in Philadelphia. CN8 went so far as to get a response from Kennedy's office, which did not deny the legitimacy document, arguing instead with its "interpretation." It was not clear if that referred to my interpretation or Chebrikov's interpretation. Chebrikov is dead.

40. See my discussion of this earlier episode in Chapter 18.

41. See, for example, Martha Bebinger, "Edward Kennedy, the Senate's Last Lion, Is Dead at 77," wbur.org, August 26, 2009; and Peter S. Canellos, ed., *Last Lion: The Fall and Rise of Ted Kennedy* (New York: Simon & Schuster, 2009).

42. In March 1983, speaking at a "nuclear freeze" rally in Washington, Senator Kennedy said: "I wish that we had an administration that was more concerned with preventing nuclear war and less concerned in preparing for nuclear war." Frank Warner, "New Word Order," *Morning Call* (Allentown, PA), March 5, 2000, A1.

43. Edward M. Kennedy, "A State of Disunion," *Rolling Stone,* March 15, 1984, 11–12. It is not clear whether Kennedy meant a "wider war" in Central America, which he mentioned in the previous sentence, or a "winnable nuclear conflict" generally, which he referred to in the next sentence.

44. "Soviet Treaty Violations: Hearing Before the Committee on Armed Services," United States Senate, 98th Congress, Second Session, March 14, 1984 (Washington, DC: GPO, 1984), 1.

45. Steven R. Weisman, "Now, Talk of New Strains Among the Top Aides," *New York Times,* March 31, 1983.

46. Reagan, "The President's News Conference, January 9, 1985," *Presidential Papers,* 1985, vol. 1, 26.

47. In addition to Helen Thomas at UPI, *Washington Post* White House correspondent Loy Cannon used the phrase. See, for example, Lou Cannon, "Too Many Simple Answers," *Washington Post,* October 28, 1985, A2.

48. Reagan, "The President's News Conference, January 9, 1985."

49. See Kengor, *The Crusader,* 66–68.

50. Adelman quoted in Knott and Chidester, *At Reagan's Side,* 105.

51. Here I am drawing from pages 182–84 of *The Crusader.*

52. "Moscow TV's 30 June 'Studio 9' Program," transcript published in FBIS, July 3, 1984, CC6.

53. Viktor Olin, commentary for Moscow World Service, December 18, 1984, transcript printed as "Olin Views U.S. Signing of 'Star Wars' Contracts," in FBIS, December 19, 1984, AA4.

54. The two TASS statements are published as "Concern Over 'Star Wars' Plans Expressed," in FBIS, February 1, 1985, AA8–9.

55. F. Aleksandrov, "How the 'Star Wars' Are Being Prepared," *Krasnaya Zvezda,* March 8, 1985, 5, printed as "U.S. Preparation, Research for SDI Discussed," in FBIS, March 12, 1985, AA5.

56. "'Studio 9' Program Discusses 'Star Wars,'" May 25, 1985, transcript printed in FBIS, May 29, 1985, AA1–12.

57. See Valentin Falin, "Fact and Fancy," *Izvestia,* April 10, 1985, 5, printed as "Izvestia's Falin Muses on SDI Issue, Part 1," in FBIS, April 15, 1985, AA3–5.

58. TASS statement in English, October 28, 1985, printed as "Reagan Takes 'Simplistic' Attitude to Problems," in FBIS, October 30, 1985, A5.

59. The author that the *New Times* quoted was Thomas S. Powers, a frequent contributor to the *Los Angeles Times* on foreign and security policy. Yuri Gudkov, "False Promises and the Nuclear Reality," *New Times,* September 1985, 3–5, printed as "U.S. Strategic Doctrine Encourages Arms Escalation," in FBIS, October 7, 1985, AA5–10.

60. TASS statement by Vladimir Matyash, October 16, 1985, printed as "Reagan Uses 'Clever Tricks' to Explain SDI," in FBIS, October 16, 1985, AA5.

61. Moscow Domestic Service statement by Boris Adrianov, October 23, 1985, printed as "Commentator Sees 'Nothing Defensive' About SDI," in FBIS, October 28, 1985, AA1–2.

62. Reagan quoted by Philip B. Kunhardt Jr., Philip B. Kunhardt III, and Peter W. Kunhardt, *The American President* (New York: Riverhead Books, 1999), 296. Reagan also protested that the term "Star Wars" conjured "an image of destruction," when, in fact, "I'm talking about a weapon, non-nuclear . . . [that] only destroys other weapons, doesn't kill people." See Reagan, "Interview with Morton Kondracke and Richard H. Smith of *Newsweek* Magazine, March 4, 1985," *Presidential Papers,* vol. 1, 1985, 261.

63. Reagan, "Interview with Morton Kondracke and Richard H. Smith of *Newsweek* Magazine, March 4, 1985."

64. Reagan, "Remarks in an Interview with Representatives of Soviet News Organizations, Together with Written Responses to Questions, October 31, 1985," *Presidential Papers,* 1985, vol. 2, 1332.

65. Reagan, "Interview with Representatives of the Wire Services, November 6, 1985," *Presidential Papers,* 1985, vol. 2, 1349.

66. Interview with Bill Clark, February 28, 2008.

67. Keyworth interviewed by Donald Baucom, September 28, 1987, RRL, OHT, folder 37, box 8, 40.

68. Lukhim quoted by Robert McFarlane in his memoir, *Special Trust* (New York: Cadell & Davies, 1994), 235.

69. See Trofimenko in Hofstra conference, 138–45; and Andrew E. Busch, "Ronald Reagan and the Defeat of the Soviet Empire," *Presidential Studies Quarterly,* Summer 1997, 455–62.

70. For a compilation of quotes from these individuals, see Kengor, *The Crusader,* 300–2.

71. George Shultz, *Turmoil and Triumph* (New York: Scribner, 1993), 264, 690, 699, 709.

72. Viktor Olin, writing for the Moscow World Service, December 18, 1984, stated that some sensible American authorities protested the militarization of space that the rash "hotheads" in the Reagan administration were allegedly pursuing. Among them were "the former Defense Secretaries [Robert] McNamara, [Harold] Brown, and [James] Schlesinger; disarmament expert Gerard Smith; diplomat and historian George Kennan; and many others [who] have warned that attempts by the administration to secure superiority in space are doomed to failure because they will inevitably cause countermeasures. As a result, the arms race will be sped up dramatically, and the war threat will take on yet another dimension." Among these experts, the Soviets especially appreciated the counsel of Carter defense secretary Harold Brown: "The former U.S. Defense Secretary Harold Brown has given a warning that if the United States deploys an antimissile defense system, it can hardly count on reaching an agreement with the Soviet Union on strategic arms limitation." Despite such prudent advice, noted Moscow, the Reagan administration had "so far given no signs of being ready to heed these warnings." This was the message from Moscow: If only Ronald Reagan's team, including Defense Secretary Caspar Weinberger, would listen to Jimmy Carter's team, especially Defense Secretary Harold Brown, then U.S.-Soviet relations would be much better. And if Reagan refused to listen to the likes of President Carter's defense secretary, there would be no missile limitations. See Olin commentary for Moscow World Service, December 18, 1984.

73. See Kengor, *The Crusader,* 198–99.

74. Seweryn Bialer and Joan Afferica, "Reagan and Russia," *Foreign Affairs,* Winter 1982/83, vol. 61, no. 2, 249–71. See pages 262–63 specifically.

75. With apologies to the occasional Columbia grad who got it right, such as Arnold Beichman—who got it right in spades. See Paul Kengor, "The Beichman Library Closes," *American Spectator,* March 1, 2010. Beichman had a bachelor's degree, master's degree, and doctorate from Columbia. See Dennis Hevesi, "Arnold Beichman, Political Analyst, Dies at 96," *New York Times,* March 3, 2010.

Chapter 21: September 11, 2001

1. President George W. Bush, "Address to the Nation on the Terrorist Attacks," Washington, DC, September 11, 2001.

2. Dinitia Smith, "No Regrets for a Love of Explosives," *New York Times,* September 11, 2001, E1.

3. Horowitz, *Radical Son,* 334.

4. As noted, the Weather Underground proudly took responsibility for twelve bombings. Among others, see Smith, "No Regrets for a Love of Explosives."

5. Smith, "No Regrets for a Love of Explosives."

6. Ayers told the *Times* that his philosophy was really more of a "joke about the distribution of wealth." He also told Alan Colmes of Fox News that this was a "joke." See "Alan Colmes Highlights Bill Ayers Exclusive," FoxNews.com, February 24, 2009.

7. Among others, see Smith, "No Regrets for a Love of Explosives."

8. Here is Dohrn's bio page at the Northwestern website, followed by her official "c.v." posting: http://www.law.northwestern.edu/faculty/profiles/BernardineDohrn/; and http://www.law.northwestern.edu/faculty/clinic/dohrn/dohrnBeCV.pdf.

9. Frederick Edwards, "Requiem for a Freedom Fighter—Corliss Lamont," *The Humanist,* July–August 1995.

10. Brickman, ed., *John Dewey's Impressions*, 110–11.

11. Congress mandates that the State Department annually report on terrorism. In its final report, in 2000, the Clinton State Department devoted more words to Iran and Iraq than any other countries. For an analysis, see Paul Kengor, "Clinton Administration to Obama: Iraq Greater Terror Threat Than Afghanistan," July 17, 2008, published in several sources, and posted at www.visandvals.org and www. faithandfreedom.com.

12. These criticisms included irrational allegations such as "Bush lied, kids died." See my discussion at the website of the Center for Vision and Values, specifically the two articles by Paul Kengor, "Yes, I Admit I Hate Bush" (January 12, 2006) and "Bush Lied, You Lied" (February 24, 2006).

13. Quoted in "Gore Says Bush Betrayed the U.S. by Using 9/11 as a Reason for War in Iraq," *New York Times*, February 9, 2004.

14. Quoted in "Senate Leader Calls Bush 'A Loser,'" CBSNews.com, May 7, 2005; and "Reid: Iraq War Lost, U.S. Can't Win," MSNBC.com, April 20, 2007.

15. *"Meet the Press*, Transcript for Dec. 5," MSNBC.com, December 5, 2004.

16. "From Congress to Union Halls, Demand Widens: Exit Iraq!" *People's World*, June 24, 2005, posted at http://www.peoplesworld.org/from-congress-to-union-halls-demand-widens-exit-iraq/. Barbara Lee, on the floor of the House, read a statement concerning alleged evidence that "Bush and his administration have lied to the world."

17. Zachary Coile, "Rep. Stark Blasts Bush on Iraq War," *San Francisco Chronicle*, March 19, 2003.

18. Stark said this on October 18, 2007. At least twice he refused to retract his remarks. Eventually, on October 23, he issued an apology, not because he regretted his accusations against Bush but because he said the controversy detracted from more pressing concerns facing the nation, like "providing medical care for children."

19. See Charen, *Useful Idiots*, 190–91.

20. See "Kerry 'Regime Change' Comments Draw Fire," FoxNews.com, April 3, 2003, posted at http://www.foxnews.com/story/0,2933,83101,00.html.

21. Not knowing that his microphone was on, Kerry was recorded saying this on March 12, 2004.

22. The quote has been widely reported. For the original source, see the *Congressional Record—Senate*, June 14, 2005, S6594.

23. Obama said this on August 13, 2007. In addition to hard-copy transcripts of the remark, a video clip of the remark is posted at YouTube.

24. Dennis B. Roddy, "Exonerated Marine to Sue Rep. Murtha," *Pittsburgh Post-Gazette*, September 25, 2008; Edwin Mora, "Some Marines Question the Navy's Decision to Honor Rep. Murtha," CNSNews.com, March 23, 2009.

25. Chad Pergram, "Murtha Says He'd Take Guantanamo Prisoners in His District," FoxNews.com, January 21, 2009.

26. Durbin's comments aired on CNN's *American Morning*, November 16, 2009, and were transcribed by CNN.

27. Kerry said this on CBS's *Face the Nation* on December 4, 2005. The quote is published in the *Face the Nation* transcript of the show, pages 3–4.

28. Kerry said this on October 31, 2006. Afterward, his spokesperson claimed that the statement had been a botched joke aimed at the alleged lack of intelligence of George W. Bush, a line quickly accepted by mainstream media sources like CBS, MSNBC, and the Associated Press. See "Kerry's 'Botched' Joke Backfires," CBS News/Associated Press, November 1, 2006; and "Uproar over Kerry Iraq Remarks," MSNBC.com, November 1, 2006.

29. Kennedy said this on May 10, 2004. Among others, see "Senate Condemns Iraqi Prisoner Abuse," FoxNews.com, May 11, 2004.

30. Kennedy made this remark on September 18, 2003. For a stinging counter-response, see Charles Krauthammer, "Ted Kennedy, Losing It," *Washington Post*, September 26, 2003, A27.

31. See "Kennedy to Assail Bush over Iraq War," *Boston Globe*, October 16, 2003.

32. John Hendren, "Kennedy Calls Iraq Bush's 'Vietnam,'" ABCNews.com, January 9, 2007.

33. "Walter Cronkite Criticizes President Bush's 'Arrogance' over Iraq," Associated Press, March 19, 2003.

34. Foner wrote this as part of a *London Review of Books* symposium/panel of reactions (by historians) to

September 11. Source: "11 September," *London Review of Books,* October 4, 2001, vol. 23, no. 19, 20–25.

35. Matthew Rothschild, "The New McCarthyism," *The Progressive,* January 2002.

36. See Paul Kengor, "Anti-Semite? Saddam Outdid Ahmadinejad," September 26, 2007, posted at the website of the Center for Vision and Values.

37. "Columbia University Faculty Action Committee Statement of Concern," *New York Sun,* November 12, 2007.

38. Tamar Lewin and Amanda Millner-Fairbanks, "President of Columbia Is Criticized," *New York Times,* November 14, 2007.

39. See "President Ahmadinejad Delivers Remarks at Columbia University," *Washington Post,* September 24, 2007; and "Ahmadinejad Blasts Israel, Denies Existence of Iranian Gays During Columbia Speech," FoxNews.com, September 24, 2007.

40. This incident was widely reported. One early source was Matthew Continetti, "Professor Mogadishu," *National Review Online,* March 31, 2003.

41. Kim died on July 8, 1994.

42. "The Carter Interview: Jimmy Carter's North Korean Notebook," *Atlanta Journal-Constitution,* July 3, 1994, A12.

43. Ibid.

44. See, for example, http://www.globalsecurity.org/military/world/dprk/dprk-dark.htm.

45. See Barbara Crossette, "Korean Famine Toll: More Than 2 Million," *New York Times,* August 20, 1999.

46. Among others, see R. Jeffrey Smith and Ruth Marcus, "White House Wary of Ex-President's View N. Korea 'Crisis Is Over,'" *Washington Post,* June 20, 1994; Michael R. Gordon, "Back from Korea, Carter Declares the Crisis Is Over," *New York Times,* June 20, 1994.

47. Carter called for renewed inspections in a January 31, 2003, statement, released by his Carter Center and posted at the website of the Carter Center: http://www.cartercenter.org/news/documents/doc1165.html.

48. Jimmy Carter, "The Troubling New Face of America," *Washington Post,* September 5, 2002.

49. Jimmy Carter, "Just War—or a Just War?" *New York Times,* March 9, 2003.

50. For the record, whether the war in Iraq met "just war" standards was hardly a closed case, as this subject was vigorously debated throughout the war period, with powerful arguments made in the affirmative by Catholic theologians/scholars like Michael Novak and George Weigel, who most assuredly had studied Augustine's doctrine. Yet Carter assumed he had the sure answer, and the *New York Times* did nothing to suggest otherwise.

51. For example, when Ronald Reagan mentioned Jesus Christ in a January 1984 speech to the National Religious Broadcasters, the *Times* denounced him. Reagan presented the speech, complained the *Times,* "not while worshiping in his church but in a Washington hotel. . . . You don't have to be a secular humanist to take offense at that display of what, in America, should be private piety. . . . It's an offense to Americans of every denomination, or no denomination, when a President speaks that way." The *Times* noted that Reagan was, after all, "the President of a nation whose Bill of Rights enjoins Government from establishing religion, aiding one religion, even aiding all religions." This was 1984, but the *Times* has remained consistent in this thinking. If anything, the *Times* editorial board is more liberal today than it was in 1984. See the editorial, "Sermon on the Stump," *New York Times,* February 3, 1984.

52. General Norman Schwarzkopf, who commanded the 1991 Persian Gulf operation, speculated that Saddam Hussein had hoped that Jimmy Carter would step into the fracas and broker a deal that would stop the United States from driving Iraq from Kuwait. See "Schwarzkopf on Hussein: Calculating 'Carter Factor,'" *New York Times,* October 13, 1994, A16.

53. Sharon Jayson, "Carter Rebuts State Dept. on Hamas," *USA Today,* April 24, 2008.

54. Ibid.

55. In his January 2002 State of the Union address Bush said of Iraq, Iran, and North Korea: "States like these and their terrorist allies constitute an axis of evil."

56. See Michael Kelly, "A Presidential Blast from the Past," *Washington Post,* February 27, 2002.

57. Sean Penn went to Iraq in 2002 and Iran in 2005; Bening went to Iran in 2009. Penn in 2005 fingered the Eisenhower administration for Iran's "anger at the United States." See Alistair Lyon, "Sean

Penn Says War in Iraq Is Unavoidable," Reuters, December 15, 2002; "Sean Penn in Iran," four-part series for the *San Francisco Chronicle,* beginning August 22, 2005; and "Hollywood's Bening Hopes to Help Mend US-Iran Ties," Agence France-Presse, March 1, 2009.
58. Transcript, *This Week with George Stephanopoulos,* ABC News, September 29, 2002.
59. Ibid.
60. Ibid.
61. Ibid.
62. See Stephen F. Hayes, "The Baghdad Democrats," *The Weekly Standard,* October 14, 2002.
63. Ibid.
64. Ibid.
65. Ibid.
66. Transcript, "Congress Debates Iraq," *NewsHour,* PBS, October 2, 2002, posted at www.pbs.org/newshour/bb/middle_east/july-dec02/iraq_10–2.html.
67. Matt Apuzzo, "US: Saddam Paid for Lawmakers' Iraq Trip," Associated Press, March 26, 2008.
68. Ibid.
69. "Prosecutors Say Saddam's Intelligence Agency Financed McDermott's Iraq Trip," *Seattle Times,* March 26, 2008.

Chapter 22: Still Dupes for the Communists

1. See, for example, Kenneth Lloyd Billingsley, "Hollywood's Missing Movies: Why American Films Have Ignored Life under Communism," *Reason,* June 2000; Radosh and Radosh, *Red Star Over Hollywood,* 243–45; and Evans, *Blacklisted by History,* 538.
2. Tony Kushner, "Kushner on Miller," *The Nation,* June 13, 2005, 6.
3. See Henry Weinstein and Judy Pasternak, "I. F. Stone Dies," *Los Angeles Times,* June 19, 1989, A1; and Charen, *Useful Idiots,* 89. To see these tributes, go to: http://www.ifstone.org/on_his_death.php.
4. *TNR,* though still solidly on the left, long ago quit carrying the water for Communists. For years, in fact, the magazine has done some of the best work countering the Communists who duped the magazine in its early years.
5. Ron Radosh, "Bohemian Rhapsody," *The New Republic Online,* March 12, 2007.
6. See Tanenhaus, *Whittaker Chambers;* Allen Weinstein, *Perjury: The Hiss-Chambers Case* (New York: Knopf, 1978); and Richard Nixon, *Six Crises* (New York: Doubleday, 1962).
7. See Arthur Schlesinger, Jr., "The Truest Believer," *New York Times Book Review,* March 9, 1997.
8. Quoted in Radosh, "Bohemian Rhapsody."
9. See, for instance, Jamie Glazov's interview with Haynes and Klehr, "Frontpage Interview: In Denial," FrontPageMagazine.com, November 25, 2003, posted at http://97.74.65.51/readArticle.aspx?ARTID=15347.
10. See Kengor, "Anti-Anti-Communism and the Academy," April 2009, posted at the website of the Center for Vision and Values.
11. James A. Miller, Susan D. Pennybacker, and Eve Rosenhaft, "Mother Ada Wright and the International Campaign to Free the Scottsboro Boys, 1931–1934," *American Historical Review,* vol. 106, issue 2, December 2007.
12. See, for instance, the journal article written by Obama's father: Barak [sic] H. Obama, "Problems Facing Our Socialism," *East Africa Journal,* July 1965, 26–33. On this, see Ben Smith and Jeffrey Ressner, "Long-lost Scholarly Article by Obama's Dad Surfaces," *USA Today,* April 16, 2008. Smith and Ressner are reporters for Politico.com, which tracked down the article.
13. Takara quoted in report by Herb Romerstein and Cliff Kincaid, "Communism in Hawaii and the Obama Connection," Accuracy in Media, May 2008, posted at AIM.org.
14. Lisa Miller and Richard Wolffe, "Finding His Faith," *Newsweek,* July 12, 2008.
15. That church was located in Bellevue, Washington, one of the areas where the family lived. Tim Jones, "Obama's Roots Are Steeped in Tradition," *Chicago Tribune,* March 26, 2007.
16. According to initial reports, this was the latter 1970s, though some more recent reports claim the relationship lasted longer than that.
17. Barack Obama, *Dreams from My Father* (New York: Random House, 2004), 77.

18. Ibid., 100–1.

19. I corresponded with John C. Drew (who contacted me after reading an article I had written on Obama and Davis) in April 2010 via several e-mails. Though the mainstream media had paid no attention to Dr. Drew, around February 2010 some conservative media outlets had begun covering his allegations, which appear completely credible. Before Drew contacted me, I had read his comments at length in print and listened to them in radio and web interviews. In one of the better interviews, in February 2010 Drew spoke with Scott Baker, a former Pittsburgh news anchor (WTAE-TV) who now does web broadcasting. The interview has been posted in its entirety on several websites. (I watched it via a February 14, 2010, post at the "New Zeal" blogspot.) At Occidental, Drew was a Marxist, as he says was true also of Obama. His main goal is to clarify where Obama stood at Occidental, which is certainly not insignificant. That said, he did tell me: "There are a lot of brands of Marxism. That was one of the key ingredients of my argument with the young Barack Obama. I see evidence of [a] continuing commitment to Marxist ideology every time President Obama traces the furor of the public to underlying economic conditions and inevitable changes taking place in society. (As he did recently with his complaints about Rush Limbaugh and Glenn Beck.) In the Marxist model, the economy is the driving force behind change in the other spheres of society." Source: April 5, 2010, e-mail from John Drew.

20. Obama, *Dreams from My Father*, 96–97.

21. In February 2010, both Columbia and Occidental were contacted for this book, specifically in order to view letters of recommendation written on Obama's behalf. The communications director at Occidental said that under FERPA (the Family Educational Rights and Privacy Act), the college needed written permission from the president himself to release his records. Columbia simply stated that the records were "unavailable" and "not public."

22. Obama, *Dreams from My Father*, 76–77, 90–91, and 97.

23. Gerald Horne, "Rethinking the History and Future of the Communist Party," PoliticalAffairs.net, March 28, 2007.

24. Quoted in Herb Romerstein and Cliff Kincaid, "Communism in Hawaii and the Obama Connection," Accuracy in Media, May 2008, posted at AIM.org.

25. Tidwell, ed., *Frank Marshall Davis: Black Moods, Collected Poems*, xxviii.

26. Ibid., xxxv. The letter was likely written around 1944. It seems no earlier than 1943 and no later than 1945. As Tidwell notes, the letter is not dated, which, as any historian knows, is quite common in biographical research. Tidwell has the letter in his possession. He includes a "Note on the Text" that discusses Davis's undated letters.

27. Kincaid told me in an e-mail that the files were released very quickly after he requested them, suggesting to him that the file had been previously processed through an earlier FOIA request, perhaps submitted by a Davis biographer like John Edgar Tidwell. Source: June 12, 2010, e-mail correspondence with Cliff Kincaid.

28. See http://www.usasurvival.org/marshall.fbi.files.html.

29. See http://www.usasurvival.org/docs/davis.FBI.File.pdf.

30. Ibid. In particular, see exhibits 6, 7, 9, 10, 11, 14, and 15.

31. See page 59 of the set of files available here: http://www.usasurvival.org/docs/Frank_Marshall_Davis_5.pdf.

32. See Herb Romerstein, "Who Was Frank Marshall Davis?" posted at http://www.usasurvival.org/docs/who.frank.marshall.davis.pdf. This information is on the first page (fifth paragraph) of Romerstein's report, following an introduction by Kincaid.

33. Quoted in Romerstein and Kincaid, "Communism in Hawaii and the Obama Connection."

34. I know this from personal experience, as Romerstein constantly so cautioned me in writing this book.

35. Bill Steigerwald, a reliable veteran reporter, was there. His article, which underscored Milbank's reaction, ran in a number of sources on June 2 and 3, 2008, including the *Pittsburgh Tribune-Review* (where he was an editor) and FrontPageMagazine.com.

36. Dana Milbank, "Obama as You've Never Known Him!" *Washington Post*, May 23, 2008.

37. Steigerwald was a witness to this particular exchange.

38. For example, I have done this extensively in spiritual biographies of Ronald Reagan, George W. Bush, and Hillary Clinton, and in a biography of William P. Clark.

39. Cliff Kincaid, "AP Lies About Obama's Red Mentor," Accuracy in Media, August 4, 2008.

40. Sudhin Thanawala, "Writer Offered a Young Barack Obama Advice on Life," Associated Press, August 2, 2008. The other AP piece, by the same reporter, was titled "In Multiracial Hawaii, Obama Faced Discrimination," Associated Press, May 19, 2008.

41. Press Release, "The Honolulu Community-Media Council Condemns Shoddy Journalism and Smear Tactics by the *Pittsburgh Tribune-Review* and the Accuracy in Media Website," Honolulu Community Media Council, July 22, 2008.

42. David Maraniss, "Though Obama Had to Leave to Find Himself, It Is Hawaii That Made His Rise Possible," *Washington Post,* August 22, 2008.

43. Quoted in Cliff Kincaid, "Obama's Red Mentor Was a Pervert," Accuracy in Media, August 24, 2008. This article is cited because it was the only source that bothered to seek a response from David Maraniss. As the title suggests, there is quite a bit of information on Frank Marshall Davis's sordid sexual life. This, too, has been ignored by the mainstream news media, but has been covered by a few respectable sources, such as London's *Daily Telegraph.* I have chosen not to address this issue, given that my focus is the matter of Communism and dupery.

44. Jon Meacham, "On His Own," *Newsweek,* August 23, 2008.

45. David Remnick, *The Bridge: The Life and Rise of Barack Obama* (New York: Knopf, 2010), 97.

46. In fact, it was Quentin Young who confirmed the meeting to *Politico.* Sources for this include Ben Smith's articles in *Politico,* most notably: Ben Smith, "Obama Once Visited '60s Radicals," Politico.com, February 22, 2008 See also Shane, "Obama and '60s Bomber."

47. There are a number of references to this in the newsletters of Democratic Socialists of America. There is also a photo of Debs at the podium receiving the award at the 1992 dinner.

48. Young often says that national health care "isn't the best solution; it's the only solution." See Karen Ide and Clinton Stockwell, "An Interview with Quentin D. Young, M.D.," *Physicians for a National Health Program,* May 2004; and Julie Appleby and Richard Wolf, "Few Solutions on the Horizon as Health Costs Rise," *USA Today,* September 1, 2005.

49. The exact date of the meeting, to my knowledge, has not been reported. My estimate is that it was June–July 1995. See Smith, "Obama Once Visited '60s Radicals"; and Shane, "Obama and '60s Bomber."

50. Shane, "Obama and '60s Bomber."

51. The word "coffee" was a direct quote from Rabbi Wolf, whereas the longer quote, "one of several such neighborhood events as Mr. Obama prepared to run," were the words of the *Times* reporter paraphrasing the rabbi.

52. Ayers has briefly addressed the subject in other contexts. He admits "we had him [Obama] in our home," but adds that Obama "was probably in 20 homes that day." See Rex W. Huppke, "Bill Ayers: 'Secret Link' with Obama Just a Myth,'" *Chicago Tribune,* November 14, 2008.

53. Shane, "Obama and '60s Bomber."

54. Scott Fornek, "Foot Soldiers for the '96 Elections," *Chicago Sun-Times,* October 29, 1995.

55. See Aaron Klein and Brenda J. Elliott, *The Manchurian President* (Washington, DC: WND Books, 2010); and "The Obama-Ayers meeting: What You Haven't Been Told," WorldNetDaily.com, May 2, 2010

56. It typically takes at least two years to earn a master's degree, meaning that Ayers probably began his master's program in 1982. See Faculty Profile, William Ayers, University of Illinois at Chicago, available at http://education.uic.edu/directory/faculty_info.cfm?netid=bayers

57. David Horowitz interviewed Ayers at the Manhattan nursery school in 1982, where Ayers was working as a teacher. See Horowitz and Collier, "Doing It." See also Horowitz, *Radical Son,* 333–34.

58. The *Wall Street Journal* has called this Columbia period "Obama's lost years." See the editorial, "Obama's Lost Years," *Wall Street Journal,* September 11, 2008.

59. Cliff Kincaid of Accuracy in Media has reported this in his online reports and articles. This period might also overlap with Bill Ayers's time at Columbia and possibly some period when Obama was living in New York. Again, much of this is unclear—and unnecessarily so.

60. See Shane, "Obama and '60s Bomber."

61. Ibid.

62. The *New York Times*'s Scott Shane ("Obama and '60s Bomber") reports the period as 2000 to 2002, with "about a dozen" meetings between the two in that three-year period. This is incorrect. The website of the fund reports that the two began serving together in 1999.

63. Jennifer Vanasco, "Close-up on Juvenile Justice: Author, Former Offender Among Speakers," *University of Chicago Chronicle*, November 6, 1997, posted at http://chronicle.uchicago.edu/971106/justice.shtml.

64. Rorty was bracingly candid in his message to parents: "We are going to go right on trying to discredit you in the eyes of your children, trying to strip your fundamentalist religious community of dignity, trying to make your views seem silly rather than discussable." See Robert B. Brandom, ed., *Rorty and His Critics* (Oxford: Blackwell, 2000), 21–22.

65. A photo of Obama next to the endorsement was posted by a number of conservative websites during the 2008 presidential campaign, though the mainstream media almost completely ignored the matter. One of the most frequently visited such postings was at HotAir.com. See http://hotair.com/archives/2008/10/20/the-blurb-that-never-was/. See also Shane, "Obama and '60s Bomber."

66. Brian Friel, Richard E. Cohen, and Kirk Victor, "Obama: Most Liberal Senator in 2007," *National Journal*, January 31, 2008.

67. See Anne E. Kornblut and Dan Balz, "Obama Pressed in Pa. Debate," *Washington Post*, April 17, 2008.

68. Robin Abcarian, "Stephanopoulos Defends His Questions to Obama," LATimes.com, April 17, 2008.

69. Quoted in Huppke, "Bill Ayers.'"

70. Maki was interviewed and is quoted by Cliff Kincaid. See Cliff Kincaid, "Communist Party Backs Obama," Accuracy in Media, July 3, 2008, posted at AIM.org.

71. Kincaid, "Communist Party Backs Obama."

72. The photo of the Che Guevara flag at an Obama office in Houston was widely circulated on the Internet. It was captured by a Fox affiliate in Houston and immediately picked by conservative print and web sources like *Investor's Business Daily* and *WorldNetDaily*.

73. Editorial, "Eye on the Prize," *People's Weekly World*, July 15, 2008.

74. For a mainstream source prior to the election, see Paola Messana, "U.S. Communists Say Their Time Has Come," Agence France Presse, October 14, 2008.

75. Kincaid, "Communist Party Backs Obama." Another conservative who has written openly on these connections is Joseph Farah of *WorldNetDaily*. Most conservatives, however, are afraid to touch this.

Chapter 23: 2008: A "Progressive" Victory

1. Throughout most of the writing of this book, the website that lists the signatories for Progressives for Obama has been http://www.progressivesforobama.net/.

2. Daniel J. Flynn, "Obama's Boys of Summer," *City Journal*, June 2008.

3. These four reportedly signed online petitions calling for an "independent grassroots effort" to strengthen Senator Obama's presidential campaign. In addition to the signers who hailed from Progressives for Obama, like Mark Rudd, these petition signers included Howard Machtinger, Jeff Jones, and Steve Tappis. See Aaron Klein, "4 Weathermen Terrorists Declare Support for Obama," WorldNetDaily.com, October 2, 2008.

4. "Jane Fonda Endorses Barack Obama: There Goes His Crossover Vote," *Los Angeles Times* blog, posted as http://latimesblogs.latimes.com/washington/2008/04/jane-fonda-endo.html.

5. This data is taken from MSNBC exit polling posted the day after the November 4, 2008, election.

6. Tom Hayden, "Obama and the Open and Unexpected Future," CommonDreams.org, June 8, 2008.

7. Barack Obama used the terms "economic justice" and "redistributive change" in a 2001 interview with the Chicago Public Radio station, WBEZ, 91.5 FM. According to a short article posted by WBEZ, the interview was done in January 2001. See http://www.chicagopublicradio.org/Content.aspx?audioID=29792.

8. Thomas Good, "MDS Conference Elects Manning Marable Chair of MDS, Inc.," *Next Left Notes*, February 20, 2007.

9. Rudd said this at an April 22, 2009, press conference on his book release. See Cliff Kincaid, "Terrorists on Tour," Accuracy in Media, April 23, 2009.

10. Rudd posted this on November 27, 2008. See www.markrudd.com/organizing-and-activism-now/lets-get-smart-about-obama-nov-2008.html.

11. The Gallup poll was released June 15, 2009, and conducted from January through May 2009, when "Obama mania" was believed to be at its peak, advanced not only by an ebullient politician but also by a massive liberal-Democrat majority in both the Senate and the House of Representatives. Gallup surveyed 160,000 people, which is far and away a large enough sample size for an accurate representation of the country as a whole. Gallup found 40 percent calling themselves conservative and 21 percent opting for liberal, an almost identical two-to-one (roughly) margin to its findings over the past two decades, including during the 2004 presidential race (40 percent to 19 percent) and the 2000 presidential race (38 percent to 19 percent). Also, Gallup once again reaffirmed that conservatives are far and away the single largest voting bloc in America. It found far more conservatives among women (37 percent to 23 percent) as well as men (44 percent to 20 percent). See Lydia Saad, "'Conservatives' Are Single-Largest Ideological Group," *Gallup,* June 15, 2009.

12. Brian Friel, Richard E. Cohen, and Kirk Victor, "Obama: Most Liberal Senator in 2007," *National Journal,* January 31, 2008.

13. Rudd posted this on November 27, 2008. See www.markrudd.com/organizing-and-activism-now/lets-get-smart-about-obama-nov-2008.html.

14. "Duncan Praised as 'Bona Fide Reformer' of Chicago Education System," FoxNews.com, December 16, 2008.

15. Ibid.

16. Ibid.

17. See William Ayers, Jean Ann Hunt, and Therese Quinn, eds., *Teaching for Social Justice* (New York: Teachers College Press, 1998); and William Ayers, Michael Klonsky, and Gabrielle Lyon, eds., *A Simple Justice* (New York: Teachers College Press, 2000). More recently, see William Ayers, Therese Quinn, and David Stovall, eds., *Handbook for Social Justice in Education* (New York: Routledge, 2008).

18. See Sol Stern, "The Ed Schools' Latest—and Worst—Humbug," *City Journal,* Summer 2006; and Sandy Rios, "Billy Graham Meets Bill Ayers," *Townhall,* February 26, 2010.

19. "Duncan Praised as 'Bona Fide Reformer' of Chicago Education System." Klonsky has also written blog posts on Duncan at http://michaelklonsky.blogspot.com/. See the Klonsky and Ayers piece in the February 1, 2006, issue of *Phi Delta Kappan.*

20. Andrew C. McCarthy, "Another Communist in Obama's Orb," *National Review,* October 22, 2008.

21. Flynn, "Obama's Boys of Summer."

22. Ibid.

23. Ibid.

24. Carl Davidson, "The Right Wing's assault on Van Jones and the Progressive Left," *The Rag Blog,* September 6, 2009, posted at theragblog.blogspot.com.

25. In October 1970 Jones, Bill Ayers, and Bernardine Dohrn signed a letter taking credit for an explosion that destroyed a statue of a policeman in Chicago's Haymarket Square. They wrote: "A year ago we blew away the Haymarket pig statue at the start of a youth riot in Chicago. Last night we destroyed the pig again." See "Weathermen Take Credit for Bombing," UPI, October 7, 1970.

26. See Juliet Wittman, "Memoirs: Radical Parents, Red Shoes and a Poet Up Close and Personal," *Washington Post,* November 21, 2004; and Carl Swanson, "Radical Take: Two Former Weathermen Cut through the New Documentary *The Fog of War,*" *New York,* December 15, 2003, posted at nymag.com.

27. Quoted in: Phil Kerpen, "NY's Tax-Funded Ex-Terrorist," *New York Post,* September 9, 2009.

28. Ibid.

29. See Keith Schneider, "Recovery Bill Is Breakthrough on Clean Energy, Good Jobs," Apollo Alliance, February 17, 2009, posted at apolloalliance.org. According to the Apollo Alliance, Reid said: "This legislation is the first step in building a clean energy economy that creates jobs and moves us closer to solving our enormous energy and environmental challenges. . . . The Apollo Alliance has been an important factor in helping us develop and execute a strategy that makes great progress on these goals and in motivating the public to support them."

30. See my article "Communicating Obama's Fiscal Disaster," March 23, 2009, posted at the website of the Center for Vision and Values. There is debate over the precise amount of the final Bush deficit,

given the fiscal disaster in the fall of 2008 and, more specifically, given which government spending (in response to the disaster) should be included in the final "Bush deficit." Either way, the Obama "stimulus" immediately added $800 billion to an already record deficit left by Bush.

31. Credit for this find goes to the hard work and diligent digging of Mary Grabar, which is published in Mary Grabar, "Did Bill Ayers Get His Teaching Job 'the Chicago Way'?" *America's Survival Inc.*, August 2009, 7. This report is posted at www.usasurvival.org. Dr. Grabar has done a review of the syllabi used in Ayers's courses.

32. Editorial, "Ayers Has Not Left Radicalism Behind," *Investor's Business Daily*, October 9, 2008.

33. Chavez was elected president in 1998 and reelected in 2000 and 2006. Ayers, in his November 2006 speech at the World Education Forum in Caracas, Venezuela, said it was his fourth visit to the country. The speech is posted at Ayers's website at http://billayers.wordpress.com/2006/11.

34. See Ayers's 2006 World Education Forum speech, posted at http://billayers.wordpress.com/2006/11. See also the editorial, "Ayers Has Not Left Radicalism Behind."

35. See, for example, Jon Lee Anderson, *Che Guevara: A Revolutionary Life* (New York: Grove Press, 2010), 633.

36. "Chavez Says Smell of Sulfur Replaced by Smell of 'Hope,'" FoxNews.com, September 24, 2009.

37. This was the description of Boudin listed in the tagline to a March 3, 2009, article posted by Boudin at the website of *The Nation* magazine.

38. Braudy, *Family Circle*, 384.

39. The bio is posted at www.columbia.edu/cu/ssw/faculty/adjunct/boudin.html.

40. This is data from MSNBC exit polling, posted November 5, 2008 It is consistent with other exit polls.

41. Rudd, *Underground*, 175–76.

42. "Doctors Call on Obama, Congress to 'Do The Right Thing' on Health Reform," PoliticalAffairs.Net, November 9, 2008; and "Steps Toward Health Care Reform," PoliticalAffairs.Net, November 13, 2008.

43. The speech was excerpted by Aaron Klein, "Communist Party Official Shares White House's Ambitious Agenda," *World Net Daily*, May 24, 2009.

44. Stanislav Mishin, "American Capitalism Gone with a Whimper," *Pravda*, April 27, 2009.

45. Manning Marable, "The Four Legged Stool That Won the US Presidential Election," *Socialist Review*, December 2008.

46. The actual quote reads: "The American people will never knowingly adopt socialism, but under the name of liberalism they will adopt every fragment of the socialist program until one day America will be a socialist nation without ever knowing how it happened."

Postscript: Bogart at the Workers School?

1. "Guide to Subversive Organizations and Publication (and Appendices), revised and published December 1, 1961, to supersede Guide published on January 2, 1957 (including Index)," 175–76.

2. This is the testimony of Manning Johnson. See "Investigation of Communist Activities in the New York City Area—Part 5," Hearing before the Committee on Un-American Activities, U.S. House of Representatives, 83rd Congress, First Session, July 6, 1953, Washington, DC, 2277.

3. "New York Leads Country in Socialist Competition," *Daily Worker*, November 3, 1934, 6.

4. This is a different district number (#2) from the district number for the Bogart at the Workers School (#5). Importantly, however, the *Daily Worker* and Workers School used different district structuring, as is immediately evident when comparing the two sets of districts.

5. "John Bogart, 80, Dies; Was Times Executive," *New York Times*, October 12, 1992.

6. "Marjorie Goodell Wed to J. A. Bogart," *New York Times*, April 18, 1937.

7. "Miss Jacqueline Branaman Is Married to Philip J. Halla," *New York Times*, November 27, 1966.

8. "Jacqueline Branaman Bogart: Tribute & Message from the Family," Tributes.com, retrieved March 5, 2010.

9. Such an eyewitness is my good friend and colleague Charles Wiley, who in 1934 was a New York–based child actor rehearsing the 1935 award-winning stage hit *Old Maid*. The female lead in that play was Humphrey Bogart's ex-wife, Helen Menken, whom Bogart remained friends with and visited occasionally backstage. Wiley was there. He met Bogart and remembers the visits well, as did Wiley's parents,

who years later, once Bogie was an established star, often reminded an older Wiley that this was the same man who had frequently visited Helen Menken backstage in 1934. Source: Interview/conversations with Charlie Wiley, April 27–28, 2010, during Wiley visit to Grove City College, Grove City, Pennsylvania.

10. Stephen Humphrey Bogart, *Bogart: In Search of My Father* (New York: Dutton/Penguin, 1995), 305–6.

11. Duchovnay, *Humphrey Bogart: A Bio-Bibliography*, 278.

12. Bogart, *Bogart: In Search of My Father*, 83.

13. Duchovnay, *Humphrey Bogart: A Bio-Bibliography*, 11.

14. Ibid.

15. According to the online Broadway database ibdb.com, these three plays by Philips were: *All Good Americans* (December 5, 1933, to January 1934); *The Pure in Heart* (which was written by John Howard Lawson, and which opened March 20, 1934, and closed the same month); and *Come What May* (May 15, 1934, to June 1934).

16. I also found John Abendroth Bogart elusive on this question. John Abendroth Bogart began working at the *New York Herald Tribune* in 1934. At the start of 1934, when the Workers School was in session, John Bogart would have been approximately twenty-one years old, which is the typical age for someone just finishing college—although most college graduates do not finish a four-year program midyear, as would have been the case here. Unfortunately, I was not able to learn whether John Bogart went to college. The announcement of his marriage to Marjorie Goodell in the April 18, 1937, edition of *The Times* does not make reference to college, whereas college is mentioned for other newlyweds listed on the page. For instance, the wedding announcement to the immediate right of the Bogart-Goodell announcement notes a groom who graduated from Yale, while the announcement immediately below notes a groom who graduated from St. Joseph's College.

17. The 150 Broadway address is listed in the 1934 New York City directory.

18. See "Business & Finance: A. B. See to Westinghouse," *Time*, July 19, 1937.

19. See Leon Morse, "TV Specs Providing Greener Pastures to Hollywood Stars," *Billboard*, July 3, 1954, 2.

20. Larry Ceplair and Steven Englund report that "Leech had joined the Communist Party in 1931, served as a paid Party organizer for two years, 1934–36, and been expelled in 1937." See Larry Ceplair and Steven Englund, *The Inquisition in Hollywood: Politics in the Film Community, 1930–60* (Champaign: University of Illinois Press, 2003), 157.

21. Radosh and Radosh, *Red Star Over Hollywood*, 53.

22. Among contemporaneous accounts: "Jury Told 43 Film Notables Are Reds," *New York Daily Mirror*, August 15, 1940; and "Tone, Cagney, March Called Gilded Reds," *New York Daily News*, August 15, 1940.

23. "Tone, Cagney, March Called Gilded Reds."

24. Ibid.

25. See Budd Schulberg, testimony before the House Committee on Un-American Activities, May 23, 1951, quoted in Nicholas Beck, *Budd Schulberg: A Bio-Bibliography* (Lanham, MD: Scarecrow Press, 2001), 81.

26. "Filmsters Blast Back at Communist Charges," United Press, August 15, 1940.

27. Bogart statement quoted in "Hollywood Stars Accused as Reds Before Grand Jury," *New York Times*, August 15, 1940.

28. Testimony of John L. Leech, "Investigation of Un-American Propaganda Activities in the United States," House of Representatives, Subcommittee of the Special Committee on Un-American Activities, Los Angeles, California, August 16, 1940, 1382.

29. Ibid.

30. Testimonies of Humphrey DeForest Bogart and John L. Leech, "Investigation of Un-American Propaganda Activities in the United States," 1375–85. Also testifying on behalf of Bogart was his financial adviser, Andrew Morgan Maree Jr., who handled all of the actor's signed checks, and who testified that he never saw one check go from Bogart to the Communist Party. Of course, the response to that defense by John Leech would be that many party members used fake names, or "party names," when dealing with the Communist Party, or used cash, and thus he would not expect a signed check in Bogart's name.

31. Testimony of Philip Dunne, "Investigation of Un-American Propaganda Activities in the United States."

32. Among other contemporaneous accounts, see "Dies Clears 3 Actors of Being Communist Sympathizers," *Washington Evening Star*, August 21, 1940; and "Dies Clears Four Accused as Reds," *New York Times*, August 21, 1940.

33. See " . . . Says Reds Sought Hollywood Cash," *New York Times*, August 7, 1940; and "Film Stars Aided Reds, Jury Charges," *Washington Times Herald*, August 15, 1940.

34. This list is also included in a report filed by the Los Angeles division of the FBI, submitted November 14, 1950, which is located in Bogart's FBI file, file no. 100–15732, 21.

35. See http://www.imdb.com/name/nm0822034/bio, retrieved August 12, 2009.

36. See Klehr, Haynes, and Firsov, *The Secret World of American Communism*, 93, 102–4.

37. Through a FOIA request, I received approximately three hundred pages of documents from the FBI on October 23, 2009.

38. David Platt, "Bogart: Anti-Fascist Film Hero," *Daily Worker*, October 15, 1944, 15.

39. See also David Platt, "Bogart and Bacall Endorse a Contest," *Daily Worker*, July 11, 1951.

40. Duchovnay, *Humphrey Bogart: A Bio-Bibliography*, 198–99.

41. Ibid.

42. A key note: Ronald Reagan personally liked Bogart and did not suggest anywhere in his first memoir, *Where's the Rest of Me?* that Bogie was a Communist or Communist sympathizer, as Reagan had done for other Hollywood Reds. Rather, Reagan noted that the members of the Committee for the First Amendment who flew to Washington from Hollywood were recruited by Communists not because they were fellow Communists but because they were "suckers." Of course, by this point, Bogart could have long since left the party or abandoned any sympathies from the early 1930s. See Reagan, *Where's the Rest of Me?* 85–86, 100–1, 186, and (especially) 200. Reagan, obviously, ended up moving much farther politically than did Bogart. Then again, Bogart died nearly fifty years earlier. Interestingly, the two men were in a similar spot politically in 1952: Reagan was still a Democrat but supported the Republican presidential nominee, Dwight Eisenhower. Bogart, meanwhile, considered supporting Eisenhower, but his very liberal wife, Lauren Bacall, persuaded him to campaign for Democrat Adlai Stevenson. See Duchovnay, *Humphrey Bogart: A Bio-Bibliography*, 29; and Bogart, *Bogart: In Search of My Father*, 140–43.

Author's Note

This book was not motivated by a desire to stir up controversy. The decision to write the book came well before the meteoric presidential rise of Barack Obama, which shocked not only me but, no doubt, even Obama's own supporters—and certainly Democrats like Hillary Clinton. (In fact, my most recent book prior to this one, published in 2007, was on Senator Clinton, whom I expected to be our president today, or at least the party's 2008 presidential nominee.)

Rather, this project was a reaction to the declassification of vast reams of evidence unavailable (even unimaginable) to scholars who studied Communism and the Cold War as recently as the late 1990s. Most notable was the release of files from the Comintern Archives on CPUSA. The Library of Congress now houses hundreds of reels of microfiche from these files—and as noted, these represent only a fragment of the full Comintern collection, which remains in Moscow. In addition to these essential resources are holdings by the Harvard Project on Cold War Studies, the Woodrow Wilson Center, the University of Virginia's Miller Center of Public Affairs, the Hoover Institution, New York University's Tamiment Library, and several presidential libraries. Adding to that, at midnight on December 31, 2006, the FBI declassified hundreds of millions of pages of secret Cold War documents on people suspected of being Communists or Communist sympathizers. The *New York Times* called it a "Cinderella moment" for researchers. Other important archives have been neglected, such as those of the Foreign Broadcast Information Service, which for decades has translated media reports from Communist countries. And that isn't even a complete list. So expansive is this material that one could spend decades poring over it and even then touch only a small portion of what is on the shelves.

When I was already engaged in this kind of research for other works on the Cold War, but on a much smaller scale, I constantly came across snippets of intriguing material, such as the May 1983 KGB document on Senator Ted Kennedy. Sometimes these documents (including the Kennedy memo) were sent to me by other researchers. Confirming their authenticity usually required digging deep into various historical archives, some long buried. Every visit required yet another visit, which brought yet another finding. Initial short visits became long-term excavations.

Excavations, like any archaeological dig, eventually yield not just broken pottery but also smashed skulls and bones. That was especially true in this case, since Communism produced more than a hundred million corpses in its wake in the twentieth century. I found further examples of unrecorded Communist criminality and brutality.

And it was that unprecedented violation of the sanctity and dignity of human life that motivated—actually, *demanded*—a response. It demanded this book. Communism produced the single greatest documentable human-rights atrocity in history. That is why I care about this issue so much, and why I think others should as well. That is why I did this book.

ACKNOWLEDGMENTS

There are so many people I would like to thank for their help that I hesitate out of fear that I will surely forget a name or two who deserve to be commended.

First off, I'm grateful to Peter Schweizer, who, like me, first got noticed through works on Ronald Reagan and the end of the Cold War. Peter and I have become good friends. A few years ago we did a book together on the Reagan presidency, an edited volume titled *The Reagan Legacy: Assessing the Man and His Presidency* (2005). We vowed to do another book together when the time seemed right. This book began as that project. We were both doing archival research on the Cold War, moving along the same path, and we both saw the need for this book. We came to this concept together, and began pursuing the work as a project through the Hoover Institution, where both of us are fellows. Unfortunately, Peter's success elsewhere caught up with him: the demand for him as an author overwhelmed him. Soon, he was under contract to produce several (significant) books simultaneously, with yet more around the corner. Thus, he had to withdraw from this project as we approached the writing stage. Still, his counsel and input during the conceptual and research stages was indispensable.

Likewise, I thank the good folks at the Hoover Institution, particularly John Raisian, Deborah Ventura, and Stephen Langlois. Among other things, they provided the administrative and accounting assistance as I sent in every record and grouping of receipts from every trip to the Library of Congress and wherever else. They were always kind and helpful.

As a professor at Grove City College in Grove City, Pennsylvania, I'm blessed with an abundance of wonderful students eager to help with research. Some of them were my student assistants, whereas others were students in classes who stopped by to see what I was researching and whether they could help. Here's where I most fear missing someone who should be acknowledged, but I will give it my best shot: Matt Costlow, Rachel (Bovard) Latta, Jonathan Riddle, Anthony Maneiro, Emily Hughes, Jessica VanDervort, Doug El Sanadi, Dan Hanson, Glen Hiler, Steve Sweet, Melissa Borza, Daniel McKrell, Dustin Heath, Julie Fox, Elle Speicher, Nicole Randazzo, Bethany Peck, David Kilburn, Brittany Pizor, Andrew Kloes, Betsy Christian, Stephen Wong, Silas Finnegan, Jordan Koschei, Sean Morris, Walter "Soren" Kreider, and Andrea Fellersen. Melinda Haring, a former student, returned from an extended stay in the former Soviet Union to suggest the photo that became the cover art for this book—no doubt moved by the spirit.

Among the Grove City College students, most critical was Matt Costlow, who was my go-to guy for just about everything with this book, especially in the final weeks of furious fact-checking, and who is generally a fabulous student assistant and young man. Also valuable were Dan Hanson, who reads Russian and was always extremely reliable; Rachel (Bovard) Latta, who was a crucial researcher here as she has been on some of my previous books (and who refused any pay in return); Anthony Maneiro, who, among other things, dug and dug until he found the Frank Marshall Davis *Honolulu Record* columns from 1949–50—no small achievement; and Emily Hughes, who worked on-site in Hawaii to confirm the electronic versions of the Davis columns that Anthony had found, as she located the original columns on microfiche at the University of Hawaii at Manoa Hamilton Main Library. How many authors can find this kind of support? Grove City College is a gift—from God and for God—that keeps on giving.

Also from Grove City College (aside from my students), I thank President Dick Jewell, Provost Bill Anderson, Dean John Sparks, Assistant Dean Dave Ayers, colleagues Michael Coulter and Marv Folkertsma, Diane Grundy and her superb library staff (especially Conni Shaw and Joyce Kebert), and my splendid team at the Center for Vision and Values: Lee Wishing, Brenda Vinton, Ray Speicher, John and Kathy Van Til, and Cory Shreckengost. Without Lee and Brenda, and their superb, devoted service, I would not have had the time to write this book, period. Cory also helped with research, as he has with past books. He is a brilliant young man, a most dependable worker, and himself a gifted author who needs a break from a publisher looking for an excellent partnership. Cory is capable of original, nicely written work.

I should add that the Center for Vision and Values has become the engine for research among Grove City College faculty that its founders—Dick Jewell, John Moore, Chuck Dunn, John Sparks, Lee Wishing, and Bill Anderson, among others—originally envisioned. At least two of the chapters (plus several sections) in this book began as white papers or conference papers for the Center for Vision and Values. I encourage readers of this book to visit the center's website, www. faithandfreedom.com, for an excellent collection of scholarly material. I'm deeply appreciative of Phil Gasiewicz for his support of the center and for our friendship.

Outside of Grove City College, I'm grateful for the help of Thomas Whittaker, a local home-school student, and his family. Likewise, three of my own home-schooled children offered input or interest—Paul, Mitch, and Amanda. I also thank our neighbor, Jim Covert, for his interest and encouragement throughout the process, as well as his friendship to my family. This is true for many other friends as well, including Tod and Andrea Reiser, Joe and Sharon Harrilla, and Father Mark Hoffman and all the other special people from Beloved Disciple Catholic Church. (Here again, there are too many to begin to list them all.) And much farther away from Grove City, I remain blessed by my special friendship with Bill Clark, who resides in Paso Robles, California, and Herb Meyer, who is in the San Juan Islands off the West Coast.

Also there with friendship, knowledge, and time-tested, battle-earned wisdom were the old salts, my cadre of Cold War veterans: Charlie Wiley, Arnold Beichman, Stan Evans, and Herb Romerstein. Herb, especially, was a fountain of information, able to answer almost any question on Communism with the immediacy of an e-mail or a phone call. When the likes of Herb and Charlie and Stan leave this world, an entire library of information will go with them—to the great detriment of historical knowledge. In fact, in that respect, the Beichman Library has since closed, with Arnold Beichman passing away in February 2010. Both Herb and Arnold were so helpful, and such giant contributors to the cause over the past fifty years, that I dedicated this book to them. Few men in the twentieth century battled so many Communists and suffered so many dupes.

Similarly, Cliff Kincaid, Mark Tooley of the Institute on Religion and Democracy, and Tim Graham of the Media Research Center were available to answer questions on certain key figures in this book. Cliff is tireless and fearless in his research on figures long past but still relevant.

I also had allies who stepped out of nowhere, some not even knowing of my latest research, to offer me old books and documents they had held forever, including thick volumes from House and Senate committees and subcommittees from the 1930s to the 1970s. They include Lawrence S. Katz, Don and Carolyn

Thomson, and Marjorie Provan. Their materials were indispensable. For that, I likewise salute all those old-school Democrats who ran the committees who exposed this information, back long, long ago when the Democratic Party was the party of Truman, JFK, and even Ronald Reagan.

Of course, I'm especially grateful to ISI Books for publishing this book. I've always admired ISI Books and the intellectual gems it produces, which no other publisher bothers to touch. The brilliant addition of Jed Donahue as the new editor lifts the product line to an even higher level. As much as I respect ISI Books, it was the hiring of Jed that sealed the deal for me. I've learned firsthand that Jed is a superb editor—truly the best in the business. Also from ISI Books, I thank the publisher, the great Ken Cribb; Christian Tappe, assistant editor and office manager; Chris Michalski, sales and marketing director; and Jennifer Fox, managing editor, who did the layout for this book—an enormously complicated endeavor that involved juggling dozens, even hundreds, of e-mails, photographs, and old documents.

Moreover, I would like to acknowledge Mona Charen, whom I met at Grove City College several years ago when I helped bring her to campus to discuss her book *Useful Idiots,* a more colorful synonym for the subject of this book. Though Peter Schweizer and I were motivated to pursue this project by the fascinating and historically significant material flowing from new archives, I'm sure that Mona's good work planted a seed in my mind prior to the opening of these archives. (Her work was very different from this one, in both style and sources, most distinctly in that it was not based on archives, which mostly were not available at the time she wrote her book.) I thank Mona for her book, which hopefully might serve with this one as a one-two punch on a subject that demands many more follow-up works; after all, many dupes and useful idiots have managed to slip through the cracks of history.

Finally, I thank my parents and brother and sister, who have always been there, and my beautiful wife, Susan, and our five beautiful children. I've been blessed beyond any reasonable expectation and truly deserve none of what I have. And for that, I thank the God who created me and continues to put up with me, ever dealing with my vices and infusing me with spiritual graces to try to squeeze out the rare inkling of virtue.

Paul Kengor
Grove City, Pennsylvania
July 1, 2010

INDEX

Page numbers in *italics* refer to illustrations.

About the Author

Paul Kengor, Ph.D., is the *New York Times* bestselling author of *The Crusader: Ronald Reagan and the Fall of Communism, God and Ronald Reagan, God and George W. Bush, God and Hillary Clinton*, and (with Patricia Clark Doerner) *The Judge: William P. Clark, Ronald Reagan's Top Hand*, among other books. He is a professor of political science at Grove City College, where he is executive director of the Center for Vision and Values. He has also been a visiting fellow at the Hoover Institution on War, Revolution, and Peace at Stanford University. A frequent guest on television and radio, Kengor has written for such popular publications as the *New York Times*, the *Wall Street Journal, USA Today*, the *Philadelphia Inquirer, National Review*, and the *Weekly Standard*, and for such scholarly journals as *Political Science Quarterly* and *Presidential Studies Quarterly*. He and his family live in Pennsylvania.